the eXile

the eXile

Sex, Drugs, and Libel in the New Russia

by Mark Ames and Matt Taibbi

GROVE PRESS
NEW YORK

This is a work of nonfiction. While all of the characters and events depicted in this book are real, certain names and identifying details have been changed.

Published simultaneously in Canada
Printed in the United States of America

Library of Congress Cataloging-in-Publication Data
Ames, Mark 1965-
The Exile: sex, drugs, and libel in the new Russia / by Mark Ames and Matt Taibbi.
p. cm.

ISBN-10: 0-8021-3652-4
ISBN-13: 978-0-8021-3652-7
1. Ames, Mark 1965- . 2. Exile (Moscow, Russia) 3. Tabloid newspapers—Russia (Federation) —Moscow. 4. Newspaper publishing—Russia (Federation) —Moscow. 5. Journalists—Russia (Federation) —Moscow—Biography. 6. Americans—Russia (Federation) —Moscow Biography. 7. Taibbi, Matt I.Taibbi, Matt. II. Title.
PN5276.A82 1999
077′ 31—dc21 99-25071
CIP

Design by Ilya Shangin and Yevgeny Raitzes
Illustrations by Roman Papsuev
Contributors: Edward Limonov, Kevin McElwee, Johnny Chen
Moscow Publisher: Konstantin Bukarev

Grove Press
an imprint of Grove/Atlantic, Inc.
841 Broadway
New York, NY 10003
Distributed by Publishers Group West
www.groveatlantic.com

08 09 10 11 12 10 9 8 7 6 5 4 3 2

TABLE OF CONTENTS

ACKNOWLEDGMENTS

We would like first and foremost to thank the members of the *eXile* staff, who put a lot of work into this book and received absolutely nothing in return:

To Eugene, the *eXile* pit bull, for killing that annoying dog;

To Konstantin Bukarev, for taking a chance on a totally unsalable product, for giving us complete editorial freedom, and for keeping us shackled to a wretched and penniless existence;

To Ilya Shangin, the Jedi designer, for his brilliant drunken innovations, and for sacrificing his health to pull all-nighters with us because we could never finish our articles on time;

To Krazy Kevin McElwee, our genuinely insane voice and uncredited managing editor, for filling holes in the paper, for filling in when we're in rehab, and for losing scores of restaurant and movie theater clients with his gratuitously vicious reviews;

To Vlad Kousraev, for putting our business back in order, for keeping us alive during the crisis . . . and for not stealing our money;

To Svetlana Negrustuyeva, for making us all that money, and for putting up with two years of relentless sexual harassment;

To Roman Papsuyev, for his great cartoons;

To Dmitri Shalya, for making us look like experts on Moscow nightlife;

To Tatiana Baklastova, for helping arrange all those barter deals we later welched on, and for bringing in wagonloads of new clients with her sexy year-round tan.

Thanks also to Dar, Nkem, Liz (for writing for free), Dasha, Tamila, our accountant Tanya, and the Ne Spat crew, Artur, Gabriel, Sergei, and Olgas 1 and 2.

To Jason Mayhew, our masterful web geek, for recording our shameless exploits on his cyber-goat skin and spreading the *eXile* Word across the globe faster than a new strain of genital warts.

Thanks also to our non-*eXile* friends:

To Claudia Cross, Jane and Charlie Bausman, Brendan Cahill, Richard Emery, Calvin Walden, and Morgan Entrekin, for their invaluable assitance, patience, support, and hygiene; also, to David Johnson, for his dedication and backbone.

And to Rick Stevenson, Mitch "Blood" Green, the Reverend Sung-Y'ung Moon for his insights, Drew Anderson, Wilbur McGillicutty, Sparky the pet fire ant, Mo Snideman, Helen "One Brow" Schwartz, John Loopman, Jennifer Butterknees, and the late Jonas Bernstein, whose loving memory we cherish, for all the nutty times.

FOREWORD

To the charming city of Paris an American literature is obliged of formation such exotic international writers as Henry Miller and Ernest Hemingway. Both men in some way may be defined as non-American American writers. (In fact they wrote exclusively about Exiles.) In same way Mark Ames and Matt Taibbi may be defined as non-American (or even totally anti-American) writers. Both men been formed by Moscow, our ugly lady of frost, concrete, and macabre violence.

To become big an American should leave America?

Both Ames and Taibbi have agreed that to publish the eXile *on American soil would be virtually impossible task. If such newspaper as* eXile *will ever occur somewhere on territory of United States, its publisher and writers will be arrested in space of three days by FBI agents, I guess. Also probably that Ames and Taibbi will be taken away by crowd of psychiatric hospital attendants. Obscene, rejecting, screaming, howling,* eXile *is totally unacceptable for common sense people, in other words, for majority of U.S. population. Poisonous newspaper* eXile *can be compared to only one publication in European history: to radical* L'Idiot International, *edited in French by Jean-Edern Hallier from 1989 to 1992 in Paris. I was a member of editorial board of* L'Idiot. *Every week I wrote an article in broken French for that illustrious publication. It was really "bad" newspaper. We were first to find about extramarital daughter of Ive Montan, we managed to oust out of power French Minister of Defense Claude Herrue. . . . Now, in broken English, I am writing for* eXile *while editing my own newspaper,* Limonka, *in my beautiful, gorgeous Russian. So, you see, I am a veteran of poisonous, extremist publications. And as a veteran, I am asserting with all qualification given to me by time and experience, "Yes,"* eXile *is really "bad" newspaper. No, Ames and Taibbi are not pretending, they really hate common folks, they are perfect anthropologists, they are dangerous.*

The irony of sort and uniqueness of position of eXile *consist in fact that they are victimizing entire population of Moscow's expatriates, without asking their permission. They are forcefully given, distributed not amongst the brothers-in-soul, but amongst the enemies and amongst few friends. It looks like a forceful distribution of Saddam Hussein's anti-American pamphlets to the staff of White House. I believe poor victims look at freshly printed issue of* eXile *with some horror when they notice it on some bar's counter or restaurant table, or worst—in his or her letterbox.*

Speaking about "her"... female condition in eXile is worst than in poorest Bedouin family wandering in the deserts of Israel. Women are badly beaten, raped, and mocked of. The eXile's crew is also arrogant, and making fun of authorities. They have questioned Russian men: How much money would you have to be paid before you'd fuck Madeleine Albright? Russian men declined proposition.

What are political beliefs of Ames and Taibbi? They are totally politically incorrect. They are extremists of a new brand: leftists and right-wingers in same time, they are racist red communist agitators worst than three-key people, bloodthirsty as Chikatilo, about women you know.

Logical thing would be to ask now: Why such dangerous people are not yet arrested? Ames and Taibbi are not yet arrested because they act on the small neutral territory between two laws. An American law is not applicable on Russian land and Russian law doesn't read an American publication. (I doubt that Mister Laptev, head of a State Committee for a Press, knows English. He is an old Communist functionary.) But if somebody reads English, anyway Russian law didn't give a damn. Because English readers are not Russian voters. Because only a voter's brain purity is bothering Russian law and its lawmen.

Dirty newspaper the eXile is extremely rare phenomenon. Like "yurodivi," or "holy fool," the eXile in its obscene language says the very truths that normal, "sane" press would avoid to tell. Long before financial crisis, the eXile's lonely voice screamed that Russia is fucked up economically, that we live here in monstrous, ruthless, bloody world of catastrophe. Life in Russia is a horror movie, says the eXile (Mark Ames compared it to the climate of a Blade Runner). But it is real, so real that everyone who falls under the spell of that macabre beauty will never leave Russia, charming land of Chikatilo and police violence.

Story of the eXile is worth a book. It is like a diary of a German lieutenant, what he kept in Stalingrad's ruins.

Edward Limonov
March 14, 1999

the eXile

Bigger!
Faster!
Ames-ier!

ISSUE#0 [000] •FEBRUARY 6, 1997•FREE

Will They Ever Pay Me?

NEW! Living Legend! Page 4!

Mark Ames tells the whole, sordid truth.

Living Hell

MUTINY AT LIVING HERE! Why everyone jumped ship for the eXile.

Mark Ames 2-3

BAR-DAK 5

LIMONOV'S COUPS D'ETAT 15

BY MARK AMES

CHAPTER ONE: INTO EXILE

"There's nothing more boring than a man with a career."
Alexander Solzhenitsyn

he *eXile* was the perfect name for our newspaper. I consider myself an exile from California. I wasn't forced out of my homeland in the classic, victim-of-tyranny way, but I was forced out nonetheless. "The *eXile*" also carried an ironic meaning, especially considering that most Western expats in Moscow spend their off-hours whining about the lack of Western conveniences, the surface ugliness of the Soviet architectural remains, the vulgar decadence of the new rich, the lazy and unreliable work habits of the natives, the rude service —everything that their cozy native lands trained them to resent.

They're the kind of people who actually prefer the predictable, convenient lives they left behind, and so for them, Moscow was a punishment, only a grossly overpaid punishment.

There is also a very unhumorous side to the word "exile." To most Russians, few words conjure as much tragedy and cultural/historical pain. Most of the great figures of Russian literary and philosophical history were forced into exile, from Pushkin to Lenin to Solzhenitsyn. Even Limonov was tossed out in 1974. The entire aristocracy, what was left after the butchery and counterbutchery in the Civil War, was exiled. With Stalin, exile was socialized, taken to the masses. It didn't matter how clever or rich or dangerous you were—all were welcome! Entire nations were exiled: the Crimean Tartars, the Ingush and Chechens, Volga Germans, Baltic peoples, Jews. . . . And here we were, a pissy, free, biweekly English-language newspaper, selling the national tragedy as a joke, with the kitsch e.e. cummings lower case "e," and the uncool appropriation of the capital "X" from Generation X just to hammer the point home. We wanted to start off on the wrong foot with our readers. All of them.

The name "The *eXile*" was part of a list of about ten or twenty suggestions emailed to me by Dr. John Dolan, from his dungeon at the University of Otago, on New Zealand's South Island. He sent the list to me when the newspaper was just starting up, in January 1997. Whereas I loved my place of exile—Moscow—for Dr. Dolan, exile retained its classic, painful meaning. He always referred to the South Island as "Alcatraz." He's been cooking up failed plans to escape New Zealand ever since he landed.

I knew Dr. Dolan from when I was a student at Berkeley in the late Reagan years. We had a lot of ideas back then, big dreams about getting famous and destroying the "Beigeocracy" that we thought stifled and controlled American Letters. We were going to impale the "Beigeists"—another Dolan coinage—on the very pens they wrote on. We were sure we were going to prevail. Everything seemed possible then: world war, literary fame. . . . Anyway, something Really Big, with us at the center of it all. He was a local cult poet, whereas I was sort of a conscript, part of a small circle of reactionary intellectuals at Berkeley. We'd ridicule the boring lefties, our enemies. We'd drop all sorts of drugs and go to the underground shows: Scratch Acid, Hüsker Dü, Sonic Youth, Big Black. It felt like something might happen, and soon.

Then something happened. As in, nothing happened. At all. And then I graduated.

The Bush years marked my decline, the Fall of my empire of dreams. When Bush and his golfing buddies got tossed out in '92, I started thinking, hey, Bush and I have a lot in common, getting overrun by progress and all. Except in one small respect: Bush was a filthy-rich historical figure, whereas I was an unemployed, barely published, aging zero. I'd written screenplays that ended up in unmarked piles. I had an agent in Hollywood, but he insisted that I move down to L.A. if I wanted to succeed—something I didn't have the stomach to do. My short stories were said to be too undisciplined and violent for a market that expects subtlety and epiphany. "Read Raymond Carver or Alice Munro," they'd advise me. I could never get past page two of their cringing, careful stories.

My circle of reactionary friends did what all reactionaries do: they either enlisted in the corporate world, since to do otherwise would be hippie-ish; or they became epic losers. Dr. Dolan, who wrote his dissertation on de Sade, wound up in New Zealand, on the South Island, teaching English Composition to freshman med-students. One friend became a corporate lawyer; another, the smartest of our circle, who peaked too early, went on welfare, became a crack addict, and joined Pat Buchanan's Crusade For America. He fell off the radar screen a few years ago. We think he's dead.

I began to notice something during those years of sliding insignificance. Strangely enough, even though I lived in California, the yardstick by which all cultures in the world measure themselves—even though I was a citizen of Pericles's Athens and Augustus's Rome, my country was, paradoxically, becoming increasingly inaccessible to me. I felt more and more foreign as the months went by. Spending five years in Berkeley can give you a pretty skewed, useless understanding of America. When you get out, the rest of the country is a real shocker. Berkeley isn't winning anything, never did: it's just a tiny nature preserve, a showpiece of dissent, a summer camp, a Potemkin Village of harmless radicalism, a campus stacked with college DJ quippers. I took a belated trip to Europe, which included a two-week stay in Leningrad, just after the failed August coup in 1991. That fourteen-day, Homeric adventure on the streets of Leningrad really made an impression—I briefly fell into a world of prostitutes, pimps, petty thieves, and high embassy officials who had to fight with the OVIR police to extend my visa and allow me to leave the country. Several months after returning home, my slow-working mind began to process it all. I didn't yet realize, consciously, that I belonged in Russia. I didn't understand that I had the right to move there. So instead of staying in Leningrad, I returned to the Bay Area in late 1991, and, in one of those classic career moves that marked my pre-Russia life, I checked into a care home for old women.

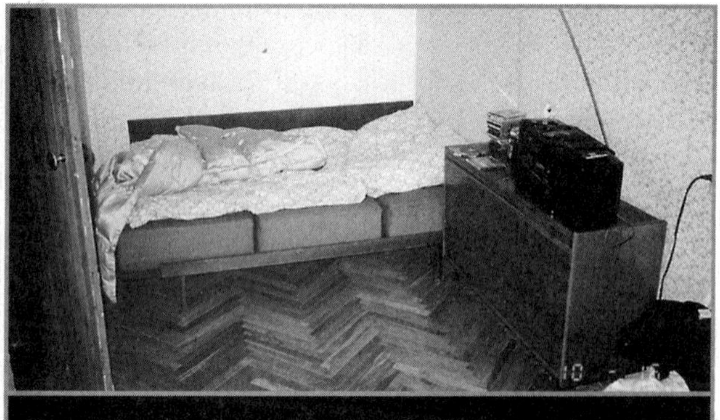

The apartment bedroom in which all the bitterness and frustration that fueled the *eXile*'s inception was born.

The care home was also the residential home where my Czech émigré girlfriend and her mother lived. They'd turned the back wing of their house into a care home, and named it "The European Care Home." It was about as close to Europe as I dared to move. I didn't have a place to live when I returned from my trip to the Soviet Union, and I didn't have the money to rent. Jobs in California were hard to come by in 1991. Also, I'd contracted an epic case of scabies sometime during my vacation, an infestation that would define the next nine months of my life.

I spent almost an entire year holed up in the European Care Home, in Foster City, a decaying 1970s suburb built on landfill on the peninsula south of San Francisco.

At this point, I'd like to take you on a little tour of suburban California. By reminding you of the bland hell that exists before your eyes on a daily basis, you will better understand why I defected to Russia.

Foster City was a scary place, even by suburban California standards. On the west side, closest to Highway 101 and San Mateo, Foster City had a cluster of '80s-style 10-story iridescent-green glass skyscrapers. It looked like a brochure for a "new high-tech industrial park," complete with watercolor-drawn humans in suits and beige skirts and sleek American midsize cars in the parking lots. It was the result of a failed attempt to remake Foster City from a commuter suburb to a high-tech center.

When I moved there in 1991, Foster City was neither high-tech mecca nor residential dreamland. You saw it when you drove past the half-abandoned silicon-chip midrises, and into the one-story, residential eastern half, closer to the bay. Every garage seemed to have a second-rate sports utility vehicle with "Ross Perot for President" bumper stickers plastered on the bumpers or on the smoked hatch windows. This was the "angry middle class," and they didn't look all that angry to me: just dull and stingy. In spite of the constant heat, you never actually saw people. And even when you did, they avoided looking at you. They'd check their mail or work on their cars while listening to classic rock. But they'd never look at you.

The European Care Home was located at the end of a cul-de-sac deep within a maze of lanes and streets. Ours was called Sand Hill Court. The care home was really just a suburban house, not too different from the seven suburban houses and condominiums I'd lived in from birth until defection to Berkeley. Only, everything was older and sun-aged, like the people inside. The European Care Home's lawn had been overrun by crabgrass, with the occasional sprout of sour grass jutting out. The swimming pool in the care home's backyard was unusable: brackish, leaf and bug-filled. The pool sweep was upside down and rusted, like a dead kelp monster.

We had two old patients living in the European Care Home. I lived in one of the five bedrooms with my girlfriend. Her mother lived in another, next to ours. Four patient beds lay empty.

The money earned from the two patients barely covered the care home's mortgage payments. I was no help: in fact, I'd moved there in large part because I had no money. Meanwhile, my scabies infection only got worse and worse. It baffled the doctors. First I was told it was a simple rash, and prescribed Cortisone. That made it spread. So I was given stronger Cortisone. I'd squirt the white cream on my ass, but the relief was only temporary. As I later found out, there's nothing scabies mites love more than Cortisone-treated skin. It makes the flesh softer, chewier. Applying Cortisone was like tilling the soil: all the mites had to do now was fuck, and they'd create one of the largest human scabies settlements on planet earth. And fuck they did. When I couldn't stand the itching anymore, I took my ass to another doctor. He diagnosed me with scabies, so he gave me a tube of Elimite. I spent the next week in itch-agony. That Elimite was like napalm. I couldn't tear my skin off. I was like that Vietnamese child from the war posters, crying and running naked down the rice paddy avenue, only I wasn't in a rice paddy. I was in the European Care Home, on Sand Hill Court, and no weeping hippie was going to hold up an anti-arachnid protest placard of me scratching myself.

The world was caving in on all sides of us. The bank called my girlfriend's mother every week, and soon, every day. The telephone's long distance service was cut off. Once they even cut off our gas. Then one of the patients, Lydia, who looked like a dehydrated old hippopotamus, collapsed and couldn't stand up. She shat all over her room. She must have weighed 250 pounds. Even I had to pitch in to help her up, although I wasn't allowed to get too close to anyone, due to my scabies.

I might have felt more sympathy for Lydia, but my scabies infestation had entered a new, unprecedented stage—and so had my selfishness. They transformed into what are called "nodal" or "Norwegian" scabies. My mites were the Albert Speers of the arachnid world. They constructed about thirty or so bunkers on my ass: hardened, red nodules which rendered the Kwell lotion and Elimite lotion useless—mere defoliants, causing my ass-hairs to fall out. Each bunker-node, as I later learned, could house up to a thousand mites.

We needed a new patient, before Lydia croaked on us. Mrs. Klausova, my girlfriend's mother, was willing take anything that still twitched, so long as it had deep pockets. She hit up some shady agency that locates potential care home patients. They reached for the bottom of the barrel and came up with two insane "clients." No other Peninsula care home would consider these two. They should have had those electric-shock collars locked around their necks and kept in a basement under a trap door; you'd throw them a raw piece of meat every so often, and that's it.

The minute they moved in, Lydia was tossed out. She was demoted to a nursing home in a neighboring Peninsula suburb, Millbrae, where she later died. I would have hugged her goodbye, but I didn't want to give her my scabies. Living in that care home made me meaner than ever.

So now we had three patients: two new ones, and the old reliable veteran, Joanne. One of the crazy new patients suffered from some kind of advanced form of emphysema. She needed an oxygen tank in her room. There was a red plastic "No Smoking" sign pinned outside of her bedroom door, on orders from her social worker. She smoked anyway. When she talked, it sounded like she was gargling broken glass. She had a way of escaping the European Care Home with regularity. I couldn't understand it. It wasn't like she was Papillon or anything. You could give her a ten-minute head start from her bedroom to the front door, and you'd still be able to stick her midway down the hallway and put her on injured reserve for 4–6 months. But somehow, she'd slip out, only to be brought back by her social worker, who'd lecture us all.

The other patient, Doris, suffered from an extreme case of Panic Attack Syndrome. I'd never heard of Panic Attack until she moved in. She'd wake up almost every night in fear. Her attacks began with a long, drawn-out moan, like some *Exorcist* demon. That went on for the first hour or so. Then she'd call for my girlfriend's mother. "Eva . . . Eva . . . Eva? Eva? . . . Eva! Eeee-Vaa!!!"

Mrs. Klausova handled it all pretty well at first. She'd been a nurse back in Czechoslovakia. She'd probably seen much worse out there. Her only problem was that she didn't understand America too well. She couldn't fathom the concept of "patients' rights," for example. As in, "Thou shalt not beat thine patients."

CHAPTER ONE

I almost never left my bedroom. I put on about 30 pounds, and lost all my color. I'd read Russian novels, dream about that two-week vacation in Leningrad, about the street punks I'd hung out with during that two-week incursion, or the girl, Olga, who became my temporary girlfriend and with whom I'd traded love vows. Olga, the half-Estonian, petite redhead. We met at some metal-head's party on Vasilyevsky Island. She asked me to dance, which was strange: his apartment was just one room of a communal flat. And the music was something like Slayer or Megadeth, blasted so loud that the speakers distorted. But I danced with her anyway. The next time we met there, Olga took me into the corner for sex. My friends were in the the same room; the "bedroom" was really just a corner of the room partitioned off by some cheap shower curtains. He and his friends blasted his television on the far side of the room while Olga and I fucked in his bed. I think I caught the scabies from her.

One thing I learned about Russians during that vacation was that they made every day count. They weren't looking to relax in front of the television and watch ESPN and talk about their mutual funds and eat at ethnic restaurants. They were looking for action. It seemed as though there, in Leningrad, in 1991, things were possible. You were always on the street, running into someone who'd just had some problem with so-and-so; girls would bump into you, and you'd make plans to meet up later; your bandit friends would hassle you, then split without a word. It was so alien, and yet, I felt more at ease there than anywhere I'd ever been. The air was cold and wet in Leningrad. They didn't oppress you with their pod-people smiles and affected self-confidence the way they did in California. In fact, they looked every bit as miserable as I'd felt inside for, oh, as long as I could remember. And yet, oddly, they were so much more alive than, say, the neighbors in our cul-de-sac on Sand Hill Court. In Foster City, you just never saw those people.

With the addition of the two new patients, the European Care Home looked solvent again. After about six months, my scabies infection began to recede. My dermatologist prescribed a tar ointment to apply to the node-bunkers on my ass. We'd dissolve their armor, then gas the nest.

We tried sedating Doris. Nothing worked: not lithium, not Valium, not Xanax, not Lorazepams. Every night, she'd panic.

Once, at about three A.M., Mrs. Klausova barged out into the hallway and slapped Doris in the face. And slapped her again. I remember hearing everything go quiet.

Then Doris, with a hurt tone, said, "You just hit me."

"Yes I did!" Mrs. Klausova said. "Now, go back to your room!"

Doris quietly returned to her bedroom.

Two days later, a social worker arrived with a police officer. Then another social worker came. They evacuated all three patients and closed down the European Care Home. Mrs. Klausova was threatened with criminal prosecution. My girlfriend and her mother were a mess. Not since they escaped Communist Czechoslovakia, spending two days and nights sneaking through the northern Austrian forests, slipping into Germany, had they been so frightened. Not since the Czech interrogations that Mrs. Klausova had endured had authorities put her through so much hell. She didn't know that in California, there was an equally evil, insidious Securitate: social workers. She threatened to commit suicide. So did my girlfriend.

The bank foreclosed the house and put it on the auction block. It sold for less than they'd bought it for three years earlier. They were ruined. We all were ruined.

The only good news was that I'd finally killed off the last of the scabies settlements on my ass, some nine months after they'd first colonized me. The flesh was pockmarked and scaly; the hairs brittle and dead. It looked like Verdun. Verdun in victory.

My first aborted attempt at fleeing California was a nine-month stint in Prague, from mid-'92 to early '93. After the European Care Home was closed down, Mrs. Klausova borrowed money from her friends in the Bay Area Czech émigré community, and packed up for her homeland. Not like they were UNICEF, these Czech émigré friends of hers. When the European Care Home was seeing good times, the Czechs did everything to destroy her. They spread ugly rumors about Mrs. Klausova and her daughter. Now that she'd failed, they were all willing to finance her humiliating return to Czechoslovakia, a country whose very name made these immigrants cringe in shame. That should have said something to me about Czech culture, but I didn't pay attention. I figured that anything—literally *anything*—had to be better than Foster City.

Prague sounded like a great option: it was cold, alien, polluted, lumpenprole-ish, and yet European—ingredients for a minor epic. With my connections through my girlfriend, I was bound to find some success! I even decided that I didn't mind working a "job" there to make money. We'd cooked up a few schemes. We were going to import used, broken cars from West Germany, fix them up using mechanics from Mrs. Klausova's village in Nova Poka, in northern Bohemia, then resell them in Prague for a profit. The whole thing seemed foolproof. Not because I knew anything about business, but because they made it sound foolproof. I bought a Berlitz book to learn Czech. I read up on the history. It didn't compare to Russia, but I tried to be enthusiastic. I thumbed through travel books at the local bookstore. I read some of Marina Tsvetaeva's poems from when she was an exile in Prague. I began imagining myself, anonymous, wealthy, bundled up in sweaters and an overcoat and gloves. . . . Cold, alone, wealthy. That sounded nice. I'd be able to write in peace. It would be a kind of minor epic exile. Lonely, true, but at least I'd finally get away from the country that gave me so little.

Then we arrived. My girlfriend found us an apartment in the center, in an artist's attic studio, on the seventh floor of a turn-of-the-century Art Deco, late–Austrian Empire building. We bought a two-inch foam pad, laid it on the floor, and used it as a mattress. Once again, we were together. Like a couple. That's when I realized how little I cared for her. In fact, she sickened me. Her evil femme fatale stance had excited me at once, way back when, before all the scabies mites got between us. Then it bored me. And now, it plain sickened me. Every night in that Prague attic I found myself cooking up newer and newer ways of avoiding having to fuck her.

It wasn't just Radka who was at fault. There was something about Prague I began to detect, something that didn't quite jibe with the intelligence reports I'd submitted to myself back in Foster City. For one thing, there were tourists everywhere. The more I looked, the more I was shocked. Then the shock turned to terror. I was sure that I even saw American students. Must be tourists too, I thought. But I was wrong.

Half of America's youth had already moved to Prague before me. They'd scooped me. I'd not only NOT escaped America, I'd landed smack in the condensed thing-in-itself, everything horrible about my generation and the generation about-to-be, the generation named after Billy Idol's bubblegum punk band from the mid-'70s: the I'm-like-lost-you-know? Generation X. There were an estimated 30,000 young, nose-ringed, torn-jeansed English-speaking students squatting in the center of Prague, and there weren't a thang I could do about it. I'd come there to make a quick, hot buck with my Czech girlfriend, and wound up getting squeezed out by grunge-hippies half my age. I paced our attic, cursing, "They've gentrified my paradigm! They've gentrified my paradigm!"

It was as if they'd taken a huge needle, sucked the genetic material out of Foster City, and injected it straight into the nucleus of Prague. As for the Czechs: mere groveling Uncle Tomaš's, West German wannabes.

Nothing was going to happen here, in Prague. It was the anaesthetized '90s. The European Care Home of the world.

My obsession with Russia only grew. The difference between Prague in 1992 and Russia of 1991 was the difference between some silly art house film and *Terminator.* I'd tell that to the few bohos I met, and they were shocked in a condescending way: Why would anyone want to go to Russia? was their unanimous reaction. That only made me more determined—because I realized that, if everyone in Prague shuddered at the thought of heading to Russia, where the people were cruel and savage and gunning each other down in the streets, where food couldn't be found and phone calls couldn't be made, then . . . that would mean . . . these people WOULDN'T BE THERE! Every day, my anger grew, anger at myself for fucking up yet again, and at these people for gentrifying my paradigm.

I took it out on my girlfriend. Her used-car scheme fell apart. Her mother had run off with an abusive ex-boyfriend from Germany. I resented her and I resented her insignificant dump of a country.

She was no angel herself. Nearly every Václav in town was tapping into her the second I'd turn my back. I even met a few of them. One had a ponytail and tried emulating the American grunge-hippies. Another bragged about his Audi car and the shopping sprees in Stuttgart. I dumped her and

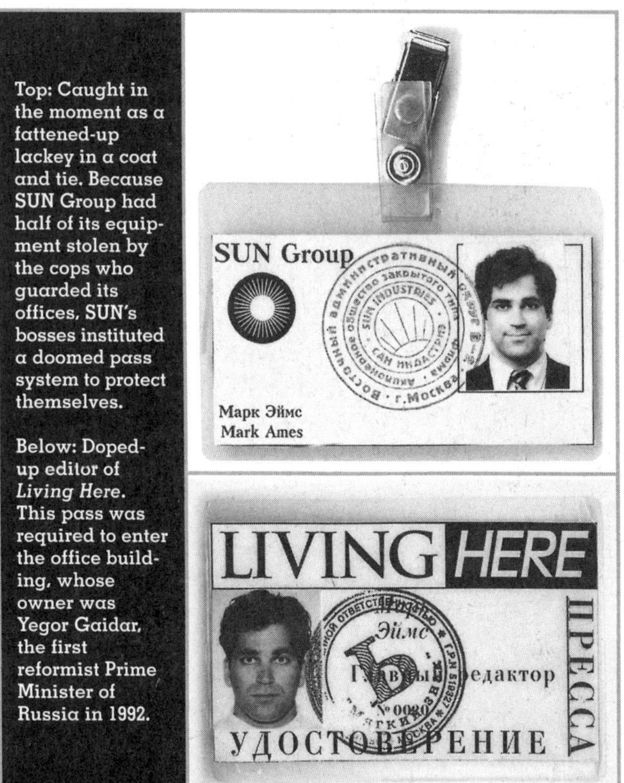

Top: Caught in the moment as a fattened-up lackey in a coat and tie. Because SUN Group had half of its equipment stolen by the cops who guarded its offices, SUN's bosses instituted a doomed pass system to protect themselves.

Below: Doped-up editor of *Living Here.* This pass was required to enter the office building, whose owner was Yegor Gaidar, the first reformist Prime Minister of Russia in 1992.

moved out on my own, into a dark, ugly apartment that reeked of urine and old tea. I'd go out to teach English to Czech businessmen. They wanted to impress upon me how Westernized they were, which made me loathe them even more. They all stank of beer and cheap deodorant. Then I'd come home and dream about Russia: violent, sexual, chaotic, too authentic for these fucks. Russia had become legendary in my mind, the more my own life diminished. The memory of those two weeks in Leningrad transformed into epic poetry: the all-night drinking and pot-smoking, the young petty criminals who took us into basement hangouts for more pot-smoking, the beautiful girls in their cheap clothes, sitting quietly. . . . Russia was the antimatter that the physicists of my mind had been searching for all those years. I had to get back there. But how?

Do you know how difficult that was to imagine—that "I" had the "right" to "move" to Russia?! It may seem easy to a lot of people, but not to me. I couldn't imagine that I had that right. So I moved back to California, to a situation far more frightening than even the European Care Home.

Unable to imagine that there was an easier way, I figured that the door to Russia led through the burning fire of California.

Russia . . . Russia was like the deep ocean floor. Almost totally undiscovered, inaccessible, and unappealing to the crude, space-obsessed Western mind.

My stepfather was diagnosed with brain cancer, giving me the perfect cover for retreating from central Europe and regrouping in the south Bay Area.

Glioblastoma, the most lethal brain cancer of all: tumors that grow as if in a sped-up time-elapsed film, ensuring a quick and ugly death. About 13,000 die of it every year in America. And he'd been chosen.

I moved into my father's house, in a suburb in San Jose, and commuted ten minutes away, up into the foothills, where my dying stepfather and my mother lived. I offered to help as much as I could, on the understanding that somehow, fate would pluck me from that baking-hot, smog-stuffed valley, out to Russia.

My stepfather and I never got along. I resented his successful crawl up the middle-class rungs. For him, it was an escalator ride. Now he was pretty much at the top, in a two-story house on the valley side of the rolling Santa Cruz foothills—God's own real estate.

He never liked me either. As far as he was concerned, I was an arrogant intellectual, a morbid creep. Then he got sick, and, suddenly, he wanted to understand me. When I returned from Prague, he greeted me with that new, radiation-sculpted mohawk, not all that different from the half-assed mohawk I once had in my punk days, a haircut he'd once mocked incessantly as proof that I'd never amount to anything.

Shortly after I returned home to help him, it seemed that he was on his way to a quick death. Then, miraculously, he pulled out of it and went into remission. His cocky instincts resurfaced and told him that he'd licked the glio. Recovery made him the same selfish, crocodilian bastard I'd always remembered him as. The first thing that upset him was that I was driving his Jeep Cherokee. He wanted it back. He accused me of running up 30,000 miles on it in a single month, even though all I did was drive back and forth between the flatland suburbs where my father lived and his hillside manor. One day, he took the Jeep keys from me and told me that if I wanted to drive a car, I'd have to get a job and buy one for myself. Until the tumors started to bloom again, my only wheels were a borrowed ten-speed.

I'm recounting all of this to put my defection into context. In America, it wasn't so much that life was boring and I

standard, sauna, videointercom, concierge. DELIGHT, 926-4222.

OKTYABRSKAYA, 120 sq.m., Westernized, jacuzzi, 549-5385, 961-0687.

PATRIARSHY, Western, unfurnished, equipped kitchen, concierge, 915-4000.

KROPOTKINSKAYA, concierge, Western, furnished, 915-4000.

TVERSKAYA, Western, unfurnished, intercom, 915-4000.

ARBAT, 180 sq.m., luxury family residence, two bedrooms, sauna, $8,000, 155-7901/7702.

ARBAT, 130, 180, 200, 260 sq.m., new prestigious building, 956-2461.

BEATRIX.

OPPOSITE MARRIOTT, 150 sq.m., 2 bathrooms, $6,000. EVANS 232-6703/04.

ROSINKA: 3 bedrooms, 2.5 baths, a/c, pool, garage, $6000, 940-5838.

SIX ROOMS AND UP

KROPOTKINSKAYA, BEST!, 6 bedrooms, 956-2461.

KUTUZOVSKY PR., 150 sq.m., after renovation, quiet, $3500, 916-3182.

CHISTIYE PRUDY, 260 sq.m., 2 levels, Western standard, 3 bathrooms, sauna.DELIGHT, 926-4222.

My mouse-infested $150-a-month dacha where I lived before returning to Moscow to start up the *eXile*. Above: a sample of apartment prices in Moscow in spring 1998.

needed something exciting—"boredom" isn't something I've ever suffered from. You don't have time to be bored when you're afraid and failing. It was so cold. Cold and terrifying. And the worst part of it all was that everyone around me seemed to think that nothing was wrong, that this was all NORMAL.

Those Berkeley dreams I once had of shaking up the Beigeist world were long gone. I may as well have declared war on dust. I'd given up. I just wanted to get the fuck out of this inverted madhouse. Out to Russia.

My stepfather's close friends couldn't deal either, but for different reasons. Seeing their golfing buddy slumped in a wheelchair with the fear of death scrawled on his sallow face was too much to bear. They couldn't "deal," as we say in California. There was always this odor around him, a metallic odor, that smelled like death. It was, to use another local expression, a real bummer. One was too busy with his start-up software company. Another, who had followed my stepfather out from North Dakota to California with Control Data Corp, didn't see him more than three or four times. He lived in the maze, down the hill, a five-minute drive away. He may as well have been living in Tasmania.

My stepfather's eyes developed this creepy glaze. They looked fake, like gag-store marbles. That was partly from drugs, but also from fear. His breath had a sour, metallic odor—a cocktail of tumor-shrinking steroids and death.

As for my mother . . . all of her friends had abandoned her; her husband's friends disappeared; his company downsized him and slashed his health benefits. She was really alone. My mother's way of dealing with it was tennis, and her golden retriever, Nicklaus Palmer.

My stepfather grew to hate Nicklaus Palmer—even though he'd bought it and named it. He'd try kicking the dog when he had the strength. The dog didn't really care. Nothing bothers a golden retriever. Even when the dog lost 20 pounds from a pancreatic disorder, he was still happy. And hungry. Niklaus Palmer would always sit next to my stepfather at the kitchen table, knowing that he was too sick to finish his meal. Mammals have that sixth sensc; they can smell weakness in a fellow mammal. The cancer killed my stepfather's appetite. Once he'd leave the table, Niklaus Palmer would lean up and swipe the barely eaten food. He was a real ham, that dog.

For all of my own mean, selfish traits, one thing I was equipped for was tragedy and death. When it came to the theory side, I was a Ph.D. I'd always been attracted to the grotesque, to human ugliness, everything that the suburbs hid. Not like I had much practice. In fact, I'd never seen a corpse before my stepfather's. CalTrans road crews work quick. They don't even have the courtesy to leave a few bloodstains on the center divider after a head-on car crash. Everything unpleasant gets sandblasted.

My stepfather's death didn't horrify me the way it did everyone else. What scared me was how effortlessly he'd been pushed out of their world. That part was impossible to prepare for. I just figured that in some way, I deserved to be marginalized, whereas he—he was the embodiment of California: successful, cocky, a die-hard 49ers fan with framed watercolors of the 49ers and golfers and yachts in piers hanging on the walls . . . . As it turned out, even my stepfather was expendable, and that really scared me. You couldn't just argue that life was some beret-capped, meaningless Camus novel anymore.

The accumulation of this suburban nihilism led to a severe mental breakdown, about the worst I've ever suffered. As I later learned, I'd come down with Panic Attack Syndrome. Doris from the European Care Home had moved into my mind, scratching at my skull. For about two months, I couldn't breathe or look anyone in the eye. I had to bottle it up. I drank a lot and read a lot: especially about serial murderers. Russia's gold-medal mass murderer, Andrei Chikatilo, loomed large in my reading and rereading habits.

It's funny, but as I'm writing this chapter, the trendy Russian magazine *Ptyutch* has asked me to write an article about the "craziest" day or experience in my life, and I know what they want to hear: something to do with sex, drugs, or death. But I look back at those six months I spent in the solitary confinement of my mind, in the boiling-hot suburbs of Silicon Valley, cooped up at my father's—twenty-seven years old, unemployed, unemployable—and I know that few could survive that. On the crazy-scale, nothing could compare to those long, baking-hot days in the San Jose suburbs, taking a bottle of milk over to my stepfather, listening to him blather, demanding from me an accounting of the mileage I'd put on his Jeep Cherokee, then groaning from pain and groveling for forgiveness for the way he'd once treated me . . .

For the most part, I did my best to help out my stepfather. I'd walk him to the toilet to piss. That wasn't easy: he weighed about 210, though his wilted legs looked like Gandhi's. I'd drive him to his chemotherapy appointments in Palo Alto. He'd sit in a small room hooked up to an IV that slowly pumped some kind of toxic Hawaiian Punch into his arm. It took about six hours to drain the chemo bag. By the end, he'd be wiped out and in pain. As if bees were slowly stinging his arms, as if wasps had crawled into his veins. I'd walk him to the Cherokee, and drive him home. I'd buy him his protein chocolate drinks and cartons of milk from Long's. That was all he could keep down, even if he popped fifty Zantacs. I'd battle his company and health insurers to keep them from cutting his benefits. He appreciated it. When his tumor popped up again in his frontal lobe and quickly mushroomed, pushing him back onto his deathbed, he gave me back the Jeep Cherokee keys and told me to drive it as much as I wanted. It was his way of repenting.

I was good, but not selfless in the least. See, Control Data (renamed Ceridian Corp after the "restructuring") was famous for its Carter-era détente business relationship with the Soviet regime. They were one of the few companies, particularly in the high-tech area, willing to and allowed to work with the Soviets. There was, as they say, a connection.

My stepfather made his living selling defense electronics equipment to corrupt Southeast Asian generals, but his friends had started up a few small-time ventures in the Soviet Union, which meant . . . which meant if I help stepdaddy through his death, he could lean on his friends and help deliver me to the Promised Land. A classic "I scratch your back, you scratch mine"; or, in this case, I mop the piss up from your bed, and you line up a Russian visa for me!

From the minute I came back from Prague, my stepfather used his contacts to try to line up a Russia-based job for me. He hooked me up with a shyster named Bob Winfrey, some flashy right-wing Southerner who sometimes snared government funds for his ventures, owing to his 1/16 Native American blood. Winfrey went so far as to fly me out to Virginia to meet his Russian counterparts. He had charisma, the gift of the gab. Silk hankies and three-piece suits, even in the middle of the swamp-humid D.C. summer.

I failed him badly. He'd assumed I already spoke Russian, and asked me to interpret a meeting between himself and three Russian scientists on a deal, using U.S. government funds, to set up a computer-aided design lab in Moscow. I'd barely even cracked my first "Learn to Speak Russian in 40 Days" book open when I arrived. The only word I understood was when the little red-bearded fascist referred to me as a "*zhid*." At night, we ate at the Mannassas, VA, Red Lobster. The Russians all ordered three lobsters apiece, tearing them apart like rabid sea otters. I hid my admiration, and quietly endured the American side's condescending whispers.

Within a month, Winfrey's project died.

Then I was introduced to Al Parker, my stepfather's childhood friend. He had a stake in some small wine-trading company in Russia. He couldn't understand why I'd want to move to Russia. He thought they were a bunch of fuck-ups and savages. Then again, you could sucker an easy buck out of them, he told me, laughing. Ah, that was music to my ears: please, God, let them be fuck-ups and savages! My kinda people!

My stepfather finally died. I'd avoided him the weekend before, because I had gone half-insane myself. He spent the last weekend of his life screaming in pain. He begged my mother not to let him die—he was afraid.

When I finally got my courage up to see him, he was already in a coma. By that time, he was just a gurgling torso. The barrel-torso convulsed with every breath. He'd contracted pneumonia from being bedridden so long. Breathing in, he gargled lightly. When he exhaled, the gargling was amplified, a water bong of lung fluid, like the *Eraserhead* baby. He died while I was in another room calling Delta Airlines to book my ticket to Moscow.

Out of sympathy for me, Al arranged my Russian visa. He got me the necessary letters, which I took up to the Russian Consulate in San Francisco, in Pacific Heights. I was sure they'd deny me. But they didn't. In fact, it went as smoothly as possible, smoother than most American government agencies I'd dealt with. I finally had it: a lavender visa, with the Cyrillic letters, specifying actual dates that I was allowed to enter.

That was how I finally got into Russia. From my first trip there in September 1991, to my move in September 1993.

Of course, it all could have been done a bit easier. I didn't know at the time that all you had to do was contact a local travel agent, pay a $200 fee, and you'd have a one-year, multi-entry visa. One or two simple phone calls, with the words, "Hello, I'd like to purchase a visa." I thought I was cunning, even coldly ambitious, by taking that 2-year roundabout scheme, from the European Care Home to Prague, then back to my dying stepfather, in order to secure a three-month single-entry visa. I thought that suffering a needless mental breakdown, those long Panic Attacks, were the war wounds necessary in order to achieve my objective. No pain, no gain.

Two weeks after I moved to Moscow, Yeltsin disbanded the parliament and civil unrest began. By chance, I happened to move to a dirty little apartment only five bus stops from the White House. The administrative parliament in my district, Krasnopresnensky, voted to side with the rebels. That meant I was living in rebel territory, in the very center of the Russian empire! I lived in a dirty Khrushchev-era apartment building, one of zillions of block-buildings planted as if haphazardly on any open piece of land in Moscow. There were no suburban zoning Nazis in Moscow. Just build 'em where you can! My neighbors warned me about the Azerbaidjani refugees, who'd jump and mug me if they knew I was an American. They were ashamed of the decaying state of their apartments.

The courtyard was a mess of weeds and ditches with exposed pipes, and a broken monkey-bar set.

"It must be so much more beautiful in America, in California," the old Tatar woman next door would tell me with a mixture of sadness and shame.

But it wasn't. This was the surface life that I dreamed of. While the few expats I knew sneered at how the Russians fucked everything up and spoke of Western beauty—the kind of familiar, clichéd beauty of European travel books and suburban development brochures—I treasured these sites, these Socialist ruins. And then a week later it snowed—in my neighborhood, outside my window, covering the monkey bars and the sickly birches and the courtyard blemishes. Snow in September!

A week after that, in my very own neighborhood, civil war broke out. It started on October 3, my 28th birthday. The rebels stormed out of the White House and seized surrounding territory, disbanding and beating Yeltsin's riot troops. They fanned out from the Novy Arbat, down to Smolenskaya Ploschad, then raced down to the Ostankino TV tower. I was watching the television as the battle there began. The announcer was terrified. And suddenly, just the way it happened in *Dawn of the Dead*, my TV went blank. The old Tatar woman from next door invited me over. She couldn't stop crying. I couldn't understand a word she said. She had a full set of metal teeth that wouldn't stop crunching. Through those teeth, she went on about World War Two, I think . . . something about having to evacuate Moscow to Kazan . . . her dead husband. . . . That night, I could barely sleep. It wasn't just my birthday—it was as if I was finally born on that day.

The next morning, October 4, I awoke to the sound of a cannon boom. Tanks! I stuck my head out of my window. The weather was warm and sunny, with a light breeze. All the snow had long since melted. I dressed in very conspicuous California clothes: shorts, T-shirt, hooded top, and black beat-up Nike low-tops, then headed outside, into the symphony of gunfire. I figured that my Nikes might act as a sort of foreigner-shield, a medieval cloak. I only intended to "check it out," but I wound up spending the entire day touring the war zones in the Krasnopresnensky Park, the naberezhnaya, the Sovincenter, the deserted Sadko Arcade shopping mall. Everywhere around you, there was a choir of small-arms fire, sometimes picking up, sometimes subsiding. A gun battle breaks out, somewhere behind a building . . . the cracking of small-arms is followed by an answer—then the whole orchestra picks up, subsides, then builds into a crescendo, before disappearing, only to reappear in another zone. Tank fire boomed from down the road, at Kutuzovsky Most. Helicopters flew overhead. Nervous militiamen manned posts on the streets. Some retreated to their stations. I couldn't stay indoors. It was as if Russia was offering me this reward as compensation for all the bland hell I'd been through. I'd waited twenty-seven years for this. I spent the entire day, heart pumping, walking from one end of my district to the other, watching the BMPs fire their machine guns and the trucks carrying troops.

On the naberezhnaya, I gathered with a crowd of Russians to watch the tanks fire into the White House. Snipers took aim at us. Bullets were ringing off the lampposts and the heavy cargo trucks parked on a lot behind us. We scattered for cover, although I was the last to actually hide. Meaning . . . I was tougher than the Russians! Or stupider. Either way, I was proud. At one point, while war-strolling in the park, I stood next to a crack OMON soldier as he knelt behind a half-finished cement wall, firing his automatic. He had to be the coolest-dressed soldier I'd ever seen: silk-black jumpsuit uniform, with the yellow "OMON" patch on his back, polished black boots, and spotless Kalashnikov in arm. I had no idea what he was firing at. There must have been infiltrators in the park. I wanted to get a better look. I stood up on the slab, and balanced. The OMON soldier looked up at me, in shock, grabbed my shirt, and pulled me down, swearing. Elsewhere in the park, while gunfire rattled, a group of men drank vodka and played chess. On a bench farther down, a woman lay on her back, reading a book.

Within a month, I saw my first dead body, lying in the metro. People passed it as if it was mere trash. Then, later, on the streets, more corpses. Two in one day!

Besides corpses, I began to notice a sexual pulse that I'd never experienced. The girls were stunning in their cheap imitation Italian-style clothes, their lace see-through blouses and garish pink or purple coats, and the overdone makeup on their faces. They looked at you —actually *looked at you*, invitingly. No one looked at you in the Bay Area.

Kara's ass: seen here cut off from the picture frame, nevertheless you can make out almost 1/8th of its volume. The bald, shriveled man in the foreground, photographer John Reynard, is afraid to look up.

People stumbled on the streets, drunken. Police

openly beat the weak and extracted bribes, even from me. Nights were dimly lit: the headlights were dim, the storefronts dim, the apartment-block windows a dirty gold-yellow of cheap lighting. No more cheap sentimentality, no cover-ups or impressions of a brighter future.

In early December, I went with some friends to a concert by the punk band Grazhdanskoye Oborona. The minute we arrived, three busloads of low-rent OMON riot police pulled up. A crowd of perhaps a thousand punks crowded on the far end of a long field between some darkened apartment blocks and the concert hall. The OMON troops were carrying shotguns and truncheons. Everything was sloppy and careless. Even the rickety buses looked like they'd been commandeered from some junkyard lot. Then they lined up and fired the shotguns. The punks backed off, and retaliated by launching bottles. A riot broke out. We almost got the shit beat out of us by the cops. One threatened me with his truncheon. My friend Vova ran up and convinced the OMON soldier not to crack me over the head.

The punks attacked, got beaten to a bloody pulp by the middle-aged redneck troops, then hurried away. Trams were set on fire, windows smashed. I saw one kid get beaten literally unconscious, his nose exploding like a thin balloon from a blow of the truncheon. Another held his snapped arm, but didn't cry. It was such a contrast to the poseurs in the punk world of San Francisco, with their harmless, body-pierced stances and kitsch nihilism. The evening ended in failure, but a kind of heroic failure.

I had finally arrived home. This was it: the anti-California. True exile.

There is no meaningful, linear time graph to trace the period between my defection from California to the *eXile*. In between, there were "jobs." My first job was selling wines for Al Parker's company. I soon quit, then went into trade with a Mauritian Indian who lived in southern Russia, in Krasnodar. He knew buyers; I knew some expats who were importing goods like medical supplies and stereo equipment. I'd put on a suit, fly down, and act like a serious American businessman. That snowed over the local Russian buyers. We'd tack on 50 percent margins, kick part of it back to the Russian purchaser, then split the rest for ourselves. Then I spent almost two years as the whipping boy of a Pakistani entrepreneur who'd set up a big investment operation scam in Russia. I'd signed up to be his personal secretary, thinking it would give me a steady income while I wrote; instead, I wound up dedicating my every waking hour to his needs. The job was a wild, painful ride through the worlds of investment banking, conferences, petty scamming, social climbing, and lackeydom. Heavy on the lackeydom. Somehow I put up with it all and then some. I had to do things like make sure that his maid had cooked him dinner, or that his witch-mother was escorted from the airport to her apartment. I'd take a verbal lashing almost every day. I learned something about myself: I'd make a damn good slave.

I finally quit when a startup newspaper called *Living Here* offered me a job as their feature columnist. It was my way out. The main expatriate newspaper, *The Moscow Times*, had just printed an old article of mine, "The Rise and Fall of Moscow's Expat Royalty," which caused a minor scandal among the colonialists. *Living Here* didn't really have any direction, but they thought that if I wrote more articles like that, they'd at least have some readers.

Living Here was an accident. The idea for starting up a third expat newspaper in Moscow to compete with *The Moscow Times* and *The Moscow Tribune* came from Manfred Witteman, a failed Dutch musician who had spent years slogging around the *Moscow Times*' offices, fixing computers and playing the feckless alcoholic comic relief. Somehow he convinced his rich, squat 23-year-old ex-girlfriend, Marina Pshevecharskaya, to pony up $10,000 to start up a newspaper. Marina was a classic "Westernized Russian," a squealing suck-up to any expat. Marina drove a Volvo and hung out at expat parties. She made her money quick and easy, acting as an agent for expats seeking apartments. She'd take a month's rent in commission, in a city ranked as the third most expensive city in the world, after Tokyo and Osaka.

Living Here was originally conceived as a real estate and community newspaper for expatriates—that way, Marina would get an immediate return via free publicity for her agency—but the idea was lame, and it fizzled. It just didn't make much sense. Manfred finally hooked an editor, a young Oxford-grad journalist desperate to be hip, who turned *Living Here* into a kind of rudderless *Time Out*–style nightlife guide on the inside, and a real estate newspaper on the outside. He quit after a few issues, and I took over as editor.

Under me, *Living Here* transformed into both a sniper's nest from which to pick off personal enemies, and an irresponsible chronicle of everything vulgar and grotesque. The one thing *Living Here* aggressively lacked was straight journalism. I had a prejudice against the very concept—and I was too lazy to give it a go. The newspaper was a totally uncensored, sloppy, irresponsible take on the violent culture of modern Moscow. Since no one covered that side of the story—everyone was too interested in top-level politics and economics—we wound up claiming a little chunk of turf. I was pretty sure there was nothing like Moscow in the world. Everyone who lived here felt that; and yet, for some reason, the official Western-reported version of events always made it seem more familiar than it really was. Simple, decent people's struggle to transform Russia into suburban California. And the difficulties they encountered.

You only dreamed of places like this back in California. You listened to your Lou Reed albums and read your Philip K. Dick books and watched *Blade Runner*, trying to scrape some of the experience off the edges of the medium. But from out there, in the flattest, cleanest, most comfortable coastline on earth, a Moscow wasn't even imaginable. The only Moscow imaginable was the Moscow as measured by the American/European yardstick: how close or far, and at what rate, Russia was approaching Palo Alto. From my point of view, Russia was to be celebrated for everything outside of those measurements.

Before quitting *Living Here*, I'd moved out to a small village about 1 1/2 hours outside of Moscow. I had to get away from Manfred and Marina, and their incessant petty squabbles over money and title. I rented an *izba,* a dilapidated old cottage on an unpaved dirt road, just across the street from a crumbling white church. I'd take two-hour baths in the tub in my kitchen, next to the gas-fed heating pipes, while snow collected outside the windows, covering all the rusted debris in the backyard. No one bothered me except for the mutts in the neighbor's yard, always yelping, or the huge construction trucks making a racket on their way out to a new site, where they were building grotesque million-dollar dachas for bankers and customs officials. Those construction trucks would tear up the road, churning up mud and spitting it in every direction.

Weekends, I'd bus into Moscow and stay with my friend Andy. It was a bus ride from peasantry to baronhood. My *izba* cost $150 a month to rent. Mice gnawed on the floorboards at night, and usually wound up dead in the bathtub in the morning. The windows didn't open. There was no toilet, just a Porta Potti that I kept in the kitchen.

Andy's place couldn't have been more different. He was on the expat package, living in a huge one-bedroom apartment in the Dom Na Naberezhnoy, where Stalin had set up most of his top officials, right across the river from the Kremlin. A lot of slumber parties were ruined by the ol' knock-on-the-door here during the '30s. The building must be jammed full of Bolshevik haunts. From the outside, all you saw was this massive block of Constructivist granite and concrete and gray. But inside, at least in Andy's apartment, it was pure Western luxury. Freshly lacquered hardwood floors. Gaudy black leather Italian couches. Late-'80s industrial-black halogen lamps. A home theater surround sound stereo system (Andy was a consumer-electronics pedant with bad spending habits). Even a $13,000-dollar Jacuzzi. All thanks to his hilarious expat package at his investment bank, a package based on the theory that Russia is such a miserable, uncomfortable place to live that you have to sweeten any offer in order to attract even vaguely qualified experts. So the $3,500-a-month rent was picked up by his bank.

Andy and I would laugh about his "hardship" package: he also had no intention of returning to America. He was a colonialist of the most nihilistic sort: he wanted to milk his package for everything it was worth, fuck as many young Russian girls as he could, then retire as early as possible to some undiscovered Southeast Asian island and drink himself to death, Russian teenage wife chained to the hut. As he often explained, the disadvantage to marrying a Russian teenager is that they're bound to cheat on you; but because Russians (particularly girls) are so congenitally prejudiced against *uzkiglaziye*, or slant-eyes, he wouldn't have to worry about his teenage wife cheating on him if she was stuck on Gilligan's Island. That way, he could drink himself to death with peace of mind.

For most of the Christmas holidays, Andy was out of the country. He gave me the keys to his apartment, and I took full advantage. I should have been writing and working, but instead, I'd found, for the first time in my life, a steady supply source of some of the finest china white I've come across in my life. I took a major step: I went from sniffing to shooting. You had to, just for bragging rights. And it was easy. You could buy needles at any corner store or kiosk.

Kolya, one of my first close Russian friends, whom I'd met a few years before in his alterno-kiosk on the Novy Arbat, was the one who shot me up. He was an expert at hitting the vein, whereas I could barely stand to watch. But I had to do it—snorting heroin was getting annoying and wasteful, especially after watching Kolya shooting and getting that direct heart-pump rush.

Shooting clean china really put you in the penthouse of the drug world. We'd pop a *tchek* of china, tightly wrapped squares of paper that held about a tenth of a gram, then we'd melt into one of the gaudy Italian black-leather couches, while thick white flakes of snow fell outside the row of windows, and the snow-powdered Kremlin cupolas and domes and crenelated red walls and pine-green towers melted to create a kind of religious background, a song. . . . As if this was staged just for us. So few people, particularly postcard-brained Westerners, appreciate Moscow's beauty. Cold beauty,

CHAPTER ONE

with a volcanic pulse underneath: that's Moscow. The quaint, harmless familiar of Prague's Old Town: that's what most people are trained to worship.

But Moscow—there is no city like it in the world. Half-ruins from the cruel dreams and super-wills of the century's most successful tyrants: all granite and severe. The later, kinder socialist block apartments from the Brezhnev era. Massive turn-of-the-century imperial government buildings and office blocks, with pink and green candy colors. All mixed together on one block. All officially failures, and yet all somehow working. And inside these buildings, a people far warmer, far more naive, than calculating, Quicken-brained Americans.

If California is, to use a Russian expression, "honey on the tongue; ice underneath," then here was its inverse: "ice on the tongue; honey underneath." Sometimes, after that first knock-down rush, I'd stand up against the windowpane and stare down below, just for a few minutes, and focus my pin-pupiled eyes across the east end of the Kameny Most on to an abandoned late-Tsarist building. Abandoned real estate at the very center of the world's last, great empire! How can you resist feeling a chill! Someday, if the West has its way, all of this will be gone. Nothing will be wasted. There will be corner stores and monuments and reconstructed Disney World Tsarist ruins. But not now, not for a while, anyway.

To the right of the abandoned building, a simple, severe "park": just some tall birches and poplars, frosted over. A simple rectangular square, with a frozen fountain. A few pedestrians. Cars with their headlights on, even though it's only midafternoon. . . . To the right, the river, frozen and covered in a blanket of snow, like a bed of cotton. And then, kitty-corner to the Dom Na Naberezhnoy, across the river, another imposing central Stalin building, with its gray granite dungeon tower. And the best part—the part that's always good for a sneer from the expat colonist—is the huge, gaudy "El Dorado" neon sign, yellow and blue, with a massive video screen below, advertising the supermarket and restaurant for the new rich banditay. Here it is, *Blade Runner.* The real thing.

Kolya and I spent a lot of time banging jones and watching vids. I must have watched *Army of Darkness* and *Apocalypse Now* twenty times in the last week of 1996. I was sad to see that year evaporate. It was the best year of my life. I had acquired a tiny plot of fame from editing *Living Here,* and dividends of that little plot were paying off in the form of long afternoon-evenings floating a few inches above the Italian couch, the Kremlin lights filtered through the flurries. I was working on a novel that was going well; I'd just broken up with my girlfriend of six years. A new year was beginning. It was as if everything was possible.

Then *Living Here*'s publisher, Manfred, fucked me over. It's a petty story, I guess, the culmination of a lot of lame shit that I couldn't deal with anymore. It began months earlier with the bitchy sniping and attempts to "put me in my place" with little comments about how I'd screw this or that up. It got worse when Manfred, once the clown of the expat community, would show up to parties, hog someone's liquor, then say, "I'm the publisher of *Living Here.* What makes you cool?" Then he dicked me in the last issue. He attached my byline and picture to a piece he'd written. He did it just to piss me off. When I saw that issue, with my annoying picture in that article, I freaked. It was the last straw.

Andy was out of town the day I quit. And it's a good thing. After I quit, I was jarred awake from that long opium slumber I'd fallen into over the previous few weeks.

I'd made a wreck of Andy's apartment. Needles scattered on the living room carpet, blood squirted in the kitchen sink basin, wads of bloodied cotton. . . . Kolya had this habit of taking his used needles, dipping them into a pinkish glass of water, then squirting the diluted, infected blood across the room from the syringe. It always made me cringe, and when Kolya was later diagnosed with Hepatitis B and C, my cringe-reactions were justified. Luckily, I never shared my needles with him or anyone else. That's from my California training. Good training. Californians generally have a lower tolerance for death than Russians.

When I left *Living Here,* I hooked up with their last sales manager, a young American named Kara Deyerin, and her Jell-O-spined boyish husband, Marcus. Kara and Marcus had quit *Living Here* a month before me out of frustration. We also stole my replacement at *Living Here,* Krazy Kevin McElwee, who hadn't been paid for several issues, and Tanya Krasnikova, the shy, apple-faced journalism school student from Tula who had been with *Living Here* from its inception. That was the entire staff.

We had several potential investors: everyone from the famous liberal weekly *Moskovsky Novosti* to the trendy-techno magazine *Ptyutch* to a couple of rich expat entrepreneurs. Kara and I whipped up a business plan—just a bunch of false promises backed with numbers and graphs. We settled on a Russian nightlife guide publisher, *Ne Spat',* or Don't Sleep. The reason was simple: their publisher, Kostya Bukarev, was ready to pony up the money and staff and print right away. He didn't get too involved with the details. He just said, "*Davai!*" "Let's go!"

The weekend before our first print run, I found out that Manfred had assembled a new team of scabs, along with help from friends of his who published the Russian version of *Elle*. The reconstituted *Living Here* was threatening to sink us even before we started. I panicked. What if they won? What if, in this ugly public battle, my newspaper was sunk? I'd never—and I mean literally *never*—work in this town again. The columns and articles I'd written for *Living Here* had made me the town villain, particularly among expat directors and expat human resource managers. I'd have to tuck tail and run. But where to? Not California. Never. I began to consider Belgrade: a pariah city for a pariah guy.

It was the middle of winter in Moscow, my favorite time of the year—the time when I don't sweat. It gets dark by 3:30 in the afternoon. The snow covers many of the city's blemishes: unfinished construction sites, weeded parks, dilapidated Soviet ruins. . . . The pedestrians wear a kind of weary expression during the wintertime, dragging themselves along the ice-layered sidewalks, doing a kind of Marcel Marceau mime act to keep from falling on their faces, or into the piles of blackened slush. My spirits are highest when it's darkest and coldest outside. Unlike the German or French armies, my own armies fight best in the winter.

Even though I was boiling with adrenaline and rage, I'd still crash every few hours. In my moments of dejection, I'd play back the tapes of my pre-Moscow life. Fear. That was how I rallied my mind's troops. I knew that if I lost, it meant I was through in Moscow, and I'd have to return to that horrible plot that I'd fought so hard to escape.

Now the question was which newspaper would survive to tell the horrible, blood-and-semen-soaked story of life in the center of the last apocalypse of the 20th century: *Living Here*, or the *eXile*. Everything came down to the wire, in the first week of February 1997. Whoever put out their newspaper first basically won the war, and we both knew it.

At first Manfred and his partners at *Elle* didn't believe that we could design a new newspaper, print it up, take it to the printing press, then arrange to have it driven around to distribution points across Moscow. They focused mostly on me: I was just a fucked-up, egotistical, spiteful junkie, in their estimation, who had no idea what he was doing. They didn't believe that we could get the registration, that we knew who to speak to at the massive Pressa printing plant to allow an "O," or unregistered first issue, to run. They didn't believe that we could maintain contacts with advertising clients that Kara knew from before, or that we could write articles. This, in spite of the fact that we had the entire editorial staff, the production manager, the sales manager, and a Russian publisher with two years' experience and a team of the best computer designers in town.

We weren't dealing with geniuses here.

Our new designer, Ilya Shengin, a gray-bearded '70s intellectual whose crack always poked out of his cheap jeans, is, to this day, the greatest designer any alterno-newspaper could possibly dream of. Our publisher, Kostya Bukarev, had been doing nothing but starting up, registering, and distributing newspapers for the past three years. These minor details were left out by our competitors in the planning sessions. They were like the Germans on the eve of Operation Barbarossa: "It will be over in a few weeks."

Here I better introduce Manfred Witteman. If you've been abroad, you might know his type: a Dutch bohemian with an affected slouch and a flat Cabbage Patch doll face that masked a cold, cunning soul. When he was younger, he'd wear an "A" with a circle around it. Now, at age 30, he showed his disdain for authority by, for example, not combing his hair, riding the bus without paying, or breaking his empty beer bottles on the sidewalks.

On Monday, February 3, Manfred and Marina suddenly got nervous. So they did what they thought everyone in Russia's business world does when they get nervous: they began to wage a dirty campaign. They called the printing press—the only press in Moscow that we could use, Pressa—and warned them not to print us, or else they'd file a lawsuit. They called the Moscow City registration office for printed press and warned them not to register us. We countered with a few bottles of Martel V.S.O.P. to the right people, and it worked.

Then Jennifer Biggs, marketing manager for a top local advertising company, threw her hat in the ring.

Like many expats in Moscow, Jennifer was playing way above her head. Aged 35, former state agency employee from the English Midlands, she had transformed herself into a typical Eurotrash yuppie with the trademark tight leather pants and the requisite cell-phone in her front pocket, and the requisite chop-stash in her back pocket. . . . Those leather pants were a fucking embarrassment. You just can't wear leather pants with a middle-aged woman's saggy ass, especially when that ass leads directly northward to a turkey neck.

Jennifer and I had known each other for three years out here. Her boyfriend was my junkie-friend Kolya, whom she met through me. Jennifer and I argued a little bit about the *eXile*/*Living Here* war just as it was heating up. She'd become a real arrogant twat ever since she'd climbed the ladder from issuing driving licenses to Big Swinging Tit in the local advertising world.

CHAPTER ONE

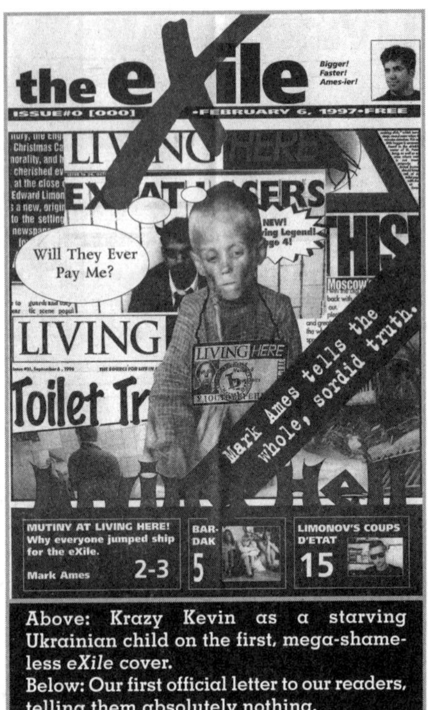

Above: Krazy Kevin as a starving Ukrainian child on the first, mega-shameless *eXile* cover.
Below: Our first official letter to our readers, telling them absolutely nothing.

Feb. 6-20, 1997 • P. 2

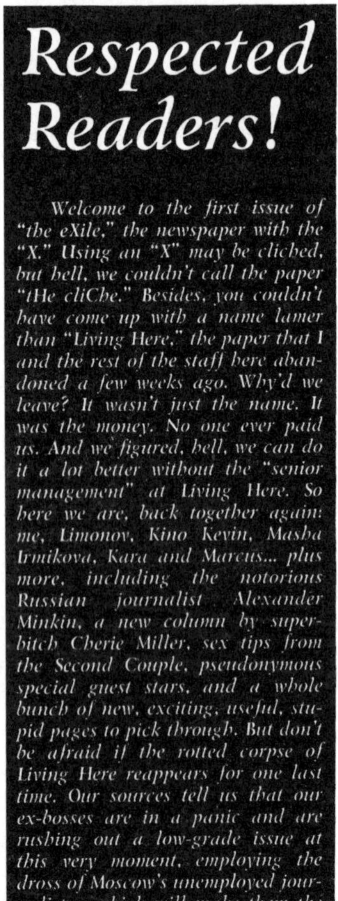

Respected Readers!

Welcome to the first issue of "the eXile," the newspaper with the "X." Using an "X" may be cliched, but hell, we couldn't call the paper "tHe cliChe." Besides, you couldn't have come up with a name lamer than "Living Here," the paper that I and the rest of the staff here abandoned a few weeks ago. Why'd we leave? It wasn't just the name. It was the money. No one ever paid us. And we figured, hell, we can do it a lot better without the "senior management" at Living Here. So here we are, back together again: me, Limonov, Kino Kevin, Masha Irmikova, Kara and Marcus... plus more, including the notorious Russian journalist Alexander Minkin, a new column by super-bitch Cherie Miller, sex tips from the Second Couple, pseudonymous special guest stars, and a whole bunch of new, exciting, useful, stupid pages to pick through. But don't be afraid if the rotted corpse of Living Here reappears for one last time. Our sources tell us that our ex-bosses are in a panic and are rushing out a low-grade issue at this very moment, employing the dross of Moscow's unemployed journalists... which will make them the

"I mean really, come on," she said. "Manfred is a publishing *genius*."

There were a lot of expats just begging to see me take a fall, after all the shit I'd written. They objected to the very concept of *Living Here*. Since it was distributed for free, they'd had no choice but to read me. The only way to shut me down was . . . well, to shut me down. The last thing they wanted was to see me succeed on my own.

Our new shared office with *Ne Spat'* was way too cramped with all of us there. The office was located on the fourth floor of a turn-of-the-century five-story building across the river from Red Square. One part of the building was owned by an arm of the Defense Ministry. There was always some gaunt young recruit in a spiffy two-tone green and lighter green Defense Ministry uniform standing outside. When you walked by, they'd either stare you down or beg for a cigarette. Usually the latter.

The far side of the building, facing the canal, housed a department of the GAI, or traffic cops. Twenty or thirty beat-up Lada cop cars always crowded into that side's entrance, along with the odd Ford Taurus or Volvo cop car. Those were for the lucky cops who successfully racketeered a local Western car dealership.

Our building wasn't kept up well. Rats ran up and down the stairs in the late hours. The interior had changed little from the early Brezhnev days: cheap beige and faded gold colors, worn thin carpet, cheap walls, cheap old doors with plastic handles that had snapped at the ends. . . . In one office, a tiny space partitioned in two, we gathered on a Monday for the final countdown, and literally didn't emerge until Thursday morning.

There were enough intrigues those three days to keep us from sleeping. On Monday afternoon, Kara's husband came running into the office, holding a fax.

"Did you read this?" Marcus asked, handing it to his wife. "I got it from Jake at Gold's Gym. He was shocked, so he gave it to me. Don't worry, honey. He didn't believe a word of it." Marcus sat down, cupped his hands, and put his fingertips to his lips, as if meditating. Kara took the letter, hid her fear, and sat down next to the computer to read.

Kara and Marcus Deyerin. Maybe back in America they make sense, but out here, they seemed like the creepiest couple I'd ever met. Not "strange" in an interesting or cool way, but rather in an icky Generation X personals-ads in the back of an alterno-newspaper sort of way. They both came from the same Seattle suburb. She went to college at some midranking small private school, while he served in the army. They married at age 21. After two eventless years in Seattle, dreaming of opening their own funky coffee shop, they skipped to Moscow.

Among other things, they were real pedants about their names. Marcus couldn't be just "Marc," while Kara always made a big deal about how you pronounced her name. Not Kara as in "*Care*-ah," like most Americans would pronounce it, but rather "*Car*-uh." As in "car." As in, you know, European. Different.

I remember people—mostly women—having those dull suburban identity crises manifested through their first names. They'd either change their names to something "unusual," or else force you to pronounce it in some obscure, difficult way. One girl from my high school officially changed her name from Renee to "Jenee"; college fling changed her name from Rosetta to Brianhan. Nothing upsets them more than when you mispronounce their name. Euro-packaging over the same bland product.

The three of us would hold our strategy meetings at my apartment. I took a tiny, spare, Brezhnevian two-room on the top floor of a brick apartment block building in Oktyabrskaya Square. We met at my place almost every night. They were like a pair of Northface mannequins in their matching midnight blue and black Gore-Tex parkas, matching Timberland boots, and matching midnight blue Gore-Tex gloves. Whenever they entered your apartment, you had to endure the ripping of Velcro tabs for like twenty minutes. There were tabs on the sleeve ends, then on the necks, on the pants, on the hats, on the gloves, on the boots, the pant cuffs, the gaiters . . . everywhere. The ripping and tearing didn't stop. It would build into a crescendo at about the ten-minute mark, then slowly subside as the layers of Gore-Tex were removed. It made you want to take a board with a rusty nail sticking out, and swing it wildly until the stuffing and Gore-Tex shreds filled your hallway. . . . Manfred, to his credit, used to refer to them as "the Mormons." He didn't get them at all.

Kara and Marcus worked at *Living Here* for a little over a month, then quit after enduring the storm of pettiness that raged between Manfred and Marina. They stuck around Moscow, trying to put together financing for their Seattle-style coffee shop idea. And then we began the *eXile.*

Actually, only Kara was my official partner. Marcus was too much of a community-college moron, and Kara ruled over him with an iron fist. He was an invertebrate, a disgrace to the male gender. At first Marcus attended our *eXile* business strategy sessions, but we must have lost half our time having to humor his baloney-brained suggestions. I could never tell if Marcus made those suggestions out of the absurd American ideology that you should always try to "pitch in," but it was getting painfully annoying.

He'd sit in our meetings, hands clasped thoughtfully in prayer, deep in concentration, then suddenly blurt out, "Why don't we try . . ." He even began making editorial suggestions and telling me what was wrong with the newspaper. In his view, we should appeal to everyone, give all points of view, and reach out to the community more. When Marcus even opened his mouth, you knew that the next twenty minutes were gone forever in the waste bin of time.

Kara finally banned her husband from attending our meetings during the crucial last two weeks. She'd send him on errands instead. It was embarrassing.

They came to Moscow with dreams of opening up a Seattle-style coffee shop, the kind where you sell Afro-Costa-Samarian coffee in those glass filter jars, where artists hang their quasi-primitive Swatch paintings on the walls for sale, where you have open-mike readings, to the background of world beat music or some lesbian folksinger. . . . Part Indigo Girls, part *Friends.* . . . A quaint dream that died along with the tales of other dead dreamers in Moscow, all those stories of expats who'd had their businesses requisitioned by bloodthirsty flatheads and Chechens. . . . I sometimes imagined Kara and Marcus's quaint little coffee shop getting visited by a Mercedes full of Chechens. . . . A group of five unshaven, leather-coat-wearing Chechens kick open the café door, grab the first flannel-shirted customer by his scraggly goatee, and snap his little Swatch neck like a stick of incense. Screams, aromatic coffee spilling off the tables, bran muffins flying across the room. . . . "Ze owners. Bring zem to us." A small, bespectacled folksinger with a stud in his eyebrow approaches the Chechens, hands up. "Hey, come on. Let's talk this out—" The head Chechen, half-confused, punches the

Moscow Tribune of the alternative newspaper world...

So why call our revamped Living Here "the eXile"? Well, first and foremost, we get to exploit the overused "X": as in, you know, Generation X. Or, Generation X-Pat. Or, Generation Malcom X-Pat. It's called merchandising. (Also, we'll have a field day mixing our name up with The X-files.*)*

We've read our Business Weeks and we came to the startling conclusion that there's a huge, untapped market out there for young, semi-alienated Westerners... and we'll be damned if we aren't going to X-ploit it! But there's more to the name than that. It's also the derivative thing we like. "Generation X" derives from the name of Billy Idol's late-70s bubblegum punk band, Generation X. Billy Idol was known as the Neil Diamond of spikey-haired rebels: a glitzy, cheesy Elvis-in-leather. Fifteen years later, Douglas Coupland (notice the "coup" in Coupland!—just a coincidence?) swiped the name of Idol's defunct, derivative band, and wrote a quirky book about semi-alienated Westerners called "Generation X." The subject? Yep, you guessed it: another lost generation. The author? Right again: a citizen of Canada, the only derivative nation on earth. The whole Generation X thing is derivative so many times over—the adulterated "X" passing like a yellowing baton from one tattooed band to the next with each succeeding lost generation—that you need an engineering calculator to make sense of it all. Either that, or a newspaper. A newspaper? What a great idea! Let's call it "the eXile"!

So we did.

But let's be fair, the name fits our situation here in Moscow. We eXpats are in effect eXiles... post-Cold War eXiles. We eXpats are sort of the free market Solzhenitsyns of our time. Like him, we've suffered in our own special, Western way. Consider the facts. Whereas the Nobel Prize author couldn't get his books published in his homeland, we couldn't find grossly overpaid jobs which we were totally unqualified to handle; whereas he was reviled and persecuted in the official Soviet press, we were ignored at bars and clubs in our native lands; whereas his basic human rights were severely restricted, our rights to such base human desires as male chauvinism and sexual harassment were so oppressed that we had to keep it all to our sick little selves. So we did what the great author, and so many dissidents like him, did: we became eXiles. We packed our bags, loaded up the truck, and moved to Beverly. Not the city, of course—but the Chuck Norris nightclub...

CHAPTER ONE

singer in the eye, tearing the entire stud out along with a flap of eyebrow-lined flesh. . . . The folksinger screams, hitting notes he'd never dreamed of, like an early Robert Plant, silenced only by the irritated Chechen, who unloads an entire clip from his TT pistol. Marcus crouches behind the espresso machine, trying to channel his tai chi master to offer some kind of nonevasive advice. "Bend like the reeds in a slow-moving stream . . ." the irritating ghost-voice whispers. Marcus struggles in vain to make sense of one single haiku-aphorism, but nothing works. Kara, after some quick thinking, decides that the best way to tackle problems with men is to confront them with resolute confidence. It's worked with Marcus, it'll work with these punks too. She marches out from behind the kitchen door, but is stopped midway past the glass display case for muffins and croissants by a burst of Kalashnikov gunfire. Marcus recoils, crawls from the espresso machine to the milk steamer, then crouches beneath the steel sink. He thinks he's safe, but then . . . *Khwwwwrp!* His Velcro sleeve cuff catches on a table leg, tearing open at 100 decibels. He reaches to stop the tearing, but then *Khwwwrp! Khwwwwwrpppp!* The entire Velcro apparatus is coming undone. It's too late. Once it starts, nothing can stop it! First the sleeve cuffs, then the under shell cuffs, then the gaiters. . . . The Chechens perk up. Out of sheer impatience, they fire a rocket-propelled grenade over by the milk steamer. Hours later, when the investigators arrive, all they find is a streak of pink milk foam, leading from the espresso machine, through a burned-out hole in the wall, and straight back into the kitchen, where a blob of unidentifiable flesh is topped by a twisted pair of wire-rimmed glasses.

. . . No, opening up a coffee shop in Moscow just somehow lacked that *Friends* je ne sais quoi.

Kara, with her squat, hirsute body, was no catch. Her ass was something to behold: it'd already consumed half of her back when I first met her, and was poised to conquer the bottom half of her thighs. When you're about five-foot-one like her, and your ass looks like something from a Mardi Gras float, you've got to move quickly to marry. What really gave me the heebie-jeebies, though, was her body hair. Ugh, even now, when I think about it: those white stockings she was fond of wearing, smearing her thick, vinelike shin-hairs: like hundreds of fly's legs smashed into her stockings! I never understood that white-stockings thing of hers. Was it a kind of Beauty Myth rebellion? Naïveté? A desire to sicken—I mean *physically sicken*—everyone within eyeshot of those legs?

They figured they'd come to the Wild East to take advantage of the opportunities that they'd read about in their cheery, eco-friendly Seattle daily. When the coffee shop idea lost its luster, the newspaper idea caught their attention: it was small-time enough to confuse any Mafia-type, yet it had the "intellectual" appeal of a coffee shop with enough salary thrown in to make it worth it. They realized as well that the newspaper could get them connections in the restaurant biz to get it up and going if they lost interest in the newspaper. It was, as those people say, a no-brainer, a win-win.

But for all their alterno-Seattle pretensions, Marcus and Kara wanted nothing more than respect in the local business community, just like every other yuppie and shyster that came to Moscow.

For that reason, a smear letter sent out to the expat community blackening Kara's reputation meant ruin. She read the letter Marcus had brought her with muted hurt, even shock. When she finished reading, she looked up at me with the chalkiest mulatto face I'd ever seen. Even her notorious mustache blanched. She tossed the letter aside, smiled, then sat back down at the computer to design an ad. I'd never seen her crack before—she had balls of steel. Hairy balls of steel. At least I'd thought so. I admired her balls. I was sure hers were eight times the size of mine: all bristle pad and hormones.

I could see that she was on the verge of tears. She was an ally of mine at the time. I've always viewed life in quasi-military terms, and she had to be defended.

So, to prepare for battle, I picked up the letter and read:

"Moscow Business Alert! This letter is being sent to you as a WARNING not to do business with Kara Deyerin. She is leaving a trail of destruction in Moscow, destroying Westerners' businesses that she works with. Deyerin seems nice and professional on the outside, and has earned the trust of some expatriates, but her Hitler-like ambitions lead her to try to steal other people's businesses. Foreigners remember what happened to Paul Tatum. Deyerin is like the people who killed Paul Tatum: she uses foreigners to learn about their successful business, then she steals it from them and ruins their lives. Foreigners, haven't we suffered enough from people like Deyerin, stealing OUR businesses that we worked so hard to build up? It is time to draw the line. We are asking you DO NOT DO BUSINESS WITH KARA DEYERIN or her new newspaper *The Exiles.* The author of this letter would sign it, but Deyerin once told us that she had good connections with the Chechen Mafia, and so we are keeping anonymous out of fear."

We knew exactly who wrote that Moscow Business Alert. Martin MacLean—a sleazy expat from Tempe, Arizona, with a greasy forehead that receded so far back it had nearly joined the greasy bald spot on the back of his head. He had been ostracized by even the lowest rungs of Moscow's expat community, and not just because he was such an obvious fraud, but because he was simply hideous to behold. Martin had a lot riding on the success of *Living Here*, since a coupon business that he and Manfred set up used the *Living Here* bank account. They drained money from the coupon business for personal use, then funneled *Living Here* profits into producing the coupon booklet product. The whole pyramid would come crashing down if *Living Here* collapsed.

Martin was the type of guy who watched those cable-access programs about how to get rich quick in real estate. He was a sucker's sucker, the kind who paid $125 fees to attend those seminars they hold in Ramada Inns, in low-ceilinged banquet rooms that reek of stale cigarette smoke. He wore these Ross Superstore suits and cloth ties and carried a fake leather briefcase. He always dabbed the beads of sweat on his boil-infested forehead. He used to leave these sales cassettes in our *Living Here* offices when I was there. "Selling Made Easy" and "Selling Against Adversity" were some of the titles.

Somehow MacLean managed to marry a Russian girl—that "somehow" was his passport, which canceled out the forehead and then some. She was fairly cute in a malnourished sort of way. On the day she went into labor with their first child, Martin had a meeting with a client for his coupon book. He put her in a taxi, tossed his pager onto her lap, and sent her off to the hospital alone.

MacLean can only be understood in the context of the expat community. Calling us "expats" is another one of those linguistic whitewashings, just as snappy catchwords like "reforms" and "shock therapy" have masked utterly sinister events. We were in fact somewhere between colonialists and an occupying force, a force made up almost entirely of losers so fourth-rate that we didn't even have the guts to commit real crimes and wind up in jails back home. We forced upon the natives our ideology and threatened them with economic ruin whenever they didn't satisfy our demands. Even when they acceded, we ruined them—but always with the best intentions.

On a micro level, in the workplace, Russians were forced to adapt to the American "can-do" attitude. It was no less sickening than the missionaries breaking the backs of native populations until they accepted Christianity, all the while turning them into slaves and destitute town drunks. What sort of people were Moscow's colonialists? A good half were low-rent eels like Martin MacLean. Moscow's colonialists could only read one thing: bank statements. And even that was difficult for most.

Martin composed and circulated the letter to all the top expat businesses in Moscow, hoping to destroy us with his petty villainy. Why not? There was no way Kara could sue. This isn't America. You can do whatever you want here. That's what the Russians are like—lie, steal, cheat, and kill if you have to—right? This is the Wild East, where savagery is the rule. Here is another feature of the expat-colonialist: at once pious, and yet, crudely adopting degraded versions of the worst of the native people.

Just a few months earlier, assassins had pumped eleven bullets into Paul Tatum's ass for not giving up his business interests in the Radisson Hotel. Frankly, Tatum had it coming: he'd taken advantage of Russian gullibility in the early '90s to land himself a deal that was far sweeter than what he deserved. Paul was a hustler and a middle-aged tanning-booth pervert, frequenting striptease bars and whorehouses; moreover, he thought he understood "the game." He couldn't believe that an American could get capped, especially in such a high-profile fight with the Mayor's office over an international hotel. We were barons, gods, immune to Russian savagery.

Murders, plunder, libel, insider-dealing. . . . What's a little smear letter in the big scheme of things? Everyone was doing it.

"We have to kill Martin MacLean," I suggested. "We have to get ski masks and lead pipes and beat that fucker's greasy head in."

Kara looked up to me from her computer with big wet eyes.

Her husband, Marcus, purported ex–82nd Airborne, wiry, tai chi expert . . . declined. "No, I have a better idea," Marcus said, adjusting his round wire-rimmed glasses and adapting the tone of a wise Zen master. "I want to talk to Martin in person. I'm supposed to meet him soon anyway."

"What?!" I was ready for blood. I'd barely slept for a week already. I was dizzy with so much paranoia about our paper failing that popping one of Martin's forehead boils with a crowbar seemed to be the perfect solution to all my problems.

"No, I want to talk to him first," Marcus persisted. He paused, smiled, and said, "I want to hear him admit it."

Marcus smiled knowingly, as though he was cooking up something a thousand times more vengeful than crowbars. Some kind of Confucian death ray that would pierce the core of MacLean's alleged conscience.

I guess that's what this Northface generation is all about: "honesty is the most painful medicine." Uh, no it isn't, guys: *pain* is the most painful medicine, far's I can tell.

"Watch this: I'm going to call Marina," Marcus said, keeping that calm, Zen smile of his. "I'm going to ask her where I can find Martin." He dialed. We gathered around to listen. The Russian employees in our office were

Feb. 6-20, 1997 • P. 3

A Triple Dose of Dumb & Dumber:

Coincidence, or Russia's Fate?

The last Tsar and Tsarina of Russia are known to have been a pair of comically dim-witted figures, sort of like Dumb and Dumber... and a lot like—according to staff that fled—the "management" team at Living Here. In these weird times, we've got to believe that there's more to it than mere coincidence... something strange and mysterious is going on: sort of like in the X-files... oops, we mean the eXile! Check out the following graph, and see if you don't get a few goosepimples!

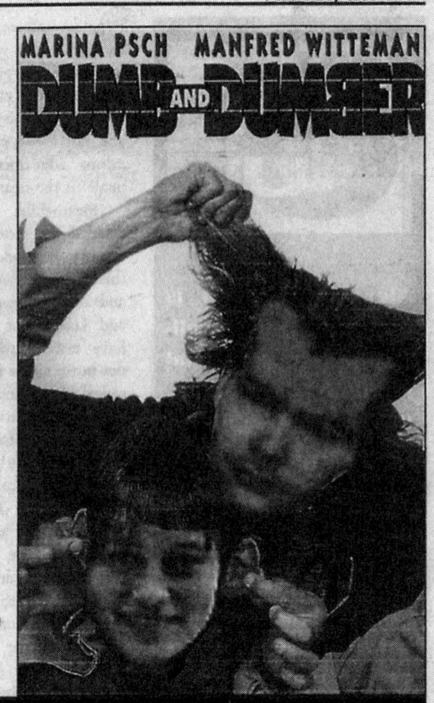

	ROYAL RUSSIANS	LIVING HELL	DUMB AND DUMBER
TRANSPORTATION	Royal couple rides royal train to Crimea every year for holidays	Witteman rides train from Moscow to Odessa in order to renew his multi-entry visa	Dumb and Dumber ride 1984 sheepdog to Aspen in order to return heroine's briefcase
WITLESS	Tsar Nicholas II said to be dim-witted, made several bad decision which led to his overthrow	Witteman said to be dim-witted, made several bad decisions which led to his overthrow	Dumb and Dumber known to be dim-witted, made several bad decisions which led to side-splitting comedy.
BAD ADVICE	Empress Alexandra relied on the mystic Rasputin for advice, which had disastrous consequences	General Manager Marina Psch-relied on dim-witted Dutchman for advice, which had disastrous consequences	Dumber relied on Dumb for advice, which led to side-splitting comedy
ZION	Lenin rumored to have a Jewish mother	Ames' mother's maiden name is "Schwartzreich"	"Dumb and Dumber" executive producer named Aaron Meyerson
WRATH	Tsar crushes 1905 revolution, thousands die	Manfred storms out of Living Here offices on several occasions, threatening to quit	Dumb gets mad at Dumber, dumps turbo laxitive in his drink
REPRESSION	Tsar's infamous secret police rounds up political opponents, has them shot	Manfred hangs up the phone on Marina, calls her a "fucking bitch"	Dumb and Dumber put "atomic" hot chilis in bad guy's hamburger, hurting his tongue
RULERS	Tsar and Tsarina rule over a vast Russian empire	Witteman dreams of ruling over a vast publishing empire	Dumb and Dumber dream of owning a worm farm
MONEY	Tsar wastes Russia's vast natural wealth to uphold lavish lifestyle	Witteman coaxes money out of his ex-girlfriend to start a newspaper	Dumb and Dumber take heroine's money and buy $250,000 Ferrari
RANSOM	Tsar and Tsarina arrested by Bolsheviks, no chance for ransom	Marina's hard drive and $6,500 held for ransom by Witteman, no chance of getting money back	Heroine's husband held for ransom, Dumb and Dumber inadvertently help win his release
THREATS	Tsar threatens revolutionaries with harsh measures, crackdown	Marina threatens Marcus Deyerin with an unnamed "phone call"	Dumber threatens to leave Dumb, hitchhike back to Providence, Rhode Island
VICTORY!	Lenin wins!	the eXile prints!	"Dumb and Dumber" earns a sequel!

shocked and surprised by it all. They didn't get it. We were Americans, after all. What the fuck was going on?!

"Hi Marina, this is Marcus," he said in that cheery Northface voice of his. When I think about Americans and their honey-tongued voices—I don't know how I'll ever return home. "Yeah, this is Marcus. I'm wondering if you can tell me where Martin is, I need to speak with him."

"I don't want to speak to you," Marina snapped.

"That's fine," Marcus said. "If you could just tell me where Martin is."

"I want you to stop spreading rumors about *Living Here*," she said. "You're ruining our reputation."

"Marina, I think you're ruining your own reputation."

"I want you to know that some people will be contacting you about this," she said, adopting a menacing tone. We all heard it—Marcus looked up and smiled, as if he'd won something.

"Excuse me—what?" he asked. "Could you—I didn't quite understand that, Marina. Could you repeat that clearly?"

"Some people will be contacting you, and you won't like that," she said.

"What exactly do you mean?"

"You'll find out soon enough!" Marina hung up the phone.

Marcus kept that Seattle coffee-shop Zen calm, while the others, including our Russian coworkers, laughed nervously.

Expats in Russia. Fighting over a small newspaper, circulation 25,000 . . . an investment of $35,000, a potential profit of about two or three thousand a month, max. And it was already turning into a game of death threats and slander. It was hard to know if Marina meant it. On the one hand, she works in real estate, which everyone knows is dominated by flatheads—those crew-cut, thick-headed Russian thugs. . . . I asked our publisher Kostya if our *krysha*, or roof, could protect us. He laughed and told us not to worry. Kostya's a big linebacker-sized guy. He's seen a lot. He takes a blase attitude toward everything, including my death. Nothing upsets Kostya. Ice-K.

Marcus somehow got Martin MacLean's phone number, called him up, and arranged to come by and pick up a VCR he'd loaned him when they worked together at *Living Here*. Later, Marcus proudly recounted how he'd calmly showed up at Martin's, without fear, and asked Martin if he'd written the letter. Martin denied it. Then, as Marcus narrated with quiet satisfaction, he told Martin that if he'd ever found out "for sure, and without a doubt," that Martin had written the smear letter, that Marcus would make him "answer for it." And that was it. I found out later, conclusively, from insiders, that Martin wrote the letter. Even Manfred told me. I relayed that to Marcus, but Marcus would just smile, nod his head quietly like a wise old kung fu master, and say, "But I want him to *admit* it. That's when it will really hurt."

That evening, Jennifer Biggs paged our production manager, Tanya. Jennifer had already been hard at work sabotaging our sales. She'd called all of our potential clients, asking them not to place ads in the *eXile*, and now she was going to deliver the final coup de grâce. Stealing our production manager, Tanya.

Tanya was only 19 years old, a student at the Journalism Faculty at Moscow State University. She came from Tula, a midsized town about 200 kilometers south of Moscow. Tanya was a bespectacled, quiet, apple-faced nerd. I really liked Tanya. Life must have been difficult for her: to come to Moscow and eke

Break A Leg

by Mark Ames

I'll write stories that will make them come from the ends of the earth to kill me... then at last it will be over, and that'll be fine with me.

Celine

I have a contract out on me. Not an employment contract with all kinds of expat benefits and a $3000 apartment—but the other kind of contract. The bad kind of contract.

At first I was told that "they," or rather a "she" and a "he," wanted to have me killed. Then my sentence was reduced to having my legs broken. Not as in, "Break a leg, Mark! Good luck with your new 'paper.'" But as in, "I'm a-gonna break yo' fuckin legs!" She can have it arranged, as she let one too many persons know. See, she's in the real estate business, which in Moscow means, flat-head central.

The threat is so serious, that two well-known journalists have even placed a ghoul-pool bet on my legs. They each put fifty bucks on the line over whether my hairy drumsticks will be snapped sometime in the next four weeks.

Only fifty?! Jesus Christ, do you know how much pain I'd have to endure for a lousy fifty bucks, guys! Fifty dollars barely gets you a couple of Provencal pizzas at Jack's! I'd be screaming like a newborn baboon as the IMC doctors drill stainless steel rods into my shins, and all that's on the line is a goddamn pizza?!

Breaking someone's legs isn't an easy job, and for that reason alone, I deserve a higher wager. The femur, or thigh bone, is an especially large, Fred Flintstone soup bone protected by layers of muscular padding. A six foot three, one hundred and ninety-pound target such as myself would require more than the average thrashing just to produce a slight hairline fracture. You'd need to get things like pulleys, ropes and heavy cement blocks to really snap my thigh bone. In Peter the Great's time, they would have tied me to a rack and pulled on my leg until the hip joint snapped; then, they would have cut deep incisions into my dislocated joint, and poured in molten lead, while taking heavy mallets to my thighs. A horse and a pair of heavy logs would have been employed to snap the femur—marrow and blood would spurt out of the compound fracture, and I'd likely pass out sometime around the twenty-minute mark.

Times have changed, and so have the methods. I've been spending my free moments trying to imagine how a pack of flat-heads will break my legs, and here's a partial list of what I've come up with: pinning me down to the asphalt and slowly driving over my thighs with a Volvo; tying me down to a table and taking a pair of baseball bats to the top of my thighs until the repetition of blows causes the bone to crack; dragging me to a sports gym, isolating a leg, then dropping 20kg bench-pressing plates edge-wise, to concentrate the force on the femur—but the truth is, my methods would probably take too much time, and too much energy.

If my assailants are in a rush, and they're obliged as per the contract to "break any said bone in that area between the pelvis and the ankle, commonly known as 'the leg,'" then they'll probably go for my tibia—the "shin bone"—or else its even-thinner neighbor on the outer part of the lower leg, the fibula. As leg bones go, these two are far more vulnerable than the femur. I've heard a fibula crack during football practice in high school. It actually sounded like a dry twig snapping, which was scary, considering that the wounded guy was a nose guard nick-named "Fireplug." Fireplug fell down on his back screaming and grasping at the air; then he started doing the wiggly bacon dance, while the rest of us stared in horror, thinking, "Thank god it was him and not me."

The sickest thing ever shown on American television was when Joe Theisman, the former Washington Redskins quarterback, had his tibia snapped completely in half by a rolling, 300 pound defensive end. One lineman had fallen down on Theisman's foot, trapping his leg in an awkward, vulnerable position; then a defensive end came hurtling out of nowhere, slamming into Theisman's isolated shin. The laws of physics just didn't work in the quarterback's favor. When Bubba tumbled onto Joe's leg, the center of his shin whipped around like a well-greased hinge; it was as though the quarterback had suddenly grown a joint where no joint had ever existed on man—a joint that allowed the lower half of his shin to bend ninety degrees *forward*, and not just backwards, like its more primitive cousin to the north, the knee. Thankfully for American sports fans (and me), ABC Sports had just introduced its Super-Slow-Mo Cam, so that you could actually watch Theisman's tibia bursting out of his grass-stained sock like the bloodied snake-thing in *Alien*... over, and over, and over, and over, and over. Until even people like me began to get nauseous. "Let's get another shot of that career-ending injury, Frank. Oo, gosh! That's gotta hurt, huh?" "Yep, that'll do it, Dan. Hey, can we get a rewind on that, I want to show our viewers out there just one more time..."

Still, the award for the most savage way to fuck up someone's legs for life has got to go to the Hell's Angels. Like a lot of things the Angels do, their method is crude and audacious—and highly effective for those very reasons. The Angels seat their victim in a chair, then secure his heel onto a second chair placed in front of him, so that his leg is suspended and perpendicular to the floor. The entire area between the hip and the heel hangs high over the floor like a creaky old bridge just waiting for King Kong to smash it apart. Which he does. An Olympic team of 220-pound grease bags get up on a table, and jump onto the victim's knees, thighs and shins, one after the other. Over, and over, and over, and over, and over. Four or five beer-bellied, graying goons in steel-toed boots jack-knifing feet-first onto the victim's legs. Until the ligaments and cartilage and tendons pop out of the joints like springs in a cheap mattress, and the bones snap and splinter, and the hip cracks, leaving the leg so mangled that even Peter the Great would be impressed.

...The most horrible thing about this contract hanging over me is how cool everyone thinks it is. Which makes me realize that I've missed out on the best pick-up line going in this town. You wouldn't even have to have a real death threat hanging over you. You could just fake it. People are so desperate to be part of the drama here that they'll eagerly employ the old fiction reader's "suspension of disbelief" and buy anything you say. So that they can claim some of the drama from you, head to the next party, and go, "Yeah, a friend of mine, some guy I know? He like, he has a contract out on him. I feel so awful..." That one always gets a sympathetic ear from the opposite sex. I keep forgetting what a brilliant strategy faking it is. As usual, I'm too slow and too late to pick up on that fact. Instead, I had to do the Ames thing and wait until a real contract was put out on me before I realized I could've just faked it. Story of my life.

I can see the ending to all this even now. Once my legs are hammered into pretzels, my friends will have a great story to tell... and they'll walk off with all the female leads, while I'll become the Christopher Reeves of Moscow, curled into my wheelchair, groping for my nurse's skirt. She wipes the drool from my mouth, slaps my hand away, then calls her expat boyfriend to tell him how sad she is that it all had to turn out this way.

out a living working with people like us, while studying at school and keeping your small-town head high in the cruel Big City of money-grubbing babes.... Underneath her naive, large gray eyes, though, there was always something else going on. You could tell that she kept a lot bottled up. Several months later, when the *eXile* was already on the road to success, she discovered sex and flew off the deep end. She started fucking anything that moved, especially African students. She traded in her poorly fitting brown nerd slacks for a pair of tight red-silk hooker pants, gold halter top, and black platforms. She looked like a street ho' from the Tenderloin in San Francisco. She'd take long cigarette breaks in the design room, and talk fashion-talk with the gay designers who worked with our Russian partners. That phase lasted about three months. Then Tanya withdrew into a kind of bizarre catatonia. She dropped 20 pounds. She developed these scabs on the sides of her face, near her ears. We told her to take a paid leave and go back to Tula. She checked into a sanatorium and was diagnosed with some nervous disorders, anorexia.... But all that came much later. When the *Living Here–eXile* war was at its peak, Tanya was still easily manipulated and among the sane. As much as she was loyal to Kara and Marcus—for reasons I could never figure out—a small-town girl is going to look up to the marketing manager of a top French ad agency like a god. Tanya came running to me after Jennifer paged her.

"What should I do?" Tanya asked after telling me that Jennifer had paged her.

"Call her back," I said, suspecting what might happen.

I sat next to her during the phone conversation. I couldn't hear what Jennifer was telling her, but I had a good idea by reading Tanya's face. She was half-breathless, but trying to contain herself as well. You could see she was being seduced. She didn't say a word, just "uh-huh" and "I understand." The conversation lasted five minutes.

"What happened?" I asked.

"She wants me to meet her tonight," Tanya said. "She said there's a job opening." You could see in her eyes that she'd been completely snowed over. It wasn't difficult to read. So I repeated to Tanya exactly how I imagined Jennifer's spiel went: *I'm sorry about all this business with Mark and Manfred—they're both friends of mine, and I don't want to get caught in the middle—but anyway, we need to hire someone as marketing assistant, we can pay you really well—the only thing is, you'd have to start tonight. We can't wait until tomorrow or another week, so I have to meet you tonight.....*

Tanya nearly burst out crying. "You mean she *lied* to me? I can't believe she did that to me," Tanya repeated. "I've always looked up to her so much. Working for her company is my dream. I can't believe she'd do that to me, Mark. I mean she's ... she's a *foreigner*."

I apologized to Tanya on Jennifer's behalf. She was really devastated. She went home early, stunned that an adult, a Westerner, would play with her life like that.

Brits—congenital back-stabbers and arrogant schemers, all of them! You'd think their dismal 20th-century record would inspire them to change their ways, come up with new tactics. But no—like Al Davis, they'll never change, no matter how many losing seasons they have.

We got our revenge on Jennifer: we threatened to out "that marketing manager with the nosebleed" in the second issue of the *eXile*. When our first issue came out, she had something akin to a mental breakdown. She turned to heroin as a source of relief. After a few weeks, Jennifer found she couldn't just walk away from the heroin. She kept doing more. And more. Until she became a full-fledged junkie. It got worse and worse. Nothing would help. She finally had to quit her job. She tried and failed to seek help. In the end, she abandoned Russia. She will never be the same again. All because of getting involved in the smallest little war in 1997.

If *Living Here* suffered from one thing, it was that it lacked any noticeably serious journalism. It was wild and sloppy and grotesque, but lacked meat. So we decided to beef up our newspaper. The *eXile* expanded from 12 to 16 pages, and added more writers. In order to try to gain some respectability, I tried to land one of Russia's best-known journalists, Alexander Minkin. Minkin has a reputation as an insufferable prick, but I liked his writing style. Of all the angry-disillusioned-liberals in the Russian press, he at least had an edge. And he was well-known, which meant that if we landed him, we'd look good. His exposés on corruption had to be admired for sheer balls. There were all kinds of rumors as to why Minkin was even still alive for the things he'd written: some said that the FSB, the KGB's successor, kept him alive as a conduit for compromising articles on enemies. Others said that it was because of squeaky über-villain Boris Berezovsky, who, it was widely alleged, also used Minkin. When trying to judge who protected which journalist in Russia, you first looked to who that journalist attacked. In Minkin's case, most of the attacks were on Berezovsky's enemies, the so-called young reformers.

I met Minkin the first time in the lobby of the Baltchug Kempinski Hotel, the very center of activity for EBRD, IMF, World Bank, and every other useless, overpaid schmoozer who made a living by offering Russia economy-killing advice.... The lobby and upstairs restaurant are what I imagine to be a modern equivalent to the Raj. Packed with manicured young Westerners exchanging business cards and holding power lunches, served by an overcompensating Russian staff overseen by strict German managers. . . . Outside, cringing Russian doormen in green and gold lackey costumes, with those flat-topped monkey hats, beam obsequious, gold-toothed smiles at anyone speaking a foreign language. For the European or American, stepping out of his Russian-chauffeured car under the portico, the heated glass doors are hurriedly opened with a welcoming, heavily accented "Good day, sir!"

The Westerner doesn't notice a thing as he enters the hotel, except perhaps the pasty hair or sallow, malnourished complexion of the Russian face that holds the familiar monkey cap in place. For Russian visitors, it's a little different. If a Russian tries entering the Baltchug, the lackeys stiffen up like henchmen. Their expressions turn to scowls. Those lackey-suits suddenly aren't so comic, not to the Russian. The doormen step in front of the Russian—easily identifiable by his poorly knotted tie, or his cowering, guilty slouch—and coolly ask their fellow countryman if he is a guest of the hotel. Usually, at that point, most Russians will scurry away, even if they've arranged legitimate meetings in the lobby with their Western partners. I've seen parties of Russians stopped and led off to the side, while Western businessmen, laughing and slapping each other's backs, are escorted right past by lackeys speaking ungrammatical, bootlicking phrases learned during their video training sessions . . . .

Once, when I worked for the Pakistani banker, I was supposed to interview a potential Russian recruit at the Radisson-Slavyanskaya, the hotel favored by American businessmen. Ruslan was half-Russian and half-Georgian. Unfortunately for him, his swarthy Georgian complexion dominated the pale Slavic blood. I waited for him in the lobby. And waited. And waited another forty minutes, then left, figuring he'd shined because someone had warned him that my boss was a two-bit swindler masquerading as an Eton-accented banker. A day later, I heard what had happened to Ruslan: The doormen stopped him, asked him why he was entering, demanded documents. . . . Ruslan, who had spent a year at Harvard and who once made a hobby of roundhouse-kicking guys who didn't respect him, argued. That led to a quick whistle-blow, a rush of *militsia* men, under pay from the hotel to club and jail any Russian undesirables. . . . Which is exactly what they did to Ruslan. He only got out of jail the next morning, with a broken nose and torn suit.

The only Russians who get by the door-hops are the most threatening ones. The lackeys don't dare to do anything: they neither obsequiously open the door, nor ask to see their documents. Instead, with threatening rich Russians in Italian boutique overcoats, they take the Sergeant Schultz approach: *I see nuh-tzink! I hear nuh-tzink!* The trick is simple: If you're really threatening, if you can really cause problems and make someone disappear with the snap of a finger, then you don't even acknowledge the doormen's existence. You breeze not past them but through them. Understanding that, the doormen step aside and, assuming the worst, look the other way. If, however, a Russian trying to enter were to even graze the eyes of a doorman, or if, like nearly all Russians, his face betrayed a slight lack of confidence or fear that he'd be stopped, it was hell to pay.

Most Western hotels, and even the Russian hotels like the Intourist, have a similar policy. Once, a friend of mine and I took a pair of gauche Russian dates into the Intourist for a dinner date at their top-floor Mexican restaurant. Just as we were being served our margaritas, two flathead doormen interrupted us, leaned into the girls' ears, and accused them of being whores who didn't pay their cut to the door. They grabbed the girls' elbows and tried lifting them out of their seats. If I hadn't intervened, the girls would have been taken into a basement office, beaten, raped, then arrested and hauled off to jail.

So I wasn't sure why Minkin, a bearded, natty journalist, thought he'd get through the lackey-gauntlet . . . unless he really was some kind of star.

Minkin stood out in the lobby. He was the only guy in the hotel with a beard—a big, messy beard. His cheap wool pants and Warsaw Pact synthetic down parka stood out among all the pressed and ironed and groomed plutocrats. Minkin loomed over a table of free breakfast snacks. There's nothing a Russian journalist loves more than free food. He must have used his fame-voodoo on the doormen to get in, I thought.

We met. He quickly called his bodyguard on his mobile phone, told him that everything was okay, then followed me out the door, across the street, and to our building. When we left the hotel, the doormen turned their eyes.

Minkin and I mostly talked literature. He wanted me to know that he wasn't a "yellow journalist." He'd started out as a theater critic with literary ambitions of his own. Nabokov was his hero. I mentioned my love for Platonov, especially *The Foundation Pit*, calculating that a literary snob like Minkin would be impressed. He bit.

I was worried that Minkin would be frightened off from our newspaper, especially since our style was unashamedly "yellow." I couldn't explain to Minkin's raw intelligentsia ego that yellow, irresponsible journalism was a better path to the truth than following J-school rules. So instead, I played on my sensitivity to Russian literature as a way of hooking him. And after a long talk in our offices, he was convinced. He even asked me to call him "Sasha," although I still used his full name and patronymic.

We already had another widely hated Russian writing for our newspaper, Edward Limonov, leader of the fascist National-

Bolshevik Party. When his banned book, *It's Me, Eddie*, was finally published in the Soviet Union in 1991, it sold over 1 million copies. Limonov wrote for *Living Here*, and he'd agreed to continue on with me at the *eXile*.

The coupling of the bitter ex-liberal Minkin with the extremist Limonov into one newspaper was a coup by any standard. We kept it a tight secret, even from our own friends and staff. There were too many rumors and leaks going around. Including the rumor that Manfred was cutting a deal with my publisher Kostya and *Elle* magazine to drop me and back him. It was a preposterous rumor, but that didn't keep me from puking more saliva noodles and wasting a lot of time panicking.

The last piece in our puzzle was the design. Our vodka-sucking designer, Ilya, gave the newspaper a far busier and more tabloidish look than *Living Here*. Shengin was a monster: he slept even less than I did those last three days, and drank himself into a garrulous frenzy. Ideologically, he was one with us. When we designed our first cover, about the collapse of *Living Here*, I wanted it to feature an emaciated Ukrainian child, photographed during the famine in the early '30s. It was supposed to represent Krazy Kevin, and the fact that *Living Here* hadn't paid him for four issues. At first, Ilya was a little shocked that we'd dip to such tasteless lows for a quick laugh. But then he quickly apologized, scanned the picture, and hammed it up. He unscrewed another bottle of vodka, and gave the concept two bottles up. Ever since, Ilya's always been a step ahead of us in the area of yellowness.

We finished the newspaper early Thursday morning, February 6, and delivered the hard disks to a Macintosh design and development center in the same building. The designers all had pointy beards and ponytails, which made me nervous. Their job was to take our Quark files and print them out onto films. At around noon on Thursday, Tanya picked up the films from the design people, who stayed up all night especially for us just to get them perfect, and ran them down to the massive Pressa building on Ulista Pravdy. I'd doubt that printing presses get any larger than this building. It's where they printed up the old *Pravda* newspaper, as well as *Komsomolskaya Pravda*, which had the largest circulation of any newspaper in the world. The equipment and building are all very heavy 1950s industrial revolution; the people look and smell Soviet. The women who run the presses are all generally older, wearing faded blue aprons and scarves over their heads . . . .

I should have slept that day, but I couldn't. I was burning filthy, low-grade adrenaline fumes.

When we arrived at the printing press with the films, the director told us that he'd received a call from an American warning him not to publish our newspaper. I brought a fifty-dollar bottle of Martel Cognac to the director, just to warm him up.

"Please take this gift," Kara and I told him.

He smiled, took it without looking at it, and placed it in a locked drawer. That sleight-of-hand was real smooth. It looked like he'd done it a few times before: grabbing a bottle, opening a drawer, and slipping it in, all the while staring straight into your eyes. Like some kind of ventriloquist trick, where they drink water while the puppet talks.

"You didn't have to do this for me in order to get the paper printed," he said, mildly reproachful.

"Oh no!"

"I'm going to share this with all my employees. It's for everyone."

"Of course, *gospodin* . . . !"

"Just so you know. I like you both, and I wish you luck. Don't worry about problems from our side."

"Thank you, *gospodin*!"

They printed up a test run of ten copies. It looked fine. Then they went to press with the 25,000. We returned to our apartments for a nap. Our distributor was expected to come by later with a truck, load up the 25,000 copies, take them to a storage shed, then distribute them to his fleet of six Volga cars, which were sort of like '60s Goofy cartoon/Soviet gas guzzlers. The Volgas would then spread around Moscow. We'd heard rumors that Manfred's last-ditch act of sabotage was to find all our distribution points, grab our papers, and throw them away.

Again, I tried to rally Marcus for some violence if Manfred tossed our papers, but Marcus always gave me that quiet Zen smile of his.

We allowed ourselves a few hours of sleep, then returned to the Pressa building, to the large docking stations where they store the printed newspapers, at around five o'clock on Thursday evening. I still expected something to go wrong. We hoped to have all our bases covered. We arrived at the printing press, and went looking for our bundled and packaged *eXiles*, the very first *eXiles*. One woman led us in one direction, another in another direction. They took us on a catwalk, up above the printing presses, green and rust metal above the clunky, clanging machines . . . then up another catwalk and ladder to the loading docks, where they store the *eXiles*. We searched around. In the far corner of the storage area, we spotted a lone packet of newspapers wrapped in brown paper. We tore it open . . . wait . . . there's only 200 copies here. Where are the rest?!

Kara and I ran downstairs into the offices and nearly tore the floor manager's head off.

"What happened to our newspapers!?"

The woman suddenly went pale. "A man came in saying he worked for your newspaper. He took them all away in a truck!"

I nearly collapsed. It couldn't be. "Wait, what did he look like?" I asked.

"I don't exactly remember," the floor manager said, blushing. Now she's trying to save her ass.

I described Manfred to her: blond hair, about five-foot-nine. Manfred could have done it, too: foreigners get away with all kinds of shit in Russia. All he'd have to do is demand that this old Russian give him the newspapers, and she'd have to concede. Russians allow foreigners to walk all over them, especially at a place like this.

"Did the guy who picked up our newspapers have blond hair?" I asked. "About this tall?"

"Yes!" she eagerly agreed.

"Oh shit!" Kara and I stared at each other in shock. He could have shown up, speaking English, and claimed that he worked for the newspaper. Then loaded all the *eXiles* in a truck, taken off for the outskirts of Moscow, and dumped an entire sleepless month's worth of work in the forest—an entire month of plans, meetings, intrigues—all down the drain!

"Was he a foreigner or a Russian?" I asked.

"I don't know," the woman said, terrified. She was afraid to answer—she didn't know which would be safer. So she gave us the familiar "I don't know, it's not my fault."

We panicked, then called our distributor, hoping it was him. He wasn't available.

I ran to the toilet, the familiar toilet, and puked more saliva noodles, mixed with orange juice. Then I started thinking about murder. Real murder. The kind that makes a "Self" headline.

A long, long half-hour later, we heard good news: it was indeed our distributor, who, I remembered, was blond and Manfred's height. He'd already started delivering the first *eXiles*.

One packet was delivered to the Irish Supermarket, a popular Western-style supermarket located in the building where *Elle* was located, and where *Elle*'s publisher, George Nikides, lived. Word reached him that the *eXile* had come out. Suddenly, all hell broke loose! After he saw a copy, he called Manfred and let him have it. Manfred had lied! He said we could never do it! Nikides demanded to have his name taken off the *Living Here* masthead for the edition that Manfred was still preparing, a day late . . . a crucial day too late. The acting editor of *Living Here*, Ben Aris, bailed as well. There was no one left.

A couple of journalists who were at *Living Here*'s office the night the *eXile* came out told me about the mad circus that followed our publication. Manfred was slumped over the computer desk, sucking down cheap vodka. Marina paced back and forth, slamming the door, screaming and crying in hysterics. She called her *rebyata* friends in the real estate business to see how she could arrange to have me killed.

"I'll have his legs broken! I don't care what it costs! I'm going to kill that fucking Ames!"

That confederacy of desperate losers, holed up in their unheated office on Gazetny Pereulok, was like Hitler's bunker in the final days, as Zhukov closed in on the Reichstag: Manfred, Marina, Martin, alone with their dumb plots, doomed. . . . I'd have paid anything to have seen the video.

In a way, I couldn't blame her for wanting to kill me. Worse than her lost investment was the lead story I wrote about our split in the first issue, titled "Living Hell," in which I portrayed her as a willing, mango-brained rape victim, and Manfred as the greedy rapist, detailing all the mistakes, the thefts, the insults, the threats, down to the last. It lost me a lot of respect in the community, but it lost her everything. Just in case anyone was wondering whether or not I was a spiteful prick, I made a chart comparing Manfred and Marina to the characters in *Dumb and Dumber*, scanning their faces into Jim Carrey's and Jeff Daniels's. The whole expatriate community had a laugh at their expense. Well, not really. I still hear it from people about how gratuitously mean that was of me.

I usually don't start these things, but once they get going, I believe you scrap the Geneva Convention and aim for total victory.

Two nights later, I bumped into a cleaned-up Manfred at the nightclub Ne Bei Kopytom. I tried avoiding him. I'm a real coward when it comes to low-grade face-to-face confrontations. I ran back into the club and hid, even though I'm about six times his size. Don't ask me why. Anyway, my ride home was waiting for me on the other side of the Manfred moat. I had to face up, be a man. . . . Jesus, what was I thinking? It would be like MacArthur being afraid of the Japanese Emperor during the surrender-signing ceremonies! I walked back towards the exit, hoping not to be seen, when . . .

"Mark!"

God, I hate socially adjusted people. Don't they ever feel fear?

Manfred graciously shook my hand and congratulated me. "I didn't zink zat you could do it," he said. He was considering leaving for home. I was exhausted and exhilarated and ashamed. I couldn't stand and I couldn't sleep.

Kara, Marcus, Tanya, the designers, the publisher, and I all celebrated. It was over. We'd won.

In the run-up to the *Living Here–eXile* war, Kara and I had spent a couple of weeks drawing and redrawing business plans and meeting with potential investors and publishers. Her inclination was to use "conservative" figures in terms of sales revenues and profits. I didn't quite understand all the details of our business plan, but from my limited experience in the business world, I understood one thing: A business plan is an advertisement meant to sucker greedy people into believing that their wildest fantasies will come true.

Kara thought that a business plan should be conservative, so as to avoid problems later. But that's not how businessmen attract money. I convinced her to ratchet up the revenue and profit projections by a good 50 percent. The investor would be committed to a cash investment of a mere $13,000. We estimated that the paper would see profits of about $50,000 in the first year and $150,000 in the second year. It was a bit high, but if we'd said the "conservative" numbers, I figured they'd cut them in half in their heads anyway and assume that the whole thing wasn't worth it. Investors expect you to lie on your business plans: they factor that into their decision. For us, we worked out a profit-sharing plan with the investor that vested over time according to profit earned.

I'd held a few jobs already in Moscow: as a sales manager for a liquor distributor, as a middleman in trade of electronic goods and medical supplies, and as the personal assistant to a megalomaniac Pakistani businessman who was stripping Russia of its third-tier assets—broken-down provincial breweries, butter factories, confectioneries. . . . I learned a good deal from the Pak on how to draw up a business plan. He'd succeeded in suckering the Western investment banking community into buying his beer holding company, raising tens of millions of dollars from Russia's first-ever Global Depositary Receipt program. I was with him all the way on that. In mid-1995, the Paks snowed the Luxembourg stock exchange into listing the stock, whose price was based on assets that the holding company owned only on paper.

In my various jobs in Moscow, I've been involved in everything from theft to kickbacks to bribery. I'll write about it someday, just my personal experiences. A handbook: *Your Guide 2 Business in Russia.* It may land my ass in jail on two continents, so I'll wait for the right time. America has a law forbidding its citizens to engage in bribery or kickbacks overseas, punishable by jail. . . . It's absurd, of course, and would land 95 percent of the American expats in Russia in Lompoc or some minimum security joint if they really meant it. Someday, I'll give them all the evidence they need.

Most Western businessmen in Moscow are dirty. I mean caked-in-shit dirty, filthier than even the most savage Russian *biznesmyen,* who at least has a frame to work within. The expat has no context, just hearsay, a crash course in corruption. They didn't grow up with a set of unspoken rules of conduct and combat; our rules are very clear in the West. Once we're here, where it seems that anything goes, the expat loses all sense of proportion; his moral rudder is swinging wildly. He's never sailed in these seas, and even as he's about to capsize in a storm of bad decisions, he's convinced that he's the most clever, cunning little cracker that Eurasia has ever seen. It's the arrogance of a colonialist. That's what makes him so reckless and idiotic: that mixture of undeserved hubris, inexperience, and neophyte evil, projected through the average mind of the average expat.

Later, even my own partners, Kara and Marcus, who went through so much with me to start up the *eXile,* who were there through thick and thin, built up a deep resentment toward me and my editorial partner. They left our paper thousands of dollars in arrears with four issues' worth of uncollected receipts, turned our publisher against us, then abandoned Moscow. Russians grow up scheming and cheating each other, to the point where it has a logic and morality of its own, a sense of justice. With expats, it's an affectation.

The Moscow expat is a creature who should be regarded with extreme suspicion by the border police of any Western country. The expat can't bring any good back home with him. He should be treated like a monkey with Ebola—seized, boxed, locked up, and incinerated . . . then take those ashes, seal them in a titanium container, and fire them off into space, somewhere beyond Saturn, so that mankind will never be infected by us expats.

I once suggested this to Moscow's U.S. Embassy spokesman Richard Hoagland, but he just laughed. "Why Saturn?" he said. "I think the remains should be fired off into a black hole. That way, they won't even infect our dimension. It's mankind's only hope."

Dick knows what he's talking about. He's seen how Moscow attracts the dregs of America, who come here to strike it rich, and transform into low-rent Huns in double-breasted suits. He's seen the perverts that have come and gone. Dick understood where we were coming from. In mid-1998, when he packed up for a stint at the U.S. Embassy in Pakistan, he requested an *eXile* subscription.

"To the various uses of the paper you offer," he wrote us, "I'd add that I'll be able to roll it up to use to plug cracks in the window frames to prevent radiation. Cheers, Dick."

Even Americans who came here young, green, and full of idealistic enthusiasm leave a year later with hair on their knuckles, fangs, and yellow eyes. It's Russia's revenge on the latest invading force: poison that will eventually filter its way back to the West, and corrode the alleged victors from within. They brought down Hitler and Napoleon; they can bring down anyone.

We won the war, and it looked like everything was over with *Living Here.* I expected Manfred to split town with his tail between his legs, go on the dole in his annoyingly liberal little Holland, then drink himself to death. But people like him never go away and die. Too selfish.

Two days after he'd conceded, I ran into him at the Hungry Duck, the most notorious, disgusting bar in the world. The Duck was just beginning a new Monday night program called "Countdown Nights." Between eight and nine, you got five drinks for the price of one; between nine and ten, four drinks for one . . . and so on. A dangerous formula in a country where alcoholism is a national religion. We were on our third cheap whiskey cola, then up walks Manfred, a mischievous grin on his face. I couldn't believe he'd show himself in public, not after what I'd written about him, calling him a rapist with the IQ of a hagfish. But he had an agenda.

"Mark, I have very, very bad news for you," he said, savoring this moment. There was something too confident in his voice. I could tell that he wasn't bluffing—that at least he believed what he was saying.

Kara whispered in my ear: "Manfred's already been talking to me and Tanya—he told us that he was going to hire us back in a couple of weeks, that we had no idea what was going on."

I got nervous. That stomach-acid paranoia returned.

"God has blessed me," Manfred said, with viscous, beer-soaked irony. "You have no idea. I got ze phone call from someone just last night, asking me if he could be my new editor. And Mark, he is thousands times better zan you! You are through."

"No one is better than me, Manfred," I said.

He laughed drunkenly, then put his hand on my shoulder to comfort me. "You have no idea who's coming, Mark. You have no idea vhat's going to happen to you. You're through. Your publisher Kostya and I unt ze *Moscow Times* people . . . you're through. You're going to have to leave zis town in two weeks, it will be zo embarrassing. He is ze best editor in ze world."

I later found out that the owner of the Hungry Duck had told security not to interrupt us if we should break out into a fight. I should have clubbed Manfred. I could have used a bottle, a weapon of some kind, to keep his blood from getting in my eyes. But I didn't. Maybe I'm the one who's all bluff . . .

Only after he left did the real paranoia kick in. Deep, stomach-enzymes paranoia. When I found out that my rival would be Matt Taibbi, who had written for us at *Living Here*, my paranoia went into overdrive. I knew Matt fairly well. I had an idea what to expect, and it didn't make me happy. I assumed that I was doomed. I didn't know why, but I assumed the worst.

We put out a second issue. The feature story was about how easy it is to kill or maim an expat, and how common such contracts were. Most people agreed that you can hire some *rebyata,* young punks, to bust a cap in an expat for about a thousand dollars, and have his legs broken for about half the price. I thought it was relevant to me, since Marina's contract on my legs still held firm. Two journalists even put a 50-dollar wager on my femurs. One of those journalists was supposed to be my friend: the balding, potbellied 24-year-old Brit, Owen Matthews. He took loud delight in his friends' misfortunes.

My sensors detected and collected more and more grist for the paranoia mill. The week of our second issue, Kara and I got a strange phone call from a couple of Americans who wanted to meet us and discuss investing in the *eXile.* I thought the whole thing was strange. For example, they called us just before our planned meeting and asked Tanya for our passport details. They asked her for everything: where the passport was issued, date of expiration—really weird stuff. When Kara tried to take the phone, they backpedaled, said there was no need, and agreed to meet us at a restaurant. If someone has your passport details, he can arrange a payment in the foreign ministry to have your visa revoked. Or he can refer you to the tax ministry. I called the American embassy. By then, they'd already opened up a file on me, because they agreed that I was in some danger.

"It is very strange that anyone should ask for those kind of passport details," I was told. "Don't give them out."

The two American investors turned out to be pretty typical fare: young, arrogant, in starched white dress shirts, matching wire-rimmed glasses, matching TV-anchorman voices. . . . They claimed to want to invest in the *eXile*, that they were media experts themselves. To this day, I'm sure something was behind them. Either the *Moscow Times*, Manfred, Marina . . . or maybe the expat community was taking donations to take over the newspaper in order to shut it down. I wouldn't be surprised.

D-day was ticking down for Taibbi to come to town. I started hearing more and more rumors. Manfred had hired a top-flight designer from the *Moscow Times.* He had money. He and Marina were telling clients that they'd worked out a deal with the *Moscow Times.* Clients were starting to leave us. Even Krazy Kevin was planning on bailing, at least temporarily. He had his reasons. Manfred owed him $1,400. They bumped into each other at a bar. Manfred promised to pay him back everything if he joined *Living Here* again. He was slobbering drunk and he told Kevin that he was going to sink me and drive me out of town. He'd gone insane with the desire to crush me.

I was losing my will to fight. No sleep, and all that post-adrenaline exhaustion, had sapped me. And now Taibbi was coming. People were calling me, asking me if I was nervous. Hell yes I was! I'd lost twelve pounds just from fear. I still couldn't sleep. I didn't know what Taibbi had up his sleeve, but I was sure he was going to produce the greatest newspaper in the history of mankind. The very print would be like nothing ever seen before.

CHAPTER ONE

I was even contemplating surrender. Of fleeing to a pariah state, like Serbia, or Serbian-held Bosnia. . . . I was serious. I'd even called the Yugoslavian Embassy to start making preparations.

The week before Taibbi arrived, I ran into one young American woman at the opening of a new club, Parizhskaya Zhizn.

"I heard that Matt's coming into town," she said with a vengeful grin.

"Yeah, it's exciting, isn't it?" I said.

"Aren't you worried?"

"Of course. Matt's very talented," I said.

"Well, the difference is, he's a *real* journalist," she said, looking away as if suddenly distracted. "I'd be worried if I were you."

Matthews told me roughly the same thing. He enjoyed it, though: the thought that his two friends might tear each other to bits. He told me that he "had to" help Matt out, since he knew Matt before me. He was angry that I didn't include him more in the *eXile*. And he enjoyed, in that cheesy Oxford way, playing the double agent.

I began to hate Taibbi. I remembered his jockish looks and backslapping good-guy demeanor, and it drove me nuts. I even recalled a particularly painful memory, one of the few times we'd hung out together before he left Moscow to play basketball in Mongolia. It happened the previous summer. I was at my studio apartment, having just finished some very unsatisfying sex with my always-dissatisfied half-Belgian girlfriend, Suzanne. Matt stopped by unexpectedly with Owen. They brought some pot with them, stuffed it into a papirosi cigarette, and smoked us out. Then we "chilled," as they say.

Although I far from chilled. In my THC-induced paranoia, I observed Suzanne taking an interest in Matt. They sat on my bed and talked. The very bed-couch where we had just had our unsatisfying sex. The bed of shame. She softened her voice, and laughed at everything he said. I was on the far side of my studio apartment, sitting on a chair, trying to pretend that I wasn't noticing, nodding my head as Owen recounted some alleged orgy he'd had with two 16-year-old Russian teenagers from Archangelsk.

Matt and Owen soon left, in a cloud of youthful laughter. Before leaving, Owen had made a quip that Suzanne didn't look satisfied. "Aren't you fucking her well?" he sneered. Suzanne and Matt were saying good-bye at my door. "She doesn't have that look on her face, Ames. She doesn't look like she's been taken well care of." He snickered, and they were gone.

Suzanne and I were alone, and I was stoned. I hate pot—the most terrifying of all drugs, worse than acid. But it was too late. I'd have to ride out the three-hour paranoia marathon.

Suzanne suggested walking to the McDonald's on the Arbat. She was starving and bored, stuck in my apartment. On the way there, on a warm summer night, she kept asking me questions about Matt. What does he do? Why hadn't I introduced them before? Does he have a girlfriend?

Finally, she blurted out, as if ironically, "God, he's so good-looking."

I tried arguing with her. Him? He looks like a caveman! A jock!

But she was persistent.

"Nooo, not at all. Matt looks like Elvis Presley," she said, giggling. Then, softening her voice, she added wistfully, "And he seems so nice. In a simple way."

Yes, I had good reason to hate Taibbi. When he left for Mongolia a month after that humiliating stoner-session, I breathed a sigh of relief, knowing that there was at least one less guy in town to cuckold me. In Mongolia, he came down with what some thought was tuberculosis. He dropped 40 pounds and lost his voice. When he was medi-vac'd to Boston, I was even sad. He was a truly gifted comic writer and a decent guy, and by then Suzanne and I had broken up.

Now that he was coming to Moscow to take my job, the resentment returned. I shook my fist at the sky and demanded an answer to a burning question inside: *Why the fuck didn't he die in Mongolia?!*

The Sunday before Taibbi arrived in Moscow, I got a call from Kara. It was three in the morning. I'd lain awake in my bed, twisty-black scribbles of paranoia going from my face up to the cheap Soviet overhang lamp above the bed. It took me three hours to fall asleep. And then the phone rang.

"I'm sorry to wake you," she said, "but . . . well, maybe I shouldn't say this, Mark, but I'm really worried."

"Why?" I asked.

"Because Matt's a *real* journalist. He's going to be able to add a serious journalism side that you . . . won't do. And that's going to hurt sales. People complain about one thing: it's that we don't have any real journalism. I think that unless something goes wrong, they're going to beat us."

That phone call really pissed me off. My own partner, getting ready to desert me even before the battle began. I told her not to worry, that I'd rise to the occasion.

She didn't sound convinced. She apologized, in that affected business tone of hers, then hung up. And panic set in again. Three more excruciating panic hours, staring up at the weak light above me, thinking, this is it, it's all over. Even Kara doesn't believe.

What scared me wasn't so much that Taibbi was a *real* journalist, even if I personally loathed the concept. What scared me was this: He was a likable person who'd probably write likable articles. I always tried to make readers pay in some way. At my age, it was a little late to change. Age: that was another problem. I was already 31, and he was a tender 27. That's a lot of years, body-wise. And, worst of all, I knew that he was a workaholic. And he'd be fresh from a two-month rest. I, on the other hand, was exhausted. I couldn't even write the stupid Gore-O-Scopes, a cheesy fake horoscope column written supposedly by Al Gore, as if he'd suddenly been demoted to emceeing a failing Vegas comedy club. Nothing seemed funny anymore. Funny? There was another area that Taibbi excelled in. His last pseudonymous Don Kipines piece, a column he wrote about me for *Living Here*, was devastating and about the funniest thing our newspaper had ever done. I hadn't seen that side of Matt, and now that he was going to compete against me in public, I realized that I was fucked: he had my troops surrounded.

Yes, I thought: I can hate him. No problem. Just wait till I'm on my Aeroflot flight to Belgrade, bags and boxes in tow, grumbling to myself like Yosemite Sam, whiskers singed from the dynamite sticks of failure . . . I'll hate 'im real good-like then!

I tried calling Matt in Boston to dissuade him from coming, but he was standoffish. He didn't understand all the shit we were going through, and probably didn't care either. He'd figured, if it worked out, great; if not, he'd find something else. It wasn't a life-or-death thing for him.

Limonov's latest book, *Anatomy of a Hero*, traces his revolutionary activity from Bosnian-Serb partisan to Russian radical.

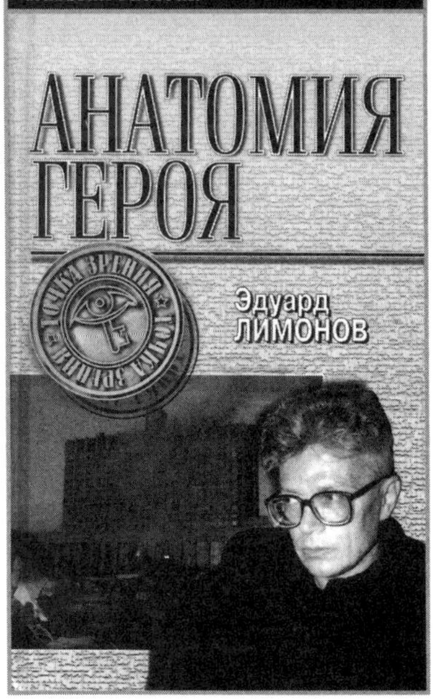

The week our third issue was coming out, our spies confirmed that *Living Here* was putting out a rival issue on the same day. I tried motivating, but it was hard. Two days before printing, we suffered another blow. Alexander Minkin left a message on my machine telling me that he was "imposing an embargo against the *eXile*." He was fuming pissed. His colleagues at *Novaya Gazeta*, a liberal-minded newspaper, were shocked that he'd appear on the same pages as their nemesis, Edward Limonov. And we had naked women plastered on a page next to his. Minkin's complex about being taken seriously as a modern-day Nabokov had been stirred. And lastly, what really irked him was that we didn't thank him at the beginning of each article in large enough print, nor did we clearly specify that these were reprints approved by Minkin, by his graciousness, and offered to us for free. I tried convincing him not to pull out, but he hung up on me.

Alexander Minkin's collected works, which he modestly titled, *I Merely Enlighten*.

. . . So this is how the ship sinks, I remember thinking.

Our third issue of the *eXile* was a disaster. The lead—a Women's Day article about how an American woman woke up and found herself transformed into a Russian girl—sucked so badly that we had to make it all pictures and cartoons. Even the cover, featuring a 30-year-old American pseudo-diva, was nauseating. If this was how we were going to compete against real journalism, we might as well close up shop and head for the hills.

We came out on the same day as the new Taibbi-run *Living Here*. It wasn't the blowout that I'd feared. Their cover was better, and they had some better articles, but otherwise it was a mess. It looked like the old *Living Here*, only with more text and a messier design. Still, I was completely exhausted from two months of sleeplessness and paranoia. I wanted to cut some kind of a deal. This was only Taibbi's first issue, and I'd heard that he barely had time to put it together.

The next issue would be ten times the work for both of us, and I wasn't capable of much more.

Matt agreed to meet me when he came into town. I was ready to cut any deal possible with him just to end the sleepless nightmares and Defcon-4 paranoia. I was exhausted, plain exhausted. I was ready to retire, like some sad old emperor. I was ready to offer him anything he wanted. Just let me retire to my little column in the corner of the *eXile*, a small pension, the odd concubine drawn from the villages, the occasional ceremonial appearance. . . . Anything but ignominious exile.

о

ОГ

нбаатар
й самбар
самбар
Баярсүх
39), Да-
лд 2(3),
тоглог-
он хуга-
І.Алтан-
дсэн тул
ун хий-
тоглол-
д таван
рдугаар
(туу) 17
энэ үед
лага авч
нарыг
тактик
Бүргэд»
, Мөнх-
талбайд
арч ирж
хэлээр
ун» гэж
логчоор
ийн со-
дутуугаа
сан бол
чөлөөт
І.Отгон-
о 57:56
бас л
Эдгээр
ас 19.20
оруулаад
нийг нь
энэ бол
Яг ийм
ва байж)
зогсож
чихдэг.
й байсан
ар гурав
, хувийн
о нударга

Basketball

Монголчуудад хачирхуулахын тулд үсээ Родман шиг засуулсан

«Алтайн бүргэдүүд»-ийн гэртээ буцсан легионер Мэтт Тайби Оросын «Комсомольская правда» сонинд энэ өгүүллийг нийтлүүлжээ

Д.ГАЛ

Гэрэл зургийг С.ЭНХЖАРГАЛ

Өнгөрсөн жил Москвад ерөнхийлөгчийн сонгууль болж өнгөрсний дараа гэнэт уйтгар төрөөд явчихсан. Бичих сэдэвгүй тул зугаагаа гаргах зүйлгүй болов. Тархиа гашилтал бодсоны дараа хаашаа ч юм нэг тийшээ явахаар шийдлээ. Ингээд Монголыг сонгож авав. Яагаад гэвэл тэнд сагсан бөмбөг шинээр үүсэн хөгжиж байгаа тухай надад найз маань нэгэнтээ ярьсан юм. Ер нь би сагсан бөмбөгт сэтгүүл зүйгээс илүү хайртай юм л даа. Ингээд «Москоу Таймс» сонинд хамт ажиллаж байсан нөхөдтэйгөө салах ёс гүйцэтгээд галт тэргэнд суун Улаанбаатарыг зорилоо. Монголын тухайд өргөн их тал, гэр, хонины мах, инээд хүрмээр малгай өмссөн намхан хүмүүс гэсэн төсөөлөл байв. Бусад нь нэг л толгойд буухгүй байсан гэдгийг нуух юун.

Гэтэл монголчууд сагсан бөмбөгөөр жинхэнэ өвчилчихөөд байсан үетэй таарлаа. Майкл Жордан, Чарльз Баркли, Хаким Олажьювон нарын нэрийг андахгүй юм. Гэвч тэдний чихэнд өөрийнх нь үндэсний баатрууд буюу Монголын сагсан бөмбөгийн холбооны «одуудын» нэр нь арай илүү дотно байлгүй яахав. Уг холбоог товчлон МБА гэж нэрлэдэг. МБА-гийн «дарга» нь парламентын гишүүн (Мэтт түүний албыг андуурчээ. Б.Одонжил УИХ-ын тамгын газарт ажилладаг. Д.Г) Банзрагчийн Одонжил бөгөөд тэрбээр Колумбийн

гавихгүй байгаагийн гол шалтгаан нь тэдний намхан нуруу. Манай багийн хамгийн өндөр тамирчин 194 см нуруутай байв. Хэрвээ Америкийн сагсан бөмбөгтэй зүйрлэх юм бол молтогчин туулай л гэсэн үг. «Бүргэдүүд»-ийн удирдлага өөрийнхөө багийг нэлээд хүчтэй болгохыг эрмэлзэхдээ Монголын хамгийн өндөр бөх Оргилболдод санал тавьсан. 208 см өндөр түүнийг Монголын Шакил О'Нил болгохыг хүссэн хэрэг. Гэвч Оргилболдтой хийсэн хэлэлцээ амжилтад хүрээгүй. Тэрбээр өөрийгөө тийм ч орчин үеийн хүн биш, сагсан

юм. Ингээд өөрийнхөө ивээн тэтгэгчдийн хүсэлтээр би багийнхаа албан ёсны бус алиалагчийн үүргийг гүйцэтгэх болсон юм. Тоглолт болгоны өмнө Деннис Родман шиг үсээ янз бүрээр будаг болов. Талбай дээр өрсөлдөгчидтэйгээ түлхэлцэж, заримтай нь зодолдож эхэлсэн. Үүнийхээ зэрэгцээ хараал урсгаж ялангуяа орос ярианы нарийн ширийнийг ойлгодог нэгнийг нь бүр ч муухайгаар хараана. (Бараг бүх монгол хүн орос хэл мэднэ) Бага бөмбөг цагариганд хийх тоолонд би цамцаа тайлж толгой дээгүүрээ дуугүүр мэт эргүүл-

хүрчихнэ. Ийм нөхцөлд эрүүл байх асуудал тун эргэлзээтэй биз дээ. Хүмүүс тоос залгиж, бис биедээ ханиад хүргэчихгүйн тулд амандаа хаалт хийж явна. (1996 онд нийслэлд тахал, холер өвчин дэлгэрсэн). Өвчний улмаас «Алтайн бүргэдүүдийн» сагсан бөмбөгчдийн шүд унаж , ихээхэн турж эцсэн. Талбай дээр гарах нь ч их цөөрсөн. Биднийг ялалтаа тэмдэглэн архи уун, тамхи баагиулж суухад эсрэг багийнхан маань бэлтгэлээ хийсээр л байлаа. Үүний дараахнаас бид хожигдож эхэлсэн дээ. Би 100 кг жинтэй байснаа 85 кг хүртэл

BY MATT TAIBBI

CHAPTER TWO: TRAITOR FOR HIRE

"As most of us know, the flight and fight response is a natural response in humans and animals. In times of danger the response is automatically activated and hormones, including adrenaline, are released into the blood stream. The hormones help the body prepare either to stay and fight the danger or to run away from it. This is the body's normal response to danger.

As the hormones move through our body it 'shuts down' the nonessential organs including the bowel, bladder and stomach. Our heart begins to beat faster and we begin to breathe more rapidly to help get oxygen and blood to the lungs, brain and muscle groups. This is all done so we can either stay and fight the situation or to get out of it quickly. Other physiological sensations of the fight and flight response include shaking, trembling, excessive perspiration. As a result of the bowel and bladder being 'shut down' some people feel as if they are going to have an attack of diarrhea or may feel an urgent need to urinate. Some people may feel as if they are going to be sick.

Fear as we all know is a huge part of our Anxiety Disorder. We may fear that we are having a heart attack, that we may die, go insane or lose control in some way. The fear may center around social concerns, obsessions or compulsions. It may be part of an ongoing memory of some traumatic experience or it could be constant worry about a particular personal situation.

Whatever our fear is . . . the more we think about it, and the more we worry about it . . . the more we are automatically turning on the fight and flight response. And the more we turn on the fight and flight response, the more our symptoms increase . . . as a result the more our fear is increased . . . the fight and flight increases . . . symptoms increase . . . and around and around it goes. It is no wonder so many of us feel out of control."

Pamphlet distributed by the Panic Anxiety Education and Management Service
Fullerton, South Australia

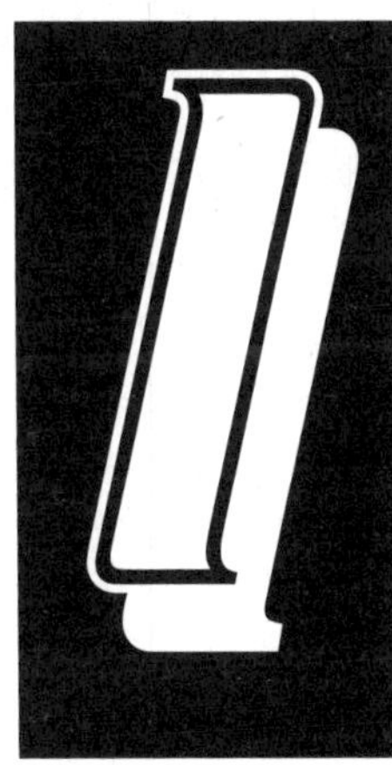

I'd been out of surgery for three hours when two doctors in pink gowns entered my room. My parents, who had been slumped in chairs on either side of my hospital bed, exhausted after a long week, spun around in fright. Something was obviously wrong. Not only had the doctors not knocked, but they were wearing ominous plastic face shields—a type of mask I had never seen before, like a salad-bar guard that extended over the forehead straight down to the chin.

"We have to talk," said one of them—the male one. They'd sent one of each sex, which in my paranoid state I thought had been done on purpose, as though to soothe me.

I'd just had a radical thoracotomy, a traumatic invasive surgery to correct an empyema, which is a life-threatening buildup of infected fluid in the chest cavity. The empyema had developed as a result of complications from pneumonia, which I'd contracted halfway around the world while playing professional basketball in Ulan-Bator, Mongolia. I'd been evacuated from Mongolia to Boston, where the world's finest diagnosticians had spent a fruitless week trying to figure out what was wrong with me. They knew I had a pneumonic condition and an empyema which needed to be corrected, but they hadn't found the bug that had caused it. Now it looked as though they finally had the answer.

"You have bacterial meningitis," said the face-shield male. "A fatal strain. We may be able to correct it with antibiotics—and we may not. We have to do some more tests."

"It's highly contagious," piped in the female. "And a potential public health problem. We may have to track down all the people who were on the plane with you."

At the last news, my mother instinctively released my hand for a moment. I looked up at her in horror. Never in my life had I felt more alone. Then the doctors left, promising to return later.

After the operation, which had been extremely painful, I'd managed to cajole the nurses into improving the quality of my pain medication. The spoils of that victory—Dilaudid, or pharmaceutical heroin—were now my sole defense against the reality of impending death. When my parents left I popped a few extra pills and raised my hospital bed to a more upright position. The room was dark and there was a tripleheader of Clint Eastwood spaghetti Westerns on television—the perfect catalyst for gradual, painless mental readjustment. By the third movie, *A Fistful of Dollars*, the drugs had lost their force and I was making desperate vows with myself as I watched the blue predawn light break through my window.

Never again, I thought. Never again would I be so careless in making my life decisions. Family, friends, and security would, if I made it through this illness, now and forever be my top priorities. No more asinine self-promoting trips to the middle of nowhere. It was time to say *yes* to health insurance and *yes* to gainful employment; it was time to say *no* to freelancing and *no* to bacterial disease. I regretted not having been married, not having a family of my own. I cried for the wife I didn't have, then I started crying for myself. It was time for a change. It was time to clean up my act.

Late into the morning I fell asleep, only to be woken up by the face-shield infectious disease specialists. This time they were shieldless. Shieldless man was apologetic and shuffling his feet; he left the talking to Mrs. Shieldless.

"We made a mistake," she said. "It turns out that fifteen percent of all people are carriers of that meningitis. You've probably had it for years. We'll take care of it with antibiotics today."

Reprieved!

I waited for the doctors to leave, then reached for the Dilaudid. It was time for a little recreation. When I saw my dose had been halved, I hit the buzzer to call for the nurse. Wasn't there any *service* in this place?

A month and a half later, all those post-Eastwood vows were old history. I got on a plane out of the United States again, this time headed for Moscow.

The expatriate mentality is a tough thing to explain easily. Any affluent or even middle-class American who renounces the good life of sushi delivery and 50-channel cable television to relocate permanently to some third-world hole usually has to be motivated by a highly destructive personality defect. Either that, or something about home creates psychological demons that in turn create the urge for radical escape.

I'd moved overseas straight out of college and been a classic expatriate ever since. I had all the symptoms: periodic unsuccessful attempts to repatriate (I had tried twice to move back to America since I first moved to Russia in 1992), a tendency to try to make grandiose foreign adventures compensate for a total inability to accumulate money; bad teeth; unhealthy personal relationships, etc. I'd been aware for years that my passion for uprooting and completely changing my lifestyle and even my career was like a drug addiction—not only did I get off on it, but I needed to do it fairly regularly just to keep from getting the shakes.

For instance: I'd missed my own college graduation. I finished my work midsemester, moved to my father's place in New York, and spent two miserable months waitering and begging my father for money to fly overseas to Russia. During that time I was feeling down and called an old girlfriend whom I liked a lot for being bright and cheerful. We met, but I fell into a paralytic midcoital depression after a disastrous date in which I'd lost sixty of her dollars playing three-card monty in Times Square. After that afternoon ended psychotically, with both of us convinced that we would never see each other again, I quickly called another old girlfriend and, trembling, asked on a whim to revive a serious relationship I'd just broken up. It was a mistake and I knew it, but by then I was on a roll and couldn't stop. Meanwhile I was having trouble even keeping my waitering uniform clean, and yet I was planning this trip overseas, which theoretically was supposed to be an alternative to looking for a job at home. And while speeding tickets and other old bills were rapidly accumulating, I managed somehow to weasel about $1,500 out of parents and other sources and finally got on a plane to St. Petersburg.

The instant I set foot on the plane, my life changed. I was charged with adrenaline, alert, positive, full of plans, inner demons palliated by a need to cope with new and unpredictable logistical problems. It was a high I would have to keep coming back to, and after a while I knew exactly where to find the vein.

Seven months after that first flight my life spun out of control again and I moved to Tashkent, Uzbekistan, where I finally started selling news articles with some regularity. In another five months I was kicked out of Uzbekistan by the Uzbek secret police after a passing critical characterization of the President I'd written appeared on the AP wire, and I moved back to St. Petersburg. Six months later my life was a mess again. Racked with loneliness and insecurity, I moved to Moscow to take a job as a sports editor of an English-language newspaper there. Five months later, calmed by the experience of regular employment, I figured my foreign trip was over and moved home. At home, where I found myself alone and doing part-time landscaping work in the country, I quickly had a howling-on-the-bathroom-floor, ten-alarm nervous breakdown, started to lose my hair, then moved north and had an affair with a married woman, broke up her marriage, became restless again, and moved back to Russia to play pro baseball for the Red Army. Five months after that the divorcée and I moved back to the East Coast. I took a job as a private detective, gained twenty pounds, bought a metallic blue Oldsmobile and commuted 3 hours every day to work. There, at the detective job, I briefly developed a passion for searching public records to find welchers and hidden assets. But after seven months of listening to National Public Radio during the commute and sampling Blockbuster video selections, I freaked out again, quarreled with the divorcée, and moved to Russia to write a book about serial murder, simultaneously taking a job with my old newspaper, the *Moscow Times*, as a news reporter. After five months I returned to the divorcée and went through a long and agonizing breakup, at the end of which I left America once again and returned to the *Moscow Times* for the third time. Right away I reconsidered my decision and tried to go back to her, and she broke up yet another meaningful affair she'd developed in the meantime as we agreed that I would move home in the summer. But then when summer came, and I found myself in the middle of covering a mini-coup in the middle of a presidential election—this was Moscow, 1996—I couldn't bring myself to go home, and a few harrowing phone calls later that affair was over and I was soon after finding the vein again and heading for Mongolia, where I went completely nuts and became a professional basketball star in the MBA, the Mongolian Basketball Association. I dyed my hair different colors before every game, shaved messages in the side of my head, drew scores of technical fouls, and became known as the "Mongolian Rodman." A local radio station made me their morning rock DJ for an English-language program. And shortly afterward I saw, but didn't speak to, a beautiful Indonesian girl at a party at the British embassy. Two days later I went to the opera alone and she appeared out of nowhere and asked me to take a picture of her and her friends. I got her address—not everyone had home phones in Mongolia—and when I went to see her a few nights later, she answered the door in a black silk robe. *Score!* But then the whole house of cards fell: I got sick, began to sweat feverishly, lost 15, 20, then 30 pounds, watched our team fall apart and out of playoff contention, finally began to cough up blood, and just days after New Year's, when I nearly beat up a short bald Frenchman who was trying to take my girl away, I was evacuated to the States for the operation and lost touch with everyone.

By the time I recovered from the operation, I knew I had serious problems, but that wasn't much incentive to change. Even just out of a serious illness and marked with a nasty fresh ten-inch scar, fleeing was still less frightening than anything else. After all, what was I supposed to do—stay in sexually inert, suffocating America, where I couldn't get anything going for myself, and *work things out?* No. It was better to roll the dice on another wild strike overseas and hope I got closer to getting the monkey off my back before the next crash.

After a few weeks of phone calls from home, what I finally settled on as a next move was the editorship of an alternative newspaper in Moscow called *Living Here*, a publication that was currently dead but would, my weird Dutch publisher promised, revive on a shoestring when I came back. This was a new kind of risk, a business risk and a creative risk, a job for which there would probably be no guaranteed salary and a very high likelihood of failure. So I had a final checkup and just after my 27th birthday in March I got back on a plane again.

There is a common misconception that people who lead Bohemian lifestyles are more dependable as friends than people leading respectable, rat-race professional lives. It makes sense on the surface: Bohemians don't have money, so naturally they have to value friendship more. In fact, nothing is further from the truth. The *Living Here–eXile* fiasco, which was the source of much amusement in the expatriate community, was a classic case of low-tech people acting, well, low-tech. The key figures all spent a lot of time screwing one another in the pettiest ways possible, over a very small amount of money and attention.

The short version of my complicity in all of this was that, once I got well, I called an old friend, *Living Here* publisher

Manfred Witteman, secretly hoping to hear that former editor Mark Ames had left, so that I could take the editing job. Manfred complied with good news. Ames was no longer with *Living Here.* I was in.

You had to have been there when I arrived to understand what a desperate group of losers I was joining up with. It was an absurd *class* of people: a bunch of jobless expatriate fuck-offs, scraping around to start a threepenny "alternative" newspaper in a city where practically anyone who spoke English and could keep from drooling in public could make $50K almost overnight in a variety of professions. . . . Since I'd met him years before at the *Moscow Times* (he was the computer systems manager while I was sports editor), I hadn't ever wanted to know what Manfred's problems were, but he clearly had them. First and foremost, he was strange-*looking:* he had a pinched, bright-red face and a permanently tousled head of short, thinning blond hair atop a wobbly, gelatin body, with a narrow chest and short arms that were, as Gogol once wrote of a character in the story "The Coach," "less like arms than like elongated potatoes." Constantly scheming, thinking up new entrepreneurial ideas, Manfred was always a little ahead of himself—looking at income projections instead of his less forgiving current account statements, or else starting up oddly unexciting projects, like a crossword puzzle magazine in Russian. . . . I knew all of this about him when I signed on, and I knew that his talk about finding $6,000 in start-up money was wishful thinking at best, but I was anxious to have my own project and had my own problems anyway, so I went for it.

Shitfaced and in disguise as the "Mongolian Rodman" at a party with high-flying sports superstar Batzaya (left), the Mongolian Basketball Association's reigning slam-dunk champion.

Manfred had somehow made a deal to put out a paper the day I arrived—some money must have depended on this somehow, I never quite heard the full story—so when I arrived I had to go straight to his apartment, which at the time was also doubling as the offices of the new *Living Here.* When I got there we had seven hours to deadline and a full newspaper to put out. Panic reigned. Manfred was already bickering with the owner, a tiny shrieking twenty-something basket case of a Russian girl named Marina, who bore a face like a canker sore and was liable to burst out crying at the drop of a hat. When I got there, they were arguing about when to take the films to the print shop—Marina wanted to stay to finish an ad, even though it looked like we were going to miss deadline.

"Come on!" Manfred was screaming, showing her a clenched potato-fist. "I'll punch your face!" he said.

"Just shut up!" she shrieked, tears rolling down her face. "I hate you! Shut up!"

While listening to this, I was sitting in horror trying to edit the pages, which were a mess. For contributors I had people like one Keith Gessen, who a week before had called me in America to pitch the idea of reviewing classic books like *Crime and Punishment* in the book review section. He'd been very put out when I insisted on reviewing new books, because that's what you did at a *news*paper. Then there was Vijay Maheshewari, a slithery and unpleasant schmoozing Indian-American, whose copy possessed the rare quality of being both pretentious and ungrammatical.

"Vijay edited some of the pages for you, since we knew you were going to be late," Manfred said, placing a hand on my shoulder and trying, I guessed finally, to reassure me. Meanwhile I was filling in huge gaps in the paper with raw text that was both lame and completely unfunny, feeling used and ashamed.

A few days later, when the chance arose to bail on this crew and join up with Ames, who was both sane and a friend, I jumped at the chance. Marina wept, Manfred sank into a deep depression, Vijay tried to reconnect, and, meanwhile, the rest of Moscow went about its business without noticing. It was the sort of slimy, low-rent intrigue that you would have found in a Bolshevik party cell meeting in 1909—a scandal that was totally meaningless except in the context of the bloated egos of the lazy twentysomething "revolutionaries" involved.

My meeting with Ames, in which I discussed the terms of my betrayal of Manfred, was a semisecret. We held it in the Starlite Diner, a glitzy prefab American hamburger joint near the center. The Starlite was originally designed to be a sort of culinary/architectural joke, a tiny slice of high-budget over-the-top Americana smack in the middle of big bad foreign Moscow, but the humor was a bit problematic. It was, after all, hard to be quaint and imperial at the same time. The management apparently didn't see the contradiction. . . . Whatever: in early 1997, there was nowhere else to get a good breakfast in the city, since expat Americans were still the only people around who ate out in the mornings.

Ames and I sank low in our booth. I think we were both a little embarrassed. By an amazing coincidence, the covers of both my first *Living Here* and Mark's most recent *eXile* had come out almost exactly identical, both featuring platinum blondes in leather bodysuits. We looked like assholes: two tall, swarthy, sweaty white Americans, sitting a few feet away from identical self-promoting publications.

I'd known Mark for a little over a year through *Living Here*, which I had contributed to under the pseudonym "Don Kipines" while working for the *Moscow Times*. I'd always gotten along with him. Although he made me nervous—extensive nerd experience had trained me to be deeply suspicious of tall, handsome males who affect tragic personalities in public—I admired the fact that he was so universally loathed in the Moscow foreign community. It wasn't hard to see why people hated him. During his career with *Living Here*, he'd published a notoriously offensive column under a cheesy, grinning beefcake photo of himself, a column in which he made a habit of taking nasty gratuitous shots at otherwise respectable people in town. There was a tremendous uproar, for instance, when Ames published a vicious article dissecting the conspicuously unattractive face of *Moscow Times* and *Independent* correspondent Helen Womack. He took

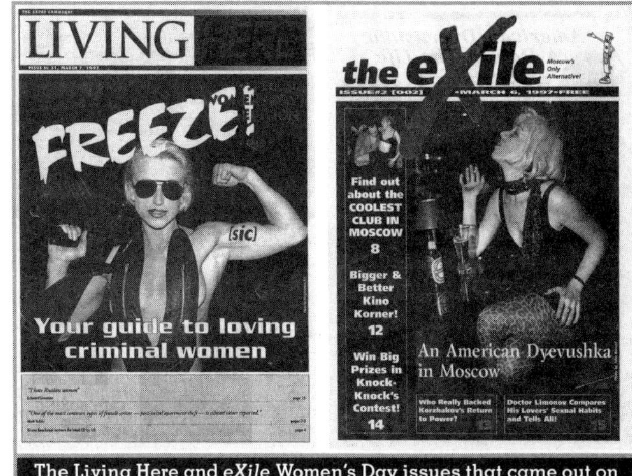

The Living Here and *eXile* Women's Day issues that came out on the same day, looking suspiciously alike.

Womack's column photo, blew it up, and scanned in arrows and circles highlighting the uglier parts of Womack's face.

It was, of course, a totally irresponsible use of the press, and as a working professional I might then have been turned off by it too—except that I'd never really liked Womack's columns all that much. . . . Another one of his targets was the aggressively menopausal Jean MacKenzie, my news editor at

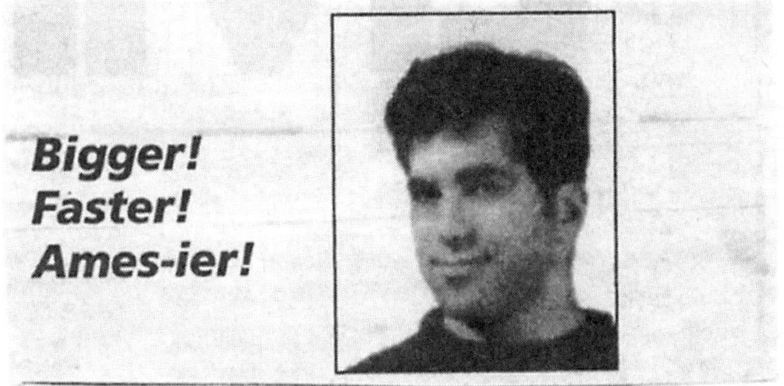

the *Moscow Times*, who was not only an office tyrant but a frankly awful writer who punished the Moscow community for years with a column (complete with grim photo) that revealed far too much about her disappointing and certainly physically abhorrent love life. Ames predicted in a "ghoul pool" list of likely upcoming fatalities that she would soon be stoned to death by her writers. There was an implicit sincere hope in this prediction's fulfillment that everybody felt and most people were probably horrified by. What no one understood, though, was that it was the very sincerity of the article that really upset Jean, which I could clearly see was

CHAPTER TWO

worth something, even if it turned public opinion in her favor.

Our experts agree that the hairline is showing signs of recession, unless her wig was suddenly pulled back by one of the many children she hangs out with.
The eyes betray either an enormous amount of Kazakh gashish-smoking, or else
ing her sex columns.
Actually, our panel of experts found her chin to be rather sexy. Sort of Sharon Stone meets Winston Churchill.
MT
Source: Panel of Experts

Before I returned to Moscow, when I thought I was going to be editing *Living Here*, I'd conceived a diabolical plan to destroy Ames. My plan was to be extremely friendly to Mark, and then make sure it got back to him that I was working round-the-clock and totally abstaining from alcohol, drugs, and girls, except for the occasional theater or ballet date. Then I would put out a newspaper that was witty in a socially acceptable way, cheerful, professional, at least slightly duller than his, and error-free, with heavy emphasis on the type of straight-news reporting that I knew he couldn't bring himself to do for his own paper. My own photograph would not appear anywhere in the paper, nor would any soul-searching or lengthy first-person testimonials. In short, I would be selling the very *absence* of Ames-ian human qualities to my readers. And I knew they would buy. More importantly, I knew that a prolonged-enough barrage of this kind of treatment would so demoralize Ames that it would send him careening into a Prozac prescription, if not outright suicide. Don't get me wrong, I really liked Mark and valued his friendship. But my ego was at stake.

Now none of that was necessary. Everything made sense now. No Manfred. No Marina. No playing "adult" to win market share. All I had to do was surrender and the world would be beautiful. As for the other consideration—the fact of joining the Ames operation to be the straight man, the hired journalistic square slipping on the "darkly trenchant" banana peels of Ames's "brooding artist" persona, that was fine. After all, why not. . . . For a manic-depressive like myself, playing the square might even be therapeutic. Besides, I had other things to worry about.

Mark didn't know what I'd gone through my first night with Manfred and therefore wasn't aware, as we sat there at the Starlite, that he held all the cards. He seemed shocked when I quickly accepted his offer of a coeditorship of his paper, with a raise of a full *one hundred dollars* over my *Living Here* salary. He didn't know that I'd been nervous even to ask for that much, or that I probably would have worked for free rather than go back to Manfred.

"So that's it?" he asked, stunned.

"Sure," I said, nervously extending my hand across the table. I'd never in my life made a "business" deal before and wasn't sure whether people shook hands to complete them, or whether that was something I'd picked up from cartoons. Maybe people just snapped their briefcases shut and got up—who knew? Ames didn't care. He shook on it and then just glared at me, waiting for me to pay my half of the check.

You have to really be able to put things in perspective, to have an instinctive grasp of the weird flow of history, to understand how quixotic and absurd it was to have two men our age negotiating a $100 raise in the secret setting of a pink hamburger joint in Moscow, 1997. This was the city where, six years before, commercialism—the "American Way"—finally vanquished its last, weird, menacing and somehow nerdly competitor. The Soviet mind-set, what Russians call *sovok*, seemed now to exist as a living emasculated souvenir, in the form of elevators that didn't work and plumbers who went on three-day vodka binges on their way to your emergency repair call. All of that was now just a charming little memory. There was a new sheriff in town—money. He was efficient and ruthless. He fixed your toilet before it was broken. And he had no tolerance for anyone who didn't want to live well.

That being true, why were two capable, well-educated Americans—members of the very imperial race that had laid the new greed ideology on Russians—haggling over play raises in what was essentially a play business? Were we kidding, just taking the piss out of someone? No, no way. No one could possibly be that obnoxious and worthless simultaneously. Something else, something much more private and sad, had to be going on.

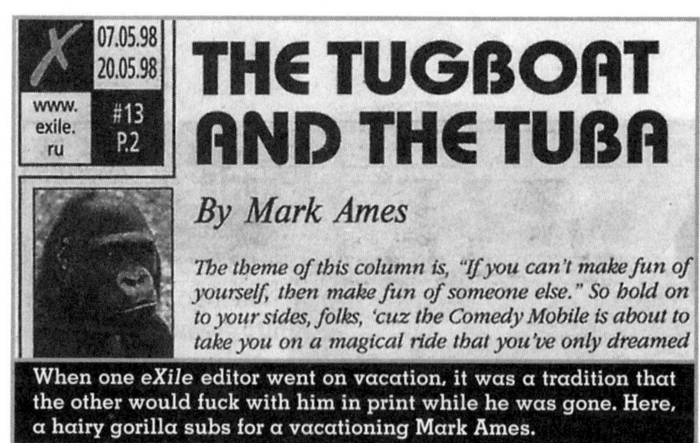
X 07.05.98 20.05.98 www.exile.ru #13 P.2

THE TUGBOAT AND THE TUBA

By Mark Ames

The theme of this column is, "If you can't make fun of yourself, then make fun of someone else." So hold on to your sides, folks, 'cuz the Comedy Mobile is about to take you on a magical ride that you've only dreamed

When one eXile editor went on vacation, it was a tradition that the other would fuck with him in print while he was gone. Here, a hairy gorilla subs for a vacationing Mark Ames.

For my part, I was like Mark in that I'd originally come to Russia because of Russian books, which had been my chief retreat in life since I was about eighteen. That was when I got the first hint that I might eventually need to flee my native country.

At NYU, my first college, I only had one friend—my Brazilian roommate, Roderigo Lopes. Tall and sandy-haired, immensely likable, with a million-dollar shit-eating Latin smile, he was happy and willing to play any part in order to keep the flow of women to his room steady, taking advantage of incredible acting range. He even hit it off with suburban big-hair metalheads in sweatpants, a type I knew his old-world mentality secretly reviled. In less than a year, what seemed like hundreds of girls shed their sweatpants in Roderigo's bed while I waited outside in the hall with gritted teeth. And it wasn't just those dirthead girls. He also sampled pompous lit majors in black clothes, adopting a troubled soul and an occasional smoking habit to make himself credibly countercultural. There were also some repressed women's studies majors in there whom he argued with half-earnestly, half-jokingly (just the way that type likes to) before skillfully calling their bluff and feigning respectful but still uncontrollable passion for a few minutes or hours, depending on his class schedule. And despite my obvious envy and contempt for him, we got along famously, which depressed me even more. I couldn't even hate him. All I could do was marvel at his incredible patience and his total lack of angst. He was the happiest American I'd ever met, and he wasn't even American. At the time, I didn't see the significance of that.

Roderigo's presence spooked me into retiring from life for a while. I spent most of my time at my father's place in the West Village, building a fearsome arsenal of loser credentials. I spent so much time indoors that whenever I came out and tried to joke with anyone, they'd just politely laugh and leave immediately, frightened by my dark-ringed eyes and my way-too-intense laugh, which was becoming a cackle, my first adult affectation. By November of that first year I was totally paranoid and unfit for any human company. I gave up even trying to talk to girls, parting so completely with hope that I wasn't even afraid of them after a while.

So I spent a lot of time reading. And since I'd learned by then to associate almost everything in America with failure, I made sure to read books set far from the States. What drew me first to Russia were the stories of Nikolai Gogol. Gogol himself had written his stories as an escape from a personality problem like mine. As a lonely clerk in nineteenth-century St. Petersburg, he made it through his sleepless panicked nights by, as he put it, "thinking up the funniest things I could imagine." I remember reading "The Nose," his nightmarish story about a petty official who wakes up with his nose missing and chases it all over town, and thinking that I had found for the first time someone who was capable of laughing at the kind of depression I was feeling. And not only that, I was able to find that solace in a place that, since it had been crafted by a great master, made a lot more sense and was a lot more aesthetically attractive than the world I was living in at the time.

I imagined Gogol's Russia as a place that was dirty and corrupt and backward, but also charged with mischievous and malevolent life—the exact opposite of the cheery, sanitary world of beer-guzzling "young people" I lived in. I imagined happily that these same frat boys and film school poseurs would not have had it so good in Gogol's world. They would have existed as grotesque mediocrities, human mustaches, trapped in endless inane conversations about the price of snuff or their chances of being promoted to chief assistant clerk. They would never have had sex, or been permitted a single decent human quality. It was a just and beautiful world and I much preferred it to real life.

For years after that I buried myself in Russian books, and finally went away to Russia to study.

Leningrad in 1990 was obviously very different than Gogol's Petersburg, but there were enough things that were the same—the rotting buildings, the grime and the mud, the mindless, intractable bureaucracy, the seediness—that I knew right away that I'd found home. The people in my exchange program were very much like the people at NYU, cheery, with stonewashed jeans sewn into their skins, always happily planning out their next beer run. Most fell into black depressions in the absence of material comforts and that total lack of friendliness on the faces of everyone around them. They couldn't believe that the stern Russian guards at the dorm door, or the fat exhausted maids who washed the stairs with handmade mops, or the cafeteria workers who cleaned their dishes, didn't break out in gushing welcoming smiles every time they walked through the door. It was something they'd always taken for granted, while I, a self-hating geek, hadn't. I was thrilled. The place was made for me.

Russia back then was a real panacea for a depressed person. Back then, it was still grim and poor enough that almost no one thought about getting ahead or looking fashionable. Get ahead where? Fashionable how? There was no place to go in life and no one to look fashionable for. The only people who had the option of moving up were people ambitious enough to voluntarily become grotesque, i.e., people who either joined the party or were real ball-busting Soviet bureaucrats.

Those types were loathed by most everybody, though, which made for a weird sort of balance—unlike the States, where the grotesque people were in the majority and zealously determined to be liked.

And unlike the States, the nongrotesque and the unambitious were allowed to have lives. There was no pressure or fear of failure—failure was the guaranteed right of every citizen. Being a loser wasn't so bad, because everybody else was, too. And despite the gray uniformity of the communist architecture, there was more of a human face on day-to-day life than there was in the States. When my computer broke, I didn't—and, at the time, couldn't—go to a clean, homogenized computer-repair center. I just asked around and found out who knew how to fix hard drives. Then I walked across campus and met a freakish amateur computer geek named Slava, who hadn't been out of his room except to buy bread in nearly six months, and drank vodka with his more mobile roommates while he did the job. It wasn't that great of a time, but it earned more points, on the scorecard of life memories, than a trip to Computer City.

I returned home that year with a Polaroid photo showing a delicious brunette lying supine and totally naked in her bathtub. This was Lena, a girl I'd dated there. Lena taught me Russian. I'd met her at a friend's birthday party and subsequently visited her house every day after class, staying in her room until about six o'clock.

We sat there with a dictionary, having extremely painful conversations—"English lessons"—until finally she'd passively lie down and let me screw her. She didn't ever seem to be enjoying herself too much, but she also didn't seem to care. It was great every time. And afterward I always got hurried out the door. She had some kind of low-level gangster boyfriend she saw at night, a guy who sold hard currency. He wasn't the kind of gangster modern Russia produces, who might have killed me with a machine gun or cut off my head, but the old-fashioned kind, who would have beat me with a pipe—a sweeter, more romantic figure.

The States would never allow me a quiet, gentle girl with an exotic face and a perfect body who would give me naked pictures of her as a heartfelt, sentimental going-away present. With time I realized that an American girl would only do something like that as a joke, or as a way of being "sexy." Americans don't do anything without irony.

Six years later, in 1996, that beautiful world I'd studied in was vanishing. That had been ensured by the arrival of the conquering expatriate community.

This was the same crowd that had driven me to Russia in the first place—the same beer-drinking, sweatshirt-wearing "think-positive"

W O R K I N G   H E R E

Traitor For Hire

"Working Here," a new regular feature in this space, will also be published in the Russian daily "Trud," where it is tentatively entitled "A Correspondent Changes Professions." It catalogues eXile editor Matt Taibbi's experiences in the Russian workplace—a new job each week, in the journalistic style of Jack London, minus the snowshoes and political convictions. This first column will not appear in "Trud."

"I can't do it, Mark. I gave them my word."

- from a conversation with eXile editor Mark Ames in February.

I said that from my home in New York a month ago, just after I'd taken a job as the editor of the then... and now... defunct "Living Here." Mark Ames, an old friend, had called me at home to slander my new employers and try to hire me away from them to work for his new newspaper, a thing called "eXile."

My response was unequivocal. I detested the lazy morality in the modern business world. I loathed corporations which laid off long-serving employees to please shareholders, and was repulsed by sports agents who convinced players to leave teams that were already paying them millions. *I would take a different path.* After hanging up on Mark, I shook my head and thought: why can't we all just get along?

Of course I'm now with eXile. It didn't take much. A little more money. A few more job security guarantees. A carpeted office.

Regrettably, this first installment of "Working Here" is about Living Here. Thematically it doesn't quite fit into the column, since the editors of "Trud" and I agreed that I would only write about Russian workplaces. Timewise, however, it's appropriate. The "Trud" people thought two shifts at any workplace would be enough material for an article—a pair of eight-hour hauls at a slaughterhouse, a roundtrip stint as a airline steward, etc. That's about how long I lasted at Living Here. A day of editing, another day of schmoozing, and then I was gone.

When I arrived two weeks ago, Living Here was in chaos. My picture had been lifted from a fax of a copy of my passport and stuck over my byline, giving readers the impression that the paper was being edited by a Rorshach test. One page was empty, the classifieds had not yet been written, and, in a sudden and extreme new symptom of the paper's psychosis, the erstwhile "Dr. Rajneesh" had renounced his ethnicity, opting instead for the odd species-ist pseudonym "Thirsty Dog."

None of this bothered me—I knew what Living Here was all about and admired it. But then eXile called me out of the dugout over the weekend, and before I knew it I was saying goodbye to these good times and going to the show.

Living Here was a great concept that came along at the right time. It was an experiment in non-journalism by non-people: not only did its writers use juvenile pseudonyms, but even some of its founders worked in the shadows, preferring to this day to remain anonymous, in order to protect their day jobs. It was committed to a policy of bad taste, being predicated on the notion that most ex-pats don't actually go to the theater and the symphony, and instead spend most of their time, as one local media mogul recently put it, "getting pissed and getting laid".

Somewhere along the line—ironically, just about at the time it started making money—Living Here had an identity crisis. The same amateurish attitude that helped it distinguish itself from Moscow's other "respectable" English-language publications was now preventing it from being a viable business. There were fights about money, petty editorial disagreements, and problems with disgusted clients and advertisers (LH writers were known to complain to restaurant owners about not getting free beer after they had already been given a free meal for a review). Take that set of circumstances and add in the fact that nearly everyone involved with the paper was a borderline delusional narcissistic personality *before* he started working there, and you have a business that was bound to collapse in an earthquake of invective and bitterness, as LH did this winter and again last week.

My part in this was the selling of my soul for a little more money; as punishment I will now spend eternity sharing an office with Mark Ames, of all people. Ames's eternal punishment, incidentally, is his own column.

Having sold ourselves down this river of "professionalism," eXile now has no choice but to become the next step after Living Here in the evolutionary ladder. eXile will now seek to become a streamlined, market-first, corporate-friendly humor *machine*. We will have a *sales team*. For our sordid practical jokes, we will use sophisticated *hi-fi technology*. Before running each childish, pseudo-pornographic issue, we will consult *attorneys*. That upper-case "X" in our name? We hate it. It fucks up our headlines. But it's perfect for selling T-shirts, and that's what we're about now.

types whose keg parties had given me panic attacks all through college. They'd invaded Russia in enormous numbers since my student days, working as lawyers, accountants, stockbrokers, and government consultants, working in unison, with the help of massive amounts of Western aid, to help build the new Russia in their image. They announced to the poor that being poor was now officially their own fault, and that they had been mistaken if they thought they'd been having fun before. They also purged the city as best they could of the very dirt, grime, and gloom that had made me fall in love with Russia in the first place. They even got rid of the unfriendliness, flooding the airwaves with Western-made commercials full of grinning, happy Russian consumers, and preaching customer service skills, mostly by way of loudly demanding, in English, better service everywhere. Those fucking Russians would like them whether they liked it or not!

I put in a long stretch working for the *Moscow Times*, a placid publication which read like the Lincoln, Nebraska, *Neighborhood Gazette* and cheered the expatriate community's campaign against the old unfriendly days. Then, finally, I realized that the only way I could feel free again—the only way I could keep from impurifying myself with visits to McDonald's and gleaming new "Western" supermarkets—would be to move even farther away from the advance of "progress." So in a panic I quit and moved to Mongolia, which I rightly guessed would be more unspoiled than the new Russia.

But even there, in that remote Asiatic valley where the plague visited every summer and beautiful golden eagles perched on your balcony, I saw the same process beginning . . . cellphones, corporations moving in to teach Mongol goatherds to gather cashmere more effectively, lots of rah-rah Uncle Sam talk about "progress." In fact, I'd been forced to write a lot of that talk myself, as the head of the English-language department in the Mongolian state wire service—acres of blather about how wonderful it was that Mongolia was gaining all of our wonderful Western values, how copper and oil deposits would finally be exploited by beneficent transnationals, how Mongolia might become the "next Kuwait."

Only occasionally did news of the old idiosyncratic Mongolia creep out on to the wires I managed. Sometimes I was allowed to send out state news releases exactly as they had appeared in the Mongolian press. A few were gems, beautiful relics of the lost world. I remember the lead of one piece:

"President Mendsaikhany Enkhsaikhan today met with his cabinet of ministers to announce to them the upcoming unavoidable fact of a total eclipse of the sun."

I sent that piece on to the wire and was reprimanded for it. My boss, an Oxford grad named Amarsanaa, sensibly decided that he didn't want his country to look backward around the world. Economically, there was too much at stake now, given the new necessity to present a "professional" image, to let that happen.

When I was evacuated out of Mongolia and left in the hospital to ponder my bad luck, I realized I was in trouble. Mongolia, the most remote place on the planet, a place where sheep were still occasionally used as currency, was no longer safe from the mind-set that I'd fled from in the first place. There was really nowhere else on the map to hide. So the only solution was to drop off the map entirely.

That's why I was joining the *eXile*. It was the end of the road. Doing just about anything else would mean getting a real job, with a boss committed to upholding all the values I'd spent so many years fleeing in despair from. It would mean total surrender. At the *eXile*, on the other hand, I would at least be able to say my piece for the short period of time we'd be able to survive financially. I didn't think it would be very long. I anticipated going home and throwing myself at my parents' mercy in half a year.

Ames, for his part, had cut the cord long ago. He had been thoroughly unemployable in Moscow for more than a year, due to his column. All he wanted now was to keep airing it out in print as long as possible, at the expense of my reputation, if necessary. I wouldn't have to worry about him selling out, anyway.

Although there was nothing really to lose, we were both frightened for ourselves. If the paper collapsed now, after we'd gone through the public comedy of joining fringe forces to earnestly pursue some vague quixotic goal of global vengeance against the "community," in the process openly taking ourselves seriously as voices who deserved to be heard, we'd be ruined—the biggest losers the city had ever seen.

That was what we thought then. But what we didn't know at the time was that circumstances greatly favored us. What eventually lifted the *eXile* above the level of an inspirational tale for a slacker group therapy session was the fact that our little effort at nerd redemption was taking place at a very specific time: alongside one of the most violent periods of social change in this half of the century.

Moscow 1997 was not only the site of some of the most Byzantine corruption the world has ever seen—with literally billions of dollars in government money being stolen more or less openly out of the budget on a routine basis—it was also

Official Rules of Oligarchy

George Soros says: I love this game!

Welcome to OLIGARCHY, the new board game of Russian politics, brought to you by eXile Brothers. Playing OLIGARCHY, you will feel like a real-live Russian oligarch! Just follow these easy instructions and you too can preside over a vast criminalized empire!

What You Need

Aside from the board, cards, and game figures provided by the *eXile*, players will need the following items to play: two six-sided dice and, for game-playing purposes, at least 500,000 rubles (but preferably much, much more), particularly in denominations of ten thousand rubles or smaller. For denominations of 10 rubles, use coins, poker chips, or any other objects. Players will also need a paper and pencil for recording property ownership.

Starting

All players start by choosing one of the provided GAME FIGURES (a Mercedes symbol, a TT pistol, a cell phone, etc.) and placing their figure on the USAID square. Each player will begin with the following amount of money, in the following denominations: one 10,000 ruble note, one 5,000 ruble note, three 1,000 ruble notes, three 500 ruble notes, one 200 ruble note, two 100 ruble notes, and ten units of 10 rubles.

After a die roll to determine the order of play (player who rolls the lowest amount goes first), players begin play by travelling clockwise from USAID.

Object of the Game

The object of the game is to acquire as much property as possible through legal and illegal means, control commerce and the press, bankrupt your opponents and finally seize the entire board. In pursuit of this goal, players buy properties, and try to obtain each of the properties in the seven Financial-Industrial Groups on the board. Once players own a whole Financial-Industrial Group, they can develop each of the properties by buying additional Newspapers and Banks, which increase the value of their properties, and, accordingly, the cost of the bribes other players pay when they land on those properties. Players also attempt to gain influence by buying the four Members of Cabinet on the board. A player wins when each of the other players is bankrupt.

Buying Properties

If you have the money, you may buy any property on the board, if it is not already owned by anyone else. Once you own that property, other players must pay you a bribe every time they land on that property. The cost of that bribe is indicated on the property itself. Each player must keep track on paper of which properties he owns.

Financial-Industrial Groups

The board is divided up into eight Financial-Industrial Groups. When one owns all the properties in a financial-industrial group (i.e. Oneximbank, Norilsk Nickel, and Svyazinvest), bribes for each of those properties automatically double. Players may also then develop each property by buying additional newspapers and banks and placing them on those properties. Newspapers cost 500 rubles, banks 1000 rubles. Players may have a maximum of four newspapers on each square, and a maximum of two banks. Corresponding rises in bribe prices are indicated on the property itself.

Cabinet Members

Players may attempt to secure influence by purchasing one or more Members of Cabinet. As with properties, ownership of Cabinet Members guarantees bribe revenues for the owner. Furthermore, ownership of all four Cabinet Members allows the owner to block the purchase of any property by any player once. For instance, if Player A owns all four Cabinet Members, he may block the purchase of LogoVaz by player B the first time player B lands on that property. The second time, however, Player A may not object. However, he may object the first time Player B attempts to buy, say, Alfa Bank. Also, a player owning all four Cabinet Members may, if he chooses, not pick up a Kompromat card when he lands on the Kompromat square.

Bribe prices for cabinet members are as follows: 500 rubles, if you own one official, 1000r for two, 1500r for three, and 2000r for four.

Insider Dealing

Players may sell any property or cabinet member to each other at any time, agreeing on a price amongst themselves. The price may include such items as "Pass Through Your Podyezd Alive" cards.

Your Podyezd

When you land on "Go to Your Podyezd" or pick up a "Go to Your Podyezd" Decree or Kompromat card, you must place your figure in the podyezd at the corner of the board. You may not leave alive until you roll doubles. You may also leave by paying 500 rubles to Switzerland. If you do not roll doubles by the third turn, you MUST pay 500 rubles to Switzerland.

Switzerland

All fines and taxes incurred on the board and through Kompromat or Decree cards must be paid to Switzerland, in the middle of the board. When a player lands on the Switzerland square on the board, he collects all the money in Switzerland. Note: bribes and money paid for property or cabinet member purchases also go to Switzerland, unlike the game of Monopoly, where rent is paid to the bank. In OLIGARCHY, no money is ever paid back to the Central Bank.

Parliament

Players landing on the State Duma and the Federation Council may buy them for the indicated prices if they are not owned. If a player owns both houses, the bribe for each house doubles, but otherwise there are absolutely no other benefits to owning these properties.

USAID

Players collect 2000 rubles every time they pass USAID. The only exception is when a player is sent to his podyezd, or sent to a square by Kompromat or Decree; in this instance he does not collect 2000 rubles.

Decrees and Kompromat

Decree and Kompromat cards are self-explanatory and may affect all players or only the card bearer, as indicated.

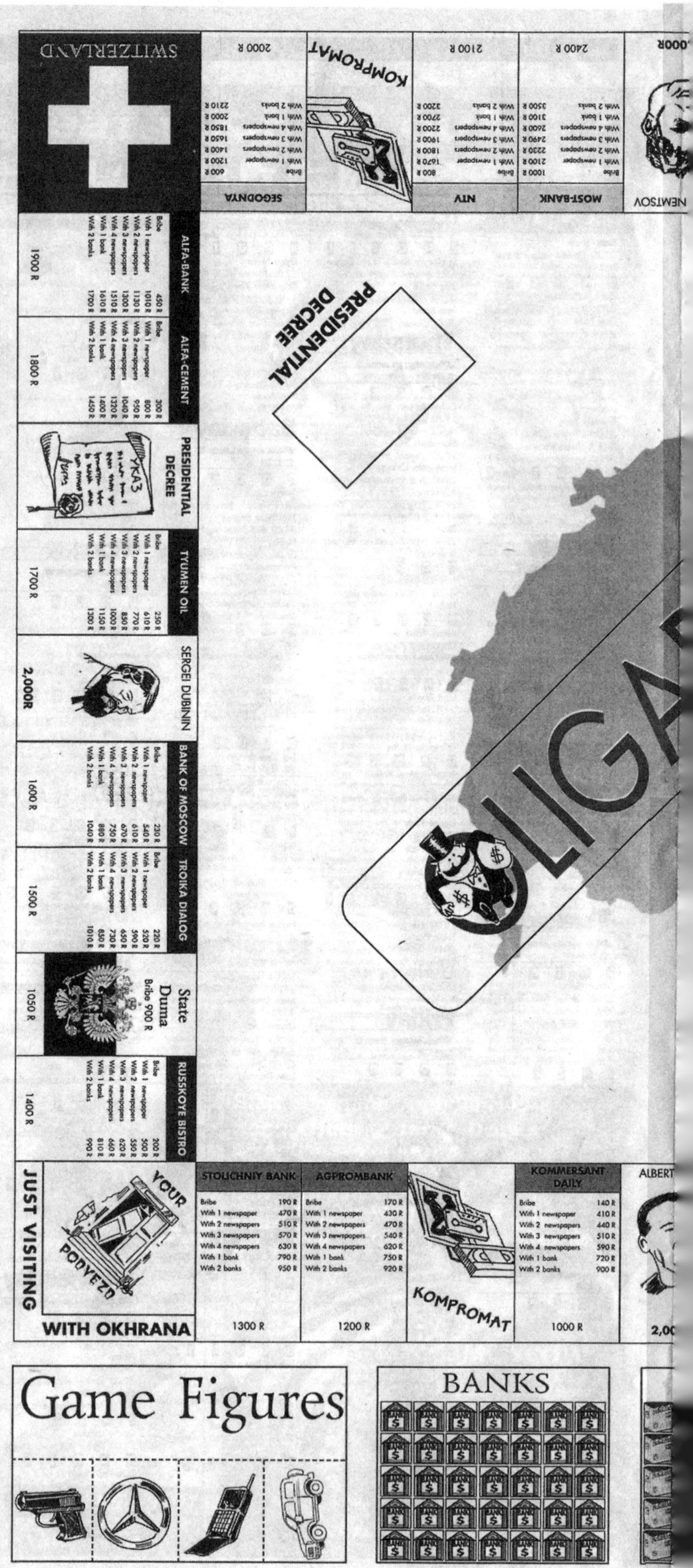

SWITZERLAND

SEGODNYA — 2000 R

Bribe	600 R
With 1 newspaper	1200 R
With 2 newspapers	1400 R
With 3 newspapers	1650 R
With 4 newspapers	1850 R
With 1 bank	2000 R
With 2 banks	2210 R

KOMPROMAT

NTV — 2100 R

Bribe	800 R
With 1 newspaper	1670 R
With 2 newspapers	1800 R
With 3 newspapers	1900 R
With 4 newspapers	2200 R
With 1 bank	2700 R
With 2 banks	3200 R

MOST-BANK — 2400 R

Bribe	1000 R
With 1 newspaper	2100 R
With 2 newspapers	2230 R
With 3 newspapers	2490 R
With 4 newspapers	2600 R
With 1 bank	3100 R
With 2 banks	3500 R

NEMTSOV — ,000R

ALFA-BANK — 1900 R

Bribe	450 R
With 1 newspaper	1010 R
With 2 newspapers	1130 R
With 3 newspapers	1300 R
With 4 newspapers	1510 R
With 1 bank	1610 R
With 2 banks	1700 R

ALFA-CEMENT — 1800 R

Bribe	300 R
With 1 newspaper	800 R
With 2 newspapers	950 R
With 3 newspapers	1040 R
With 4 newspapers	1320 R
With 1 bank	1400 R
With 2 banks	1450 R

PRESIDENTIAL DECREE

УКАЗ

TYUMEN OIL — 1700 R

Bribe	250 R
With 1 newspaper	610 R
With 2 newspapers	770 R
With 3 newspapers	850 R
With 4 newspapers	1000 R
With 1 bank	1150 R
With 2 banks	1300 R

SERGEI DUBININ — 2,000R

BANK OF MOSCOW — 1600 R

Bribe	230 R
With 1 newspaper	540 R
With 2 newspapers	610 R
With 3 newspapers	670 R
With 4 newspapers	750 R
With 1 bank	880 R
With 2 banks	1040 R

TROIKA DIALOG — 1500 R

Bribe	220 R
With 1 newspaper	520 R
With 2 newspapers	590 R
With 3 newspapers	650 R
With 4 newspapers	730 R
With 1 bank	850 R
With 2 banks	1010 R

State Duma — Bribe 900 R — 1050 R

RUSSKOYE BISTRO — 1400 R

Bribe	200 R
With 1 newspaper	500 R
With 2 newspapers	550 R
With 3 newspapers	620 R
With 4 newspapers	660 R
With 1 bank	810 R
With 2 banks	990 R

YOUR PODYEZD

JUST VISITING WITH OKHRANA

STOLICHNIY BANK — 1300 R

Bribe	190 R
With 1 newspaper	470 R
With 2 newspapers	510 R
With 3 newspapers	570 R
With 4 newspapers	630 R
With 1 bank	790 R
With 2 banks	950 R

AGPROMBANK — 1200 R

Bribe	170 R
With 1 newspaper	430 R
With 2 newspapers	470 R
With 3 newspapers	540 R
With 4 newspapers	620 R
With 1 bank	750 R
With 2 banks	920 R

KOMPROMAT

KOMMERSANT DAILY — 1000 R

Bribe	140 R
With 1 newspaper	410 R
With 2 newspapers	440 R
With 3 newspapers	510 R
With 4 newspapers	590 R
With 1 bank	720 R
With 2 banks	900 R

ALBERT — 2,0

PRESIDENTIAL DECREE

OLIGA

Game Figures

BANKS

Late in the summer of '97 we created a post-Soviet version of Monopoly, based on the actual structure of the Russian oligarchy. Board walk and series of intrigues and scandals. In this game, players bought Deputy Prime Ministers instead of railroads, picked up compro mising information

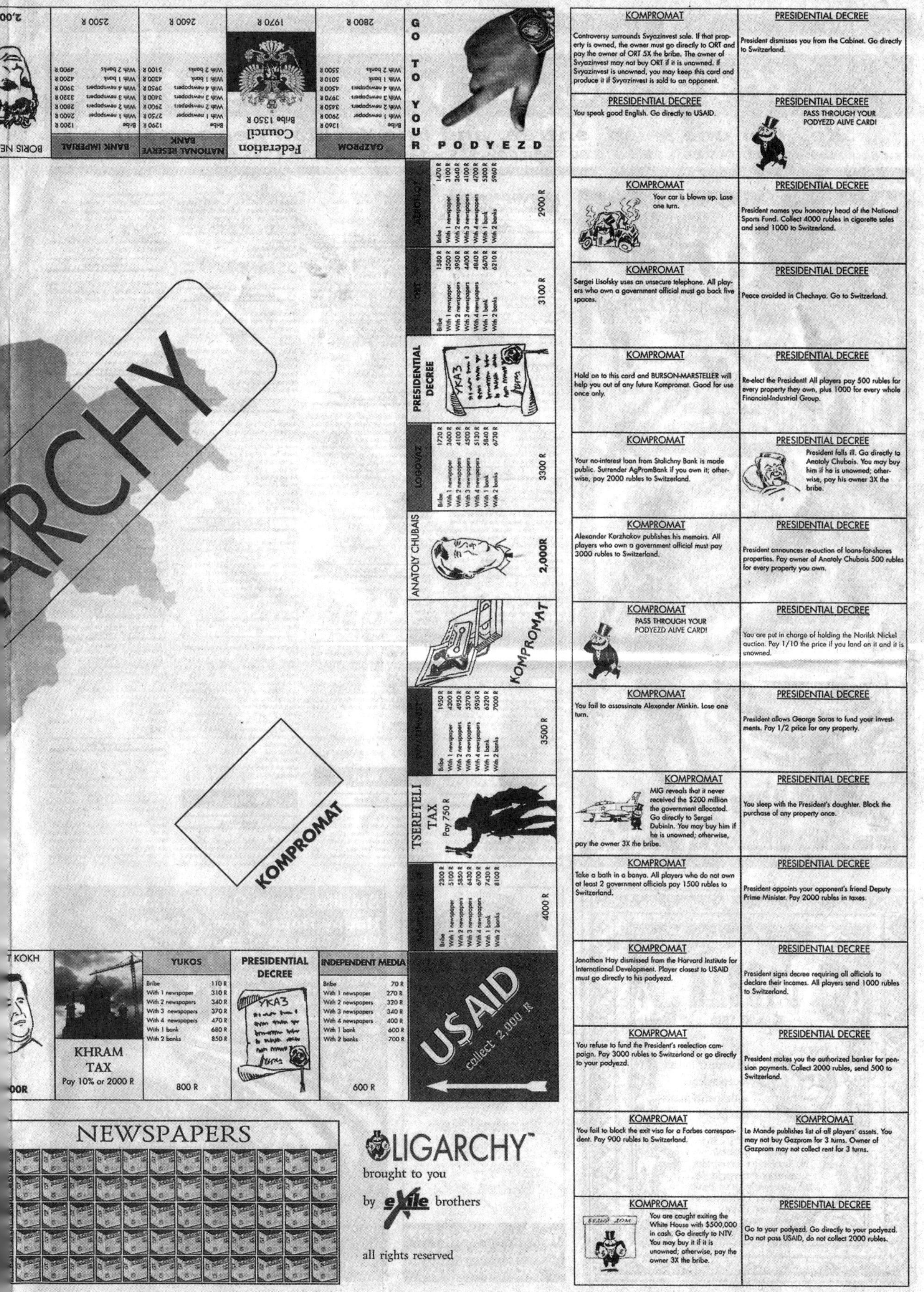

Park Place in our version were Norilsk Nickel and Svyazinvest, the two major corporate properties that were auctioned off that summer amid a instead of Chance cards, put money in Switzerland instead of Free Parking, and collected funds from USAID instead of GO.

the place where the Western global economy had come to finally sell its soul.

The well-publicized Western aid effort to build law-based capitalism in place of communism had fooled no one in Russia. The very people who'd been put in charge of setting up the new rules, specifically a brilliantly cynical English-speaking minister named Anatoly Chubais and his supporters, had turned out to be thieves and villains of a type that the world previously had seen only in James Bond movies.

Beginning at the end of 1995, Chubais and co. had masterminded a series of auctions of state properties which had resulted in the instant state-funded creation of an oligarchical billionaire class. In just a few years virtually all the wealth of communist Russia had been turned over to a pocket-sized group of bankers and tycoons—seven men, nearly all bald and with shady if not overtly criminal pasts. They were gangland auto distributor Boris Berezovsky, ex–black market antiques dealer Alexander Smolensky, ex–Soviet trade apparatchik Vladimir Potanin, Alfa-Bank heavy Mikhail Freedman, ex–theater agent Vladimir Gusinsky, youth communist chief and probable ex-spook Mikhail Khordakovsky, and Inkombank head Vladimir Vinogradov. They were all winners of oil companies, mineral deposits, media holdings, precious metals conglomerates, and other properties at cut-rate auction prices—prices they themselves often set, when Chubais designated them in charge of the auctions they participated in.

By the time I met with Mark in the Starlite, these guys wielded so much power in Russian life that virtually every Russian newspaper or magazine was controlled by one of them. They had latched on to the press as new sources of political power, and as they girded up for the fight for the last remaining public scraps to be "privatized"—shares in the state telecommunications company Svyazinvest, a few remaining state oil companies, etc.—they began to use the press to attack one another. A side effect was that a paper controlled by bald thief A would suddenly never print information beneficial to bald thief B. Thus, the newspaper *Izvestia*, for years the showpiece of post-communist press freedom, went totally in the tank for Vladimir Potanin's Oneximbank over the summer of 1997 after its editor, Igor Golombiyevsky, was fired for printing information harmful to Potanin.

Law and civil liberties, the very things we were supposed to have been fighting for during the Cold War, were being rolled back in Russia. Now, if a newspaper wanted to be irreverent, it could only be irreverent in one direction—against the interests of its owner's enemies. Even NTV, "Independent Television," had shed its independence a year before, during the presidential election, when it shut the communists out of its coverage entirely and campaigned openly for Boris Yeltsin. After the election, the station was rewarded when the state dissolved "Russian Universities," an educational station it had shared airtime with, and handed the whole channel to NTV. By 1997, it was a mouthpiece for the government, with its news programs clearly written or at least cowritten by political advisers, instead of "independent" journalists.

What's more, the people who had created this swamp of corruption and coercion had very clearly demonstrated their willingness to kill anyone who didn't agree with the nature of things. A few years before, a young reporter for *Moskovsky Komsomolets* named Dmitri Kholodov had been assassinated by an exploding briefcase while investigating corruption linked to Defense Minister Pavel Grachev. In one of his most cynical and deplorable moves as president, Yeltsin came out days after the murder and hailed Grachev as "his favorite minister." Berezovsky, the LogoVAZ auto distributor, had survived a car bombing that had decapitated his chauffeur and was himself a key suspect in the murder of Vladislav Listiyev—the director of the ORT television station Berezovsky had a controlling interest in. Muckraking reporter Alexander Minkin of *Moskovsky Komsomolets* and then of *Novaya Gazeta* was repeatedly beaten for writing vicious

Александр ХИНШТЕЙН

"БОРИС АБРАМОВИЧ, МНЕ ПОРУЧЕНО ВАС УБИТЬ"

"Boris Abromovich, I've Been Ordered to Kill You" read the headline in the yellow Moscow rag *Moskovsky Komsomolets* after slithery oligarch/underworld heavy Boris Berezovsky survived a car bomb that beheaded his chauffeur.

columns about public figures—once by a pair of thugs in Ninja suits who crashed through his bedroom window at night and attacked him with a crowbar.

Now, it was true that this wasn't 1937, and there was no longer a policy of political mass murder in effect. It was also true that bribery and the use of compromising information were the preferred currency for managing day-to-day political and business affairs. But the glue that held it all together was violence. By 1997 the powers that be in Russia had decreed that the press should be controlled, and one had to assume, given the history of these people, that they meant it.

It was in this atmosphere that the *eXile* planned on flipping its giant, 25,000-copy middle finger in all directions all over Moscow. I had a feeling, even before Mark and I started working together, that we were going to write things out of simple adolescent resentment that might, if we had been Russian reporters, cost us our lives, or at least our unbroken knees. We weren't going to write that Russia was "on the right path," as an official U.S. government editorial put it in September of that year. We were going to tell the truth, which was that the country was being run by killers and swine who had stolen everything they could get their hands on, and sent the whole country reeling into such total chaos that people in the provinces were eating one another out of boredom and desperation.

This was going to piss people off. Not because it injured the vanity of Russan thugs—they were too busy making money to be vain, and they weren't going to read us anyway. It would, however, hurt the feelings of the "community"— the tie-and-business-lunch expatriate crowd with the all-purpose happy smiles.

As a college student, it had always seemed to me that the lie that kind of smile had concealed was the social desperation that brought students back over and over again to those keg parties they secretly knew were twisted and sad. Here in Moscow, the smile concealed a desperation to make money so great that they were willing to support any delusion which facilitated it. In this case that delusion was that Russia was a developing democracy and they, the Westerners, were here to spread the gospel of fair play and law-based economics. Unlike the Russians, who six years into their neocapitalist history were refreshingly unabashed about their greed and unscrupulousness, Westerners still found it necessary—both for public relations purposes and, surprisingly often, for their consciences—to put a happy face on their drive to make money. I'd seen that at the *Moscow Times*, when virtually any business conflict between a Russian and an American was depicted as a struggle between crooks and honest, principled businessmen. In order to keep that nervous smile on his face, the expatriate couldn't be open about having nakedly commercial interests, or about the necessity of making Machiavellian deals with corrupt officials in order to take part in an auction bid. Instead, he had to package every struggle as a fight between right and wrong, between progress and reaction, between democracy and communism.

And every time he did that, he robbed those big words of their meaning—at a time when, following the Soviet collapse, they were very much under the world microscope.

Looking back now, when I try to figure out how it was that the *eXile* changed my life so much, I see that it had a lot to do with accidentally latching on to those big words. The *eXile* started off as a blind, spiteful crusade to wipe that smile off the community's face, an extension of a common high school hang-up, but it quickly turned into something else. It became

Below: The actual text of a U.S. government editorial which proclaimed Russia "on the right path" less than a year before the country experienced a total financial collapse.

ANNCR:
THE VOICE OF AMERICA PRESENTS DIFFERING POINTS OF VIEW ON A WIDE VARIETY OF ISSUES. NEXT, AN EDITORIAL EXPRESSING THE POLICIES OF THE UNITED STATES GOVERNMENT.

VOICE:
ACCORDING TO A LEADING AMERICAN ECONOMIST, MARTIN FELDSTEIN, THE RUSSIAN ECONOMY HAS MADE REMARKABLE PROGRESS. HE SAYS THAT OFFICIAL STATISTICS UNDERESTIMATE THE RATE OF GROWTH IN RUSSIA BECAUSE AS MUCH AS FORTY PERCENT OF ECONOMIC ACTIVITY MAY BE UNREPORTED.

SINCE THE COLLAPSE OF COMMUNISM IN 1992 -- AND THE END OF PRICE CONTROLS -- THE RUSSIAN STANDARD OF LIVING HAS IMPROVED IN MANY WAYS. THE DEMISE OF THE COMMAND ECONOMY HAS ENDED WIDESPREAD SHORTAGES OF CONSUMER GOODS, AND ANNUAL INFLATION RATES HAVE BEEN REDUCED DRAMATICALLY. FROM 1992 TO 1994, INFLATION SOARED TO MORE THAN EIGHT-HUNDRED PERCENT. REFORMS BROUGHT INFLATION DOWN TO ABOUT TWENTY-TWO PERCENT IN 1996. THE INFLATION RATE IS EXPECTED TO BE FIFTEEN PERCENT THIS YEAR.

PRIVATIZATION OF BUSINESSES AND HOUSING HAS BEEN A KEY FACTOR IN RUSSIA'S ECONOMIC TRANSITION. OWNERSHIP OF INDUSTRY HAS BEEN TRANSFERRED FROM THE STATE TO SHAREHOLDERS, WHO ARE FREE TO SELL THEIR SHARES TO PRIVATE INVESTORS. PRIVATIZATION HAS NOT YET PRODUCED A SUBSTANTIAL INCREASE IN INDUSTRIAL PRODUCTIVITY, IN PART BECAUSE THE TRANSFORMATION IS SO RECENT. BUT THERE ARE OTHER FACTORS AS WELL: A SHORTAGE OF SKILLED MANAGERS, INADEQUATE LAWS, HEAVY REGULATION, AND WIDESPREAD CORRUPTION.

THE GOVERNMENT IS STARTING TO TAKE STEPS TO REMEDY SOME OF THESE PROBLEMS. BANKS ARE BEGINNING TO PROVIDE COMMERCIAL CREDIT. THE LEGAL SYSTEM IS BEING REFORMED TO ESTABLISH PROPERTY RIGHTS AND TO MAKE BANKRUPTCY AND MORTGAGE FORECLOSURE POSSIBLE. THE GOVERNMENT HAS PROPOSED AN OVERHAUL OF THE 1992 TAX CODE TO ENCOURAGE INVESTMENT AND PERSONAL SAVING, AND EFFECT A REDUCTION IN THE MARGINAL TAX RATE. IN RESPONSE, THE RUSSIAN STOCK MARKET HAS JUMPED ONE-HUNDRED FIFTY PERCENT THIS YEAR.

IN SIX YEARS, RUSSIA HAS TAKEN STEPS TO PRIVATIZE, FREE PRICES, OPEN THE ECONOMY TO INTERNATIONAL TRADE, AND BEGIN THE CREATION OF THE LEGAL AND INSTITUTIONAL CULTURE NECESSARY TO A MARKET ECONOMY. WHILE A GREAT DEAL REMAINS TO BE DONE, THE U.S. BELIEVES THAT RUSSIA IS ON THE RIGHT PATH. BY PERSEVERING WITH FREE MARKET-REFORMS, RUSSIA'S PEOPLE CAN BEGIN TO ENJOY THE FRUITS OF PROSPERITY.

ANNCR:
THAT WAS AN EDITORIAL EXPRESSING THE POLICIES OF THE UNITED STATES GOVERNMENT. IF YOU WOULD LIKE TO BE HEARD ON THIS ISSUE, PLEASE WRITE TO EDITORIALS, VOICE OF AMERICA, WASHINGTON, D-C, 20547, U-S-A. YOU MAY ALSO SEND US A FAX AT (202) 619-1043. YOUR COMMENTS MAY BE USED ON THE AIR.

From the Editor

Don't Pooh-Pooh this Bear

Wasn't it Bismarck who warned of the dangers of waking 'the Russian bear'? Seemingly a sound foreign policy principle. Yet, apparently Bismarck also said that, in foreign policy, there can be no principles, just circumstances. It is interesting to consider what Bismarck would have made of our present post-Cold War circumstances, and how the West should relate to the Russian bear.

Of particular salience is the US-led drive for the expansion of NATO, to include some of the states of Eastern Europe and the Baltics. While talking heads inside the Washington beltway (and inside the Clinton administration) are calling NATO expansion a done deal, pooh-poohing potential adverse effects on US-Russian relations, the view from Russia is quite different. Here, the expansion of NATO is increasingly seen as a very ominous threat to Russian security and to US-Russian relations. It is seen as an effort to 'kick the bear while it is down,' to encircle it once again with a hostile alliance.

In this context, even moderate Russian politicians, such as Duma deputy Alexander Shokhin, don't rule out an alliance with China as a possible reaction to the expansion of NATO.

the weird, unaccounted-for variable in a complex historical Hegelian equation—the valve through which all the moral energy of the Western "reform" movement first began to flow when it finally began to sell out its principles.

t was our first practical joke, and it was working. Hunched together in our first office, which was about the size of a Coke machine, Mark and I were giggling like schoolkids and listening in on the phone receiver.

The guy on the other end of the line was a stuffed suit named Mikhail Ivanov, editor of a pathetic English-language magazine called *Russian Life*—a publication with so little going for it that one of its employees had already taken the drastic step of coming to *us* to look for a job. Ivanov had come to our attention from the very first moment we'd opened the glossy, aspiring-to-be-serious magazine. He was impossible to miss: Apparently anxious to join the ranks of the self-serious blowhards who dominated the debate about Russia in academic/journalistic circles, he'd plastered a striking tie-and-grimace photo of himself (practice for his book jacket?) over his "Letter to Editor" on the inside page. And next to his ominous portrait was the headline to his obligatory cliché "whither Russia" editorial, which limped sadly across the page to read, incredibly: "Don't Pooh-Pooh this Bear."

Mark and I both recoiled from this photo as from rotting cheese. Like Mark, I had a fierce aversion to daffy mediocrities who schemed to get photos published of themselves standing in suits and ties with their arms folded; a lifetime of watching Republican Party operatives and anchormen had ensured that. And now here was a guy who was playing Russian nationalist on the one hand, but bringing with shameless cocksucking zeal the Western tie-and-folded-arms disease to Russia. He had to pay, this guy.

Within minutes of seeing this photo, Mark and I had composed a letter to Ivanov in which we represented ourselves as overpublicized liberal-establishment Russia guru (and *Lenin's Tomb* author) David Remnick, looking for work. If Ivanov's own people were willing to submit to the professional humiliation of writing for the *eXile*, it would be interesting to see just how high Ivanov thought the standards for his own publication should be. In the letter we had a subtly vicious Remnick propose a series of "compare'n contrast" editorial pieces that would be written by Remnick and his buddy Marshall Goldman of Harvard University. Goldman was American academia's leading hurrumphing Sovietologist, the man whom every hack political scientist in the world wanted writing his preface, and dropping his name meant we were bringing an awful lot to the table.

"*Russian Life* seems to fit the format I'm looking for," we wrote. "Of course, it is a new publication, but I don't think newness is any reason to 'pooh-pooh this bear'!"

After we sent the letter we'd had Remnick's "secretary" (actually our own frightened teenage employee Tanya Krasnikova) call, explaining that "Dave" was away on business in Volgograd but wanted to know Ivanov's answer.

Amazingly, Ivanov's answer was that he was "interested," but that he "didn't want" Goldman—he thought the other writer should be Russian! Here was a first: an editor of one of the least-read publications in the world, turning down the world's leading Russia commentator. It was a demonstration of business sense we'd have to share with the community.

In any case, after Goldman's rejection, we had "Dave" come back from Volgograd ahead of schedule and, despite a fictional yet still terrible case of diarrhea, call Ivanov personally to go to bat for his unexpectedly downtrodden buddy Marshall. That's what we were doing, sitting there hunched over in the office. I took notes while

DAVID REMNICK

March 25,1997

Mikhail Ivanov, Editor
Russian Life
Pokrovsky Blvd. 8
Fax: 917-9148

Mr. Ivanov:

We've never met, but I'm intrigued by your publication and have decided to write you. My name is David Remnick; I am a journalist who worked in Russia for many years and even wrote books on the subject, including *Lenin's Tomb* and *Resurrection*. I have contributed to a number of newspapers and magazines, including, on occasion, the "New Yorker."

I'm writing to you because I am considering returning to Russia after a long absence and have been looking for a local outlet for my articles. I feel it is important to write for the community one lives in. *Russian Life* seems to fit the format I'm looking for. It is glossy, thoughtful, and topical. Of course, it is a new publication, but I don't think that newness is any reason to "pooh-pooh this bear!"

What I had in mind for publication would be a series of "one-on-one" style editorial pieces presenting my views of Russian politics in contrast with those of another writer. My close friend and colleague Marshall Goldman has tentatively agreed to be a contrasting voice in such a format. Please let me know if this would be acceptable to you. I can provide clips or examples of my work, should you find this necessary.

I will be leaving for a trip to the provinces this week, but I would appreciate a prompt reply by fax sometime this week, as I like to have ample time to prepare my material. My secretary Yuliya can answer any questions you may have about my schedule.

Thank you for your time, and I hope to speak with you soon.

Yours Sincerely,

David Remnick

Our letter to Ivanov from Remnick. We used the same letterhead we'd used for a phony Donald Trump letter.

Mark played Remnick, using a weird East Coast health nut accent. Ivanov was fooled. We had him nailed. As the call unfolded, Mark and I both felt that something incredible was happening. For once in our stupid slacker lives, we were *winning*—finally giving it back to these people.

The transcript of that call, as it was eventually published—to Ivanov's great embarrassment—went like this:

Ivanov: Hello?
eXile: Hello, this is David Remnick. I sent you a letter . . .
Ivanov: Yes, I spoke to your secretary.
eXile: Yeah, I got a message from her. I was out of town. I just got back from Volgograd.
Ivanov: Oh, yeah? How was it?
eXile: It was interesting, but I'm not feeling so well. I've got a nasty bug . . .
Ivanov: Yeah?
eXile: A really bad case of the runs, you know . . .
Ivanov: Right, so we spoke . . .
eXile: Running back and forth, if you know what I mean. The runs . . . Jesus . . . anyway, I understand you're not interested in working with Marshall.
Ivanov: No, it's just that I think it would be better to have a sort of Russian-American exchange, instead of two Americans.
eXile: Yeah, but the thing is, I know Marshall pretty well, we like to do this sort of swinging-back-and-forth thing . . .
Ivanov: Yes, but I think it would be better, from a contrast point of view, to have somebody, you know, else.
eXile: But we do contrast. I mean, I guess Marshall's more of . . . more of a hard ass. And I was looking forward to doing a sort of Remnick-Goldman thing . . .
Ivanov: Well, that's an idea. We could do a sort of hawks-and-doves thing—not that you're, ah, one of them. [!] But still, I'd like to do something more with someone else . . .
eXile: Maybe a right-left thing.
Ivanov: Exactly. Right-left, hawks-doves, something like that. Maybe it would be better with somebody like a Solzhenitsyn.
eXile: Yeah, Solzhenitsyn would be good, I guess.

Here Ivanov tried to steer us into an intellectual discussion, but Mark wasn't having any of it:

Ivanov: By the way, did you see Solzhenitsyn on *Itogi* Sunday?
eXile: No, I didn't. How did he look?
Ivanov: Look?
eXile: Yeah, I mean he looks so good for a man his age.
Ivanov: I guess he looked good.
eXile: Gosh, what's his secret? I mean, really, a man his age.
Ivanov: I don't know . . . Um, so listen, why don't we meet?
eXile: Sure, we should meet. And we'll talk about Marshall.
Ivanov: Sure, but we should meet.
eXile: Okay, let's say next week. And hopefully these fucking cramps of mine will be gone by then. Ow, Jesus!
Ivanov: My God, what did you drink there in Volgograd?
eXile: God knows what I drank in Volgograd!
Ivanov: Did you drink the tap water?
eXile: No, actually I try to drink only French mineral water.
Ivanov: (pause) Uh . . . okay. So we'll talk later.
eXile: Okay.

We published this call under the headline, "Your Investment Is In Good Hands, Mr. Richardson"—a reference to Ivanov's publisher, Paul Richardson. A spy in Ivanov's office informed us that the reaction over there was everything we could have hoped for: mute rage, unnecessarily vicious and hurtful interoffice bickering, sagging morale. A correspondent from *Time* magazine even told us that David Remnick had written him to complain about the prank. Pulitzer Prize winners don't like their diarrhea cramps discussed in public.

Before we made that call, I'd never known that it would be possible to experience such a predatory thrill as part of a paying job. I liked it. It felt like something I wanted to do over and over again.

Now I was anxious to find more twerps like Ivanov. Even investigative journalism, something I'd always avoided, suddenly seemed like a tolerable occupation if it meant getting even with these assholes.

And the deeper I looked into the community and the politics behind U.S. aid, the World Bank, and the whole structure of the Western money flow in and out of Russia, the more people I found who were worth going after. I had reasons for disliking, even hating these people, but the reasons weren't what motivated me. It was the hostility. Hostility felt good. It was better than self-loathing, anyway. And there were so many people in this city who were long overdue for some hostile treatment.

NEW WEEKLY FORMAT!

the eXile

FREE 26.02.98 05.03.98 ISSUE #05/30

DOES ANYTHING MATTER?

LAST MONDAY wasn't supposed to be the lovely, sunny, warm spring-like day that we all remember fondly. Monday was supposed to be that day that Russia exploded in a mass uprising led by the armed forces, overthrowing the Yeltsin regime.

Lev Rokhlin, the former "hero" of Chechnya, had set the date of February 23rd himself, leading to all sorts of wild speculation in the media and a government commission meant to quash "extremism." This isn't the first time Russia has been threatened with a violent cataclysm.

/Continued on page 2/

DR. UMONOV'S TIPS ON HOW TO STAY YOUNG P2

MISTRESS SUKI RETURNS, MORE BITTER THAN EVER P6

TWO HEADLESS DEAD OLD MEN KISSING P.14

CHUBAIS SCORES IN CHAT ROOMS P.13

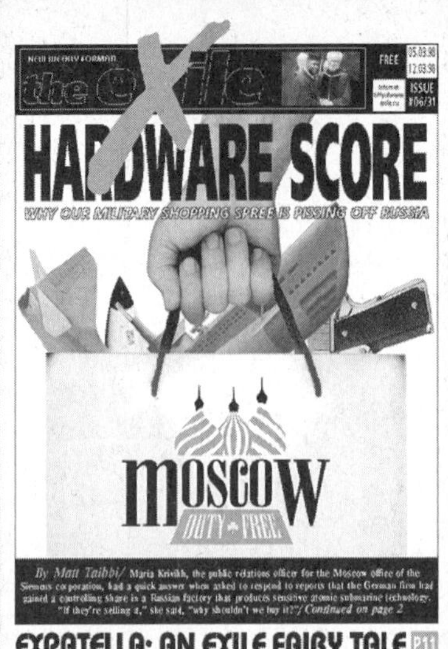

NEW WEEKLY FORMAT!

the eXile

FREE 05.03.98 12.03.98 ISSUE #06/31

HARDWARE SCORE

WHY OUR MILITARY SHOPPING SPREE IS PISSING OFF RUSSIA

By Matt Taibbi/ Maria Krivikh, the public relations officer for the Moscow office of the Siemens corporation, had a quick answer when asked to respond to reports that the German firm had gained a controlling share in a Russian factory that produces sensitive atomic submarine technology. "If they're selling it," she said, "why shouldn't we buy it?"/ Continued on page 2

EXPATELLA: AN EXILE FAIRY TALE P.11

Moscow's Only Alternative!

the eXile

ISSUE#23 [024] •DECEMBER 4, 1997•FREE

GUILTY!

How a new Moscow law punishes the ugly

Great privatizing minds look alike: special photo archive discovery 4

Come sit on our laps at Moscow's *phattest* Christmas party 7

Death Porn adds new icon, shocks readers, critics, self 21

"THE STREET SMART ALTERNATIVE"

the eXile

FREE 19.03.98 26.03.98 ISSUE #08/33

The Bribefather

Russia as a Mafia Movie in Progress

By Matt Taibbi/ Attempt after attempt has been made by journalists and academics alike to deconstruct the New Russia, to grab it by the throat and shake the essence of its politics out on paper for the whole world to read and digest, and do you know what? In seven years, not one person has gotten it right yet. It isn't a fledgling constitutional democracy with elements of monarchy; it isn't a despotic city-state; it's isn't Chicago in the 30s, Paris in the 20s, or America in the age of the robber-barons. All you people who think that way, you're all aiming too high./ Continued on page 2

IS VECHERNAYA MOSKVA DEAD? P.3

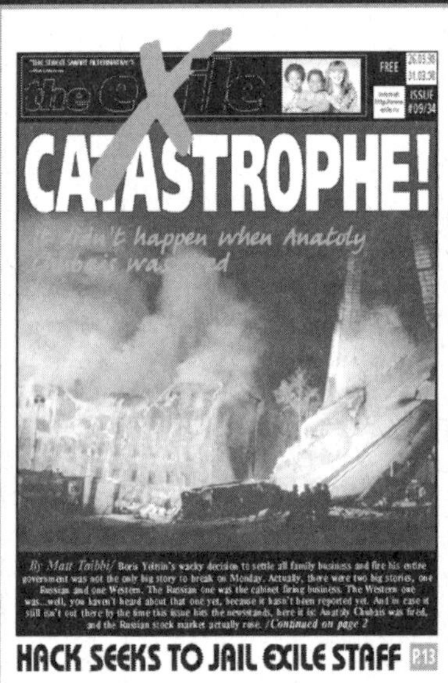

"THE STREET SMART ALTERNATIVE"

the eXile

FREE 26.03.98 31.03.98 ISSUE #09/34

CATASTROPHE!

It didn't happen when Anatoly Chubais was fired

By Matt Taibbi/ Boris Yeltsin's wacky decision to settle all family business and fire his entire government was not the only big story to break on Monday. Actually, there were two big stories, one Russian and one Western. The Russian one was the cabinet firing business. The Western one was...well, you haven't heard about that one yet, because it hasn't been reported yet. And in case it still isn't out there by the time this issue hits the newsstands, here it is: Anatoly Chubais was fired, and the Russian stock market actually rose. /Continued on page 2

HACK SEEKS TO JAIL EXILE STAFF P.13

"THE STREET SMART ALTERNATIVE"

the eXile

FREE 09.04.98 22.04.98 ISSUE #11/36

GIRLS of the INDUSTRIAL DECLINE

...le pictorial p. 8

SEPARATED AT BIRTH???

Your guide to spoofing the Moscow Times on April Fool's Day p.14

NEWSDAY GETS EVIL-ON TAPE P.13

"THE SOURCE FOR NIGHTLIFE"

the eXile

FREE 23.04.98 06.05.98 ISSUE #12/37

BULLSHIT!

By Matt Taibbi/ Reporting the news before it happens is always a dangerous business, but when waiting for the inevitable loses its thrill, it's all a real journalist has left to do. And with Russian parliamentary politics, the thrill has been gone for ages now. Though this paper hits the stands on April 23, we're pretty sure it's already safe to report the following: Sergei Kiriyenko was confirmed as Prime Minister this Friday, April 24, on the third State Duma vote on his candidacy since he was nominated by President Yeltsin last month. It was a close vote, 226-124, and it passed on a secret ballot./Continued on page 2

EXILE STEALS MT EDITOR'S PEN P.21

SOMOS POCOS, PERO LOCOS

the eXile

FREE ISSUE #14/39

5 Reasons

By Matt Taibbi/ A few weeks ago Ames and I went out on one of the weirdest evenings either of us has experienced here in Russia. We'd been invited to a striptease party by a couple of punks named Sasha and Andrei, old friends we'd met at the Titan squat near Mayakovskaya Ploschad. /Continued on page 2

LENIN'S BRUSH WITH EXILE DEATH P.21

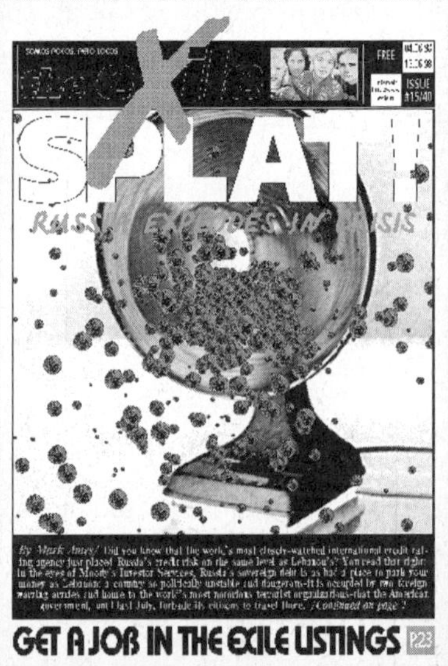

SOMOS POCOS, PERO LOCOS

the eXile

FREE ISSUE #15/40

SPLAT!

By Mark Ames/ Did you know that the world's most closely-watched international credit rating agency just placed Russia's credit risk on the same level as Lebanon's? You read that right: in the eyes of Moody's Investor Services, Russia's sovereign debt is as bad a place to park your money as Lebanon: a country so politically unstable and dangerous—it is occupied by two foreign warring armies and home to the world's most notorious terrorist organizations—that the American government, until last July, forbade its citizens to travel there. /Continued on page 2

GET A JOB IN THE EXILE LISTINGS P.23

BY MATT TAIBBI

CHAPTER THREE: THE *EXILE* MEETS THE EXPATS

fter Ivanov, the first people we went after were our competitors, the *Moscow Tribune* and the *Moscow Times*. From ten paces they looked identical, with the same A3 tabloid paper and blue banner, but there were huge differences. The former simply sucked, while the latter was fast becoming a tyrannical corporate mini-Godzilla, stomping on the expatriate community's communication lines with its high production values and aggressively banal news coverage.

Undermining the extravagantly staffed, liberally funded *Times* was going to be a long-term project; putting the *Tribune* in place would be easier. This was a two-bit copycat publication run by a British mama's boy named Anthony Louis, son of Victor Louis, the well-known English correspondent and reputed Soviet double agent. Years ago, Louis Sr. had brought the text of Khrushchev's secret speech and films of Sakharov in exile to the West. Now Daddykins was dead and twentysomething offspring Anthony wanted to follow in his journalistic footsteps, using the platform of an English-language paper in Moscow.

Louis's paper had actually been the first such paper in post-communist Russia, but it quickly lost almost the entirety of its market share to the *Moscow Times* through mismanagement, editorial ineptitude, and the conspicuous lack of an overall publishing concept. Historical forces had also played a role in squeezing it out. The *Trib* was a hokey British cold-warrior leftover of the mind-set which had created faux-friendly projects like Apollo-Soyuz and the Goodwill games; it had been the big paper in town when "Joint Venture" and "Cooperative" were the hot new words on the street, and people like Grigory Yavlinsky put forth pie-in-the-sky fantasies of revamping the Soviet economy in 500 days, and were taken seriously when they did.

The *Times*, on the other hand, was a product of the next, more lasting era, in which armies of American consultants virtually took over Russian government, and smooth-talking Western corporations moved in to replace that hokey Cold War atmosphere with the efficient, calculating feel of "professional" Russia. Everything about the *Times* was corporate: the American style and spelling (despite Dutch ownership), the gleaming new computers, the high-rent start-up office in the Radisson hotel, the confident, libertarian editorial slant. . . . If the *Trib* was ratty tweed, the *Times* was creased collar and power tie, which by 1992 was the chosen uniform of much of the can-do expatriate community.

The *Trib* couldn't compete. Within a few years after its inception, its entire marketing strategy was geared toward clumsily copying the *Times*, which had brought on a core staff of experienced hacks in its start-up stage to compete with the *Trib*'s low-cost editorial staff of wire services and Upper Voltan grad students. The *Trib* was shameless. Every time the *Moscow Times* did a redesign, the *Trib* did one, seemingly copying every last detail (*Times* decisions to go weekly or insert a color banner, for instance, were quickly countered by the *Trib*). This was the kind of business you only see Westerners daring to run out in the open when they're far away from home; it was a newspaper in the same vein as "Leevi's" jeans, "Naike" sneakers and Starter jackets with "Atlanta 49ers" emblems.

By the time I arrived at the *eXile*, the *Trib* had already started to copy us. They'd put out a nightlife guide which was a naked copy of our own "Bardak" pullout section, a thing which had already gained some renown around town for rating clubs according to your chances of getting laid at them, using copulating stick figures as graphics. The *Trib* answered with a guide that used eXilian words like "whores" and "E-ed out"—all in the wrong places, of course, but there all the same.

This was a low-tech version of something we were going to come across over and over again—Westerners operating under a thin cover of "Western" respectability, ekeing out tiny profit margins by running athsmatic little rackets with public or private money, and hoping no one would notice amid the general chaos of modern Russia. After all, the logic went, there were plenty of Western corporations and governments doing big-time good in the new Russia—what's wrong with a little racket or two on the side, as long as they're kept relatively quiet?

We were small-time, too, but we were going to take a different tack, choosing to dispense with the pretense and be openly nasty in our attempt to get a little piece of the pie. Living as we were in a country where government officials unapologetically stole in the billions, we figured our readers would at least appreciate our honesty. The *Trib* was a good place to start. Mark and I took a quick glance at their new guide and decided to turn around and shove their editors' subtle parasitism up their asses.

Posing as independent marketing consultant "Sam Weiss" —the first in what would be a long line of mischievious, fictitious *eXile* Jews—we called around Moscow's leading Western p.r. firms and said that we were working for Anthony Louis and wanted help in refashioning the *Trib* concept. In a peculiarly contemptuous twist, we pitched the idea of a "scratch 'n sniff" *Tribune* to every company we called.

The results were brutal. Every company in town declined our business, regardless of how large a fee we offered. A company called Friedman and Rose gave a typical response, explaining in a written response that "the challenges facing the *Moscow Tribune* are more substantial than any promotional 'gimmick' can instantly resolve. . . . The problem does not lie exclusively with its marketing. The publication has a 'me, too' look which does nothing to set it apart from its competition. The *Moscow Times* and (to a lesser extent) the new lifestyle tabloid, the *eXile*, have re-positioned the *Tribune* into a tenuous middle ground position—rather than as a true alternative to either."

That company even included in its rejection letter a free copy of an inspirational self-help book (*Disruptions: Overturning Conventions and Shaking Up the Marketplace*), whose jacket cover we published along with all the letters and phone coversations accumulated in the course of the prank, which documented the *Tribune*'s pathetic standing around town. Advertisers reportedly called the *Trib* in a rage, demanding to know if it was true, as we'd claimed, that their papers languished in stacks for weeks. The *Trib* had no defense. There were holes in its deniability at every major distribution point in the city.

In any case, nine months later, the *Trib* was down from five issues a week to two, and was being run on the editorial side by a guy who had gone from entry-level copy editor to editor-in-chief in the space of six weeks. Anemic ad revenues and rising rent in the diplomatic office space his late father's spook friends had found him forced him to squeeze the staff that he'd kept on two whole floors into half of one floor. And after a year of hounding his paper, we were expanding, from 16 pages biweekly to 24 pages biweekly and finally to 16 pages weekly, largely by swiping away his advertisers.

The *Times* was a tougher call. This was a paper backed up by a big corporation called Independent Media, which was headed by my former boss, the diminuative Dutch ex-Maoist Derk Sauer. Sauer had started with just the *Times*, but now also had Russian versions of *Cosmopolitan*, *Playboy*, *Good Housekeeping*, *Marie Claire*, *Harper's Bazaar*, and *Men's Health*, in addition to business publications like *Kapital* and *Skate Press*, which were staples of the Western financial community. There was no way we were going to put these people out of business, but we could at least embarrass the newspaper.

Although the *Times* had been very indulgent with me throughout my stay there, rehiring me no less than three times during my many years of frenzied flight between jobs, countries, and nervous disorders, the company leadership had been unaccountably nasty and condescending when I told them of my original plans to edit *Living Here*. The most obnoxious of the lot was editor Geoff Winestock, a dour, reactionary Australian with a weaselly, suspicious face and a notorious lack of interpersonal skills. Geoff had been wearing the same tight maroon turtleneck for about four years, and it appeared to have cut off the blood supply to his head; he always looked half-asphyxiated and pissed off. I'd known Geoff for years and never liked him. The year before, he'd tried to talk me out of leaving the *Times* to move east, arguing with a straight face that playing pro basketball in Mongolia was a disastrous career move compared to staying with his paper to rewrite wire copy. He'd sweetened that pep talk by informing me that if I went through with my basketball plans, I'd never be welcome back at my dull job at the *Times*. Tactics like this had caused turnover to skyrocket at the *Times* since Winestock took over from his more straightforward and professional predecessor, Marc Champion.

In any case, when I returned to Moscow to edit *Living Here*, Winestock promptly banned me from the *Times* offices—where I still had friends—then refused to let one of his employees publish his book serially in my paper after he himself had rejected it, telling the reporter he'd be fired if he wrote for me. After that, Winestock swiped away another contributor of ours, a Russian journalist who was writing under a pseudonym, by threatening to tell the writer's publisher about his extracurricular activities unless he switched from the *eXile* to the *Times*. It was a crude power play, the first of its kind I'd ever encountered, and it set the tone for future *eXile*-*Times* relations.

But personal considerations were really secondary when it came to my attitude toward the *Times*. As a literary organism alone it made for a very conspicuous villain. Though former *Times* editor Marc Champion had chided me, when I returned for Moscow, for joining up with a "shit paper" like *Living Here*, the truth was that the paper

Svalka Right outside metro Profsoyuznaya. The place looks dead on weekdays but Fridays and Saturdays here are undoubtedly one of the best in the city. Good bands, reasonable prices, nice looking girls, extraordinary interior and dances till you drop will drive crazy anyone.

The *Trib's* Time Out section. Above: The *Trib* seeking to "drive crazy anyone" with its eXilian club guide. Right: Sam Weiss's letter.

The Moscow Tribune

Sam Weiss, Independent Media Consultant
tel/fax: 252-5628/9

The Moscow Tribune is Moscow's oldest foreign-owned English-language newspaper. We began publishing in 1989, more than two years before our competition, The Moscow Times. We believed that the then-Soviet Union was poised to become one of the world's leading energing markets, which in turn would require news and information in English, of which there was little at the time. We expected an influx of foreign businessmen and consultants to take advantage of this situation, all potential readers. We believe our predictions have borne truly.

Since 1992, competition has eaten away at our readership, and, subsequently, at our client base. This has had several negatory effects, including of which has been our difficulty in attracting "blue chip" journalists and editors. While we are very proud of our staff and the product we produce, we believe that there has been major damage to our IMAGE. The IMAGE of the Moscow Tribune is that of the "third" newspaper, after the Moscow Times and "The Exile" newspapers. This is frustrating, considering that The Exile only started a couple of months ago, while we, the "third" newspaper, has been in Moscow for SEVEN YEARS! Specifically,
1. Newsstands across Moscow regularly reveal that readers are picking up the Times and the Exile, while ignoring the Tribune
2. This has led to clients complaining that people aren't reading our newspaper

Last summer, the Moscow Tribune conducted an extensive reader survey, which lasted almost two months, and culminated in a free trip giveaway. This period was perhaps the best period for our readership in terms of pikcing up the newspaper period, which we believe is partly attributable to the contest. For that reason, we would like to emphasize, as a short-term solution to our problem,, GIMMICKS which will ATTRACT READERS. We unfortunately didn't learn too much about our readers, except that they seem to like GIMMICKS. Otherwise, we estimate that over 80 percent of what remains of our readership are expatriates with high salaries.

Consider the graph below. Our readership has been falling for roughly the past six years, and is in danger of EXTINCTION, besides perhaps a few of our friends and families. This dangerous situation has led Anthony Louis, editor and owner of the Moscow Tribune, to hire me, Sam Weiss, as his PR consultant in order to remake our image, and to come up with weekly gimmicks which will attract readers to pick up our newspapers. I am presently collecting proposals from several of Moscow's leading PR and advertising firms. We need our first proposals no later than Friday, April 18, for my presentation to Mr. Louis on Monday, April 21.

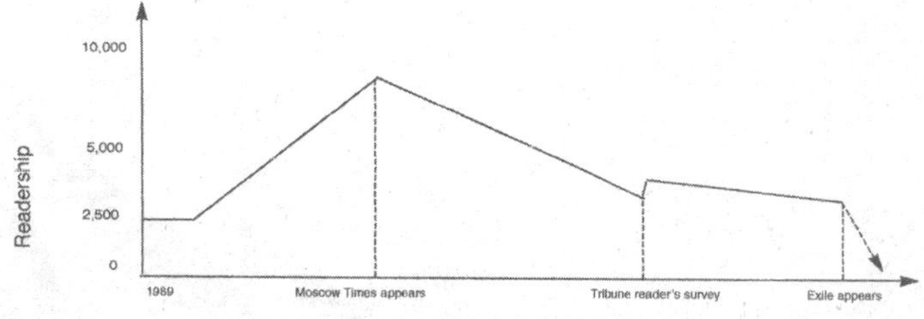

The Moscow Tribune

Sam Weiss, Independent Marketing Consultant
tel/fax: 252-5628/9

Dear Rory, April 15, 1997

Following up our telephone conversation today, I am sending to you the brief that Mr. Louis, the editor/owner of the Moscow Tribune, approved for me today. I hope it is satisfactory for your needs. I look forward to receiving your proposal by the end of the day on this Friday. As I explained, we need, in the proposal:

* General ideas on gimmicks which you think would help move the newspaper off the stands (giveaways, scratch 'n sniff, etc)
* General ideas on image makeovers which would distinguish us from the Times or Exile, or else help us to steal away their audience
* A brief history of your firm and your firm's client base
* Pricing

Thank you for your time and work.

Sincerely Yours,

Sam

he'd helped build was, in my view, a much bigger disappointment. His *Moscow Times* hadn't even been modeled after major Western dailies, which at least tended to boast, at the community level, a staff of investigative writers who acted as watchdogs over their own readers.

Its coverage of Russian politics and issues was first-rate by straight journalism standards, but the part that concerned its own readership read more like a suburban community newspaper, sponsored by the local Jaycees and Elks Club—the kind that sells hardware-store ads around grainy photos of local Little League games.

Which might have been appropriate for some Third World backwater expat paper. The *Moscow Times*'s readers, though, were a huge army of about 50,000 representatives of the richest and most powerful companies and governments in the world, relocated temporarily in post-communist Moscow to act as architects for possibly the hugest social transformation the century had ever seen. The very banality and dullness of the *Times* was a huge boon to these people, providing soothing cover and a benevolent public face for the high-stakes business deals and cutthroat subterranean politics that, right or wrong, they were here to carry out.

The *Times* was proud of its "professionalism." Even I had been, when I worked for them. I remember working there and saying all the time that, for an expatriate rag, the *Times* "was a really good paper." But now its condescending attitude just pissed me off.

A few weeks after Champion laid his "shit paper" speech on me, a brief appeared on the *Moscow Times* sports pages entitled "Wilt the Stilt to play for CSKA?" It reported that Wilt Chamberlain had fallen in love with a Russian girl, converted to Russian orthodoxy, and decided, at age 58, to move back to Moscow to make a comeback with the Red Army basketball team. The source on the piece was a report in the "Santa Monica Daily Bugle," which quoted Chamberlain agent "Jerry Steinblath" as having confirmed the story.

The story, of course, was a plant. "Steinblath" was one of our guys, sitting in his fictititous Maccabee locker room next to Sam Weiss. We'd foisted the whole story on both the Red Army and the Russian sports daily *Sport-Express* as part of an April Fool's Day prank, never guessing that the *Times* would reprint the thing. And not only reprint it, but not identify its true source (*Sport-Express*), fuck up Steinblath's name (they wrote "Steinblatz"), and blow Chamberlain's age. All in the space of three tiny paragraphs. So much for professionalism.

This was just the beginning of our attacks on the *Times*, but it was a good start. In our gloating post-factum account of their fuckup, we named all the culprits by name, in particular sloe-eyed *Times* sports staffer Gennady Fyodorov, who'd copied the story almost verbatim out of *Sport-Express.* This was, incidentally, how a lot of *Moscow Times* articles got written: a staffer would spot a story in a Russian paper, make a phone call or two, then rewrite the thing in English, knowing that most of his readers wouldn't guess the source. Expat journalism 101. Fyodorov's only mistake was that he hadn't made the one phone call.

For obvious reasons, the sportswriter didn't appreciate being used to expose the *Moscow Times* journalistic method. In fact, he was so peeved that he made it a point to search me out and harangue me on neutral territory, in the dark, alcohol-stained halls of the Russian daily *Komsomolskaya Pravda.*

I got a thrill just looking at his wounded, harried face wobbling toward me in the hall. He was practically wearing the chewing-out he must have gotten from the loathsome Winestock.

"I read what you wrote," he said, waiting for me to finish the sentence.

I said nothing, surprised suddenly to find myself radiating the aura of being busy and having better things to do.

"You were so out of line," he said. "I mean, not like anyone cares, because no one reads your paper. But, I mean, you know how the newspaper gets written. You can't check every little thing."

"No, I don't know that," I said. "In journalism school I learned that everything has to be verified."

I'd never been to journalism school.

"But," he said, "you know, you've done it yourself, take something out of a newspaper."

"Never once," I lied. "My conscience wouldn't have allowed me to disgrace the *Moscow Times* like that."

I threw my hands in the air and stared at him. Finally Fyodorov left in a huff, disappearing down the hall. My friends at *Komsomolska*, who, like most of the paper's writers, only moved from their state-subsidized chairs a few times a day, pointed angrily at him.

"Fucking jerk," said one. "He's always hanging around here."

But the *Times* and the *Tribune* were little fish. The real big targets were the cream of Moscow's expatriate society—the leaders of the aid community.

Aid was a difficult subject to cover. It was complicated and frequently very boring. But if you had the patience to learn the details of the politics involved, you couldn't help but be shocked. The expatriate community's dirtiest little secret was its official reason for being there.

On May 22, the United States Agency for International Development (USAID), the government agency responsible for distributing foreign aid, announced that it was canceling the remaining $14 million left on its contract with Harvard Institute for International Development—the body mainly responsible for implementing Western-funded capitalist reforms in Russia.

The reason was that HIID's Moscow chief, Jonathan Hay, and the HIID Russian program chief in Boston, professor Andrei Schleifer, had been caught violating Institute policy regarding investments in their host countries. Hay had

Courage Crunch

Solzhenitsyn's Book is No Bestseller
—Moscow Times headline, June 4
Solzhenitsyn's Book Sells Out
—Moscow Times Headline, June 5

Fasten your seatbelts and brace yourself for the following incredible piece of Moscow Times commentary, published on June 4:

"For all his greatness, Solzhenitsyn offers no solutions and lacks the moral courage to name names or take a political position on concrete issues."

Are you laughing yet? No? Go back and read it again. That's Geoff Winestock, the wiry little Australian interim editor of the Moscow Times, saying that Alexander Solzhenitsyn lacks moral courage.

Geoff Winestock earns in the high five-figures. He has a pleasant wood-paneled office which he reached mainly by skillfully demonstrating the absence of a personality over the course of about eight years of cautious business reporting. Developing a hangnail or being served a slightly overcooked hamburger would normally be enough to constitute a bad day for Winestock. In his editorial messages, he is consistently pro-status quo and pro-authority, and seldom takes a stand on anything at all.

Alexander Solzhenitsyn spent eight years in a concentration camp for having made a derogatory remark about Stalin. Shortly afterwards, he was diagnosed with terminal cancer, which he miraculously survived. He then spent much of his adult life in open opposition to one of the most brutal governments in history, a government that, until he was exiled, had absolute control over virtually every aspect of his life and the lives of his family members. Somewhere in there, Solzhenitsyn's passionate, splenetic prose also won him a Nobel Prize for Literature.

Geoff Winestock telling a gulag survivor—and one whose voice first broke the mystique of Soviet communism—that he lacks moral courage? Are you all kidding me, or what?

God knows why, but the debunking of Solzhenitsyn has become one of the favorite pastimes of the Western press and the Moscow Times in particular. Brownwyn McClaren's gloating June 4 "Not a Bestseller" article even went out of the way to point out that biographies of phocine pop queen Alla Pugacheva, seedy thug Alexander Korzhakov and even Queen Elizabeth II outsell books by Solzhenitsyn.

Well...no shit. And Sue Grafton would have outsold Tolstoy. Leave it to the Moscow Times to judge a writer by how much money he makes. After all, even if Solzhenitsyn hadn't become the windbag that he now is, he'd have had a tough time selling even a masterpiece to a country raised on violence, bad disco music and Brazilian soap operas.

But that's beside the point. The real question is, why is it necessary to debunk Solzhenitsyn? Where's the page 1 urgency? Why not just leave the guy alone? You almost get the sense that no matter how much lip service they pay now, people like Winestock have resented Solzhenitsyn's anti-establishment moralizing all along. Like they thought maybe he should have been quieter about being a martyr. These kinds of people tend to favor reform from the top down; they don't like Solzhenitsyn's way of doing things.

For what it's worth, Solzhenitsyn still is relevant, despite what Winestock thinks:

"But after his expulsion and decades of exile in France and the United States, Solzhenitsyn apparently lost touch with Russia. He sacrificed much moral authority by dismissing the changes begun by Mikhail Gorbachev and Boris Yeltsin. When he eventually returned to Russia in 1994, the crucial moment had passed and the new Russia had other heroes and concerns.

"Solzhenitsyn has tried to maintain his position as a voice in the wilderness, but since his return he has failed to adopt any clear public stance on any issue."

Um...actually, Geoff, it was Solzhenitsyn who first called the modern Russian state an oligarchy. He did it in June, 1994, when he first returned to Russia. That was about three years before you dared to use the word yourself. But then again, maybe he just didn't have the moral courage to wait the way you did...

In the spring of 1998, *Moscow Times* interim editor Geoff Winestock set new standards for expatriate hubris when he wrote in an editorial that writer/gulag survivor Alexander Solzhenitsyn "lacked moral courage."

invested money in Russian stocks through his girlfriend, Beth Hebert, while Schleifer had invested through his wife, Nancy Zimmerman.

This was the first big public blemish USAID had really suffered in Russia, and for a few weeks it was diligently reported all over the Western press as a shocking isolated incident of corruption. A few papers even ventured to do longer features tamely questioning the efficacy of USAID policies toward Russia in general. But almost nobody bothered to report the monstrous and extremely obvious failure of the Western aid effort to live up to the inspirational white knight role it was supposed to be playing—a story that was obvious long before the HIID scandal broke.

The HIID scandal broke at a fortuitous time for us. At exactly the moment USAID was making its Anouncement canceling the contract, we were sending an exposé on USAID to press. The article was based on a report by George Washington University professor Janine Wedel, and argued that United States aid money had really been used not for reform, but as financing for the political career of Western-friendly Deputy Prime Minister Anatoly Chubais, who sat on the board of most of the organizations which received U.S. aid. As head of the state property commit-

Winestock Through the Ages

Extensive research by the eXile has uncovered evidence of a storied journalistic tradition in the Winestock family. At first we thought the whole business of saying Solzhenitsyn lacks moral courage (see below) was a real novelty, but it turns out we were wrong. Winestocks throughout the ages have been pushing the edge of that envelope for centuries now:

1. "The teachings of Jesus Christ...lack the resonance to take hold among citizens of the Roman Empire. Christ's message of love and tolerance is way off the mark. What the people want these days are rituals and new forms of animal sacrifice."
*** Winestockius, 1st century Roman Historian of Greek origin**

2. "Napoleon hath no armie... (He) shalle not crosse the Rhone or see Italie. His military tackticks lacke boldnesse and innovatione. No pastrie shalle be named after him."
*** Jeffe Winestocke, 18th century British military historian**

3. "The so-called Whitechapel murderer will not strike again...If he is not captured he will simply cease his efforts once he realizes the public is not interested in his crimes. Put another way, these incidents lack...the power to terrify."
*** Scotland Yard constable Jeff Winestock, after the second of five Jack the Ripper murders**

4. "The Kaiser will never the Germanic Provinces unite. He the inclination to do so lacks."
*** Jiefer Winestauch, 19th century Prussian General**

5. "Hitler...lacks the will to solve the Jewish question."
*** Richard (Zip) Winestock, Times of London guest columnist, 1937**

tee in 1994–95, Chubais had also overseen the U.S.-led privatization effort, itself practically a second '90s revolution.

I hadn't done too much original reporting for that piece, but the more I learned about how the community worked, the more I saw the general lack of public contempt for the aid effort as a scoop in itself. So when we ran a cover with a big headline that read "BogUSAID: How the eXile #24 • December 18 - December 29, 1997 • P. 19

In Search of the Perfectly Inane Editorial

We here at the eXile have often been accused of being overly critical, while leaving the great question of how to be constructive untouched. "It's easy to tear things down, but harder to build them up," they say.

This issue, we've turned our attention to our friends over at Ulitsa Pravdy, who seem to be finally tackling the great issue of how to create the perfect editorial. On December 5th, we received a slew of phone calls after the Winestock-penned classic "Gorbachev Should Not Sell Pizza," which most of our readers thought was a practical joke we'd played on the *Moscow Times*. "How did you guys slip that fake editorial into their newspaper?!" cried more than one bemused reader.

The embarrassing fact is that we didn't. They—or rather, interim editor Winestock—composed that editorial all by his whacky, interim self. We were nearly struck with jealousy that he had penned such lightly humorous asides as, "the great man's image will tarnish fast once he starts exhorting people to visit the salad bar at their local Pizza Hut," and in the next paragraph, adding fuel to the fire of comedy, "But Gorbachev risks [...] his halo as the man who ended the Cold War when people start seeing him as a pizza salesman," and of course who can forget the rousing finale of cymbal-crashing humor when Winestock concluded with the surprise punchline, "... the [Gorbachev] foundation's reputation will suffer once its guiding light starts doing Pizza Hut ads..." This is a knee-slapping, sides-a-hurtin' example of how Winestock is expanding his reach into high comedy.

Oddly, the comedy came to a screeching halt, although the will to experiment took a mind-bending turn. On Wednesday, December 10th, the interim editor published his first-ever "must" editorial, as opposed to the innumerable "should" editorials that have marked his brief tenure. Headlined "Law MUST Root Out Bad Police," Winestock shocked his readers by actually taking a clear stand. Not that he'd find too many sane human beings who would disagree with his argument that bad policemen should be fired, but we figured that this was a first step, a big toe dipped in the lake of commitment, and there's nothing more we'd like to do than to run up behind him at full speed, lower our helmet, and stick him in the lower back, sending him deep and far into the lamprey-infested waters of Lake Take-A-Stand.

So we at the eXile, sensing change in the *Times'* editorial-writing department, decided to lend a helping hand. Posing as Bernie Schwartz from the *Moscow Times* marketing department, we called various expat organizations—particularly local journalists—to find out just what it is the reader wants and expects from a Winestockian editorial. Each of the callers was given a short spiel on how the *Moscow Times* is working on a new experimental program to fine tune its editorials to the readers' expectations. Callers were given the alleged topic for the next day's MT editorial, then asked to recommend, based on a series of choices, which type of editorial should be written on that subject.

Our first call was to the Business Week news desk:

eXile: Hello, my name is Bernie Schwartz, and I'm calling from the marketing department of the Moscow Times.

Business Week: Hello.

Exile: What's your name?

Business Week: John Crawford. I'm the deputy bureau chief.

Exile: Nice to meet you, Mr. Crawford. We're doing a new reader's response survey to help us with our editorials, in which we ask readers of our newspaper some questions about what they expect in an editorial. Maybe you've heard of this kind of thing? They do it a lot in the States.

Crawford: Uh-huh.

eXile: Why don't I just get right down to it? Tomorrow's editorial is supposed to be about the Rosneft loans-for-shares thing, about how they floated the idea, then withdrew it, and now they're floating it again.

Crawford: Uh-huh.

eXile: My first question is, should this editorial be humorous, serious, or a "points-to-a-larger-problem" type of editorial?

Crawford: Uh, let me see. (Pauses) Points-to-a-larger problem editorial.

eXile: Okay. Next question. Should we make this a "there-they-go-again" editorial, a "the-idea's-not-bad-if-it's-fairly-held" editorial, or should we use the phrase, "we should not rush to condemn it"?

Crawford: H'm, that's a tough one. What were the three options?

eXile: (repeats)

Crawford: I would say "we should not rush to condemn it."

eXile: Okay, and the last question. Should we end off strongly in favor of the Rosneft loans-for-shares, strongly against, or remain ambiguous?

Crawford: Ambiguous. That way you cover your options.

Wow! He didn't even blink! Like minds think alike. Moving on, we called the New York Times to see if that ultimate paper of record might do its part to help pull Winestock onto the conveyor belt of "objectivity." To our surprise, we were lucky to hook up with one very helpful Marina Lokhman, an American researcher.

Lokhman: I'd be more than glad to do this survey. It's part of my job, you know, to read your editorials.

eXile: Oh that's great. We're happy that you read our newspaper. Things have been getting tough lately, and that's why we're doing these reader-response surveys for our editorials.

Lokhman: Oh, what a great idea!

eXile: We're doing an editorial on the Rosneft loans-for-shares thing.

Lokhman: Uh-huh, yeah.

eXile: Do you think our editorial should be serious, humorous, or "points-to-a-larger-problem"?

Lokhman: Oh definitely "points-to-a-larger-problem." I really like those types of editorials. Usually economic issues point to a larger problem, you know? Especially here, where it's like, make-up-the-rules-as-you-go-along, you know? In this instance you always need to point-to-a-larger-problem.

eXile: I see. The next question concerns the body of the editorial. Do you think that this editorial should a). have a "there they go again" angle, b). idea not bad if it's fairly held, or c). we should not rush to condemn it?

Lokhman (pauses): Okay, well. H'm. Okay, I'm not too familiar with this particular issue. I can only tell you what I'd expect. I always expect in this circumstance a "here we go again" type of editorial.

eXile: Okay, good. Now the last question. Should we be strongly for, strongly against, or ambiguous?

Lokhman: H'm, against or for? You want *me* to say?

eXile: Well, yeah. That's what this survey's about. We're finding out how people respond, then we'll fashion tomorrow's editorial based on polled reader responses.

Lokhman: Interesting. It notes a lack of independence... but you guys are entitled to that if that's what you want. You guys will probably come out against the loans-for-shares thing. I mean, you guys are real rabble-rousers in your editorials. I really like them—like what you wrote about the Moscow Duma and how they should have an opposition? I totally agree. In fact, I don't know the last editorial you wrote that I disagreed with.

eXile: (baffled) You think we're "rabble-rousers"?

[Editor's note: If the New York Times's idea of "rabble-rousing" is that a municipal legislature should not be a rubber-stamp body for an authoritarian mayor, then we'd be curious to see what they think is tame.]

Lokhman: I don't mean that's bad! But like, for example, you really came out against Chubais. That was good.

eXile: We did? Oh. Anyway, we're also planning on doing a web site soon.

Lokhman: Oh great! I'm so excited!

eXile: We're going to do a sort of reader interactive editorial page, where we'll put up the next day's editorial topic, then have readers vote on how we should write it.

Lokhman: That's so exciting! I think reader-interaction is great to get people involved.

eXile: No, I mean we're going to take the average reader response then base our editorials on that.

Lokhman: Well, so long as people know that your editorials will be based on reader response, I guess that's really great.

eXile: Actually, no. We're not going to tell our readers anything. We're just going to leave it the way it is, as a regular editorial. The only difference will be that our position will be generated by the average reader's desires.

Lokhman: (pauses) If you do, it's weenie.

eXile: Why is it "weenie"?

Lokhman: It's weenie because you're representing the readers' opinions as that of the newspaper.

eXile: Well, it's all part of the restructuring at the *Moscow Times*. We're also thinking of getting rid of the MT Out section. They're saying that it can't compete with the ***eXile***.

Lokhman: No, I like the MT Out. I mean the ***eXile's*** guide is geared towards people who want to drink or go out to clubs or something, but the MT Out is more... intellectual.

It's downright impossible to argue with that!

Next on our list were our old friends at Burson-Marsteller, the renowned PR firm which once gained fame in our newspaper for jumping on our proposal to try to cover up St. Petersburg's image as a city whose brutal treatment of foreigners and undesirables was earning it the ol' "violation of human rights" tag, which might cut into profits in their Eurobond issue. For the folks at BM, this wasn't a problem; after all, they're the same guys who were hired by Exxon after the Valdez spill, Union Carbide after its Bhopal disaster killed tens of thousands, the Argentinean military junta, the Indonesian despot, and just about every other ne'er-do-well in the global village who needed someone to lie for them after they'd hit the proverbial baseball through the neighbor's window. Like the Wolf in La Femme Nikitia, who cleans up assassination jobs by dissolving the bodies in tubs of acid, Burson Marstellar can clean up a bad mess like no one!

eXile: We're trying to do reader-survey editorials to make sure that our editorials are in line with reader expectations. It's kind of the new thing in the States.

Marstellar: Uh-huh.

eXile: So if you have a minute-

Marstellar: Go ahead!

eXile: Well, we're doing an editorial tomorrow on the Rosneft loans-for-shares. My first question is, do you think the editorial should be humorous, serious, or points-to-a-larger-issue?

Marstellar: I think that, uh, it should be serious.

eXile: Okay, next question. Should we make it a "there they go again" editorial, a "the idea's not bad if it's done right" editorial, or a "we should not rush to condemn it" editorial?

Marstellar: (serious tone) That's a good question. H'm. (pauses) I think the last one, "we should not rush to condemn it."

eXile: Okay, and the last question. Should the conclusion be strongly for the loans-for-shares, strongly against, or ambiguous?

Marstellar: Strongly *for*, definitely!

eXile: Okay, good. By the way, I'll need to get your name again.

Marstellar: Jim Vail. I'm a senior account executive.

eXile: Wait, haven't I seen your name somewhere?

Marstellar: Yeah! I used to write for you guys! I wrote for the Moscow Times last year!

The *Moscow Times's* reputation for moral flexibility was so firmly entrenched in the expat community that people actually believed us when we spread the word that the paper would, from now on, be fashioning the opinions in its editorials based upon the results of reader surveys. In this joke, we conned employees for *Business Week*, the *New York Times*, and Burson-Marsteller into giving the *Times* a little friendly advice.

USAID Helped Anatoly Chubais Screw Russia," it was news before people even started to read the text. No one in the city had ever publicly questioned the essential righteousness of the aid mission, much less dared to imply that its heroes had "screwed" anybody, even their own wives.

Which didn't make sense, since there was plenty of evidence out there to show that the key protégés of U.S. policy within the Russian government had marauded the budget and state property for personal gain with all the subtlety of an attack on Masada. The key event there was the "loans-for-shares" auctions, in which shares of state enterprises were auctioned off to private investors in exchange for cash loans.

In retrospect, it might not be an exaggeration to call these auctions, which were masterminded by Chubais in the fall of 1995, the biggest thefts in the history of the human race.

[T]imes

WWW.MOSCOWTIMES.RU

All's Well

Kremlin reassures foreign investors about reforms. Business, Page 10.

MICEX RUBLE RATE 6.2780 0.0025

MT INDEX 2.92 111.13 DOLLAR 8.38 313.15 RUBLE

The *Times* had a charming habit of keeping things nice and simple in the midst of complex phenomena like the 1998 financial crisis.

The scheme worked like this. In the fall of 1995, in what would subsequently become a pattern in the increasingly ghettoized world of Russian politics, the Russian federal government found itself short of cash. The Yeltsin regime needed money to pay foreign debts and, so it said, pensions and state salaries. So it devised a scheme to raise short-term money—the loans-for-shares auctions. The scheme was devised by the State Property Committee (GKI), a body within the government which for years had been in close cooperation with the U.S. government–funded Russian Privatization Center (and had, incidentally, worked with the RPC to hold the voucher privatization program). Their idea was to auction off shares in private enterprises to private banks (who would then hold them in trust) in exchange for cash loans to the government. Eventually, if the private investor wanted to keep the property, he would have to win a reauction of the same shares.

The Moscow Times

I N B R I E F

Wilt the Stilt for CSKA?

■ MOSCOW (MT) — According to American newspaper the Santa Monica Daily Bugle, one of the greatest players in the NBA's history, Wilt Champerlain want to resume his basketball career in ... Russia.

Jerry Stainblath, Chamberlain's agent, told the newspaper that he wants to come to Moscow to marry his fiancee Larisa Kazakina and to convert to the Russian Orthodox Church.

Stainblath said the first option for his client would be joining Russian champion CSKA Moscow. Chamberlain, 58, retired in 1973.

10 ❖ Friday, March 13, 1998

E D I T O R I A L

Downgrade By Moody's Badly Timed

Credit rating agencies like Moody's Investor Services are supposed to warn investors about risks ahead. But in its recent decision to downgrade its appraisal of Russia, Moody's is lagging well behind the times.

Russia's finances have indeed endured a crisis in the the wake of the collapse of Asian financial markets. Spooked by the realization that emerging markets are risky, international investors lost faith in the Russian treasury bill and stock markets.

This in turn put pressure on the Russian currency as rubles were repatriated into dollars. The Central Bank was forced to spend billions of dollars of reserves to prevent a sharp devaluation in the currency.

All this placed a huge strain on the Russian government, which suddenly found it could not borrow to cover its budget deficit,

There was probably no better example of the *Times*'s habit for boosterism than its March, 1998 editorial blasting a Moody's downgrade of Russia's credit worthiness. Six months after the *Times* in this article insisted that there were no "risks ahead," Russia defaulted on its domestic debt and suffered a near-total collapse of its banking system.

Santa Monica Daily Bugle March 25, 1997 • 17

Chamberlain May Play in Russia, Rumors Say

by James Milkie
STAFF WRITER

Is 58 too old to play professional basketball? Not for a man in love, say friends of NBA great Wilt Chamberlain.

"Wilt's coming back. He feels great. He can't wait to get out there on the court," said Lloyd "World B." Free, one of Chamberlain's closest friends. "And he can't wait to move to Moscow."

According to Free and other NBA insiders, Chamberlain has asked his agent to arrange trouts with professional basketball teams in Moscow, Russia, the home of Chamberlain's new beau, Larissa Kazakina.

Chamberlain, sources say, has dispensed with his legendary womanizing habits and is "hanging it up" to grow old with Kazakina.

"He's in love. I can't believe it," said Elgin Baylor, reached in Los Angeles yesterday. "I've never seen him like this before."

Chamberlain himself has not been available for comment, but his agent, Jerry Steinblatz, has confirmed that "discussions are underway" with Russian teams, most notably the league-leading "Red Army" club.

Baylor and Free also confirmed reports that Chamberlain is partly motivated by a new religious spirit. Both men say that the "Stilt," who once averaged 50 points a game, is mulling a conversion to the Russian Orthodox Church.

"Larissa has him believing in God," said Baylor. "I went to his house, and he spent an hour showing me all his icons."

Steinblatz would not confirm the reports of Chamberlain's religious conversion, but said that his client is "still viable" and would be a major contributor to any team below the NBA level.

"Wilt can still play," he said. "I would have preferred Italy, because of the weather. But he's the boss."

This phony *"Santa Monica Daily Bugle"* article was enough to convince the Russian sports daily *Sport-Express* that Wilt Chamberlain had decided to make a comeback in Moscow.

It sounded simple, but there were a lot of catches. For instance: somehow, 38 percent of the state mineral magnate Norilsk Nickel fell into the hands of giant Russian bank Oneximbank for just $171 million, or $100,000 over the starting auction price. The company, which controls 35 percent of the world's nickel reserves, is worth a lot more—in fact, it is said to clear more than a billion dollars a year in exports. All in all, although huge chunks of about a dozen of the biggest state enterprises were auctioned off, the state only earned about a billion dollars total in cash from the whole process. It was as though the upper crust of the Fortune 500 had been bid out for the price of a couple of NFL expansion teams.

The amazing thing about the auctions, though, was the way they were held. Oneximbank, for instance, had been assigned by the GKI to regulate, itself, the auction for Norilsk. The bank was therefore given license to exclude a much higher bid for Norilsk by rival Bank Rossissky Kredit on the grounds that it had "insufficient financial guarantees." Another giant Russian bank, Bank Menatep, was given license to regulate a tender for 78 percent of the oil firm Yukos, and won the auction after excluding a rival on the grounds that its representatives had been 24 minutes late for the auction.

Worse still, the State Accounting Chamber, a body roughly analagous to our own General Acounting Office, later found that Oneximbank, Menatep, and other loans-for-shares winners had used government funds to purchase the auctioned shares. How? Well, as "authorized banks," Oneximbank, Menatep et al. were holding government funds designated for other purposes, i.e., payment of state salaries. The problem was that Russia did not yet have a sufficiently developed treasury system to allow the government to do all of its own banking, so it held similarly

CORRECTIONS

A chart on Page 2 of Wednesday's paper labeled "Crime Statistics" should have noted that the statistics were for the city of Moscow only.

A story on Page 14 of Wednesday's paper headlined "Wilt the Stilt for CSKA?" saying that former NBA star Wilt Chamberlin might play basketball in Russia was a hoax and should not have appeared.

An article on Page 9 of Tuesday's paper headlined "Cash-Strapped Lenfilm Goes to the Car Wash" should have described St. Petersburg Governor Vladimir Yakovlev as a political independent.

ПИСЬМО ОТ АГЕНТА ЧЕМБЕРЛЕНА - НЕ ШУТКА

По словам генерального менеджера ЦСКА Юрия Юркова, в адрес армейского клуба на днях пришло письмо из американской адвокатской конторы с предложением провести переговоры со знаменитым центровым Уилтом Чемберленом, который, как уже сообщал «СЭ», выразил желание выступать за один из московских клубов. Однако до обсуждения конкретных деталей возможного контракта дело пока не дошло.

ЧЕМБЕРЛЕН ХОЧЕТ ИГРАТЬ ЗА МОСКОВСКИЙ КЛУБ!

Как сообщила газета Santa Moniça Daily Bugle, один из лучших
ков за всю историю НБА Уилт Чемберлен намерен вернуться в ба
бол и хотел бы выступать... в России! Американская газета утвер
(ссылаясь на другого известного в прошлом баскетболиста Уолд
Фри), что Чемберлен уже дал указание своему агенту Джерри Ш
блатцу подыскать для него подходящий клуб в Москве. Штайн
подтвердил, что начал переговоры, рассматривая ЦСКА как наи
благоприятный вариант благоустройства своего 58-летнего кли
«Уверяю вас, он еще может играть, хотя и не на уровне НБА», - с
агент Чемберлена.

Желание Чемберлена поехать в Россию объясняется тем, что
скве проживает его невеста Лариса Казакина, утверждает газета
влюблен по уши! Я никогда раньше его таким не видел», - сказал

"Chamberlain Wants to Play For Moscow Team!" screamed the headline of the Sport-Express article eventually picked up by the *Moscow Times.* The Russian paper later wisely went on the offensive and announced (see left) that "the letter from Wilt Chamberlain's agent is not a joke" and that no retraction was necessary.

bogus auctions for the right to manage government money. The winners of those auctions then went on to use government money to bid on state companies. Menatep, for instance, won the Yukos bid at a time when state Academy of Science workers—whose salary funds were held by Menatep—stopped receiving their pay.

The loans-for-shares auctions were conducted according to the same principle of clan tribute and cronyism that had reigned in Russia during the Soviet years. The only difference was that the scheme punished the average Russian economically in a way that was much worse than the Soviet system had. If Soviet economics placed ordinary people in a state of near-indenture in relation to their bosses, the economics of privatized Russia reduced them to more or less outright slavery. By 1997, it was no longer unusual for employees of companies like Norilsk to go 6 months to a year, if not longer, without receiving their meager salaries. Russian newspapers even reported scenes of people collapsing from hunger in the streets in the towns surrounding the industrial centers. Meanwhile, the banks like Oneximbank which controlled these companies were leveraging them to the hilt to make bids on other properties—and this was after using public money to buy their stakes in the first place!

There was another insidious angle to the auctions. As 1995 came to a close, and key parliamentary elections as well as the next year's presidential election approached, both the Yeltsin regime and the West noted with alarm that the Communist Party was leading in the polls, and antigovernment sentiment was rising. Catastrophe seemed imminent and something needed to be done. That's where the auctions came in. Though it has never been openly admitted or conclusively proved, loans-for-shares was almost certainly also designed to create a super-rich propertied class that would support the regime against any political movement to renationalize the economy. It was hardly a coincidence that the biggest loans-for-shares winners were Yeltsin's most important allies in his reelection campaign the following year. As very recent owners of Russia's key national television stations and newspapers, almost the entire national media, actually, their support virtually guaranteed a public relations sweep that the doddering incumbent rode to victory.

The scope of loans-for-shares was breathtaking. It wasn't just that millions of Russians were having their livelihoods taken away. With the help of the Russian Privatization Center and the State Property Committee—both places that were packed with people who were on a first-name basis with the leading American aid consultants—Russians had actually paid tax money to instantly enrich a small group of bankers, who in turn performed the service of making their labor unpaid. It was a scam that most criminals wouldn't have considered trying, simply because it was too improbable. Even the Gambino family never sank that low.

All of which was reprehensible and sick, but what was most offensive were all the Americans in town who were apologizing for the corrupt officials in the Russian government who'd pulled heists like this off. If they'd come to town in Viking costumes, or with swastika armbands, it probably wouldn't have bothered either Mark or me so much. But to come in and preside over the rape of so many people with a big smile on your face and an attitude of benevolence and righteousness . . . it was almost too offensive to comprehend. A lot of these people sincerely believed that their North American birth and their superior dentistry made them the arbiters of public morality by default. Growing up, I'd been taught that that sort of attitude had died out of American life with King George.

It hadn't. Russia, for instance, was full of consultants on the public dole who worked for a company called Burson-Marsteller. This is a Canadian firm that grew to be the largest public relations company in the world through its skillful prosecution of public smoke-screen campaigns on behalf of the very biggest swine on the planet. Their client list reads like something out of Madame Tussaud's chamber of horrors: the Indonesian government (hired during its brutal suppression of the independence movement in East Timor), the Three Mile Island nuclear plant, Union Carbide (responsible for the deaths of thousands following the chemical plant explosion in Bhopal, India), Exxon (following the *Exxon Valdez* oil spill), A. H. Robbins (after the Dalkon Shield I.U.D. disaster), and the Mexican government, which paid B-M $8 million during the Chiapas rebellion to shield American and Canadian voters from the fact that the Zapatistas were revolting against the planned passage of NAFTA.

Amazingly, Burson-Marsteller was one of the companies hired by the United States government to propagandize good capitalist values to Russia. Among its many tasks was providing p.r. for the disastrous Russian voucher privatization program, which gave Russians shares in public companies (and preceded the loans-for-shares scheme). B-M had a massive public contract, and when they weren't actively doing evil, they were just sitting on their hands collecting checks while their clients went around pillaging the country.

A former coworker of mine, Matt Bivens (who was now the editor of the *St. Petersburg Times*, the *Moscow Times*'s sister publication up north), had taken a job with B-M in Kazakhstan a few years before. Before he took the job, he'd been just another kid like me, freelancing for the *Los Angleles Times* up in St. Petersburg. But when he got married and started a family, he decided to try to make some real money.

So he made one phone call to the USAID office in Washington, and on the basis of that one call landed a B-M contract job package—complete with housing, a maid, a per diem, and a restaurant allowance—worth about ninety grand in total. Not bad for a 26-year-old. Then he went to the Kazakh capital of Almaty and presided over asinine projects like the publication of "Privatization calendars" and the production of privatization soap operas, racking up massive bills that were, perversely, rewarded by more funding.

Bivens, who later outed the whole scheme in *Harper's* magazine, also reported that B-M had a thing called a "cost-plus" policy running with AID. This was a classic example of a phenomenon we would run into over and over the more we reported on the expatriate community: publicly funded businesses and organizations that were guaranteed profits, independent of any competition or accountability for performance, while supposedly furthering the capitalist virtues of competition and fair play. B-M's "cost-plus" arrangement, according to Bivens, meant that "USAID reimbursed all our costs, and added 7 percent on top of that—our profit margin. In other words, the more we spent, the more we made."

I knew some of B-M's Moscow consultants, or knew of them, anyway. Many of them weren't much older than me. I'd see them at the Starlite Diner sometimes on weekends, dressed in college sweatshirts and faded jeans. Looking at their bright, happy faces, you'd never guess that these were the people who'd had the balls to tell millions of Russians that their jobs and benefits needed to be sacrificed for the sake of "competitiveness." On the contrary, they looked like they'd never left the keg party.

There was no point in fighting fair against people like this. Humorless lefties like Ralph Nader had been doing that for decades, much more effectively and with much greater attention than we ever could, to very little result. Besides, from where we sat, people like Nader were missing the point. The important thing was to loathe corporate henchmen not for what they did, but for who they were. As one of Gogol's heroes said, "Coat a frog all over with sugar and I still won't eat it." People like Nader were going after the frog—corporate abuses. But the real thrill in attacking people like these would be to take the sugar coating away—embarrass them socially, pick on their looks and their mannerisms and speech, expose them as *people.* We had to at least make it tough for them to maintain their public superiority complex while they went about their business of fucking up huge historical missions like the reform of post-Soviet Russia.

We went after B-M in our USAID article. They turned out to be pathetically easy to dupe. All we had to do was make up some phony stationery and claim to be representatives of the St. Petersburg mayoral office, who were interested in engaging their services. Posing as "Alexander Rublev," we sent a letter saying we needed help in quelling bad p.r. over the city's notorious police brutality problem.

Some background on this joke: It was a well-known fact that one of the reasons St. Petersburg had been turned down as a site for the 2004 Olympic games was its policing problem. Prior to the Goodwill Games in 1994, then-mayor Anatoly Sobchak had been so determined to keep riffraff out of the eye of the international press that he used Russia's reactionary visa registration laws as an excuse to deport practically every dark-skinned pedestrian (mainly Azeris, Armenians, Chechens, and other Caucasus peoples, whom Russians call *chernozhopiye*, or "blackasses") his police could find to the city limits.

A friend of a friend of mine, a hairy Italian-American, had even been detained once in a local Petersburg police station and had to watch in horror as a succession of Caucasian drifters ahead of him in line were led into another room and beaten savagely for no reason. He escaped only after digging through his bag and producing an expired California driver's license, which so impressed the precinct chief that he not only decided to let the kid go, but broke out in a smile and sang "Hotel California" from beginning to end—while in the next room the blows still rained percussively on the Chechen-of-the-moment.

None of this mattered to B-M. When bubbly American B-M rep Jennifer Galenkamp got ahold of our letter, which expressed the hope that the city's reputation could be cleared up in time for an upcoming Eurobond issue (which was actually due to take place), she jumped all over it with giggly cheerleaderish zeal.

We clicked on the tape recorder function on our office phone as she announced to "Rublev's" assistant, in reality our virginal Russian secretary Tanya Krasnikova, that:

"We contacted the London office . . . because this is a

European issue you would need work done there, and we can do that. Our London office is eager to support us, so I think that everything will be, you know, okay."

She also sent us a letter expressing her willingness to work with us, which we also published.

We heard some feedback from B-M through mutual acquaintances. Basically the consensus over there was that we were in the wrong, because we had misrepresented ourselves. "They can't do that, call up and say they're who they're not," one staffer reportedly said. "That's not fair."

We had a big laugh at the idea of B-M complaining about misrepresentation. This was the same company that had been commissioned by the U.S. government to make a privatization commercial for Russian TV which was supposed to say, "Your voucher, your choice." But when it came out, the slogan read "Your Voucher—Your Choice, Russia!" The latter half (*Vash vuibor, Rossiya*), in Russian, was actually the name of Anatoly Chubais's political party, Russia's Choice (*Vuibor Rossii*). It was a blatant manipulation of public money for political purposes, but these were the kind of people who were all over the place in the aid community.

As far as I was concerned, we didn't have to trick Burson-Marsteller into doing anything to make our point. Their very presence in the entire aid effort should have been shocking enough to anyone who'd had to live through the Cold War period on either side.

Just think about it: For more than forty years, Americans were told that we were fighting the Cold War—at enormous expense—to defend the cause of personal liberty, fair play, and openness. Then we win the fucking thing, and we hire a bunch of half-bright bloodsuckers like these idiots at B-M to come over and finish the deal. It was sickening.

Not long after we ran the USAID piece, I called up a Russian reporter named Leonid Krutakov, hoping to get some more information about the ins and outs of privatization. He gave me some, but also gave me an education into the life of a top-flight Russian investigative reporter—a story very interesing in itself.

We met in the first week in July, just after Krutakov had volunteered for the honor of being Russia's latest "Most Likely To Be Assassinated" public figure by publishing an article called "*Kreditui Ili . . .* " in *Izvestia.* The article revealed that Chubais had received a no-interest $3 million loan from Stolichny Bank chief Alexander Smolensky, and strongly implied that the loan was in return for the successful rigging of a tender for a state agricultural bank.

If that wasn't a dangerous enough thing to publish—especially considering that he'd conspired with his editor to slip it into the pages of a newspaper controlled by a powerful Chubais ally—Krutakov brought some extra anguish upon himself by pulling off a shocking *eXile*-style adolescent stunt in addition to his reporting. When he learned that the official reason for the $3 million loan was to help Chubais "spread good democratic values," Krutakov put on his one shabby tie and decided to try something out. He walked into a small Moscow branch of Stolichny Bank, took a seat at a customer service desk, and with a completely straight face asked if he could have a $3 million loan to spread good democratic values.

"Without interest," he added sternly.

They tossed him out, but not before they took a few hours nervously humoring him while security ran a check on his ID. In Russia, you can never be sure that even a guy as shabby-looking as Krutakov isn't secretly running the country, or worse.

In the days following the publication of the piece, Krutakov was hauled in by several different branches of the Russian secret services and grilled at length. All of them wanted to know who'd put him up to writing the article—the piece had taken them by surprise, since it was published in a Chubais-friendly newspaper. Russian government officials, of course, don't like surprises. They still remember the old days, when the sudden demotion of a middle-level party functionary in some small factory town today might turn out to mean the disappearance of an entire department in Moscow—maybe even theirs—tomorrow.

So Krutakov was raked over the coals until they realized with surprise that he was merely an individual malcontent acting alone, at which point they heaved a sigh of relief and let him go. In the old days they would have shot him as an afterthought, but that isn't done in Russia anymore. Which is one sign of progress, I suppose—although it might also mean that the individual simply isn't dangerous anymore to anyone in power in Russia. I tend to think the latter is true.

In any case, Krutakov, when he came to see me, was bright and smiling, having just been fired. It was the third time that year he had been fired from a newspaper. The other two firings were for similar offenses, although the official reason for his first dismissal, from the giant daily *Komsomolskaya Pravda*, was that he had been paid by his sources. *Zakazniye materiyaly*, or "commissioned articles," are standard practice among Russian investigative journalists. The way it usually works is that some spookish middleman from a bank, or a ministry, or in parliament, or wherever, comes to the reporter, hands him a packet of documents full of compromising information (called *kompromat* in Russian) about a certain competitor, then pays him to publish it.

Since Russian journalists *a)* make almost nothing in the way of regular salaries, and *b)* have virtually no other way of penetrating the weird, secretive, deadly labyrinth of Russian commerce and politics, they often take the money and run with it. Virtually every Russian reporter is on somebody's payroll, and most have just one patron. With one patron, you can stay at one newspaper, which normally is controlled, influenced, or owned by a friend of your patron.

If you're like Krutakov, though, and you hedge your bets and write scandalous garbage about everybody, including people who only yesterday you took money from, you find yourself without a job pretty fast. Krutakov by the time we met was the absolute champion of this method of career advancement. In fact, he went on later that year to set a new standard by being fired by a new newspaper before it had even published its first issue. He'd written an exposé about the new paper's owner, banker Boris Berezovsky, and published it in a rival paper just after being hired.

I asked him what he knew about privatization, whether any Westerners had been involved in any particularly egregious shenanigans the world should know about.

"What do you mean?" he asked, startled. Until that point he had been quietly registering, without much interest, the giant rubber alligator head, garish multicolor carpets, and rank month-old yogurt containers which littered the *eXile* office.

"You know," I said, "were there any Westerners up to no good during that time?"

"What do you mean?" he repeated. "They all were. Which person in particular are you interested in?"

"I don't know," I said, shrugging lamely. "Maybe you should tell me?"

Krutakov gaped at me, then sputtered out a few things here and there about loans-for-shares and the GKI and insider dealing, never really getting into specifics. Then he looked up suddenly and said, "Well, actually there is one figure I've always been interested in. Jonathan Hay—I've always been interested in him. I even did a thing on him a few years back."

I sat up, interested. This was the same Jonathan Hay who had just been fired from the Harvard Institute and caused that little scandal in the press.

I expected to hear more about HIID and Hay's private investments, but Krutakov laid a different and more amazing story on me. Two years before, he'd run a story in *Komsomolskaya Pravda* entitled "Did the CIA Privatize our Military Factory?" The thrust of this piece—based, incidentally, on unnamed sources—was that Hay had invested, through a Vietnamese middleman, some $700,000 into a Moscow factory called NII Grafit, which developed Russian stealth technology.

"Nobody ever picked up the story," he said. "But you know, I saw Hay the day that story ran. We were in the Radisson Hotel, at a press conference. He was smoking. I'd been watching him a while, and I'd never seen him smoke before."

If any of this was true, it would raise the privatization mess from mere criminal stupidity to the level of sinister, premeditated criminal stupidity. At the same time, the idea of a tweedy Harvard grad, too dumb to avoid being caught investing spare change in his girlfriend's mutual fund, acting as bagman for daring cloak-and-dagger deals in secret factories—it was almost too goofy to imagine.

It was after this meeting that I learned one of the first rules about brilliant espionage exposés: they don't happen. When I tried to track that story down, I ended up interviewing a graying, slit-eyed "retired scientist" who was a shareholder at NII Grafit and confirmed that, yes, Jonathan Hay was an investor in the factory. As this weird old man with conspicuously careful dress led me slowly up the stairs to his office—an immaculate, mostly abandoned gray office building near the Butirka prison—his eyebrows kept leaping upward on his head after every word he spoke, as if to express some deeper meaning to every action, even the opening of his door. In the interview, when I tried to pin him down on where I could get documentary verification on the Hay thing, he plunged into a cat-and-mouse game that lasted for almost an hour. "You can't prove this thing," he said.

"Then why did you agree to meet with me?" I asked.

"I am interested," he said, "in seeing this news get out."

"Well, then," I said, "I need to get some documentary information."

"Not possible," he said. "Although, on the other hand . . . "—again the eyebrows—"something might be arranged."

"Okay," I said, contemptuously by then. "'When?"

"You understand," he said, "that if you publish this story, you'll be out of Russia in 24 hours."

"Okay," I said. "So when can we make this arrangement?"

"You will be contacted."

Our letter to Burson-Marsteller in which we represented ourselves as officials in the St. Petersburg mayor's office who were seeking to engage their services.

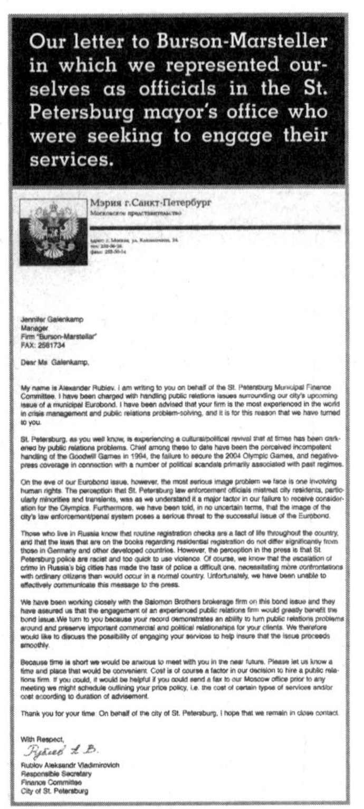

Мэрия г.Санкт-Петербург

Jennifer Galenkamp
Manager
Firm "Burson-Marstellar"
FAX: 2581734

Dear Ms Galenkamp,

My name is Alexander Rubiev. I am writing to you on behalf of the St. Petersburg Municipal Finance Committee. I have been charged with handling public relations issues surrounding our city's upcoming issue of a municipal Eurobond. I have been advised that your firm is the most experienced in the world in crisis management and public relations problem-solving, and it is for this reason that we have turned to you.

St. Petersburg, as you well know, is experiencing a cultural/political revival that at times has been darkened by public relations problems. Chief among these to date have been the perceived incompetent handling of the Goodwill Games in 1994, the failure to secure the 2004 Olympic Games, and negative-press coverage in connection with a number of political scandals primarily associated with past regimes.

On the eve of our Eurobond issue, however, the most serious image problem we face is one involving human rights. The perception that St. Petersburg law enforcement officials mistreat city residents, particularly minorities and transients, was as we understand it a major factor in our failure to receive consideration for the Olympics. Furthermore, we have been told, in no uncertain terms, that the image of the city's law enforcement/penal system poses a serious threat to the successful issue of the Eurobond.

Those who live in Russia know that routine registration checks are a fact of life throughout the country, and that the laws that are on the books regarding residential registration do not differ significantly from those in Germany and other developed countries. However, the perception in the press is that St Petersburg police are racist and too quick to use violence. Of course, we know that the escalation of crime in Russia's big cities has made the task of police a difficult one, necessitating more confrontations with ordinary citizens than would occur in a normal country. Unfortunately, we have been unable to effectively communicate this message to the press.

We have been working closely with the Salomon Brothers brokerage firm on this bond issue and they have assured us that the engagement of an experienced public relations firm would greatly benefit the bond issue.We turn to you because your record demonstrates an ability to turn public relations problems around and preserve important commercial and political relationships for your clients. We therefore would like to discuss the possibility of engaging your services to help insure that the issue proceeds smoothly.

Because time is short we would be anxious to meet with you in the near future. Please let us know a time and place that would be convenient. Cost is of course a factor in our decision to hire a public relations firm. If you could, it would be helpful if you could send a fax to our Moscow office prior to any meeting we might schedule outlining your price policy, i.e. the cost of certain types of services and/or cost according to duration of advisement.

Thank you for your time. On behalf of the city of St. Petersburg, I hope that we remain in close contact.

With Respect,

Rublov Aleksandr Vladimirovich
Responsible Secretary
Finance Committee
City of St. Petersburg

The guy certainly sounded like an ex-spook, but that didn't mean much. For all I knew, he might have been a simple metallurgist who wrote bad spy novels in his spare time and answered personal ads. You meet a lot of people like that in Russia—nondescript middle-aged men who act like heavies, but might just as easily be grubby onanistic nerds. Six months later, I found out, from the State Accounting Chamber, that the NII Grafit story was true. But at the time, the story sounded so far-fetched that I dropped it, settling for a different story on Hay—one that perfectly symbolized the dim-witted cynicism and corruption of the expatriate community.

Not long after I interviewed Krutakov, I scheduled an interview with Yevgeny Nikulishev, an inspector for the Accounting Chamber. Analagous to the American General Accounting Office, the Chamber was a government body that had been responsible for uncovering most of the dirt on the loans-for-shares auctions, and the people who ran it were loathed by nearly everyone in the country who had any power. Fortunately for those people, the Chamber had no prosecutorial authority, and its inspectors could do nothing more than advise the parliament and the prosecutor's office when they uncovered improprieties.

The gloating article we eventually published exposing cheerleadery Burson-Marsteller moron Jennifer Galenkamp.

#8 • May 22 - June 4, 1997 • P. 4

Busted, Marstellar!

The *eXile* dupes USAID's favorite public relations firm

Soon after its creation in 1995, the Chamber's inspectors began to notice that no one in government ever listened to any of their recommendations. When installments of their meager budgets stopped arriving on time, coming in sporadic bursts, the inspectors temporarily found themselves without money to keep up their offices. For a while many of them worked out of their homes.

By the time I walked into Nikulishev's office, their financial status had improved somewhat, but bitterness over their continued impotence to get anyone in their own government to listen to them had left a undeniable scent of urgent, semireligious inquisitorial fervor hanging in the Chamber hallways. These were guys who were expending an enormous amount of energy, grief, and stress not to make money but to make a point—something that almost no one in the entire country could say at the time.

Nikulishev was practically twitching with anticipation when I walked into the office. He even dispensed with the xenophobic gruffness one generally observes in an ex-communist government official when he receives a pampered Western guest. When I walked into his office, he put chocolates and cookies on the table and served me tea himself, waving off his secretary.

The Chamber is frequently described, particularly by IMF/World Bank people and Western reporters, as a hotbed of raging red communists. Jonathan Hay himself said as much, calling them "communists" and "a totally unreliable source" when I finally spoke to him in the winter of 1998, long after he was out of the aid community and editing a business newsletter. While there's clearly a heavy concentration of Zyuganov voters in the Chamber—and among these probably a good two or three key members who still keep Lenin or even Stalin busts in their studies at home—the truth is that the inspectors' political leanings cover a pretty diverse range.

The Chamber's most visible public figure is an inspector by the name of Yuri Boldarev, who was better known to Russians as one of the founders of the liberal political party Yabloko, headed by Grigory Yavlinsky. Yavlinsky and his party are probably the closest thing to a Western bleeding-heart liberal political party that exists in Russia, a coalition of touchy-feely PC/Green types and economic libertarians. Yabloko means "apple" in Russian: the name is also an anagram of letters representing the names of the party leaders. "Ya" is Yavlinsky; the "B" was for Boldarev.

Burson-Marsteller **MOSCOW**

International Trade Center, Office 1402
12 Krasnopresnenskaya Naberezhnaya
Moscow 123610 Russia
Tel.: (7-095) 258-1752
(7-095) 258-1733
Fax: (7-095) 258-1734

TeleFax

Date:	**May 22, 1997**
To:	**Aleksandr Vladimirovich Rublev**
Company:	**Finance Committee, City of St. Petersburg**
From:	**Jennifer Galenkamp**
Re:	**Today's Meeting**
CC:	
Total number of pages including this page:	**1**

Dear Mr. Rublev:

I hope all is well - we were expecting you at 3 p.m. this afternoon to discuss possible public relations support for the St. Petersburg Eurobond issue, per my conversation earlier this week with your secretary. I'm sorry you weren't able to make it.

As I hope your secretary passed on to you, we are delighted that you have contacted us with regard to this project, and very interested in working with you and the city to help achieve the desired results. Burson-Marsteller has extensive experience around the world working with and communicating to the financial community.

I am eager to discuss the parameters of the project with you, the city's needs, expectations, goals and desires, as well as the specifics of the bond issue. I have already prepared, in coordination with my colleagues in London, some estimated figures for what this project might cost, and am ready to discuss those as well. Obviously, without knowing all the facts, it is impossible to give you exact figures, but I imagine that I will be able to do so shortly after our first conversation.

Please do phone me to let me know when we might reschedule a meeting; I do look forward to meeting you.

Burson-Marsteller employee Jennifer Galenkamp's letter to the *eXile*, complaining that our fictitious Alexander Rublev had missed a meeting

Boldarev split with Yavlinsky a while back over disagreements over party strategy (and, reportedly, frustration with Yavlinsky's famously large ego), then went to work for the Chamber. Since then, his frequent articles in the liberal weekly *Novaya Gazeta* newspaper about his investigations have been practically the Chamber's only public voice, as the controlled-from-above Russian press increasingly shut the Chamber out of its coverage.

In any case, the point is that no communist organization would have allowed Boldarev to be its public mouthpiece. The idea is as ridiculous as the John Birch society hiring Jesse Jackson as its press secretary. Yet this is the way reform proponents countered Chamber investigations.

Nikulishev, a soft-spoken academic type in glasses and a checked green sportcoat, was clearly in the middle of the Chamber's libertarian-communist spectrum. He was an ex-party member, but when he sat down to talk he confessed that his true model for economic development was Sweden, or "one of those countries." He seemed to be a good accountant, whose goal in life was to find a job quietly snorkling through streams of numbers, make a few corrections here and there, and then go home to a dull family and a Saab. It was a perverse twist of fate that a mild personality like this had to be exposed on a daily basis to vast, ingenious criminal conspiracies like loans-for-shares.

The Hay story Nikulishev told me revolved around a thing called the Investor Protection Fund. This was a public-relief program created by the government to compensate defrauded Russian investors, who made news when they emerged as the world's biggest suckers after the collapse of the MMM investment company—a pyramid scheme that had robbed millions of Russians, many of them pensioners and veterans, of hundreds of millions of dollars. That company's founder, Sergei Mavrodi, escaped punishment by using his financial gains to get himself elected to parliament, where he experienced immunity to criminal prosecution, before the police could assemble a case on him. To countermand that impressive demonstration of justice, the government in 1996 created the Investor Protection Fund, which was supposed to take 2 percent of all privatization revenue—a huge amount of money, considering the massive properties the state planned to auction off—and distribute the money to victims of MMM-like schemes.

All of which sounded fine, until you got to the nuts and bolts of the operation. The schematic diagram for the money flow that Nikulishev showed me was very complicated. The actual money that was to be paid to defrauded investors moved first from the auction winner's accounts to the Russian Privatization Fund, the holding tank for all revenue raised through privatization, then went into the account of the actual Investor Protection Fund. From there, it was to be sent out to a private investment contractor, who would hold and invest the funds—thereby adding to pot—while the Fund processed fraud claims. That private contractor would itself have contractors —for instance, the private depository that would hold the physical shares of the companies the investment contractor invested the Fund money in.

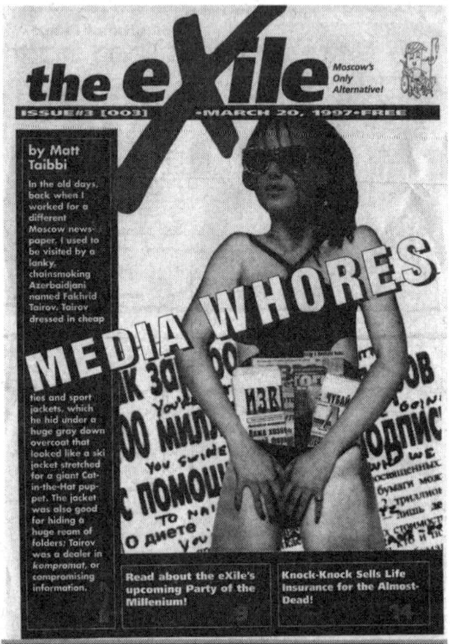
the eXile
Moscow's Only Alternative!
ISSUE#3 [003] •MARCH 20, 1997•FREE

by Matt Taibbi

In the old days, back when I worked for a different Moscow newspaper, I used to be visited by a lanky, chainsmoking Azerbaidjani named Fakhrid Tairov. Tairov dressed in cheap ties and sport jackets, which he hid under a huge gray down overcoat that looked like a ski jacket stretched for a giant Cat-in-the-Hat puppet. The jacket was also good for hiding a huge ream of folders; Tairov was a dealer in *kompromat*, or compromising information.

MEDIA WHORES

Read about the eXile's upcoming Party of the Millenium!

Knock-Knock Sells Life Insurance for the Almost-Dead!

Just as the *eXile* started up, every Russian newspaper had been taken over by one oligarchical interest or other.

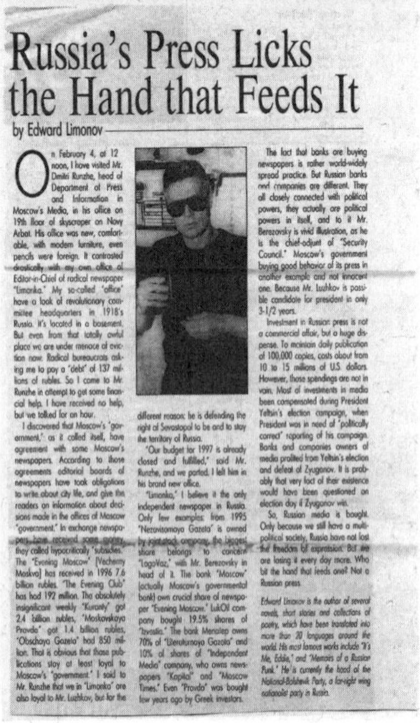
Russia's Press Licks the Hand that Feeds It

by Edward Limonov

On February 4, at 12 noon, I have visited Mr. Dmitri Runzhe, head of Department of Press and Information in Moscow's Media, in his office on 19th floor of skyscraper on Novy Arbat. His office was new, comfortable, with modern furniture, even pencils were foreign. It contrasted drastically with my own office of Editor-in-Chief of radical newspaper "Limonka." My so-called "office" have a look of revolutionary committee headquarters in 1918's Russia. It's located in a basement. But even from that totally awful place we are under menace of eviction now. Radical bureaucrats asking me to pay a "debt" of 137 millions of rubles. So I come to Mr. Runzhe in attempt to get some financial help. I have received no help, but we talked for an hour.

I discovered that Moscow's "government," as it called itself, have agreement with some Moscow's newspapers. According to those agreements editorial boards of newspapers have took obligations to write about city life, and give the readers an information about decisions made in the offices of Moscow "government." In exchange newspapers have received some money, they called hypocritically "subsidies." The "Evening Moscow" [Vechemy Moskva] has received in 1996 7.6 billion rubles. "The Evening Club" has had 192 million. The absolutely insignificant weekly "Kuranty" got 2.4 billion rubles, "Moskovskaya Pravda" got 1.4 billion rubles, "Obschaya Gazeta" had 850 million. That is obvious that those publications stay at least loyal to Moscow's "government." I said to Mr. Runzhe that we in "Limonka" are also loyal to Mr. Luzhkov, but for the different reason: he is defending the right of Sevastopol to be and to stay the territory of Russia.

"Our budget for 1997 is already closed and fulfilled," said Mr. Runzhe, and we parted. I left him in his brand new office.

"Limonka," I believe it the only independent newspaper in Russia. Only few examples: from 1995 "Nezavisamaya Gazeta" is owned by joint stock company, the biggest share belongs to concern "LogoVaz," with Mr. Berezovsky in head of it. The bank "Moscow" (actually Moscow's governmental bank) own crucial share of newspaper "Evening Moscow." LukOil company bought 19.5% shares of "Izvestia." The bank Menatep owns 70% of "Literaturnaya Gazeta" and 10% of shares of "Independent Media" company, who owns newspapers "Kapital" and "Moscow Times." Even "Pravda" was bought few years ago by Greek investors.

The fact that banks are buying newspapers is rather world-widely spread practice. But Russian banks and companies are different. They all closely connected with political powers, they actually are political powers in itself, and to it Mr. Berezovsky is vivid illustration, as he is the chief-adjunt of "Security Council." Moscow's government buying good behavior of its press in another example and not innocent one. Because Mr. Luzhkov is possible candidate for president in only 3-1/2 years.

Investment in Russian press is not a commercial affair, but a huge dispense. To maintain daily publication of 100,000 copies, costs about from 10 to 15 millions of U.S. dollars. However, those spendings are not in vain. Most of investments in media been compensated during President Yeltsin's election campaign, when President was in need of "politically correct" reporting of his campaign. Banks and companies owners of media profited from Yeltsin's election and defeat of Zyuganov. It is probably that very fact of their existence would have been questioned on election day if Zyuganov win.

So, Russian media is bought. Only because we still have a multi-political society, Russia have not lost the freedom of expression. But we are losing it every day more. Who bit the hand that feeds one? Not a Russian press.

Edward Limonov is the author of several novels, short stories and collections of poetry, which have been translated into more than 20 languages around the world. His most famous works include "It's Me, Eddie," and "Memoirs of a Russian Punk." He is currently the head of the National-Bolshevik Party, a far-right wing nationalist party in Russia.

The private investment contractor for the Fund turned out to be the Pallada mutual fund, the one run by Beth Hebert, Jonathan Hay's live-in girlfriend. The depository was the First Depository, run by Julia Zagachin, a former coworker of Hay's.

But back to that in a moment. There was other money involved with the Fund.

A fund is a physical entity: it's housed in an office, and has employees. Under the system worked out by Federal Securities Commission chief Dmitri Vasiliyev, the salaries for the Fund employees were to be paid with money loaned by the World Bank as part of a broad $31 million investor protection program (which also funded, incidentally, Burson-Marsteller p.r. campaigns on the safety and efficacy of private investment). The World Bank money traveled first to Vasiliyev's Securities Commission, then from there moved to the Harvard Institute of International Development (yes, the same one) before moving to the Institute for a Law-Based Economy (ILBE), a body Hay created and ran. ILBE was the body that was ultimately responsible for paying the salaries for the employees of the Investor Protection Fund.

If this sounds complicated, it's because it is. To make things simpler, you can concentrate on two things: one, that the money that was going for Fund employees was loaned to Russia by the World Bank, meaning that Westerners were going to make a profit on that end of the operation. Secondly, both the Pallada Mutual Fund and the First Depository, by managing the massive Fund holdings, stood to make a huge profit there as well.

Already you have two sets of Westerners making money off of what is essentially a charity program for the very poorest, weakest people in Russia. So far, so good. But by summer 1997, a year into the Fund's existence, we've already hit upon the key catch to the whole story: not one of these poor, weak people had yet received a single kopek.

That's right; according to Nikulishev's documents, which the Fund and Vasiliyev ultimately admitted to have been correct, more than $3.5 million dollars accumulated in the Fund's first year of existence, yet not one defrauded investor had filed a successful claim.

Meanwhile, Nikulishev had discovered in his investigation that Hay's girlfriend had won her contract without a tender, a seemingly outrageous conflict of interest, considering Hay's key position in the scheme and his close advisory relationship with Securities chief Vasiliyev.

I called Pallada for comment before I ran this story. Press spokesman Vadim Soskov (Hebert wouldn't speak to me) balked when I told him that I was about to run a story that Pallada had won its contract without a tender.

"Of course there was a tender," he said.

"Okay," I said. "Who were your competitors?"

"Well," he said. "I don't remember. But we definitely had some."

Had such a tender been held, of course, the preparations for it would have consumed the entire company's attention for weeks, even months; everybody's job in such a situation would be on the line; stress would reach such a high level that something as small as the absence of Styrofoam coffee cups in the office kitchen would move even the most imperturbable employees to near tears and fits of hair-pulling; wild-eyed interoffice romances would spring up because of it and then break down disastrously, resulting in strained or even destroyed marriages. . . . The entire collective would have been consumed with just one thought: *How can we destroy company X?*

A year after the fact, Soskov was trying to tell me he didn't remember company X. Pallada later admitted that there had been no tender.

In any case, all of this so far sounded like a straightforward case of corruption—very interesting mainly because it involved Hay, the Big Swinging Dick of the aid community, but still just another story nonetheless.

But Nikulishev had more than just a simple corruption story. Far beyond a precise grip on the ugly paper trail, and the revelation of the impressively sickening scheme by which affluent Westerners cashed in on public sympathy for poor suckers and then suckered them some more, Nikulishev had rare documentary evidence of the bumbling, heartless, unbelievably cynical psychology behind the entire aid effort. He had proof not only of how little good these people did, but how little they *cared.*

After the State Accounting Chamber finished the Pallada/Fund investigation, it sent a letter with its conclusions to President Yeltsin. Yeltsin, in what was either a spontaneous burst of conscience or (more likely) a result of being temporarily dissatisfied with Chubais and his allies, quickly sent off a short and ominous letter to Prime Minister Viktor Chernomyrdin which demanded that Chernomyrdin immediately bring Chubais ally Vasiliyev, the Securities chief, in for a reaming.

"I request," the letter read, "that you review the activities of the Federal Social-State Fund for the Defense of Investors' and Shareholders' Rights and take active measures to correct the problems uncovered by the Accounting Chamber of the Russian Federation. B. Yeltsin."

Chernomyrdin must have done his job, because a little more than a week later, Vasiliyev sent a groveling 10-page mea culpa to Chernomyrdin in which he agreed to all the suggestions asked for by the Accounting Chamber, while trying vainly to defend the Fund's record.

There is a lot that is strange and illogical in this document, but the most striking is Vasiliyev's means for excusing the Fund's failure to pay out any of the 22.5 billion rubles it had acquired over the course of its 18 months of existence.

While it was true that the Fund had not actually compensated any defrauded investors, Vasiliyev wrote, it had performed a valuable service by "receiving 27,192 letters, answering 17,143 telephone calls, receiving 25,440 visitors, and granting free legal advice to 2,568 persons."

You have to admire Vasiliyev. It takes balls to tell thousands of destitute people that they should say thank you for keeping a phone line open to tell them to fuck off with.

Vasiliyev went on to list eight critical measures that he planned to introduce in order to satisfy Yeltsin and the Chamber. Measure number 4 read, "Documents are being drawn up for a tender for the transfer of Fund holdings to a Russian Company in possession of the proper license."

This passage was clearly inserted to answer charges that Pallada had received its contract without a tender. Soskov may not have been able to remember whether or not there had been a company X—but Vasiliyev could.

Vasiliyev in his letter also agreed to draw up incorporating documents for the Fund, which hadn't existed previously, to make a list of Fund employees, which hadn't ever existed, to provide a detailed list of Fund expenses, which had not ever been handed over, and to fire all leaders of social organizations who were supposed to be lobbying on behalf of defrauded investors but who had instead been put on the payroll of either ILBE or the Fund and kept quiet while no payments were made.

And yet, after tacitly admitting guilt to all of these wild improprieties, Vasiliyev turned around at the end of the letter and complained to Chernomyrdin that "the conclusions of the Accounting Chamber are absolutely politicized." It was a conclusion that gibed nicely with a long passage at the outset of the letter, in which Vasiliyev himself defended the Fund on political grounds:

"The realization of a complex program for the defense of investor's rights, as well as the formation in April 1996 of the Federal Social-State Fund for the Defense of Investors' and Shareholders' rights, made possible the significant weakening of social-political tension in the population and the wrecking of the plans of the leftist opposition to use the issue of 'defrauded investors' for its own political ends."

Translation: It was okay that the Fund hadn't actually

compensated anybody, since its very creation had accomplished the sought political objective.

This was what "aid" was all about. It was never about accomplishing anything. The Fund for these defrauded investors had only been created as a political necessity. No one used it to compensate any victims, because that wasn't what it was for. What it was for was to help reelect Boris Yeltsin. And so long as it was there, it also served another purpose—to help a few government stooges and their girfriends make a little spare change. That was the level of moral commitment of these people.

Curiously, the Hay/Vasiliyev story was not the ultimate proof of the intellectual bankruptcy of "reform." For that, we had to wait for a higher authority to step in—the World Bank. For comment on the Hay/Pallada story, I'd called up Charles Blitzer, who for two years in the mid-1990s had been the Moscow chief of the World Bank. Blitzer was now working as a financial consultant in London and enjoyed a cozy patriarchal relationship with the Moscow press, forever lending his stodgy wisdom in the form of doctrinaire quotes presenting the World Bank/IMF viewpoint on virtually any issue connected with Russian development, whether it was relevant or not.

Most reporters loved him. So did we, but for different reasons. He gave our lives focus. Through his own self-promotional efforts, Blitzer had become more or less the official mouthpiece of the Western reform effort in Moscow. If the expatriate aid community in Moscow had the same sweatshirty, Nazi-oid feel of a major American State University, the vain and doddering Blitzer was its Dean Wormer—a near-perfect caricature of a bullying mediocrity religiously devoted to the cause of a narrow, careerist society with himself at the helm. With Blitzer around, we came into focus as the community's Delta House. By the time we were through with him, you could almost hear him shouting "I *hate* those guys!" all the way from London, as our own print version of the Deathmobile bombed its way through the reform parade.

Blitzer came to our attention when I called him for comment on the Investor Protection Fund story. We had a long interview that was remarkable for its poisonousness on both sides. I had been prepared to let him get away with just trotting out the World Bank party line and refusing any specific comment on the Fund story, but Blitzer shocked me when he not only defended the entire program right down to the ugliest details, but viciously berated me for even researching the story in the first place.

This is outrageous," he said. "You shouldn't publish that. It's extremely irresponsible."

"Why?" I asked.

"Because that would play right into the hands of oligarchs like Chernomyrdin and Berezovsky," he said. "All the people opposed to reform."

"What do you mean?" I said. "What about all of these investors that weren't compensated? That isn't shocking to you?"

"But look at your source," he growled. "The Accounting Chamber. A bunch of communists."

Blitzer's comment turned out to be the first of many times that serious advocates of reform would dismiss my reporting by calling either me or my sources communists. I found repeatedly that if you dug deeply enough into the abuses of reform, that if you had your facts straight enough to force an interview subject to confront apparent flaws in reform policy or implementation, the answer you inevitably got was just a bunch of name-calling.

The idea that the *eXile* might have been a vehicle for communist propaganda was ridiculous, of course. Ours was a publication so gross and outspoken and pornographic that it would not only not have been tolerated under communism, but would have earned imprisonment or death for anyone who tried to publish it. If Ames and I had been born in the 1930s as Russians, the NKVD would have worked us to death in coal pits in Vorkuta and used our bones to make veterinary soap rather than let us live ten minutes as free adults. Even under Brezhnev, we would have ended up in psych wards. We knew that.

Blitzer didn't care. As far as he was concerned, anyone who didn't support the World Bank was a communist. When I made it clear to him that I trusted my sources and was going to run the story, he tried to scare me with a different set of bogeymen, the oligarchs.

"You just can't do this," he said angrily. "It's not right. It plays right into the hands of people who don't want our kind of capitalism. You're helping create an oligarchy."

"But these people are allies of Chubais," I said. "And Chubais pretty much created the oligarchs, wouldn't you say? Certainly he's still a strong ally of Potanin."

"Well, yes," he snorted, "I admit that in the past year or so, Chubais has been working on behalf of Oneximbank about ninety percent of the time, and for reform only about ten percent of the time. All the same, you can't print this."

"Well, I'm going to, so if you'd like to comment on the

actual story, please say so. Otherwise, I'll just leave your point of view out of the piece."

"But you can't run this," he repeated.

"Of course I can," I said. "I can run anything I want to. It's my newspaper."

"I'm telling you, you can't run this!" he shouted. "Aren't you listening to me?"

The amazing thing about all of this wasn't the fact that Blitzer seemed genuinely to believe that there were laws prohibiting the publication of obnoxious news pieces, but that he couldn't even take the time out to say that it was too bad those defrauded investors hadn't gotten their money. The guy's mind was built on the binary system—reform in, reform out. A story implicating Jonathan Hay in wrongdoing was "reform out." It didn't compute, not even on a level of instinctual decency.

Blitzer couldn't even evince disgust on behalf of capitalism. When he insisted that aid programs were run efficiently because they were contracted out in competitive tenders, I reminded him quickly that the crux of the whole story was that Pallada had won its contract without a tender.

"Well," he said, "in some cases, contracts are distributed without a tender, depending on the size of the award."

In any case, we tried after that to keep an eye on Blitzer. Unlike many of the smooth-talking spokesmen for "reform," Blitzer had one obvious weakness which we knew might very easily be taken advantage of: his love, even greater probably than his love for money, of seeing his name quoted in newspapers.

A few months after we ran our first Hay/Pallada story, we spotted Blitzer's name quoted in a *Moscow Times* article about the Asian stock market crisis. This was just after the Asian markets first started to crash, and two days before Russia crashed. Russia was due for a crash, of course; it had been the world's best-performing market for almost two years, despite having one of the most atrociously performing economies in the industrial world. Worse still, a reputable British think tank called Control Risk had just rated it the most corrupt country in the entire world, ending a long Nigerian reign.

Nonetheless, the *Moscow Times* article trotted out the predictable line that the Asian business was a temporary correction, and that there was nothing to worry about. Blitzer was quoted as follows: "In the coming days the nervousness of the markets will begin to calm down."

In fact, in a single "coming day," the Russian market crashed twenty percent. Panic ensued, and the exchange closed for the first time in Russia's history. By the time we ran our next issue a week and a half later, the market was 40 percent lower than it had been when Blitzer pulled his spin-doctor act in the *Moscow Times*.

After the Russian crash, we decided to call Blitzer back and see if he'd changed his mind. Mark called and left a message on Blitzer's machine identifying himself as "Sam Weiss" of "*Moskovskaya Svoloch*," a financial newsletter.

Now, "*Moskovskaya Svoloch*" translates literally as "Moscow Bastard." This was a control question. We were pretty confident that Blitzer had never even bothered to learn the language of the country whose economy he had once more or less administered for years. If we were wrong, there was no way he'd call us back.

Blitzer called back straight away. "Is this *Moskovskaya Svoloch*?" he asked our Russian secretary. She was new but had been instructed that this kind of thing might happen from time to time. She answered in the affirmative and put him through to Mark.

Once he got Blitzer on the line, Mark adopted his usual cartoon-Brooklyn-Jewish Sam Weiss voice, and immediately threw Blitzer another curveball, asking him a slew of questions about the Mongolian stock market.

Mongolia had been the only country in the world to avoid the effects of the Asian crash; its market had risen 6 percent the same day Russia's fell by twenty. Blitzer's responses showed the former World Bank Moscow chief's financial acumen at its best: he couldn't even predict events that had *already happened.*

Blitzer: Hi, I'm calling for Sam Weiss. You left a message on my voice mail.

eXile: Yes that's right. I'm working on a piece about the market disturbances for a new financial newsletter, *Moskovskaya Svoloch*, and I was wondering—do you have some time to take a few questions?

Blitzer: No, I don't have much time, but go ahead. [Note: the interview lasted some ten minutes, all on Blitzer's bill.]

eXile: Okay, I'll try to be brief. What sort of lessons do you think we've learned from the market crash here in Russia?

Blitzer: Movements in equity markets are now linked globally.

eXile: Is that why other small markets in the region such as the Mongolian market also collapsed?

Blitzer: Of course, in small or illiquid markets like the Mongol market, the effects will be larger than in more liquid markets.

eXile: Do you think the Mongol market will bounce back?

e d i t o r i a l

The eXile applauds the recent announcement that the leadership of the Pallada mutual fund is negotiating the sale of a significant stake of the company to the giant Boston-based bank, State Street Global Advisor. Should the deal go through, it would be encouraging evidence that Americans have finally learned to hold their own in the rough-and-tumble world of Russian business.

It seems like only yesterday that the Pallada Fund was heading in a nosedive for the dustbin of history, hounded by sensationalist news exposes and forced by a stern and disapproving Duma committee to rebid for its lucrative contract to manage the assets of the state Investor Protection Fund. Once again, it seemed, Russia's xenophobic inferiority complex before the West would strike down an honest American effort to engage in meaningful trade.

Western business observers who followed Pallada's troubles reacted universally with shock and outrage. Particularly troubling was the fact that the Duma committee and the Russian press had even ignored Pallada's efforts to conform to local cultural norms by winning its contract not through fair competition, but through a direct award without a tender. American business was bending over backwards to do things the Russian way, and still being shut out. Was there any hope at all?

Well, it turns out that there was. What Pallada director Beth Hebert discovered, and what a host of other American firms in town have yet to learn, is that the real money to be made in Russia isn't even Russian. It's American. And all you have to do to get at that American money is set up shop here, then turn around and do business with American companies— who themselves are likely to be weighed down by old concepts like due diligence that will keep them earthbound in Moscow while you soar through negotiations to financial nirvana.

When Pallada was in trouble not long ago, stuck with lingering accusations of cashing in on the hardship of destitute and mostly elderly defrauded investors who for some mysterious reason had not received any of the compensation the government had promised them, Hebert did the smart thing. She took her company's main weakness—its American management and the nationalist loathing it aroused in Russians—and turned it to her advantage. If well-connected Americans on the ground in Moscow couldn't communicate successfully with the locals, she probably figured, a gang of stuffy M&A brokers perched in a cozy office next to the Boston Harbor Hotel, just over the outdoor harbor seal tank at the Aquarium...well, they'd do still worse. And she picked up the phone.

That's good business. That's horse sense. That's an example of a company taking the best from both cultures and just running with the ball. That's what America is all about. 3rd and 26 on your own 8 yard line? Take a deep drop. Go for the end zone. There are fans on that side of the stadium, too. And they're not booing.

As any good NFL football coach knows, you might as well hold the defensive tackles on the line when you go for a long bomb from deep in your own end. If you get caught holding on a 3rd and 8 on your own 8, you end up punting from your own 4. No big deal. It's worth the extra second or two of protection for your QB and his million-dollar arm. You've got nothing to lose— and seven points to gain.

Holding off the DTs at the line is an even better idea if the referees are all blind and stumbling along the field with canes. That kind of refereeing is a little bit what doing due diligence in Russia is like for Bostonians whose usual daily routine involves looking out their office windows at the Aquarium's outdoor harbor seal tank below. If you can't see the game, you might as well stick your hands out and search out the penalty by touch—or make a phone call to check a few references across town at Harvard, as the case may be.

Pallada's road to salvation was paved with a few obstacles, of course. Due to the miracle of fiberoptic technology, virtually anyone these days can call directory assistance and learn the telephone number of State Street Bank, meaning that any party so inclined could still revive the troublesome due diligence process. But that state of affairs would only present a problem for a company operating in a city that's also home to a meddlesome English-language nightlife weekly staffed by mindlessly vengeful people with absolutely nothing better to do than send fax after fax after fax all night long to strangers overseas.

Fortunately for Pallada, there is no such publication in Moscow. Its secrets will never escape the Russian capital. Particularly not the part about it possibly losing most of its assets under management in an upcoming rebid. We at the eXile are glad that's so. As it stands, Pallada's brilliant maneuver will, once it comes to a successful conclusion, usher in a new era in Russian-American commerce. After all these years, we won't be at a disadvantage anymore.

Pallada Deal is Well-Timed

One of the chief beneficiaries of the so-called Investor Protection Scandal was the Pallada mutual fund, which was headed by Beth Hebert, the live-in girlfriend of major American aid figure Jonathan Hay. Hebert and Pallada won a contract to manage the money of the State "Investor Protection" fund—a Hay-run project ostensibly designed to compensate Russians defrauded in phony investment schemes—without a tender. When word leaked out that Hebert was trying to sell her company to State Street Bank in Boston, we felt a responsibility to try to wreck the deal. In the meantime, we used the *eXile* to try to make Moscow resident Hebert as nervous as possible during sale negotations.

Blitzer: Typically, after a slump, there's a rush to get out. In Mongolia, foreign investors did everything to pull out when the market fell, because of the . . . illiquidity. But it's all a correction, and these markets will bounce back.

Here Mark threw Blitzer yet another curve. This one was in the dirt, but Blitzer swung anyway:

eXile: Some people are saying that the movement in the Russian market is linked to the weather. Last winter was warm, and the market rose. This winter it's supposed to be a lot cooler, and the market's falling. Is there any connection?

Blitzer: Well, I won't get into hypothesizing about that. Uh, the market is illiquid, the volume's low . . . but I don't know how the market links to the weather.

eXile: Do you think it's going to be a cold winter here in Russia? President Yeltsin does.

Blitzer: I have no idea what kind of winter Russia will experience. I do know that with the return of El Niño, the weather patterns are changing around the world. The weather is getting warmer, the ocean—it's warmer in the Pacific region, and this is having have some impact on Russian weather.

El Niño? What the fuck was Blitzer talking about? We called Timur Ivanidze at

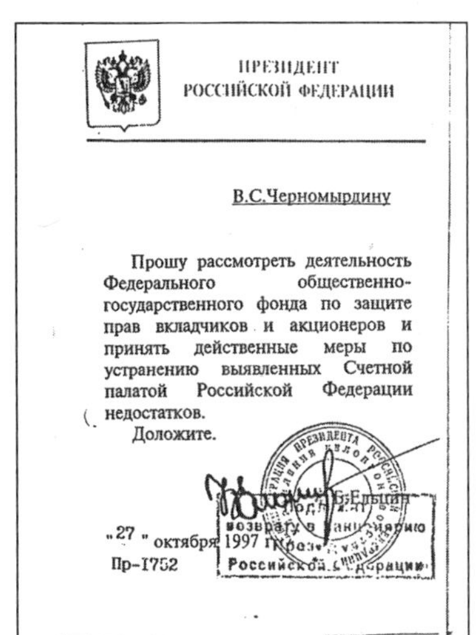

ПРЕЗИДЕНТ
РОССИЙСКОЙ ФЕДЕРАЦИИ

В.С.Черномырдину

Прошу рассмотреть деятельность Федерального общественно-государственного фонда по защите прав вкладчиков и акционеров и принять действенные меры по устранению выявленных Счетной палатой Российской Федерации недостатков.

Доложите.

Б.Ельцин

„27" октября 1997 г.
Пр-1752

the *Gidrometsentr*, Russia's state meteorological center, to set the record straight:

eXile: Does the El Niño phenomenon have any effect on Moscow?

Ivanidze: No, not at all. It only affects tropical areas of the Pacific Ocean, specifically the Western Pacific.

eXile: Because the former head of the World Bank in Moscow says El Niño has an effect on worldwide weather patterns, including Russia. His name is Charles Blitzer. Maybe you've heard of him?

Ivanidze: No.

eXile: He's sort of an all-around expert.

Ivanidze: I can only tell you that there is no worldwide effect from El Nino, only in the tropical regions of the Pacific. Russia is not affected by it.

eXile: There's a theory going around that the Russian stock market is linked to the weather. When it's warm in the winter, the market rises, and when it's cold, the market falls. Is there any truth to that?

Ivanidze: (laughs) I can't comment on that. I don't play the market.

eXile: Well, do you think that one can even make predictions about the stock market?

Ivanidze: I think it's all speculation.

After we published the transcripts of these calls, we got a letter from an EBRD executive in London, asking for a copy. We figured it was an interorganizational rivalry at work—Blitzer must have had some enemies back in England, who probably faxed the thing all over the place. For all we know, the piece is now taped over every World Bank copy machine in the world.

The joke certainly got around in Moscow. A few months later, we called the Legal Attaché office at the U.S. embassy as part of our "Vox Populi" man-on-the-street feature, in which we asked really dumb questions of really smart people. We got FBI agent Gary Dickson on the phone and laid the question of the week on him: "Are there other life forms in space, and if so, will the Asian Stock Market Crisis affect their economies?"

"No," Dickson quipped, "but El Niño might."

Stunts like the Blitzer call and the Burson-Marsteller prank put the community on guard. By late spring, Mark and I were both hearing pretty regularly, from friends and non-friends alike, that people they knew were openly expressing a desire to stay off our bad side. Whether or not the pranks we pulled actually met with anyone's approval, there was increasingly an awareness around town that any time the phone rang, it might be us calling—no matter who it sounded like on the other end of the line.

Obviously, we liked to hear this. It was the first hint we had that the paper might be able to find a way to survive. In the beginning, before we started to make money and before our investigative pieces started to be taken seriously, the ability to make people nervous was the only leverage we had in the community. Taped phone calls and copies of letters in which well-known people in town made fools of themselves were the only proof we could offer to people that we existed anywhere except in our own heads.

Awareness of that fact put us constantly on the lookout for ways to demonstrate our capacity for high-tech nastiness. In our desperation to stay alive, we sometimes picked people to make examples of who didn't even deserve it. They were just there—old decommissioned ammo dumps, just waiting to be exploded by controversial new test weaponry.

That was how the Gorbachev thing happened.

One night during the summer I woke up in a cold sweat. I'd had a terrible dream and for a moment had no idea where I was or what day it was. I had a cup of tea, went back to sleep, then woke up again an hour later with an idea. Why not try to hire Mikhail Gorbachev to be an assistant coach for the New York Jets?

On the surface, the idea made no sense. Mikhail Gorbachev hadn't done anything to anyone lately. He was an addled old man whom nobody took seriously. In fact, in a weird way, I liked him, particularly since I'd had to cover his presidential campaign the year before, when he had more or less gone publicly insane on several occasions. He was like a Soviet version of Don Quixote—potbellied and completely devoid of personal warmth, lacking the charm to attract even a Sancho Panza.

During that campaign, when an illiterate drunk in the Siberian city of Omsk rushed him in a crowd and punched him in the neck, Gorby-Quixote quickly made him into a windmill of state conspiracy, claiming that the drunk was actually a crack paratrooper who was trying to kill him with his open hand. I was at the press conference when he laid that theory on the Russian press and had watched in awe as he was nearly laughed out of the building—possibly a first for a Nobel Peace Prize laureate.

Since then I'd had an odd kind of sympathy for him. I was even proud that we shared the same birthday, March 2.

Business is business, however, and when I woke up that summer night I knew immediately that the joke was doable, that it was possible to hire Mikhail Gorbachev to be an assistant to Bill Parcells, and right away that eliminated any moral qualms I might have had about going through with it. In a way, it was out of my hands. We *had* to do it. It was like the atomic bomb: you couldn't uninvent it.

When appraised of the idea, Mark and the rest of the *eXile* were grave and skeptical, but cooperative. Without much in the way of conversation, our designers set to work making phony New York Jets business cards, while Tanya contacted the Gorbachev Fund (the General Secretary's think tank) and made an appointment with a Gorbachev aide to discuss the idea. Meanwhile Kara sat down with me and made up Jets stationery, upon which I wrote a letter to Gorbachev's office from "Samuil Belov," a Jets talent scout.

"Samuil Belov" was a Russified version of Sam Weiss, who had performed so well for us in the *Tribune*/Blitzer business. The mechanism I'd worked out centered around Belov, the American son of Russian and Italian immigrant parents, who had recently retired from pro football due to injury ("my ACL") and had gone to work as an assistant coach to Bill Parcells. Belov's unusual biography was necessary for the purposes of explaining his fluency in Russian, in which he would negotiate with the Gorbachev people.

In Belov's original letter to Gorbachev aide Vladimir Polyakov, he explained that the Jets, which in 1996–97 had been the NFL's worst team, were going through a period of "restructuring," which in Russian is *perestroika*. The team, Belov explained, needed an expert in the reform of "stagnant institutions." For this reason, they'd turned to Gorbachev in the hopes that he would consent to give some inspirational talks to the team.

A good practical joke should always contain a slight element of total absurdity, so that the victim has no excuse for not knowing better when he is finally exposed. Of course, the very idea of a former Slav emperor collecting a fee to give pep talks to a crowd of mostly black football players was ridiculous enough, but we added another detail for emphasis. Belov went on to propose that, for an additional fee, Gorbachev consent to allow the Jets to name him as an honorary member of the coaching staff—the "*perestroika* coordinator."

Having sent this letter, Tanya then scheduled an appointment for "Belov" to meet with Polyakov personally. But then, as always happens in large projects, we hit a hitch. The business cards were held up at the print shop due to a computer error. No one discusses six-figure deals without a business card. So we had to stall.

In the end, the hitch actually helped. We had Tanya call Polyakov back and explain that the world-traveling Belov had been recalled on urgent business first to Egypt (to recruit a Nile Valley nose tackle), then to Prague, and finally to Kuala Lumpur. With each phone call, Polyakov grew more impatient, but he seemed more and more to buy into the idea that Belov actually existed and meant business.

Finally, when the business cards were ready, we scheduled the meeting. I put on what at the time was my only blazer and tie and headed off to the Gorbachev Fund, hoping that no one would recognize me—I'd been there on several occasions as a reporter. But then, when I got to the door, catastrophe struck. You couldn't get into the building without a passport. I had mine, but didn't, for obvious reasons, want to use it . . . so after five minutes of frenzied haggling with the guard, I skulked away in defeat.

Back in the office, I quickly called Polyakov to apologize for missing the meeting, explaining that my flight had been delayed. The conversation with Polyakov was extraordinary:

eXile: So I understand that Maria explained to you on the phone something about what we had in mind.

Polyakov: Something, yes.

eXile: Please let me explain a little bit first about who I am. I'm an American of Russian heritage and a former football player. I played on defense for the Jets for years, but then I injured my knee—an injury called the "ACL." It still hurts.

Polyakov: Uh-huh.

eXile: In any case, I work now in the team administration. And here's the story. The Jets, you understand, are one of the unluckiest teams in the country. They haven't won anything in more than twenty years. This year, the team decided to take extraordinary measures to turn things around. We hired a guy named Bill Parcells, a very famous coach. He's sort of like an American Tikhonov, you know?

Polyakov: Okay.

eXile: Anyway, a few weeks back, I was talking to Bill, and he was saying to me that he wished he could communicate to the fans how long it takes to rebuild a business like ours, how drawn out the restructuring process is.

Here, with that "restructuring process" bit, I'd dropped the magic word—*perestroika.*

Polyakov: All right.

eXile: So I said to Bill, as a joke at first, that maybe we should hire Gorbachev—there's no better expert at restructuring!

Polyakov: (sternly) I see.

eXile: Anyway, we thought we could invite Mikhail Sergeyevich to give a series of speeches, and maybe perform some other nominal services for us. We think he could really help our defense. Obviously, this would have a demonstrable public relations benefit, and . . .

Polyakov: When would this be?

eXile: Well, the season starts this fall, so we're looking at mid- to late fall. I understand Mikhail Sergeyevich was once connected in some way to Columbia University, and I thought if he were in New York anyway, it would be an easy way for him to pick up a few extra dollars, and it would be interesting for him.

Polyakov: He's not only going to be in New York. He's got a big trip planned all over the States this fall.

eXile: I see. So you think it would be possible to arrange this?

Polyakov: I think we'd need to discuss it. But he is planning an American trip, anyway.

eXile: Does he know anything about football?

Polyakov: I'd have to ask him.

Polyakov seemed onboard with the idea, but we needed something on paper. So a few days later I had Tanya call him and ask for a fax of his fee expectations. He hesitated, and after a week or so of not hearing from him (despite repeated phone calls), we were about to give up. But then one afternoon, while Mark and I were engaged in the usual office business of sexual harassment and Nerf basketball, the phone on the fax machine rang.

Because radio silence was still in effect—while we waited for practical jokes to play out, we never identified ourselves when we answered the phone—our secretary Yulia let it ring. Autoreply kicked in and before we knew it a message was spitting out of the machine. Tanya saw the letterhead pop out first and called out to us, and quickly we all crowded around and watched the following letter roll out:

Dear Mr. Belov,

Thank you for your letter dated June 26, in which you made a series of proposals with regard to the president of the Fund. It presents a certain interest and should be discussed with yourself and with the administration of the team in the next few days. The reason for this is that we are currently finishing our preparations for the president's upcoming trip to the United States, a trip that is going to be extremely busy and demanding. The schedule for this trip must be completed and confirmed by the president. In the event that you and the team administration are prepared to meet with a representative of the Fund, he would be prepared to fly out on the authority of the president in the next few days.

With Respect,
Vladimir Polyakov

After we published a long and detailed account of this joke, even plugging it on the cover under the headline "Mikhail Gorbachev Goes Deep for the *eXile*," we spent a nervous week or two waiting for the worst. This sinking feeling of impending catastrophe was something we'd had to get used to. The fact was, we were risking very serious trouble with stunts like the Gorbachev–Jets thing. Russia wasn't, and isn't, like America, where trouble comes in the mail, in the form of a letter from a lawyer. This is a country where there are thousands of people walking around you every day who'd be willing to break your legs for a hundred bucks and kill you for five.

You can ignore people in America when they threaten to do things like break your legs, but we couldn't ignore them in Moscow, not with so many people, even Westerners, getting leaned on and threatened as a matter of business routine. In the absence of a functioning civil court system, the only question that mattered in business disputes was which side had the more powerful *krysha,* or roof—meaning the person providing paid protection, usually either a criminal gang or its close relative, a police precinct or government office.

We didn't know anything about our publisher's *krysha,*

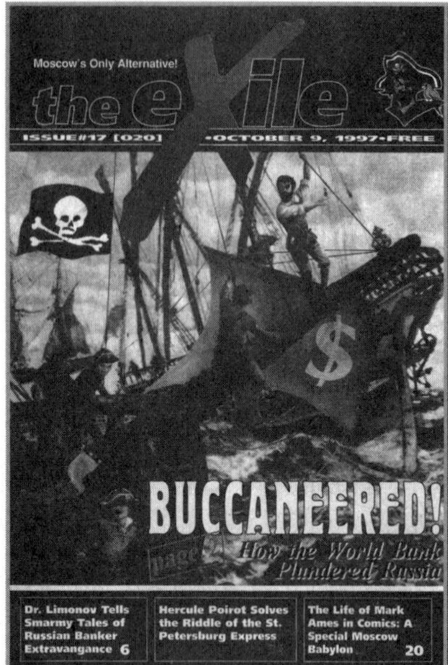

Our fall 1997 cover story on the World Bank prompted a flood of letters and firmly established our reputation as wrong-thinking, anti-market naysayers who had the gall to favor protectionism in Russia. A year later, when Russia's economy collapsed, commentators suddenly started to suggest, timidly, that perhaps the World Bank and USAID had been wrong in insisting that Russian industry be immediately ex-posed to Western competition.

and had to assume we would come out in the losing end of any dispute that reached that level. For this reason—and particularly after I had a real scare following the publication of a semislanderous article earlier that spring (see chapter 4)—Mark and I by midsummer were figuring the possibility of death or dismemberment into the equation every time we we decided whether or not to run a potentially troublesome story.

There were certain Pandora's boxes neither of us would ever dare open in print. There was the one containing the name of the person everyone in town knew had killed American hotelier Paul Tatum, or one containing a too-explicit connection between sinister banker Boris Berezovsky and certain no-longer-alive television personalities. At times, we didn't even know how much danger we were in. In September, Mark ran into a richly dressed girl at an expat party who turned out to the daughter of a very powerful and scary (read: we are still afraid to mention his name even here, years later) member of the Russian government. She had read our paper. "I know how you write," she said to Mark. "If you write about me, I'll have you killed. And I can do that, you know," she said seriously.

That incident came after I'd already written a long burlesque piece in which I'd identified myself as another scary government honcho, Anatoly Chubais, contributing a special guest practical joke to the *eXile*. The piece lampooned Chubais's successes in schmoozing funds from USAID, and hinted that he'd arranged the entire HIID scandal as a means of embarrassing and subduing Securities chief Vasiliyev, who'd come out in opposition of Chubais's vision of a securities market. A week after it came out, I ran into Kristen Staples, a Burson-Marsteller employee who worked for Dmitri Vasiliyev and conferred frequently with Chubais. She told me she'd shown the Vice-Premier the piece, and said he'd read it silently, then burst out laughing. "He said he'd never read anything so funny," she said.

I was raving drunk at the time (we'd run into each other in a pretentious nightclub called Four Rooms late on a Saturday night), and when she told me this story I at first very obnoxiously couldn't contain my excitement. Coming from a criminal genius like Chubais, that reaction was a great compliment, one I could always be proud of—like getting a laugh out of Louis Farrakhan by calling him a nigger.

But in retrospect, I might have been in serious trouble if he'd been in a different mood when he read it. All a guy like Chubais had to do was make one phone call and the newspaper would have vanished from the planet instantly. There were any number of ways he could have done it, but the one that came to mind first was a sudden production-night raid on our offices by a gang of masked tax police. I'd seen it often enough on television: they'd have sent the rottweilers in first, then marched in in their camous and dragged out the bodies. Even if he didn't have a legal reason to do so, we'd have been dead. We had no *krysha*, which meant we were automatically wrong ahead of time in the eyes of the law. In fact, any enemy who wanted to pay off the appropriate office could have shut us down overnight, for a fee.

As goofy and obviously deranged as Mikhail Gorbachev was, there was no doubt that he headed a *krysha* with instant death capability. After all, the guy had once commanded the world's largest and most deadly secret police force. He'd certainly sentenced better people than us to lengthy and exotic basement tortures. So we waited for the worst. Poor innocent Tanya suffered the most. She was worried for weeks that she would be arrested or disappeared.

But in the end we never heard a thing from Polyakov again, and moved on to other things. A few months later, Gorbachev announced that he'd done a television commercial for Pizza Hut.

As hard as we worked to be an antagonist to the expatriate community, the *eXile* wasn't exactly a pro-Russian paper. Our coverage generally sympathized with the ordinary salary-collecting Russian who'd been screwed over by people like Hay and Blitzer and Chubais—the scientist who'd been privatized into a career as a cab driver—but in nine out of ten cases,

Our July 1997 cover story described how the World Bank lent money to Russia so that it might hire high-priced Western consultants, while at the same time insisting, as conditions of these loans, that "excess" staff of state enterprises (i. e., farms, hospitals, elementary schools) be fired *en masse* in order to keep budget expenditures low. In other words, Russia fired its own workers in order to borrow money to pay Western consultants exorbitant salaries.

that same person probably would have been horrified by our depiction of his country. Between the "Death Porn" section and our pornographic club guide, the *eXile* reader came away with a vision of Russia as a sort of Rwanda with a high cover charge.

Which it was, of course. What we wrote was hyperbolic, but true. Reading about Russia in the *eXile* was like wearing pink sunglasses in a pink room. We were doing our readers a legitimate public service by informing them in our capsule review of the menacing whore-gangster hangout "Marika" that "if you ask someone to dance, you will die." We had an illustrated scoring system for clubs and bars which rated, on a scale of one to three stars, your chances of getting laid and of walking out alive. If a place had two or three stars in the latter "flathead factor," it generally meant that we knew someone who'd had a gun pulled on him (the club Paris Life) or who had been beaten up in the bathroom (myself, in the Hungry Duck). Of course, as the party/alternative paper, it was in our interests to make the scene seem as a wild as possible, but our vision of "wild" wasn't exactly flattering to your average Ivan—even though it was true.

Another problem was our practical jokes. Russians have great senses of humor, but the kinds of jokes we were pulling were a new phenomenon in the Russian press. Krutakov's prank in *Izvestia* was about the only other instance of a really vicious practical joke, one intended to embarrass someone, making it into print in Moscow. For obvious reasons, that tradition simply didn't exist in Russia. Although, contrary to popular belief, Soviet Russia even in the darkest times had been home to all kinds of unruly, pseudo-criminal behavior and naked adolescent disobedience—our own Edward Limonov wrote about that best in *Podrostok Savenko*—doing this kind of thing for publication had always been totally out of the question.

If a reporter in Soviet times had even jokingly suggested forging the stationery of the St. Petersburg mayor's office for a gag and admitting it in print, his editors might have shot him for their own protection. Things had changed since then. Still, not that much time had passed—and there was still no one out there in a position of editorial responsibility quite ready yet to be as stupid as we'd been all our lives.

We were on virgin territory. Jokes that wouldn't have had a chance of getting off the ground in the States were here mowing over Russians like Nazis in June. When we decided to call around town to arrange a fact-finding tour for deceased president Richard Nixon, not one person called our bluff. Most were having a hard enough time getting used to the new language of the free market without having to worry about crap like this.

"Well, what exactly does Mr. Nixon want to do?" snapped the gruff Sovietish p.r. director at the Moscow Meat Factory, momentarily forgetting her customer service skills. You could almost see her through the phone, sneering, hugely overweight, surrounded by accounting papers and an abacus.

"You know," we said. "Just walk around, see things, talk to the people."

"Absolutely not," she said. "We can't arrange for someone to just 'walk' through our factory. Our security certainly will not let him through. If there's some kind of specific offer that he has, for example to deliver our meats, then of course he can come."

We were hassling everybody. When dictator Mobutu Sese Seko finally got tossed out of Zaire, we called up practically every hotel in Moscow, in the guise of Mobutu aides, in order to see how many would be willing to take the butcher of Kinshasa as a guest in exile. Not suprisingly, all the obsequious wannabe "Westernized" Russians in the swanky new business hotels jumped at the business ("We have for him nice suite," the clerk at the Radisson said in broken English, "and our hotel is very nice—five stars!"), while only the old-fashioned Soviet-style "House of Fishing and Hunting" told us that they had no room.

In another case, we convinced the administration at the old communist organ *Pravda* that they had been bought out by a blind, Jewish dwarf from Florida named Barry Apfelbaum, who planned on using the paper to promote a chain of Sears and Roebuck stores in Moscow. The paper had already been bought as a curio by a pair of rich Greeks, and its staff was willing to believe anything. Representing myself as a *New York Times* reporter calling for comment, I laid the bad news on them.

"He plans on renaming the paper the 'Sears and Roebuck *Pravda*,' " I said.

"What's 'Sears and Roebuck?' " the *Pravda* woman asked.

"A big store that sells playground equipment and blue jeans," I said.

"Oh, God," she said.

As proof of the story, I sent her phony copies of Florida news articles containing Apfelbaum's biography.

"Apfelbaum, who is congenitally blind and a dwarf," read a "*St. Petersburg Times*" piece we'd made up, "made his name as a fiery courtroom orator who won large settlements for victims of accidents on Disneyland rides. He was later hired by Disney to defend against similar suits."

"American, Greek, it doesn't make a difference," the woman at *Pravda* snapped, when I called her back. "They're all the same."

The interacting we were doing with the domestic population wasn't exactly constructive. While other Western reporters were writing glowing portraits of new Deputy Prime Minister Boris Nemtsov and helping him attract foreign investment, the *eXile* was calling up Nemtsov's press service in the guise of a Japanese businessman named Hashimoto Godzilla and annoyingly demanding tee times and a recommendation for a good sushi restaurant in Moscow. It didn't matter that Nemtsov was a fraud who deserved to be exposed (our cover in that issue showed Nemtsov's face over the headline, "Reformer My Ass!"), or that Nemtsov, in a comical Soviet-style gesture, had actually given out his cellphone number in Tokyo and told Japanese businessmen to call if they needed help with anything. The point was, times were tough, and the last thing pretty much any Russian needed was to be mooned in print by a couple of suburban American yo-yos with too much time on their hands.

The only people we connected with were the ones who didn't understand the paper. Late in the summer, we ran an editorial entitled "Africa: At a Crossroads, Facing Tough Choices." It was a piece we had been proud of because it had elevated us to new levels of frivolity. Among other things, it expressed our support for the fact that Africa is completely surrounded by water, and in a part about war-torn African nations, asserted that "certainly a strong international presence would give these nations a strong international presence."

A few days after that ran, I got a call from Kester Klomegah, a Ghanian with whom I had worked at the *Moscow Times*. Kester was a gentle, subdued guy and we'd always gotten along very well, even cowriting a few pieces about African issues together. Still, I didn't know him very well, mainly because I was never sure exactly what he was talking about, since he spoke in a strange whisper in both English and Russian. I knew he rented a room from an elderly Russian woman somewhere and had been studying toward some kind of degree for about seven years. But I didn't know much else. And when he called, I didn't know what to think.

We scheduled a meeting. Two days later, he showed up at my office with an African friend, a DJ at a Portuguese radio station. Like most of the Africans who lived in Moscow, Kester's usual costume included a shabby, yellowing, artificial fabric button-down shirt, ill-fitting slacks (frequently of Arab make), and, most characteristically, a subdued, unobtrusive posture.

Most Russians, when they visit the United States for the first time, inevitably make a frightened comment about how big black people are in America. The ones they're used to—mostly all students on public-exchange programs, like Kester—are almost all ill-nourished, poorly dressed, and so accustomed to constant denigration (it's not uncommon for a Russian to call an African a monkey to his face) that, out of habit, they become bent and mute. Russia is a bad place to be black. And it's a terrible place to be black and poor, as most of Moscow's Africans are.

Kester and his friend sat down and folded their hands on a desk.

"It's about your editorial," Kester said.

Fuck!

"Oh, that," I said, through clenched teeth. "Listen, I'm sorry. It was just a joke, you know, a spoof . . . "

"No, no, I wanted to thank you," he said. "What you wrote really does make sense."

"It does?" I said.

"Yes," he said, scratching his beard. "Because you see, Africa really *is* at a crossroads, facing tough, tough choices . . . "

Kester and his pal weren't the only ones who had trouble understanding the paper. Actually, no one in the expat community could figure the paper out, not even the minority that was inclined to like it. There was a core readership out there, mostly young people and student/lefty types, who were clearly looking to us to be the Righteous New Voice whose views they could support. These people agreed with our politics and cheered our early attacks against Burson-Marsteller, Hay, Blitzer, and other henchmen of The Man, and in our early stages, you could almost hear them hoping that we'd assume the mantle of a responsible "alternative" paper, a sort of edgy *Village Voice* with red ink instead of blue.

But there was a psychotic, highly personal side to the paper that these people soon realized weren't just growing pains. Mark and I seemed to be right on all the issues, but . . . we weren't exactly normal people, either.

DEATH PORN LEGEND

low-yield murder	cries for help ignored
"skull-brain trauma"	"investigation continuing"
podyezd	carved up like a Turkey
really stupid criminal	killing "connected with professional activities of victim"
cannibalism	riddled with bullets
children	old people
Russian Sports Connection	murder-suicide

There was the Death Porn section, for example. The *eXile*'s version of a crime diary, the Death Porn section took Russia's most gruesome rapes and killings and used them as fodder for a sort of campy print variety show, complete with a laugh track—Ted Bundy narrated by Rich Little. There was no shortage of material, of course. Russia was a yellow journalist's dream. Not only did it have one of the highest crime rates in the world, it was simply overrun with Dostoyevskian lunatics who were constantly outdoing one another in their efforts to be more disgusting, more bloodthirsty, and more disturbingly, ingeniously evil. Jeffrey Dahmer in Russia would have made the news, but on any given day, he'd have to share the page with about three other serial killers and a couple of *Chainsaw Massacre*–style sadistic provincial gangs.

In the spring of 1996, I'd interviewed Alexander Bukhanovsky, the criminal psychiatrist whom many Americans know from the HBO movie *Citizen X*, about the Russian serial murderer Andrei Chikatilo. Bukhanovsky was the country's leading expert on sex crime, and after a sinister lunch of vodka and home movies—tapes of murders that Bukhanovsky's patients had filmed—he let me in on a secret. "In Russia, at any given time, there are one hundred serial killers operating," he said. "And those are only the series that are conspiciously series. I'm not talking about people who have killed twice, three times. We've got *tons* of those."

Russia was a massive industrialized country that had suffered an absolute economic and ideological collapse. Outside of Moscow, there were hundreds, maybe thousands, of communities that no longer had industry, government, or law. There were just masses of people hustling change here and there and waiting it out in grim concrete housing projects. Nothing to live for. Nothing to do. In these circumstances, people went crazy. They were killing and raping and eating one another at an alarming rate. It was mayhem. Absolute nihilism. This was the "state of nature"—maybe even the first signs of the end of civilization.

Whatever the right way was to approach covering that subject, most people felt pretty sure it wasn't "Death Porn." Readers turning to that page were generally met with a very gratuitously disgusting photo of a mangled corpse, underneath which there was usually a nutty game-show-host caption, i.e., "Hey, pal, can you lend me a hand? And a leg? And a head?" Each Death Porn story came affixed with little cartoon pictures, which told you what kind of story elements to expect in the tale you were reading: a Far Side-ean screaming old woman to indicate "Cries For Help Ignored," a piece of Swiss cheese to indicate "Riddled With Bullets," a turkey for "Carved Up Like a Turkey." Worse still, the stories were narrated with an unabashed voyeuristic glee that even the most progressive of our readers couldn't endorse publicly. Whoever was writing this stuff clearly got off on what he was doing. It was creepy, and didn't at all gibe with the do-gooder tone of our political coverage.

I was the Death Pornographer. Although most people blamed Mark for the paper's excesses, the truth was that the sicker parts of the *eXile* were a joint effort. The paper was really a two-front operation. On the one hand, it entered the public debate on its terms, sourcing stories,

CHAPTER THREE

following basic journalism rules, genuinely trying to persuade. On the other hand, the paper was uncomfortably personal, conspicuously written for the most part by two specific people who self-aggrandizingly made themselves characters in the text. There was a lot of stuff in the paper, stuff like Death Porn, that was clearly in there because the editors got a kick out of it, and not because it had any audience appeal or was attractive to advertisers. Worse, as time went on, readers realized that the things the editors got a kick out of were usually very morbid and disgusting.

Mark and I wanted to make a publication that people like ourselves would enjoy reading. Which meant, in essence, a paper for paranoid depressives with very twisted enthusiasms. Since we weren't likely to get rich with it, satisfaction from the product itself was the only return we expected to get out of the *eXile*.

A lot of the things the *eXile* published looked like mental malfunctions; they had the same strangely ordered and yet somehow embarassingly inappropriate quality of dreams. There was a Bugs Bunny comics version of the crucifixion, an ode to the late Mexican poet Octavio Paz featuring an overtly racist full-page portrait of Speedy Gonzalez, candid and cheerful discussions of rape and drug abuse in our contributor columns, and viciously threatening and usually totally uncalled-for responses to letters to the editor, so extreme that we were likely to tell an admiring writer from suburban California that we were going to hunt him down and fuck his kids, be they male or female, it didn't matter.

Once in the spring of 1997, for instance, Mark and were I lounging around in the office when we suddenly started discussing, as a kind of amusing intellectual exercise, potential suicide plans. Not actual kill-yourself suicide, but suicide articles—ways to horrify our readers so totally that we'd put ourselves out of business overnight.

The idea we eventually came up with was a cover with a giant close-up of a puzzled black face, accompanied by a banner headline: "NIGGERS: Where Did They Come From? And What Are They Doing Here?"

Well, *that'd do it,* we thought.

Out of consideration for the black community and for everyone else we knew would be permanently turned off by it, we sat on that joke for a full year. But finally, in the spring of 1998, we gave in and ran it—although not on our

NEW YORK JETS

Владимиру Анатольевичу Полякову
Фонд Горбачева
Ленинградский проспект 49

Уважаемый г–н Поляков,

Благодарю Вас за то, что Вы уделили время нашему вчерашнему разговору. Еще раз прошу прощения за опоздание на нашу запланированную встречу. В следующий раз я обязательно организую свое прибытие в Москву на день раньше.

Как мы уже обсудили в нашем телефонном разговоре, наше предложение Михаилу Сергеевичу достаточно просто. Наша команда переживает реорганизационный период, и на всех нас, а в особенности нашего тренера, оказано большое давление с тем, чтобы все изменения произошли как можно скорее. Одна из особенностей пребывания в Нью–Йорке – гораздо более нетерпеливое отношение общественности к достижению успеха, чем в других городах. По этой причине, тренер Парселлз решил, что было бы полезным использовать часть нашего обширного бюджета на консультантов и специалистов по связям с общественностью, которые помогли бы сгладить это общественное нетерпение во время реконструкционного периода.

Как я уже сообщил Вам вчера, идея предложить Михаилу Сергеевичу выступить с обращением к команде изначально была легкомысленно предложена мной, но тренер Парселлз, который в течение долгого времени восхищался бывшим Генеральным Секретарем, воспринял ее достаточно серьезно. Он верит, что ряд речей Михаила Сергеевича оказали бы огромное влияние на улучшение морального состояния как наших игроков, так и сотрудников нашей администрации, в особенности тренерский состав защиты. Более того, как специалист в реформации застойных структур, Михаил Сергеевич смог бы подать команде глубокое ее понимание.

Связь с Михаилом Горбачевым, конечно, принесет безусловную пользу для общественных связей Нью Йорк Джетс. Естественно, мы, хотели бы компенсировать г–ну Горбачеву все дополнительные услуги.

Мне сообщили, что я в праве распоряжаться бюджетом в размере $150 000, выделенным на приглашение г–на Горбачева выступить перед командой. Я предвижу 2 выхода (примерно по одному часу каждый) перед командой в течение этого осеннего сезона, мы могли бы организовать их согласно расписанию г–на Горбачева. Команда заплатит за каждое выступление по
$50 000. Я предполагаю дополнительную оплату за услуги г–на Горбачева по общественным связям, в особенности за предоставление нам привилегии назвать его почетным членом администрации команды, возможно в качестве «Реорганизационного координатора», в размере дополнительных $50000. Никаких дополнительных услуг под этой должностью не подразумевается.

Я надеюсь, что Михаилу Сергеевичу будет приятно предстать перед одними из его самых горячих поклонников. Бил Парселлз, владелец Джетс Леон Хесс и остальные члены команды видят в г–не Горбачеве одного из самых выдающихся людей этого века. Как Американец русского происхождения я относился к генеральному секретарю с глубочайшим уважением с те пор, как он открыл мне двери для более частого посещения моих родственников в Москве. Его появление перед командой – для нас большая честь.

Я запланировал вернуться в Москву в этом августе, возможно, мы могли бы тогда обсудить все более подробно. До этого времени, вы могли бы связаться со мной по моему телефону в Нью–Йорке (как указано на моей бизнес–карточке), но т.к. я буду в Европе в течение еще 2–3х недель, Вы могли бы связаться со мной по телефону в Москве (я веду еще одно дело здесь и работаю с секретарем, которая принимает звонки и держит со мной постоянную связь), если у Вас возникнут какие–либо вопросы. Телефон: 252–5628

По вопросу распределения бюджета было бы полезно узнать, что для Михаила Сергеевича является обычной оплатой гонорара за выступление, и имеет ли смысл наше предложение. Я был бы Вам ужасно благодарен, если бы Вы могли послать мне короткое письмо или факс (номер моего московского факса – 252–5054) относительно этих вопросов примерно в течение недели.

Еще раз благодарю Вас за уделенное время, и я надеюсь, что в следующий раз нам удастся встретиться лично. До этого времени остаюсь

Искренне Ваш,

S. Belo

Самуил Белов
Ассистент персонала
Нью Йорк Джетс

"Samuil Belov's" letter from the New York Jets to Vladimir Polyakov of the Gorbachev foundation.

NEW YORK JETS

SAMUIL BELOV

Special Assistant
Personnel Department

435 W 43RD ST
NEW YORK, NY 10019

Tel.: (212) 695 4454

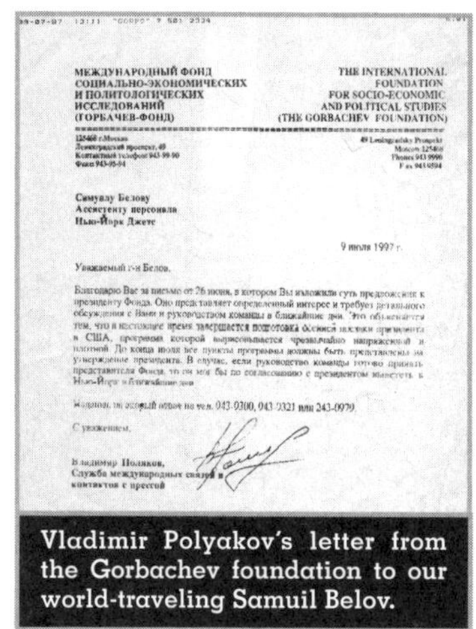

МЕЖДУНАРОДНЫЙ ФОНД
СОЦИАЛЬНО-ЭКОНОМИЧЕСКИХ
И ПОЛИТОЛОГИЧЕСКИХ
ИССЛЕДОВАНИЙ
(ГОРБАЧЕВ-ФОНД)

THE INTERNATIONAL
FOUNDATION
FOR SOCIO-ECONOMIC
AND POLITICAL STUDIES
(THE GORBACHEV FOUNDATION)

125468 г.Москва
Ленинградский проспект, 49
Контактный телефон 943-99-90
Факс 943-95-94

49 Leningradsky Prospekt
Moscow 125468
Phones 943 9990
Fax 943 9594

Самуилу Белову
Ассистенту персонала
Нью-Йорк Джетс

9 июля 1997 г.

Уважаемый г-н Белов,

Благодарю Вас за письмо от 26 июня, в котором Вы изложили суть предложения к президенту Фонда. Оно представляет определенный интерес и требует детального обсуждения с Вами и руководством команды в ближайшие дни. Это объясняется тем, что в настоящее время завершается подготовка осенней поездки президента в США, программа которой вырисовывается чрезвычайно напряженной и плотной. До конца июля все пункты программы должны быть представлены на утверждение президента. В случае, если руководство команды готово принять представителя Фонда, то он мог бы по согласованию с президентом вылететь в Нью-Йорк в ближайшие дни.

[illegible] на тел. 043-9300, 043-9321 или 243-0979.

С уважением,

Владимир Поляков,
Служба международных связей и контактов с прессой

Vladimir Polyakov's letter from the Gorbachev foundation to our world-traveling Samuil Belov.

own cover, but on the cover of a spoof copy of the locally published *Russia Review* that we were designing for a parody of the magazine.

A sister publication of the *Moscow Times*, the glossy boosterish business mag had a banal, colloquial, stupidly confident style that fit the joke perfectly—in some other dimension, they might actually have run a cover like that in earnest.

When we finally designed it, it looked exactly like one of their own ads. By now giving up all hope of maintaining discretion, Mark added a text to the ad that was even more horrifically inappropriate. It took a vicious dig at 6'9" ex–Boston Celtic forward Marcus Webb, who was now playing in Moscow for the Red Army (CSKA) basketball team after having been tossed out of the NBA following an indictment for forcible sodomy of a girl in Boston. Using the usual cheerleading tone of the *Russia Review* ads, he plugged a fictional *Review* feature on Webb's success as a new black entrepreneur in Russia, lauding a "jelly and lubricant" factory we claimed he'd opened.

When I saw Mark typing that up on the screen, I sighed. Great, I thought. It wasn't enough that we were alienating the entire black community for no good reason. No, Mark had to go one step further and single out the very biggest and browniest black man in Russia for unprovoked attack. Now we were marked men: you could practically start the t-minus for the inevitable humiliating beating. I could feel the Reebok sole patterns rising on my neck already.

As usual, there was no second-guessing, no last-minute spasms of caution. We closed our eyes, sent the thing to print, and went home to hide.

We paid for it immediately. As it happened, we had some problems with distribution of that issue, and as an emergency measure, Mark and I had to bring packets of the paper by hand to a pair of bar/restaurants in town. The two places we hit were the Hungry Duck and a place called Hola Mexico. Both places had black doormen. I dropped my packet at Hola Mexico and hit the ground running. Mark did the same at the Duck. We met on the street. On the way home, we backtracked past the door of Hola Mexico, and glanced in: both doormen there had picked up our paper and were staring squarely at the offending page with intense expressions on their faces. We hid our faces and fled. There it was, the first miserable installment in a lengthy payment plan.

Soon afterward, we went to the opening of a club called Gentleman Jack's. The owner was a black guy named Elijah whom we knew from his other bar, a well-known expat hangout called the Sports Bar. We got along well with Elijah, and were relieved to find him in an *eXile* hat when we showed up at the opening. But there was a surprise in store for us. Elijah had invited Marcus Webb. I saw him first. I was standing near the entrance, meekly sipping a Diet Coke, when he walked in. Webb is your standard massive, scary-brother type: ill-fitting baggy jeans, multicolored Hilfiger sweatshirt, about a pound of gold around his neck. I stashed my *eXile* hat deep in my back pocket

The phony practical joke which Burson-Marsteller employee/Dmitri Vasiliyev press secretary Kristen Staples showed to Anatoly Chubais.

Knock-knock! Who's Theeerrrre? eXile special guest prankster Anatoly Chubais, taking America for a ride...

In its endless attempts to gain credibility with its readers, the *eXile* has long sought to attract the very best writers and contributors Russia has to offer. We were obviously thrilled when Alexander Minkin and Eduard Limonov agreed to work with us, but words simply cannot describe how happy we were when First Deputy Prime Minister Anatoly Chubais called us up with an idea for our "Knock Knock" section. "Listen, I've got this thing, you've absolutely got to run it," he said, giggling over the phone. "I spent years on it. What's your fax number? Oh, wait, here it is—same as the [sic] page, right? By the way, are those letters fake, or what?"

"They're real, all of them," we said. "Nobody believes us."

"Whatever," he said. "I'll send this right over. Don't worry about the money, there's no rush. I'll pick it up later."

A few minutes later our fax machine started spitting out paper. After a quick read we all had to admit—it was a pretty good gag, definitely worth dropping a hundred bucks on. So here it is, a special guest Knock-Knock, stamped with the seal of quality of the government of Russia:

By Anatoly Chubais
the eXile

How gullible is the United States government? A few years ago, as the deputy mayor of St. Petersburg, I decided to find out. Posing as a westernized new Russian "reformer," I contacted officers of the United States Agency for International Development (USAID) about the possibility of setting up pro-privatization, pro-market reform organizations in post-perestroika Russia. To my surprise, all it took was a cell phone, a laptop, a command of English, and a few other "reformist" affectations to ring up millions of dollars in grant money:

Chubais: So, how about those Redskins?

USAID: Oh, don't even ask. Things just haven't been the same since Gibbs retired.

Chubais: Yeah, he was a great coach— really knew how to get the running game going.

USAID: Just move the chains, that's what it's all about.

Chubais: Yeah...so anyway, we're looking at about fifty million for the privatization center.

USAID: Oh, okay...will you be running it alone, or should we invite some others to participate?

Chubais: Well, I...Tic Tac?

USAID: Oh, no, no thanks, I've got gum.

Chubais: As you like. No, I think we can handle it ourselves, we've got free time.

USAID: Okay, well, we'll have that money transferred—

Chubais: Banque du Geneve, acct. # 314519578—

USAID: Wait, wait— one, nine, then what?

Chubais: I'll start over.

American policy, it turned out, was relatively easy to dictate. The people who held the most sway with the U.S. State Department proved remarkably open to suggestion, particularly the tweedy types in the Harvard Institute of International Development:

Chubais: So, listen, professor, you've got the wrong idea about the Securities Commission. If we let the Duma play a role in its structure, we'll never get an open securities market! We'll just create the whole thing by decree. Don't worry, we can do that here, it's a Russian thing.

HIID: Sure, but...

Chubais: Hey, listen, what do you drive back there in Cambridge?

HIID: Me? A Saab.

Chubais: Good mileage?

HIID: Fine, but it breaks down. It's an '83.

Chubais: It's yellow, right? I'm really good at guessing car colors.

HIID: Orange, actually.

Chubais: There, see, I was close! Listen, we really need more consultants here. Why don't you get yourself a bigger staff and a couple of Lincolns? We can find you a driver.

HIID: Well, I don't know. Money's tight, we were thinking of maybe building a hospital here...

Chubais: No, see, the thing is, you've got to teach us to build hospitals ourselves. (Beating breast). The Russian people will never be able to rise up out of poverty until Americans teach us how to be more efficient, you know? I know it's difficult for you to spare the manpower, but...since conditions are so difficult here, you really ought to be well paid. Maybe that way you can attract the right people. I mean, something along the lines of a $5000 a month housing allowance, a per diem, you know. I mean, you personally, a Harvard professor, you're well off, I'm sure you don't need it. But others might respond to that kind of incentive.

HIID: Well, maybe...

Chubais: And don't worry about that decree thing. We'll take care of that. By the way, did I show you this idea we had for our state auctions?

HIID: Uh, no.

In addition to being pliant and servile, the U.S. turned out to be an extremely useful political ally. I used their consultants and their legal experts to draw up the framework for the redistribution of property from the State to a selective group of banks. Believe it or not, the Americans were so convinced that the Communist opposition in government was the main stumbling block to progress that they didn't notice that they had virtually financed and written the plan for the extragovernmental transfer of power to an oligarchical clan of corporate raiders. Even funnier, they and the Uncle Toms they planted in places like the Federal Securities Commission were sure up until the very end that we were all close buddies. Even Commission chief Dmitri Vasilyev didn't guess that I'd gone behind his back to rat out that pair of Harvard losers I caught making themselves a little lunch money by trading on the inside on the Russian securities market:

Vasiliyev: I just don't understand this whole investigation. It just makes us look terrible!

Chubais: Gee, I know, it's awful.

Vasiliyev: This could sabotage everything we've been working for! If the public gets ahold of this, it'll give those bankers every reason to move in on the securities market. We won't have fair competition anymore!

Chubais: (Weeping) Our dream of creating a free and fair market will be ruined!

Vasiliyev: But USAID must know this. So why are they doing it? Who tipped them off? Who could possibly convince them to pursue this in public?

Chubais: It must be those darned Republicans in Washington! They always hated us.

Vasiliyev: (Sighing) Yeah...Maybe if we'd spent less money on per diems...Those Republicans are such penny pinchers.

Chubais: They just don't understand that you need to spend money to get a result.

Vasiliyev: Break a few eggs to make an omelet!

Chubais: Exactly!

The HIID investigation I set in motion finally gave me the excuse to cut the cord with Uncle Sam. The self-satisfied snobs in Washington who for years had treated me as their little junior capitalist whipping boy were shocked when they received my one-paragraph letter, which effectively told them to take their six years and their hundreds of millions of dollars and shove 'em:

TO: Brian Atwood, USAID chief

Dear Mr. Atwood!

I request that you terminate all existing contracts between USAID and the Harvard Institute for International Development relating to market reform in Russia. Because of changing conditions, the agreement is no longer consistent with Russian interests.

I'd almost have been willing to hold a fair auction just to see the look on their faces when that rolled in over their fax machine. The letter, of course, could have included a thank you, but why bother? After all the things they'd helped me and their own staff get away with, they weren't in a position to give me a hard time in public or anywhere else, for that matter.

After that letter, all that was left of the prank was the icing on the cake— hanging that boy scout Vasiliyev out to dry. After I announced that Russia was abandoning its policy of keeping the Securities Commission separate, Vasiliyev found himself on the fast track to a job as a junior accountant in Arthur Andersen:

Vasiliyev: Tolya, please, think this over.

Chubais: Look, that's my final offer. I'll give you twenty bucks to do the whole lawn. If you rake the leaves I'll toss in a Snickers.

Vasiliyev: Man...

Chubais: Alright, time's up, I'm out of here. (Grabs laptop)

Vasiliyev: Wait! Okay, I'll do it.

Well, hey, Uncle Sam—thanks for the memories! I'll get lunch next time, I promise (wink wink!). In the meantime I'm going to catch up on some reading I missed in the last few years. I'll start with Lenin. I find something in his life story inspirational...

and stealthily backed into a shadowy corner. Then I saw Ames heading our way and intercepted him.

"Marcus Webb!" I shrieked.

"Oh, Jesus," he shouted, instantly stashing his hat away.

We both backed up against the wall, then slowly crept sideways, unblinking, like crabs, around and out the door. I remember thinking: Noam Chomsky never went through this.

My hard-to-please girlfriend Masha was waiting outside, in addition to the entire female staff of the paper, and some of their friends. The girls' club was treated to a textbook display of cowardice in action. We refused to go inside, hid around the corner, screeched in terror when the girls tried to put on our stupid multicolored company propeller hats. Finally we relocated to a restaurant across town and joked around as though nothing had happened, but the girls didn't really buy it.

Sales dipped, and a few white liberal readers gave us a hard time for the joke, and then things went back to normal.

Most people thought that the rampaging-id aspect of the paper was its main flaw. *Boston Globe* bureau chief David Filipov, who was a friend of mine and a sometime admirer of our more serious stuff, was constantly hounding me about Death Porn. He implored me to repackage the section somehow, at the very least remove the horrible pictures and change the title. "It's like you're announcing to the world, 'Don't take me seriously.' That's all you're doing," he sighed, clearly irritated that I was fumbling away the kind of editorial freedom he didn't have at the *Globe.* "It doesn't accomplish anything."

Many academics and journalists felt the same way, but what most of these people didn't realize was that our sick material was also part of a conscious marketing strategy. We quickly learned that the more contradictory we were, the harder we'd be to pin down. Of course it was absurd that a paper which appeared to celebrate serial murder and sexual abuse would rant righteously about things like free speech and the rule of law. But we also knew that if we didn't have those conspicuous moral deficiencies, we'd have been just another "right-thinking" left-leaning alternative paper—the dog of dogs in the post–*End of History*, post-Clinton publishing world. As in, a humorless, predictable, easily dismissible nag like the *Village Voice.*

Well before we came on the scene, there were plenty of people who were saying many of the right things about Russia in print—*Green Left Weekly*'s Renfrey Clarke, for instance, or *Hindustan Times* commentator Fred Weir, or George Washington University academic Janine Wedel. But we knew that, with all due respect to these people, the truth is that nothing scares the powers that be less than an opposition of bearded lefties and nitpicking academics. They

the eXile decoding key:

= Fahkie Factor! will you "do it tonight"? ★ = no dice ★★ = if you wear sunglasses indoors, maybe ★★★ = like being in a dog kennel in late spring—you'll have to pry the patrons off your leg with a crow bar.

= Flathead Factor! will you walk out alive? ★ = probably ★★ = just don't bump into anyone ★★★ = if you so much as flinch, you're dead

= Brewski Factor! Will even the cheapest, most selfish eXile reader afford the beer? ★ = $2-$3 per beer ★★ = $4-$5 per beer ★★★ = $6- $60,000

actually welcome them. When you're rich, confident, and in charge, you actually find being opposed by cautious, low-earning, poorly dressed intellectuals flattering. They cut a nice figure for you.

We were different. Nobody who tangled with us came out looking good. To begin with, even being mentioned in the same breath as the *eXile* was an automatic minus for most respectable people. We were like the obscenely drunk party guest whose very presence casts aspersions on the host. You can be sure Jonathan Hay hated seeing his name written in boldface over and over again just a page or two away from the "fakhie factor." This was a no-win situation for a guy like Hay. He would never be able to respond in kind. And even if he had responded, he would have lost there, too.

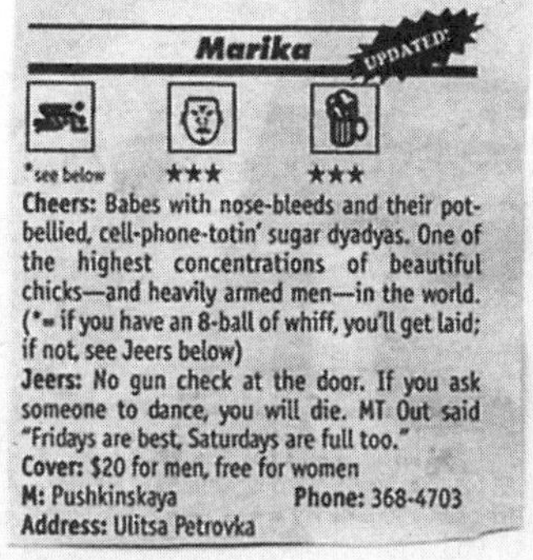

Marika UPDATED!

*see below ★★★ ★★★

Cheers: Babes with nose-bleeds and their pot-bellied, cell-phone-totin' sugar dyadyas. One of the highest concentrations of beautiful chicks—and heavily armed men—in the world. (*= if you have an 8-ball of whiff, you'll get laid; if not, see Jeers below)

Jeers: No gun check at the door. If you ask someone to dance, you will die. MT Out said "Fridays are best, Saturdays are full too."

Cover: $20 for men, free for women

M: Pushkinskaya **Phone:** 368-4703

Address: Ulitsa Petrovka

Here was another way we differed from bearded lefties; we had no compunctions whatsoever about lowering any debate we were engaged in to the level of vicious schoolyard abuse. And at the schoolyard-abuse level, we were tenacious and unbeatable. When Stanford University professor and heavy-hitting ex-USAID consultant Michael McFaul tried to get us banned from an influential Internet list, even writing us personally to chew us out, we hounded him mercilessly, sending him such a fearsome barrage of invective that he soon retreated into his cyber-hole and never said a peep about us again. McFaul just couldn't compete with us. He was out of his league on our turf, and we didn't respect his. While Mark was debating him on the issues (mainly a free-speech argument)—and winning—I was hanging on his every written word, pettily berating him at every turn for his surprisingly atrocious grammar and spelling.

After a steady enough dose of this, McFaul started to lose control of his writing entirely and make horrifically comic gaffes, leaving him open to still more annoying corrections. At one point, in a letter to Mark, he referred to someone on the aforementioned Internet list as having "stepped to the plate and delivered" a key argument about something. Mark emailed the thing to me, and I instantly wrote to McFaul to remind him that in baseball, you deliver from the *mound,* not the plate. To which he quickly the eXile #20 • October 23 - November 5, 1997 • P. 22

Knock-knock! Who's Theeerrrre? The eXile's C.R.E.E.P.-y dead president's promo agency, helping Dick Nixon get popular in Moscow

Political has-beens lead a tough life. It's not just that they've lost their perks, their power, their status. No, worst of all are the snubs they have to endure. And no political has-been is more rudely snubbed that that has-beenest of has-beens: a dead political has-been.

We decided to test this theory by arranging a Russia tour for long-deceased has-been and former slimeball Richard "Dick" Nixon. The pretext was that he was combining yet another fact-finding mission—one of many Nixon World Tours he took long after his forced retirement to give the impression that he was an "elder statesman"—with a book-signing promotion for his newest work, "Notes From the Other Side."

To test the former president's has-been status in Moscow, we tried to see what his chances would be of getting into the most eksklusivny restaurant in town, the ElDorado (yes, it's spelled without a space). See, to get into their restaurant, you need to be a member of the ElDorado club, which isn't easy for plebes like you and me. How difficult is it for the late architect of detente?

eXile: I'm calling on behalf of Richard Nixon, the former president of the United States.

ElDorado: Yes.

eXile: Well, he's coming to Moscow soon and he would like to become a member of your restaurant so that he can get in any time he wants.

ElDorado: It's possible to do this, but he needs a member of our club to recommend him for membership first. I hope that your people know someone who is a member of our club who could recommend Mr. Nixon.

eXile: Well, actually we don't know anyone. Is it really necessary to get that recommendation even for Mr. Nixon?

ElDorado: If you want to reserve a table, just call in advance.

eXile: No, I want to get a membership in your club for Mr. Nixon.

ElDorado: Well, you can come to our club, and if there are any free tables, of course we'll seat you.

eXile: No, that's not what we want. So he really needs a recommendations, even if he's the former president of the United States?

ElDorado: Yes.

eXile: Well, h'm, okay. Thank you very much.

ElDorado: Not at all.

With that snub-o-la, we backed off and realized that even a dead Tricky Dick can't get no respect, even here in Moscow. Better to try setting up the book tour instead.

We called Rubicon Books to see if they would be interested in hosting a Nixon reading and book signing. We were afraid that given the fact they are an English-language bookstore, they might remember that Nixon had died a few years back.

eXile: Hello, Rubicon Books?

Rubicon: Yes.

eXile: Can I speak to your director?

Rubicon: His name is Ernst Bonchunovich Yan. He's Korean.

eXile: Oh. Uh, does he speak Russian?

Rubicon: Unfortunately, yes.

(later)

eXile: Hello Ernst Bonchunovich, I'm an assistant for the former president Richard Nixon. He would like to come to the Rubicon to promote and read from his new book, "Notes from the Other Side." Sort of based on Dostoevsky's "Notes from the Dead," but with a twist. Would this be possible?

Rubicon: This sounds wonderful! Call me at home. (gives his home telephone number) We'd arrange everything so that Mr. Nixon's reading would be properly arranged and beautifully done. Please call back so that we can arrange it. When is Mr. Nixon coming?

eXile: Probably early next week.

Rubicon: Well, that's wonderful! Call me back at home and we'll arrange everything.

Gosh, Dick, there IS a Santa Claus! Next, we worked on arranging a place for the deceased former president to stay while in town. A hotel, we decided, would be too obvious, and keep the late president far from the ground-level. Better to have him sleep among the filthy, jansport-totin' backpackers, to get a sense of "what the kids are feeling." First, we called Traveller's Guest House, then Bed & Breakfast.

eXile: I'm calling on behalf of former American president Richard Nixon. He's coming to town on a fact-finding mission and a book tour and we'd like to book some rooms at your hostel.

Traveler's Guest House: Uh, really? How many?

eXile: There'll be about twenty-five in his entourage.

Traveler's: Well you know, this is a small hostel. Mostly foreigners stay here.

eXile: Mister Nixon is a foreigner too.

Traveler's: I know. The thing is, we have space, but our rooms are simple. There's a a bed, a chest and a window. And that's all.

eXile: Well, Mister Nixon wants to lie down and be with the people. He's tired of being around charlatans. He wants to get a pulse on the youth.

Traveler's: I see. Well, we have space if he's interested.

Richard Nixon rushes from Traveler's Guest House to Rubicon Books in a hectic day.

Bed & Breakfast: O moi god (in Russian)! 20 person entourage?! With the president?! You understand, we have apartments in the Belorussky Vokzal area. These are typical Soviet-style apartments. Five days a week a maid cleans up, and there are food items in the refrigerator. I would be more than happy to warm up my apartments for President Nixon, but the problem is that the apartments aren't all in one building or in one podyezd. I can only tell you what would be. You probably have 2 minivans and you'd need an hour to get everyone together from our apartments.

eXile: That's true. Thanks a lot. I'll call back when we decide.

B&B: Oh no, thank you! And please tell Mr. Nixon that I'm a very big fan of his.

eXile: Well, he's putting out a new book so you can buy it.

B&B: I most certainly will!

Now that we found a place to stay, the deceased former president will naturally need to find facts to make the whole trip worthwhile. What better venue for a corpse to visit than one of Moscow's top meat factories, the "Moskovsky Myasa Kombinat 'Mikoms'.

eXile: I'm Richard Nixon's assistant—you know, the former president of America?—and he's coming to Moscow next week for a fact-finding mission and a book tour.

Mikoms: (annoyed) Yes.

eXile: He'd like to visit your meat factory to learn about the changes in post-Soviet Russia, as part of his fact-finding mission.

Mikoms: But what exactly does he want to do?

eXile: You know, just walk around, see things, talk to people.

Mikoms: We can't arrange for someone to just "walk" through our factory. Our security will certainly not let him through. If there's some kind of specific offer that he has, for example to deliver our meats, then of course he can come.

eXile: But this is the former president, and he'd like to just see your factory and walk around.

Mikoms: Absolutely not. We don't have time for that. We want concrete proposals.

A dead president dissed by a meat factory? Now that's hitting an all-time low if we've heard of one. But perhaps the biggest dis of all is that NOT ONE SINGLE PERSON even remembered Nixon's death. Oh well. It's tough being a dead president, especially if your chances of winding up on a coin or dollar bill are about as high as... well... as getting into the Mikoms Meat Factory on a fact-finding tour.

The results of an *eXile* survey around Moscow gauging enthusiasm for an especially tricky fact-finding tour by dead president Richard Nixon.

responded, exasperated, that it was late at night and his baby was screaming, etc., and, damn it, it didn't matter if he couldn't keep his metaphors straight.

This was part of the reason why Mark and I never took the high road people like Filipov urged us to take. For a no-name, underfunded, antiestablishment paper like ours, the high road was a dead end. It was a one-way ticket to permanent marginalization. But as morally ambiguous brutes, we could march right into the middle of the debate, take center stage, and really get under the skin of people like McFaul.

The *Moscow Times* was another obvious target for unfair play. We knew better than to counter editor Winestock's insidious colonialist editorials with polite, reasoned *Moscow Times*–style editorials of our own. That was equivalent to surrender, as far as we were concerned. No, what we did instead was hire a mole in the *Moscow Times* newsroom to steal things off of Winestock's desk, then publish gloating photos of the bounty. Among other things, we stole his ballpoint pen, offering it as a reward to anyone who wrote a Winestock-style editorial condemning the theft. We provided sneering headline possibilities: "Theft of Pen Poorly Timed," "*eXile* Must Return Pen," "Pen Theft No Laughing Matter." To have people thinking about the fact that we'd stolen Winestock's pen and imagining his pinched, livid face while they read his stupid editorials was more damning and more effective than having people read us and agree with us. It was also more satisfying, of course.

Our lack of a real protective *krysha* exposed us to a little-publicized but extremely ugly truth about small business in Moscow: the legendarily corrupt Russians were actually more trustworthy as business partners than expatriate Westerners.

We were in a position to know. Since none of our advertising space was prepaid, we always ran the risk of taking on deadbeat clients—an unpleasant situation to be in, since we really had no recourse if someone chose not to pay his bill. There was no point in going to court over $800 of lost ads. In fact, about the only thing we stood to gain even by threatening to sue was a host of new problems, not the least of which being a deadbeat client so irritated at the thought of a lawsuit that he would sick his *krysha* on us in addition to not paying up. In short, we were totally vulnerable to anyone who wanted to screw us. But as it turned out, the only people willing to play that wild card were Westerners.

Getting screwed by expats was actually instructive. It proved that despite having grown up in the system their whole lives, Westerners still often had a weaker instinctual grasp of capitalism than Russians did. The bulk of our Russian clients—most all of them small entrepreneurs who'd had to make Faustian deals with gangsters and pay exorbitant bribes to bureaucrats just to stay afloat—seemed to understand that even if no one can stop you from doing so, it's just bad business to cheat someone. They'd had enough experience with life to know that what goes around, comes around. And after all, when things come around in Russia, they really come around.

Never Trust an eXpat

by Mark Ames

When I lived in a communal apartment in my first year in Moscow, my neighbor came to me once with a distressed look on his face. We rarely talked except for the usual pleasantries. But that day, he'd heard something that shocked him.

"Are there bad Americans?" he asked, with a hurt look on his cragged, alcoholic face.

I laughed and asked why.

"My best friend and a few others were just swindled by an American who collected money from them, saying he was going to send their children to America to learn English. He took their money and disappeared. I thought only Russians did these things. Is it common with Americans?"

This was 1994, the beginning of the end of Russia's infatuation with the alleged Western ethic. And it's no one's fault but our own.

For incoming expat businessmen, this country is like a giant horror house: the proverbial door creaks open ever so slowly at Sheremetyevo, a terrifying smell and sight greets you, then suddenly, from the depths comes a voice-a squeaky American voice-warning you, "Get out of Russia... GET OUT!!! M-m-m-ha-ha-ha!" It's not just the corruption, the Mafia, the laws, or the possibility that you'll get turned into human confetti by AK-totin competitors. The main thing everyone warns foreigners about is that, when it comes to business, you can never trust a Russian. Just read any issue of the Moscow Times business pages: have they ever once insinuated that a joint venture dispute was the fault of the Westerners? I'll offer a free eXile T-shirt to anyone who can show me such an article.

From my experience, Russian untrustworthiness serves as a patsy to throw you off the scent of the real threat to anyone doing business here. You're warned in-advance about Russians, so you're on your guard. But there is a far more savage creature hiding behind the cloak of Russian amorality, and that is the eXpat huckster.

A majority of eXpats, after just a few months here, start to play what they think is "the game." No one takes a contract seriously? Fine, then I won't take contracts seriously either. Run up debts and tell my creditors to screw off, just like the government does? Why not, no one will touch me. Steal assets at cut-rate prices by bribing the right people? Hey, if finance ministers and oligarchs can do it, why not me! Insider deals? My name is Jonathan, and you can count me in!

I have a proposal for lawmakers back home. Any eXpat who has spent more than six months here should undergo rigorous psychological and moral examinations when he returns home. A council of priests, rabbis and town elders should have the right to deport any eXpat deemed to be morally unfit for life in his or her home country. If an eXpat has spent more than 18 months here, he should be locked up in a re-education camp in North Dakota, and held there for a period of no less than six months while authorities examine and re-assimilate him, using brutal methods if necessary. If he has been here longer than 18 months, than he should be treated like the Ebola virus: as he crosses the border, a platoon of armed men in plastic space suits should roughly detain him, strip him of his citizenship, and deport him.

Last week, Masha and I went to visit a deadbeat client, a certain Mister Mufid, who owns the Sheherazde restaurant. He's also in the car importing business, so he may ram a cap up my ass for writing about him... if they find my limbless torso bobbing in a bloodied icehole in the Oka, then please, reader, do your Christian deed and burn Sheherazde to the ground.

We'd signed a contract with Sheherazde about four months back. Week after week, they kept coming up with reasons why they weren't paying us. And each week, we foolishly trusted Mr. Mufid.

Finally, I went with our own Masha to surprise Mr. Mufid at his restaurant/auto parts store at the end of December. We stopped him right in front of his employees and customers and confronted him with the invoices, asking when he'd planned to pay us. He promised to pay the following Monday, but we were persistent—we knew he was full of it. He then brought us down into the unlit restaurant, using candles to light the basement... it was a cheap attempt to frighten us. When we didn't budge, he gave up all pretence and told us that he believed the bill was "our fault" and not "his fault." There was nothing we could do, short of resorting to methods that no eXpat should get involved in, at least not over a thousand dollars. Sorry, bub.

I got that queasy feeling which reminded me of the worst eXpat villain of all here, the pair of British slimebags who run Quasar. We have a contract with them, signed by their director at the behest of general manager Guy Barlow. When Quasar first started, they placed ad after ad in our paper. Each ad was carefully designed based on material which was sent and approved personally by Barlow and then-marketing manager Rob Kelley (and that's no blarney). After a few issues, Barlow tried to back out of the contract. It was incredible: here was an eXpat, a citizen of the allegedly civilized West, doing things according to the alleged rules of "the game": sorry, we don't need your contract anymore. Fuck you.

It always sucks hitting up a deadbeat. You feel you're confronting the dull mass of amorality itself—in this instance incarnated in the sweaty, unpleasant, wart-covered form of Guy Barlow. Like Mr. Mufid, he avoided our calls, so we cased Quesar and jumped him with copies of invoices. Finally he agreed to begin making payments. No payments came. We met again, this time with his accountant, and agreed to a schedule. But as we found out later, the minute we walked out, Barlow told the accountant to disregard everything he'd promised us. Nice fucking guy.

It's not like all eXpats are swindlers. We have many other clients, both expats and Russians, who are professional, honor their contracts, and lodge legitimate complaints about our nauseating pictures in Death Porn...But the greatest East Bloc myth of the 90s—that Westerners are inherently more ethical than Russians—is dying a hard, bitter death, thanks to people like Barlow.

Perhaps if you go to Quasar and you see that lying jerk, or his nerd sidekick Marty, you'll remember that you're patronizing the low end of the eXpat community, spineless twerps who only needed to find the right environment in order to let their true slippery characters shine in all their glory. We know that we'll never see that money—and because of Russia's tax system, we had to pay taxes on those ads anyway. So thanks a lot to Guy, Marty and the gang for holding onto your Western values. It's a good thing you're in a management position. Your Russian underlings have a lot to learn from people like you. And so will your Russian investors, when the time comes for them to see just how you've been spending their money.

This column Mark wrote about expat debtors reportedly sank a deal to sell the Quasar laser-tag club, one of the deadbeats in question.

May 11, 1997 • Tampa Bay *Register-Bulletin* • p. 9

Orlando Millionaire To Purchase *Pravda*

By Hugh Jassets
Register-Bulletin

Sources close to Orlando personal-injury attorney Barry Apfelbaum say that the millionaire has brokered a deal that will make him the chief financier of the communist daily newspaper *Pravda*.

According to Tampa Bay banker Wallace Beck, Apfelbaum, who retired from his legal practice in 1991 to buy a chain of Sears-Roebuck franchises, has finally come to an agreement after months of top secret negotations with Christos Yiannikos, the the Greek general director of Pravda International, the Greek company which owns *Pravda*.

Beck, whose Florida First National Bank brokered the deal, told the *Register-Bulletin* that Apfelbaum was a lifetime admirer of "world history" who wanted *Pravda* as a "trophy to add to my collection of holdings."

The storied communist organ has experienced great financial difficulties since the collapse of communism in 1991. It was purchased by Yiannikos' firm in 1993.

Apfelbaum is well-known to Orlando residents as the former director of Apfelbaum Associates, a personal-injury firm whose colorful television commercials in the 1980s helped the owner amass a huge personal fortune over the course of the decade.

Apfelbaum, who is congenitally blind and a dwarf, won a cult following as a fiery courtroom orator who frequently won huge settlements for blue-collar workers and for victims of accidents on Disneyland rides. He was later hired by Disney to defend the company against similar suits.

Both Apfelbaum and spokesmen for Pravda International in Athens declined to comment on the story, saying that reports were "premature."

Beck said that the two sides would make a formal announcement in Athens next week.

He added that Apfelbaum was considering opening a Sears franchise in Russia.

He said the attorney planned to advertise his business by striking a sponsorship agreement with *Pravda*, whereby Sears would cover printing costs in exchange for free advertising space in the paper.

Pravda in Russian means "truth."

The phony *"Tampa-Bay Register-Bulletin"* article we sent to the newspaper *Pravda* in an attempt to convince them they'd been bought by a blind, Jewish dwarf.

The classic expat fraud, on the other hand, was a shabby little nerd who'd moved overseas to escape the very laws of physics which had made him a failure at home in the first place. He didn't understand cause and effect, because he tended to be in heavy denial to begin with, having spent a lifetime developing strong mental defenses against the acceptance of blame.

Dwarf to Buy *Pravda*

How low can the once-mighty communist daily *Pravda* sink? To about four-foot two, according to a report in the Tampa Bay *Register-Bulletin*.

The *Register-Bulletin*'s Saturday edition, citing sources in the Tampa Bay First National Bank, reported that celebrated Orlando personal injury lawyer Barry Apfelbaum has closed a deal with Greek-owned Pravda International to purchase the legendary socialist organ, based in Moscow, Russia.

Apfelbaum, a blind dwarf, became famous in the 1980's for the wacky TV commercials he made for his personal-injury firm, Apfelbaum and Associates. The best-known spot pictured the quick-witted attorney pacing in front of a witness stand, saying, "If the jury can see me, they'll believe me!"

Apfelbaum, the *Register-Bulletin* said, is a history buff who is buying the paper to add to his "collection of holdings."

Pravda, founded in 1919, is Russia's oldest newspaper. It has struggled financially since the collapse of the Soviet Union in 1991.

More materials, this one from the *"St. Petersburg Times,"* backing up our story about the blind, Jewish dwarf owner of *Pravda*.

Godzilla Versus Nemtsov

Boris Nemtsov stunned the world two weeks ago while on a visit to Tokyo by offering his personal mobile telephone number to a delegation of Japanese businessmen. "Call me if you have any problems, guys," he told them, to the cheers of the Western press. Was this gesture a sign of a New, Improved Russian reformer? Does this mean that corruption will end, companies will become more transparent, competition will become more fair, and Russia will finally enter the family of civilized, law-abiding nations? If yes, then does the handsome young Deputy Prime Minister know just how painfully annoying his life could become if indeed he intends to listen to the petty, frivolous problems of each and every Japanese businessman? We decided to test the New & Improved credentials of Boris Yefimovitch. Disguised as regional manager "Mr. Hashimoto Godzilla" of "Mothra Electronics," the eXile called a government press secretary, Nikolai Vasilyevich Prosin to see just how literally the reformer meant his words to be taken.

Godzilla: Hello, my name is Hashimoto Godzilla from Mothra Electronics. Not long ago, I met with the esteemed Vice Premier Boris Naumin-ovitch [sic] Nemtsov. I want his phone number because when I was in Tokyo, he gave us his mobile telephone number, and I need to ask him some important questions. Please tell me how to get his mobile telephone number.

Prosin: I understand everything. Your secretary who just called me understood me very well. I don't know the mobile telephone number of Nemtsov. Please call his personal press secretary.

Godzilla: And please tell me again, who are you?

Prosin: I work in the department of information for the government.

Godzilla: Ah, I see. Then could you please help me. Do you know the mobile telephone number of Boris Nauminovitch Nemtsov?

Prosin: I don't know, I don't know! I'll give you the phone number of his personal press secretary. 205-5208.

Godzilla: Excuse me, Nikolai Vasilyevich. Maybe you can help me too, because I noticed at the meeting in Tokyo that Mr. Nemtsov is a very new, good Russian, a kind of Western businessman-type of person, and I respect him very much for this. So I have a few questions for him that could help me. For example, well... you see I had his mobile telephone number, but I lost it.

Prosin: I understand, but I don't have it—

Godzilla: But maybe you could help me, because I wanted to ask Boris Nauminovitch, for example, where in Moscow you can find a good golf club, because golfing is very important for business. For Japanese it is particularly important for the soul as well.

Prosin: I know that a club opened up not long ago in Moscow. You should call your colleagues or accredited journalists. They should know.

Godzilla: But there are two clubs, right?

Prosin: I don't know how many golf clubs we have in Moscow. I don't play.

Godzilla: Do Russian businessmen play it a lot?

Prosin: No, no. It's a new sport.

Godzilla: Considering that Boris Nauminovitch is a New Russian reformer, maybe he plays golf?

Prosin: I don't know that.

Godzilla: Maybe just one more question, then I won't bother you any more. Where can you find here some good sashimi, unagi, sushi, because I can't get used to your Russian food.

Prosin (getting more annoyed): I don't understand, what do you need?

Godzilla: Sashimi, sushi, Miso soup. Japanese food.

Prosin: I think there's a restaurant here serving Eastern food.

Godzilla: Do you think Boris Nauminovitch eats sushi?

Prosin: Oh, I don't know.

Godzilla: Because maybe I would like to invite him to sushi.

Prosin: That telephone number I gave you, they'd know better. (repeats name and telephone number of Nemtsov's personal press secretary).

Godzilla: And, just one last question. Uh, karaoke: do you have that in Moscow.

Prosin: Probably, yes.

Godzilla: Ah, excellent. I love to sing.

Prosin: I understand.

Godzilla: Thank you so much.

Prosin: All the best.

Godzilla: Goodbye.

Our first run-in with expat shysterism involved a schmoozemeister named Dominique Berhout, who'd bounced around several restaurants and businesses as a promotions manager and director before landing, by the time we met him, at Le Gastronome, one of Moscow's most elegant restaurants. This was a jittery working-class guy with the face and build of a minor league hockey coach who in Moscow had somehow reinvented himself as a high-society gourmand. His chief affectations were a snappy

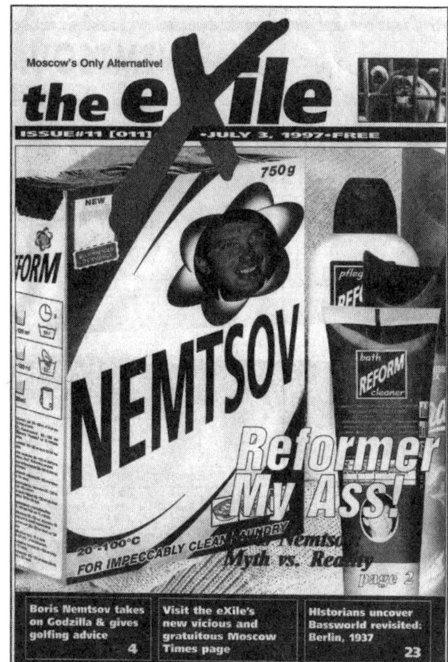

blue suit and a right forearm permanently twitching from the urge to give somebody, anybody, an earnest handshake.

Dominique gave Mark a call in late March and invited him to Le Gastronome for a night of what in Russian is commonly called *khalyava,* or "free stuff" (although Dominique himself certainly wouldn't have known enough Russian to call it that). In this case the *khalyava* was a free meal at a real four-star restaurant, complete with fine wines that would have put a massive dent in Mark's monthly salary had he been given a bill. The food was so good that Mark almost didn't notice Dominique's incessant schmoozing and paranoid insistence on asking every ten minutes if the food was okay. Mark also paid little attention when Dominque dropped the name of scary Chechen gangster Umar Gimbrailov, or when he mentioned that he was on good terms with a Dagestani restaurant owner who was rumored to have recently killed his Western manager for embezzling money, or when, ridiculously, he bragged that he'd once been a boxer. Mark didn't register, at the time, the not-so-subtle implication that Dominique ran with very heavy hitters, and maybe even was one himself. . . . In any case, Dominique subseqently struck a huge deal with us to advertise both Le Gastronome and a new restaurant/nightclub called the Zoo, which his company was planning on opening. The Zoo deal involved half-page ads on a semiregular basis, which was a big deal for us at the time. We were so grateful for such a high-class client, in fact, that when the Zoo finally opened, we made the biggest mistake of the paper's existence: we blew it in a review, even though the place sucked.

The obvious blowjob review prompted a flood of disgusted letters from restaurant people around town, and though we admitted our mistake in our letters page, our reputation suffered a severe blow among other advertisers. Meanwhile, the outstanding Zoo/Le Gas bill was quietly growing in size. When we complained, Dominique kept insisting everything was okay and ordering more ads. We went along, stupidly and chauvinistically believing that an American working for two of the best-financed restaurants in town wouldn't screw us. But when the bill reached $7,000, Dominique stopped returning our phone calls, forcing the entire company to mobilize in an effort to track him down in person.

The typical debt collector/debt evader scenario ensued. Mark, our mustachioed business manager Kara, and I hovered around Le Gas and the Zoo morning and night, and quickly discovered that the managerial staffs

e d i t o r i a l

Africa: At a Crossroads Facing Tough Choices

We know that it isn't in the news and that it has very little to do with expatriate life in Moscow, but the eXile editorial board has decided to devote this space in this issue to discussing Africa. We have very strong opinions about Africa and we feel they should be aired.

Obviously, Africa is entirely surrounded by water. We support this wholeheartedly. It has been a known fact for thousands of years that access to sea routes is a great boon to human civilization. Sea travel allows people to exchange goods and ideas. And Africa, as much any other continent, has a right to enjoy these advantages.

Of course, these days, Europe lies north of Africa. As we all know, this continent has been home to many of humanity's most prosperous civilizations over the course of the past five centuries or so. Now the countries of Europe are talking about uniting.

All of which only indirectly affects Africa. In Africa, African affairs take preference over non-African ones. Chief among these issues are trade, the political sovereignty of African nations, health and longevity of African citizens, the environment and the more abstract issues of family and sociological relations. In each of these areas, Africans have cause for both optimism and concern.

Africans have every right to be concerned about their own affairs. To ask them to be concerned about our affairs would be unfair. It also probably wouldn't do any good. What do they know about our problems?

Very little. And some Africans are Nigerian. Nigerians are distinguished from other Africans by their Nigerian citizenship. Nigerians have their own official language and the Nigerian treasury prints its own currency. You can't use that currency to buy anything in neighboring Ghana!

Still, if you were to take the whole Western part of Africa and just chop it off, Africa wouldn't have that funny "q" shape anymore, but would be more like a big rectangle. And if you were to take all of the people out of Africa, it would be totally unpopulated.

The eXile has no intention of supporting any external effort to chop off the Western part of Africa. However, should Africans undertake this project themselves, we feel it would only be fair to support their right to self-determination.

Furthermore, it is well known that Africa now is home to a great many ethnic conflicts, none of which take place anywhere outside of Africa. These conflicts must resolve themselves if they are to be resolved. Certainly a strong international presence would give these troubled nations a strong international presence.

The leaders of the Western world should not be shy about recognizing the existence of Africa. As time goes on, our relations with African nations will depend more and more on our ability to locate them. Be they in the north, south, or western part of Africa, our diplomats should make it their duty to be awake and physically present at all negotiations held with African officials.

This will take time. But time, unfortunately, is something that most Africans without it do not have. Therefore it seems prudent to recommend that all ineffective aid programs be canceled and replaced with effective ones. Only such a course will allow Africans to take charge of the destiny that is their own.

Hopefully, some good will come out of our ephemeral awareness of Africa. For too long our insistence upon leading lives totally independent of Africa have left us with a completely chartorial revacuation with our own fratratial inseams. The closseted subterchange of multilateral encrimony ensures that last year's bold hegefinal Pan-African surgetiative may yet subscond the stark macchalian bortinines that so characterized our previous relations with these countries.

Overall, Africa's young reformers face many tough questions, which they alone can answer for themselves. Will they be able to muster the courage to face their problems bravely? Will they take the time to understand the mission that is theirs? Only time will tell.

It was not unusual for Death Porn to feature three or four identical stories in one issue, each describing the shooting of a "commercial director" in the doorway of his apartment building.

Murder by Numbers

After a while, the news stories all begin to sound the same. Victim X was director of company Y. Travelling along street Z, he exited foreign car of A make and was finally shot in the head in his podyezd by automatic weapon of make B. Ineffectual police department in C city closes the case by announcing that the investigation is continuing. Hired killer D remains on the loose. For this story, fill in the following blanks: X=Alexander Kolesnikov, Y= "AO Interstroigazkomplekt", Z=Moskovskoye Shosse, A=Mercedes 600 series, B=TT pistol, C=Smolensk and D, as always, remains unknown. It all happened two weeks ago; look for the same story to happen again soon in a different city. Just hold on to our eXile algebra murder equation, and everything will be as E-Z as ABC.

of both restaurants had developed a habit of having just stepped out any time we were around. As long as we were around, both places were ghost ships, manned entirely by waiters and sous chefs.

After enough of this, we tried a new tack. I called Dominique's home number and left a message on his answering machine asking him if he was going to pay, adding that the "editorial content of the next issue" depended on his answer. We'd just run a very ugly exposé on another Dominique-esque figure, *Moscow Tribune* columnist/restaurant promoter Michael Bass, and we were hoping Dominique's paranoia would get the best of him.

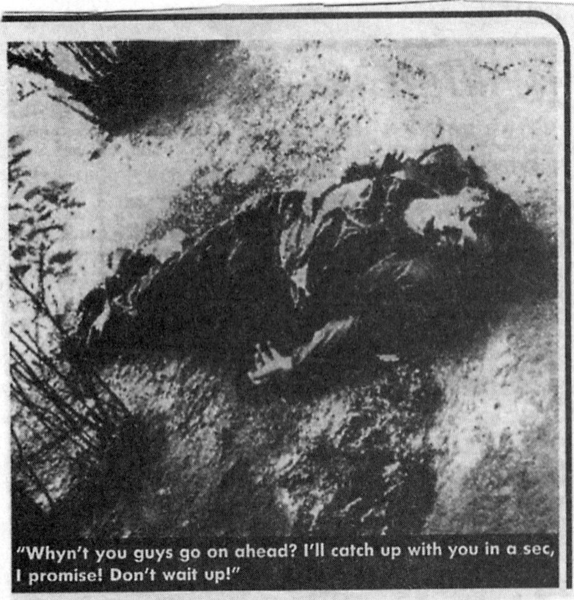

"Whyn't you guys go on ahead? I'll catch up with you in a sec, I promise! Don't wait up!"

Vadim Yershov thinks sadly: "Damn! I only killed nineteen people. I thought I was on my way up..."

Yet Another Serial Killer

Hear about the guy from Krasnoyarsk who killed 19 people? We didn't think so! Yet another p.r.-challenged killer seeped into the middle pages not of Izvestia, not of Moskovsky Komsomolets even, but of Kriminalnaya Khronika, Russia's only national newspaper devoted exclusively to crime. Nosferatu-lookalike Vadim Yershov, a deserter from the Far Eastern army group, returned home to Krasnoyarsk a few years ago and set about raping and killing women. This past summer he made the mistake of diving on a woman in a podyezd in broad daylight whose husband, an FSB officer, happened to be just a few yards away. The chekist beat Yershov to a pulp, tied him up, and sent him to jail. His court case winds up next week; he's already confessed to 19 killings and seven attempted kidnappings, so his chances of escaping heavy time or even death despite the 99% conviction rate of Russian courts are slim, although Charles Blitzer has not yet made the authoritative prediction.

The Death of Raisa Gorbacheva

We don't know enough about this story to even be funny about it, but here's what we do know from various Russian press reports: a 47 year-old woman by the name of Raisa Gorbacheva was murdered last week in Bishkek, the capital of Kirgizia. Gorbacheva, a journalist and a poetess, was strangled in what police describe as an apparent robbery. She has no relation to Raisa Maximovna, although her death, according to local police, has allowed her to eclipse her living namesake in political relevance.

Yet Another Serial Killer And Still More Good News From Nakhodka

Looking for a new home to move to? Try sunny Nakhodka! Just last issue we told you about a group of boys in notorious Nakhodka who were caught playing soccer with a human skull. This time, Kriminalnaya Khronika reports, two dismembered female bodies were found there— in an area where those same boys were playing soccer again! The paper concludes: "It is logical to conclude that Nakhodka now has its own serial killer, just to round out completely its criminal portfolio."

He called back right away. "Why didn't you tell me you were anxious about the bill?" he said. "We'll settle this right away."

We quickly realized what was going on: Dominique was on his way out at the restaurant, and no longer had any pull with the Russians who controlled the money. We couldn't even be sure that the über-bosses had approved the original ads. Whatever the real story was, Dominique clearly had no intention of telling it to us. We set a deadline for him to pay up or suffer the consequences in print, and it wasn't until past midnight on production night that he broke down and told us that he was about to be fired, that there was nothing he could do.

"I don't understand," I said. "Are we supposed to care about that? We still want to see that money by noon tomorrow."

Dominique was shocked. Apparently he'd been so sure that we would have appreciated the sheer bravery he'd demonstrated by admitting his highly embarrassing professional situation that we would have let him off the hook out of pure admiration.

"I can't believe this," he said. "I can't believe you're threatening me like this. I was straight with you."

"Noon tomorrow," I repeated. We were bluffing, but what the hell.

"Look," he said. "I give you my absolute word that this will work out. Just hold off tomorrow."

"No way," I said. "We've waited long enough."

exile.ru P.14
"Hey Rosita, I have to go shooping
Down town for my mamma
She needs some tortillas and chili peppers
La la la, la la la la la la la la
La La La la la la la la, la la la la la la la la

Your dog is gonna have a puppy
And we're running out of coke
No enchiladas in the ice box
And the telebision's broke
I saw some lipstick on your sweat shirt
I smell the purfume in your ear
Well, if you're gonna keep on messin
Don't bring your business back here

Hey Rosita, come quick, down at the cantina
They're giving green stamps with tequila
La la la la la la la la ....."

– 1990
OCTAVIO PAZ
POET
1914-1998

Sometimes we got a little out of hand in abusing our readers, but they didn't stop sending us letters.

WE'LL FUCK YOUR KIDS

Dear [sic],

I have been reading your website for some time now and I have to say that I find it very interesting. As a married criminal defense attorney in Southern California with three kids, two mortgages, etc., I read about your lives in Moscow with shock, horror, and of course barely controlled envy.

Keep up the good work! At least we suburban drudges can live vicariously.

... sort of.

Anyway I really did want to say thank you for one of the most unusual publications on the net. "Unusual" is probably an understatement, I suppose.

Keep on truckin' and avoid the flatheads!

Jeff ███

Dear Jeff,

You want to introduce us to that wife of yours? Think she'd mind if we ass-fucked her? How about your kids? Any of them have pubes? Male or female, it's the same to us.

He called several more times through the morning and night to complain, but at 11:55 A.M., a fax spilled out of our machine. It was a copy of a wire transfer receipt for $5,800. Apparently, there was still *something* he could do.

We had similar problems with other expats. A fat warty Brit named Guy Barlow, the manager of the "Quasar" laser-tag bar, tried to weasel out of a $6,000 bill, stalling and making excuses all along the way even while bragging around town about how he'd never intended to pay us. Like Dominique, he figured we had no recourse, and we wouldn't have—had not fortune intervened. When Mark finally got fed up and published a savage column berating Barlow and other expat deadbeats, we didn't expect a response.

As it turned out, though, Barlow was in the middle of negotiations to sell his bar—and our column sabotaged the entire deal. As a result, Barlow was torn a new asshole by his corporate superiors in London, and another Quasar rep called us immediately to settle the debt in order to put the p.r. fire out and keep the deal alive. Unfortunately, Mark was whacked out on speed when the time came to do the deal, and he angrily refused their initial offer of $3,000 in cash, having become fixated for some reason on collecting the full amount or nothing at all. They went out of business shortly thereafter, and we never saw a dime of that money.

Our few other assorted deadbeats were also all expats, providing still more evidence in support of one of our central hypotheses about the expat community: namely, that a great many of the foreigners who came to Russia felt that the country's obvious sociopolitical chaos gave them an excuse to dispense with their normal standards of behavior. A lot of them were swept away by the shiny-suit-and-tommy-gun gangsterish feel of the city, and began to forget their backgrounds as dweebs raised in the American suburbs and feel like tough guys. Not having any kind of experience with this kind of thing, they began to see angles all over the place even when they weren't there, and started to assume that playing things straight was automatically a dumb move.

Our own business manager, the aforementioned Kara Deyerin, was a classic example. Short and squat with a freakishly fat ass and a copiously hairy body she stubbornly refused to hide (she frequently wore translucent white tights over her shaggy unshaved legs, resulting in a lower body covered with garish patches of matted black hair), Kara was a deeply resentful and prematurely bitter woman who used Russia as an excuse to see conspiracies rather than cope with her own multitudinous and doubtless very daunting personal problems. She grew to loathe Mark and me and eventually quit out of resentment.

In any case, when she finally quit in a rage, she did so suddenly, with just two weeks warning, dropping a series of bombs on us which suggested she'd been planning her departure for a long time. She somehow managed to convince our publisher to let her keep her 15 percent share in the company, despite the fact that her contract specified that she was only entitled to it if she stayed on for two years. She'd convinced the publisher that we were planning to steal the paper and move to another publisher. Apparently we needed to be stopped, and she offered to play the role of the heavy for him. "This is what Kostya wants," she

Lawrence Summers once called for more pollution in poor countries: he would have liked our phony Moscow Times brief.

Poison Gas Irks Indians

■ CALCUTTA, India (AP)—A DuPont mustard gas chemical plant outside of Calcutta exploded into flames yesterday, releasing a toxic cloud that authorities say may have led to the asphyxiation deaths of millions of Indians, while forcing tens of millions to evacuate the region. Also yesterday, a bus packed with 42 people, mostly women and children, crashed into a ravine in the southern state of Jaffa, killing all on board.

Markets in India reacted positively to the news, rising 3.3 percent in early trading.

The toxic cloud is expected to drift across the entire Indian subcontinent before settling into the atmosphere over the Indian Ocean. World Bank officials believe that the cloud will pose no threat to the region.

said. "And he's serious. If I were you guys, I wouldn't cross him. He knows some pretty serious people. I only recently found out how serious. Keep that in mind."

This was incredible. Here was a 24-year-old American woman, raised in the cradle of Seattle's coffee shops, essentially threatening us with a gangland hit if we didn't swallow her breach of contract.

Like a lot of Americans who started trying to pull these kinds of power plays after moving to Moscow, Kara was a person who would have been afraid to jump a subway turnstile at home, much less threaten anyone with murder. But a year and a half of living in Moscow had convinced her she knew all the moves. It was laughable. But it was really happening.

By March 1998, the *eXile* office was beginning to feel like Verdun in 1915. There were huge losses all over the place, and no one was winning. On the plus side, most of the people on our short list of usual suspects had taken a beating over the course of the last year. Jonathan Hay was out of government, under investigation by the U.S. Attorney's office in Boston for mismanagement of government funds, and writing some kind of semiannual newsletter out of his girlfriend's office and ducking our phone calls. Hay's girlfriend, Beth Hebert, had been told by a Duma subcommittee (which had called the *eXile* for assistance in its investigation) that she would have to rebid for her Investor Protection Fund contract. Anatoly Chubais had been fired and four of his closest aides were under investigation; the very term "young reformer" had become a joke in the Russian press. The bureau chiefs of the *New York Times*, *Los Angeles Times*, and the *Times of London*, all of whom had been repeatedly brutalized in the *eXile* press review, had packed up and left town. The pathetic *Tribune* was teetering on the verge of bankruptcy. Whether or not we had anything to do about it, it seemed like everyone we'd written about had met a bad end. At the same time, though, the *eXile* was in crisis. An ill-considered decision to go weekly in February sent Mark, Krazy Kino Kevin, and me careening into severe substance abuse. Toward the end of the winter, we were each

Below: The *eXile* version of a Russia Review ad.

WE'VE GOT IT, YOU CAN GET IT.

Western companies have long wondered about the presence in Moscow of black Africans, and their importance in developing marketing and consumer-targeting strategy. Now, Africans are catching on.

The number of Africans in Moscow has grown exponentially in recent years—and their combined spending power has soared to over $100 million dollars in Moscow alone. Geoff Winestock, the newly-appointed editor of *Russia Review*, takes you behind the scenes to show how Western consumer companies are adapting, and how Russian companies are not far behind, recreating their marketing campaigns. We also bring you an exclusive interview with Marcus Webb, star forward for the CSKA basketball team, who has recently branched out into testimonials for consumer products such as jellies and hemorrhoidal creams produced at a plant in Khimki.

From the latest trends in the stock market to an analysis of maverick reformer Anatoly Chubais's Montes Auri investment firm, we bring you all you need to know about business in Russia.

COUPON FOR WHAT YOU WANT TO KNOW

✓ Yes, I will subscribe to *Russia* Review for 12 months for the price of $295.

✓ Yes, I want to receive the Red October Box full of chocolates. FREE.

ADMT141000

Name Mr/Mrs ______ Position ______

Company ______ Industry ______

Address ______

Code/City ______ Country ______

Telephone ______ Fax ______

Payment (Equivalent US$ and Eurocheques accepted)

☐ Bank Transfer ☐ Cash ☐ Check enclosed, payable to Independent Media

Credit card: ☐ Amex ☐ Eurocard/Mastercard ☐ Visa ☐ Diners

Card Number ______ Signature ______

Valid thru ___/___ Credit card charges will be made in US$

Please fax or mail this coupon to:
- For USA/Canada: fax 802-223-6105; or mail to RIS, 89 Main Street, Suite 2, Montpelier, Vermont, 05602-2948.
- For Russia: fax 095-232-1761; or mail to Russia Review, Ulitsa Vyborgskaya 16, Moscow, Russia 125212.
- For Europe & rest of the world: fax 31-20-676-0701; or mail to Van Eeghenstraat 93, 1071 EX Amsterdam, The Netherlands.

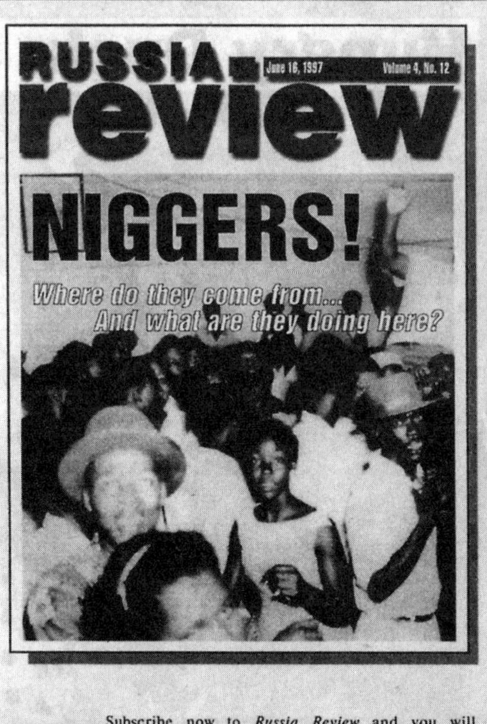

Subscribe now to *Russia Review* and you will receive a free box of "Friends" cappuccino-flavored candies from America. It may be your hippest investment of 1998.

FREE

snorting enough speed every week to cause heart failure in the entire pan-African wildebeest herd. We spent our few waking off-hours waiting out heart palpitations and calming our nerves with hot chocolate and PG movies. At night our pillows were damp from uncontrollable sweats. For the first time in my life, I considered seeking help for a drug problem.

After about six weeks of this, the line between reality and paranoid fantasy had become so blurred in our office that we were no longer sure what exactly it was we were doing. The huge piles of refuse, gigantic yellow-press headlines, and frantic faxes all over the city pointed to some determined, aggressive purpose, but by mid-March we no longer knew what that was. Personally I began to wonder whether we were just hurling invective out of inertia. I started to wonder: Was all of this worth it? Could well-fed middle-class people like ourselves really have enemies terrifying enough to justify this much aggression and self-destructive energy? What was the point?

We got our answer late on a Saturday night in March. Ames called me from his apartment. We'd both been off drugs for something like 36 hours, and the phone call was unusually lucid. There was no point to any of this, we realized. We had to go back to biweekly or else we would die. We were both relieved. Privately, I started having thoughts about making the post-amphetamine *eXile* a "nicer" publication.

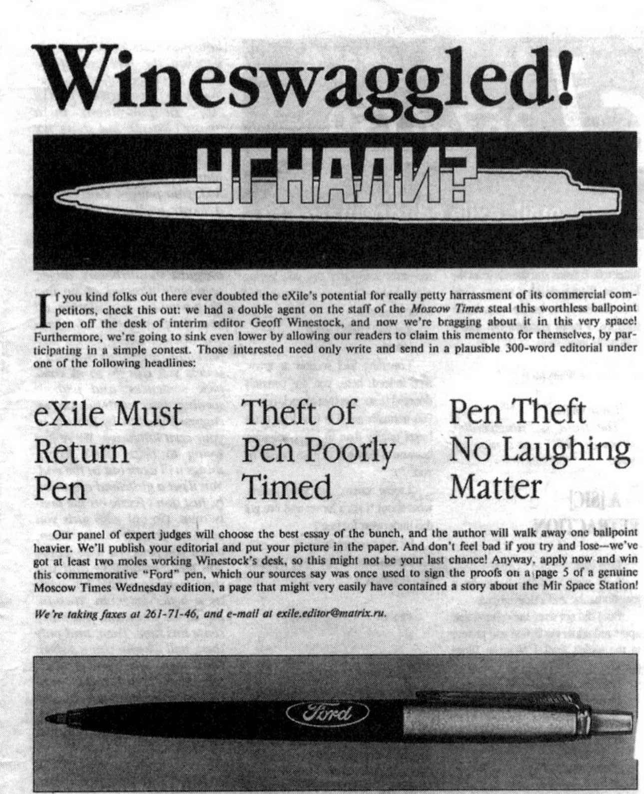

Wineswaggled!

УГНАЛИ?

If you kind folks out there ever doubted the eXile's potential for really petty harrassment of its commercial competitors, check this out: we had a double agent on the staff of the *Moscow Times* steal this worthless ballpoint pen off the desk of interim editor Geoff Winestock, and now we're bragging about it in this very space! Furthermore, we're going to sink even lower by allowing our readers to claim this memento for themselves, by participating in a simple contest. Those interested need only write and send in a plausible 300-word editorial under one of the following headlines:

eXile Must Return Pen	Theft of Pen Poorly Timed	Pen Theft No Laughing Matter

Our panel of expert judges will choose the best essay of the bunch, and the author will walk away one ballpoint heavier. We'll publish your editorial and put your picture in the paper. And don't feel bad if you try and lose—we've got at least two moles working Winestock's desk, so this might not be your last chance! Anyway, apply now and win this commemorative "Ford" pen, which our sources say was once used to sign the proofs on a page 5 of a genuine Moscow Times Wednesday edition, a page that might very easily have contained a story about the Mir Space Station!

We're taking faxes at 261-71-46, and e-mail at exile.editor@matrix.ru.

That Monday, Yeltsin fired the entire government. Just what we needed. Exhausted, we went back on drugs and put out a nearly unreadable issue. By the time we woke up, it was Friday, March 27. Things looked bad. We were a humor magazine, and we had no plans for April 1. Our stock in the expatriate community had fallen sharply. We were looking like losers again.

So we got together and quickly came up with an idea. This awful period in our lives was going to end with a bang. If we were going to go down, we were going to bring some people with us.

Early on the morning of Wednesday, April 1, the guards at the North gate of the U.S. Embassy followed their normal daily routine and brought about 200 copies of the *Moscow Times* into the embassy cafeteria. The *Times* was distributed for free, and diplomats and other embassy staff generally read it over breakfast to start their day.

According to the paper, March 31 had been a busy news day. The headline on the lead article read "Sex Scandal Rocks Kremlin" and told a spectacular story: new Prime Minister-designate Sergei Kiriyenko had been fired by Boris Yeltsin after being arrested in a midnight fracas at a gay nightclub over a beauty pageant tiara. This was huge news for the embassy staff, particularly since Russia had already been teetering on the verge of a political crisis as a result of the March 24 firing of the entire government. Now, with the new PM shot down in a sex scandal that even the staid *Moscow Times* was calling a "new round of hostilities in the so-called banker's war," Russia would be lucky to escape widespread pandemonium. Word spread quickly around the embassy, and an emergency meeting with Ambassador James Collins was convened to discuss the crisis.

Meanwhile, at hotels and restaurants all over the city, expats and anglophile Russians alike were scratching their heads. Expat American sports fans got up early to check the results of the NCAA basketball final, but their morning edition of the *Moscow Times* neglected to tell them the score, reporting only that the game had been a hugely entertaining double-overtime thriller. *Nezavisimaya Gazeta* reporter Boris Kagarlitsky read the *Moscow Times* report about Kiriyenko's dismissal and bounded into action, calling the State Duma and the government press office for details of the firing. As usual, they told him nothing. Press colleagues he contacted reported similar frustration in unraveling the story. By 11 A.M., phones in the *Moscow Times* newsroom were ringing off the hook with complaints and desperate requests for further information. The calls were in vain. Editor Geoff Winestock was on vacation, and the early-morning arrivals at the MT offices pleaded total ignorance before hanging up on each of the callers.

While all of this was going on, Mark and I sat hunched over in a booth in the Starlite Diner at Oktyabrskaya Square, watching customers flow in and read the news. We were dressed to the nines, each decked out in brand-new night-sky-blue $18 Belarussian sweatsuits that were made of an artificial fabric so rugged that even our knees were pouring sweat from trapped heat. Twice during breakfast I had to excuse myself to sponge my knees off in the bathroom.

The suits were symbols of our changed luck. The night before, Mark and I had held a late-evening meeting to discuss how best to receive a reporter from *Rolling Stone* magazine who was traveling all the way from America to interview us, and would be arriving the next day. Ultimately, the only thing we could really come up with was the need to buy matching night-sky-blue track suits with raised white stripes, so that we could receive him in appropriately idiotic dress. So we went outside at the end of the last workday before his arrival to search for the suits.

There were no sporting-goods stores within a one-mile radius, but within five minutes we came upon an old woman standing near the metro station. She was selling night-sky-blue track suits, in size 56. Our size. We'd passed by that spot every day for months on the way to work, and never seen her. Now, on the one day when we really needed two size-56 night-sky-blue track suits, she was standing there, holding *exactly two* size-56 night-sky-blue track suits, and nothing else. We paid her and went to our respective homes to sleep.

The *Moscow Times* that had been distributed to the embassy was, of course, actually a special April Fool issue of the *eXile* that we had spent the previous three days laboring over. If you looked closely, you could see the words *EXILE #35* written in fine print under the banner, but otherwise it was an exact copy of our competitors—and quite a vicious one at that. It wasn't the "Moscow Slimes," or "Moscow Time," or any other friendly send-up, but the *Moscow Times.* With the *Times*'s fonts, graphics, layout format, even the bylines of real *Times* writers. A key element of the joke was its clear libelous illegality.

The Kiriyenko lead story was meant to be taken seriously at first glance, and it had taken a fair amount of planning to create all the story elements. Filling the rest of the paper, though, was no problem, mainly because we had a set format: the real *Moscow Times* filled its news pages with exactly the same stories every day. In fact, we knew, putting out a paper like the *Moscow Times* is mainly a matter of dressing up a preselected assortment of clichés—photos of rock-throwing Arabs, alarmist headlines about the "creaky" Mir Space Station, very big adjective-rich articles telling us what kind of weather we're having, insufferably boring op-ed pieces by hurrumphing laissez-faire realists, a sports section, and Dilbert cartoons, all capped with a letter from the editor which shows the pros and cons of

Our April 1 parody of a typical *Moscow Times* editorial. Editor Winestock was known to describe some of his columns as "waffly."

6 ❖ Wednesday, April 1, 1998

EDITORIAL

A Difficult Choice For Yeltsin

President Boris Yeltsin faced a difficult choice last night when he received news that new Prime Minister Sergei Kiriyenko had been detained in an embarrassing nightclub fracas.

Yeltsin had no reason to be dissatisfied with Kiriyenko's work: under Kiriyenko's watch, the economy finally began to show signs of real growth, with industrial production rising three-fifths of one-tenth of a percent last week. When the history books are written, Kiriyenko's commitment to reform will be duly noted.

Nonetheless, Kiriyenko was hardly the ideal choice to lead Russia's economy into the 21st century, and his detention in a violent imbroglio at a Moscow nightclub may yet be seen as a fortuitous break in the country's ongoing search for a real dynamic young reformer to head its government.

Following Kiryenko's tenure at the White House, Russia is finally stable and at peace. Nonetheless, the bespectacled young technocrat never once displayed the kind of tough mettle in pushing through reforms that so many people had hoped he would when he was first named Prime Minister. Instead, he seemed content to remain in relative anonymity, allowing key decisions about the economy to be made by people who actually held power.

Certainly, the speed with which Kiriyenko was dismissed is a sad reflection of Russia's continued intolerance for the personal lifestyle choices of its citizens. This is a shame.

There has been some talk that Yeltsin may attempt to place American investor George Soros in the post, but it is unlikely that the Duma would ratify such a choice. Although he would doubtless put a stop to the type of robber baron capitalism which has kept Russia relatively isolated from the world economy, Soros would inevitably become a lightning rod for nationalists and hardliners seeking an excuse to put up obstacles to reform.

Bank Menatep President Mikhail Khodorkovsky has also been forwarded as a possible replacement, and there are certainly many salutary aspects to his candidacy. However, [illegible] be desirable in any case.

Yeltsin may be thinking of the other "young reformer," Boris Nemtsov. It has long been no secret that the former Nizhny Novgorod governor is the apple of Yeltsin's mind's eye. The naming of ally Alexander Braverman as acting prime minister would seem to favor Nemtsov's candidacy.

A year of internecine battles in the rough-and-tumble world of Kremlin politics have exposed some weaknesses, but Nemtsov remains the country's most articulate spokesman for reform and is the only true democrat in the President's inner circle. Of the available candidates, Yeltsin could do a lot worse.

Will Russia's mercurial President finally decide to give his government a leader truly determined to give reform a one-and-for-all test drive? We can only hope for the best. As it stands, only one thing is certain: it is a difficult choice.

The *eXile*'s defeatist letter from the editor, explaining why the weekly format was abandoned.

26.03.98 31.03.98 www. exile. ru #09 P.4

editorial

In a move that is sure to gladden the hearts of people everywhere who hate this newspaper, the eXile is switching back to its old biweekly format. Beginning in mid-April, the paper will again publish 24 pages every two weeks, rather than 16 pages weekly.

Greed Not Funny

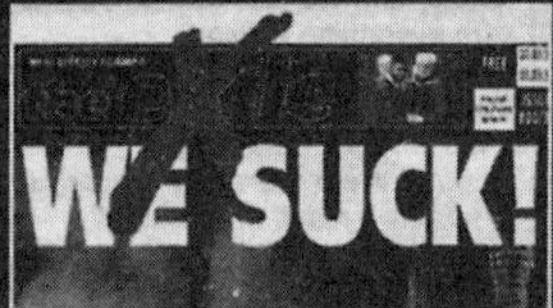

We'd like to say the reasons are financial. They're not. The issue here was quality. The weekly format sucked. It wasn't funny. When the first print runs came off the press, we didn't want to see it. The only things the writers ever looked at later were the comics, and that's only because they didn't draw them ourselves.

The weekly launch of the eXile is a classic example of what happens when people who have no business trying to make a lot of money get greedy. There wasn't a single creative reason to lay twice as many eXiles on the eXpat community as before, but we did it anyway, because we had this dumb idea that it would make us more money. We never calculated how much money—we just knew it would be more.

Bohemian people are pretty poor at economic planning. They're so unused to financial rewards that all you have to do is say the word "raise" to them, and right away they're bracketing in car payments and a sauna. It doesn't matter if the raise in question is only enough for a couple of dinners out a month. For these people, a raise is one size, fits all.

It wasn't worth it. By the third weekly issue, no one on the staff was talking to one another. Long-buried resentments rose to the surface and flared out in ugly production-night spats. We were pulling three all-nighters a week, and every hour of lost sleep inevitably got blamed on someone who didn't feel like he deserved it. And by the time a paper went to press, we were all waking up and realizing that it was time to go back to work again with all of those people we hated so much.

In the midst of all this, we made an amazing discovery. No one wanted to read the eXile once a week. At biweekly, we were all under the illusion that the public appetite for our genius was limited only by the conviction that no more could possibly be expected of us. We figured that by going weekly, we were just throwing a pebble in a Grand Canyon of demand.

We were wrong. As it turns out, we're pretty annoying. It took going weekly to realize that in the first year of our existence, people were only moved to read us by the numbing banality of ten consecutive issues of the Moscow Times. Five issues didn't cut it. For the vast majority of English-language readers in this city, our act was just barely tolerable for eight minutes or so out of every 14 days, despite the fact that we were distributed free and stacked in front of your face every time you went out to eat anywhere.

And that was when we were working at optimum efficiency. In the weekly regime, we quickly developed substance abuse problems and were soon struggling even to retain the motor skills needed to transfer the few consumptive ideas we had left onto paper. We lost weight and developed cavities. When we pretended to laugh at our own jokes to try to keep up morale around the office, we exposed mouths full of black teeth.

Readers could tell. As part of a "consumer survey" someone in the greed-minded end of the company thought up, we polled readers and asked them what they thought of the new format. A full 87% said the old format was better, a distressing statistic given the fact that only 19% of those same readers classified the old format as "good" or better in a four-point scale. A full 37% of readers said the eXile staff "should not quit their day jobs," while a good 11% said we "suck." Worse still, more than 94% of those who said they read the eXile only did so for the ads.

Anyway, we're going biweekly again. We apologize deeply to our readers for overestimating our ability to deliver a good product. It won't happen again. We will still suck, but we will do it less frequently, and with much greater humility. The one thing we regret is that we can't go out of business entirely. We're scheduled to keep going for at least a few more years. Things are so bad, we might even settle down— and start families.

both sides of an issue before instructing readers that "time will tell."

We did all that, making the clichés as grotesque as possible. There was a "rock-throwing Arab" story about Israeli Prime Minister Benjamin Netanyahu's decision to relocate the entire Palestinian population into a single condominium, a "Weather Returns" headline, and so on. For our "hurrumphing" op-ed piece, we were surprised to find that it only took a very gentle edit to make the Unabomber manifesto into a believably staid pro-IMF editorial about the benefits of reform to post-communist Russia. There were also lots of nasty little barbs directed at individual MT writers, even an article about the resignation of editor Winestock (whom we'd harassed all year by constantly referring to him as "interim editor Geoff Winestock"), but the most obnoxious thing about the issue was its absolutely perfect resemblance to the *Moscow Times.* Mark, Kevin, Ilya, and I—four people—had done in 72 drug-addled, sleep-deprived hours what the *Moscow Times* employed over sixty people to do in a

The Moscow Times

SINCE 1992

THE EXILE NO.35 WEDNESDAY, APRIL 1, 1998 WWW.EXILE.RU

Investor Lashes Out At Russian Cheaters

Local miners battle junk bond whiz over embattled mine. Page 12.

NCAA Hoop Tourney Ends in 2 OT Thriller

Utes and Cats clash in unforgettable final. Page 14.

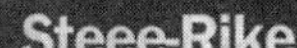

Steee-Rike!

Meet the lycra-clad king of Moscow's burgeoning nightclub scene. MT Out.

RUBLE RATE

MT INDEX

DOLLAR RUBLE

Sex Scandal Rocks Kremlin

By David McHugh

STAFF WRITER

Just days after he was permanently nominated to the post of prime minister, Sergei Kiriyenko was fired after being arrested in an embarrassing early-morning nightclub fracas that analysts say may signal a new round of hostilities in the so-called "Banker's War."

Kiriyenko, 35, was one of 17 men detained by special police forces in a wild early-morning fracas at the "Chameleon" nightclub in the Krasnopresnensky region. Deputy State Property Committee Chief Yury Medvedev and former Presidential Advisor Boris Kuzik were also reportedly arrested in the commotion, which police say broke out after midnight following an argument between the officials and a group of unidentified men.

Presidential spokesman Sergei Yastrzhembsky issued a curt statement to the Interfax state news service late in the morning indicating that President Yeltsin had dismissed Kiriyenko and Medvedev from their posts "in connection with assignment to other duties."

Alexander Braverman, also of the State Property Committee, was named acting Prime Minister by Yeltsin, Interfax reported.

No reason was given for the dismissal, but the site of the arrest is almost certainly at the heart of the controversy. Chameleon is known as a popular nightlife haven of Moscow's gay community.

Analysts said that Yeltsin may have dismissed Medvedev and his new protege Kiriyenko after deciding that the incident had rendered both men politically non-viable.

"Yeltsin's only reason for nominating Kiriyenko in the first place was to have his own person at the reins of government," said Andrei Piontkovsky of the Center for Strategic Studies. "Now, following this incident, Kiriyenko's authority in government will be automatically compromised by his perceived political weakness."

Moscow police spokesman Andrei Kiselyov said that all three officials were released shortly after

See SEX, Page 2

Nightclub Fracas Too Much For Yeltsin

By Dmitry Zaks

STAFF WRITER

Even as President Boris Yeltsin was publicly toying with the idea of making Sergei Kiriyenko his permanent choice for the post of Prime Minister, observers wondered whether or not the relative

NEWS ANALYSIS

anonymity of the young Fuel and Energy ministry graduate might turn out to be as much a handicap as a benefit to the President in his efforts to retain control over his government.

Nearly all observers thought that Kiriyenko, 35, was chosen as acting Prime Minister precisely because of his neophyte status in government, and not because of any particular personal qualities he brought to the post. Analysts said that Kiriyenko's lack of a political power base made him totally dependent on Yeltsin, making it possible for the aging President to head off potential threats to his authority throughout the remainder of his term.

But following an embarrassing incident in which Kiriyenko was detained at a nightclub known as a popular haven for Moscow's gay community, it appears that Yeltsin may have failed to properly calculate the disadvantages of naming an

See ANALYSIS, Page 2

ELIZABETH SCHWARZKOPF / REUTERS

Moscow police securing the premises of the nightclub "Chameleon" following the brawl involving Prime Minister designate Sergei Kiriyenko.

Customs Officials Target U.S. Travellers

By Bronwyn McLaren

STAFF WRITER

Most passengers who wait in the incoming passport control line at Sheremetyevo 2 Airport don't even notice the beige, unassuming door adjacent to the diplomatic passport control booth. Brian and Pearl Edwards, a retired American couple from Florida, learned exactly what that room is for last Saturday evening, when customs authorities detained them on suspicion of mulling narcotics.

"It was horrible," said Brian Edwards, 67, who came to Moscow on his first-ever vacation outside of America. "They yelled at my wife and me in Russian, and we couldn't understand a thing of what they were saying. And then they made us undress."

According to the couple, customs authorities brutally forced them to strip in the room, which they said was cold and packed with eleven officials, many of whom laughed and smoked. Both Americans say they were subjected to full cavity searches, including Pearl Edwards, who just a year ago underwent a hysterectomy. Russian customs officials reportedly did not take heed of the 65-year-old former nurse's pleas not to perform a cavity search, leaving her distraught. The couple was transferred to a detention center on the airport

See STRIP, Page 2

The cover page of our April 1 phony Moscow Times issue.

day. The *Times* had over 25 staff writers, kept dozens of freelance contributors in tow, and subscribed to every major wire service to fill its pages; on the other hand, we wrote all 95 article entries ourselves and even had time to design some of the ads. The *Times* had reportedly spent tens of thousands of dollars and months of research designing its bland "MT OUT" clubbing section: Ilya did it in six hours, lifting the fonts from a can of air freshener. The whole thing was a monument to the childish simplicity of the straight-news newspaper business.

But the cruelest indictment of the *Moscow Times* on April 1 hadn't even come as a result of anything we'd done. It was their own doing—a tiny item on page 4 of the actual April 1 edition of the *Moscow Times*, which for some reason had been poorly distributed that day and only occasionally could be found sitting in stacks next to its evil *eXile* twin brother. The item was a small, 300-word story at the bottom of the page which announced that a tiny breakaway Russian republic had declared war on the Vatican. The byline on the story belonged to a heretofore unknown freelancer named "Babar Glupov," whose name translated as "Babar Stupid," the leader of the breakaway republic, as reported in the article, was a certain Mr. "Durakilov," a name oddly reminiscent of the Russian word "Durak," or "fool." This was, of course, the *Times*'s own effort at an April Fool's

No parody of an Independent Media publication like the *Moscow Times* could be complete without an ad for a fictional Independent Media launch of a Russian-language version of *Juggs* magazine.

WE'RE HIRING!

Independent Media is proud to announce the addition of a new publication to its growing family of monthly magazines. In conjunction with the Bob Guccione Group of the United States, Independent Media will shortly be launching *Djags*, a Russian-language version of the successful Guccione publication *Juggs*. It is our hope that *Djags* will help fill the gap in the Russian market for magazines devoted to men's issues. Hunting, fishing, snowboarding, and photography are among the many relevant issues that will be tackled by the staff of promising young writers we hope to attract to *Djags*.

In accordance with our company's stated goal of maintaining the highest professional standards possible, we plan on hiring people at our own expense to work on the new magazine project. We are currently seeking to fill the following positions:

- **Managing Editor**
  Responsibilities:
  Holds photographer's leash
  Makes aesthetic adjustments
  Provides cover story to parents
  Receives served process
- **Talent Scout**
  Requirements:
  Own car with trunk
  Contacts in the state orphanage system
  Immunity to clofeline
- **Models**
  Requirements:
  Humongous Honkers
  Dyed blonde hair with roots showing
  Lobotomy, with certificate of attestation

If you feel you have what it takes to be a candidate for any of these positions, please apply to our offices before April 21, 1998.

ДЖАГС
май , 1998 №1
Да Здраствует
Гравитация!

Our address: 24 Ulitsa Pravdy tel: 257-30-10 fax: 257-32-11

W O R L D The Moscow Times

Housing Plan Irks Palestinians

By Muhammed Goldberg
THE ASSOCIATED PRESS

NABLUS, The West Bank—Palestinian sources reacted negatively yesterday to a new peace proposal by hardline Israeli Prime Minister Benjamin Netanyahu, calling it "insulting and demeaning."

Netanyahu's bold plan envisages moving the entire autonomous Palestinian authority into a single two-story house in the West Bank town of Nablus. Netanyahu claimed that Israeli security concerns led it to revise the Oslo Accords and to take back all of the land thus far ceded to Yasser Arafat's control, leaving the Palestinians with a 2,350 square foot house on the outskirts of town.

The house, which is in need of minor repairs, also boasts a small garage and cable television access.

"Israel is a small nation surrounded by enemies," Netanyahu told reporters outside of the Knesset. "For security reasons, it is impossible for us to cede more of our territory."

While Palestinian leaders decried the proposal as yet another example of Netanyahu's lack of commitment to the peace process, the U.S. State Department remained cautious. "We are studying the details," said a spokesperson.

Dennis Ross, the U.S. representative for peace talks in the Middle East, is said to be proposing that Netanyahu modify his plan and allow the Palestinians to set up a semi-autonomous state in a 2,880 square foot town house closer to the central square, but Netanyahu is reportedly defiant.

"If we offer them a duplex, then why not offer them an entire apartment block?" Netanyahu angrily told a conference of Likud Party members. "And if not an entire apartment block, then what is to stop them from demanding all of Israel, including Encino?"

DIETRICH FISCHER DIESKAU / REUTERS

The winner of the Be the Millionth Arab Photographed Throwing a Rock contest.

Markets reacted positively to the announcement as shares on the Tel Aviv stock exchange rose a modest 1.1 percent. Traders said that there was likely to be further upward movement in the belief that the Palestinians would eventually accept a "duplex compromise," although the issue of how an entire government, not to mention the 1.7 million Palestinians who live in the West Bank, could fit into a single duplex has yet to be worked out.

"We're still hammering out the fine print," said the spokesperson.

Jewish groups in America are said to be backing Netanyahu publicly, although privately, they are said to be in favor of Ross's duplex proposal.

Colin Powell, considered by many to be a leading candidate for the Republican presidential nomination in 2000, denounced the Clinton Administration's attempts to pressure Israel, while former President Jimmy Carter is said to be preparing a peace mission of his own.

Meanwhile, militant Jewish settlers denounced Netanyahu's proposal as a sell-out to the Palestinians. Eiten Sachs, a leader of the right-wing Tsimodet Movement, vowed that his group would never allow the Palestinians to set up a sovereign nation in the house, located at 38 Khalil Lane.

"That house where the so-called Palestinians are planning to set up their state is a sacred site to all Jews. Bernie and Mildred Finkelstein built that house more than forty years ago, before being forced to sell it. We will never allow that house to become Arab land."

One of the permanent features of the *Moscow Times* was its page-5 "Rock-Throwing Arab" story. In our April 1 version, protests had erupted over a proposed Israeli move to put the entire Palestinian population in one half of a duplex.

joke—delivered with all the wacky corporate wit of a tampon brochure, and the subtlety of the emergency broadcast system. It was the work of an organization terrified to its core that its clients might suspect it of having a genuine sense of humor.

Mark and I made the rounds that day, hanging out anywhere newspapers were distributed. Everywhere we went, total strangers approached us to offer congratulations. Even the stuffiest of businessmen winked at us and patted our backs. We didn't pay for a meal or a drink all day. For a few hours anyway, the expat community—the same people we'd been slamming for over a year—made us the toast of the town. We were assholes, and we stood for all the wrong things—but at least we weren't bores. And that counted for something.

SC Johnson wax
Glade

A can of air freshener...

MT out

...and a bad nightlife guide?

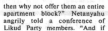

Our mad publisher, Ilya, came running out of the bathroom one day holding this can of Glade and pointing to the MT Out section of our rivals.

I N B R I E F

Isles Threaten Russia

■ MOSCOW (MT)—If Russia achieves less than 7.5 percent year-on-year economic growth over the next 47 years, it will soon drop behind Tonga and Reunion Island in terms of gross domestic product, a senior Russian analyst predicted Tuesday.

Andrei Illarionov, director of the Independent Moscow Institute for Economic Analysis, told reporters that Russia ranked 14th in the world for absolute gross domestic product in 1997, and would slip down in the rankings if it did not achieve at least 7.5% annual growth.

He said, however, that that figure was not reachable, indicating that Russia would soon fall behind Fiji, Tonga, and a host of other tropical islands. Reunion, the nearest threat to Russia in the rankings, has advanced in the course of the last year due to increased trade in sea shells.

Illarionov was presenting his new book, *Russia Below Your Feet.*

Metals Set to Go

■ MOSCOW (MT)—Russia's State Reserve for Precious Metals is prepared to start selling platinum group metals and other commodities for cash, changing its previous policy of simply giving them away for nothing, officials said Tuesday.

Reserve official Valery Goncharov said that the sales would go through as soon as the government grants the appropriate licenses. Those would most likely be given out after the 1999 budget is passed.

While Russia has not exported metals for months, Goncharov denied that . Russian stocks were depleted. Rather, he said, the metals had been distributed to reserve officials for their own use.

Markets Respond

■ MOSCOW (MT)—Markets reacted favorably Tuesday to news that the entire world had been fired.

The Dow Jones jumped 2000 points as investors rewarded companies that had committed to putting a lid on spending.

The CAC-40 rose 73% as France welcomed the news that there would now be more time for lunch.

Our phony *Moscow Times* "briefs."

Moscow's Only Alternative!

ISSUE#18 [019] •SEPTEMBER 25, 1997•FREE

Meet Michael Bass

All About Vladimir Zhirinovsky's New Imagemaker

page 2

BY MATT TAIBBI

CHAPTER FOUR: MICHAEL BASS

y first contact with *eXile* archenemy Michael Bass wasn't even contact. It was a missed meeting.

It was the spring of 1996. I was working on the news desk at the *Moscow Times.* Mine was an important strategic seat in the newsroom. I sat directly behind and to the left of then news editor Robin Lodge, facing reporter/revolutionary orator-descendant-and-namesake Patrick Henry, and to the left of politics reporter and chain-smoking hypochondriacal conspiracy theorist Jonas Bernstein, who was 40 years old—30 if you didn't count the ten years in the sixties and seventies that he'd missed while he was doing acid and listening to Led Zeppelin and Cream albums in his basement.

Bernstein's desk was always covered with a huge pile of newspapers and notebook sheets covered in indecipherable pencil scratches. He'd sink lower and lower in his chair as the workday progressed, and his face would turn blood red from stress. While other reporters focused their energy horizontally, in a direct beam between their head and their computer screen, Bernstein was operating in both longitude and latitude on a perilous mental sea—trying desperately to keep his pile of highlighted newspapers, audio tapes, and notes in line long enough to coax something intelligible on to his screen before it all spun out of control.

Bernstein's daily struggle was the only thing that made my workday at the *Moscow Times* bearable. Every day I would watch him closely out of the corner of my right eye, keeping close track of his rising stress level. After a long day of reading magazines and playing video games, I would at about 4 P.M. make a few phone calls, then ostentatiously write my vapid article with a minimum of effort and worry in what would seem like a matter of minutes. Then I'd push a button on my keyboard to send it to the editor, turn slightly in Bernstein's direction, and wait.

Somewhere between 7:00 and 8:00 P.M. every day, Bernstein would reach critical mass. His papers would begin spilling off of his desk in a panic: deadline would come and go and he would always be hopelessly late, well past the point when the article could conceivably be finished in time to get into the next day's issue; shame and despair would begin to creep across his face, and, worse still, you could see that a faint trace of a snappy sentence would occur to him as he was hurrying to finish up, only he wouldn't get it right away—he'd freeze, struggling to

The *Moscow Times* newsroom, circa 1996. Beleaguered hack Jonas Bernstein (center, in glasses) sinks his in chair, struggling to write his lead. Taibbi seated at far right.

wrest it out of the drug-addled corners of his mind as the clock ticked away, and . . . not get it.

And at exactly that moment, when the reality of failure and missed opportunity and age met him face to face, I'd lean over with a friendly smile on my face and say:

"Hey Jonas! How're you doing, pal?"

"Fuck you!" he'd scream. "You always do this! Fuck you!"

On the day Michael Bass called I was perched in my seat, article finished, staring at Bernstein and waiting. It was already dark out and Bernstein looked about 40 minutes and a couple of bags of potato chips shy of his Old Faithful act.

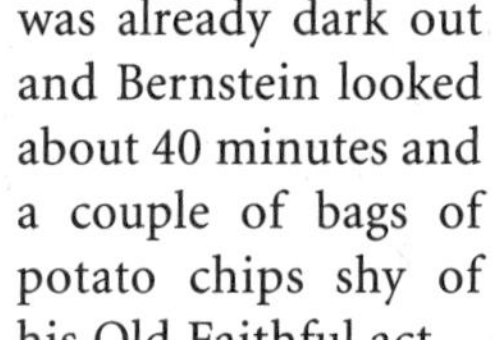

Then, behind me, the phone rang. The seats behind me were occupied almost exclusively by female reporters. That side of the newsroom was where phone calls that were from people in search of a sympathetic ear went to. No one was around, so I hesitatingly crossed into that territory and picked up the phone.

"Hello, this is Michael Bass," the voice said. "Who's this?"

I frowned. Michael Bass was an American and a strange nightlife figure who had some kind of job in a couple of casinos in town and had been hassling every reporter on the staff to help publicize some charity program he was apparently involved with. I knew through notorious MT features reporter and degenerate friend Owen Matthews that the completely bald, white, and round, Bass also had some kind of connection with prostitutes; he'd taken Owen out on a docked cruise ship once and offered him a selection of whores, and nothing had happened because Owen was broke . . . it was one of those stories you never quite remember the details of, but of which the essential slimy memory sticks.

Bass pitched his charity story to me. It was a "women's shelter" which he said was being unfairly shut down by the city. He wanted to rally the foreign community behind him with the help of the *Moscow Times.*

I listened closely to Bass's plaintive, even voice. If this story was bogus—and from what I'd heard, the "women's shelter" was actually a brothel—his sanctimonious good-guy act was really impressive. For sheer balls alone, he deserved some credit. I shrugged and agreed to meet him the next day.

The next day I ordered a driver and headed over to the building just off Tverskaya Street in the center of town that housed Bass's shelter. But when I got there I realized that I'd left the exact address back at the office. I paused for a moment, then in a sudden burst of contempt and irresponsibility decided to leave Bass hanging.

"Fuck it," I thought.

A half hour later my driver and I returned to work, shrugging as we walked through the hall.

"Bass didn't show up," I told my editor.

"Asshole," he said.

Bass called almost immediately. He screamed and yelled, but I took the strong position that I had actually been there and he hadn't showed up.

"Never in my life have I missed a meeting," he said in a wounded voice. "I'm shocked."

But I insisted, convincingly, that I'd been there. Then I somehow managed to pawn him off on another reporter and snuck back to my own comfortable work routine. I was safe. Bass was known as a pain in the ass. No one would believe his story over mine. And no one would care enough to listen to him anyway.

year later, I was fleeing the city on account of Bass. As editor of the *eXile*, I'd published a brutal exposé on him, and afterward he'd called up and threatened to kill me, a threat that caused me to consult with the FBI and split town. And that was just the beginning.

The story of the 1997 war between the *eXile* staff and Michael Bass is a sordid, absurd, and tragic tale of what happens to foreigners when they are allowed to operate outside their culture's usual moral and ethical standards for any significant length of time. Michael Bass was a bona fide criminal who came to Russia to become respectable, while we were American kids from the suburbs with an unhealthy curiosity about the sleazy underworld people like Bass came from. We shared a flair for self-promotion that caused us all to become public figures in the foreign community in Moscow—and when we clashed, it got a lot more serious and a lot uglier than either side would have expected.

Bass was a convicted felon; he'd done time in California for mail fraud in the 1980s. How and why he had arrived in Moscow was a mystery to a lot of people, but by the time I went to work for the *eXile*, I'd heard what just about everyone else who'd been in town seemed to know already, which was that he'd been working as a peculiarly Muscovite form of "modeling agent" for many years. Eventually I would even be shown a stack of "résumés" for his modeling agency "Karin." The holder of that stack was a friend of mine who'd been passed them by a Bass associate on the understanding that any of the girls in the pictures were available for a price. In any case, Bass formally made his living as a consultant to clubs and casinos, which he kept packed full of his teenybopper models, and privately he appeared to be making money off those stacks of résumés and various special "excursions," about which more will come later.

Well . . . so what? The world is full of sleazebags. Only a few of them, though, have the gall to try and become respectable public figures, which is what Bass did by engineering a column for himself in the *Moscow Tribune.* "Bassworld" was, at the time of its creation, the only society column for the expat community. The column read like a newsletter for a Beverly Hills rehab clinic, which may in fact have been where Bass's style originated from; the protagonist playing the role of the group therapist in every weekly installment was Bass himself, whose eerie bright white head, puffy body, and purplish lips appeared smiling alongside the patient-subjects of his society notes.

Despite his syrupy prose and saccharine good-guy therapist voice, Bass apparently had a temper. He was the type of guy who went around town demanding free drinks, hassling women, and abusing doormen and security guards, and along the way he made a lot of enemies. Within just a few months after joining the *eXile* I was inundated with requests from what few readers we had at the time to do something on Bass. Mark and I weren't against the idea. After all, Bass wrote for a competitor, and he brought in a lot of business for the *Trib.* Nauseating as it was, his column was the only thing in the paper worth reading. And after all, it was offensive that a guy who made his living packing nightclubs full of destitute Russian girls would host dinners for ambassadors and worm his way into photo opportunities with people like Bill Clinton, Benjamin Netanyahu, and King Juan Carlos of Spain.

So when one of our clients gave us the idea to reprint a chapter of a book called *You'll Never Make Love in This Town Again* that showed Bass in a very

Sculpted At Birth?

Cowed and bloodied Casanova restaurant manager Michael Bass...

...and an ugly discarded statue behind the Dom Khudozhnika?

unflattering light, we had no objections. Although that client, who unfortunately has to remain nameless, offered to publish the thing as a paid advertisement, we stupidly said we'd just enter it in as straight unpaid editorial, since we thought it was a legitimate story.

The book, which had been a *New York Times* best-seller, had been written by rock groupies who described their sexual experiences with people like Don Henley and George Harrison. It contained a chapter about Bass that was written by "Liza," one of the four authors of the book. Liza had met Bass back in he days when he was still living in Beverly Hills and was working as a modeling agent; the chapter told a story of how he'd offered her a job as a runway model in Paris. The Paris job turned out to be as a sex slave for an Arab prince, and when the girl refused the work, Bass locked her in a hotel and kept her doped up on Quaaludes. . . . The story wrapped up in semicomic fashion when the model tied sheets together and lowered herself in her bra and panties out of a second-story window onto the Paris street, where she was indifferently rescued by a local bartender who let her use his phone.

In short, it was good stuff—the kind of thing we all felt had to be shared with the *Tribune*'s readers.

Mark was on vacation when the Bass piece came out on Thursday, May 8. Almost immediately, on Friday, I got a frantic call from Jane Butchman, a friend of ours who worked as the food and beverage manager at the Beverly Hills Club. Liz was a young American divorcée with cropped hair who loudly advertised her s&m leanings. Her defining character trait was an inability to keep phone calls short. Mark and I both got along well with her, but for fear of hearing all about her latest bad date, we almost never answered our phones.

Liz, however, was our main link to Bass. Bass did promotional work for the Beverly Hills Club, and the two saw each other all the time. Liz and Bass didn't get along, probably because Bass suspected that Liz was trying to get the club owners to get rid of him. Also, I think, the two of them frequently fought over the right to use the club limousine.

"Matt," Liz said, "I spent hours last night talking to Michael Bass. He's thinking about having you killed."

"What?" I said.

"I think I have him calmed down. . . . But he was saying that his roof wants you dead, and he's not sure what to do. But I think I've convinced him that it would be a bad idea."

"*What roof?*" I shrieked. "What's he talking about?"

"His roof. . . . He says that when they saw the article, they wanted to kill you right away. Bass was really crazy last night. He'd be nice to me half the time, then all of a sudden he'd start screaming. He kept talking about how everyone says I was always sucking cock in the kitchen when I worked at Azteca—can you believe that?"

I cut her off. "What did he say about me again?"

"He said he's not sure what to do. His people apparently want you dead. I just couldn't believe that thing he said about me sucking cock. What an asshole!"

After I got off the phone with Liz, I called Bass right away. I told him that, while I wouldn't print a retraction, I was willing to publish his side of the Paris story. He hedged, diving straight into his creepy rehab-therapist voice:

"I don't know, Matt," he said. "I just don't know what to do. I mean, I'm really hurt about this. I cried. And you know, the worst thing is that my charity programs are going to suffer. That's the thing that hurts the most."

Was all this really happening to me? Was he serious? "So what are you planning to do?" I asked.

"I don't know. . . . My roof wanted to kill you right away, but I really don't know what to do. I mean, what are my options? I can have you killed, or I can pay someone a couple of hundred bucks to have your legs broken, or I can just let it go. And I don't like any of those options."

"Michael, I can't believe you're threatening me like this. What is this, the Solntsevo gang? You're talking about having me killed."

"I'm not threatening you," he insisted.

"You're sitting here, saying you don't know what you want to do, and talking about having me killed as one of your options! That's a threat from where I sit."

"I'm not threatening you."

"Michael, if I understand it as a threat, then that's the only thing that matters. I'm the subject of the threat. Can't you see that distinction?"

"No, I'm not threatening you. But listen." He laughed. "You have to understand, Matt, I travel in the kind of crowd where. . . . Well, it's dangerous for me if you do this and I let you get away with it. You realize that, right?"

I said nothing.

"I mean," he continued, "did you ever think about what might happen to you if you do something like this in this town? People get hurt for things like this."

Bass eventually refused my offer and hung up. In a panic I called the U.S. Legal Attaché office at the embassy—the FBI. I knew that they had no arresting power in the city, but I thought that if I could arrange a sit-down between them, the Moscow police, and Bass, then I would be covered. That way, if something happened to me, Bass would know he'd be picked up right away.

Agent Dennis Cosgrove agreed to meet me in a half hour at the north gate of the embassy. I raced over there and found him waiting. He was a tallish man with slightly thinning wavy hair, a mustache, and a stiff, proud, sheriffy walk. Back straight, hands swinging confidently at his side, he led me into the embassy and into a cafeteria next to the swimming pool. As a courtesy, he bought me a diet soda. We sat with our two cans of Diet Coke, two decent Americans, talking against the white concrete cafeteria wall.

Cosgrove listened to my story carefully. They'd had complaints about Bass before. He began asking me if I'd ever heard that Bass was dealing in pornography. I said I didn't know anything concrete. He frowned and leaned back.

"So, you're with the *eXile*," he said.

"Yes," I said. "I'm the editor."

"You go out to all those clubs?"

"Sure," I said.

"You know what's amazing?" he said. "There are so many beautiful women in this city. I mean, I walk around town, or sometimes I'm on the subway, and it's like, I just can't believe it. Where do they come from?"

"I don't know," I said, shrugging. "The provinces?"

"And the other amazing thing is that they all turn into such monsters when they get older. You see those older women? They're huge!"

"Yeah, I know." I said.

"Amazing," he said, shaking his head and then sipping his soda.

"So," I said, clapping my hands, "what should I do about Bass?"

"Well, I would say, at this point, just take normal safety precautions," he said, looking away.

"Okay," I said. "But . . . wouldn't I just get shot in the back of the head in my doorway, if something was going to happen? I wouldn't have any warning."

"Well, yes, I guess that's true. But I don't think you have anything to worry about . . . "

After I left the embassy I decided to leave town for a while. Not wanting to be alone, I packed my things and went straight to Bernstein's apartment. Now retired and happily freelancing in the comfort of his own home, his stress level had dropped significantly. When I showed up at his place, he was lazily playing his guitar and smoking a cigarette.

"You look tense. Want some tea?" he said.

He made tea. I sat in his living room staring out the window. Soon he poked his head in from the kitchen.

"Sugar?" he said.

"Sure," I answered.

He laughed. He knew the whole story. "Sure, have some sugar," he said. "You know—*live a little!*"

That weekend I did all of the things easily rattled people do after getting a threat from a would-be serious source. I worked out elaborate plans for leaving the country and suffered bad hypochondriacal episodes. Why was I sweating at night? Was I sick? And what was that pain in my abdomen? It made some eerie kind of sense that I would get a lymphoma by chance just exactly at the moment I had imperiled my life by design.

I missed my family. One thing about being home: You never feel farther than a phone call away from having all

#13 • July 31 - August 13, 1997 • P. 4

TOP TEN
WAYS TO AVOID APPEARING IN BASSWORLD

1. Mention you know his parole officer
2. Ask him to sign a copy of "You'll Never Make Love in this Town Again"
3. Wear garlic around your neck
4. Tell him that Sean Penn is in the other room, and Sean doesn't like flashbulbs
5. Ask him to put an apple on his head and to stand 100 meters away
6. Cancel your subscription to "Pre-Teens in White Panties"
7. Follow him around and pat his head
8. Hire Beverly Hills Club security staff to follow you to restaurant opening parties
9. Have hair
10. Carry a copy of the eXile with you at all times

* if you are female and under the age of 15, sorry, there's nothing we can do to help you - seek professional help immediately!

your worries taken care of. I considered performing some awful mea culpa before Bass in Moscow, then hurrying back to my parents' homes in New York and Boston. Apologize, cry on my mother's shoulder, and start over, with a smarter, safer life plan.

But I just couldn't imagine it. The idea of going home, to the awful "real world," made me want to cry. I felt trapped. So after a few days I went back to Moscow on a night train.

At the time I was living with that old *Moscow Times* friend of mine, Owen Matthews. I was pulling a Kato Kaelin in his luxurious apartment just south of the police headquarters on Petrovka Street. Owen and I went way back, but our relationship had changed lately. Two years before, we'd been the staff fuck-ups on the *Moscow Times.* He was a prematurely middle-aged Oxonian with slicked-back thinning hair and tight stretch slacks, while I was a dopey American who wore sneakers to work and didn't know who the Prime Minister was, and together we spent a whole summer loudly not getting laid. We had all kinds of ideas, some as dumb as just walking up and down the fabled Arbat street at night, politely leering at passersby, and hoping for a random act of God. But nothing worked, no matter how much Owen in his nervous lilt talked about "parking porky in the pigpen" in the MT stairwell where we all hung out smoking cigarettes.

Back then, Owen had been constantly broke and we'd both often borrowed money from each other when we had nothing left to buy food (or, in Owen's case, pay for cab fare—Oxonians don't take the subway). Now, however, Owen's operating nut was much bigger. His schmoozing skills had soared in those two years and he was inundated with pricey freelance assignments from splashy European magazines. And during the Bass affair, he was just about to be given a job on the bureau of *Newsweek*—the coveted reporter job in the city. He had a big stuccoed two-bedroom apartment with tasteful paintings he'd bought at auctions, delicate sugar bowls and other kitchen accoutrements, and a hardworking maid who came three times a week; Owen hadn't done a dish in over a year. He'd also honed his technique in two years and now had a fairly steady flow of not entirely ugly women who entered his apartment wary and doe-legged on weekend nights and sometimes gave in under heavy rhetorical pressure. Meanwhile my cash flow was next to nil and I was sacking out in his second bedroom for free, smoking his dope and burdening his maid with my filthy underthings. And my social life was limited to a couple of disastrous low-sex entanglements with hysterical Russian teenagers, whose sloppy denouements reflected the excessive amount of time I'd been spending worrying about my newspaper.

"You shouldn't have done that to Bass," said Owen, when I came home. "He's really upset."

I stared at him. Was it possible that my *roommate* had been talking, socially, to someone who had just threatened to kill me? Dressed in a green silk robe, Owen leaned back in his chair and took a drag on a Gitanes. I knew him well and knew he had a weird Moriarty-esque flair for moral ambiguity—an admiration for poisoners, plotters, and turncoats, for stylish and desperate scoundrels. It was some sort of literary pose he had picked up at Oxford, and it freaked me out. I knew he liked to hedge his bets and play both sides of the fence, but I wouldn't have guessed he would have done that here. I was caught totally by surprise.

He kept laughing at me, trying to explain to me that Bass wasn't going to kill me, but the reasons he was giving were very conspicuously *reasons*—like that Bass was too much of a coward—not arguments that the whole thing was ridiculous, or even meaningless reassuring phrases like, "You have nothing to worry about," which I guess was what I wanted to hear. Then he'd get farther down on his cigarette and try to convince me to apologize to Bass, or print a retraction.

After that, I no longer felt safe at home.

Days passed, nothing happened, and finally Mark came back. A true friend, he jumped immediately into my corner, answering the phone when Bass called and telling him that he had okayed the piece, that it had been a joint decision. Now both of us were responsible.

By now the next issue was looming. Mark, Bass, and I entered into negotiations, which were annoyingly arbitered by the conspicuously unwelcome Owen, who kept calling the office late at night to press Bass's case. Bass wanted a retraction at most and a chance to tell his side of the story at the least. I insisted that, in light of the death threat, I would no longer publish his side of the story, unless I could publish a piece detailing the threats he'd made against me.

Bass hedged, then finally agreed. And here's where the story became really comic. The would-be assassin suddenly, on the phone, transformed into a meek freelancer.

"Does it need to be typed?" he asked.

"That would be nice," I said.

"Because I like to write by hand," he said.

"Well, whatever," I said. "We can type it in."

"What about spelling and grammar?" he asked. "My spelling isn't too good."

I paused. "Well," I said. "Try your best."

"Okay," he said brightly. "I'll get this right to you. It'll be there in a jiffy. I'll enjoy this!"

Three hours later a handwritten letter spilled over our fax machine. Mark and I read greedily. Filled with atrocious spelling and grammar mistakes, it was manna from heaven. The text was the work of a stone-cold obvious sex criminal. No one who read it could doubt that Bass belonged on a warning poster in every battered women's shelter in the world. My favorite part is his reference to the "alledged [*sic*] 1983 trip to Paris with a girl who in the book pretends to have never met me in Kansas but only [*sic*] in her imaginary trip of 83. [Eds. Note: If the trip was imaginary, that was strange, since Bass had contended to me that one of the holes in "Liza's" story was that she was on the 15th floor of the Paris Hilton, not the second.] She was tripping that's [*sic*] for sure."

spotlight and realise how easy it is to get
burned this tale about tails is considered
fiction. [illegible] my own mother [illegible] YES
Mom I could have found a better way to
entertain the [illegible]. I hope to receive
a quick settlement and appology letter
from the publisher and my [illegible] who
probably would sign it just that way
I of course appologize to everyone
who came in contract with me these
last two weeks. I was upset about
being singled out without you the
reader getting the benifit
[illegible] laughing through the juvenil[illegible]
set [illegible] Whore er stores by
[illegible] un HAPPY Hooker
who [illegible] earn 300 at night
flight lying down and turned
to lying the most pure form
of prostitution. Most humiliating
for me was comming from
The girl who came close to stalking
me for over four years calls me
1) an ugly nerd [illegible] with 2) no personality
and 3) claims we never had sex.
I hope most will agree she's
probably at least 2/3 wrong.

In any case, here is the whole text:

"Who Says I'll Never Make Love in This Town Again?"
by Michael Bass

"On Monday my legal team of Joseph J. Perrini and Raymond Markovich filed a $70,000,000 libel suit in N.Y. Supreme Court against Dove Books, its distributor, lawyers and private investigative firm which are all supposed to vet the book for at least obvious slander. And of course let's not forget Liza Greer Journalist/Hooker and of course my X lover who's intro reads under goals 'to finish high school and become a counselor to help other prostitutes and drug attics.' Well maybe she was Claudia Schiffer in appearance and Jethro Boden in brains but she was appealing to me in the late 1970s when I was in my early twenties Looking back she was like a boomerang which kept returning to my door step. Finally in late 1982 I refused to see her. Enter the tale of 1983 recreated 15 years later with the exact recall or flash back of Dorothy in the Wizard of Oz and full of imaginary people taking an imaginary trip. Lots of characters in this book Rod Stewart, Olivia Newton John, Vanna White, James Caan, Timothy Hutton, Jack Nicholson, Warren Beatty, Don Henley, Dennis Hopper, Sylvester Stallone, Stephano Caserachi, George Harrisson and Hugh Hefner to name drop a few.

"For those of you who have a life and are unfamiliar with Dove Books they are devoted to publishing smut written by X wives of personalities etc. Although I am about the least known figure in the book I am unfortunatly the olny one living in Moscow. Most o what is written is not contested by celebrities who prefer to ignor such books as this one in order not to further promote the lies contained inside. However since the book couldn't get any more publicity than the *eXile* already provided I will respond. Let's face it these girls did Oprah and every other talk show. Most of what was written about the others was behind closed doors and very difficult to contest. However I hope to lead the way by filling the first suit and calling everyone to join as a plaintif or witness. My case is supported by solid facts the chapter devoted to me makes reference to an alledged 1983 trip to Paris with a girl who in the book pretends to have never met me in Kansas, but only in her imaginary trip of '83. She was tripping thats for sure

"1) I was in America all of 1983

"2) I stopped seeing Liza in late 1982

"3) I never had the pleasure meeting the King of Saudi Arabia, King Fahd

"4) I never stayed in the Paris Hilton, I prefer the Ritz

"5) I never had Armed Arabic security guards dressed in tradditional attire wondering the champs ellysee with me—defiantly bizarre and Anti-Arab in nature!

"6) The whole chapter was written for illiterate housewives from Nebraska who think Naked Gun is a movie based on facts, Oliver North was telling the truth and corn should never be eaten off the Cobb.

"7)a) I am wondering why no one checked Liz's passport, hotel registration, plane ticket, immigration record, or I.Q. before print.

"b) How could she have yelled from the room and no one spoke English in Paris.

"c) Or maybe Inspector Cues should have questioned her tying two bed sheets together and then crawling from the third floor window like cattleman

"d) Eating lumpy oatmeal in a cheap hotel near the Champs Elise

"Maybe when your goal is cash accuracy and truth don't count.

"For those of you who have been in the spotlight, you realize how easy it is to get burned, and this tale about tails should be considered fiction. For my own mother I answer yes Mom I could have found a better way to entertain the king. I hope to receive a quick settlement and apology letter from the publisher and my x who probably would sign it just that way I of course apologize to everyone who came into contact with me these last two weeks. I was upset about being singled out without you the reader getting the benefit of laughing through this juvenile set of whore ER stores by this most UN HAPPY Hooker who couldn't earn 300 at Night Flight lying down and turned to lying the most pure form of prostitution. Most humiliating for me was coming from the girl who came close to stalking me for over four years calls me 1) an ugly nerd with 2) no personality and 3) claims we never had sex. I hope most will agree she's probably at least 2/3 wrong.

"If I ever wind up in a sex scandal again I hope I can be present and at least enjoy mycelia when I get screwed. As for Stallone, Nickolson Beatty and company. You'll never make love in this town and probably have to give up your careers. For me since I never made love in the book I hope next time I at least get the girl and more respect then Rodney Dangerfield."

We got his piece at 1 A.M. on production night. I was thrilled and had no intention of altering it. Bass's own text was my best defense. But then he called me, like any other freelancer would, and asked how I liked the article.

"So, what do you think?" he said. "Was it good?"

"It . . . had something," I said.

"Was it funny?" he asked hopefully. He was like a schoolkid.

"Yes," I said honestly. "It was."

"Listen," he said. "Can you clean up the grammar and the spelling for me? I know there are a few mistakes."

"I . . . what? No way!" I said. "Michael, you're a professional writer. You also threatened to kill me not long ago. Did you forget that? There's no way I'm going to edit your piece. You're a grown man and you can handle it."

"But I'll look illiterate," he said, dejected. He sounded shocked that I would betray him like this.

"Well," I said. "There's not a whole lot I can do about that."

"Look," he said. "I'll get someone to clean it up for me, and then I'll send it back to you, okay? Just give me a minute."

"It's pretty late," I said.

"Just hold on."

Two hours later a conspicuously cleaner, but no less demented, version of Bass's letter spilled over our fax. I looked at my watch, consulted with Mark, and together we decided to fuck him. The first version was funnier. And we wanted whoever had helped him—and we were pretty sure it was Owen—to have wasted those after midnight hours. We ran the first letter, then didn't speak to him for months.

But Bass wasn't done. Later that year, toward the end of the summer, he somehow managed to get himself hired by Vladimir Zhirinovsky as an imagemaker. Shunned by almost everyone in the foreign community after years of shenanigans and public scandals—including the *eXile* affair—Bass suddenly arose from the dead and started zooming around town in a Russian ZiL limousine (including a friendly stop at an *eXile* riverbank party), organizing press conferences and getting Zhirinovsky in the news. The whole thing was surreal; Bass spoke almost no Russian at all and was, very conspicuously, an American Jew, a strange partner for an ultranationalist anti-Semite like Zhirinovsky. It was the kind of thing that only made sense if you'd been living in Moscow for years.

Meanwhile, life had been moving steadily along at the *eXile.* We'd kept after Bass since the death-threat incident, feeling that he was game as long as he was still employed by the *Trib.* His sickly-sweet column had become more lovey-dovey than ever, and even featured pictures of Bass siding up to terrifying LogoVaz chief Boris Berezovsky—one of the most feared men in Russia—and describing him as being "in fine form" at a function at the Radisson-Slavyanskaya hotel. We responded with our own version of "Bassworld": The paper, in that time, had been growing; the Bass issue had caused us to be an eagerly anticipated scandal sheet, and as the summer progressed our revenues steadily rose as Kara stormed around town on her giant haunches extorting ad revenue out of restaurants and clubs. Owen and I reconciled after I matched his treachery by coming home drunk one night and hurling his visiting elderly father, a pretentious and irritating former British spy, across the room into the wall. The father-beating incident left us even and on good terms.

Bass's hiring as a Zhirinovsky aide made it inevitable that we would cross paths with him again. When the popular daily *Moskovsky Komsomolets* ran a feature of Bass with a shocking photograph of him, we found ourselves scrambling to find any story that would support putting that photograph on an *eXile* cover. We set to work digging up old and new Bass material, and in the meantime an angel visited—and arranged a guest spot for me on a new talk show.

The show was called *Akuli Pera*, or Sharks of the Quill, and was intended to be a forum for young political activists and journalists to ask questions of leading Russian political figures. When I was invited, through a contributor to our sister publication, *Ne Spa*, I was told the guest was going to be Gorbachev. But when I arrived at the set on a Saturday morning, word filtered around that the guest was going to be Zhirinovsky.

Sick and twisted as he was, I liked Zhirinovsky. I knew that, for the greater good, he should probably be shot, but he's at least funny—really funny, funnier than anyone in American public life. Once, years before, after he'd announced an intention to reclaim Alaska, I'd approached him at a press conference and asked him if he really planned to take Alaska back.

"Where are you from?" he quipped.

"Boston," I said.

"We'll take Boston too," he said.

Now, here I was, dressed in a new suit early in the morning, waiting to face Zhirinovsky at a talk show—and for once, in my whole career of press conferences, I had a *real* question to ask. About midway through the show, after the other young panelists had fired away a few questions about politics and started the great bullshitter rolling, I reached for the mike.

"About your new imagemaker Michael Bass . . . " I said.

"Michael, right, I've got one of those," he said.

"Did you know he'd done time in America for fraud?"

"Of course," Zhirinovsky said. "So what?"

"But that doesn't bother you, right?" I said, knowing the answer. A few years back, the Interior Ministry had released a report showing that Zhirinovsky's party, the LDPR, had over a dozen convicted felons in it. His party was the Oakland Raiders of politics—the place you go when you've fucked up one too many times. Its Duma headquarters had a great reputation for parties.

"No way," Zhirinovsky said, smiling. "Michael has fulfilled his societal obligations. . . . And in general, there's no such thing as a clean family. Dig deeply enough into any family, and you'll always find someone who's done time. It's normal."

The crowd applauded. I smiled. The exchange was shown on national television a few months later.

After that exchange Mark and I scrambled to get 2,000 words' worth of material on Bass ready and handed Ilya, our mad-scientist designer, a special picture of Bass, which had been taken at the Beverly Hills Club/casino a few weeks before.

This was a serious photograph. It had been taken after Bass had tried to force himself and Zhirinovsky into a banquet for ambassadors at the club. When security had denied them entrance—mainly because Zhirinovsky archenemy Boris Nemtsov was expected to dine at the event—Zhirinovsky called every news network in Moscow to cause a scandal. Once they were inside the club, Bass got into an argument with Ivan X—I can't and won't use his real name here—a fearsome local heavy in the Moscow gaming world. X, a giant hippopotamus-sized monster of a man who wore a size-56 suit, eventually lost his patience with Bass and smashed a whiskey glass on the American's bald head, crunching the splinters into his skull. The victim ran shrieking out of the restaurant, where he was met by a patiently waiting *Moskovsky Komsomolets* photographer who took the fateful photo.

There was an ugly undercurrent to this story. After the incident, Zhirinovsky and co. pushed Bass to press charges against Ivan X for assault. The problem there was that X was said to be a very heavily connected member of the Izmailovo mafia gang—some of the scariest people in the

the eXile — #11 • July 3 -

Bassworld Retrospective: Berlin, 1937

Like many people in the eXpat community, we were startled last week to read the entry in the Moscow Tribune society column "Bassworld," where favorite eXile suspect Michael Bass hinted at a friendship—and a set of mutual personal problems—with scary LogoVaz chief Boris Berezovsky.

"**Boris Berezovsky**," he wrote, using his trademark bold key, "was in great form as he entered the Sad-Sam Summer Solstice party.

"While enjoying the BBQ, he fielded questions regarding everything from **Anatoly Chubais** to his slander suite [sic] against *Forbes* Magazine. We agreed to meet soon as it was difficult to hear over the West African band **Melange**..."

Bass's flattering name-drops of figures like Berezovsky and others struck us as strange until we received word that he's done this for years. Many years, in fact. Professor Sam Weissov at Moscow State University sent us a note and a copy of a rare newspaper clipping: the society column from the 1937 Berlin expatriate newspaper the Berlin *Tribune*, at the time the third-leading English-language paper in Berlin. It seems Bass, who at the time was still a mere 47 years old, learned his journalism skills in a very fertile environment.

By Moenkle Basse

IMAGE REICH

SS Colonel Karl Koch finally held his posh ribbon-cutting at the sparkling new **Buchenwald** camp. **S.D. chief Reinhard Heydrich** organized everything, from the largest ice carving of its kind to a limbo contest with camp guards. **S.S. chief Heinrich Himmler** did not disappoint us, coming in his trademark black shirt, and even entertaining us by grabbing a watermelon and doing a very funny impersonation of Jesse Owens after the ceremony. **Franz von Papen**, fresh from declaring a state of emergency in former **Prussia**, was in fine form as he tested the nozzles in Buchenwald's swank new "shower" room.

Herr Goebbels and Herr Goering relaxing

While enjoying the buffet, he fielded questions regarding everything from the planned annexation of **Austria** to the Reich's grievance suit against the League of Nations, though it was difficult to hear over the 178-piece band commissioned by stylish state architect **Albert Speer**, who added very high pillars of light. We had hitched a ride with Soviet Foreign Minister **Vyacheslav Molotov**, who was in town for talks with Reich Foreign

Admiral Doenitz at the helm

Secretary **Herman Ribbentrop**. "Vyach" tasted sauerkraut and kartofelpuffer and confided in us that he and Herman were planning to study Polish together, which made us feel bad that we had never studied in school. The **4th annual Berlin Book Burning** was hosted at the **Herrenhof** by one of our favorite government members, **Propaganda Minister Josef Goebbels**. We warmed our hands by a fire which consumed the books of Thomas Mann,

Keitel looking sharp

Erich Maria Remarque, Jack London, H.G. Wells and many Jewish writers. The gathering was a good opportunity for the Minister to educate us about the goals of the **Reich**. He said the flames not only illuminated the end of an old era, but they also lit up the new. We wish him every success. **Julius Streicher**, editor of **Der Sturmer**, dropped by the ceremony in his new Mercedes. In 1923 in Munich we were invited to drink at the beer halls by **The Fuhrer** almost every evening. In those evenings Julius was always very aloof. Only in Berlin did I realise it wasn't attitude, but a combination of shyness and thoughts of more important things, such as religion, family, and literature.

Brau at the Herrenhof

We should have realised Julius was not a Bertoldt Brecht type. Julius has been helping the effort to protect Christian children from having their blood used to make matzoh in Passover ceremonies. His effort in distributing Der Sturmer to Palestine has saved thousands of Christian children there. As Julius told us, "It just got in my gut. I felt I had to

3 - July 16, 1997 • P. 23

do something." Julius, we're glad you came out of your shell. We received a lovely invitation from **S.D. researcher Adolf Eichmann** to a trial for 17 attractive young "race defilers." Sad to say but in this country many young women go astray. Of course they were all found guilty and that's what they deserve. Finally we were treated to a very special visit to the Eagle's nest with **the Fuhrer, Adolf Hitler,** his lovely young companion **Eva Braun, Magda and Josef Goebbels, Herr Himmler (again!),** and **Lutwaffe head Hermann Goering.** We had an excellent Crepe Suzette which many said we would all be eating more of very soon. After dinner the **Fuhrer** invited us to watch a new screening of **Lefi Reifenstahl's** excellent film **The Triumph of the Will.** The Fuhrer, as always an excellent critic, said the well-shot film was very good but maybe showed him in too flattering a light. But we all quickly reassured him that there could never be too flattering a light for the deliverer of our nation from sensational Yellow journalism.

The Fuhrer, Himmler and Mr. Basse hangin'

The *eXile*'s pardy of "Bassworld."

city. Pressing charges against him was like asking to be assassinated. And if any American in Moscow was going to be killed, it was Bass. Already his friends Paul Tatum, a partner in the Radisson hotel project, and Joseph Glotser, the director of the strip club "Dolls," had been killed in the previous twelve months for various reasons, and those two people both had had many more friends than Bass.

Bass was playing a dangerous game. He was probably banking that Zhirinovsky and the LDPR would protect him, a near-delusional assumption given Zhirinovsky's crew's attitude toward American Jews. And it was at the peak moment of his stress that we blindsided him with our cover story—25,000 copies of his bloodied head, seen in the beginning of this chapter, plastered in every hotel and restaurant, every place that Bass did business in town.

The text was unsensational, although we outed his criminal record and added a few other choice anecdotes, such as the story of his brief tenure as the manager of boxer Julio Cesar Chavez—Bass in the eighties had tried unsuccessfully to swipe Chavez away from Don King (accusing the multigazillionaire King of cheating Chavez out of a whopping $4,700) and been quickly moved out of the boxing world. In any case, after it came out, we sat in our new office—since the death-threat story, we'd moved to a bigger, cleaner, more modern facility on the other side of town—and waited by the phone.

Finally, a few days after the story came out, Bass called. He sounded tired and dejected on the phone—in fact, he was too down even to threaten me. All he did was take issue with a few lines in the piece.

"You write here that 'even otherwise-intelligent basketball star Kareem Abdul-Jabbar allowed himself to be photographed' with me," he sighed. "Why say that? Am I so disgusting that you have to use language like that?"

"The piece was written . . . from a certain point of view," I said.

He sighed again. He was sighing two or three times between every sentence. Next he complained that I had published a picture of his handwritten letter.

"It really hurts me that you pick on my writing," he said. "I don't see why that's relevant."

"It wouldn't be, except that you do it for a living," I said. "You write for a competitor. You use your column to gain access to ambassadors and all sorts of people."

"But, you know, I'm a dyslexic," he said. "How could you pick on me like that? I can't help it that my grammar is bad."

"Michael," I said. "I'm sorry you're a dyslexic. But you don't see any midgets playing for the Knicks, do you? Being a midget doesn't make someone a bad person. But it certainly rules out his playing pro basketball."

"That letter I wrote to you, I wrote under duress," he protested. "I didn't have time to edit it. That's why it came out like that."

"Michael . . . " I said.

I hesitated, beginning to feel sorry for him. He had that effect because he was so obviously weak and vulnerable. But then I remembered everything I knew about this guy. He would promise sixteen-year-old girls trips to Europe, if only they'd blow him in his limousine. He went to clubs and rang up thousand-dollar bills and walked out. He was violent and vicious with women. And he had, of course, threatened to kill me in the spring, and was probably thinking of doing it again now. Worst of all, he wrote for the *Moscow Tribune.* I shook my head and pressed ahead.

"When I have to write fast, I don't make mistakes," I said. "That's because I'm a professional writer. You're clearly not."

A REAL BASSHOLE!

THIS ZIPPERHEAD'S A WINNER! When we first spotted this Michael Bass costume at the giant GosOrgHalloween party at the planetarium two weeks ago, we thought it *was* Bass, it was so convincing. Turns out it was just a great costume— and the first reason we've had to give away one of our prized propeller hats. Brian, if you see this, and we're sure you will, give us a call at 267-41-59 and arrange to pick up a hat you could probably use. And by the way, we were too drunk to get you a t-shirt that night...

"But I'm funny, aren't I?" he said, hopefully. "I've got style, don't I?"

"You've got personality," I said. "But you can't say you're a good writer, because you're not. And I'm in a position to judge. I'm sorry."

He was quiet for a while. Then, finally, he spoke up.

"You know I'm pressing charges against Ivan X," he said.

"I know," I said. "I'm sure you know what you're doing. I wish you luck."

"It would make a pretty good story if I got killed, wouldn't it?" he said. "Wouldn't it?"

I paused. "Well, no one wants to see you get killed," I said. "Why don't you just leave the country?"

"Because I believe in sticking up for what's right," he said.

"Really?" I said.

"Well . . . " he said, sighing one more time. I thought he might cry. "I don't know. Anyway, I was very upset by your piece. It ruined my charity efforts."

"I'm sorry," I said.

"Good-bye," he said, and hung up.

A few weeks later it was Halloween. Mark had again left the country, heading off to France to gorge himself on rich food and visit with his weird Californian family; when he came back, Kara and Marcus announced that they were leaving the company. A period of intense stress followed, with the result that we hired a beautiful, daffy American blonde, Nicole Mollo, to replace the scheming husband-wife duo. Sales dipped, then Mark's old rhetoric professor, John Dolan, dropped in from New Zealand for a visit; we all snorted a lot of drugs in semidarkness, in front of a flickering television, for about a week, then the two of them left me alone to emcee a giant Halloween party that Mark had weaseled us into.

Prior to the party, I'd written a bit in our gambling page about Bass, daring our readers to come to the party dressed as our archenemy. The costume, I said, was simple—shave your head, stick a bunch of zippers on it, and enter the party trailed by hired assassins.

Raving drunk, I ascended the stage at the party in a toga and gave away a bunch of T-shirts, bobbing and weaving to avoid flying tomatoes (I'd distributed a bunch to the audience).

"Fucking queer," someone in the band said, behind me.

"Have a T-shirt," I said, tossing him one.

There had to have been 500 people at the party, which was called GosOrgHalloween—the wildest thing I'd ever seen in Moscow. It was a shock for me; I don't get out much. And I'd come to Russia in the first place precisely because it was grim. In any case, I didn't have too much time to think; the crowd screamed for the band, and it was time to get down.

When I got down, I saw a bald head leaning over the bar. Michael Bass! Or was it? I walked over and looked at the figure. It wasn't Bass, but a guy named Brian whom I knew because he'd moved into my apartment when I'd left for Mongolia the year before. He'd shaved his head and stuck zippers on it, and drawn bloodstains all over himself.

"Nice costume," I said.

"Thanks," he said.

Nouveau pop-icon Bass himself was nowhere to be found. He'd been keeping a pretty low profile lately. He was still alive, but the Ivan X thing had him really rattled. Club owners reported not seeing him at any of the major hangouts. And Zhirinovsky quickly dropped him. But he didn't go home: there were all sorts of rumors about why he wouldn't, or couldn't, go back to the United States, and he had apparently decided to stick it out in Moscow.

the eXile

Death Porn

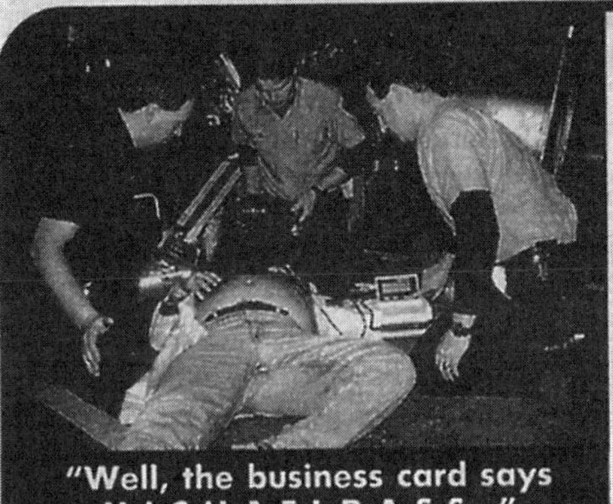

"Well, the business card says M-I-C-H-A-E-L B-A-S-S..."

Boy, Was He Pissed!

The *eXile* award for most twsited crime of the year so far goes to 46 year-old Alexander Petrov of the Tombov oblast, who left six people charred and burnt in the hospital after a freakish botched murder-suicide. A veteran mechanic at a sovkhoz in the tiny village of Verkhnyaya Yaroslavka, Petrov, like just about everyone else in the provinces these days, was pissed over not having received his salary for months. Unlike most others, however, he decided to do something about it. On the afternoon of May 16 he entered the office of the sovkhoz administration, poured gasoline all over the floor and over himself, and dropped a match to the ground. Within minutes the entire first floor of the small building was in flames, and the five workers who were at their desks on the second floor came barreling down the stairs to head for the exit. The only problem was that Petrov, by now himself engulfed in flames, was blocking the one door to the building. When a woman attempted to move past him, he stabbed her with a plastic-handled knife. Eventually, however, the remianing four managed to overpower him and burst out the door. Farm firefighters arrived quickly enough to put out the fire and the flaming Petrov, who by then had passed out in shock on the first floor. All six people were taken to a hospital in Tambov and remain in serious condition. Petrov, if he lives, will be charged with attempted murder and arson.

Just before Christmas, Mark and I met with a guy named Andrei Alexandrov, the director of *Kak Bui*, a new club near our office. *Kak Bui* had previously been a gay club called "Exit," and previous to that been a gay club called "Banana." It had been shut down in both incarnations for various reasons, and in the latter stages of its existence as "Exit" had been the emptiest, saddest club in Moscow. It had since been redone in loud spray paint and had a new straight, "funk" image it was hoping to project. Alexandrov was a nice guy, but the club seemed doomed, and as a business it had the desperate, expectant feel of a kids' lemonade stand.

"I had a visit from a guy named Michael Bass," Alexandrov told us, laughing in the quiet of his empty club. "He told me that he could come in, be my general manager, and take fifteen percent of my profits. I said to him, 'No Thank you.' What a weirdo!

"Anyway," he said, "I think things will pick up around here. Once I have a sign made for the outside, anyway."

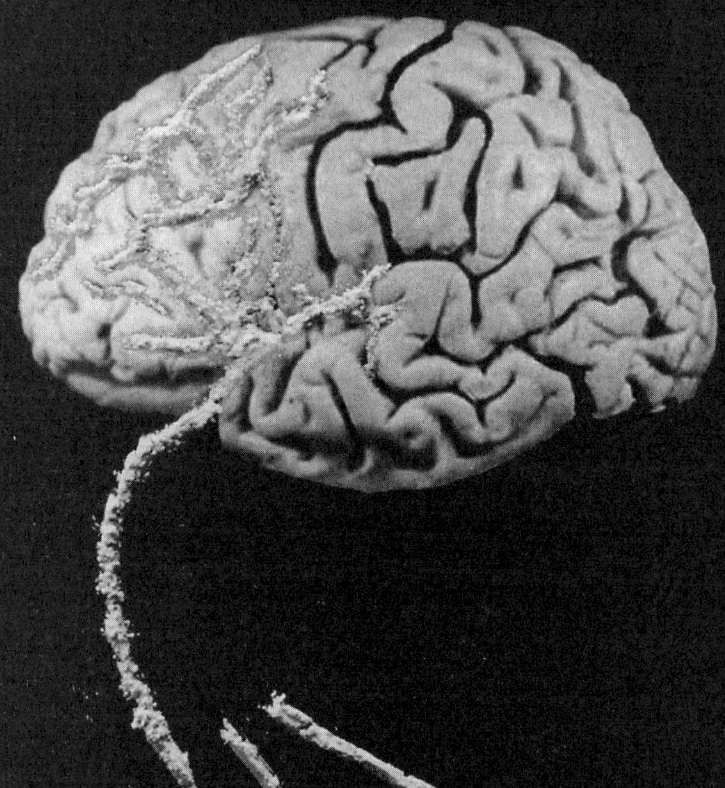

+ дорожка
– извилина

the eXile

BY MARK AMES

CHAPTER FIVE: OUR GOD IS SPEED

"Our God is Speed"
Vladimir Mayakovsky

e took a vote. Should we skip an issue in August, when business is slow and half of Moscow is on vacation? How to take advantage of the expected advertising boom coinciding with the garish, $150 million celebration of Moscow's 850th birthday in early September? . . . I voted to skip a week in August and readjust our publishing schedule so that we'd have an issue coming out the week of the "party of the century," as Mayor Luzhkov's people were calling it. Kara wanted to stick to the normal schedule. Matt had an even better idea: Why not *really* cash in by putting out three issues in a row, week after week, back-to-back, without the usual one-week interval? That way we'd have one issue coming out the week *before* the birthday bash, one the week *of*, and one the week *after*. Kara liked the idea: they heard cash registers ringing . . .

I was staunchly against it. It was mosquito-muggy that day. The mere mention of extra work made me break out in one of my famous Sephardic sweats. I argued against it as best I could. My economics ratio is fame:work. How can you squeeze as much fame out of as little work as possible? But Kara and Matt outvoted me. Two to one. And then, to my horror, they both split for vacation during that same three-week period. Taibbi chased his girlfriend back to Yale, while Kara and her husband were secretly plotting to sink the company. Like all embittered partners, she wanted to see the paper die in her absence. She was all for me running the newspaper alone. As I later learned, the gist of their plan was to run up arrears with our printing press and our film developer, while not collecting on any of our bills, leaving us choked of funds and without any favors to call from the people who we had to pay to keep the paper going. She had counted on the fact that our operation was so feckless—and Kara was so on top of everything—that we wouldn't figure out the scheme until it was too late. It almost worked.

But before then, when phase one of the sink-the-*eXile* plan first kicked in, I didn't see the storm clouds coming. Actually, I waited until the roof of my cozy little house was blown off and I stood in four feet of water before I realized, Fuck! I'm going to have to do this ALL BY MY FUCKING SELF! The selfish American shitheads had abandoned me for their vacations RIGHT WHEN I NEEDED THEM MOST!

There was only one other person who could possibly help me through.

I called up Krazy Kevin to beg him for some editorial assistance. I'd pay him anything.

CHAPTER FIVE

"Oh no, man," he said in his lazy, slacker way. "I'm going to Ukraine and the Baltics. Didn't Matt tell you?"

So I was alone.

Before leaving, Taibbi joked that my hair would turn white before he returned . . . like Leland Palmer's from *Twin Peaks.* I didn't laugh—the possibility was too real. I'm getting up there in age. My brother, who is only two years older than I, has whitened temples.

But I was lucky. I got ahold of one secret aide, my little Santa's helper: an old snowman who's been bailing me out of trouble ever since college finals first pinned me up against the wall.

If it wasn't for the speed I'd scored in Estonia while renewing my visa that summer, I don't know how I'd have made it through. It wasn't very good speed—in fact, it's about the worst speed I've ever snorted in my life. Way too ex-lax white for my tastes: white means baby powder and laxative. The really good speed is yellowish or crystal-brown. My friend Lee always has a rock of pure crystal when I visit him in Hollywood. He takes a razor and scrapes a few rails off the crystal for me every time I see him. He calls his speed "glass"—he gets it before they even wash it down with whatever chemicals they use to dilute it.

The Estonian shit—you can tell you're the very last sucker in the drug chain pyramid—you're the last scavenger to the corpse. What's left is fur and bone, the odd ligament. But you don't have a choice. When it comes to drugs, you takes what you can gets.

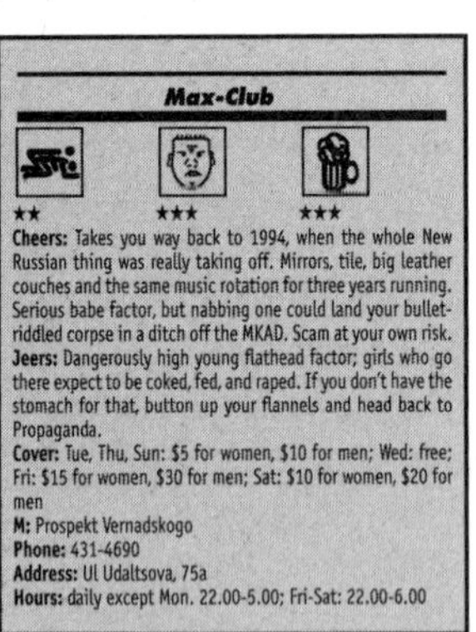

Max-Club

★★ ★★★ ★★★

Cheers: Takes you way back to 1994, when the whole New Russian thing was really taking off. Mirrors, tile, big leather couches and the same music rotation for three years running. Serious babe factor, but nabbing one could land your bullet-riddled corpse in a ditch off the MKAD. Scam at your own risk.
Jeers: Dangerously high young flathead factor; girls who go there expect to be coked, fed, and raped. If you don't have the stomach for that, button up your flannels and head back to Propaganda.
Cover: Tue, Thu, Sun: $5 for women, $10 for men; Wed: free; Fri: $15 for women, $30 for men; Sat: $10 for women, $20 for men
M: Prospekt Vernadskogo
Phone: 431-4690
Address: Ul Udaltsova, 75a
Hours: daily except Mon. 22.00-5.00; Fri-Sat: 22.00-6.00

When I was working on the second solo issue, I got a call from Jeffrey Tayler. He'd been commissioned by *Spin* magazine to write an article on drug abuse in Russia. In the fall of 1997, it had become the new fashion among foreign correspondents to write harrowing, chilling accounts of young drug addicts in the former Soviet Union. The *Los Angeles Times*, the *New York Times*, *Newsday* . . . they'd all run harrowing-Russian-drug-abuse stories that fall.

Tayler called me for help because he figured, reading our newspaper, that we knew everything there needed to be known about drugs. I was flattered, as I easily am. We agreed to meet. I had a preconception of what a *Spin* writer should look like: earring, stringy hair, leather jacket . . . a kind of deceptively lazy-voiced ex–college radio DJ type.

On the day of the appointment with Tayler, some absolute nerd arrived in his place: tweed jacket with elbow patches, pressed slacks, loafers, perfectly coiffed hair, cartoon square jaw, and soft voice. Was he looking for an art gallery party? *Here?*

"Hi, I'm Jeffrey Tayler," he said, introducing himself.

I hid my shock, the way you try not to show your revulsion when you meet someone with a birth defect—a glass eye, a bionic hand, a jaw destroyed by flesh-eating bacteria . . .

In the hope that the *eXile* would get some publicity, I spent a few weeks helping Tayler. He admitted to me almost straight off the bat that he'd never tried drugs in his life. He told me that he'd previously written for *Atlantic Monthly* and *Harper's Magazine.* "I don't even understand the drug language, so I hope you can help me," he modestly pleaded. "I usually write about culture and that sort of thing." Tayler tried ingratiating himself to *eXile*-y decadence by telling me about the time he spent in Morocco.

Tayler needed training wheels. He didn't know that you "snort" coke, or what "banging" heroin meant. It was embarrassing. I myself felt like some washed-up hipster with an earring, using that kind of language. He was looking for the real dark, harrowing angle as well.

"*Spin* wants me to write about some other kinds of drugs," he said. "I'm not sure what they're called, but not the regular stuff, you know. I need to find drug addicts shooting up dirty needles, that kind of thing. They want a real gritty, dark story, with a Russian angle."

I wasn't going to let his annoying idiocy get in the way of my own literary ambitions, so I introduced him to a drug addict friend of mine, under the pretext that he'd be protected. I told Tayler clubs to visit, places to go, things to watch out for. In return, he was going to blow the *eXile* in *Spin.*

One night, I got a call from an astonished Tayler. He asked me, in a whispered, nervous voice: "Is it . . . is it true that you can *snort* heroin?" he asked.

I laughed. "Uh, yeah, of course. Everyone does. Why?"

"Wow, I didn't know. I was at Marika, and these girls were snorting something in the bathroom. I asked them what it was, and they said 'heroin.' I thought they were just teasing me."

Another time he told me about going to Titanik and seeing a group of young techno types in sunglasses passed out on couches with blank expressions. "What do you think that is?" he asked.

"I don't know. Coming down from E, or else heroin."

"Yeah, I think it was ecstasy," he said. "That's what my friend said. I have an escort showing me around. I'm going to a kislotechny (acid) club tonight. You wanna come with me?"

"I'll meet you there."

"What time?"

"Don't wait," I'd say.

I'm still not sure what the guy's deal is. How could someone in their mid-30s never have tried drugs? It was bizarre. He spoke a flawless, almost accentless Russian. Only CIA spooks and Mormon evangelists have stats like that. He just didn't make sense.

I finally saw the article a few months later. I was shocked. I thought I'd trained this bitch up, but he'd let me down. It was nothing but a collection of every harrowing-tales-of-drug-addicts-doom-apocalypse cliché you could ever imagine. And worst of all—the fucker didn't mention me once! Me, his OB-1 Kanobe, without whom . . . ah, fuck it.

Journalists aren't just professional liars, propagandists, and pickpockets—they're also the lowest, most shameless careerists and ingrates on Planet Earth.

The accumulation of drugs=despair articles in the fall of 1997 spoke more of a conspiracy among careerist hacks than anything remotely resembling the truth. What people forget in every article ever written about drugs is one simple, basic fact: PEOPLE TAKE DRUGS BECAUSE THEY'RE FUN. That's it. It's the most basic premise of all. There's no mystery to the drug thing. People drink water to quench their thirst; they have sex because it feels good; and they do drugs because they're fun. Is it really that difficult a concept to run by the reader? Is this obvious fact really so dangerous and censored that we can never utter it in the printed public?

Even Hunter S. and William Burroughs couldn't state it that plainly: they elevated drugs to the mythical level, keeping mum on the single most obvious, dangerous fact. So I'll repeat: PEOPLE DO DRUGS BECAUSE THEY'RE FUN. It's no different from alcohol or roller coasters, except that drugs are A LOT BETTER.

If everyone would admit that people do drugs because they're fun, then suddenly, the whole 30-year war on drugs thing would seem savage and bizarre: the war on fun. Which is exactly what it is.

Drugs are also incredibly practical. They can help you get through rough times. They can numb you to horrible circumstances. They can improve your social skills. Or they can increase your work efficiency. Sometimes coffee just isn't enough, just like sometimes beer isn't enough.

When I was stuck doing three issues back-to-back, all alone, it was the speed that stepped in as deputy editor, copy editor, ideas-man, and gofer. I went days without sleeping, just railing out one *strelka*, or arrow, after another. True, each issue was worse than the previous one. The last Taibbi-less issue was almost a complete editorial disaster. Readers were beginning to complain about the decline in quality. It could have been worse, though. There could have been no newspaper at all, with me hanging from the ceiling, a scrawled note pinned to my body: "I didn't have what it takes. Go on without me. M"

Muscovites rarely take speed. It's one of the few truly baffling things about this place: an enigma wrapped in a zipper lock wrapped in a nose-bleed. It's not like Russians don't love their drugs as much as the next guy. They vacuum up overpriced, heavily cut cocaine, they bang heroin and Special K, they drink shoe polish and paint thinner, they sniff glue and gasoline, they drop countless tabs of cheap Polish acid, they pop Latvian ecstasy like it's chewing gum, they score rank opiate substitutes and poppy straw from babushki at Lubyanka and bang it in basements, they chow mushrooms, they spark up Kazakh shake that takes 20 hits to get a buzz from, they smoke Afghani hashish, drop tranqs . . . they even take drugs I'd never even heard of before I arrived. Like vint, an amphetamine developed by the Germans for the Luftwaffe. I'd like to try it, but I'm sure it's a filthy high, full of awful speed-hallucinations. I don't want to have one of those Prince Myshkin wiggly bacon seizures in the middle of someone's floor, spike-in-arm.

Ketamine is another drug I didn't know about until I came to Moscow. The Russians say that Ketamine was developed as an anaesthetic for abortions. It works differently on men and women. Women experience a kind of sweet, euphoric high, lolling on the puffy clouds, passing through heaven's petting zoos. For men it's a bit different. There are no petting zoos and puffy clouds. It's more like an H. P. Lovecraft world of terror, fish that are all bear-trap jaws. . . . Your body becomes a pilotless slab of concrete in low-gravitational flight, paralyzed but awake, recklessly careening above the stratosphere, in the darkness, without any brakes or headlights . . . just burning out of control into a physical place called Terror. A poet friend of mine, Andrei Turkin, shot Ketamine a few times and told me all about it. At the time, I was desperately searching for drugs, coming up empty. With Turkin, I thought I might have finally found a "Drug Crowd," that secret underground clique that lurks in every city, town, class, etc. . . . Since Turkin was a poet—a

Russia Turns Trendsetter

by Mark Ames

Almost two years ago, on the eve of the 50th anniversary of Russia's victory over the Nazis, I experienced the quintessential evening of Moscow Decadence. It began at around midnight in the parking lot of the Young Pioneer's stadium. My friends, a mixture of Europeans and techno-Russians, spread the goods atop a mirror: an 8-ball of whiff cut into rails as long as asparagus stalks, 6 caps of X, and some diazapams to smoothe the ride.

Inside the club, you could tell us apart from the others: we had the largest eyes and the weirdest smiles... and we pounded the most water.

As the evening wore on, the doses were boosted. People drifted in and out of our circle. Then a group of us split off to go to a friend's apartment, where, I was assured, I would witness "group sex." The idea of "group sex" didn't appeal to me—in fact, it embarrassed me—but I went along for the ride. I didn't want to miss out—a sin in suburban mentality: the fear of "missing out."

At Stas' apartment, some of the guys based over the stovetop, little gray-white rushes of smoke shooting up from the tin foil. Then another round of caps were offered, although I threw in the towel. It was five thirty in the morning, and I had a meeting with my boss in two and a half hours. Also—I don't know how else to say it—I was reaching a stage where I didn't feel involved anymore. I was starting to make mental notes of the whole thing, trying to find relevance, preparing the column in advance. That's always a bad sign.

Then the "group sex" began. Yulia, Tanya, and Svyeta, feeling the boost kick in, launched into an annoying techno-dyevushka dance (early morning TV aerobics step with a vacant expression) right there in the living room. The guys sat around, staring with jaws open, while Stas reassured me that the "group sex" leg of the program was just around the corner. With a lecherous grin, Stas crossed the room, dancing in rhythm, moving up close, rubbing Tanya's ass, kissing her... they fell to the floor, real Wild Orchids-like... On the other side of the room, Yulia jiggled harder, then took Sveta onto the floor and started dry humping her. The European next to me got excited; he crawled next to the sapphites and started rubbing Yulia's back as she humped Sveta. If only I had a camera, I thought, this would make some seriously good comedy... real Don Knotts/Jack Ritter meets Pia Zadora... I don't know what it was—it just all seemed so fucking *healthy.* There was a strange, practiced, zombie-like quality to it all that, while interesting, certainly wasn't erotic. Still, I stayed on, afraid that if I cut out, I'd offend someone. Finally, at around 7:30 in the morning, I slipped out, just in time to meet my boss for the Victory Day parade. At the time I was living on Kutuzovsky Prospekt, which served as the runway for the military parade: all kinds of APCs, tanks, howitzers, jeeps and so on were rolling under my window as the spell of the previous evening wore off, and I was forced to confront a few questions: a). Did 20 million Russians die so that their progeny could become wigged-out techno heads engaging in some kind of flat "group sex"; b). why didn't I get excited?; and c). are these questions mere seratonin-soaked attempts to "get to the bottom of it" or to "see a pattern" where one doesn't exist? The only answer I could come up with was that yes, indeed, 20 million Russians did lay their lives down exactly so that a few thousand kids, on the 50th anniversary of that tragic victory, could inhale imported drugs and engage in "group sex." What the hell did they expect anyway? I got mean and nasty and as the seratonin washed away, and the rumble of tanks below my window kept me from much-needed sleep, and if my boss hadn't come banging on my door at 8, I would have spent all morning brooding about the meaninglessness of war and life.

Okay, now here's the twist. See, that was two long years ago. The winds only blew from west to east then. But I've been back to California, and I've seen something... so awful... could it be? "Chemical Brothers and Orb Headline the Henry J. Kaiser Auditorium!" "Techno Music Takes Youth By Storm!" "From 'Ambient' To 'Jungle': The San Jose Mercury Guide to Techno"... In the listings, you can choose your night out based on what kind of music you're into: garage has about 10 listings in San Francisco; Progressive, House and Hardcore have a few, and so on. So it's finally happened to America, only FIVE YEARS AFTER IT HIT RUSSIA: America has gone techno! What scares me the most is that I'm beginning to detect a trend of America following the lead of Russia in a lot of things. For example, in the film Fargo, the kidnappers offer the cop fifty dollars to forget about a registration violation. True, the cop refused, and wound up getting his head blown off... but still, it means Russification has reached the far north of Minnesota, not to mention popular culture, and it could only lead me to ask, what in God's name is next? Group Sex? No—one thing I realized about Americans is that they stopped having sex—heterosexual sex, at least. You can see it in all the surveys they publish. Americans are fascinated with lesbians right now—they've gone bonkers over dykes, who are all over the TVs, movies, magazines—even my mother's talking about them—it's the closest thing we get to Group Sex, only it's far cleaner, clean enough for the whole family. But conspicuous consumption—that one trait expats have sneered at most—is definitely in. Not only has the Next Generation gone techno and bribery, but they're also into expensive cigars, golf and quirky cars that cost a lot. It may not be the Golden Palace, but it's a step in that direction, and it makes me sort of glad that I'm heading back to the land where trends are set. Russia—the trendsetting nation of the late 90s. I can see the doubly ironic leads now: "The Times They are a Cha-a-a-ngin'" or "If Reagan was dead, he'd be turning in his grave knowing that America's youth takes its cue from Russia's." Kind of makes you wonder who really won the Cold War after all, doesn't it?

Not really.

well-known Moscow poet—it seemed natural that he'd have access. It's understood that one of the few perks in the art world is access to drugs. I was trying to get him to hit up his avant-garde friends for some good drugs, but Ketamine was all he could offer me. I considered it. I was so desperate for a vacation in the mind that I even considered banging Special K with him until he told me what to expect. It sounded like PCP, and that's got to be about the scariest substance on earth. I would rather die—I mean literally DIE—than endure a night on PCP—or Ketamine, for that matter, although the Ketamine "high," if you can call an awake nightmare a "high," mercifully only lasts an hour. Once Andrei told me that he saw God while on Special K, and it was horrible. He didn't get into details. But he did continue popping the shit, right until he moved to Austria, when the government gave him a grant to write a novel. I asked Turkin why he took it, and he'd just laugh, twist his finger to his forehead, meaning to say, "I am crazy Russian poet, hee-hee!"

Turkin and his ex-jock girlfriend were a pair of obscene alcoholics drinking themselves to death every night. As a protégé and member of Dmitri Prigov's postmodern poets' circle, I thought Andrei would have access to something better than liquid panic. He made a few promises to find me speed—he kept calling it "phedrene"—but they never came through. The drug world seems to follow the same script in any culture. Ten empty promises for every bad score, and five rip-offs for every decent score. Not very good odds.

Who else could I turn to for speed? Vova, my banker friend, only wanted to drink vodka and smoke that shitty Kazakh shake. He introduced me to a locally famous, but painfully bad, punk band, DumBo, whose lead singer, the Armenian Jew "PoZr," couldn't come up with anything better than weed either. I smoked a few joints with him before the DumBo concerts at the old Sexton and Bunkr clubs, where metalheads, punks, and bikers hung. I didn't even catch a buzz—just got tired and scared.

Once, I almost got stomped at a DumBo show by some bikers, the Night Wolves, who are the local Hell's Angels. I was drunk and I slapped one of their girls' asses. It was idiotic—I deserved a good knifing for it, but she mercifully pulled them away from me. So I was humiliated, and straight. Jesus! If even a popular punk band can't score anything better than fucking weed, I'm doomed.

In late '93 and '94, I had to rely on the *apteky*, or pharmacies, for my scores. The real coup was the Stary Arbat pharmacy, a newly remodeled pharmacy, dom 25. The walls were painted fresh white. The display cases looked like they'd been imported from Austria, all clean and glass, with painted strips of metal. I cruised inside once when Dr. Dolan was visiting me in Moscow. In one of the sparkling glass display cases,

The War On Pleasure

by Mark Ames

A truly terrifying incident happened last week to a close acquaintance of mine.

He'd scored two grams of smack from a young African woman—she sold it to him in her podyezd while holding her five month old baby in her free arm—and made a straight B-line to a friend's house nearby. For the next six hours or so, the group of smacking-buddies binged themselves into a numb, groggy stupor. Three snorted, two jammed. They watched movies, talked (or rather drawled in half-sentences), nodded off in chairs... it was harmless fun by any standard.

By five in the morning, two of them —both expats—decided to leave for home. They stood out on Leninsky Prospekt trying to a flag a car down to get back to the center. No one stopped, perhaps because, as my friend put it, "I'm like you, Ames—they take me for a blackass."

Finally, one enterprising driver took a chance: he made an illegal U-turn to pick them up. They agreed on a price, then got in. As they headed towards the center, a militsia car pulled up beside them, on the passenger's side. The cops stared menacingly at my friend, then blew their horn and motioned for them to pull over. Right then, my friend realized that he was holding one and a half grams of china white—one ball in his inside coat pocket, and the other in the front pocket of his pants.

"I thought about pulling the shit out and dumping it on the floor of the car," he told me, "but I realized that they were probably watching my movements. I had to gauge which would be riskier. I just had to hope that they wouldn't haul me in and frisk me."

The driver got out and showed his documents. There was still hope they'd quickly get away. Then one cop came up to the side of the car and banged roughly on the backseat passenger's door. The guy in the backseat didn't have any smack on him, but he'd forgotten to bring his passport. He nervously got out of the car. That's when my friend's paranoia reached a peak: he thought, "Why did they pull everyone out of the car but me? Is this some kind of Soviet mental torture?"

To give the impression that he was a confident Westerner, he got out of the car himself and approached the cop, offering his passport. The cop asked him what he did in Moscow, and mocked his answers. He mocked his job, his citizenship, his bad Russian (my friend affected the bad Russian, hoping that naivete would put the cop off)... Then the cop noticed a minor fault in his visa, and said, "Davai v militsiu." That was it: they were taking both of them into the station. Where, for sure, they'd be frisked. And where, for sure, the smack would be found.

"My legs started shaking uncontrollably," my friend told me. "I kept this stupid American smile on my face, but me knees were like Shaggy's from Scooby Doo. I've never shaken that hard before."

If he'd been busted, it would mean nine months in Butirka waiting for a trial, and another two to three years time in a foreign labor camp in Mordova. The chances of getting tuberculosis in that time are about as high as the chances of getting raped in Folsom. Official statistics claim that ten percent of Russia's prison population has TB, but the real figure is far higher. No man, and particularly no milkfed Westerner, can possibly survive such an ordeal without serious and permanent damage to his health and mind. And all for what? For a completely victimless crime; for trying to momentarily relieve the pain and boredom of "reality" via a natural substance that happens to be less filthy, and more appealing to the senses, than alcohol and cigarettes. Alcohol: how many murders, rapes, assaults, auto accidents and the rest happen each year in Russia, or any country, because of alcohol? One estimate I heard is that up to a third of Russia's crimes are alcohol-related. Ah, but it's all so fun and whacky, all that alcoholism, isn't it?

I have since asked around what the sentence might be for someone carrying one and a half grams of heroin for personal use. The court in the Novocheryomushki region told the eXile that such a person would "sit for three years." Sergei Zabarin, a lawyer who is fighting for clarity and sanity in Russia's drug laws, told me that Russia's drug laws are unconstitutional, and yet he has several clients sitting in holding cells for carrying amounts even less than half a gram of heroin.

"It is uncivilized and inhumane," he told me. "But I don't have the money to fight it in the World Court."

The Russian criminal code separates drug offenses into three categories: small amounts for personal use, large amounts, and very large amounts obviously intended for sale. However, there has never been an official list published which spells out what a "small amount" is, although the Ministry of Health, which is in charge of naming that amount, has privately listed a "small amount" of heroin as .005 grams—in other words, about one microscopic granule, which could implicate frankly anyone who's ever bumped into a druggie. The obvious intention is that this gives wide leverage to the cops to bust who they want—and to extract massive bribes at whim.

"The Russian constitution forbids prosecuting a citizen for a crime that has not been properly disseminated through the media," Zabarin told me. "Since no one knows what a 'small amount' of heroin is, by our own constitution, they should not be prosecuted. However, I have one client who has sat in Matrosskaya Tishina for eight months after they found .4 grams of heroin on him. He's still waiting to hear his sentence."

Expats are not at all immune. I remember hearing about a black American who last year was caught with a gram of coke and sentenced to two years, but this has never been confirmed. The Chereyomushki court told the eXile that an American woman was busted in August at Sheremetyevo, having stuffed seven kilos of smack into her daughter's barbie dolls en route from Lima, via Moscow, to Ljublijana. It's hard to feel sorry for her, though: her bust has more to do with social Darwinism, weeding out the mongoloids, than anything else...

What happened to my friend? As they were about to put him into the back of the militsia car, he feigned surprise while masking his terror, and said, "Wail, why jail? Can't we just pay a fine?"

The militiaman's expression suddenly changed. He motioned my friend to follow him to the side of the street, then turned around and whispered, in English, "One khandred fifty."

My friend sighed in relief, but again feigned surprise and shock. "One hundred fifty? You mean, uh, sto pyatdesyat' tysich rublyei?"

"Da!" the militiaman sneered.

My friend shook his head, then pulled out the bills. It was business, that's all.

Never again will my friend leave his house with drugs in his pockets.

Nor will I.

we spotted a bottle of German codeine cough syrup. I couldn't believe my eyes, but it was true. Regulations were lax when I first arrived. The cough syrup was a real find: I'd buy about four jars of the stuff for twenty dollars a bottle. I'd come home, strip naked, light a candle, then gulp down a half a bottle at a time.

The high you get from codeine cough syrup is fairly close to a heroin high, if you drink enough: that same numb, low hum in the ears. I'd lie in my bed in the communal apartment I lived in, play my Breeders cassette, and pass out. . . . My neighbors, a pasty alcoholic and his obese architect wife, quietly avoided the American junkie in the apartment. I selfishly blasted my music and ignored them. But after fifteen or so bottles, the codeine effect wore off. After a few months of sucking that shit down, I was starting to look like a bleached, thin poet. That really scared me. And then, just like that, they pulled the codeine cough syrup off the counters. The revolutionary chaos from '91 to '93 was quickly fading, a rippling effect that began with the tanks shelling the White House, sound waves that rippled into the pharmacies, onto the streets, until it spread across Moscow: random order was replacing chaos.

So I was back to square one. By mid-'94, I was ready to give up on Russia as a source of vascular decadence. I was despondent, and my inflated opinion of Russians began to wane. Here's a nation of proud maximalists, living on the footsteps of nature's very own opium poppy preserve (Central Asia), and of all things, they choose to stick to vodka—dirty, filthy, piss-in-your-underwear vodka. It seemed to me that the idiots only wanted to drink, that they couldn't imagine drugs that took you to far more interesting places than Ketamine, pot, or alcohol. I tried defending Russians in my mind for their bad taste: such as, life here was already so intense that the kind of drugs I was looking for would only send them over the edge. Of course you need speed, E, or heroin in suburban America—NOTHING HAPPENS IN SUBURBAN AMERICA. But that excuse didn't wash—it's all a matter of taste, and in this area, the Russians, I was sure, had bad fucking taste.

There was another, possible source. It was the expat world. From what intelligence I had gathered, they were a very unlikely source of drugs. Moscow's American expats in particular were a grotesque caricature of Middle America: part Tim Allen, part Jerry Lundergaard. They'd have had bar-b-ques on their lawns if Moscow had lawns—they did, in fact, practically every weekend. They had proverbial bar-b-ques on their proverbial lawns every weekend.

On my first day in Moscow in 1993, I was dragged to an expat softball game just outside of town, where they tried bar-b-queing uncooked McDonald's hamburger patties. This is the truth: on my first day, about a hundred expats took two U.S. Embassy buses out to a field in a village outside of Moscow for a foreigners-only softball tournament. And among the sponsors was McDonald's, which delivered hundreds of uncooked hamburger patties and a couple of hibachis. I was dragged there by Al Parker's local American manager, Ted Krashenko. Since Al had lined up my visa, and Ted had picked me up from the airport when I arrived, I complied. And was shocked. The expats there—almost all Americans—told me with wild-eyed joy that this was the best day of the summer.

"You're really lucky," several of them said. "It barely feels like Russia here. It's great, isn't it!"

I'd come to escape the American paradigm—and here it was, transplanted in its entirety! I thought I'd made a huge mistake in coming here, and I briefly considered fleeing to somewhere more remote—Novosibirsk, Irkutsk, Tomsk-7 . . .

As expat communities go, Moscow's has to boast the shoddiest bunch of losers of all. Hands-down. It's as though, no matter how young they were, they couldn't wait to be middle-aged—that is, the type of middle-aged people who, trying to show their youthful spark, dress in college sweats and baseball caps. And just in case you didn't get it the first time around, the Americans created an intramural ultimate Frisbee league, and a softball league, and a tag football league. They took over the fields and parks of Moscow for their sports, and chased locals away when they bothered them.

Later in the evening they happily drank beer at expat parties, or expat bars. *Beer!* And they did a lot of worrying about their careers. *Careers!* And they were and are an incredibly ugly community, physically speaking. *And I mean U-G-L-Y!* Especially compared to the Russians—well, the female Russians—who are the most physically attractive gazelles on earth.

For expats, in 1993, Moscow barely even existed, and to this day barely exists—Moscow might at times be conceded as a cinematic backdrop to their career-climbing, hotel-lobby-lurking, insulated lives. And yet, Moscow didn't even provide a cinematic backdrop—it couldn't, in fact: because the expats here were the least cinematic people alive. They were the triumph of genetic blandness, beige-blooded. It took me a while to understand. The whole setup was too bizarre; it's never been described before in literature or film, this incongruous blandness upholstered over the chaos of a collapsed empire. At first, I couldn't quite verbalize it; I thought somehow it was I who was misreading things; it was I whose romantic expectations of Moscow were not only wrong, but perversely distorted. I had expected savagery, nihilism, and romance when I arrived. And I knew those things were going on, in every nook and cranny of Russia that hadn't been sterilized by the presence of an expat. They tried to recreate familiar episodes—moving, in seatbuckled transport, from Rosie O'Grady's Irish bar to the Western-furnished apartment to the Western supermarket to the Western restaurant . . . it just made no sense.

What were they doing here?! These types don't just pack up from America and head to Moscow. Damaged people like me go to Moscow—we flee, we take refuge in the anti-America, or so I'd thought. Instead, they came here and took refuge in an insular simulation of the familiar.

So what about the "unconventional" expat? Where did he go? As far as I know, the ever-so-slightly, temporarily unconventional types go to Prague. They spend a year there. They write a little poetry. They dabble in a few things they never had the guts to try in college: ecstasy, bisexual sex, whacky hairdos and body piercing. . . . Then they go back home. But Moscow as magnet for boring careerists? There was something truly bizarre about this expat community desperately trying to force a bar-b-que morality on the most violent, corrupt, anarchic city in the world. Like Ned Flanders packing up for Goa to sell processed cheese, avoiding the giant raves and hippies, cowering in his Goa-Sheraton hotel room, glued to a Tony

Alina, Will You Marry Me?

by Mark Ames

Last week, I sent the following letter home to my family:

Dear Everyone,

I have some good news and some bad news.

The good news is that I'm finally getting married.

The bad news is that my wife-to-be is sitting in jail.

Don't worry: I'm not marrying for love. This is purely humanitarian.

They were shocked. I'd never done anything humanitarian in my life—they remember me cheering when the French busted a cap in a Greenpeace activist during one of their Nouveau-Beaujolais-mushroom-cloud festivals in the South Pacific. My joke at the time: "Q: What do you call a dead Greenpeace activist? A: A dead Greenpeace activist." It really bowled them over in Peoria... had 'em rolling in the aisles in Kalamazoo... But that was back

Out here you're faced with enough road kill, cop beatings and gonorrhea—that is, the stuff black humor is made of—to rattle your average cynic. Once in awhile, you even have to shed your cynicism, to do something to fight against the horribleness of it all, or else you feel you'll lose your right to comment on anything. Sometimes those black jokes seem as defiant as singing Christmas carols on Christmas Eve.

The trial of Alina Vitukhnovskaya is one such injustice that has inspired me to utterly futile action, and not mere quips. She is the victim of vicious persecution from renegade FSB agents, a rigged legal system, and hypocrisy on the part of American writers and human rights activists, who once beat their breasts in support of Soviet dissidents, but now keep obediently quiet.

I went to her trial way out in northwest Moscow. You sit in this worn beige and yellow room on the fifth floor of a severe granite building... an empty cage awaits the defendant on one side, and three dilapidated Alice In Wonderland high-backed chairs on the far end, where the judges sit. You realize, just by looking at this perversion of a grammar school detention hall, that there's no way the accused will be judged innocent. You could sit Mother Theresa in that cage, and she'd look like guilty.

Taibbi and I came to watch Vitukhnovskaya's trial, which has reminded many here of the repression against writers and dissidents during the Brezhnev era. The State went after Vitukhnovskaya in 1994 in a highly-publicized trial in which she was accused of selling seven dollars of acid to a pair of rent-a-junkies who, everyone admits, had been brutally beaten by a team of eight FSB goons to force a «confession.» After an outcry by famous Russian writers and leading human rights activists, she was freed in 1995, but not after spending over a year in Butirka prison, one of the most savage dungeons in the northern hemisphere.

This year, her case was reopened. The judge signed a secret order in August to re-incarcerate her based on a rarely-invoked Russian statute, article 96, which allows re-incarcerating someone based on the "dangerousness of the crime." He called Vitukhnovksaya in for a hearing on October 23rd, and unexpectedly, without warning, had the five foot two poet seized, arrested, and thrown in Women's Prison number 6 for the duration of her trial. To imagine what her days were like there, remember that each prisoner is allotted an average of .7 meters of space. Often they have to sleep in shifts. The harsh, cramped cells are hostile to humans to the same degree that they are luxury suites for parasites. Prisoners become little more than a human salad bars for lice, fungi, bacteria, gum disease, tuberculosis, and worse.

The judge presiding over her case is a 30-year-old ex-cop from outside of Moscow; his two "consultants" are a pair of barely-breathing white-haired Soviets, one of whom spent most of the trial asleep.

After the first trial, I left for home feeling utterly defeated. You can write an article about it, make some phone calls, but you know you'll have no effect. Something else had to be done. Something to draw attention to her desperate plight. Something... *stupid.*

That's when I realized that if I married her in jail, thus making her an American citizen, then perhaps the American press would decide that she "counts." We all know that if the American press cries, the Russian government listens. It even worked during Soviet times!

Even though every Russian and West European human rights group has condemned her trial as a farce, the Americans won't touch it because of drug allegations. The local head of the PEN writer's association, Alexander Tkachenko, admitted his frustration.

"Even the American PEN backed away when they heard that there was a drug accusation," he told me. "I showed them evidence that the accusation was unjust, but they didn't care—the accusation was enough to scare them off."

My stepsister, who is an intern at the New York branch of Human Rights Watch, agreed. "The Russians are tricky," she wrote me. "They must know that people here are afraid of looking like they support drug use."

Just last Thursday, the judge made an unbelievable decision: he transferred Vitukhnovskaya to the Serbsky Psychological Institute to decide whether or not she is insane. This is exactly the same judgement handed down to countless Soviet dissidents, and this is the very same psychiatric ward where the same Soviet dissidents were held. Only now, it's worse: today, Serbsky holds the worst, sickest maniacs and serial killers in Russia. This is where the "Red Ripper" Chikatilo underwent his examination. And now this innocent young poet is stuck in there with them. Her sentencing is set for January 26th, unless the psychiatric expert assigned to her case decides he needs more time. Incredible, but it's happening. Now there's no other choice but marriage.

So here goes. I'm on my knees, Alina. Sure, I've got a few blemishes on my record. I was denied a few weeks back by a disfigured provincial girl; I hate children, and I will strangle you with a pair of cheap stockings if you if you dare threaten me with kids. All in all, I'd make a shitty husband. But I have a few pluses. I'm tall, for one thing; I can score free eXile drinks. And most importantly, I have American citizenship.

Lately, I've tried imagining what our married life would be like. You'd fry up some meat and potatoes, toss up a little tomato and cucumber salad with mayonnaise... I'd be watching some cheap porno in the other room. We'd talk about our day at work—how the eXile is going downhill, or how you're becoming more famous and more respected than me—as Mr. Nasty groans in the background... when we make love, you insist on wearing the famed eXile propeller cap. We're a team. And the most important thing is that you're free. You're out of that madhouse that they're holding you in. And they won't hurt you any more, because Carol J. Williams and Michael Specter have decided that your oppression counts. They've written you up, so the same people who intervened to free Richard Bliss have intervened to free you.

Even the thought of your freedom is enough to cheer me up. And that's all that matters.

Robbins special. . . . The chasm between expat world and Moscow reality was so great that it created something psychotic. The expat community reacted as any individual might react to such a disparity between one's inner, familiar world and the outer, inexplicable world: they got a big-time disease. The expats became grotesquely demented and didn't even know it. They suffered from a mass psychotic episode of Foliea Deux, although instead of imagining themselves as emperors and tank commanders, they adopted the blandest delusion possible—that of commuting careerists living back in suburban Atlanta, occasionally passing a depressed industrial district over the freeway bridge . . . a delusion that could only be punctured by bad weather and occasionally malfunctioning telephone lines.

Moscow was not real for the American expats. It was ignored, the way these people have learned, through solid American upbringing, to ignore a lot of unpleasant things they don't want to know. They even have a propaganda organ, the *Moscow Times*, to reinforce that delusion, successfully superimposing white Atlanta microbrewery culture over savage Moscow, and making everyone feel all the more comfortable for it.

I was willing to engage in psychotic episodes and mass delusion, so long as it was artificially induced. But these rock-climbing types didn't need or want drugs. They just wanted more beer.

They were no help to me.

I wanted drugs, even if Moscow was providing its fair share of natural excitement. The shelling of the White House was great, I have to admit. I spent the whole day wandering around the gun battle. Once, when I passed a barricaded police precinct station, two cops pointed their AKs at me and threatened to make human confetti out of me if I didn't take a long, circuitous route around them. That day-long adrenaline rush was the closest to speed I'd had in Moscow. The killings, the corpses that litter the streets, the odd bomb that went off in the night. They were good for a rush. But I wanted drugs because I need that vacation in the mind every so often. After my first year, I thought I'd come to the wrongest place on earth for drugs. The Russians only wanted to drink, and I don't care for alcohol; and the expats were duller than Belgians, Homo Sovieticus perfected, Brezhnev's wet dream.

Then I met James.

James is the guy who dropped something called Marilyn. I still don't know what the fuck Marilyn is, and I haven't

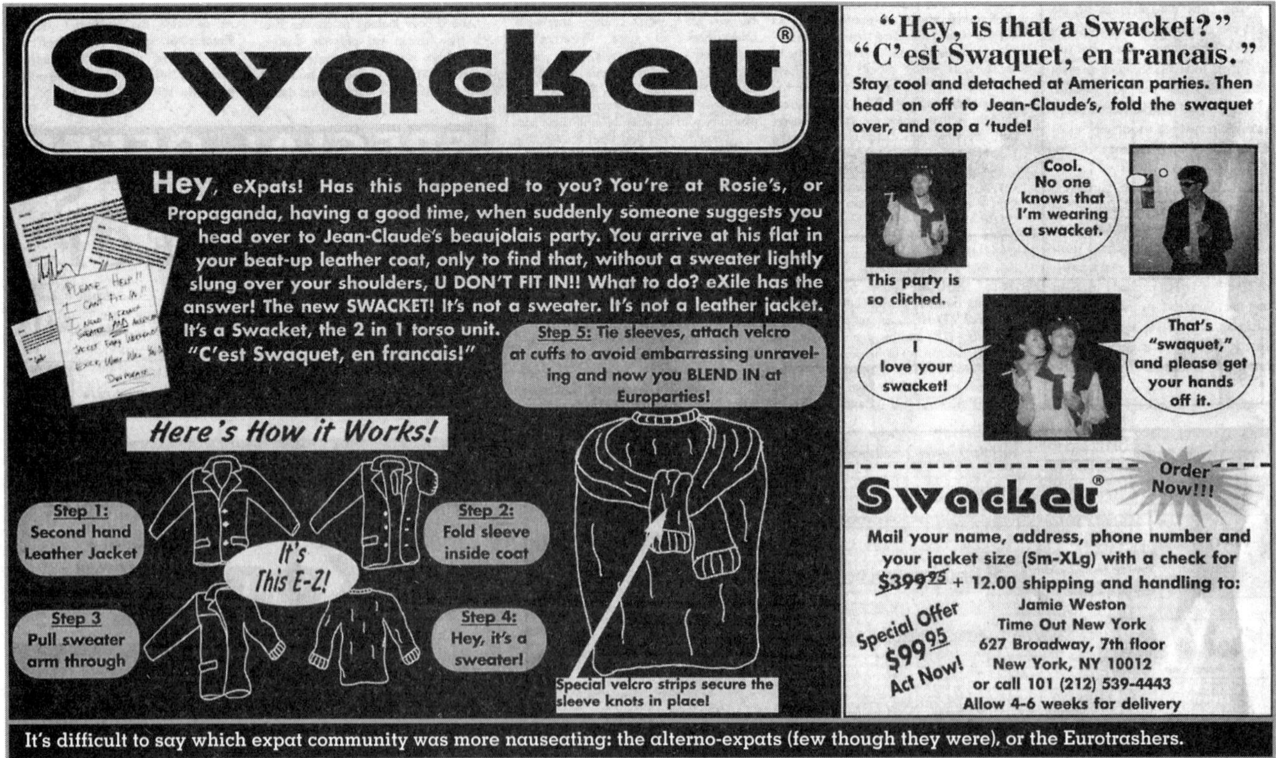

It's difficult to say which expat community was more nauseating: the alterno-expats (few though they were), or the Eurotrashers.

heard of it since. It looked horrible, but James insists to this day that Marilyn was the best drug he'd ever tried, and you could only get it in Moscow. I'd try it just to try it, but I wouldn't go into the ride with an eager smile and my hands up in the air—I'd clutch to the safety bar and scream like a bitch.

All I remember is that James did a lot of twitching when he was on Marilyn. We were in Ptyutch, the infamous (and overrated) underground rave club that survived until mid-'96. I saw James there, sitting alone on a couch. Twitching and trembling. The left side of his face looked like it was melting off the bone. A filthy-rich 25-year-old Russian cigarette distributor named Igor, decked out in Day-Glo techno uniform and metallic platforms, had scored James the tab. He couldn't explain to me what Marilyn was because he couldn't verbalize a complete thought that night. He kept slouching in his chair, with a blind smile on his face.

This flyer announces perhaps the last ever Moscow July 4th bash, which generally means a "Whites Only" bland-o-rama held at some historical Russian landmark. On the center-right, note that "All Ex-Pats, families, and friends" are welcome, and "Passport or other identification required when purchasing a ticket." That is, if you're Russian, fuck you, get off your historical landmark! Sasha, our last production manager, furiously glued a swastika on this flyer and hung it on our wall.

"Mark," James repeated, trying to throw his arm around me. "I really . . . I really . . . what? Did . . . did you say?" His eyeballs vibrated back and forth like figures on a slot machine, and his hands shook so violently that he couldn't pull a cigarette out of the pack.

"Are you okay, James?" I asked.

"Yeah," he drawled. "It's really great. This guy . . . he gave me Marilyn. He gave me . . . " James fell asleep in the middle of his words, then suddenly jolted awake, turned and smiled, then tried throwing his arm around me again. He couldn't lift them high enough to get them around my shoulders.

I worried about James that night. But I was pretty high myself, which made me selfish in a numb, distant sort of way. I'd done my first lines of Russian heroin, and they weren't that bad. A creepy young junkie, Misha, invited me to go with him and his girlfriend into their car, parked around the corner from Ptyutch. He poured some china white on a face mirror, quickly cut it into rails, and passed the mirror to me. Within twenty minutes, I was happily buzzed. Things were looking up in Russia.

James never could figure out what Marilyn consisted of, and I've never heard of it since. I would guess that it was some kind of cocktail of ecstasy and heroin. I'd heard about a Russian girl who OD'd on such a cocktail. She popped one E/heroin cocktail, but didn't feel anything. So she popped another. She waited, but got impatient, and wanted to show off her Russian nonchalance. So she popped another cocktail. And then another. She finally felt a rush, but being drunk and Russian and predisposed to taking things to the limit, she thought she'd pop another one for good measure. And one more. About an hour later, her heart stopped. They rushed her to the hospital. She survived, but she lost that chirpy glow of hers forever.

James had been overindulging in ecstasy over the previous year, and he had a few physiological glitches resulting from a meningitis attack as a child. Maybe his nervous system couldn't handle the sensation overload of an E and heroin cocktail—if that's what the Marilyn was. Perhaps Marilyn was just some bizarre KGB psychotic, who knows. But it fucked James up. Ecstasy was doing enough damage to his nerves. The last time I saw him on E, his eyes dripped down to his lips, and his lips were pouring off of his face. It didn't look fun or funny; just horrifying.

I thought about James as I lay in my bed that night, floating weakly from the last residue of heroin in my blood. It was the first time I'd scored heroin in Moscow, and it lived up to its promise. The danger to James seemed abstract to me at the time, and my sincere worries were equally as distant. The next afternoon, James met for a Sunday brunch with some local executives. He told me he felt great, and although he still couldn't describe Marilyn's effects, it was worth the ride.

"I was really worried about you, James," I told him. "I was seriously considering calling an ambulance."

"No, I was fine," he laughed. "I really enjoyed it. But if you were so fucking worried, Ames, why did you abandon me? Great friend you are."

"Sorry."

James comes from a freakishly wealthy, yacht-owning English family. It was through James and his Eurotrash friends that I finally found the Drug Crowd in Moscow. When all else fails, always go with the rich. Careerist middle-class Americans are guaranteed bummer-'bots. They won't even do drugs in private. They've been so successfully co-opted by the Reagan propaganda machine that they actually *believe* drugs are immoral; and what's worse, they're convinced that they came to this sick, perverse conclusion *all on their own.*

Russians at least don't judge you morally, particularly not when it comes to self-abuse. It's one of the main reasons I feel so much more free here than back home. They don't judge you, and they aren't hypocrites.

Before James I'd never hung out with Eurotrash types. In fact, I'd barely even believed that they were real. One thing I noticed right away was that his crowd liked to be around beautiful Russian women—unlike either my poet friends or American expat acquaintances. Or rather, beautiful Russian girls liked to be around James's crowd. In any event, it was a sign that unlike the mainstream bar-b-que expats, these guys were looking for maximum sensual pleasure.

There were some drawbacks to the Eurotrashers, however. They listened to techno music, talked lovingly about Ibiza and modeling shows, and dropped a few coded hints that, at the very least, cocaine was part of their weekend. . . . Okay, I could tolerate the coke part. To coin a proverb, where there is coke, there is the catalogue.

One night, when James felt safe enough, he invited me to a party his Eurotrash friends were throwing in an huge apartment on the Novy Arbat. It was the night I was first introduced into Moscow's drug world. I can't remember exactly how it went, but I think James said something jokish and disparaging about people who drop ecstasy, but the disparaging was so obviously ironical to my ears that I decided to up the coded ante by mentioning drugs in a morally neutral sentence, which he then seconded in his own way, which I then peeled open by admitting that I'd "tried" a few drugs, which led to a few jokes about pot and hash, then a mention of ecstasy . . . a few minutes later, I followed him into a closed bedroom, where his friend Ben sold me a hit of E for $35.

There were probably 40 people at the party, including a few Russian DJs in leather coats and Caesar hairdos. Every single one of us was flying. Sometime later, the cops broke it up and even threatened to haul us in. They were responding to complaints about the music, and looking for a little bonus. They made us line up against a wall. A couple bottles of vodka solved the problem.

After that, I went on a wild coke-and-ecstasy spree with James and the Eurotrash gang. At the time I was working as a personal secretary to the hyper-ambitious Pakistani investor. He drove me like a scabbed mule. I worked more hours than anyone I knew, and made less than anyone I knew. I'd go days without sleeping, just to keep the Pak from screaming. I'd work through the weekends. Those weekend nights I got off, I was so desperate to escape even the residue of the business world that I'd gorge myself on James's coke and E.

The Eurotrash circle was fairly international: British, French, German, two Americans, and a lot of Russians, particularly female Russians. They were all lifestyle, and they were doing it right. They distinguished themselves from the conventional American expats in almost every way, from being physically beautiful to being Russian-speaking, not overly concerned with their careers outside of office hours, and by their healthy attitude toward corporeal pleasure. It was understood that none of us would reveal to "the community" what we were doing on weekend nights; we all pretended that we were beer-swilling, bar-b-queing expats. But when we got together, it was all pills, powder, techno music, and model girls. We were living almost like rock stars—well, they were, actually. I was only getting the scraps when it came to sex. I got the leftovers, but that was fine. They tolerated me, although they thought I had a screw loose—or else I was somewhat nerdy in their eyes, out-of-code, awkward.

I was willing to sell out, sell out everything. Fuck the punks and artists, who couldn't score me anything better than banana peels! Call me Mr. Techno, so long as they can get me high! I listened to and—get this—even DANCED to their techno music, clumsily of course. After watching the Eurotrashers a few times, I started getting the steps right (hooking thumbs in belt loop and thrusting pelvis; cocking arms and holding index finger out like revolvers, pointing everywhere while shaking head with a cheesy techno smile, and other assorted embarrassments). I hated the music more and more after having initially decided to ignore it; I snorted coke with greed, dropping my hard-earned money on gram after gram in the hope that I'd be invited into the heroin penthouse; I popped caps of E well after they stopped making me feel good. It was still better than the alternative: beer and bar-b-ques on the lawns of Moscow.

It got to the point where we were dropping E and snorting coke almost every weekend. That and 80-hour workweeks for a manic, ambitious young Pak were wiping me out. But I pushed on. I'd read about these *ubermenschen* business types who never slept at all, and I figured I could do it too. I had to somehow nullify those 80 hours of pain and waste with a few good hours of bliss, even if it meant I paid more later.

On the eve of the 50th anniversary of the Red Army's victory over the Nazis, I slipped out of my boss's apartment at eleven in the evening on a Saturday—we were putting together a kind of employees' manual to define our alleged corporate culture—and met up with James at the Titanik club, which has reigned as the king of flatheads-on-ecstasy disco since it opened.

Titanik is massive, two-floored, like something from a Hollywood movie. Buzz-cut security in *Die Hard* costumes and ear mikes keep order and occasionally rough up a drunken flathead. It's all smoke, eardrum-mangling techno booms, and sweating nouveaux riches. In the parking lot, James, his girlfriend Ira, her sister, and I snorted several lines of coke in his Saab. Then we each popped an E tab and headed into the club.

It had been a few weeks since I'd taken anything. Work was beginning to drive me insane. My Pak boss dragged me up and down his stairwell of ambitions and complexes day in and day out.

But on this night, for some reason, the E and the coke didn't work their magic. There's a law of diminishing returns with drugs. I was exhausted. Exhausted from work, from drugs, and from faking it, faking that I belonged to this Eurotrash crowd.

That's how you start a-feelin' when it's five in the morning, dawn breaks, and that mental decathlon takes its toll, one too many wipe-outs. You want to retire in peace. You start thinking about sitting by a fire, in your bathrobe, with a John Grisham book, dog on the carpet. . . .

A couple of months later, James took me to a party at Bogdan's apartment. Bogdan was a Russian techno pop star. He was always on TV, prancing around in sunglasses and gaudy techno Elton John outfits. And he was the darling of the rave underworld, mostly because of the infamous parties he threw in his apartment.

I was grateful, if a little perplexed as to why I'd been invited to what was supposed to be the coolest of the cool in the techno Eurotrash world—a party at Bogdan's private flat. But I didn't ask questions. The apartment was huge and cleared of most furniture: there was a massive sound system, a huge projector TV projecting onto the side wall, and a side cubbyhole area for DJs. Behind the TV projector were two couches and a long, low table. In the center of the table, a kind of traditional Russian party bouquet of Soviet champagne, wine, cognac, grapes, and mandarins. . . . On the edges of the table, rows of pills—ecstasy. There must have been about forty people who showed, half of whom were teenage girls.

I was in awe—I kept my mouth shut. Everyone dropped a tab—except for James and me. It was a Sunday night, and I couldn't physically or mentally take the strain any longer. I figured I wouldn't get laid anyway. I'd only end up paying at work the next day.

James withheld too, which surprised me. I regretted it

then as I regret it now, but I can't argue with my general frame of mind, which was that I couldn't fake it any longer. Even though this neo-'70s disco drug scene was better than no drug scene, I wasn't really enjoying myself. It was beginning to feel like work, as though I had to come to meet them not halfway but all the way. Selling out wasn't all it was cracked up to be. A constant effort, a constant pushing and masking.

Secretly, I was hoping for something better, ideologically up my alley. Time, as it turned out, was on my side.

By 1996, the drug scene had exploded and democratized. The government claims that drug use exploded by 300 percent between 1992 and 1997, and that there are now 2 million addicts. Another statistic claimed that heroin imports increased by five hundred percent in 1998 alone—continuing one very wonderful vertical X-Y graph slant that began when Yeltsin took power. If anything, they're probably underreporting it a thousand percent.

Which was good for me. I no longer had to sell myself just to get high. After *Living Here* established itself, I stopped hanging out with the Eurotrash crowd completely, and spent time with journalists and quasi-arty expats.

Later, as a manner of bragging, we listed Bogdan's apartment in the *eXile* as the top "Ho-ing" place to visit. We bragged about the wild ecstasy parties and tripped out teenies and Euro-decadence. But we didn't give away the address. We must have received hundreds of phone calls and letters from desperate readers, begging us to let them know where Bogdan's was. They were looking for fun.

Kolya couldn't tell me where to get speed. He was an ex-junkie from northern Kazakhstan who used to bang boiled opium extract from the age of 13 to 15, out of sheer boredom from living in the steppes. His geologist father moved his family there as a child. He told me that the boredom was unbearable: just a flat, moonlike, dusty steppe, and a city plunked in the middle of nowhere. Block Brezhnevian apartment buildings, grim schoolyards. . . . You either fought the rival punks, or banged poppy straw.

The word "speed" in Russian means AIDS. So you don't go asking junkies, with an eager smile, where you can score some AIDS. Most junkies here share their needles. They don't want to hear about AIDS. Hepatitis B and C are bad enough. When AIDS comes to Moscow—and it's just about here—"speed" will be the evil incantation. . . .

The closest equivalent word for speed is "phenamine," although some also talked of "ephedrine," a ma huang Chinese herb which, like ginseng, is pure fiction.

I met Kolya at the only pirate music kiosk in Moscow that

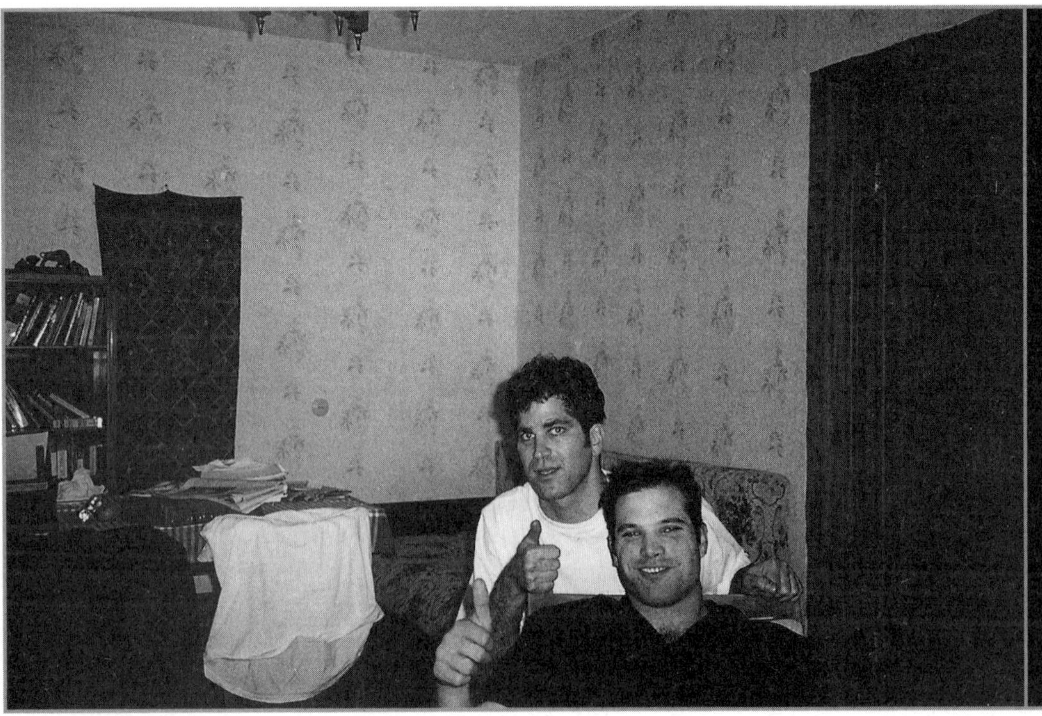

Heroin first started trickling in around late '94, started to become popular with the cool crowd in '95, and sent a generation of super-cheesy/hip techno kids into a vomit-drenched slumber of coolness in 1996. As always, the *eXile* jumped on the heroin-Xploitation bandwagon way too late, and when we did, we faked it, got it all wrong, and sold it back to the reader as cutting-edge journalism. The truth, however, is that our senior staff wisely abstained from whiffin' Burma's finest, and we wouldn't be caught dead doing cheesy drug rituals like getting high and snapping self-timed photos of ourselves.

sold punk and alternative tapes. He couldn't believe that an American would be interested in avant-garde music. The few Americans he'd met were all of the Ned Flanders lawn-set. The bar-b-que crowd had really fucked up things for the rest of us.

Kolya invited me to sit with him in his kiosk, drink beer, abuse the customers, and steal tapes and money. Actually, he stole the money, while I just stole a few tapes here and there. We had fun, although in the summer it was a fucking pressure cooker inside that kiosk. You could barely move one way or the other without worrying about tipping over a stack of pirate cassettes, and you sweated like a 300-pound noseguard during training camp.

Kolya pocketed every third sale. He needed the money for his wife and child. They rented an apartment so far out of town that, by train, bus, and metro, it took him over an hour to get into the center. I started spending some time at Kolya's kiosk after I heard that he was an ex-junkie. This was in 1994. As it turned out, he was even less connected than I was.

By the summer of '96, I didn't need Kolya. Through *Living Here*, I'd come into a second, somewhat more interesting and intelligent group of dopeheads, including journalists, investment bankers, and regular hangers-on. They were neophytes for the most part, but the drugs were real enough. They'd even cracked the speed enigma: one had scored speed in Estonia and brought several plastic gram packets to Moscow. It was pretty weak, heavily cut with baby powder or something, but if you took enough you could make a chattering fool of yourself.

It was heroin I was after most by now. After Misha's little gift at Ptyutch, I went seven long, dry months without it. I finally found the wormhole to Luang Prabang at the Water Club, which in the summer of '96 was considered the hippest "underground" techno club. It was built into a Soviet river-port building, but done up sort of like an MTV video: earth-gray curtains and sheets hanging, the requisite Day-Glo wall murals . . . rooms cut out of nothing . . . and an outdoor chill out in a colonnaded space, perhaps an old waiting area for riverboat travelers. Water Club was the successor to Ptyutch, the now-mythical underground bomb shelter where I'd seen James twitching on Marilyn.

Not that Ptyutch was all that interesting: just another dark disco, only every single kid was guaranteed fucked up. The authorities closed Ptyutch, probably because at any given time about half of Moscow's MDMA was bursting and popping in the brain canals of Ptyutch's patrons. Water Club, although more impressive in design, never took off. In mid-'96, the drugs were beginning to take their toll on the first wave of chemical gluttons. People like Kirill and Stas had been devouring drugs for a solid year now. Not in a measured, American way, but like raging alcoholics in charge of a vodka warehouse. They had the money and the connections, as the children of the old Soviet elite—and thus, the New Russian elite. So they did lots of drugs every single night, and slept it off in the day. They lived like vampires.

But their supply of serotonin and dopamine had depleted. By the time Water Club got off the ground, the usual faces were starting to drop off. A couple had gone to dry out. One lost her husband to jail for a minor possession infraction. Someone—a young blond ex-model—got raped and killed while out on a score. There were overdoses. We heard about another person dying. Others tried to stay away from the Water Club just to save themselves. They'd become heroin junkies. They'd been blindsided. It just happened.

A word about the Russian attitude toward drugs. In 1994, drugs began to appear in Moscow like never before, and by '95, the distribution networks were falling into place. The youth—particularly the sons and daughters of the new elite, who generally had a lot of money, good instincts for what was cool, and a love of techno culture—consumed everything without prejudice. Because they came so late in the game, Russians don't carry the baggage of old, false preconceptions. All are equal before the Russians' eyes!

In America, the hippies somehow got control of the drug-ranking levers, and little has changed since. So we have these dated moral values attached to each drug, such as:

Marijuana: benign, the Corona Beer of the drug world
Mushrooms: relatively benign because they are "natural" or "organic," next logical step up from pot
Cocaine: can be a bad scene, but good for conversation
Ecstasy: fun, positive, mostly benign, just don't take too much
Acid: a requirement for mind expansion, just don't abuse

And a separate category:

Speed: dirty, bad. As Allen Ginsberg wrote in a manifesto in 1967, "Speed is antisocial, paranoid-making. It's a drag—bad for your body, bad for your mind, in the long run uncreative and a plague in the whole dope industry."

And a third category:

Heroin: E-V-I-L

My own pyramid would be the complete inverse. I've

never been more terrified than on mushrooms and marijuana, whereas heroin has taken me into its down pillow den many times, and never once hurt me.

Speed is everything the hippies said it wasn't: it *is* social, confidence-making, creative, and a bright spot on the whole dope industry. Marijuana, on the other hand, is absolutely paranoia-inducing, bad for your mind, antisocial, and not just uncreative, but responsible for some of the dumbest music, lyrics, and album-cover art in the history of man.

All drugs hit the market in Moscow at roughly the same time. So the Russians judged each as it made them feel, discounting hippie lore. No doubt ecstasy is still by far the most popular drug in Moscow, along with coke, but heroin is not far behind. More often than not, the complaint about heroin is that it's unsociable. But there is no social/moral stigma attached to a person who takes that plunge "down" into heroin, which in America puts you into a kind of prison uniform.

This made Russians far more enlightened than Americans in their attitude toward drugs, but also created a lot of unwitting junkies very fast. If you have a weakness for heroin, or an addictive personality, you may as well buy heroin a diamond wedding ring.

Russians as a race are prone to excess. I mean extreme excess. They consume 80 percent of the world's vodka. You can see them wobbling drunk on the streets on any evening, helping each other into metro cars and at crossings. It's considered a right here. Even centuries ago, foreign travelers reported seeing not just drunken peasants, but smashed aristocrats and clergy, stumbling down the morning streets naked, in the

BOOK REVIEW

You Were On Ecstasy, You Stupid Dickhead!

The Ecstasy Club
by Douglas Rushkoff
Sceptre Press London 1997
315 pp. UK retail price 10 quid

by Mark Ames
the eXile

I won't lie. I'll admit it right off: I didn't finish this book. I couldn't. I mean I literally, physically couldn't. It sucked so bad that it didn't even warrant a mercy laugh. I mean, look at the 5th grade science textbook cover: would you call it "trippy, man," or just plain stupid? Trust me, Masha Gessen was like Hunter Thompson compared to this; at least she had a subject to work with. Her book was grotesquely affected and false, but at least, on the basic physical level, you could turn the page without screeching out loud from raw pain. In fact, a lot of really bad books can be valued for their unintentional humor: take Rick Furmanek and Jennifer Gould as examples. The eXile offices sounded like they'd been taken over by a pack of pot–smoking hyenas the night we read Gould excerpts out loud to each other: her book was kitsch non–fiction, a sort of Toxic Avenger of the journalism world. The terrible, shocking thing about Gould was that she actually found a publisher and an audience who not only didn't laugh, but took it very seriously, at face value—including her airbrushed pinup photo.

This book, despite the blurb by William Gibson, was a literary root canal: like being chained to a dentist's chair, eyes tweezed open like the guy from Clockwork Orange, forced to watch a ninety–foot Bill Clinton on a movie screen groveling with tears in his eyes for eight hours straight. Telling you, "All is bliss. All is bliss."

That line constitutes a pivotal, deep, intense moment in the novel, by the way. I didn't just make it up. Douglas Rushkoff did.

So why are we even bothering to review *The Ecstasy Club* way out here in Moscow? First, it is considered by many to be the hippest book of the year, and the first and only authentic piece of fiction on rave culture. The young rave chick who loaned me the book struck me as intelligent and cynical, so in spite of my natural revulsion for things–techno, I really didn't expect the book to suck this bad. I expected to swallow the bitter taste of literary envy. Instead, I got a whiff of pure, liquid shite—that's right, "shite," and not "shit."

As the first "voice of a new generation" book since Douglas Coupland's boring, middle–brow novel *Generation X*, *The Ecstasy Club* simply had to get a review in our newspaper, since we ourselves claim to be the voice of a new degeneration. Well folks, one thing I can say pretty confidently as that our voice and his voice ain't got nuttin in common, and ho daddy am I glad.

Now I'm assuming that *The Ecstasy Club* authentically represents the zeitgeist of the rave/techno generation. And lemme tell ya, folks, they're as stupid as I'd always feared. Which is why, I suppose, this book—or what I read of it—was the most terrifying reading experience since, well, Douglas Coupland's *Generation X*... another novel, by the way, that I couldn't finish.

The massive, crater–sized flaw in Rushkoff's first novel is that he didn't follow basic drug codes. There is an understanding among experienced hands in the drug world that, excepting speed, drugs make you dumb. You may have a lot of fun and you may experience sensations more intense than anything you'd known... but those sensations do not translate back into the world of the sober as anything but embarrassing outbursts you'd rather forget. Probably for that reason, almost none of the huge body of 60s hippie literature survives.

No drug makes a person more stupid and sentimental than ecstasy, with cocaine running a close second. Remember what Denis Leary said about coke? Even Jews would sneak into the bathroom with Hitler if he had an eight ball to share...and, after whiffing out, the Jews, in their coked–out enthusiasm, would say, "You know Adolf, I think you had a lot of really neat ideas." But hey, at least they'd feel pretty damn embarrassed the next day. That's no reason not to sniff coke. Just remember all that empty chatter was purchased with your own seratonin and dopamine...

Rushkoff is no different from the Jews of Leary's joke, sneaking into the proverbial bathroom with a bunch of morons and popping ecstasy, then writing down such inane reflections as, "Their tension dissolved into the smooth lines around them. People began swaying in the waves of energy..." That was a scene when an outdoor rave was almost broken up by a bunch of mean black kids who, in typical white suburban niceguy fantasy, only needed to understand and be understood, and of course, get drawn into the rave party. What calmed the blacks down? The alleged genius/leader of the rave pack, who softly whispered, "All is bliss. All is bliss." That was all it took to soothe the generations of racial tension, discrimination and hardship. Some wiry little cracker whispering, "All is bliss. All is bliss." A few pages later, there's even a deep, pitiful homeless man whom the ravers adopt. We're supposed to be impressed that the ravers take him in and understand him. Of course, nothing is mentioned about the bum's lice, crabs, urine–and–shit–soaked underwear, or tuberculosis. I had to imagine it myself–imagine the characters wincing every time their little homeless cloud of fungus and bacteria sat down to chat.

Thirty years ago, Charles Manson thought he heard something profound in even the dumbest Beatles songs. As Sam Kinison screeched, "YOU WERE ON ACID, MANSON! You would have heard messages in the Monkees songs, and they weren't even a real band, you fuck!"

That's exactly how I felt reading The Ecstasy Club. "YOU WERE ON E, YOU FUCK! I took that shit too, but I always felt embarrassed the next morning. I just hoped no one would remember how stupid and affectionate I was the night before–I didn't go writing my impressions down like they mattered!"

It hit me a couple of days ago that maybe I was missing the whole point of The Ecstasy Club. A novel couldn't possibly have lines as stupid as, "He had that whole working–class–British thing about him. Those are the people who wore Doc Martens in the first place–before the punkers and then the ravers decided they were so cool." Leaving out the fact that it was skinheads who first popularized Docs, I began to get the queasy feeling that maybe this novel was working on a meta–level, as in meta–satire, or meta–parody. A parody of rave culture and ecstasy thoughts. A post–modern cyber–novel that both exploits and laughs at its subject at the same time.

So I rushed to the internet to find out if my hunch was valid. Nope. Not a chance. The book was meant to be taken at face value. The only satire, according to the author himself, was to show that the raver characters, in their "attempt" to free themselves from the chains of conventional life, wind up creating oppressive institutions of their own. I swear to god, it really works on that grammar school level of cheap morality.

Apparently Rushkoff has touched off a lot of controversy lately. Not because he wrote a bad book so painful that it could paralyze a man. But rather, because he was accused by "leftists" in America of having "sold out"; ie., he charges speaking fees. It's like being back in high school and arguing over whether or not REM "sold out" after Murmur, or after Fables of the Reconstruction. The only positive impression I kept after abandoning this novel fifty pages into it was relief–relief that I live 6,600 miles away from the Bay Area, where the novel takes place... 6,600 miles away from that incredibly vicious, pointless paradigm of utter stupidity.

The book confirmed most of my suspicions about the techno culture. Such as how desperate they are to prove that they are cool (or underground), and how they stole all the idiotic mysticism and cheap slogans of the hippies without adapting what made the hippies truly interesting: active confrontation. What these characters have learned is that you can steal all of the slogans about fighting authority or doom or death that the hippies and punks paid so dearly for, and merely repeat them in code; that for them, style is the end–all of rebellion: a nose–ring is substituted for molotov cocktails. End of discussion...

There is nothing fun, funny or kitsch about the stupidity in The Ecstasy Club. I don't doubt that this book really does authentically capture the esprit of the new generation (even though rave culture is hardly new). After getting attacked last week by a Russian nationalist who kept calling America "stupid," I've been thinking: the longer I stay away from my motherland, the more right he seems to be. This book has me convinced that the stupid genes are being successfully passed down into the young generation. If America really is stupid, however, then stupidity is a pretty damn successful national strategy. America may well be the stupidest country in the first world–no other nation is as religious or god–fearing. However, that kind of stupidity, that kind of willful self–delusion on the individual level may in fact be the necessary ingredient that makes a nation strong. America completely lacks the self–doubt and self–loathing that gripped not only the late Soviet elite, but grips all of Europe. The stupidity of this novel proves, if anything, that America will stay strong and rule the world for at least another generation.

I've spent some time over the past three years in Russia with the local rave scene. My reason is simple: They live in the body, as opposed to the life in the bitter mind I had explored to death before arriving here. I could handle hanging out in the rave world not because the music was good or the aesthetic was profound. I always blocked out the stupid parts, the pseudo–mysticism and the freshman "if a tree fell in a forest and no one was around to hear it, would it still make a sound?" level of philosophizing. No, I hung out with them because they popped pills and had sex. And now, frankly, I feel really stupid myself.

In spite of the *eXile*'s policy of trashing anything that smacked of techno culture, a techno diva named Apollonaria dropped by our offices and gave us this book to read, thinking we'd be blown away. Well, we were blown away—we nearly died from a bile overdose. After printing this review of über-moron Douglas Ruskhoff's book, we sent a copy of it to him via email. He actually responded with the usual hurt tone. So we fired off another salvo of nasty emails, to which he finally replied with deafening "bounces off of me and sticks to you" silence. Douglas, your name's on our list.

middle of winter, holding their hands in front of their genitalia and picking fights with phantoms.

During Gorbachev's failed temperance campaign, Russians found clever ways to get hammered. For example, they learned that fuel products used in MiGs, when distilled, yielded something akin to a low-quality vodka. So the MiGs—which became known as "flying restaurants"—were tapped for their break fluids and gear fluids. While Vanya and Sasha got tanked in the airfield tool shed, Sergei Petrovich, flying five miles up in the air over the empty steppes, suddenly realizes that his wing flaps aren't responding. . . . The flying restaurant suddenly starts heading in a downward tilt, and there's nothing Sergei Petrovich can do. . . . No foreigner can drink—truly drink—with a Russian. Even a teenage girl will put you under the table. But at least with alcohol, it takes a bit longer for the drug to turn to poison.

That's why a drug like heroin successfully pruned some of the weaker-willed young Russians back in 1996. The penchant for excess and addiction meant that a dabble in heroin meant jail, destruction, or death for every tenth Golden Youth-er. In a culture where people help each other and even allow people to fuck up massively, having an addictive, excessive personality is not only tolerated, but encouraged. They'll get deeper and deeper into the addiction, assuming that somehow fate—or someone—will pull them out. And even if no one successfully pulls himself out of the shit, at least all the fussing and crying makes for good social drama, which Russians can't live without.

So the Water Club got emptier and emptier, and Golbuev, the owner, got more and more desperate. Ilya looked nothing like the raver kids. He was a curly-haired, bearded, potbellied Jew who looked twenty years older from the coke abuse. Here was another thing I'd never known until now: how coke fiends get fat. I can think of about six or seven heavy coke fiends I've known in Russia, all of whom were slob-fat Belushi types. Golbuev was one of them. And as the owner of the coolest new club, he had a new worry: patrons dropping off like flies. The cutting-edge techno scene that he was instrumental in creating at Ptyutch was cannibalizing itself.

We spent a lot of time together that one summer at the Water Club. He turned me on to some shit jones one night. He took me and a few friends into his back office with a mad look in his black-ringed eyes. He pulled out a wad of cocaine and poured it onto a mirror. He pulled out two credit cards and started to chop and divide like a Benihana chef, cutting some of the hugest rails I'd ever seen. We whiffed out on those high-speed rails, Golbuev taking three for our one. Then he pulled out another packet: heroin, as per my very own request.

"This is gray. Persian gray," he chirped.

A nasal speedball. It was nice, if a bit weak.

I bought two grams of coke and a gram of Persian from Ilya. A day later, he called me up and asked if he could come over. He was over in comic lightning speed. [Ames hangs up phone, suddenly, doorbell rings, Golbuev's at the door . . .] He rushed for my stash, poured it out on my desk, and cut rails that were even larger than the ones a few nights earlier. They were six-lane freeways, those coke rails. Three of them lined up next to each other. He had good drug manners. He paid for it—he bought it all back from me, then hurried off in a taxi to someone else's house. On his way out, he shook my hand, paranoia burning in his charcoal-ringed eyes.

I didn't see Kirill any more. There was a rumor that he'd gone to a rehab clinic in England or Miami. Stas also cleaned up. As did all of James's friends. James was developing some strange disfiguration in his facial muscles, a kind of wind-tunnel polio droop that got worse every time he dropped E. So he finally gave it a break. But by now I didn't care about the Eurotrash crowd. I'd moved on to a new group of seratonin parasites who had better taste in music—Pixies and Lou Reed albums in between the techno.

Near the end of summer, word got out that the Water Club was in big trouble, that it was dying. Golbuev was having problems. I could easily imagine: with those manic coke fiend eyes of his. . . . A regular of the club was raped and murdered. A Water Club manager OD'd. The patrons were thinning out. They were dropping off like flies, this first generation of Moscow's druggies. They'd reached a limit.

And then we heard the news: Golbuev had been assassinated. He apparently had coke debts in the hundreds of thousands. It's hard to imagine someone doing that much blow, but he did.

Later the story got changed. He absconded, or simply fled and spread the rumor himself that he'd been assassinated. He snagglepussed to Argentina with his girlfriend, then eventually made his way back to New York.

I later learned a shocking fact about him. He was only 27 years old. He looked like he was 40.

Later, in early 1998, Liza Berezovsky, who was close to Golbuev, was hauled in by the St. Petersburg cops for possession of cocaine. She'd been busted at a local rave. I feel sorry for the cop who busted her. Boris Berezovsky isn't known for his warm, forgiving personality. You don't rise from controlling the mafia-run automobile distribution network to über-oligarch and survivor of car bombs that

Top: we printed Rushkoff's emailed reply to our review of his book. Below: Yet another *eXile* reader desperately trying to find out where Bogdan's apartment is, and how he can get invited.

A BAD ECTS[SIC]SY TRIP

The following is an email from Ecstasy Club *author Douglas Rushkoff, in response to last*

20 - December 3, 1997 • P. 24

issue's review of his book, which was emailed to his web site.

Ecstasy Club is a satire. I guess you're too serious to get that.

Oo, that's smarts! More ruthless satire from the vicious, acidic pen of Douglas Rushkoff.

BOGDAN'S ADDRESS REVEALED!

Alright Guys,

How's it going ??? Hopefully you can help. I am a frequent visitor to Moscow, the first thing I try and do is pick up a copy of the eXile, just to find out where all the shit is going down. There is one particular club that me and my mates want to check out, "BOGDANS". Every fucker I speak to in Moscow has heard of it (or have they ?), but no-one knows where it is.

I've gotta get to the "Sixth Dimension", & don't care if I ever leave, but none of the Gypsy Cabs know where it is.

You gotta help !!!!!!

Dear !!!!!!,

Okay, okay. Everyone's been hassling us about this, so we'll tell you exactly where Bo[illegible]s located. The addr[illegible] it a [illegible] Dom 5. Good luck, a[illegible] 'em tha[illegible]e sent you!

decapitate your drivers by holding charity raffles. And now, his little Liza was in jail, and word had leaked out to the national press.

Liza, of course, got off. The loophole was found. A little-known section in Russia's draconian, Malaysian-style drug laws allows you to get off scot-free if you turned the drugs in yourself. And now, according to the arresting cop, whose memory had probably undergone a little reediting by Berezovsky's thugs, Liza had in fact turned that coke in all by her goodie-two-shoes self. The bust was reported in *Komsomolskaya Pravda* and *Moskovsky Komsomolets*, two papers not too friendly to the dark prince of privatization.

Other drug offenders haven't gotten off so lightly.

In Tallinn, the most Western of any FSU cities, speed is the drug of choice, perhaps sharing top billing with ecstasy. It makes practical sense: speed gives you a far better value, ten times the juice of coke for less than half the price. The Estonians are Western-minded and more practical, so it makes sense that the Estonian youth, in their accelerated drug-selection Darwinism, would go for the best value.

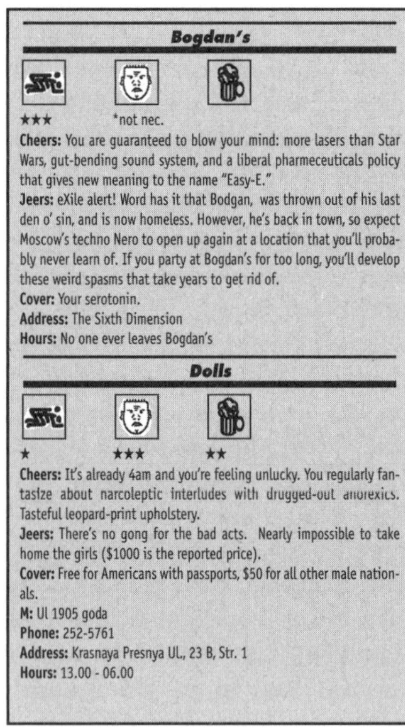

Bogdan's

★★★ *not nec.

Cheers: You are guaranteed to blow your mind: more lasers than Star Wars, gut-bending sound system, and a liberal pharmeceuticals policy that gives new meaning to the name "Easy-E."

Jeers: eXile alert! Word has it that Bodgan, was thrown out of his last den o' sin, and is now homeless. However, he's back in town, so expect Moscow's techno Nero to open up again at a location that you'll probably never learn of. If you party at Bogdan's for too long, you'll develop these weird spasms that take years to get rid of.

Cover: Your serotonin.

Address: The Sixth Dimension

Hours: No one ever leaves Bogdan's

Dolls

★ ★★★ ★★

Cheers: It's already 4am and you're feeling unlucky. You regularly fantasize about narcoleptic interludes with drugged-out anorexics. Tasteful leopard-print upholstery.

Jeers: There's no gong for the bad acts. Nearly impossible to take home the girls ($1000 is the reported price).

Cover: Free for Americans with passports, $50 for all other male nationals.

M: Ul 1905 goda

Phone: 252-5761

Address: Krasnaya Presnya UL., 23 B, Str. 1

Hours: 13.00 - 06.00

What you get in Tallinn is not the best speed or the best ecstasy, but it does the job for a price. For forty dollars, you get a gram of baby-powder white speed. I try telling my friends that real speed looks like brown sugar with small crystal glass shavings: it has a harsh, industrial look. One tiny blast will keep you going for hours. But I'm just a speed pedant in that way, and it must get old hearing me whine, the way expats always whine about sub-Western quality.

A few friends of mine—expats only—muled their own personal stashes in from Estonia by train. The chances of the customs officials checking foreigners are very slim, slim enough to warrant the risk.

But still no Russian speed. The nice thing about speed is that it can be manufactured in any part of the world—but here, you've got to import it. I've tried to understand why Russians eschew the most rigorous drug of all. My first answer would have to do with social stigma—or rather, the complete lack of a social stigma. Speed signifies nothing. It's a working-man's drug: for artists, truck drivers, late-shift operators, physicists.

But living in a country where people aren't used to working too hard kills the incentive to do speed. On the other hand, coke is exotic, expensive, and cinematic. Speed is proletarian or intelligentsia—so it's almost like snorting a concentrated Soviet Union. Drugs are supposed to be an escape, a vacation, not a return to the familiar.

People who take speed usually do so because they lack the energy and confidence to meet the daily grind. Russians have to be the most energetic race in Europe. They are a northern anomaly in that way. You can't shut a Russian up. They can talk for hours, days on end, about nothing, and make it sound urgent. People with high metabolism rates tend not to like speed that much. As for confidence, while Russian men may lack the kind of anchorman confidence of the average Western businessman, he more than makes up for it in genuine, unaffected fearlessness.

A small nation like Estonia, on the other hand, would like to feel big and vital a few times a month. As would a lot of very small American individuals who felt they were promised so much more, and rather than accept that it was all a lie, rail out on speed to feel that bigness, that vitality that is lost to nearly every American by the age of 20.

Heroin really hit big in '96, but has declined lately in popularity. The techno kids who missed out on the first Ptyutch wave started hitting clubs like Galaktika and Plasma and Les, content with dropping ecstasy, mushrooms, and acid. Those clubs have since closed, and new ones opened in their place: Chaos, Territoriya, interchangeable techno joints decked out in Day-Glo. I say they're all a bunch of fucking lunatics. Go into a techno club and watch these zombie recruits. When not slumped brain dead in a chill out, they're crowded into the dance floor, all staring ahead in the same direction like soldiers waiting for orders. The orders come from the DJs, who vary the music to try to correspond to the dominant drug of the evening and the crap stage dancer. The Return of Disco, Part 10.

The Russian drug scene is becoming more Western in that factions are starting to form. Before, heroin was on a moral par with coke and ecstasy; it's now earning a reputation as something a bit more dangerous and devilish than the others. In a culture where restraint is a totally foreign concept, heroin is indeed more dangerous than other drugs. It's just that it's capable of ruining lives faster than the others. Vodka takes about twenty or thirty years to turn your insides into ulcers and confetti. That is, if you haven't been run over by a car or killed in a fight during one of your 3-bottle binges.

Russians will develop drug rankings and morals based more on consequence, not on ideology. Russian youth are, to their credit, the most ideology-free human beings on earth. They are the only people who can look skeptically upon everything we're pushing on them—from drugs and goods to market economics and post-Christian morality. Americans must be the most ideologically rigged people on earth, after the North Koreans, precisely because they don't even see their morals as having an origin in time and history. As the victor of the 20th century, America feels its values to be natural, the base standard.

The first time I saw Kolya shoot up was in my apartment in the Kropotskinakaya region of central Moscow. This was in the great summer of '96. He'd scored one dose, or so he said, and he wanted to bang in front of me. To his credit, he did offer me a share, but I wasn't in the mood.

"Can you get me a tie or a belt or something?"

I brought him an old tie from my slave days with the Pak businessman. Kolya wiped his nose, tied the knot, proudly jacking the works, as they say. I had to turn and look away, especially when the blood was drawn up the neck. It's a little phobia of mine, needles and blood. After pulling the needle out, he rolled his eyes up and stared at my ceiling. "Wow!" he cried. Then he moaned listlessly. I was impressed by how little time it really took. "Ohhh, wow."

Six months later, in my friend Andy's apartment, we tore open the fresh needles that we'd bought from a kiosk and dipped them into spoons full of freshly cooked smack. I tightened the belt around my biceps, while Kolya slapped a vein on the inside of my elbow. He'd bought cotton and a small round bandage just for me. He leaned over and shot me up. As the heroin spread throughout my body, then slowly fanned out to the extremities, I remember thinking, Kolya was right. They've all been right, all who have walked this path. Lou wasn't lying either. You really can't lie about smack. It's like lying about love.

GUILTY: The War on Fun

By Peter Garrett

The Moscow City Duma last week passed an incredible resolution. A majority of city deputies agreed in principle to sign the following bill into law: under a new administrative statute, nightclubs and discos can be fined and even closed if invading police decide their patrons ***appear*** to be under the influence of drugs.

"It's not a joke. It's true," said Yelena Tarasova, spokeswoman for the Duma. "The law governs only the appearance of having taken drugs, not incontrovertible proof."

According to the new law, clubs which contain stoned-looking clients can be fined 500 times the minimum wage the first time, 1000 times the second time, and be closed altogether the third time.

Fined for bad-looking clients? Thanks to the Moscow Duma, face control has just entered a new, dangerous phase: this isn't about trying to be cool anymore; it's about keeping your business from being shut down. Maybe in Russia it really has come to that—where you can be punished just for looking at a cop the wrong way.

Should the bill pass into law—and it has only one more hurdle, a second reading after corrections are introduced—it will mean just one more way that the introduction of new "administrative procedures" has been used to make everyday life more repressive, less free, and less fun in recent years. While the economy has been liberalizing, everyday life is in danger of returning to the gray, dull days of yesteryear. And the administrative code has been at the heart of a lot of it. If you're an American and you remember the literacy tests for black voters, you know that there's nothing that secures a bummer faster than an "administrative procedure." Only a few of them are funny enough to bring the whole depressing phenomenon into focus. The new drug law, an inspired piece of knee-jerk anti-fun legislation, is one of them.

Club owners could have seen this coming. In the last year, a whole slew of clubs have suffered severe problems due to administrative crackdowns. The gay club Shans was raided earlier in the year and closed temporarily; rave clubs like Galaktika and Akvatoria have all also had temporary shutdowns, while Less, Moby Dick, Aerodance, Water Club and other "underground" clubs have closed for good. Jack Rabbit Slim's and Miramar have both seen their nighttime business close due to rules about commercial activity in residential buildings—a rule that ruined the infamous Ptyutch club, and ensured that Krisis Zhanra keeps a cap on the nighttime fun factor. In a country where every single high profile murder that has been committed in the past seven years has gone unpunished, someone for some reason has decided that nightclubs, and the dopey, stoned, practically brainless teenagers which patronize them, are a threat the Russian public needs to be protected from first of all.

Now we're going to get a law where beered up, buzzcutted cops from provincial holes like Voronezh and from the Podmoskoviye are going to have to walk into places like Luch, look at the sloe-eyed teenyboppers in London rave gear grinding away to monotonous techno music, and make the expert determination, on sight, as to their sobriety.

Owners of youth-based clubs who've been hit up for building code violation fines, architectural zoning infractions, and municipal rent hikes know exactly what the deal is with a law like this. This is the beginning of the end for the club scene, the first round of cultural legislation—the moment where "hip, happening Moscow" gets rolled back, leaving nothing but casinos, strip clubs, and a bunch of barely-above-freezing podyezdy as recreational choices for the masses.

"This is serious. This means the police can come in and shut down any club at any time, for no reason at all," said Andrei Alexandrov, director of Kak Biy, a club in eastern Moscow. "It's just one more in a string of stupid and savage laws."

Another club manager, who asked not to be identified, said that the new law is not intended to enforce cultural prejudices, but to help police aid partners in protection schemes. "This law gives police the excuse to shut down the competitor of any club which pays a big enough bribe," he said. "It has nothing to do with imposing new cultural standards of order. If they wanted that, they'd shut down the drug dealers at Lubyanka. This is all about money."

Many of our readers who are not fifteen year-old girls with dumbstruck looks on their faces might very well ask themselves: who cares? What does it matter if hangouts for ravers and hippies get legislated out of existence? As long as my oil deal still goes through, why should I care?

The answer is that the new drug law is very representative of an ugly new habit the Russian government has adopted lately of circumventing the law through an emphasis on "administrative" discipline. If you were one of those people who believed our propaganda when we said we wanted freedom for Russians before perestroika, this—and a few other "administrative" foibles we'll be getting to in a minute—should be the kind of thing that would disturb you. Or, alternately, if you're a businessman who believes that the value of his Russian shares will ultimately depend on the international perception of Russia as a democracy, you may want to pay a little more attention to administrative law. That's because as a result of it, the Moscow authorities already have the practical experience to control movement, behavior, public speech, and even consumer choices—all the things democracy was supposed to leave up to the individual. When the world finds out your consumer base isn't free, you may be in trouble.

While most Muscovites, including the folks at the eXile, were shamelessly cashing in on the festivities surrounding Moscow's 850th anniversary, the Helsinki Watch for Human rights released a report on Moscow that contained what would have been eye-popping statistics, if anyone had been paying attention. Among the most shocking things in its report was the fact that in the first five months of 1997, Moscow police entered apartments to make registration document checks 1.3 million times. That means that this year about one out of every five people in Moscow has been subject to random administrative checks—most of which have resulted in bribes, fines or deportations (Helsinki Watch found that 63.4% of the checks uncovered violations).

Like the new drug law, the mass registration checks are based on the use of police to enforce administrative procedure, blurring the lines between criminal and administrative violations. In fact, under Moscow municipal law, police do not have the right to enter apartments to make registration checks. Article 10 of the Law on the Militia grants police the right to unhindered entry into citizens' homes in order to pursue a suspect in a crime, in cases of accidents, and to "protect the safety of citizens and public security in times of natural disaster, catastrophe, and . . . massive disturbances." In short, for any reason you might need a policeman for—not for administrative purposes. There is a Ministry of Internal Affairs decree which allows police to enter businesses and hotels on plausible grounds that a crime or administrative violation has occurred, but that doesn't allow police to enter private homes.

Alexei Yegorov, a lawyer who has campaigned for fair drug laws, believes that the new drug law and other police behavior are creating an environment where people have come to expect and tolerate even the most ridiculously obvious types of invasion of privacy from the government.

"That new drug law is a mockery of the whole concept of law," he said. "You can't have people fined just for looking a certain way. This would be an obviously illegal procedure."

So far, there hasn't been too much public outcry about the random apartment checks or the drug law. Why? Because the majority of the people having their apartments raided are dark-skinned migrants, and the majority of Muscovites aren't all that sympathetic to X-ed out teenagers.

Russians, of course, have a storied history of tolerating just about anything as long as the majority is left alone. After all, only about a million people were repressed in 1937, a tiny minority. So it makes perfect sense that no one would get too upset about a few passport checks or a stoner law or two.

Everyone knows that police in this city harass pedestrians. But how often have you heard that it's getting worse? Here are a few statistics: in 1996, 3,098 people were deported out of Russia from the territory of Moscow—1.7 times more than in 1995. Most of those deportations came as the result of random passport checks, which have soared again in 1997. In fact, in the first five months of this year, street passport checks nearly doubled in comparison to the same period of 1996, reaching 1.4 million in addition to the aforementioned apartment checks.

This ugly person could close down your favorite club!

Given Russia's history, you'd think that when Russian police start invading privacy a million times a year, people would start having bad memories. In fact, when the Russian police do anything at all a million times in a year, thoughtful people should probably worry. But you don't hear much of anything in the newspapers—even in the Western, "democratic" press.

With the notable exception of Stanford professor and unabashed Yeltsinophile Michael McFaul, who last week made the extraordinary assertion that Russia was not an undemocratic state because the near-dismissal of Anatoly Chubais demonstrated that public officials are still somewhat accountable for their behavior, even the most conservative Western commentators have backed off the assertion that Russia is a democracy. In fact, in separate editorials in recent weeks, the conservative *Economist* and the *Financial Times* both published lengthy apologies for the post-Soviet Russian regime, speaking in detail about the progress the country has made since the end of communism. Yet although both spoke about new respect for the "sanctity of private property" and the promise of the "new market economy," neither mentioned the word "democracy" at all, except as a future goal.

A weird sort of boosterism has taken over in our view of Russia. When the club scene booms, everybody from Good Morning America to *Newsweek* rushes to publicize it. But when democracy erodes to the point where clubs can be shut down just because the people who hang out in them look funny, you don't hear a peep about it in the news.

It's beginning to look a lot like we were kidding when we funneled all that junk over Radio Free Europe in the early 80s. We talked about the free press, and when the press went in the tank for Yeltsin in 1996, nobody protested too much. Now the press is almost completely bought off, and the U.S. government still issues editorials, through Radio Free Europe, saying that Russia is on the "right path." We talked about human rights in the 1980s, but by this year we have millions of illegal home entries every year and a criminal conviction rate of 99%. The system of representative democracy has degenerated to the point where there is only one election—the Presidential election—that matters, and even the 1996 version of that was dubiously held at best.

Now, with this drug law, we've got this great example of the men

continued on p. 4

For the next three weeks we lived in those needles. I was getting careless, spending all that time in Andy's apartment. Andy was kind enough to loan me his swank pad while he was on vacation, and I was messing it up with blood and syringes and needles. There were bloodied needles on his floor, on the glass table, in the sink. . . . Kolya was worse than me: shooting bloodied water from his infected needle across Andy's floor. He'd leave his used, bloodied needles in Andy's sink. I wouldn't go near Kolya's needles. I know what he's done, who he's been with. I know how safe Russians are, how worried about consequences, how practical-minded they are. I don't think even an AIDS explosion—when it comes—will change those habits. You have to be viscerally afraid of death to change your habits, the way Westerners are. Russians aren't as terrified. That's why they make such good infantry.

One downside to maining with a poor junkie was that if he helped buy you smack, he felt that it was half his. That was what I'd call the "Kolya Tax." He'd phone at any time of the day and, after a few forced pleasantries, say, "So, is there a little bit left, man?"

I learned to just lie after awhile. But Kolya was the type who responded to sharp slaps on the muzzle like a dog begging for food at the dinner table. He didn't have a right to take a quarter or a third, let alone a half or more as he usually did, of other people's shit. He'd push to see how far he could go, how much he could take.

The best shit we bought was through a girlfriend of mine, the great Sofiya, she who has made *kasha* out of my heart, she who almost turned me into the O. J. Simpson of Moscow. Sofiya is Nexus-6, beauty incarnate: six feet tall, long blond hair, pale blue eyes, antelope legs. And not mean, not in the least. She's always up for a laugh. She slept overnight, in bed with me, on January 1, 1997. I made a move—just one. And quickly retreated back to my border posts, crouching, terrified the entire night.

The following morning, Sofiya berated me, in front of Kolya, for being "*smirny*," or meek. Later, my internal newspapers recalled that incident as, and I quote, "An evening that will live in infamy." The details remain hazy.

We got on the subject of drugs, and Sofiya told us of her old childhood neighbor, Pasha, who sold heroin. Pasha was a lieutenant in the Russian Army and a cadet at an elite school. He was also on his way to becoming a major junkie. Sofiya called him up and made the arrangements. Then we crossed town to Prospekt Mira, and hung out at Sofiya's while we waited for our man. Her apartment was cozy and cluttered with reds and golds and embroidered carpets on the walls in the old Soviet fashion. Her father is a colonel who usually serves in overseas units.

Kolya slipped on his suede wool winter coat, and we followed him out the door, leaving Sofiya behind. Sofiya doesn't like heroin. She prefers coke or E. "Heroin just makes me go plttt!" she says, splaying herself on the divan like a whacked-out zombie, then jumping up and laughing. Sofiya. . . . I can't even think about her without wanting to burst into a post office. . . .

The three of us—me, Kolya, and Pasha—catch a taxi out to Petrovsko-Razumovskaya, one of those anonymous regions of Moscow that you might never hear of in ten years. Moscow has more people than the entire Czech Republic, more than all of Hungary. It spreads in every direction. Every year it swallows up another ten villages, a few municipalities. It's like the deep sea. I've never met a single person in Moscow who knows his city well.

We agreed to meet our dealer in the central platform of the metro at an exact time, thirty minutes from now. It was snowing that day, a nice cold white snow. Somehow the gray buildings and the white snow made for a truly cinematic scene. The gray had never been more solid and stoic than right after a powdering.

We waited on the platform for about fifteen minutes. The dealers were late, just like in the song. . . . Then two well-dressed bandit-teenagers approached us, each in their *dublyonki*, or thigh-length sheepskin coats. We introduced ourselves, shook hands, then followed them up the stairs and out of the metro station. Parked beside the station was a Zhiguli 6-series, based on a boxy 1960s Fiat model, with pitch-black smoked windows. Pasha and Kolya agreed to go into the car to make the score.

I passed the money to them, hoping to get two grams for myself. One of the bandit kids opened the back door. Kolya and Pasha got in, eyes greedily fixed on the dealer. The bandit slid into the back with them, while the other young bandit waited outside with me, checking for cops, making sure I wasn't a snitch. I did my best to act cool and nonsnitchy.

I got a good look at his eyes—they were dead. I remember that he had small pimples on his chin.

"Aren't you cold?" I asked, noting his open coat.

He laughed and turned away. "Naw," he drawled.

That was the giveaway. "So how're you feeling?" I asked.

He smiled vacantly and growled, "Fuckin-A."

The score took about ten minutes. This mobile scab unit wasn't exactly the most discreet method I'd come across. I was shocked and nervous. But I figured that they had to have the local *militsia* paid off to operate this openly. Either that, or they were just taking the "*davai*" attitude. Hard to tell, even in hindsight. For those ten long minutes, I started coming up with ways to save my ass. If they bust me, I'll do like Ash in *Army of Darkness*: "Hey . . . I've never even *met* these assholes!"

Kolya came out with a shocked look on his face. "Oh Mark, it's very good, man," he said, then laughed in disbelief, shaking his head. I knew he wasn't lying. We gave two .1 gram *tchetki* to Pasha as a kind of agent's fee, then we

The Water Club, the last of the first generation raver clubs in Moscow, was already half empty a few months after opening in mid-'96. But you'd never know anything was wrong by the mirthful expressions on these dorkadent customers' faces.

23.04.98
06.05.98
www.
exile.
ru

Clampdown!

By Mark Ames

Last week, the Russian Duma passed what is easily the scariest law since the body was first formed in December 1993.

Now, a cop can stop anyone on the street and haul him into a police station if the cop even SUSPECTS that this person is under the influence of drugs. They can search not only you, but also your place of residence, just based on your facial expressions. It gets worse. If the police don't find any drugs, they have the authority to force the suspect to submit to a drug test—meaning they can jam their filthy needles into your arm and determine via questionable means if you are under the influence. Under the new law, *merely testing positive for illegal substances constitutes possession*, and possession in this country usually carries a *minimum of three years' prison.*

Russia is said to have 2 million drug addicts. Given the general ratios of addicts to casual users, perhaps 10-20 million Russians on any given day might test positive and would thus be considered felons "in possession" of drugs. The state doesn't intend to lock everyone up—it can't; rather, it wants to assert its authority over the masses through fear and arbitrary power, with the "drug war" providing an acceptable cover.

Now, it all depends on whether or not you *look* like a suspect. Which I apparently do.

Early last week I was walking with Krazy Kevin near Ploschad Ilyicha when a rickety *militsia* jeep swerved up on the sidewalk and two cops jumped out, clutching their AK-45s. They forced us into the back, hoping to scare us. After some arguing, they tossed Kevin out, leaving me sandwiched in, AK barrel lazily pointed at my ribs.

"We're gonna go for a ride," laughed the fat-faced cop next to me.

The driver was slightly nervous, but the other two cops were whoopin' it up, taunting me about the hell that awaited me at the *militsia* station. I knew they didn't really want to take me down; they just wanted some cash. I played dumb, entertaining a sick curiosity to see how far they'd take it, but I gave in after a 10-minute drive that took us to an empty storage lot.

"How much?" I asked.

"Put down what you want, and we'll see," said the fat-faced one.

I only had one 100,000 ruble note, and I couldn't very well ask for change. I laid it down on the seat. The fat cop hastily grabbed it and stuffed it into his pocket, nervously looking out the window, like... *like in a drug deal.* Then nothing happened. For a moment, I thought they were going haul me in anyway. But these guys weren't interested in paperwork.

"Where would you like to be dropped off?" the driver asked politely. He seemed almost embarrassed.

"Where you picked me up," I said.

On the way, they stopped at a kiosk to make a few purchases. It was Cosmonaut's Day. Then they dropped me off, wishing me a cheery ironic, "Privyet Amerika!"

Another slapstick skit, I thought, but four days later, the Duma passed their War on Drugs law, farce turned to fear, and now I'm not even sure if this article is legal.

After hearing from friends about the law and noticing that last week's *Moscow Times* account omitted the most menacing provisions, I called Sergei Zabarin, a lawyer who works closely with parliamentarian Yuri Shakochikin, a Yabloko representative on the Duma Security Committee, where bills regarding drug laws are produced. Zabarin, who has been fighting for some kind of sanity in Russia's drug laws for a couple of years now, was nearly out of his mind when I spoke to him last week.

"It's incredible!" he said. "This is total madness! It's completely uncivilized, and a violation of the Russian constitution." Zabarin confirmed that the new law is vague enough that local police officials and courts have broad leeway to interpret it as they see fit, which, he said, means that suspects can be detained, searched and forced to submit to blood tests *if they simply look wrong.* Most Moscow cops are from the provinces, and couldn't tell the difference between the munchies and the jones... now, they're going to decide who looks high and who doesn't. You can guess what subtle criteria they're going to use.

The law has been passed, and it's already being applied. A close friend of Ne Spat' editor Dima Shalya was detained outside his home Monday night because the cops thought he looked "pale." They accused him of being a junkie and hauled him into the station. This guy isn't a raver degenerate, but rather a typical young Russian, age 25, who works in a travel agency and has never touched drugs in his life. The cops locked him up, searched him for drugs and checked his arms for signs of track marks. They threatened to take him to a local facility for a blood test, but eventually, he was released.

Knee-jerk social liberals like the *Moscow Times* may print editorials about the need for increased education and needle exchange programs to solve the drug problem, but the fact is that drug use will never wane for the same reason that alcohol use won't: DRUGS ARE FUN. Even though this has been common knowledge since roughly the beginning of time, it's still highly censored. So let me repeat: DRUGS ARE FUN. Drugs are *more* fun than real life—real life means a lousy job, a bad marriage, leaky bathtubs, cars that don't start in the morning... But not everyone has the nerve to take drugs, so the rest, the ever-vengeful herd, insists that they be locked in jail.

When I saw Alina Vitukhnovskaya sitting in that courtroom cage six months ago, I took a selfish interest in her case because I suspected that I could be next. Now I'm more convinced than ever. Even Boris Kagarlitsky of *Nezavisamaya Gazeta* expressed his surprise recently about how many people read the *eXile*. They're not all fans, either. They include the same FSB people who locked up Vitukhnovskaya not long after she published her articles on drug culture in *Novaya Vremya*.

In Russia's darkest periods, the State treated its citizens as potential suspects. I believe that is the reason why a criminal culture is so strong today. It is impossible to create a democracy when such a relationship between state and citizen exists. The West, which claims to have fought the Cold War in the name of democratic values, doesn't seem to mind, because the stated aim of the law is to combat drugs; just as no one cares about the virtual genocide of the Russian population this past decade, a "necessary" by-product of the shock therapy reforms.

White folk can pretty well avoid looking like suspects by ditching the leather coats and dayglo stripes for respectable L.L. Bean catalogue clothes and thick horn-rimmed glasses—the thicker, the better. Glasses, even fake ones, can obfuscate your dilated, pinholed, or bloodshot eyes, while the LL Bean clothes will rightfully scare most cops away like garlic to vampires. It's an unpleasant option, but a lot better than wearing a prison uniform.

If you're a blackass or an African, then my suggestion would be to flush your shit down the toilet now, and start learning to enjoy alcohol. Cops and lawmakers drink it all the time, and look how well it has worked for them.

were off again to the *apteka* for needles, then Andy's plush apartment for movies and smack.

Then *Living Here* collapsed, and I had to go cold turkey. It was a terrifying week. Quitting smack is sheer pain: splinters in your knees and feet, nausea, and intense paranoia. You're completely aware that this world is nothing but a giant charnel house, a concentration camp, and there's no hope. All your friends are plotting against you. Even your body is rejecting you.

I was lucky to score some Valiums at the *apteka* to get over that withdrawal. Then the *eXile* had me consumed. Kolya and I saw less and less of each other. I kicked the heroin, but Kolya never left. It got worse and worse. He was jamming a half a gram a day, then more. . . . He developed nasty tracks on his inner elbow.

"Mark, I think I'm starting to have a problem, man. I think I may need help," he told me over the phone one day. He was high at the time. His voice was groggy, vaguely desperate.

I have this natural mechanism that goes off inside of me when weak people need my help: I feel a kind of contempt, and they suddenly vanish from my screen, <delete>, almost maliciously so. I have a few exceptions to that very suburban California reaction, but Kolya wasn't on that list. He'd call me, groggy-voiced, pleading through the fog of heroin. I told him I'd help him. Then he'd disappear.

He and his English girlfriend, Jennifer Biggs, couldn't decide if their junkie lives were cinematic or merely horrible. *Trainspotting* had just come out on video, so the instinct was to choose cinematic. People who try drugs late in life, like Kolya's girlfriend, get stupid ideas in their heads.

Pasha, the army lieutenant, had become such a serious

junkie that the great Sofiya told me she wouldn't even see him anymore, even though they were old friends going back to childhood. I immediately hated Pasha, on her behalf.

Pasha's military father busted him; they locked him in the house for six months, and he was cured. Compared to Kolya, he was lucky.

Kolya's brother-in-law, a longtime junkie from the suburbs of Moscow, was recently busted by the police for possession. The last person I jammed with, a strange foreign-currency trader from a top local bank with horn-rimmed glasses and a heavy-metal hairdo, somehow got hooked on speedballs, overdosed, and died a couple of months after we banged together. After that, I gave up the needle.

Just today, finishing this chapter, Taibbi and I saw a pair of junkies lying almost dead in my apartment entrance. They couldn't have been older than fifteen. For some reason their shirts were pulled up—they'd probably fallen out of my elevator. One's face was turning yellow-white—his lips had lost their color. We ran and found some cops, but the junkies had somehow reanimated and escaped. I was sure they'd died.

These are the usual heroin endings, although I have to say my own is a happy one. I haven't become a junkie. Nor have several friends of mine who dabble with it. I think this is a highly censored truth about heroin: that an overwhelming majority of those who try it don't become junkies. You have to have some inner drive to junkieness for that to happen: I'm not sure if the psychological foundation is that inseparable from the physical one. A junkie will become a junkie of something at some time: alcohol, codependence, bad relationships. . . . Anyway, I'm not, nor are my friends, several of whom have done it.

Kolya is. He cried for help several times, but wouldn't let me help him. He enjoyed the attention, the work it took to try to cure him, but not the actual cure. Like so many Russian men, he wants to be the center of a melodrama, to be worried over. Jennifer, his aging disco-hip English girlfriend, provided that better than anyone. Hell, she went straight down the junkie chute with him, because, as she'd tell me, "I worry about him, Mark, you know? And I don't want him to do this alone. I want to do it with 'im so he's not alone, you know what I mean? So that he has an anchor."

Finally, though, even they couldn't conjure up a cinematic version of their realities. Kolya needed to be saved. I got the name of a rehab center from Medicins Sans Frontiers. It was supposed to be the closest thing to a humane rehab center east of Poland. In fact, the place was like a jail, with grim nurses and doctors marching down the guarded hallways, and the odd patient being hauled from one wing to another. I escorted Kolya myself to the doctor, a stern, jaded central Asian with a clipped silver mustache, who started off by telling Kolya he had almost no hope. Kolya weakly protested. The doctor persisted.

"How much are you taking a day?" the doctor demanded.

"A gram," Kolya moaned.

"One gram," the doctor repeated. He shook his head. "Let me see your arms."

Kolya sniffled, then pulled the sleeves up on his arms. I almost gagged: pustules and scabs lined all the way up the underside of his forearm, and up the backside as well, going along the ulna. His arms were rotten Swiss cheese, no doubt about it. The doctor gave him very little chance, but he agreed to do it for free.

Kolya checked in Monday afternoon. The warders closed the door behind him and locked it. The first thing Kolya did was sneak into the bathroom, slip a stash of smack from under his shoe, and a needle that he'd hidden in his sleeve . . . and jammed it into an empty spot. The other inmates demanded their cut, so Kolya passed them his needle and what was left of the smack. They fought over it like animals, but by then he didn't care. The entire drug rehab clinic was banging Kolya's heroin! Hurrah!

Later that night, they started their rehab regime: it consisted of pumping him full of tranquilizers and keeping him under tight surveillance. Jennifer came to visit him. You weren't allowed to go in and see him in the first week. She caught a glimpse of him through the sealed glass door—she said he looked like a zombie. He yelled as well as

Plasma wasn't just another techno club. Its owner, Timur Mamedov, was constantly raided and harassed by the cops for promoting fringe rave culture among Russia's Golden Youth.

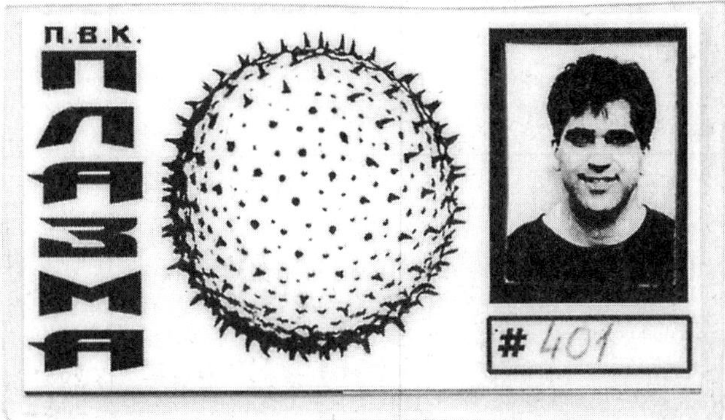

19.02.98
25.02.98

www.
exile.
ru

#04
P. 2

Moldova was all I fucking needed. I hadn't slept since our demi-skinhead party, a full five days of blood poisoning, when I boarded the flight at Vnukovo. I had to go to Kishenyov to cover a free-lance assignment, but I was hardly in the right frame of mind. This weekly eXile thing is going to lead to a ",SELF" triple-murder suicide. I'm already receiving telepathic gab-

Washed Up in Kishenyov

By Mark Ames

ber-messages from outer space to begin preparations. The galaxy's future depends on it.

...1998 has started out more depraved and dangerous than any year. Beginning two Fridays ago and ending a week later in Moldova, my memory is a blur of aimless desire, discharge and shame. The only thing I'm sure of is that I unwittingly took a snowball from one of my own best friends, who blew in my new girlfriend's mouth before I ever kissed her. In fact, he may have been the fourth or fifth guy to blow in her mouth that night, not counting the gypsy cab driver or the doorman at the Karusel Club.

I remember being in major regret-mode the Saturday morning after our skinhead party. I'd woken up dizzy and pasty-mouthed beside an ex-convict who'd hoovered half the male population of Moscow. I ran to the bathroom and brushed my teeth, but it was too late. By the afternoon, after hitting the bottle again, I was adding to my list of regrets, turning it into a dissertation on delayed-fuse teenage irresponsibility. Then on Sunday night, someone stuck a pin into my eyes and drained my pupils. That was a sweet night, floating, but unfortunately Sunday night turns into Monday morning, which turns into Monday afternoon, and it's hard to get pumped for work when your corpse is floating somewhere over the poppy-studded hills beyond Luang Prabong... I was in no shape to tie my boots, let alone write and edit for our new eXile launch. That's when I called in the chemists to construct a high speed monorail line from ganglion to retina, down to palms that had turned into a pair of abalone feet, and straight into the Big Pump. But the monorail didn't work right. The train ran wild, derailing here and there... it didn't stop to pick up a single passenger, leaving me stranded in random thought patterns. I was like Cornholio, giggling wildly to myself and blurting out disjointed bits of info while the others did their best to avoid me.

This wasn't a question of being "on da edge." When it comes to sex and drugs, those yardsticks of choice for Olympiad edge-judging, then I consider myself to be pretty standard—a kind of Ford Escort of the decadence world.

So what's my excuse? I don't know. It all began with a few cans of Miller Magnum in the skinhead basement. That's the last clear memory I have. Two weeks later, I'm not the same person. Now, all's I can do is try to recover the little black box in my head, and continue popping as many antibiotics as the local *apteky* will dispense. My lawyer has advised me to go on a strict two-week diet of Amoxicillin, Erythromycin and Ciprobay, a super-antibiotic generally reserved for what Phillip K. Dick would call *The Sixes*: politicians, movie stars, CEOs and the like—*humans that matter.* Thanks to all these antibiotics, I'm single-handedly responsible for mutating about two or three easily-curable microbes into scaly, spiny, indestructible bloodmines.

I'm not complaining though. Things could be worse. Taibbi has been on my case about gross under-reporting on my part, an affected slant towards the negative. He's right, but I can't help it—I just have a hard time imagining that I've suddenly taken a lead part in anything, even a *shite* indie film that'll never make it to video. In my last column, I mentioned a homely underage girl who had allegedly had a miscarriage at the Duck on Ladies' Night. Well, I didn't tell all the truth. I got to know her well—too well. Natasha. The good news is that she didn't actually have a miscarriage—that little polliwog in her alcohol-and-nicotine-soaked womb is still mutating into a cute little Flipper baby, right on schedule. But as things stand right now, neither Natasha nor Flipper have a daddy. Or a home. I didn't mind spending a night with a pregnant, bleeding teenager a few weeks back. But then she started calling me. And coming over. And ringing my doorbell for a half hour straight at four in the morning. I finally ripped the cheap box out of the wall and smashed it, and I don't intend to fix it soon. The last time she called me, she asked me if she could come over and see me.

"Look, Natasha, you're pregnant," I laughed.

"Nu i chto?!" she snapped.

I don't know, man—maybe I should get a caged pitbull and put it in my podyezd with a video camera... when someone rings, and I don't like what I see, I press a button releasing Scraps, whom I haven't fed in six days and who has spent his puppyhood getting regularly beaten by hired neighborhood dyevushki. "Go for the womb, Scraps! 'Atta boy!"

It's a good sign that I'm thinking these pitbull thoughts. Taibbi's right. Just a couple of years ago, I'd have put a cute golden retriever in that cage. Things have definitely improved.

Now I have someone living in my apartment with me. She'd just been released from a three year stint in prison the day we met, and she needed a place to sleep. A lot of this was her fault. I spun completely out of the orbit of responsibility and adulthood, leaving everyone else to do the work of putting the newspaper together. I fucked everything up, down to the last word. When I boarded the Air Moldova flight to Kishenyov, Taibbi and Krazy Kevin hadn't even begun to experience their literary Stalingrad. Me—I just pressed the seat release, kicked back, and tried to think of reasons why this rattling Tu-134 wouldn't explode in mid-air. Then I realized, I didn't fucking care—after five days of mental gymnastics, I was ready to surrender to any fate, including a See Page 3 story with the caption: "No survivors were found."

At least the eXile staff got its celestial revenge on me. Kishenyov is the exact topographical representation of what a heavy methamphetamine come-down feels like. This is the real gray, the end of the line. Hope was sucked from its very soil. Even the city's beggars and taxi drivers seem more dead than alive, like those weary phantoms in a Platonov novel. Coming down from a six-day serotonin-sucking binge in the Kishenyov Cosmos Hotel is just plain redundant.

The White God factor was disturbingly high in Moldova, but the swarthy, empty faces were not the stuff of even my most troubled fantasies. I understood what it felt to be a mid-ranking, pith-helmeted British official in the Raj—as the natives groveled at my feet, I wanted to swat them away with a sharpened rod, and quickly get to my hotel room.

The nicest Moldovans worked in pharmacies. For some reason they all had it in their heads that I was from the George Soros Foundation. Not bad: Soros, after all, bankrolled the California referendum that allowed marijuana houses to open. "Yeah, I'm from the Soros Foundation," I agreed, as they filled my Christmas stocking with diazepams and rohypnols and phenobarbital/codeine cocktails. "It's a lot of hard work, being a philanthropist. No sleep at all." I showed up to interviews with bankers and ministers a bloodshot wreck, nodding off in mid-answer. I assume they thought it was some kind of eccentric, Soros-like behavior on my part, and not the symptoms of a washed-up expat crying for help. Which is where I'm headed if I don't get a handle on this bronco called Moscow.

he could for her to rescue him. Then they dragged him away.

By Saturday, Jennifer and I were officially allowed to visit Kolya. The oddest thing happened, though. He wasn't dressed in a smock. He was chipper and excited, kissing the orderlies good-bye.

"All right," he said, hugging us both. "I'm out of this fucking place."

"Wait, what do you mean?" I asked. "You're supposed to do three weeks or six weeks, aren't you?"

"No fahking way, man," Kolya said. "They threw me out and told me never to return. They fahking hate me. I made their lives fahking miserable until they can't stand me anymore. They're telling me, 'Fakh you, we take care of you for free and you act like this.' And I tell them, 'Just let me the fahk out, I don't want your fahking help.'" He laughed proudly and hugged Jennifer.

"But Kolya—" Jennifer weakly protested, but it was clear by the way she snuggled up to him that she was happy to resume their little film.

On the car ride home, she boasted about her own painful withdrawals, and all the weight she'd lost from her junkie spree. Kolya called her "Babbles," and told me that everything was all right, he was cured.

The next week he and Jennifer were both back on, worse than ever before. I clicked and dragged Kolya's icon into the delete bin, certain that he was going to be dead within a month. He called, but I didn't return his messages. We ran into each other again at a nightclub, and he was high as usual.

"I need your help, man," he moaned. "Really, I need your help."

But by then, he didn't exist in my hard drive. He was communicating through a pathos-filter, meaning that as far as I was concerned, he was little more than babbling furniture.

He finally left his girlfriend and took off first for St. Petersburg, then to northern Kazakhstan, to his home village, for another three weeks. He told his parents everything, and they helped nurse him back to health. Can you imagine that in suburban California? Being welcomed by your parents with open arms when you tell them that you're a junkie, that you need their help? No way! They'd throw you on the streets and tell you "it's for your own good." That line—"it's for your own good"—has done more harm than any land mine. That middle-class selfishness cloaked in morality. What people really mean is, "leave me the fuck alone!"

Kolya returned to Moscow a month later, tanned, fit, and with his old voice back. He was completely clean. Jennifer had done the same, having moved to England for two weeks.

And then. . . . Within a month, they were back on. At first they dabbled, like regular casual users. Then, like some subatomic physics equation, they leaped up to the next orbit, the junkie orbit. It happened so quickly. They sank into a kind of slow paranoia—a very indoors, drawn-blinds and scattered-cassettes paranoia, a bourgeois Sid and Nancy. But she couldn't take it anymore. She was dying. In the summer of '98, she abandoned Moscow.

Kolya called me in a panic after she left. "I can't believe the bitch! She just left! Now where am I going to get the money? I'm fakhed, Mark. Can you help me?"

I brought two grams of speed with me from Tallinn into Moscow to help me when Kara and Matt left. I was in the train wagon with another mini-mule, Owen Matthews. When we crossed the border, we stuffed our grams into a crumpled-up cigarette box in our first-class train car. I was nervous at the border crossing—Jesus, what was I thinking? Seven years, hard labor in the foreigner prison in Mordova just for a lousy two grams of shit Estonian speed?! It was too late. The passport control checked our documents, then left.

Suddenly, two blue-uniformed customs agents burst into our cabin, one with a flashlight, the other, the hefty mustached one, moving slowly. The one with the flashlight steps onto the bed and shines his light into the cubby hole up top, where our bags are kept. He asks me to lift up the bed, to check the storage space underneath. I comply, trying my best to keep from shaking. And then suddenly, they're out. Just like that.

That speed helped me get through a rough period with the newspaper. The rest went into writing this chapter.

Later, a techno skinhead friend of ours scored us some local "phen," yellowish amphetamine imported from Latvia. Taibbi and I must have vacuumed fifteen grams of the shit from February through May 1998, when we tried and failed to convert the *eXile* from a biweekly to a weekly. Looking back, those months barely register on the memory. Just quick scenes of frantic scrambling to meet deadlines, the cut-up method put into practice. I can still hear the evolution of Taibbi's snorting habits: at first, he'd line up tiny little yellow *strelki*, snort, and screech. Within a couple of minutes, paranoia would hit him. "What? What are you looking at, Ames?"

"Nothing, dude. Don't worry."

Then he'd start to pour sweat, worse than me.

After a couple of months, Taibbi's *strelki* got fatter and fatter, while his snorting got louder and louder. You could hear him from the other side of our offices. It was like an elephant with a nasty case of the sniffles. And he'd always finish off his snorts with a loud, half-pained, half-satisfied, "Ahhhhh!"

Club Lux

★★ ★★

Cheers: For the serious, discreet gambler. No hookers, no unshaven mafiosi, no seedy chelnoki; this place is actually respectable, the clientele consisting mostly of biznesmeni.
Jeers: Don't come here looking for sex; security dressed like Giulianni cops means you have to check in your fun—and your gun—at the door.
Cover: Free
M: YugoZapadnay
Phone: 430-4393
Address: Michurinsky Prospekt 4/1
Hours: daily 13.00-8.00

Golden Palace

★★★ ★★★ ★★★

Cheers: Split floors, running stream with fish (no golden fish) swimming past the card tables, awesome New Russian interior. Got rid of the Vietnamese restaurant, so it's shed a bit of the Deer Hunter feel. Also, great selection of $500 a pop whores (though they can be talked down).
Jeers: Nervous Russian security with their shotguns pointing at your face. Have to pay the barman for the whores. Scary Vietnamese clients haven't abandoned the casino, in spite of the closing of the restaurant.
Cover: 8.00 - 20.00: 60.000 rubles, 20.00 - 08.00: 250.000. Free for ladies.
M: Belorusskaya
Phone: 212-3909/-41
Address: 3rd Yamskogo Polya, 15
Hours: 24 hours

We were lucky, again: if not for the speed, we'd have collapsed after three issues. As it was, with the speed, we crashed after about fifteen issues, but the crash was proportionately brutal.

We snorted our way through four months straight of weekly *eXiles*. And in the process, we lost track of our new, embittered sales director, Nicole Mollo, who had replaced Kara. Under Nicole, the business end began to fall into disarray. Before our incarnation as Moscow tweaks, we kept a close eye on her. She hated our newspaper and everything Matt and I stood for, and desperately wanted to be accepted by those baloney-sandwich geeks whom she imagined were the elite of the expat community.

Her background was anything but normal. Nicole told Matt and others that she had been pushed into a foster home in rural Wisconsin as a child. How she wound up in Russia is unclear. She was 17 when she arrived. One version is that she came here with her mother and ran away. The other version is that her mother brought her here and abandoned her. For Christmas, she received a box of gifts at the *eXile* from her mother: Inside were scores of kiddie world toys meant for the "Ages 3-8" segment. Nicole showed them to me and told me that this was one big reason why she wasn't going back to America. It made us feel sorry for her and, in the midst of our brain-sucking speed binge, we forgot to keep our eye on her.

Just as the phen was running out, and we made the decision to go back to our biweekly regime, I arranged to have a meeting with Nicole to go over all the cash receipts and expenses since Taibbi and I first dipped into the crank four months earlier. She skipped the first meeting. I called, and she didn't return my calls. I left messages on her pager, but got nothing. Then came the weekend, near the end of April 1998. And still she was nowhere to be found. The following Monday morning, just recovering from a weeklong dry spell, I arrived early in the office. My energy was best in the morning. My brain could only produce enough serotonin fuel to last until lunch. That's when I saw Nicole's note on her desk, next to her pager. She'd absconded.

There wasn't a lot we could do, at least not right away. She took the financial records of all the cash-in and cash-out transactions. She promised to hand them to our publisher, but never did. We've never seen them since.

We tracked her down through a friend of hers at the American Embassy. But what could we do? Only our boss could have her iced—which he wouldn't dare. Icing an American girl wasn't worth that kind of money to him. We couldn't have her arrested. Bringing this to the attention of the *militsia*, a force so corrupt that they make the Mexican police look like Andy Griffith, would only cause more problems. No, we'd have to postpone our revenge on Nicole.

Worse, we'd run out of speed. We were plunked back into reality—stripped of money, honor, and amphetamines. You couldn't find phen anywhere in all of Moscow! The Latvian labs had been raided. The punks went back into hiding. We got desperate. So desperate that we agreed to hire the techno skinhead who'd scored us our speed on a permanent basis, if he could line up another batch.

Eventually, he did. We bought 20 grams. And got a special customer discount, which we then kicked back in the form of a bonus to our skinhead. Now we've got enough phen to last us to the end of the year. It was a win-win situation for everyone.

That was my last issue.
I feel that I'm enjoying you
guy as much as you're
enjoying me!
I will fax all needed
financial paperwork by
the end of the week
incl. monies owed.
You can reach me through
956-4228. (Had a landlord problem)

Our last female American sales director skipped town on the day we were supposed to discuss the cash situation. She left this note, along with her pager, on her desk, and cleared everything out—including our cash-in/cash-out records. Despite leaving a telephone number, we were never able to reach her. However, we know where she fled to, and we plan to drop by some day.

X 26.03.98 31.03.98 www. exile. ru

Avoiding the Death-Thing

By Mark Ames

I barely leave my apartment these days. Mandarin peels and coffee grinds fill my kitchen sink. For the last two weeks, I've lived mostly on a diet of mandarins and coffee.

Since we went weekly, I've dropped almost ten pounds. Don't sleep much anymore either. All those bodily functions... They're such a waste of time. I could pump out two free-lance articles in the time it takes to shit out a Mama Zoya's dinner—and they'd look roughly the same, too. But there's no way around it, you've got to tend to the body's basic needs. Unless you want to wind up like Karen Carpenter: a shriveled skeleton, blackened at the edges. Which is where I'm headed if this weekly thing doesn't give.

Sometimes you have to wonder if you're taking things too far. I consider myself to be pretty modest in that area, especially compared to some people I know. Like my friend Layton, who has whiffed so much glass over the last three years that his teeth are falling out, his dick has shriveled into a walnut, and he can't take a shit without consuming three bars of Ex-Lax chocolate. I don't think he's left his Hollywood apartment since I last saw him over a year ago. Another close friend here in Moscow contracted hepatitis from carelessly maining. There's been a fresh hepatitis epidemic among junkies this year. Half of Moscow's krutoi youth has yellow faces and yellow eyes. I recently got my hep-A and hep-B vaccines because you never know who's popping with dirty needles and who isn't. You'd be surprised how many young Russians I've met jam drugs like it's nothing: Special-K and poppy straw... even LSD juice. It seems that almost everyone I meet has popped at least once in the last month. Not just grungy hair-dye types with nose rings, but seemingly normal people. Your girlfriend/boyfriend or receptionist or research analyst might be one of them. Unlike in the West, here, maining drugs doesn't set you apart from the pack and place you in a special, dangerous category. It's just seen for what it is: a better, faster means to a high.

You can buy needles at just about any apteka in town. The quality varies: you can get anything from Danish needles to Turkish or Indian ones. Those can be painful, leaving big greenish bruises for days. But Russian needles are the worst: thick, dull... Popping one of those into your veins is like trying to cut a tractor tire with a butter knife.

Just last Saturday night I was at an underground club, talking to some grungy teenage girl, out of school and out of work. She told me that she regularly jams Special-K and LSD, but she avoids heroin because too many of her friends have become junkies. You'd never know by looking at her that she bangs, which is why I'm just going to assume, in the future, that anyone I meet is a regular dirty-needle junkie. Which is as good a reason as any to get your hep vaccinations and—gulp!—wear condoms. You just know that Russians, with their blase attitude towards the Dying-Thing, aren't dipping their friends' needles into Clorox bleach solutions before sticking them into their arms. There's only one thing on their mind when their yellow-hued, scabbed-faced friend passes the needle, dripping with infected blood: «Davai!»

Another mutual acquaintance OD'd on a monster speedball a few months earlier. He was a FOREX trader for a top local Russian bank who couldn't get enough stimulation. You've got to wonder that feels like, ODing on a speedball: is there a thirty-second flash of Pure Bliss before the aorta explodes? Like one of those blinding white lights that makes your jaw drop, and say, "Oh... my God! It's... beautiful..." before slumping over in a pool of vomit. Or does a little voice in your head screech, "Danger, Will Robinson! Dan—..." as the battery pack in your back falls to the floor and you keel over dead.

About a month back, I was heading into my podyezd with Taibbi, when we nearly tripped on a pair of teenage corpses that had fallen out of my elevator. One was lying on his back, his shirt and sweater drawn up almost to his shoulders. His face was whitish-blue, and his lips had lost color, while his friend was curled into a ball. It was clear that they'd OD'd on some bad junk (the purity of heroin has gone from less than 50% to over 90% in the last few months, according my old housemate Lena). Right then, some babushka from my building comes storming in, yelling at the two corpses, kicking the blue-faced kid's legs and making a scene. Then she turned and asked Taibbi and me to help her drag the dead kids out into the snow. Jesus, and I thought I was a nihilist: but this old bitch made me look like Sally Struthers!...

Since I've been spending a lot of sleepless nights lately in my apartment, I've been thinking more and more about the Death-Thing. The way I look at it, it's important to avoid the Death-Thing. Seems straightforward enough. Russians, as I said, are far less paranoid about death than your average Californian—that's why they make far better infantry than surfers. Their attitude has always impressed me. But...still... not wanting to die is a pretty good strategy. And for my money, the best way of avoiding death is by staying locked up in my apartment. I fixed my doorbell recently, but I don't answer it when it rings. And I stopped answering the phone after I got a bitter, tear-drenched call from an ex-girlfriend whose abortion story I wrote up last time. "Don't you know that people I know read your newspaper?!" She's probably boiling a rabbit right now in her kitchen, a rabbit named Mark. Before her, I was getting regular calls from some OMON thug who was having an affair with Lena when she lived with me. Who knows to what lengths he'll go to find her. And speaking of Lena... she disappeared three weeks ago, her bag is still in my apartment, and I haven't got so much as a message. I wonder if she's even alive.

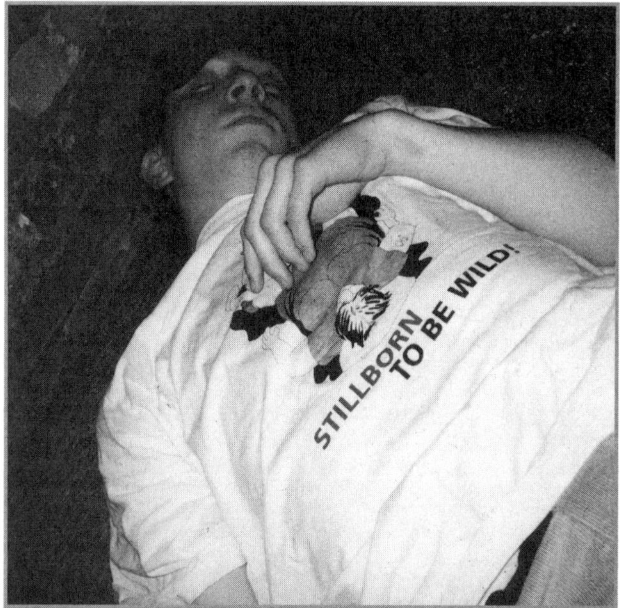

The *eXile*'s first year anniversary party was held in a basement squat for skinheads, orphans, and techno freaks. One of them, pictured above, helped organize our party, stole our beer and tranqs, and nearly died from consumption. The party was a smashing success.

I try to limit my outer-world excursions to the eXile offices. But I'm beginning to think that this is where it will all end. There's a kind of eerie, foreboding vibe going around the eXile offices these days, as if something BAD is going to happen. The weekly schedule has put an unsustainable stress on us all. Also, the unannounced-weird-assed-visitor-Index has soared to an all-time high at our offices. Crypto-Nazis hanging out in the corridors; skinheads popping in and out; and just the other day, some strange middle-aged Russian man who claimed to work for a state information agency innocently dropped in, refused to look at Taibbi or me, and proceeded to quietly gather up as many copies of the eXile as he could fit into his briefcase. Then he disappeared... We even had a former Burger Kveen burger-flipper drop off a manuscript two weeks back, and pester us with twice-daily calls. His piece was a fairly interesting account of what it meant to be a Russian "eXile" living in squats in Moscow, and the difference between these suffering, harassed Russian eXiles and the pampered, hedonistic eXpat heroes of our newspaper... when we told him that we were interested in running his piece if he rewrote it, he played the hurt, misunderstood artist, grabbed his manuscript, and split.

That got me thinking: one of these days, someone's gonna Mark David Chapman us all. The question is when, and by who.

The Kathy Lally letter to the Johnson List [see page 13] is proof positive that our days in this world are numbered. Now we've got a correspondent from the *Baltimore Sun* who not only wants us censored and banned, but who's willing to play the NKVD informant and help lock us up in a Russian prison because she doesn't like the way we write. That's not just a lapse of journalistic ethics—that's a sign that the lynch mob is reaching critical mass...

My solution to the Death-Thing is to try to stay at home as much as possible. I'm beginning to like my apartment, in spite of the awful smells that waft in from the bums who sleep and crap in the corridors. I've got my "South Park" tapes and a porno film starring a Great Dane, a water buffalo, a pony, and some Pacific Islanders to keep me company. After this issue's done, I'm going to settle down for a quiet laugh watching eight year old cartoon kid Kenny get impaled on a flag pole, and his slow, blood-greased slide down to the ground. Even if it's not funny the tenth time watching it, at least it's soothing, under the age-old theory of "Better him than me."

BY MARK AMES

CHAPTER SIX: THE WHITE GOD FACTOR

There are a lot of reasons why Kara tried sabotaging the *eXile* only nine months after she and I first drafted those business plans. Moscow is a lousy town for a young, married couple from Seattle. Her husband, Marcus, never learned more than a few words of Russian, and he couldn't figure out simple business tricks.

Marcus was a failure among failures, in a town where failures didn't fail. Most fell into wads of quick cash, climbed the corporate ladder, or, like us, started up newspapers that would never have made it off the pot-smoke-clouded drawing boards back home. When he was our "promotions manager" he was fixated on making *eXile* lighters and key chains. They were never made. So he was promoted to sales manager at Kara's insistence. He didn't sell more than two ads the whole time, while Kara ran around gathering clients and handing them to Marcus as a way of propping him up.

We even had to replace Marcus as our cartoonist. I created a kitsch '50s-like cartoon door character called "Knock-Knock" to accompany our childishly cruel practical jokes. I handed the annoying door character over to Marcus, since he drew better than me. He clung to that Knock-Knock like a Down's syndrome adult clinging to a cat's scratching post. He plastered his Knock-Knocks all over our press and sales kits. He ordered a huge vinyl banner for the *eXile*, and made Knock-Knock the centerpiece. Once, when I was in their apartment, I saw his entire oeuvre of "Knock-Knock" drawings, signed and dated, carefully stacked in a glass cabinet, in the sincere belief that some future Christie's auction would be interested.

When Roman Papsuev, a freak-talented cartoonist geek with mind-reading powers, showed up in our offices with a pen and some drawings, we fired Marcus as our artist—actually, he got the hint and, in his Zen way, offered to resign. And that was it. That was all he had to show after a year in Moscow—and if that's all you have, you're bound to start conjuring fond memories of Seattle, about how you'd left behind a paradise of aromatic-coffee-scented opportunity.

We got it into our heads that Marcus needed to be put to use, so we suggested dressing him in a 1950s Disneyland-style Knock-Knock door outfit and having him stand in Pushkin Square, handing out copies of the *eXile* and taking pictures with children. The giant foam Knock-Knock would beam its cheesy smile at passersby. Marcus would keep one hand over the mesh-grill for his eyes and mouth, waving with the other hand. He'd force copies of the *eXile* on lovers, babushki, businessmen, flatheads. He'd probably get stomped every once in a while, or rolled by Gypsies, but that'd be the price he'd have to pay to promote our newspaper.

Once, Taibbi aired our private joke to Marcus, just to test

LOOK OUT SOTHEBY'S! Marcus's Knock-Knock door character started off as a way of annoying our readers, but quickly evolved into a disturbing window into his subconscious mind.

his reaction. Marcus seemed to like it. He added that he should wear a pair of white tights with the foam Knock-Knock. We let it drop.

We often wondered how he could stay loyal to Kara, who, physically speaking, was a gnu among gazelles.

It's not as though there weren't options, even for Marcus. Moscow is packed with more female beauty per square mile than any place on earth. And not haughty, cold types, but inviting, curious beauty, always looking to try something new, trade up, succumb to pressure, fall into some wild and unexpected adventure. . . . You catch their eyes on the streets, something that doesn't happen in America. Femme fatales on every sidewalk! Vixens riding down the metro escalators! Sly seductresses pouring into the streets! Somehow Marcus managed to block that part of Moscow out. We'd often ask ourselves how long he could deny the yawning beauty gap between his wife and, well, just about every single girl in Moscow. . . .

If most expat women begin at a massive disadvantage against their Russian counterparts, then Kara was disqualified from the competition. While Marcus had the face of a 15-year-old, Kara resembled a pirate. She tried to assert her qualities—her strength of character—by being aggressively un-beautiful. That kind of shtick might work in progressive Seattle, but it died on contact in Moscow.

Taibbi and I often joked, in private, that Marcus spent the better part of his time with his pug nose wedged deep inside Kara's gorilla ass, gnawing away for hours while she surfed the Internet or ran Excel or prepared aromatic coffee or designer pasta. To this day we're not sure exactly what the fuck went on between them. Strange things, that's for sure. Everyone who knew them thought there was something creepy going on. Once, during a long night of work, Kara called Marcus into the design room and told him, "Marcus, if you want to, you are free to leave." Right in front of us. He thanked her quietly, and left.

A few months after we started the *eXile*, Kara invited an acquaintance of theirs from the Midwest, Paul Barker, to come to Moscow and take over as sales manager. Kara didn't want to be known as a salesperson—rather, she wanted to be known as the General Manager. In the aspiring corporate world, salespeople are ranked, in status, at the bottom of the heap. Marketing people and general managers are like quarterbacks and running backs, the glory folk.

So Kara wanted to hire a sales manager to work beneath her.

Paul Barker had a ridiculously innocent, puppetoon face: bright red lips, twinkling eye, greased back hair—'80s Wall Street hair. . . . His trademark was his goofy chortle. If he wasn't chortling, he was nervously bullshitting you about one thing or another.

Paul was a monstrous failure as sales manager, but not bad at trying to fuck the entire Russian female staff at the *eXile*. His first target was our sexy receptionist Yulia, a half-Estonian 20-year-old with honey-colored hair and big green eyes, and a sexy laugh that drove Paul nuts. He started off by trying to charm her, and she led him on with her inviting laugh, one hand on her chin, big green eyes looking up. From down the hallway, you could hear Paul chortling, like a barking seal during mating season. Within a month, he was literally chasing Yulia down the hallway to try to get her to kiss him. He didn't mind that Yulia's husband is a karate champion.

"What's he going to do? I'm American!" Paul would say, chortling again. He demanded her phone number. Once, Yulia screamed for me to help her. I had to pull Paul off and lock her in our publisher's office. I blocked the door and told Paul to calm the fuck down.

"I love Moscow, man!" he'd wheeze with that hand-in-the-cookie-jar expression of his. "Man, you can do anything here!"

Kara and Marcus had to watch this every day: *eXile* guys chasing women in the office up the walls, into stalls. . . . Paul fucked the first sales girl he hired, Lyuba, a silicon-lipped 19-year-old blonde. She quit a few weeks later. He fucked our production manager, Tanya. He fucked a married card dealer from one of the casinos that he'd landed as our client. He fucked a neighbor of Kara's. He fucked everyone, that is,

SHE'S ASKING FOR IT! What sane American male wouldn't mistake our receptionist Yulia's warm expression, pictured here, as an invitation to rape and pillage her?

but his ex, Kara. With her, you just asked for money.

Paul was such a failure at sales that even Kara couldn't hide it. Marcus, when he heard us grumbling, waited patiently. When it was safe, he began to openly lobby for Paul to be fired. "I could do a better job than him," Marcus complained ominously.

Paul was finally given the boot. He headed back home to America, but first, he pocketed a thousand *eXile* dollars from an overdue client, and spent them on cards and whores and coke.

Kara installed her husband in Paul's place. In her clichéd approach to business, she thought she needed that leverage to counterbalance the Ames-Taibbi Axis.

Marcus arranged a wet T-shirt contest, with Kara's approval, for the September '97 *eXile* party. Marcus, in the shadows on the far right, led the ceremonies.

Right up to the last, Kara tried to play the game and never show that she was bothered by our blatant sexism. She wasn't PC—she wanted us to be clear on that. I think that's a late '90s progressive grrrl thing, to be, at least on the surface level, anti-PC.

Kara wanted to show that she could run with the boys. She laughed at our overt sexist take on Moscow. She even encouraged it at times. She told us once that she liked to wear tight halter tops to important meetings, to show off her tits. She was proud of her little contribution to the sexist plot. It made her tougher than the other girls.

I'd look at her apple-sized breasts, then pan up to her Blackbeard face, and think . . . *Ee-gads!*

Then Kara abruptly quit, telling us that her life plans had changed, that she was frustrated, and she couldn't continue working with Matt and me. She particularly resented Matt.

The two of them had never hit it off. The night that Matt joined after our epic summit meeting at the Starlite Diner, we met over at Andy's apartment for what I assumed would be an amicable shaking-hands agreement, followed by celebration. Kara came about twenty minutes late, with Marcus behind. They took another twenty minutes to de-Gore-Texize their bodies. Velcro ripped and tore in Andy's front hallway. Matt stared at me in disbelief, but for the most part, we ignored it.

When they walked into Andy's TV room, we were already drinking champagne. Andy proposed a toast, but Kara stopped.

"I think we need to get things straight first before we start drinking champagne," she said, adopting a cold, officious tone. She went on the offensive, immediately trying to drive a wedge between the two of us. It was strange, especially coming after her warnings to me that if we didn't hire Matt away, we were

MD: what are you wearing? :)... my wife and i are into plating and golden showers lol... right now i have the laptop on my throbbing member [mmmm] :)

fucked. She saw Matt and me sitting together laughing, and she felt threatened.

A couple of months later, while I was on vacation, she tried giving Matt a back rub while he was typing an article on the computer—some kind of hippie Seattle bonding thing, I guess. But Matt's not too good at hiding his emotions; he told me he broke out in one of those shivers that sends the whole body into an epileptic convulsion, then he turned around and, with a sour, bug-eyed look, asked her what the hell she was doing. A few days later, I got a call in California from Kara that the newspaper was about to collapse. Later, she told me that "it's either Matt or me."

It was only a week or so before she actually left town that we discovered the depths of her bitterness toward us. We were in our office, near the end of the workday, when she delivered to us some ominous threats about our publisher Kostya, and her demands that we reduce our salaries (which were already about half of Kara's) and allow her to keep her stake in the newspaper even after leaving. We were in shock. We pressed her. She kept up her attack. We pressed her more. How could she threaten us like that?!

Then she broke down and told us what she really thought.

We'd never given her any respect or credit. We were glory hogs and obnoxious jerks. Worst of all was our sexism. Our sexism and sexual harassment of the Russian female staff, as well as the sexism in our newspaper, was too much for her. Watching us harass the young female staff had to be the most painful part—because we'd never, in a million years, have thought of harassing her.

"You know I'm not PC. But there's a limit. You go too far. You're always trying to force Masha and Sveta under the table to give you blow jobs. It's not funny. They don't think it's funny," Kara complained.

"But . . . it *is* funny," Matt said.

We have been pretty rough on our girls. We'd ask our Russian staff to flash their asses or breasts for us. We'd tell them that if they wanted to keep their jobs, they'd have to perform unprotected anal sex with us. Nearly every day, we asked our female staff if they approved of anal sex. That was a fixation of ours. "Can I fuck you in the ass? Huh? I mean, without a rubber? Is that okay?" It was all part of the fun. Fun that Kara was no part of.

In the end, that's the real reason why Kara quit and left this town a bitter wreck. Moscow is a hellish Twilight Zone that completely turns Seattle on its nose-pierced head. Kara, like so many expat women, wanted to see the whole thing go up in flames. She didn't just quit the job. She tried leaving a few fuse-delayed time bombs to sink the paper. She let three months' worth of clients' bills go unpaid without telling us, leaving our bank account in deep arrears. She ran our last few issues well into the red. Before she left, she assured me, Matt, and Nicole that all finances were in order and we had no outstanding debtors.

A few weeks after Kara disappeared, we needed money to wire to our printers. They told us that it was the last paper they would print, since we hadn't paid for printing for four issues. I was in shock. I went to our accountant Tanya, and she produced for me a sheet of paper showing $30,000 in outstanding debts.

"What?! Tanya, I had no idea. Why didn't you warn us? Kara told us that we had no debts!" I cried.

Tanya smiled in that pithed way of hers. Tanya's not a bad person. She's just slow. Which is why she's our accountant. Anyone clever in her position could make off with our money and have us all sitting in jail for life. . . . Better to have a doe-eyed idiot who can, on a good day, add up the figures in the left and right columns.

Luckily, we untangled the mess, leaned hard on our clients, and for the first time turned the *eXile* into a profitable operation . . . until Nicole came along, made an even worse mess, took key financial records (leaving many questions unanswered), and split for Rotterdam.

The first time I met Danielle Downing was at a let's-pretend-we're-middle-aged expat party she threw at her apartment, which meant Gypsy Kings soundtrack, chinless Americans and Brits . . . and beer. She was a big deal in the banking community. My Pakistani boss took me to meet her. Like him, Downing was a fellow Wharton grad—an elite carpetbagger.

Every American expat party in Moscow is the same. Particularly if they're thrown by American women. First, the functional interior, the middle-class "low key" prints on the wall, and simple decorations, an intentional way to distinguish yourself from the allegedly vulgar, gaudy Russians. Worse, not a drug in sight, not a single drunken Russian or even a whiff of sexual tension. It was odd, this barricaded safe house of human ugliness in a city teeming with hungry beauty. Most American expat parties in Moscow are like that: a kind of inverse *Night of the Living Dead*, where the boring, homely expat creatures lock themselves indoors to protect themselves from the pulsing, beautiful miniskirted humans on the outside.

Downing had short black hair, and was dressed in a simple gray sweater, jeans, and topsiders, with no makeup. Her harsh, mannish features weren't softened by the clothes, but then

Knowing that Nicole the Libra suffered from childhood-trauma-induced paranoia, we stuck messages about her into our Gore-O-Scopes—the one section she'd always quote—after she absconded. We were convinced she'd secretly read them, triggering a lifelong Xanax habit.

LIBRA This is a tricky one, Lib. See, you've absconded with money and financial records from people close to, and you've started to get the idea that maybe they've forgotten all about it and you're off scott-free. And you know what? You're darn-tootin' right! So don't worry about them knowing where you are, Lib, and worry about Number One. That's right: U! Take a little chunk of that dough and head over to American Express and treat yourself to a trip abroad, will ya?!

FROM : Amer.Embassy Cafe , Moscow PHONE NO. : 9564118 Apr. 27 1998 05:34PM P

267-4159

755-8296

To: Mark and Matt
From: Nicole Mollo

I have already spoken with Kostiya today about your outrageous lies. I do not appreciate you calling people and telling them the load of crap you have invented. I will return from vacation to settle this with Kostiya, as we discussed today. I purposefully left the way I did because I expected your behavior to be extremely irrational and unfair. You have exceeded my expectations. I prefer not to speak with either of you again. Since the finance question will be dealt with by Kostiya, there is no longer any need for you to attempt to contact me, or any of my acquaintances. When I have further time, I will fax you a list of the accounts which owe money. I collected money from the Duck, which was equal to the amount which was owed to me, and the balance is due to the exile, which can be collected at a later date. I hold no money which belongs to the exile. You must realize that if you persist in harassing me, or my acquaintances, there are measures I can take to protect myself.

After we realized that Nicole had disappeared with our cash-in/cash-out records and a lot of unanswered questions, we called all of her friends around town, trying to track her down. When that failed, we called several airline companies asking them not to allow her onboard. We told them that she might be carrying a highly contagious disease, and that it was vital we contact her. Only Aeroflot refused to cooperate. We also spread veiled hints that our publisher had plans for her. She barricaded herself in the American Embassy with a friend, and sent off this threatening fax.

again, she dressed pretty much the way everyone else at her party dressed. She didn't even *try* to appear sexually appealing. That's because within the frame of her party, she didn't need to. Instead, she did what all expat women do when they throw parties in Moscow: she barred all the competition—there wasn't a single Russian woman under the age of 35. This is a strategy imitated by female expat managers at restaurants, bars, and companies: They invariably hire bland support staff, weeding out all elements of potentially arousing beauty. The Starlite Diner, Video Express, McDonald's . . . everywhere it's the same. It's kind of an unstated joke in the expat world, but everyone knows it's true. The threat is real. Downing, in spite of her money and her position, was not immune to the brutal sexual humiliation that all expat American women endure in Russia.

The expat men at Downing's party were careful not to offend. It's an implicit rule in Moscow that bringing your young, leggy Russian *dyevushka* to a female expat's party is bad taste, rubbing salt in the wound, like showing up at a Vietnam vet's reunion with a slope girlfriend in a peaked straw peasant's hat, Mao outfit, and gag water gun. . . .

All American women, and practically all the European women, are socially and sexually devastated by Russia. They're at a massive disadvantage for the first time in their lives. They didn't expect it at all. None of us did. We all came here expecting to skim the top, showing the poor savages how to work, eat, dress. . . . But things started to happen to us. We—the expat men and women—veered off in wildly different directions, on to nonintersecting planes.

Eventually, all the expat women abandon this city bitter and frustrated, deeply Russophobic and devoted to the Brzezinskian doctrine of containment and dismemberment of the Russian beast . . . because the sexual strategies that they have been used to employing cannot compete against the Russian *dyevushki*. It's swords against SS-21s. American women have been raised to believe that traditional qualities of femininity—appearing as though you are trying to please the man by caking on makeup, wearing tight short skirts that show off your legs, speaking in a high voice, giggling, and deferring to his desires—as well as characteristics usually used to describe sluts—high heels, heavy perfume, sleeping

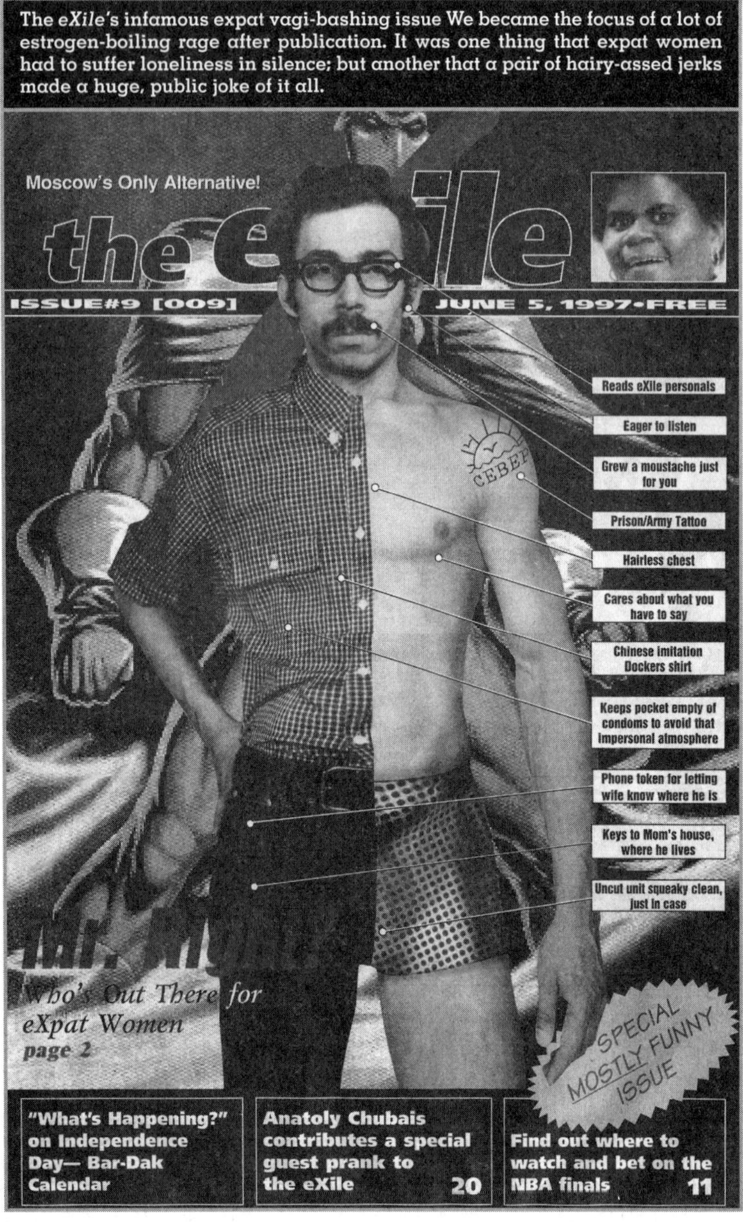

Moscow's Only Alternative!
the eXile
ISSUE#9 [009]
JUNE 5, 1997•FREE
Reads eXile personals
Eager to listen
Grew a moustache just for you
Prison/Army Tattoo
Hairless chest
Cares about what you have to say
Chinese imitation Dockers shirt
Keeps pocket empty of condoms to avoid that impersonal atmosphere
Phone token for letting wife know where he is
Keys to Mom's house, where he lives
Uncut unit squeaky clean, just in case
Who's Out There for eXpat Women
page 2
SPECIAL MOSTLY FUNNY ISSUE
"What's Happening?" on Independence Day— Bar-Dak Calendar
Anatoly Chubais contributes a special guest prank to the eXile 20
Find out where to watch and bet on the NBA finals 11

The *eXile*'s infamous expat vagi-bashing issue We became the focus of a lot of estrogen-boiling rage after publication. It was one thing that expat women had to suffer loneliness in silence; but another that a pair of hairy-assed jerks made a huge, public joke of it all.

with a man on the first night without demanding he use a condom—are not only atavistic and repugnant but, ultimately, unsuccessful tactics in the competition for Mr. Right.

Most American men are also culturally programmed to believe that what they really want is not a "bimbo" but an "equal": someone who can stand on her own two feet, earn her own coin, make her own decisions, hang with the boys, think like a man, speak in a low, monotone, ironic tone of voice—while at the same time radiate some kind of eroticism vaguely reminiscent of traditional femininity, though without implying that era's oppressive power hierarchy. . . . Just writing this down reminds me how strange and schizophrenic our expectations are. American women aren't aware that they've been handed just about the most crazed, impossible script on Planet Earth. They don't know how bad it is because America's influence is winning, the historical trend is running straight out of San Francisco and New York and Boston, and, therefore, however horrible and painful it all may be, arguing against any part of the American Way would be like arguing against history itself.

Out in Russia, you gain a little perspective, which can be dangerous. Deep down, as it turns out, even the most emasculated, wire-rimmed glasses, cigar-smoking and martini-drinking American guy fantasizes about living in world full of . . . well, I'll let you guess:

a) self-reliant women who are also your friends

b)sluts

Okay, still stuck? I'll amend it. All men—that's right, all sane men—fantasize about a world populated with:

a) self-reliant androgynous women who are also your friends

b) young, beautiful sluts

Envelope please. . . . Whoah! This is a shocker, folks! Hold on to your seats! Turns out, when you scrape away the surface implants, every single sane man wants . . . *drum roll, maestro* . . . young, beautiful sluts!

CUT TO: Young, beautiful sluts seated in third row, hands cupped over mouths in shocked surprise. . . . They stand, crying-laughing, hugging each other, then slowly make their way toward the podium, kissed by vigorously applauding men on their way there . . .

Young, beautiful sluts. It's a censored fantasy, and best kept that way: After all, in coastal America, reality couldn't be further away from that fantasy. It exists only in chat rooms, and even there, most of the alleged F18's are gay 50-year-old men with spiked five-inch butt-plugs wedged up their asses.

When I look back at America now, I shudder. All those millions of poor sad fucks who spend their lives on the Internet "meeting" people—they scare me the most. I remember my life those last six months in California. Had I stayed, I might

TOP 10 PICK-UP LINES USED ON EXPAT WOMEN

1) You know, I'm tired of women expecting me to sleep with them on the first night. It makes me feel like an object.
2) I don't know about you, but for me, my career is the most importatnt thing.
3) I think make-up makes women look cheap, don't you?
4) Hey, have you seen Legal Eagles?
5) I won't lie—I'm a lazy alcoholic, and I just want someone to take care of me.
6) Hey, are you gonna finish that?
7) I think women improve with age.
8) Oh Jesus, I'm gonna be sick!
9) Oh, so you're a speedskater? No? I just thought...
10) Right now, I'd fuck anything.

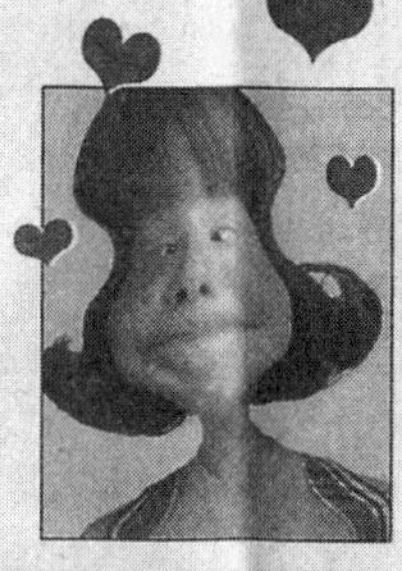

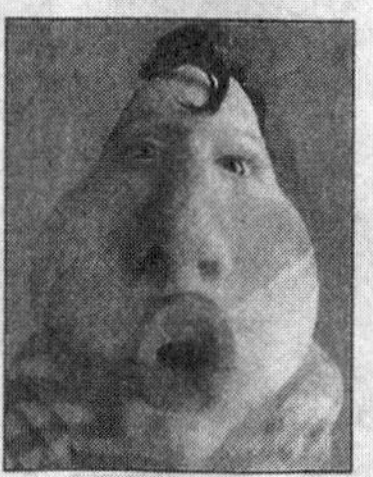

have wound up in chat room number 12 myself, jerking off with one hand, desperately wooing some socially terrified woman with the other. But now that I've been in Russia, where people aren't quite as afraid and alienated from each other, I realize that I didn't HAVE to endure that—the social/sexual script I'd been handed in suburban California is one of the bleakest in man's history. Turns out that there are several other scripts out there in the global village far superior, with far happier beginnings, middles, and endings than the American one.

For Russian girls, the stakes in sex are pretty simple: money, and/or self-destructive adventure. When American women try to tell their Russian sisters that they have it all wrong, that in fact they're being oppressed and demeaned, Russian girls invariably assume that the *amerikanka* is a frustrated spinster. *Dyevushki* value the surface far more than deluded Americans. They judge each other by how beautiful they look, how much makeup they wear, how high their miniskirts are cut . . . under those criteria, any American feminist's ethos is immediately undercut. Russia's a tough crowd, tough crowd.

The gulf between the two is unbridgeable. I remember entire feminist groups thriving in Prague—Czech women were eager to gain Western acceptance via any route. Those same Prague-based feminist organizations made a few failed attempts to crack the Russian market. I knew one of the leaders, a Canadian Jew named Rachel. She told me, after a doomed tour of Moscow and St. Petersburg, that the Russians were "primitive" and "hopeless." The feminists' main problem is that they were marketing a less attractive alternative to the wildly flawed but never-boring local sexual narrative. For Russians, there is no greater sin than a boring, safe life. Everything else is negotiable. In that frame, American feminism falls as flat as would a Russian nerd coming to a high school class in California and advising the kids that they should listen to Boney-M and wear tight Vietnamese-manufactured counterfeit Levi's if they wanted to be cool—which, if the Soviets had won the Cold War, they might have done.

But such bizarre advice wouldn't wash with the kids—and neither will a feminist's advice in Russia. The *dyevushki* have the game down pretty well here, even if it usually ends up with marrying a wife-beating, syphilis-infected, drunken loser who can't so much as change the lightbulb.

But that part comes later for the *dyevushki*. And they know it. So they live it up to the max while they have the upper hand, when nature is good to them. They know that time is working against them. Youth is a dirty word here—most go straight to adulthood by the age of 14. I can count five women I've slept with who lost their virginity at age 11; they

EXPAT BEAUTY. It's an oxymoron. Pictured here are the homecoming king and queen of Moscow's English-speaking expat crowd. If they're really nutty, they might even drink beer.

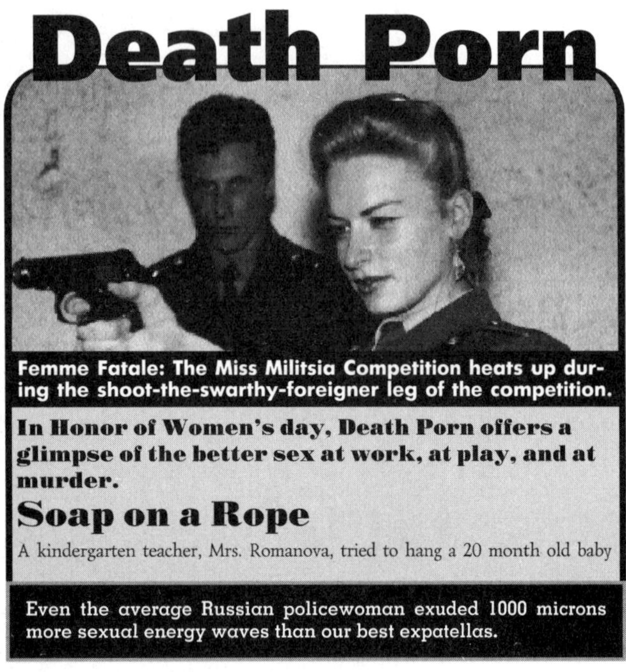
Death Porn

Femme Fatale: The Miss Militsia Competition heats up during the shoot-the-swarthy-foreigner leg of the competition.

In Honor of Women's day, Death Porn offers a glimpse of the better sex at work, at play, and at murder.

Soap on a Rope

A kindergarten teacher, Mrs. Romanova, tried to hang a 20 month old baby

Even the average Russian policewoman exuded 1000 microns more sexual energy waves than our best expatellas.

treat it as dry fact, like when their first teeth grew, and not as a psychology-loaded tragedy. A Russian woman is at the peak of her power from about age 13 until 20. After that, beauty is subjected to the cruel forces of entropy, which renders them unrecognizable beasts—Division II noseguards—by the age of 30. That's why most have been married at least once by the time they hit 20—in the provinces, the age is more like 17.

Russian girls are the most physically attractive women on earth, and they are all available to the right bidder. The Supermodel types usually wind up on the arms of some middle-aged, roly-poly businessman. Chechens and Georgians were "in" when I first arrived in Moscow; now, Slavic-blooded flatheads have replaced them. Middle-aged and rich is the key. The rest—the sevens and eights—are up for grabs. Even the whores for sale at Night Flight, Metelitsa, and Monte Carlo clubs are the kind of girls you'd only expect to see in *Sports Illustrated* Swimsuit Issues or Ratt videos. But anyone can have them—for a price (about $200 at Night Flight, from $300 to $700 or more at Metelitsa).

Nearly every Westerner who comes here—male and female—is shocked by the beauty factor. It takes a while for the brain to trust the eyes. During the Cold War, we were brainwashed to expect mustached bodybuilders and gruff-voiced fireplugs—Kara Deyerin types—not dainty, leggy teenie-vixens. Their Eurasian features (pale skin, eyes that are both slanted and large, colored gray or ice-blue, and sleek legs like a gazelle's) and exaggerated feminine gestures stir things in the expat male's primordial consciousness. Perhaps it has something to do with the gratuitous fellatio-friendly lipstick jobs girls here wear: bright red paint from nose to chin, which screams: "I am capable of sucking your dick so hard that you'll have to pull the sheets out of your ass!" In America such women are available only to producers and rock stars. In Russia, they're everywhere—they're the norm. And expat men have a leg up on everyone.

Expats represent the ticket out of the smoldering ruins of this Visa-caged East, and into the glorious, clean, civilized West. This puts nearly all expat men into a position they'd never been trained for: that of heavy-metal guitarists having to choose among potential groupies. Every bar, every restaurant, every day at work, there is some attractive Russian *dyevushka*—whose stunning beauty and tender age the expat man had always assumed was beyond his reach—distracting him from his work. He can barely contain himself. Many expat guys I know run amock here, like escaped convicts offered a free Happy Hour at the Mustang Ranch, consuming as many women as possible, in the fear that someday, this opportunity will vanish, like a dream.

Others just can't get used to the idea. They stand around in bars and nightclubs, clutching their beers, staring at the items with a dumb, scared expression. They can't believe that they have rights to any of it—they're afraid that they'll be permanently damaged if they try. Or worse, that they're being watched, tested, if not by the Feminist INTERPOL Police, then by God himself.

Russian parents encourage their teenage daughters to date men in their 30s—men who offer experience, maturity and money—preferably Western men. So teenage *dyevs* make themselves available. It takes a while for most American men to get the nerve up to sleep with a teenager. Well, not that long. He's a bit awkward at first. He's worried about social consequences. His conscience tells him something's wrong with fucking a teenager, although the rest of his body takes out a pair of two-by-fours and clubs his conscience unconscious.

Once he crosses that line, that's it, he's spoiled forever. That's why his former expat girlfriend will say about him, "He's been ruined . . . he's not like he used to be . . . " I say "former" because I don't know of a single American couple that came to Russia together and didn't split apart after six months because Biff decided he wanted to play Axl Rose while the Axl-in' was good.

My expat girlfriend, Suzanne, said the exact same thing about me. We started dating a month after I moved to

Moscow. Then she left for Belgium, and when she returned to Moscow a year later, she didn't like the New Me. I used to be shier and clumsier. I was more likable before.

Expat women like my old girlfriend get hit with a double-whammy of shit luck in Moscow: First, they're physically outclassed by the Russian girls; and secondly, the Russian men are slouched, pasty, unkempt, and, in most Western women's eyes, the ugliest men in Europe. And yet . . . *even the Russian men don't want expat women.* Which leaves—exactly no one wanting expat women. That's right: *no one.*

In order to survive, American women in Moscow try to adapt—at least those who want to keep a foot in the Darwinian lottery. Some start pouring on makeup and dressing like the local sluts, but somehow that makes them even more pathetic. Most get looser, much looser.

They'll sleep with anyone. Even the *eXile*'s villain costar, the gas-bellied, balding Owen Matthews, boasts an entire shelf of American women trophies. It's the saddest statement of expat female desperation—all those American girls that Owen conquered. They submitted the way women in conquered lands submitted to their sweaty, barbaric conquerors in days of yore. And those were the lucky ones—at least they got laid by someone.

One famous story tells of a USAID woman who complained to another friend, "It's gotten so bad here that I've resorted to licking pussy." Other American women still hold out hope. They survive by casing certain expat-only bars where they prey on fresh-off-the-boat expat men who don't speak a word of Russian—they're the only ones with whom she has a chance of building a relationship. Many just give up, focus on their jobs, sock away the hot dough like Downing, and return home to America where she's back in the driver's seat. She's comforted only by the

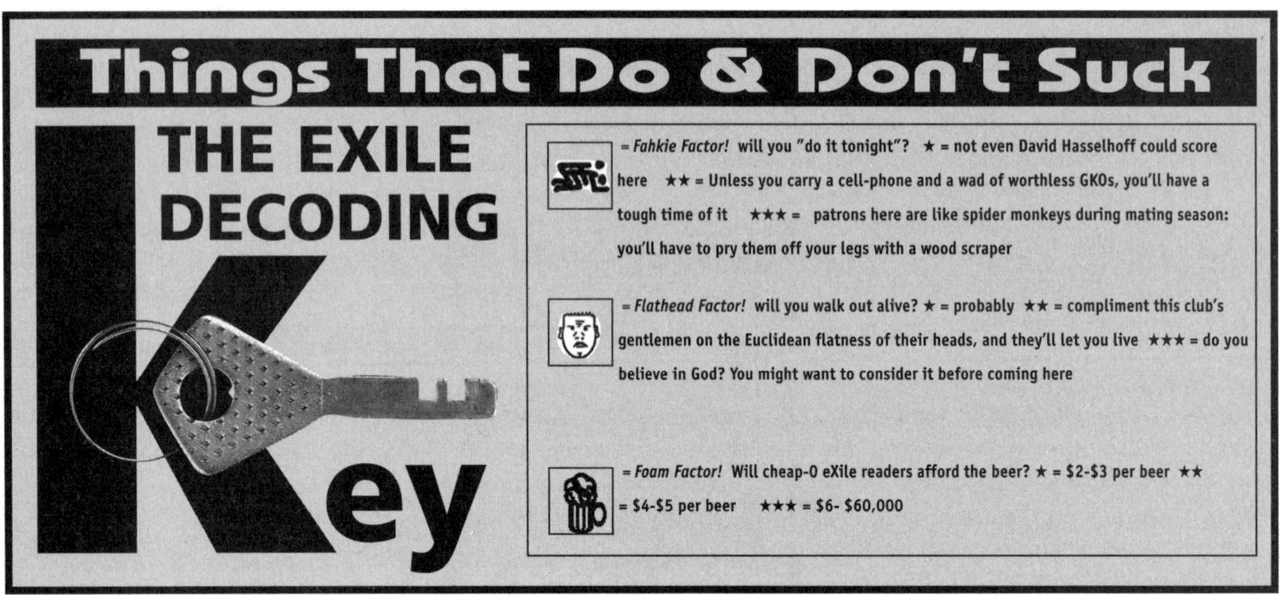

thought that when Biff comes back, vengeance will be hers. Because when Biff shows up at JFK passport control, he's going to have an ego-slashing time readjusting to America's dry, flat, sexless narrative. It's just one way that Russia, pretending to be overrun by the West, is quietly poisoning its "conqueror." The same way that other "conquerors"—Sweden, France, Germany—limped out of here squeaking in shock, emasculated forever.

Things That Do & Don't Suck
THE EXILE DECODING Key
= Fahkie Factor! will you "do it tonight"? ★ = not even David Hasselhoff could score here ★★ = Unless you carry a cell-phone and a wad of worthless GKOs, you'll have a tough time of it ★★★ = patrons here are like spider monkeys during mating season: you'll have to pry them off your legs with a wood scraper
= Flathead Factor! will you walk out alive? ★ = probably ★★ = compliment this club's gentlemen on the Euclidean flatness of their heads, and they'll let you live ★★★ = do you believe in God? You might want to consider it before coming here
= Foam Factor! Will cheap-O eXile readers afford the beer? ★ = $2-$3 per beer ★★ = $4-$5 per beer ★★★ = $6- $60,000

We published an article in the *eXile* spelling out these unpleasant truths. To this day, nearly the entire female expat community won't talk to us. Having the truth aired out in public like that was salt in the wounds—like pissing in the wounds, blowing your nose in them, and laughing the whole time. They didn't appreciate that very much.

About a month after we launched the *eXile,* I started getting a call from some kind of nervous American nerd asking how he could contribute to the newspaper, since he was a big fan. He stuttered when he spoke to me; he tried to drop hip expressions, but they came out wrong and forced. I did my best to put him off. I have a terrible prejudice about writers who cold-call me—I assume that they must be worthless if they're crawling up to me. It's the same tried-and-true formula that has led to a disastrous record in the field of long-term relationships with girls: If she wants me, something must be wrong with her.

This guy had sent a letter to our [sic] page, a place for readers to submit themselves to open abuse in exchange for an *eXile* T-shirt, and signed his name "Johnny Chen." I thought the name was a joke or a pseudonym, since few people sent us letters using their real names. About a month after that, he called me again, and asked if he could pick up his *eXile* [sic] T-shirt. I told him to come by after work that day, so that I would miss him. Another fear of mine is that anyone who comes to our office has one intention: to murder me for things I've written.

The next day, I asked Marcus, who was in the office when this "Johnny Chen" came by, what he looked like. I'd expected some nerd surfer-type with a soccer hairdo. Chen had some of that coastal California inflection, although he'd clearly been excluded from the crowd.

Marcus shrugged. "Oh, I don't know. He looked like some normal Asian-American guy."

"You mean he's really a Johnny Chen?"

Marcus turned and laughed, adjusting his gold wire-rimmed glasses. "Yeah, he's really a 'Johnny Chen.' He also asked me to leave this for you to read. I'm sure he's the writer you've been dreaming of and more."

Marcus handed me a large manila envelope addressed to "Mark Ames" in large letters.

I didn't open it for another few months, assuming that it was an attack on me. I put it on our desk, and let it serve as the bottom layer upon which several layers of paper sediment built and built, especially after Taibbi joined.

Then disaster struck the *eXile.* Owen, who wrote club reviews for us under the pseudonym "Robert Plant," got worse and worse as a writer. Not only did he never get his pieces in on time (once he handed his piece to us through the barred-window grill on deadline night—he was so late that the security guards wouldn't let him in), but he even wrote reviews on clubs and bars that he never visited. And every piece was the same: Russian-managed bars sucked and lacked taste, and Western-style clubs were signs of hope. Readers complained.

Just as Taibbi and I were trying to figure out what to do, I got another call from Johnny Chen.

"You never answered me, Mark. Just tell me yes or no. Don't you realize that you're passing up an opportunity?"

I looked through the bars in our window, across the courtyard, and up to the roof. We were located on the ground floor of a residential apartment block, a horseshoe of eight-story buildings. This crazed gook's probably Oswalding me from the roof across the way, with a cell-phone and a scope-rifle.

"Look, I understand your newspaper better than anyone," he went on. "It's basically *Revenge of the Nerds.* But you guys aren't the real thing. I've seen you and Taibbi—you look like a pair of wrestlers. You guys aren't the real thing, you know. I am. I can give you an authentic dweeb's view of Russian nightlife. All I ask for in exchange is one of your *eXile* press cards you guys have, so that I can get into clubs and stuff free, and use it to impress girls. In return, let me write your club reviews. Let me at least try. Your Robert Plant guy sucks, and you know it. Everyone I talk to thinks he's a joke, and you're losing cred. But just think: What newspaper, anywhere in the world, would ever hire a thirty-one-year-old Asian-American like me, a fucking information manager at a Big Five firm, to write their club reviews? You guys are always trying to buck convention and stuff, and you try to be hip by being unhip: Well, here's your chance to make nerd history. Think about it: If it can be proven that a guy like me can get laid and have a wild nightlife in Moscow, then literally ANYBODY can. That's what I tried to tell you in my letter you never read."

Goddamnit, he was right! I mean, only if he could write. But fuck it, even if Chen couldn't write, we'd use his persona, publish his picture, and edit the hell out of it, just to bring the Moscow Decadence myth to a new level. Chen wouldn't be the first shitty writer we'd used for the sake of using crazed, shitty writers: Bobby Brown, the totally mad New Jersey expat who runs a pirate video rental store out of his apartment, faxes us his trademark video reviews. Brown was a short Italian who always wore unbuttoned shirts showing off his gold medallion. If you went to his apartment to take a video, he'd keep you for hours recounting every Steven Segal or Jean-Claude Van Damme film, comparing them to his own experiences fighting off armed *bandity* with his feet and fists. Brown would lose a writing competition to Koko the gorilla . . . and yet, he became a literary legend in the *eXile.* Chen, therefore, had a lot of room in which to maneuver.

His first review was about a disastrous evening out to a strip joint called Rasputin. The short Chechen club manager was so sure that Chen was a fraud posing as a journalist that he set him up. He sat Chen down at a barstool and motioned one of the girls to join him for a drink. When the aging red-haired stripper-whore sat next to Chen for some light conversation, she ordered a glass of champagne, then later walked. The barman presented the Chenster with the bill: $150 for the glass of champagne, $20 for each gin and tonic that the manager had offered him.

Chen threw a fit. He told the barman that he refused to pay. The barman called a manager over, a different manager than the Chechen, who said he had no idea that Chen had been invited as a journalist/guest. The Chechen was gone for the night. Meaning, pay up, bub. Chen threw a fit. He told them he was leaving, like it or not. They could take him out back and beat him, but he wasn't going to victim to a shit Bangkok scam like that. For some strange reason, they backed down, an example of the kind of luck that Chen has had ever since moving to Moscow.

When he came into the office to deliver his Rasputin piece, I was shocked at whom we'd hired as our Voice Of Hipness: Chen's longish, parted black hair, square wire-

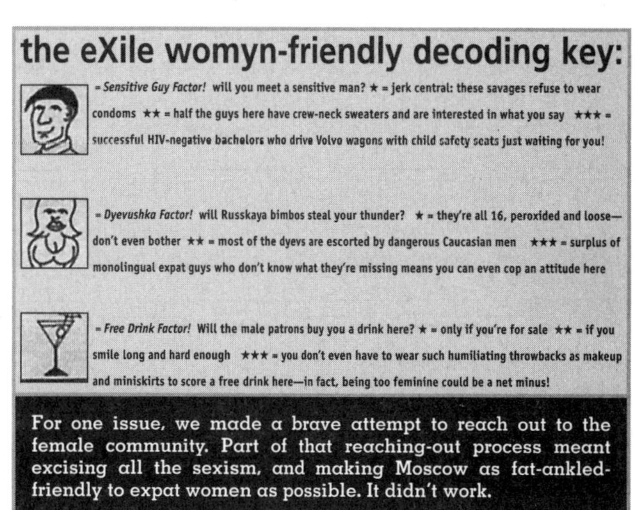

the eXile womyn-friendly decoding key:
= Sensitive Guy Factor! will you meet a sensitive man? ★ = jerk central: these savages refuse to wear condoms ★★ = half the guys here have crew-neck sweaters and are interested in what you say ★★★ = successful HIV-negative bachelors who drive Volvo wagons with child safety seats just waiting for you!
= Dyevushka Factor! will Russkaya bimbos steal your thunder? ★ = they're all 16, peroxided and loose—don't even bother ★★ = most of the dyevs are escorted by dangerous Caucasian men ★★★ = surplus of monolingual expat guys who don't know what they're missing means you can even cop an attitude here
= Free Drink Factor! Will the male patrons buy you a drink here? ★ = only if you're for sale ★★ = if you smile long and hard enough ★★★ = you don't even have to wear such humiliating throwbacks as makeup and miniskirts to score a free drink here—in fact, being too feminine could be a net minus!

For one issue, we made a brave attempt to reach out to the female community. Part of that reaching-out process meant excising all the sexism, and making Moscow as fat-ankled-friendly to expat women as possible. It didn't work.

rimmed glasses, and beige corduroy pants, and a slight pigeon-toed slouch, spoke of years of halfheartedly masturbating by the computer table. In person, he was much shier and tongue-tied, although on the phone and in print, his voice reflected at least a good working knowledge of coastal California slang.

Chen started living up to his promise as the approaching-middle-age-nerd who shamelessly groped his way into corporeal heaven. He abused his press card as much as possible. He'd flash it in everyone's face, and it paid. At first, I thought his tales of sexual conquest were exaggeration, but once, I saw him at a club crudely French-kissing two teenagers. They weren't cute, but they were alive. I found myself even getting sort of pissed off. The bastard! Leeching off our sweat and tears for his cheap thrills! Then Chen started dabbling in heavy drugs. Dabbling? More like Hoovering them off anyone and anything he could find. When Chen came into our offices, we had to hide everything. Piles of phenamine, normally sitting out by our computers on production night, would suddenly be locked into the cupboards. Even our female sales staff hid.

Later, it was Chen's famous "rape" review of a club, in which he allegedly wrote about how he raped a girl who'd fallen off the bartop at the Hungry Duck and into his arms, that sparked Stanford professor, Carnegie Endowment honcho and Clinton administration tool Michael McFaul to begin his official ban-the-*eXile* campaign. Chen made headlines in every Russian-studies academic's Internet mail programs. He became the subject of heated exchanges between journalists, and the focal point of a First Amendment debate. But more on that later. . . .

Chen ate the publicity up. "Russian girls get really excited when they see your name in a newspaper," he told me, spittle building on his lips. He'd carry laminated copies of the articles with him into clubs and show them off. "I'm really glad that McFaul jerk attacked me. I've never scored so much pussy in my life!"

hen the Hungry Duck bar and grill opened at the end of 1995, I remember thinking, *There goes the neighborhood.* America's worldwide blandification effort had just planted a seedling in the center of Moscow. Moscow was still pretty barren at the time. It had a kind of an *Omega Man* postapocalyptic feel: all those massive, heavy gray buildings, tombs of the mid-20th century. The storefronts were still mostly dead, dimly lit—if at all—after dark. City lights came from the apartments, gloomy beige backlit curtains. The real commercial explosion that Moscow is now famous for didn't take place until after the presidential elections in 1996. Up to then, it was still sort of a toss-up whether or not Moscow would succumb to the homogenizing influence of the West, or whether it would somehow fuck it up, slow it down. I had a latent fear that I'd wake up one morning, and Moscow would be transformed into Atlanta, with microbreweries on every street corner, and sport utility vehicles with child safety seats clogging the streets. The way other once-interesting European cities decayed into blandness: Berlin, Prague, Paris.

Prague is an excellent example. I saw what happened to Prague, how it became a safe, tourist-friendly, boring little addition to the global village. Prague could have gone either way after the communists were thrown out. In 1991 it was still a mess—a heavy element of the mid-20th century still suffocated the average visitor: excess cement, crude architecture, and terrible food. But Prague had one advantage from the Western point of view: good, cheap beer. Cheap Beer meant that the Germans would never leave the place alone. Cheap Beer meant that fresh-out-of college Americans would make it their home away from home. The young Czechs were desperate to rush the EU frat house, and the Semester at Sea Americans who shacked up there were effective in steering Prague away from its suspicious, time-warped past and toward the familiar: something like Haight Street meets *Reality Bites.* If they haven't already met.

There was another part—I couldn't much talk about it at the time, because when you're around Americans your whole life, you learn to censor yourself. Women. The Czech women . . . they just weren't happening. At their best, they looked like those Muppets from the film *Willow.* That *Willow* look is the more pure Slavic blood. But few had that pure Slavic blood. Too much Teutonic trash had fouled the gene pool. Bad skin, not like the baby's ass complexion that most Russians have. Worse, the Czech women were already getting attitudes. They were spoiled by the oversupply of foreign tourists, making them as inaccessible to me as—well, as America. They began to acquire that cold, determined expression.

My Czech girlfriend, Radka, didn't help much when it came to forming my opinion of her people. When I lived at the European Care Home, I'd wake up in the night to hear the loud hum of some vibrator under the sheets. She went through a dozen of them during our relationship. Mangled cucumbers collected under her pillow. She'd whisper things into my ear, playful lines that had once turned me on: "Daddy, what is this? Daddy? . . . Daddy, baby wants you to do that thing to me . . . " It made me want to puke; sex was my enemy. Only the scabies mites saved me from having to respond sexually.

We came to Prague together planning on making a quick buck, hiring some Slovak servants, but everything went bad, everything reverted to that familiar, awful Central European love-triangle script. It was a life without dignity, a small life.

Russia wasn't like that—not in 1991, when I visited as a tourist. Russian women were uniformly prettier, and more accessible. I was a kind of White God stepping onto the shores of the Neva. I didn't take advantage of that situation—nothing in my American upbringing had prepared me for it—but the memory stayed with me, and gave me Hope in those long years of sexual famine. I dreamed often of Russian women: In my mind, they were exiles in a remote, abandoned colony from which there was no escape. If I could only get transported to their distant colony—if I could find a space shuttle to get me there, I was sure that they'd appreciate me more than the females on my own planet.

I found a short-wave Russian-language radio station when I lived in Prague, and listened to the voice, although I didn't understand the words. The melody—when Russian women speak, there is a melody, a song to their speech that is unlike anything else. Almost exaggerated girlishness. I imagined the announcer: her porcelain complexion, her soft round face, and eyes of surrender.

So I dreamed of the East without telling myself exactly why. The West—that was my enemy. The West meant creeping impotence. The West meant anesthetized famine. The West meant a cozy extinction.

Reports filtered into Prague about how horrible Ukraine was, and how lucky we all had it. The bohemians' CW was that we shouldn't complain about the lack of services and food choices, because compared to people in the former Soviet Union, we were living in Paradise.

Farther to the east of the dreadful Ukraine was Russia, and Moscow. The nose-pierced CW on Moscow was even worse: crime, filth, and, again, no food. Food was all that was on these progressive grunge-types' minds. Russia's rep really put the fear of God into them. It was too authentically alien, whereas Prague was the safe simulation. Western visitors loathed Moscow, and hated the fact that the Muscovites fucked everything up (i.e., they didn't do things OUR way). From my point of view, as a refugee looking for a place to exile myself, a paradigm-refugee seeking an alternative universe,

Moby Dick Does Moscow

By Johnny Chen

Call me Chen. There I was, on a Saturday night, cruising Moscow in search of the great mythical white whale—which in our case just meant a decent new nightclub. The irony of it all was that I was cruising in a rented white 4-door Merc—the White Merc in search of the White Whale. Delicious irony, ain't it?

By now you may have guessed that the nightclub in question has something to do with the legendary American novel Moby Dick, although I'd be reaching if I tried to make a literal connection between the book and the club. Moby Dick isn't exactly a new club, but it has completely changed its schtick from a shabby bandity disco to an "underground" techno club, one of several "underground" techno clubs that dot provincial Moscow (if only those quotes around "underground" had Java script fingers curling up and down).

Here I'll have to make a quick digression so that readers out there—particularly American readers—can understand what this overused word "underground," in its current 1990s incarnation, means. The word "underground" has almost no relation to its previous meaning, which I think traces its roots to Dostoevsky's Notes From The Underground, published in the mid-1860s. Up until the grunge explosion of 1991, "underground" generally referred to a kind of aesthetic or lifestyle that literally had to hide itself underground in order to avoid serious social/legal consequences, including violence. Fetishists, punks, junkies, homosexuals, skinheads, revolutionaries, artists whose works risked censorship or imprisonment-they and their circles were, until this decade, referred to as "underground." But if the West is good at one thing it's in taking something once-considered dangerous, defanging it, and repackaging it for commercial consumption.

Hence, the 90s techno definition of the word "underground" no longer refers to that which is dangerous, but rather that which is trendy, one step ahead of the mainstream. It is a complete inverse of the previous meaning, when the underground did everything to avoid the mainstream out of fear of being found out; today's underground is similar to the Russian marketing word "eksklusivny," and therefore attracts the mainstream.

Now that you've learned your lesson in 90s technospeak, let's return to Moby Dick, one of the better "underground" techno clubs in provincial Moscow. The nicest thing about Moby Dick is that it's a funny place. It's located in the first floor on the side of a typical block apartment building; the stairwell leading up to the chillout is made up of those heavy cement steps that reek of the FSU; and best of all, the patrons can't dance for shit. All except for two. One, who wore red overalls, white gloves and sunglasses, looked just like Fred "Rerun" Stokes from What's Happening!, while another, a woman doing the robot, reminded us of Yarnell from Shields & Yarnell.

But there's another reason to go. The kids—mostly under 18 years old—are a Belgian pedophile's dream come true. My nightclubbin' companion, in his early 30s and wearing an orange linen blazer, went fly fishing near the billiards table (yep, that's right—another Moscow club with billiards) and almost hooked a 14-year-old blondinka with barely budding breasts and the cutest little nose ring this side of Seattle.

I wouldn't be fair if I didn't talk about the really bitchin DJs they had last Friday. They played some of the best house music I've heard in ages, ranging from hardcore to Tibetan chant/trance, while in the upstairs chillout, a besunglassed DJ spun some trippy experimental stuff that made us feel like we were having flashbacks to our hippie days, even though I never had hippie days.

Drinks are cheap, there are no bandity, and the entire atmosphere is somehow charming: provincial Muscovites trying to recreate the all-too-cool Water Club scene, and failing.

As one girl in the skimpiest little dayglo miniskirt said to me, "I prefer Moby Deek to Luch. It's more underground." I guess that means that skimpy dayglo mini-skirts will be the fashion this summer. That, and technodweebs imitating Rerun.

See ***Bind Your Bones*** for details

Moscow's alienness made it an ideal escape. The more crazy laws and illogical, frustrating barriers that the Russian government put up to thwart foreign investment, the better for me. The more Westerners getting shot or having their business stripped away by the Mafia or corrupt officials, the more likely I'd be able to fit in. Less competition. Moscow was so far away from Prague, so inaccessible, that it had a chance of being spared.

And now, smack in the middle of the jungle, some frat-boy podling had planted its roots and it called itself the Hungry Duck. There goes the paradigm, I thought despondently.

I refused to go to the Duck when it opened. When I heard that they were starting to advertise in *Living Here*, I was bummed. That meant I couldn't trash them in our club and bar guide, since we were desperate for advertisers. A couple of months later, a Mexican lawyer friend of mine went there and reported to me how "these fucking frat-boy idiots at the Hungry Duck were tossing coasters at everyone, including me, thinking they're back in college . . . I almost decked one dude in a baseball cap, but someone pulled me away." He has a similar disdain for ordinary people and their ordinary amusements. "I didn't come to Russia just to wind up at a third-rate Chico State frat party. Jesus fuckin-A!"

As 1996 progressed, the nightlife scene in Moscow was getting bolder in every way. Ptyutch catered to underground techno drug fiends. You could score coke or E right there. More bars and dance clubs were opening, and the Russian girls had become noticeably more fashionable, confident, and drug-wise. The radical gap between the Russian girls of James's crowd—model-types in Italian boutique clothes—and the masses of girls who had to sneak into *podyezdy* and basements or other people's apartments to party in the years up until '96 was beginning to narrow. Moscow's nightlife was becoming larger and more democratic. Normally, that would fill Americans' hearts with joy and hope—just the word "democratic." But here, that meant debauchery, drugs, and sexually transmitted diseases raised to a new level not seen since . . . well, not seen at all in my lifetime. Even the Duck was supposedly mutating into something medieval.

The democratization of the nightlife led to Moscow becoming a city-state of depravity. We milked the

A Fistful of Pain

or How Can I *Relax* with this Phist in My Ass?

by Johnny Chen

Every once in awhile it happens: a night on the town so hellish, so horrible, so full of disappointment and misery that you almost wish you were back in Milwaukee.

Last weekend, my friend and decided we'd hit the outskirts of town, but we'd do it in style. After all, this is my first article for the eXile, and I wanted to make a positive impression. So we rented a 4-door white Merc, dressed ourselves to the hilt in gold chains, shiny Italian shoes, and open silk shirts revealing hairy chests (even though my chest is as bald as a baby's butt). We were looking sharp—like nothing would stop us.

My friend and I decided to travel off the beaten path, so we headed way, way the heck out to the Sevastopol Hotel complex. The numerous towering blocks that make up the Sevastopol could easily solve the Hutu refugee crisis (assuming you forced them to live in tight, inhuman, Amnesty-report-inducing conditions). We pulled up around the back of the complex, where the bright lights of club "Relax" beckoned us.

The entrance looks like the lobby to any large Soviet block building stretching from Brest to Vladivostok, complete with seedy creeps playing slots, stale papirosi stench, and crusty garderob. To coin a paraphrase of Robert Plant's, anyone who was cool wasn't there. Which, using Chen's reverse logic, should mean a superior evening for a pair of washed-up lechers... right?

Normally, yes. But not here. We'd hoped to "Relax" and settle into an evening of quiet pedophilia, when we were obstructed by two sets of flat-heads, one in the lobby guarding the elevator entrance, and one on the fourth floor guarding the elevator exit.

We took the elevator up to the fourth floor, and, after crossing the dimly lit beige foyer, we entered the black-light discotheque that is known as Relax. The bar area was nearly empty, while the cheesy dancefloor was about one-third full of Wannabe-But-Never'llbe-New Russians, or what I call "Wabnners." We noticed about 15 teenie chicks, and about 11 Wabnner guys, some who desperately tried to grow mustaches, some who desperately tried to shape their heads into a menacingly flat shape, all of whom wore loose-fitting silk shirts. They were uniformly the worst dancers in the Moskovsky Oblast—walking stiffs, straight out of the mall scene in Dawn of the Dead, saw horses in fancy clothes, log stumps with shoes... (You better stop me—I gotta million of 'em.)

For the eXpat man-about-town, a scene like this should have said, "It's like shooting fish in a barrel." I emphasize "should have." On this theory, we made our move. The prettiest dyev of them all, who danced like a Shiva with an extremely stiff back, sauntered past us; my friend reached out to say hello, groping for her miniskirt, when she angrily knocked his hand away and told him to back off. Stunned by this unprecedented rejection, my friend decided to recover his pride by hitting up on one of the ugliest girls in the club. She had peroxided hair, heavy black eyebrows, and a chin that recalled the puppet "Madame."

"Can I get to know you?" my friend asked, pulling up a stool next to her. "No," she curtly replied, turning away. It was useless. At first we thought it was our fault, until we realized, no, it's their fault.

So we stormed off to the Treasure Island, located in the next korpus over, with the same lobby, the same junkyard dog flathead guarding the elevator, and the same hostility. We flashed the flatheads our eXile cards and told them that we had arrived to rape their women, score free drinks, then abuse their club in our newspaper. For some reason, they refused to let us in for free. We were livid. Look, I didn't give up the life of a quietly successful laundromat manager and enter journalism only to get treated like a commoner. The cover at the door was a laughable 250,000 rubles, far more than truly cool places like Titanik or Bulgakov. They must have been going on the theory that anyone stupid enough to go all the way out there was stuck, and they'd pay whatever ridiculous cover to get in, even if the club was located in the Sevastopol. The truth is, Treasure Island is more like Gilligan's Island: a far-out dump, a bad sitcom, with a few babes on the level of Ginger and Marianne, but management as whacked-out as Mr. Howell. After some hollow threats to ruin their club, we got into our Merc and sped away. All in all, the Sevastopol was a dive, a ream job. I have a solution. I say Russia should trade this Sevastopol to the Ukraine, in return for their Sevastopol. That way, Ukraine can own a piece of Russia (albeit the worst piece), while Russia would get in return what is rightfully hers.

Now would be an appropriate moment to introduce to our readers Johnny Chen's "Phist O' The Week Award." This week's Phistie goes to Rasputin, a new strip club located near Park Kultury, which we visited upon an invitation from the management. We met the manager on the second floor, the floor o' sin, after passing through the authentically seedy ground-level bar area, which features red velvet on the walls. So far, so good.

Upstairs, the strip show was already in high gear. A woman with a decent bod, but a crocodilian expression, worked the pole like a Flashdance-cum-Ed-Nasty veteran. My friend and I thought we'd arrived in Mecca. The manager offered us some gin and tonics, then mysteriously vanished, only to be replaced by one of the hoes. She sat down next to me and chatted me up, making me feel like a real man. Then, she leaned over to the barman. "Sasha, champanskoye pozhaulsto," she chirped. We watched a few more strippers work the poles (the "girls" had a kind of unpleasant "lived-in" look to them). When we'd had enough of it all, we asked for the bill. This is when Mr. Phistie arrived. The total for four gin and tonics: $222 dollars! The champagne that the 'ho ordered cost a whopping $150 for a glass, which was charged to my bill! Now as any seasoned SE Asia traveller will tell you, this is the oldest scam in the books. I spent almost a half an hour arguing the bill, when they finally agreed to strike the $150, leaving us with a $72 bill for five gin and tonics, all of which had been offered to us by the management. So to you, Rasputin, I duly honor my first Phistie. Keep up the shoddy work!

Mr. Phistie Salutes Rasputin, Moscow's Newest Strip Bar!

Robert Plant has been suspended from the eXile pending investigation into a "burgers for articles" scandal. He is currently in Windsor rehearsing for a world tour.

See *Leave Your Liver* for details

theme without shame or subtlety. It's one of the things that made us famous. Why not? It was true, and it goes hand-in-hand with the moral and political corruption. When *Newsweek* and *Time* ran pieces in September of 1997 about "Moscow Decadence," both magazines cited the *eXile* as a key source. A famous American TV correspondent came to Moscow in the fall of 1997, and stopped by our offices, allegedly to do an entire segment on the *eXile.* He repeatedly asked Taibbi whether or not clubs that we claimed were hotbeds of sexual activity actually existed. He wanted us to escort him around, to show him the ropes. He opened up our "Bar-Dak" bar and club section in the newspaper, and pointed to each club that had a high "fahkie factor." Was it true? he demanded. Was it really that easy to get laid at those clubs? . . . He asked to meet Johnny Chen, but we were under obligation to protect him from too much publicity, so we said that Chen was on vacation—even though he was probably sawing up a teenage girl who'd OD'd on his jones stash, sticking her bones in the basement incinerator.

Later, when it became clear that his *eXile* piece wasn't going to run on his network news show, a local production assistant admitted to me that the only reason he came to our offices was to find out how he could get laid in Moscow. "He read your newspaper when he got here, and he forced our bureau into a panic to arrange an interview. We had to rally everyone, get the tapes, the cameramen. All because he wanted to get laid in Moscow. He's a fucking pig." Her voice had that clenched, pent-up contempt that you often hear from American women here.

The piece never ran, but the Anchorhead came back again as the crisis in Russia exploded the following summer, and interviewed the *eXile* about . . . *you guessed it* . . . the club scene.

When the *eXile* hit the streets, our English-language competitors, the *Moscow Times* and *Tribune,* were developing plans to copy our bar and club guide. But they were at a disadvantage: they had to maintain that respectable, paper-of-record veneer. So the *Moscow Times* started up an entertainment section called "MT Out," with the club guide named "Going Out." The *Tribune* soon followed with their "Time Out" section, including a club and bar guide with short, quasi-racy descriptions to match ours.

When it was obvious they were stealing the *eXile*'s guide idea, to the point of mentioning sex and drugs in their reviews, we added a feature that no one could steal: the "fahkie factor," a three-star rating system on how easy it is to score in a given establishment. We figured the hell with it, no point in being clever and indirect: there's only one reason why people go to a bar, and that's to get laid. The icon pictured those Olympic stick figures in doggie-style sex; one star meant no chance, two stars meant that if you carried a couple cellphones or waved your passport around and offered false promises of marriage and citizenship, you might get lucky, and three stars signified that you'd have to zap the sex-starved patrons off your legs with a cattle prod if you wanted to keep yourself from getting raped. . . . There was no way to gear the guide equally toward men and expat women. I talked to several expat women and fished for advice, but all admitted that there wasn't a single club in Moscow that expatellas considered a premier spot for finding quality men. So, for the sake of professional accuracy, we airbrushed expat women out of the nightlife picture.

Because of our cynicism, I earned the rep of a common pervert (Taibbi was spared somewhat, since he covered more "serious" topics).

Once, we interviewed a potential journalist, a graduate of Wellesley College. She arrived at our offices dressed very much the part of a New England woman with a higher education: severe sweater, horn-rimmed glasses, no makeup, flat voice. . . . And black. Well, mulatto. At the end of the interview, she told me, "You know, you're really different than what I'd imagined. I thought you'd have an open silk shirt and a big medallion in your hairy chest. But you're much different."

We fired her after one issue.

It was and still is strange for me to believe that anyone could take me for even an aging skirt-chaser, a kind of Burt Reynolds of Moscow. Nothing could have been further from the truth. When I lived in America, it wasn't uncommon for me to go an entire year without sex. I never really understood the game. I just found the whole American courtship ritual terrifying. When you first meet a woman there, you are assumed to be an HIV-positive, razor-wielding stalker. Your first task is to convince her that you're harm-

05.03.98 12.03.98
www. exile. ru
#06 P. 6

By Johnny Chen

PLASMA GIVES TECHNO BLOOD

A lot of things are supposed to have died over the past year or two: Yeltsin, *The Moscow Tribune*, and techno music are the first three walking zombies that come to mind.

They were supposed to die, but they didn't. In fact, they seem to get stronger—I'm thinking of the *Trib* in particular. I mean Holy Jose Alinez, how do they do it? Crawling back from the brink of death every three months . . . If I ever have any contract disputes with these eXile pricks, I'm heading straight to Anthony Louis's office . . . then again, I'm afraid he might name me Editor-in-Chief. I mean, how do you follow in the footsteps of Howard Gethen? Or Jose Alinez? Or Vijay Maheshwari?

You don't. You don't even try.

Like the *Trib* and the Prez, techno not only doesn't die, it comes back with a vengeance, like some nasty STD.

Our newspaper has been pretty rough on techno culture. Whether rave, house, gabber, brrreakbeat, acid-goa-trance, and so on . . . it's all techno to us, because it's all blips and beeps.

Well, enough of my yakkin'. Let's hop in the taxi (no White Merc) and take a take a techno cruise.

My first stop was Kreiser, the bastard child of Moby Deek, last year's Provincial Moscow Club Of The Month. Kreiser continues the suckcessful formulae that made Moby Deek such a . . . suckcess: take a Brezhnev-era hall, spray a bunch of day-glo paint around, get a rippin' sound system, and pack it full of Oxy-10 kids. What made Moby Deek cool was the upstairs chill-out and the fact that it was never "discovered." That brought in provincial Muscovites from all over, with the average age about 16. Max. That struck a chord on the Chenster's Perv-O-Meter, but for some reason I never returned, something I half-regretted.

Kreiser, located in some kind of shipping warehouse near Paveletsky Vokzal, opened up in January and has already earned a following: Oxy-10ers with Dr. Seuss ski caps and long-sleeve striped tops. When we were there, about 3/4ths of the kids were slumped head-first into the tables, dribbling on their shirts . . . The age factor was about a year older than Moby Deek's, and a year wiser. An extra year of brain damage will do that to you. It also features the single stupidest prop in techno history: an old 14-inch TV set spraypainted in orange and green day-glo. Trippy, dude. All in all, I recommend it if you're zoning on the proper medicines, but be warned: you'll be hard-pressed to start up some interesting conversation.

My next stop is the find of the year. I'd sort of avoided hitting Plasma for a couple of months, even though I stuck it into our club and bar guide, because I figured it would be the same shit as Galaktika or Robotech. Well, Galaktika, which had a much-publicized "war" with Plasma (hard to imagine techno people at war) over who played the best bleeps 'n blips, lost. Kaput. Closed. And it's a good thing, because Plasma, the brainchild of Aerodance legend Timur Mamedov, kicks techno butt. The theme here is definitely Goa: eight-armed Indian gods and intricate Hindu spiderweb patterns adorn the black walls. The music is softer than Aerodance, although later in the night things approximated a sort of soft/hardcore. Best of all were the two bars, serving up cheap liquor, and the crowd: mainly MGU and younger students. They weren't as doped up as the Kreiser kids, and they were definitely a level higher on the beauty front.

One girl, Emila, was on the prowl for speed. She was 16, stupid, and stacked. My type of gal. Before my friend spotted her 60R for a strelka of speed, she was dead as a rock; after making the rounds with some proto-flatheads upstairs, she headed off to the bathroom and returned the spunky li'l Emila I always knew she should be. There were others of Emila's caliber, some even with brains. If you have any interest in youth culture, a cool cheap club or stacked teenie babes, then mainline some Plasma this weekend, and on the 14th, check out a cool party at Kreiser.

less. But not too harmless—that would be boring. You've got to have some kind of angle as well, something that implies you're dangerous and unique—in a safe way. I never quite got how to modulate between those two poles.

I got worse and worse at it as time went on. Being unemployed and 25 was bad; 26 and living with your Czech girlfriend, her mother, and two geriatric patients in their nursing home was worse; 27 and still unemployed made me too authentically dangerous, taking me completely out of the contest. I just couldn't fake it, and American women have excellent noses for distinguishing between affected psychopaths and real ones.

Even before, even when I was in college and viable, I still failed. If fear didn't hold me back, then logic did: I just didn't see the upside to it all. I'd been in love once—that's a long story. I had a few dates—they never lasted long, usually because I'd discover something about them that repulsed me: a rank box, budding wrinkles, bony knuckles. . . . If I got laid, I didn't feel the pride of a conqueror. In fact, just the opposite: the minute I'd ejaculate, I'd plunge into depression, often ordering my dates to leave immediately. It got to the point where I understood exactly what Soviet serial murder Anatoly Slivko meant when he described his state of mind after sex with his wife: "Nausea, despair, tears."

Slivko was executed for kidnapping young boys in their Pioneer uniforms and hanging them on meat hooks while filming, then later masturbating to those films. My fetishes were tamer, but Slivko and I were in the same ballpark when it came to post-coital depression.

I arrived in Russia after nine dry months. Two years earlier, when I visited the Soviet Union as a tourist, I had a brief affair. Her name was Olga. Memories of her kept me going during the long famine between 1991 and 1993. Even the few times I'd fuck my Czech girlfriend, scabies crawling all over us, I'd think of Olga. I'd sometimes fantasize that it was Olga who gave me the scabies, and, therefore, that her blood and mine were mixing in their mandibles. It was the only way I could live with them.

I looked to Russia as my savior, a place where love was still possible. My affair with Olga was used as evidence to convince me. I filtered her through the characters of Russian novels I'd read and reread: Dostoyevsky, Gogol, Solzhenitsyn, Limonov. . . . I consumed those novels as a means of escaping the bleak present, and, I see now, as a means of preparing my eventual move. Intelligence work.

I paid a lot of attention to the women in those Russian novels. They were so unlike the ironic, self-conscious American women that I knew—so drastically unlike them that I didn't believe that they existed. For an American, it's hard to believe that other white people could be different from us. Russian women couldn't possibly be wildly capricious or slavishly self-sacrificing or self-destructive or quietly obedient.

Even physically it was hard to picture them. I didn't believe that they could have "gray eyes" and "ruddy cheeks" as they were often described. . . . Where I came from, people had blue or brown or fake green eyes and sun-poisoned, crusty-complexioned chins. But then I came to the Soviet Union and saw for myself that, to quote from Malcolm X, "I say you been tricked! You been had! Bamboozled! Hoodwinked! Thrown for a loop! . . . "

My stepfather's friend lined up my visa, and an American contact in Moscow. The contact was the former manager of his wine-distributing business, a Californian named Ted Krashenko. Ted met me at the airport in Moscow, bless him. He pulled me out of the crowd of menacing petty criminals in cheap leather jackets, stinking of sour cigarette smoke, and rushed me to his Chevrolet pickup in the airport parking lot.

Ted was in his early thirties, slightly balding, with a pock-marked complexion masked by twice-weekly visits to the tanning booth, and slow-witted. He dressed in that post–frat boy Dockers way that clearly marked him as an American—as key to sexual success at the time as a great plume of feathers is to a peacock.

On my first night after moving here, September 9, 1993, Ted took me straight from the airport to the Arbat Blues Club, the only expat live music hangout in Moscow at the time. I didn't even have time to shower.

That Chevy pickup was Ted's own. Probably one of five pickups in Moscow in 1993. He drove me from his high-rise apartment near the MosFilm Studios to the center of town, behind the Arbat. I didn't get it at first. I expected Moscow to be completely barren and alien, and here he was, excitedly talking up this "blues club." We got out of the car, and walked a couple of blocks, past abandoned one-and-two-story 19th century houses, down narrow lanes. And then came to a club. I looked at those lopsided Tsarist-era houses and fantasized about what went on in there: a lonely daughter, a mad poet, someone smoking a bowl of Kyrgyz opium. . . .

It was a club all right: no different than, say, a blues club in Prague. White, aging, beer-bellied blues. A front room bar area, stacked with lawn furniture, serving iced beer. And a black-lit band room, with a large dance area, and a stage, with lights, sound, and an expat band belting out harmless party songs. "Riiiiide, Sally riiiiide!"

Ted introduced me to a dozen or so expats. They were kinder to me than the people back home. They assumed that I was one of them, on their side—a besieged noble living reluctantly among the savages. I tried to be polite, although I wanted out. I wanted to roam the streets, and not be stuck in this too-familiar blues bar. Ted led me into the dance-hall area. I was immediately struck by the change in Russian girls from 1991 to 1993: they were looking more familiar, more Western . . . *less desperate* . . . which was bad for me, I knew.

Ted prodded me out to the dance floor. I felt so stupid. I couldn't believe I'd traveled 7,000 miles . . . *for this.* It was like being at L.A. Rocks in my hometown suburb, or C.B. Hannigan's Bar & Grill, or a zillion other idiotic places.

"The only good thing about living in this fucking city is the girls," he told me, yelling into my ear. I smiled and nodded my head. "Usually you can score if you're American," he continued.

He pointed to a pair of girls, reasonably attractive but cold in the eyes.

"Let's dance with them," he said. I wavered, but he pressed me. "You know, Mark, I'm really glad to have someone like you here, someone my age who I can meet chicks with."

I'd come expecting just to fall into some Dostoyevsky narrative, and here I was, in a bad frat house. . . .

Ted made an obvious, almost goofy move to get in front of one of the two girls to start dancing with her. I felt I had to do it for Ted—I owed him. It was my rent payment. I started coolly dancing up around the other side, trying not to look too interested so as not to scare her away (unsuccessful tactic perfected in the 27 Years' War of Attrition back in California). I wanted to sneak up on her so that, once she found me dancing in front of her, it wouldn't be as though I'd tried to. That's the big crime where I come from: showing that you care. They'll lock you up in your room for 27 years for that! Anyway, the Russian girl looks at me—I flash what is probably an unnerving attempt at a smile that comes off more like a rabid mountain gorilla baring its teeth. . . . Immediately, she turns away, spins around, and starts dancing with her back to me, moving toward the opposite side of the floor.

Ted grabbed me with an embarrassed look on his face and said, "Don't worry, Mark, she's a bitch. Some of these Russian chicks have attitudes now. Forget about it."

I remember thinking: "Wait . . . that wasn't supposed to happen! I just failed!"

Ah, my oh my. I hadn't left California at all. The very concept of escape was flawed from the beginning. Moscow would be overrun just as quickly as Prague was. Fukayama was right. The End of History meant the End of Mark's Sexual History. Time to head to the American Embassy and turn myself in.

On my second night in Moscow, Ted took me to another party. That's where I met Polina.

The party was held at Park Place, a Western-amenities office/apartments biosphere, one of about five or six Western biospheres that dotted what was then Moscow's bleak, preboomtown *Blade Runner* landscape. I remember being shocked by a lot of things that night, not the least of which was the incredibly sub-par collection of chinless bores. The American guys were uniformly geeks—baloney sandwich and Topsiders types—while the American girls were plain, lumpy, loud, fixated on "the local market" talk. . . . One guy bragged to me about how he'd been in a barbershop quartet back at college, and he was trying to put one together here, too.

I had a naive notion before coming to Moscow that the expats here would either be high-powered suits, or brainy Slavophile types. Instead, Moscow got the sub-middle of America, the ones who weren't even trying.

Among all this bland human furniture, one corner of beauty stood out: a group of four Russian girls, one of whom was Polina.

Before I met her, I'd watched an incredible scene, the kind of thing I've seen many times since, but only here in Russia. Some pinched, chinless middle-aged American manager was chasing his tall 18-year-old *dyevushka* around—she clearly didn't care for him much. She was wearing a brand-new pair of white and baby blue Reebok sneakers, courtesy of Sugar Daddy. In 1993, Reeboks really meant something. Sugar Daddy flipped out when some younger, healthier American started dancing with his girl. Sugar Daddy had lost all sense of proportion: he slugged the luckless competitor, then tried grabbing his *dyev* for some hugging and kissing. She rolled her eyes and walked off with her friends, laughing. He had O. J. Simpson written all over his face: it was clear he was going to lose her. . . .

But what interested me was that he had had the chance to spend even one precious week, or night, with this goddess, this Titian painting. . . . She was at her prime: 18, long golden hair, bright green eyes, slender legs like a doe's. I smelled her as she walked past: vanilla and light body odor. No aging American man can allow that to slip through his fingers. I'd be surprised if today, her head isn't sealed in a glass jar, hidden in Sugar Daddy's closet, while the rest of her body has been taxidermized and stuffed under Sugar Daddy's bed. . . .

Then I met Polina. She had a wonderfully bright smile. And gray eyes. And ruddy cheeks. She talked literature with me. We went out for dinner. I was so shocked that a woman could make my heart race like that again . . . I was sure I was in love. She called me late at night after our first date and kept me on the phone for two hours, telling me that she didn't want to be alone. I didn't get the hint—even though it wasn't really a hint—it was more like an air-raid siren screaming at me to come over to her house and fuck. But . . . look, I was stupid. I was just coming out of a coma. Twenty-seven years of coma.

Polina and I dated a few more times. I wanted to take things slowly. I wanted to live out the literary romance. But I was awkward and hesitant, behavior which is supposed to win you the lead girl in the movies, but which, particularly here in Russia, is as charming to a woman as farting. After a week, Polina had had enough of me. She'd roll her eyes at everything I said. She was always distracted. I took her once to see a play, an English version of the *Brothers Karamazov* at the Chekhov theater; she walked out before intermission, leaving me alone. We went out for a dinner; she saw an old boyfriend, and left me to join him. She wouldn't even kiss me good-bye. Then she arranged to meet me on a date and never showed. I remember her snickering as she arranged our meeting place.

This is when I learned the word *dinamit.* It means to "dump"—or, as the surfers in my hometown would say, to "shine." Only *dinamit* is crueler; you shine the person by explicitly arranging to meet them at a certain place, never intending to show up, and you repeat the performance until the moron figures out that you don't want to see him.

"It was a good experience"—that's how my spin doctors described it. They kept my devastated interior hidden from the public for months, for fear of panicking the markets.

I was shortly rescued by Suzanne. She came to Moscow as a student. And was probably getting dissed by the other students in favor of the *dyevs.* But for me, Suzanne was the Savior: dolphin-tight body, smooth and well-proportioned. Two months after we started dating in Moscow, she returned to Belgium to finish her degree. That put me in a difficult position: remain true to a Westerner, thereby going against one of the very tenets of my Russia-paradigm exile, or abandon her and thus, my last connection to the West.

In the spring of 1994, when I was in Sochi trying to arrange a corrupt trade deal with my Mauritian Indian partner and a director for a local chain of retail stores, I almost had my first affair. I was in the hotel lobby of the Sochi Radisson-Lazurnaya Hotel, discussing with Ravi and Nikolai Ivanovich how we were going to bilk Ivanovich's state firm out of thousands of dollars and stuff them into our pockets. Nikolai Ivanovich, a young, blond-haired hustler who always wore white button-down shirts and white slacks, charmed our cocktail waitress into falling for me. He told her that I couldn't stop talking about her. He said that I wanted to take her to America with me. Nikolai Ivanovich had a big laugh over the whole thing. He wanted to soften up his American partner-in-crime. And like sheep to the slaughter, the *dyevushka* was charmed.

Later, the cocktail waitress met me in a park across the street, after the lobby bar closed. It was after midnight. A light breeze blew up from the Black Sea. It was warm and humid. We sat on a bench, beneath a willow tree. I made a move—she began heaving and breathing heavily. She was ready to let me fuck her right on the bench . . . but something grossed me out. Maybe it was that bolt-sized mole on her neck, or the burnt odor from her cheap platinum hair dye. I literally dry-heaved while we were kissing. I couldn't take it, and eventually left.

Nine months after I moved to Russia and just a few weeks before I was supposed to visit Suzanne in Brussels, I made my move. Her name was Stasya. She was ordinary-looking and undemanding, slightly dumpy, with a bulbous nose and a big smile—and nineteen. Gray eyes, ruddy cheeks. Stasya had that spark of life in her. She liked to drink a fruity liqueur called Misty and hang out in parks and make fun of people. And have sex. She was planning to move away from Russia to meet up with her American boyfriend. We had a month before she was set to leave Moscow to meet him—some spoiled skate rat whose rich father ran a U.S. government–funded project in Kharkov. Before moving, Stasya wanted to have fun with me. She was a good teacher. She put me into the metaphor with Russian women. I learned a few "secrets of success with Russian girls": like how to be cruel and yet impulsively romantic; and how to demand what you want from them when you want it, sex or otherwise. How to rape them, basically.

Suzanne vanished from my screen. That was that.

After that, I briefly dated a Cossack girl who loathed sex but submitted anyway. She'd lay on her back and grimace while I slithered away on top of her.

Then I hooked into James's crowd, where I met Lydia, five-foot-ten, long black hair and Cleopatra bangs—a real baroness of darkness.

I danced with her at a new disco, back when there were still few discos. We kissed on the dance floor. Later, I saw another one of James's earl-level friends, a kraut named Hakim, corner Lydia and try kissing her. She stood passively still, and didn't push him away. Then she returned to me. I pretended not to notice.

She asked me to accompany her and her friend, Tanya, home in a taxi. I agreed. We dropped Tanya off, and then, heart beating, I suggested we stop off at my place.

"Why didn't you just say that earlier?" she laughed.

We came back to my apartment, and she immediately started to undress in my bedroom. I was surprised, but I kept quiet, taking off my clothes. Naturally, my sock got stuck on my foot, and I nearly tripped over.

"One minute," she said, kissing me. She went into the shower, and came back five minutes later, towel around her body.

She lay down in bed next to me. I hesitated. Then I made a move. She heaved, breathed heavily, then pushed me off of her.

"No, I can't, Mark. I've never done this before."

But I was partially trained up by this time. I attacked her, forcing open her legs. Her resistance couldn't even be described as token. She was clearly grateful that I was coming off as the aggressor. . . . After that, we slept together a few times—I'd never been with someone who was as dramatic in bed as her, moaning and crying.

Lydia and I didn't last long.

On a boys' night out with James's crowd, the subject of girls came up. Specifically, the subject of Lydia.

James smiled mischievously, put his arm around me, and asked, "Who among us has already slept with Mark's Lydia?"

Three French guys raised their hands. Laughter.

"Okay, now: who has fucked Lydia without a condom?" James asked. Again, three Gallic hands sky-high, and more swinish laughter.

"Okay, now for the big question: who has fucked her in the ass?"

Again, three hands WAY up high, transforming into clumsy EU high fives.

That was it. I never spoke to Lydia again.

That experience depressed me. Especially when I factored in everything my Russian friends had told me about their *dyevushki.* "Never, ever trust them, Mark. They'll fuck whomever they want. Russian girls are never loyal to a man. They're only loyal to their caprices. They take what they want."

It made me miss Suzanne. Terribly. So I groveled back to her over the telephone. We had long telephone conversations. I apologized for my sins. I was a bastard. We agreed to meet in Brussels, at her parents' apartment, then from there, move to Moscow together. When we spoke, I recognized some change in her voice. She'd become more ironic. She wanted to talk about sex. About vibrators. Bisexual anecdotes. It should have clued me in—that the dolphin had swum away. But I edited that out.

We met up in Brussels. She didn't want to come meet me at the airport. I took a train to her metro stop, and hauled my suitcase up to her apartment. She coldly greeted me. We lay down in her bed. The first thing I noticed was that she'd lost her dolphin-skin compactness. Flesh moved. And her cunt—it wasn't glovelike. I finished early, and she slapped my shoulders. "No! Don't! Don't cum!"

Afterward, in the light, I saw that she had developed wrinkles around her mouth. The wrinkles of someone who had been getting fucked.

We fought bitterly. She wouldn't confess more than a few details. A German doctor was all she'd admit. A German! Jesus Christ! They were probably doing things like pissing in each other's mouths, icky bourgeois Euro-decadence! Ugh! Anyway, I caved. She moved in with me, but our relationship was bitter and unsatisfying. From then until just before the *eXile* was launched, we were essentially living out the doomed expat relationship—I had the occasional affair, and was constantly frustrated by the affairs I didn't have.

Then came 1997, the year we started up the *eXile.* Suzanne and I broke up. And I broke out. That person who was holed up in the upstairs bedroom at his father's suburban house, tugging on a decreasingly responding organ, reading books about serial murderers in order to find clues about himself . . . that person was a bad memory, packed away somewhere in the cellophane and cobwebs of my fatty brain cells.

Now, I'm embarrassed to admit sexual success—out of respect for that long famine I endured. I had grown used to my failure. I was proud of occupying the basement. Between 1965 and 1993, no one had it worse than me. It made me a one-man comic routine, although the hours were tough. When you're used to failing for so long, you wind up taking pride in it, and despising everyone who has it good. You develop an entire moral system based on the alleged benefits of failure. Failure has its aesthetic virtues, for one. But now that's changed, and while my body is grateful, my mind is a little less so: I'd spent years writing from the point of view of a failure, and now. . . . After four years in Russia, I've had to do a little editing of the memory—editing of that Failure Bible I'd penned in my head.

It wasn't my fault—all that failure. As the evidence shows, it was America's fault. Just as certain plants or animals wither and die when placed in the wrong environment, so I was doomed in America. I'm a cold-weather plant. A cold-weather poppy.

The year that the *eXile* was born, the Hungry Duck had irrevocably mutated from its humble mainstream inception into a vomit-drenched, blood and-semen-stained Gomorrah that is constantly under threat of closure from horrified public officials, rival corrupt police departments, and predatory mafia gangs who'd like to get a piece of the action.

Every night, the place is packed wall-to-wall with out-of-control Russians and thrill-seeking expats. The Russians who come to the Duck are not the most beautiful, wealthy, or educated. They are usually lumpenprole types who come with a purpose: to drink themselves blind, dance on the bar counter, find someone to fuck, and somewhere along the line make time for a fistfight or two. I have never been there without seeing some saloon-style brawl, which goes invariably like this:

Scene One: misunderstanding between two heavily inebriated Russians

CHAPTER SIX

Scene Two: skipping the usual 15-minute American-style "come on, I dare you!" fists and boots immediately fly.

CUT TO: two more fights break out, then two more—no fewer than four more fights always accompany the core fight

Scene Three: one is knocked to the floor, and begins to receive the inevitable boot-kicks to the temple, a specialty of Russian fighting

Scene Four: Hungry Duck security arrives—these guys are trained special forces thugs who handpick two or three combatants and proceed to pummel them mercilessly, usually with body blows so as to avoid leaving scars

Scene Five: unlucky combatants are pacified, dragged downstairs, and given a good thrashing in the gated courtyard in front of the Duck. Blood slicks on the floor and walls are soon washed away by flying beer and vomit.

It's all in a night's fun.

The Duck was a steady advertiser when I was at *Living Here*, and an even more solid client of the *eXile*. The owner, Canadian national Doug Steele, even offered to fund the *eXile* at its inception, but at the time I thought it was wiser to work with an experienced publisher who had the whole infrastructure set up. Nonetheless, most people closely identify the Duck with the *eXile*, which works fine for both of our businesses, even if it isn't true.

One time we managed to offend our readers so much that Doug threatened to pull his advertising. Taibbi had run an over-the-top photo in one of his mock-serious editorials, this one extolling the viability of investing in the *eXile* at a time when the Russian stock market was in a free fall. In the editorial, Taibbi printed a picture of a woman with a champagne bottle sticking out of her ass as an example of the kinds of things we are willing to print in order to ensure that people read the *eXile*, since no other publication would print such pictures. The point of the article was, invest in the *eXile*, because we'd do anything it took to get you a high ROI, return on investment.

It was a great joke that incited the whole expat community to revolt with a kind of torches-and-rakes lynching frenzy that had been brewing for months. Advertisers pulled, including, or so he threatened, Doug from the Duck. The community was momentarily bound together in their indignation toward the *eXile*. You knew that if you upset Doug, you must have really gone too far. Taibbi felt terrible about it: he fell into one of his self-hating funks, promising never to do it again, although five minutes later, he'd bark, "Fuck 'em!"

When Taibbi and I went to visit Doug to kiss-up, he laughed and said it was no big deal. He'd received about twenty phone calls from friends and patrons, asking how he could associate with or advertise in a newspaper that printed such smut.

"The problem is that everyone thinks I have a piece of the *eXile*," Doug told us, laughing.

Shortly after, Doug created a special Hungry Duck version of Ladies' Night that made our champagne bottle seem like bathroom graffiti in comparison. Ladies' Night is another word for rape camp. On Ladies' Night, only girls (generally ages 12 through 25) are allowed in, while all men are kept at bay from 7:00 P.M. to 9:00 P.M. The girls are offered free drinks, as much and as fast as they can down them. Not just offered free drinks, but pumped full of free drinks. . . . Russians aren't known for their moderation when it comes to liquor; your average five-foot-one *dyev* could put any NFL lineman under the table. The point of Ladies' Night is to get the girls as drunk as possible in a two-hour period, then to open the floodgates to the guys and let the rape camp festivities begin. It was a brilliant idea to raise the volume of vomit and semen to levels yet unseen even in the Duck.

Taibbi and I were invited to be guest bartenders at the second Ladies' Night. I'd never bartended before, and I was kind of nervous. A half hour before Ladies' Night began, we met with the night manager, Craig, a 32-year-old Southern Californian whose Joe Biden-like baldness would have severely limited his sexual opportunities at home, but who, here in Moscow, seems to have a new teenager every week in his apartment. The night we met him, he showed us two 18-year-old blond ballerinas from Siberia staying in his apartment. He described them dancing around his kitchen, giggling and prancing "like a pair of does." You can't shut Craig up when it comes to sexual braggadacio.

At 6:50 P.M., we took these bendable, neon-liquid sticks, waved them around to get them all neon-y, then passed them out to the girls, while security cleared the men from the bar and made them wait at the door. All except for the table of drunken interior ministry cops—they could stay and rape whomever they liked.

At first I was nervous, then I realized—I could do whatever the fuck I wanted. Between 7:00 and 9:00, I drank more liquor than any of my customers except one: a short 16-year-old named Alla, my intended victim. She had the Lolita factor going, with these cute fluorescent buttons pinned all over her sweater top and her hippie hairdo. . . . I found it touching, and served her up with three back-to-back triple tequila fizzes, then a straight-up tequila and a rum and coke chaser. We kissed across the bar table, much to the disgust of Taibbi, who was frantically running around the bar making sure that the customers were satisfied. He was on his way to earning an Employee of the Month plaque.

That night, I must have drunkenly slobbered into seven or

ON WOMEN'S COMPARATIVE SEXUALITY

by Doctor Limonov

Doctor Limonov studied first-hand love-making habits of different women, that he could compare their qualities, stretching from the time of 70s until now, geography of his copulations stretching across most of northern hemisphere. What follows is result of rigorous research.

Brazilian. *Fernanda,* 26, was of a Spanish blood. Black hair, darkish skin, with a heavy ass and massive thighs. Too well-educated, studied at university under professor-writer Jorge-Luis Borges. Not very good in bed because unflexible body. Complained of inconvenience of throwing legs too high and of general "cruelty" of treatment in bed. However, love-making with her was an intense experience, as she was a daughter of wealthy merchant and Edward-man was poor and unemployed. She called him with hate "Trotsky." He fucked her with hate and "cruelty." They met in the East Village of New York.

American. Next door girl, *Julie,* 22, eldest daughter of FBI agent, from a Virginian family of six children. Tall, pretty, heavy ass, slim long legs, but little bit cross-eyed. Of simple, almost peasant habits, she was a house-keeper of a rich New York City socialite, she made her own bread, and practiced belly dancing. Superb, unbeatable friend, she felt little of love-making 'cause of too big vagina and some other probably clinical reasons that her partner Edward ignored.[1]

Jewish. *Marilyn,* 21. Tall, slim, perfect tits. Have had some psychological problems, resulted in a strange phobia, in a habit to pinch out hair of eyebrows and those on her head. Sported a wig constantly, even if under a shower. Was a very good fucker, one of the best in Edward's life.[2]

French. Drug-dealer *Ellen,* 37. Aging jail-bird, in and out of prison. Skinny, wrinkled, may be too hot and sleazy inside, but very good as a love-partner. Very attentive to the man's needs, proud to be "clean French woman." She would clean her partner's genitals after love-making with a hot wet towel, saying, "I am not an American, I am French woman." Used Quaaludes/cocaine combination for love-making. Good old girl. God save her at the Ricker's Island Women's Yard. If she is still there.

Mongol *Yelena,* 20, nick-named "Tugrik." Daughter of a pure-blooded Mongol from Ulan-Bator in Republic of Mongolia and Russian mother. Mongol-faced and Russian-bodied. Pretty, tall, elegant girl with a charming drunken habit and accompanying it

nymphomania. Completely shameless, born to fuck, "everybody's darling," opening her legs after few whiskeys.

French. *Jacqueline,* Countess, 40. Tall, skinny, alcoholic, from Parisian world of high fashion. Used to drink heavily and have a habits of an alcoholic truck-driver, rather than those of countess. When drunk, would fall, would enter driver's door of her car, would exit by crawling out from the passenger door. Always kept liter bottle of a cheap beer next to bed in order to drink it at night. Good passionate lover, pissed when having an orgasm.

Scottish. *Fiona,* 31, TV star. She was recognized by the crowd when she walked streets of London, 'cause she played in popular TV soap opera. Heavy build Scottish woman. Unpleasant heavy odor of her vagina was so unbearable that have killed all sexual sentiments. Biggest failure of Edward's sexual life. She also proved to be greedy. For two years (!) she bombarded Edward with demand to pay her back some small money spent by her on Xeroxing his manuscript.

French. *Anne and Carol,* about 25, editors of known porno magazine in Paris. Anne: small, slim, tender, and nymphomaniac. She fucked in every possible way with a great enthusiasm. But Carol, oh Carol, was a real miracle. Tall, heavy long legs, animal ass, big tits, slim shoulders. Face of a village whore, defect of a speech (she lisped), she wore a terrible tasteless clothes as a concierge. Anne was a very good fucker, she wept when fucked (preferred to be fucked into her rear), but Carol, oh, Carol was above Anne and above any woman. Carol's talent of lovemaking was of a supernatural origin. She moved, groaned and excited man in such a way that all men who happened to sleep with her were charmed forever. One moment one felt he fucks the majestic queen, the next moment that obscene fat animal. Carol was a Devil or a dirty big-assed goddess of lust.

German. *Renata,* 35, artist-painter from Munich. Prussian aristocrat. Almost skeleton, very tall, pretty, well-educated, extremely literate. Strange in bed, like a big, skinny cold child, that needs to be warmed up.[3]

Serbian. *Militsa,* 17, student. Very big, of a heavy beauty. Black hair, big Turkish lips and ass, Slavic puffy face. Her cunt leaked with desire, like that of a big young animal. Too big vagina, inconvenient, but nice to feel anyway, feels like a man making love to young horse.

Russian. *Masha,* 17, National-Bolshevik Party member. Tender, big tits, fat, good-natured small child. Rosy cheeks. Feels as one fucks his own fat daughter.

Russian. *Natasha,* 19. From a "New Russian"'s divorced family. Have no tits at all, round ass, face of a girl of 13. Wears a Doc Marten's high boots, and "Naf-Naf" clothes. Her list of lovers have a name of a leading singer of known Russian rock group and at least one bandit. Funny, insolent, she fucks of desire to be adult. One fucks her as a daughter of an enemy.

Peruvian *woman.* No name, age is uncertain. From a crowd of women that God sent to Edward that is worth of mentioning separately. Peruvian woman was an American Indian pure blood, she had a narrow "Aztec's" nose, very narrow strangely long angles, enormous haunches and ass, huge long tits with a brightly red nipples. She was like an extraterrestrial, not a human.

[1]**DESERVE TO MENTION:** that good women very often lousy lovers.

[2]**NOTE:** No doubt, in general Jewish girls should be prized in a matter of fucking.

[3]**ANOTHER COMPARISON OF SEXUAL INTERCOURSE WITH HER:** Auchwitz's victim love.

Edward Limonov is the author of several novels, short stories and collections of poetry, which have been translated into more than 20 languages around the world. His most famous works include "It's Me, Eddie," and "Memoirs of a Russian Punk." He is currently the head of the National-Bolshevik Party, a far-right wing nationalist party in Russia.

eight different teenage mouths. A few of them had vomit trickling from their lips. There were puddles of vomit outside the women's bathroom, and a kind of river of vomit coming out of the stalls. Underaged girls were harshing in the men's bathroom as well. You needed galoshes to get around there.

At 9:00 P.M., the men poured in, ready to pounce on the weakened girls. Fights broke out, heads were kicked. I saw Alla get on the bar counter and make out with some sweaty Russian jerk in a Chess King silk shirt. Then she swapped spit with some 40-year-old cop, before breaking away. She tried to jump from the outer bar counter to the inner bar top, where the beer taps were. The only problem was a deep, four-foot moat, the area where the bartenders walked between pouring beers and serving customers. In mid-flight from outer to inner bar, Alla disappeared. All I saw was her head drop. About five minutes later, a bartender picked her up. She was woozy. Her teeth bled a little, but otherwise she was fine. One of the bartenders stood her on the countertop. She wobbled a bit, then right away started kissing someone else and grabbing his crotch.

I stuck with her because she was the drunkest and the youngest that I could see. We went back to my place before midnight and had a bizarre, not entirely satisfying round of sex, which left me with severe bite wounds on my stomach, chin, and tongue.

A few days later, she came to meet me with two of her friends, one who was also 16, and another, Natasha, who looked even younger.

Russian law states that any woman 16 or over is eligible; if a girl is between the ages of 14 and 16, and she looks 16, then she is still legal, so long as she didn't prove to you that she's under 16.

I needed somewhere to take these girls besides my shitty little apartment. So I called my old friend Andy Weir, the investment banker with the $3,500 apartment, $13,000 Jacuzzi, and full Kremlin view.

"Andy, what're you doing?" I asked.

"Well, I'm off to this fucking boring expat banker party. Why?"

"Night of the Living Expats again, huh?"

"I'll take any other option, Ames, if you've got one."

"Well, if you're interested, there're these three 16-year-old girls here at my place and I need someone to help me entertain them. You're the only guy I'd like to share this evening with."

He laughed, and told me to come over right away.

We took a cab to Andy's and loaded up with a few more bottles of liquor, several bottles of beer and juice, and a few packs of cigarettes. The two sixteen-year-olds, Alla and Dasha, sang songs as they got drunker. One was a ballad about soldiers in Afghanistan. They were hard to understand: they spoke in pure *mat',* Russian language's version of cuss, which is several times richer and filthier than English cuss. We could barely understand them. The word *pizda,* or cunt, can be mutated into so many different forms of speech and meanings just by adding prefixes, suffixes, changing a vowel here or there, extending it, attaching it to another word. . . . We couldn't keep up. Natasha, with her New Jersey sheepdog bangs, pug nose, and large black eyes, kept quiet most of the time, clearly the "younger sister" of the three. Dasha and Alla were really nuts—loud and careless.

At some point, Alla and Dasha stripped down and hopped into Andy's Jacuzzi. They drank, smoked, and sang. Then they started to have sex together. I snuck my hand through the curtain and snapped some photos, just to send to my friends back in America, the ones who are barred from dating any women who are happy, carefree, and young. I like making my friends suffer—it's a form of bragging, like spiking the ball in the end zone right into your defender's shoes. I can't help it—I can't enjoy my own little victories unless people I love suffer proportionately.

When I went back into the TV room, Andy pulled me aside with a worried grin on his face.

"Dude, do you realize . . . do you know how old that Natasha is?" he said.

"Sixteen?"

"No! No, she's fif-teen. Fif-teen!" Right then, my pervometer needle hit the red. I had to have her, even if she was homely. I sat down next to her on the couch and fed her another double martini with pineapple juice, and asked her to take off her clothes now, to prepare for the Jacuzzi.

"Why?" she asked, keeping her eyes to the floor, but smiling.

"So you'll be ready," I said. I was assuming the role of Rod Steiger from *Doctor Zhivago*, the classic rake. I'd really traded up literary models over the past couple of years, from Myshkin to Svidrigailov.

"Why do you want me to be ready?" she asked, sipping her drink shyly and still avoiding my eyes.

"Actually, hell: I just want to see your body," I admitted, throwing my hands up. "I'm really attracted to you, Natasha."

"What about Alla?" she asked. I could already see her weakening, knowing Russian girls and their willingness to betray friends, lovers, and anyone else. "You're with her, aren't you?"

"What *about* her?" I said. "I want *you.*"

It took very little work. Alla caught us kissing in the bedroom a little later. She protested some. She even set off a fainting fit in front of us. I'm not sure whether she was faking it, but her face and neck turned red, and she collapsed on the floor, barely breathing. Dasha ran up, made me hold Alla up by the shoulders, then she punched her as hard as she could in the heart, four or five times. Alla awoke, coughing.

We finally threw Alla out on the street, penniless. She headed over to Bell's, a rival disco to the Duck. Who knows what happened there—she probably went home with the drunkest, most diseased jerk.

I took Natasha back home with me. My elevator stinks worse than a dog kennel. I live on the top floor, where, inevitably, some bum is sleeping by the trash chute, shit in his pants. A romantic walk to my apartment. . . .

When we got to my apartment, Natasha quietly took her clothes off, then asked to take a shower. I waited in my bedroom. She came back ten minutes later, wrapped in a towel, and sat on the bed, sipping a beer. I pulled her towel off. She giggled nervously, still not looking at me. I pulled her down, and put her drink on my bed table.

After sex, she confessed to me that she had a three-month-old baby, and the father had abandoned her.

"*Svoloch,*" she said. "Bastard."

I asked her why she didn't have an abortion. We got into an argument roughly similar to the one I had almost a year earlier with Katya, one of my first *eXile*-era girlfriends. About three months after we started dating, Katya sat on my lap and told me she had some exciting news: she was pregnant, and I was the father!

I panicked. Children are my worst nightmare—worse than worst. I'd rather wind up in a Hutu death camp than father a child. My aversion to children is religious: I hate the way they look, the gurgling sounds they make, and the time and money that they require, time and money that I don't have. I told Katya that I wasn't ready to be a father—she told me that that was fine, she could give the baby to her parents, who live in Chukhotka, in the Far East of Siberia, some gold-mining GULAG town. Her parents would be more than happy to have a living creature to keep them company. Katya

CHAPTER SIX

and I could take the child back when we were ready, she explained.

"No, Katya, you don't understand. I *cannot* have a child. I *do not like* children. I *hate* them. They *disgust* me, physically."

"But I can't have an abortion," she pleaded. "I was told that if I did, I'd never be able to have a child."

I knew she was bluffing, so I countered with the RU-486 pill. I offered to fly to France, pick one up, and bring it back for her. "It's totally safe," I cheerily offered.

"I can't do that," she said. "I can't kill our child."

Right then, I stared at Katya with a look—I'm not sure how it appeared to her, but in my mind, I was starting to contemplate two courses of action: murder, or AWOL.

"What will you do, kill me?" she said, laughing nervously.

"Maybe, yeah," I replied. "I'll throw you off my balcony. I'll make it look like an accident."

She started to cry, but I was relentless. I told her that if she had the child, she would be killing me, so it was an act of self-defense. And if I didn't kill her, then I would flee Moscow and she'd never find me. Her child would be fatherless. He wouldn't have an Oedipal complex like the other kids; his complexes would be monumental, guaranteed to make her life a living hell. He would terrorize her and despise her until the day she died. I was relentless. I attacked her the Russian way: I wore her down for hours during the night, KGB interrogation-style.

Wearing down your opponent is a formula for success in Russia. Take Peter the Great against Charles XII, or Kutuzov against Napoleon or Zhukov against the Wermacht. They simply wore down their opponents.

At 5:30 the next morning, Katya, acting the martyr, quietly slipped out of my apartment, made a beeline to the abortion clinic, and sucked the little fucker out.

She called me periodically after that. I couldn't get her off my case. So, I wrote a column, mentioning her name and what she did to me, naming her the worst woman of the year. I didn't mince words—I was wired on weeks of accumulated phenamine when I wrote that column about how I coerced her to have an abortion, under threat of death. All that speed makes you throw caution to the wind—you can move mountains when you're railing.

Katya called me crying a couple of days later, asking me how I could be so cruel.

"What did I do? I don't understand," I said, playing dumb.

"Don't you know that my friends read your columns!" She hung up in an outburst of tears, and briefly, for a good ten minutes, I had one of those soul-searching moments, asking myself, *Who am I? What's become of me? Have I taken things*

e d i t o r i a l

A Crash-Proof Moscow Stock

We here at the eXile have a suggestion for all of you who got killed in last week's stock market fiasco: invest in us.

One of the major reasons the Asian markets collapsed was that the securities being traded on those markets were hugely overvalued. You won't have that problem with the eXile. Our value is nothing. Zero. Everybody knows that. Throw your money at us—even a dollar of it—and it has nowhere to go but up.

George Soros will never be able to precipitate a world sell-off of stocks by unloading his interests in the eXile. The reason? George Soros would never invest in the eXile. We think he sucks, and we tell him so. About the only thing Soros would ever give us is a quiet working over by his security guards, or a buzzing by one of his private jets.

Objectively speaking, the eXile is a great investment. We have no debts. Our revenues are steady and can easily be increased rapidly, simply by ordering an end to the honest restaurant and club reviews which have so pointlessly cost this paper so much in advertising sales. And, perhaps most importantly, we have an endless reserve of bad ideas, meaning we will never deplete our supply of natural resources.

The eXile has no competitors. We are the only publication in Russia willing to publish pictures like the one below in order to attract readers. And we are not merely sensationalist: our staff brings expertise to the table. The average eXile employee can tell from one glance what brand of champagne is featured in that photo.

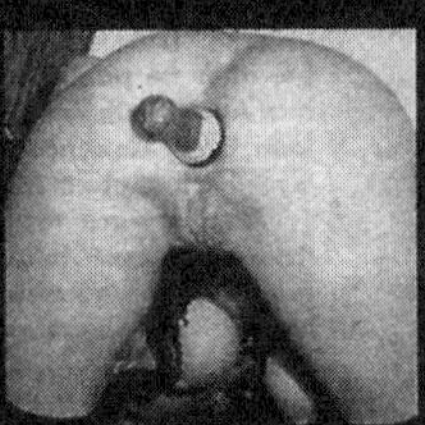

That's training. That's experience. You won't get that with your average expatriate publication, whose writers are all wet, so to speak, behind the ears. No, the eXile's is an office peopled with seasoned veterans, in whose practiced hands your investment is as safe as your bubbly.

The eXile is a company with a global outlook. It has looked all around the globe and observed that it has no potential for growth anywhere outside of Moscow. It is therefore totally insulated from international developments. And since virtually no one in Moscow takes it seriously, it is also almost completely insulated from local developments as well. In short, it is an investment vehicle that exists as though in a vacuum, neither gaining nor losing value with the passage of time, the progression of historical events, or the migration to and fro of potential readers.

The only danger for potential investors, as far as we can see, is that other investors might also begin to recognize our newspaper's value. If that happens, still more investors might hear that others have invested in our newspaper. At that point, we might become a hot commodity, and still more investors will seek to buy our shares. Then, before we know it, we'll be part of mutual funds offered to insurance salesmen in Idaho and housewives in Bourgogne. And then, suddenly—and we're not saying this would happen—one of those investors might get cold feet and back out, and we'd have a whole mess on our hands as everyone scrambled to sell. I mean, we'd just feel awful if that insurance salesman in Idaho lost his nest-egg because of us.

Still, we don't think that will happen. Because we know that in real life, the market doesn't operate that way. Traders and brokers aren't so shallow and unethical as to try to profit on the speculative rise of overvalued securities. No, what they look at are cold, hard facts—company infrastructure, real estate, revenues, and honest revenue potential. We know that even if our stock was rising, no one would invest in us if they weren't sure we were really worth it.

And we are. We promise. So send in your check today. Now, if we could only find an opener...

too far? . . . Then I popped in a *South Park* video that Krazy Kevin gave me, and forgot about it.

Funny, but that column nearly got me lynched a few weeks later by Kathy Lally of the *Baltimore Sun.* That's a long story. . . . And speaking of abortions, Natasha told me that night that the reason she didn't Hoover her baby was because the doctor had told her that if she had an abortion, she'd never have children. A familiar tale here.

It was hard to imagine that Natasha had squatted out a baby. Her cunt was as tight as a cat's ass. She was impenetrable, like prying open a mollusk. Nothing like a mother. I knew: I'd slept with mothers before—they're a lot wider. Sex with them is like probing a straw in a mildew-lined German beer mug.

A few nights later, Natasha tried coming over to my house at two in the morning. She rang the doorbell for a half hour straight. I got up, pulled the doorbell ringer out of the wall, tore the metal magnet plates out of their rubber tabs, ripped out some spring contraption, dropped it all on the floor, then went back to sleep. She called and called, but I didn't answer.

On the next Ladies' Night, I heard a story about a 15-year-old girl who'd drunk too much and had a miscarriage in the Duck's bathroom. She came running out with blood smeared all over her legs and blood on the bathroom walls, mixed with the usual vomit—other people's vomit. Doug and Craig arranged to have her taken to the hospital, where they learned she'd had a nasty cut on her leg from broken glass and from falling off the bar counter. There was no miscarriage. She was still safely pregnant.

Later, they brought her back to the Duck so that her two 16-year-old friends could take her home to her parents. They all drove back to her parents', but her mother ran out and ordered them to leave in a hurry. The 15-year-old girl's father, a *militsia* sergeant, said that he would kill his daughter for drinking and partying recklessly while still pregnant. If she showed her face, he would kill her. So the girls went back to the Duck and stayed at Doug's apartment for the night.

I saw Doug the next morning after that incident. He had rings around his eyes, and was shaking his head.

"The police are a little upset with the Duck," he told me. "But hell, it's not the first time."

The week before, a competing interior ministry police division had raided the Duck with machine guns and truncheons. A few weeks earlier, a corrupt cop had his eyeball literally knocked out of its socket in a fight with another cop from a different department. All these things get smoothed over, even when an underaged girl has a miscarriage in your toilet.

As I heard Doug recount the story, I couldn't help but think that the 15-year-old in question was Natasha.

That night, I started getting phone calls from Natasha and her friends, asking if she could move in with me.

"Why did you tell me that you had a child?" I asked her. "I'd heard from someone else that you're four months pregnant, and not that you have a three-month-old baby."

"So you figured that out," she flatly replied.

"You're pregnant, Natasha. Why didn't you tell me?"

"Why does it matter!" she snapped. "Would you not want to see me if I'm pregnant?" She wasn't even angry—she was flabbergasted that I wouldn't want to fuck her just because she was four months pregnant.

"*Svoloch', blyad!*" she said. "Fucking bastard."

I got another call three nights later from Natasha at six A.M., telling me she was at a pay phone in front of my building and she had nowhere to go.

"Leave me the fuck alone," I told her, hanging up. I figured she had to be with a friend, and she was playing the homeless girl to sucker me into letting her into my apartment. I knew what to expect once she got in the door. She'd never leave. She and the little monster growing inside would plant a flag in front of my TV. She'd clean my dishes and cook me fried meat and potatoes. She'd shower and lie down and let me fuck her. But she'd never leave.

Johnny Chen may have proved to all of Moscow that literally ANY expat could, if he so desired, live out his debauched daydreams. But before Chen popularized the notion, any number of even less attractive American men were on to the game. Among them was the late Paul Tatum, and his coterie of whore-hopping middle-aged perverts. I met some of them the week after Tatum was murdered. I was sitting in the Starlite Diner at Mayakovsky Square when a bearded Grizzly Adams type yelled out my name.

"Hey, you're Mark Ames, right? Mark Ames!" He stretched his arms, winked, and nodded his head, motioning for me to come to his booth.

I was cornered—there was no way out.

Grizzly asked me to sit down with him and another man, some sort of middle-aged Indian nerd with buckteeth whose name I think was Vik, short for Vikram. They started off by complimenting me, laughing about a very cruel joke I once played on a *Moscow Times* columnist Helen Womack. I panicked until I realized that they sincerely enjoyed it.

CHAPTER SIX

HERE'S TO THE HEROINES

My ideal woman has no womb. No tubes, no ovaries, no womb. The rest is negotiable.

Mayakovsky

By Mark Ames

Just under a year ago, we published a piece about the woes of eXpat women in Russia. Almost the entire female American community came clamoring to our offices like an angry peasant mob, with torches, rakes, and pitchforks . . .

We escaped, but a year later, as the guest editorial (I swear it's real) and comix prove, nothing has changed and no one has learned anything. Expat women are still growing anger lines around their mouths, stuck in a situation they'd never dreamed of: like consumer goods that cannot compete with the locally manufactured products, they wind up collecting dust on the shelves, marked down five times over, and finally dumped in overstock or returned to the manufacturer to be melted down and sold for scrap . . .

But instead of rehashing the sordid truth, I'd like to dedicate a Women's Day column to some of the women I've come to know over the last year.

Katya. For some reason, she still calls me. She tried pulling the oldest stunts in the book last spring. When a woman claims she can't have an abortion because her alleged doctor allegedly told her that if she does, she'll never have children again, call her bluff. Tell her you'll fly to France, pick up an RU-486 pill, fly back, and pop it in her mouth over a nice dinner at Horse and Hound. You'll accompany her to the toilet when Junior squirts out like a bowl of borscht; you'll even flick Junior's sardine eyes off her thighs, because U care.

That's when she changes her tact—she tells you she can't kill a living baby. "Kill what?!" you demand. "It's not a baby—*it's a fucking larva!*"

"But at two months, it already has hands and feet," she protests.

"And a tail!" you reply. "And sardine eyes!"

But she won't give, so you're left with no choice: you threaten to kill her.

That's what I did. And it worked. At 5:30 the next morning, Katya quietly got out of bed and left my apartment, acting like a martyr.

On a brighter note, Natasha, the 15-year-old pregnant girl who thought she'd had a miscarriage at the Duck a few weeks back, finally did the Right Thing. I guarantee that her fatherless child would have grown up to be one of those elevator rapists—he had the "really stupid criminal" icon written all over his translucent forehead; now, thanks to Natasha's sage decision, his fetal membranes are getting boiled down in some sewage treatment plant on the outskirts of town, and believe me, folks, it's better for all of us. I'd suggest sterilizing Natasha now, for the good of society, like what the Swedes used to do to their degenerates. As far as I'm concerned, this Women's Day, Natasha deserves one of those cheap trophy cups with the inscription: "World's Greatest Mom!" Signed, Junior.

Which leads me to two truly heroic women who are linked not just by their prison experiences, but by their determination to live life in that massive, depopulated continent beyond the pale of society.

Lena is insane, which is why, as much as I like her, I've been trying to shine her. She still has everything she owns in my apartment: two cheap duffel bags packed full of whore's clothes. Evidence of a big, drunken, horny mistake on my part. She had just been deported from a Western European country after serving three and a half years in jail. You had to figure . . . a young attractive Russian girl who hasn't seen the light of freedom in three and a half years, and you're the first guy she's going to spend the night with . . . as the black guy says to Clint Eastwood in *Dirty Harry*, "I gots to know..." Christ, I gots to know too fucking much for my tastes.

You don't meet too many women like Lena. It's as if each day is her last. Most people don't experience in a lifetime the kind of savage adventures she falls into on a daily basis. Since I've known her, she's been raped, robbed, beaten, detained for heroin possession, nearly murdered . . . In the scariest incident, a pair of flathead pimps who mistook her for a deadbeat whore (Lena briefly moved into a *kommunalka* with two teenage whores when I told her to split) beat her in the kidneys to extract what they thought was their rightful protection cut; they dunked her head into a bathtub full of water until she nearly fainted. They eventually let her go, having squeezed her for every last ruble she had, but the other two girls weren't so lucky; they were driven out to a forest, stripped naked, and left to walk back to the nearest road, two hours away. There are other, worse things that happened to Lena that she said she couldn't even tell me about.

Lena had some great prison stories to tell me. Like how she raped a Bulgarian girl, age 19, in the showers; and how said Bulgarka became a sort of willing slave after a few weeks. "It's strange," she observed. "All the girls I raped became that way."

The other heroine I want to honor is still sitting in jail. I'm speaking of Alina Vitukhnovskaya, the poet jailed for allegedly selling seven-bucks-worth of LSD to a pair of junkies. The junkies have already retracted their forced confessions, and all the evidence collapsed; the judge ordered her moved to Serbsky Psychiatric Ward, an infamous sanitarium where dissidents were interred during the Soviet days.

Last week, they shipped her back to Women's Prison #6, where she sits awaiting more trials and hearings. Her bogus case goes back to 1994, and no one knows if or when it will end.

Alina and I have been in correspondence recently. Her letters are really impressive: you can tell that the physical confinement has driven her already hyper-detailed inner world to develop entire cities, underground railroads, population transfers within that hyper-aestheticized mind of hers . . . There is a serenity in her written voice, reflecting a strength you don't expect from a petite poet/prisoner. I nearly grew envious of her intense focus, made manic by her confinement. When you think about all the brain cells wasted out here in civilian life, worrying about money and food and meetings and work, you get envious . . . until you remember that she's in a Russian prison. These aren't nice prisons. These are Midnight Express prisons. And yet, Alina seems to be growing stronger. "I don't want to be and will not be a victim," she wrote me.

Alina and Lena are two women who deserve to be celebrated on Women's Day because, in their own ways, they are both heroines—in the guerrilla war against blandness and ordinariness.

One thing Alina asked me was to publish her address in our newspaper so that you, readers, might send her letters to relieve her boredom. This Women's Day, why don't you write her a letter, to someone far more deserving of Women's Day accolades than any of us civvies. Her only request is that you write the letters in Russian. And please, don't bore her with maudlin do-goodie letters of how bad you feel for her. Tell her horrible stories about yourself or your neighbors or your ex-lovers. Send her naked pictures of yourself soaping down a llama. Whatever you do, just don't bore her. She deserves better.

109383
Moscow
Ulitsa Shosseinaya, dom 92
CIZO 48/6, kamere 313
Aline Vitukhnovskoi

Hungry Duck

★★★ ★★ ★★★

Cheers: eXile alert! Female Friday's boasts of almost a thousand drunken, crazed chicks and far too few dudes, while the success of the Ladies' Nite formula has led the Duck to add a new Sodom Sundays. You thought that the den of sin had seen and done it all . . . but now they're offering to get all chicks blindly drunk on FREE liquor from 7-9pm Tuesdays, Fri's and Sun's, while keeping the men at bay. Then at 9pm, the doors open, and the men pour in, and the rape camp festivities begin. Thank god for antibiotics! Mondays still feature countdown drinks. Perhaps the most notorious bar in the Northern Hemisphere. Always jam-packed. Look for Moscow's only eXpat eX-con, Stanley Williams, fresh out of jail and on the wheels of steel. You are guaranteed to see at least one teenie fall teeth-first into the corner of the bar-counter.

Jeers: Bar girls sing karaoke over dance tunes. If you're not really drunk when you fall off the bar, it hurts. High Yosemite Sam barroom fight factor. On Titular Tuesdays, chix start to bail by eleven, so Lolita-hunters better act quick.

Cover: 35 rubles (50R on Ladies' Night)
M: Kuznetsky Most
Phone: 923-6158
Address: Pushechnaya Ul. 9 (next to the Kuznetsky Most Metro)
Hours: 12.00 - 6.00

"There's something serious I want to talk to you about," Grizzly said, putting his arm around me. "It's about Paul. He was a very close friend of mine, so I'm wondering what you're planning on writing about his murder. See, cuz the *Moscow Times* and all these people are lying. You know and I know who killed Paul. But the goddamn cowards won't talk about it. Paul was a very, very close friend of mine. He was a hero. A hero. And no one wants to take notice."

I quietly nodded my head. At the time, I was planning on running a lead story mocking Tatum's murder. An assassin with a Kalashnikov had busted eleven caps in Tatum's back, just outside the Radisson-Slavyanskaya Hotel, where his disputed 40 percent stake became the eleven stakes in his ass. . . . I was considering various tasteless front-page banners: "Paul Takes a Fall!," "Bull's Eye!," "Tatum Checks Out For Good!"

"Everybody knows who killed him," Grizzly said. He lit a cigarette and curled his mouth, disgusted. "And they're keeping quiet, and pretending they don't know. We've got to do something, Mark. I want to take action. I want to get the American community involved. We're going to write a letter to the American Chamber of Commerce about those bastards at the Radisson," Grizzly went on. "We're going to arrange a boycott of the Radisson until they admit it."

"Uh-huh."

"Maybe you can help us write it, Mark? You're a good writer and all."

"I don't know, I'll have to see." I remember sitting there, stuck between these two clowns, wondering, are they serious? Do they think they're going to bring an international hotel chain to its knees merely because their whoring buddy got blasted?

"Paul was really a hero, you know. And he was a guy who loved life. He was a crusader. Wasn't he?"

The Indian nodded his head solemnly.

"He was just a guy who loved life. He—" Grizzly paused, then smiled knowingly. "You know, one of Paul's favorite things was coming out to a bar I own out in Kirov." He turned to the Indian and winked.

"Oh yeah, Paul loved it," the Indian concurred, breaking a collusive, mischievous smile, then covering his buckteeth with his hands.

"I own a bar out there in Kirov called 'The American Saloon.' Have you heard of it?"

"No."

"Well, it's the best-kept secret in Russia. I'm telling you, Mark—" He jabbed me with his cigarette finger. "*You* would love it. You've never seen anything like it." Grizzly nudged the Indian with his elbow. Then both laughed knowingly. "Yep, you—I know you'd really like it. It's your kind of place."

This column, written in the depths of a blinding crank binge, was the spark that first ignited *Baltimore Sun* correspondent Kathy Lally to call for censoring the *eXile*.

"Really? Wow."

"Am I bullshitting him?" Grizzly asked the Indian.

"No way," the Indian said sternly.

"Every month or so we get a train full of Americans and ride into Kirov to party at my bar. It's wild down there, because all the girls want to be with Americans."

"Yes, they love *us Americans*," the Indian agreed, nodding feverishly.

"Every guy who goes down there gets laid," Grizzly calmly continued. "I mean the ratio of girls to men there is like five to one. And I'm not talking whores here, Mark. These are all fine girls, not the working-types. They just come for a good time, because they like American men. People just go nuts, they really let loose. You should have seen—Vik here—the last time we were in Kirov, Vik was dancing on top of the roulette table, and he and a stripper, Olga—was it Olga or Larissa?"

The Indian bared his teeth and spat: "Both!" He wiped his mouth and laughed.

"Both of the girls were stripping Vik here until he was in his underwear. Isn't that right, Vik?"

"I was in my underwear, it's true! I was dancing in my underwear on top of the roulette table, man. And these girls were doing everything to me! I swear to god, man."

I looked at the Indian, imagining him in his yellow-stained ball-hugger underwear and Gandhi-like chicken legs dancing atop a roulette table while a pack of peroxide whores groped at him. A frightening scenario, but given the utter desperation in the regions of Russia, not entirely impossible.

"The girls there will do *anything* to be with an American, they really love us," Grizzly said.

"It's true, *we Americans* are like *royalty* down there, man," the Indian agreed.

Grizzly and I exchanged phone numbers. I figured, you never know, there might be a story there. I also decided to tone down the Paul-Is-Dead story, because I was sure that if I ran it, I'd have to duke it out with a bearded 50-year-old freak, and I just didn't see what I had to gain from that.

Every few weeks after our first meeting, I'd get a call from Grizzly urging me to join his trainload of sad, middle-aged Americans for a weekend of chasing desperate, provincial Russian divorcées. It sounded like great material for a column, at the very least.

Shortly after Taibbi joined the *eXile*, I had the time and the stomach for it. Then somehow Owen Matthews got wind of the Kirov sex train. The scoop was gone. I was going to back out, but Owen pushed me.

"Come on, Ames," Owen urged me. "You've got to go with me. This is going to be fucking hilarious. Think about it. On the one hand, you've got these loser businessmen. Fat, balding . . . " He laughed, but I don't know why—Owen, at age 25, was already "fat, balding" . . . "And then you have this miserable, depressed town called 'Kirov' full of lonely, desperate teenagers who we can just take into our rooms, mace them and use them, like farm animals in ways that God didn't intend."

The thought of spending a weekend with Grizzly, the Indian, Owen, and even lesser humans made me nervous. I'd have no escape. But I knew that the basic premise was true: girls in the provinces are far more desperate than girls in Moscow and St. Petersburg, who have been spoiled by contact with too many Westerners. Kirov is like Moscow was seven or eight years ago: the Westerner premium is high, grossly overvalued. A girl from Kirov, stuck 1,000 kilometers east of Moscow, in the middle of fucking nowhere, has two choices: either marry some drunken, wife-beating Pasha, whose factory never pays him, and never leave that miserable, snow-and-rust-stained steppe, or hook up with an American and have the chance to live in civilization. The awful knowledge that you will never, ever leave a city like Kirov would drive anyone to take extreme measures . . . even sleeping with Owen Matthews, or a drunken Indian who *claims* to be American. . . .

I arrived in Kirov with my friend Andy a day after everyone else. We drank ourselves silly on the overnight ride, then popped open a bottle of vodka when we awoke in the morning. We headed over to the hotel, a heavy gray block structure set in the middle of decaying lots and half-finished buildings, and made a straight beeline up to Owen's room.

By Doctor Limonov

How to be Mad and Happy at Fifty-Five

Considering subject for my column for present issue I have asked Mark Ames what he wants me to write. Mark suggested to me to write a piece on the subject of health care, something sounding like "How to stay fit at 55," written by Frank Sinatra or Jane Fonda. I laughed. Then I thought, "Why not, as tomorrow is my birthday, I am going to be a fifty-five, and I feel as mad and crazy as ever, as at thirty-five, so why not?"

So I will attempt to create something like "way to a good health," or, "How to stay fit," or, "How to be mad and happy at fifty-five," or "Doctor's Limonov advices to a middle-aged men."

First requirement to fulfill is: the man of fifty-five should go to bed only with young girls. For its religious orgies Tantrism have recommended usage of only very young girls, not older than twenty, as it said in a sacred book "Makhmudra-Tilaka." Jut recently I heard on Radio Liberty that scientists made an astonishing discovery: longevity of a male's life depends on quantity of orgasms he gets during his life. Man who experience many orgasms during his entire life, including old age, live longer and stay younger.

So, in order to stay young, throw away your old wife, never even look at overweight, wrinkled woman. Find yourself a pretty teenage girl and fuck her as often as you can. Don't let a complex of inferiority to overcome you. Contrary to all rules of bourgeois society, in reality young girls like to get an attention of older man, it flatters them. Many girls would be proud to go to bed with you, it will give them enormous sexual thrill that they lack in relationship with partners of their own age. Besides, some girls dream of sexual relationships with their fathers. You will be welcome as a thrilling substitute, believe me, or either I am not Doctor Limonov. Young girls will excite you better. Young girls have a tight, hot pussies, their love juice is a boiling one, on the contrary, love juice of an older woman is glue-like. Young laugh, their freshness, even their nanve stupidity will have a rejuvenating effect on you. Listen to stupid hit songs with them, get them drunk, fuck them and be happy.

Don't be upset by your age, don't let social pressure on you to become so strong that you will be choked by numbers of your age. Psychological victory over your age will open you a way to pleasurable and easy life. However, don't stay with a same girl for a long time. Change them.

Take care of your look. It's easy. Just don't eat too much. Russian middle-aged man usually overweight, American man also, as both countries have a bad eating habits. Don't eat three times a day-eat twice a day. Me, for at least twenty years now I never eat breakfast. In the morning I drink few cups of a very strong coffee, or a very strong tea. I never eat before 2pm, or even before 4pm. Second meal I eat between 8 and 9pm. I never limited myself in food consuming, I eat a lot. But for last few years I eat very little of bread, or no bread at all. I like meat, especially pork meat. From a Serbian wars I brought a habit of eating tons of raw onions. My weight now is 67 kilograms. I consume alcohol with pleasure, but sometimes I don't drink during a week or so. I never drink before 6pm.

As to sport, I have in my apartment my dumb-bells and a weight of 16 kilos. From time to time I do some exercises with weights.

To conclude I must again underline the importance of getting rid of psychological burden of your age, of those silly numbers. Behave yourself as if you don't know your age. As you don't know what behavior is required by society from a man of your age.

Transgress all taboos, be mad. That is the key to a happiness of a man of fifty-five.

CHAPTER SIX

He was miserably hungover, and offered us a bottle of his wine.

"How is the American Saloon?" we asked.

"It sucks. It's a joke," he said. "These guys are such losers you wouldn't believe it. Half of the guys are like these bald freaks, then there's this guy with a soccer haircut, and another with like this Ronald McDonald perm and a mustache. And no one—I mean no one—got laid."

I knew what that meant in Owen-speak: he'd been dissed by every chick in town.

Just then, Grizzly barged into Owen's hotel room, sighed dramatically, then dropped onto a chair. He was shirtless, dressed only in sweat bottoms and tennis shoes. He was thinner and smaller than I'd remembered, which was a relief.

"Boy did we have a helluva night last night," he said. "Whew! My wife Larissa's in there with another girl, Tanya. Man, I am wiped out. You know, these Russian girls, they really like bisexual sex."

Owen snickered; Grizzly lifted his head and squinted at me, with an almost worried expression.

"You wanna see my wife and Tanya? They're just lying in bed together, in each other's arms. You wanna see them?"

"No thanks," I said.

"Come on."

"No really, I don't want to," I said.

"Just for a second. I'm afraid maybe you guys don't believe me. Owen, tell 'em how it was last night."

"Oh don't worry, I've told them," Owen snickered.

"You sure you don't want to look at my wife and Tanya? They're sound asleep, you won't bother them. It's really beautiful, man, just seeing the two of them curled up. Man, they really tired me out."

"No really, that's okay."

Andy and I escaped, then reappeared at the American Saloon at about 9 o'clock at night. It was empty, except for the group of American and English losers. Everyone wore an ironic expression, as if the reason they came was really a joke—as if they were spectators, and not actors in this low-rent comedy with gag tuba soundtrack. One British man in his late 30s, with spectacles and combed-back hair, explained that he came to Kirov to buy some local art; he was an art collector. Another American made fun of himself. Only the guy with the soccer haircut, Chris, and his friend Ronald McDonald, were beneath self-mockery.

"Things should pick up here soon," Grizzly said, looking worried.

But things didn't pick up.

His wife did a pole dance with Tanya. I was dying to leave, but Grizzly sat down right next to me.

"You should have seen those two go at it last night," he whispered into my ear. He pointed to the British art dealer and Ronald McDonald. "Those two—I let them watch."

We finally got out of there and headed to a disco called "*Zapretnaya Zona*," or Forbidden Zone. Unlike the American Saloon, with its cheesy Wild West theme and cheap wood paneling, *Zapretnaya Zona* was a large disco, a huge dance floor with a fifty-foot-high ceiling, lasers, and booming techno music. I met a girl over by the bar who was a stage dancer. Her name was Natasha. Yet another Natasha. Natasha #6. She was eighteen, with long golden hair and a large, aquiline nose, and full breasts. She gave me her address, and told me to come by her place the next day. She didn't have a telephone—most residents of Kirov don't have telephones.

Later, Andy and I found Owen in the upstairs bar talking to a group of girls. When we made to sit down with them, Owen snarled condescendingly. "Do I have to do everything for you losers?"

I got to know one of the girls, Alyona. She was pretty, but conversation with her was tough—it was like sucking water from a brick. I couldn't tell if she was deaf. Andy talked up a blond-haired teenager with a cute, pudgy face, while Owen led his wet, doe-eyed Irena by the hand onto the dance floor.

"This girl is so in love with me," Owen told me. "She says to me, 'Oh Owen, you dance so well.' God, it's like shooting fish in a barrel here. I'm going to mace her and use her like a farm animal in ways that God didn't intend." He laughed, then scooted away.

Sometime a bit later in the evening, Owen got slapped in the face and dumped. He hit up on another girl, a sort of peroxide techno dyke whom I learned had a reputation in Kirov for boning anything with a pulse. She was the town slut.

"I don't know what's wrong with that bitch Irena," Owen told me, sucking on a cigarette. "But this other girl's fantastically sexy. She and I are going to rendezvous tomorrow at two o'clock next to Kirov's statue. It's all so devilishly romantic."

The town slut never showed. She "dynamited" him, as they say. Things aren't always easy for expats.

hen we started the *eXile*, I met a warm, honest, and slightly attractive, if dumpy, American girl of Slavic descent, Tamara. We became good friends. I tolerated her more predictable fresh-out-of-college small talk about gender politics. Tamara wasn't cold and ambitious; instead, she was desperate for solid companionship. She would attach herself to any suitor—a frat type, a degenerate like me, rich, poor . . . it didn't matter who. But then she foisted herself on me sexually. Normally, I have a pretty strong willpower when it comes to resisting sensual pleasures. I can keep a baggie of heroin or speed in my little Lao jar for months, if only to test my will, before using it up. Anyway I caved with Tamara. There's just something about a girl sitting at your feet and begging you—*begging* you—to fuck her.

It was a disaster. I forgot what Americans are like! I hadn't slept with one since 1991—six whole years. The petting part went fine, but when the panties come off, all those years of brainwashing and conditioning suddenly reveal themselves. First you get an earful of dry, half-ironic quips . . . a sort of pre-penetration negotiation . . . then the condom question is popped, followed by a reprimand . . . you try to get into position, but she's . . . she's . . . she's *talking* to you, *commenting* on things. Another ironic quip. Don't do this, but make sure you do that. Yes, that. Don't come before me. Do touch me like that. My last boyfriend did this. I've slept with Y number of guys. My childhood, let me tell you all about it. . . . I was horrified: this isn't sex—*this is therapy! . . . a job interview! . . . yard work!* . . . After a few minutes, I lost my erection, and never slept with Tamara again. I can never go back, that much is clear. Russia has taught me that American women are incapable of enjoying ANYTHING on this planet.

Moscow of the '90s will vanish, like so many enviable eras. There have been other islands of corrupt paradise driven to extinction, even in my lifetime. I'm thinking of Laos in the early 1970s, before the communist takeover, when opium dens were on every street corner in Vientiane. I envy those reporters who lived there. A quiet Lao woman, packing your opium pipe and lying supine beside you, massaging you, not asking for anything in return. All that's gone now. You have to go looking in the villages. And even there, it's vanishing. No girls to pack your pipe. Self-service. The DEA is successfully transforming Laos from a country of peaceful opium-smokers lolling in the clouds into Marlboro-smoking, wife-beating drunkards. I was there. I saw it. That left an impression on me, on the temporal nature of Eden and Sodom. Whenever Eden or Sodom appears, a DEA agent is sure to helicopter in and shut it down. A Michael McFaul or Jerry Falwell.

The DEA's best hope here is to Americanize the Russian women—to make them less desperate, to put Reeboks on their feet and shapeless Gap skirts on their legs. I know very well that an ex-nerd like myself (eleven times decorated for excessive lameness in the line of duty) has profited from an historical glitch: descending upon a defeated, ruined empire whose buildings, and girls, have been left intact. Instead of sacking the place and burning it down, expats have slowly bled it, a quiet sacking stretched out over a decade, masked as a "market transformation."

That's how a jaw-dropping goddess like Alyona wound up with someone like me.

Alyona lived in a depressed suburb of one of the most miserable, doomed cities in Russia: Kirov. Not even Kirov, but a village outside of Kirov. With the military-industrial complex finished, Kirov has absolutely no raison d'être. Just hundreds of thousands of citizen-refugees trying to keep from freezing and starving to death, stuck out in the middle of the flat, dead earth between Kazan and Nizhni Novgorod, wondering if the government will ever pay them their pensions and wages. In Vyatskiye Polyani, a small town in the Kirov oblast built around a giant defense factory, the desperation is so great that you wouldn't even bother with a "White God" factor. More like "White Galactical Emperor-God" factor. The population of Vyatskiye Polyani dropped from 80,000 to less than 20,000 between 1992 and 1994, as the factory stopped receiving government funding, and the people stopped receiving wages.

One enterprising nutcase, Alexander Komin, saw this as an opportunity to mix his own market economics theories with certain sadistic impulses. In 1996, he spent months building a complete basement-factory underneath his tiny garage-shed, then lured local women into the shed by promising them some vodka. Once inside, he locked them up and forced them to produce goods such as oven mitts and boxer shorts. He raped them, tortured them, murdered one attempted escapee by forcing her to drink antifreeze, and drilled the word RAB ("SLAVE") into their foreheads, just to get that corporate teamwork thing going. The business was going so well that he was even photographed and honored by the local chief of police, whom he presented with a gift—needlework wall art produced in Komin's "factory." Several months later, one of his slaves got pregnant. Komin was flabbergasted. "Do you really think it was me?" he asked the slave. "Who else could have done it?" she replied. He determined to do the honorable thing and marry her—but the minute he took her down to the courthouse, she turned him in.

Proving, of course, the one major drawback to having a relationship with a Russian woman: she is congenitally unfaithful.

No story better sums up "Russian Reforms" than this little heart-warmer. Someday, this will be made into a four-boxes-o'-Kleenex film, a kind of *Sleepless in Seattle* meets *I Spit On Your Grave*. Note that the women pictured have the word "Slave" drilled into their foreheads.

INNOVATIVE MANAGEMENT

There are many reasons to commit murder. There are even many reasons to spend years building an underground cavern in which to imprison and torture kidnapped strangers. If one is greedy and/or a sadistic sex fiend, these things make sense. But if your aim is to start up a low-overhead boxer short company, murder, kidnapping and torture don't seem like logical options. Nonetheless, one Aleksandr Komin of the Kirov suburb of Vyatskiye Polyani did just that. According to Komsomolskaya Pravda, Komin and a friend, Aleksandr Mikheyev, spent four years building a multi-story basement under his garage on the edge of town. Neighbors remarked at his industriousness. When he was finished, he began putting the basement to good use. He lured a series of men and women into the garage with vodka, then knocked them out with drugs and/or blows to the head and imprisoned them underground, where they were set to work making boxer shorts on sewing machines. He tattooed the word "Slave" ("rab") on his captives' foreheads, fed them on black bread and potatoes, and forced them to go to the bathroom into a 40-liter plastic barrel. For technical expertise he had to capture a seamstress who was the friend of a friend named Nikolai Malikh; Malikh's body was found in the local landfill two years after his seamstress friend disappeared. One worker named Vera Tolpayeva who lost the will to work was given a choice of suicide options: electric shock or antifreeze ingestion. She chose antifreeze and died after two days of agony; Komin had his first organized labor uprising when the remaining slaves refused to make ground beef out of her and eat her. Give 'em an inch and they take a mile, huh? In any case, tune in to the next issue of the eXile for more details on this story, which ended unhappily for the pair of Kirov slave drivers.

Edward Limonov, in his most recent book, *Anatomy of a Hero*, writes: "Russian women are usually, physically speaking, attractive, but morally—they are repulsive creatures, cripples."

Limonov has been married three times to Russians, and hasn't lived in America for almost 20 years. He remembers the loyalty of American women with fondness, perhaps rightly so. Russian women are not reliable, but then again, neither are most Russian men. At least half of the girls I met here married at age 18 or 19, and, after having a child, were dumped by their older husbands, who couldn't resist the urge to hunt down a fresh new teenager. Russians' lax attitude toward fidelity is, in my opinion, highly progressive and rational, so long as it isn't covered in lies. Since most people enter relationships in Russia expecting an affair sooner or later, you can deal with it. It's hypocrisy that scares me the most.

The Russian masses have been abandoned by their government and by the West, because they're no longer needed. And within that frame of abandonment, Russian women have to think about the man they'll marry—a man, if he's Russian, who's likely to abandon her, after beating her, infecting her with syphilis, and milking her for all her dough. Tens of millions of people live in dire circumstances, stranded in the center of the world's largest continent, with little hope of going anywhere. Which means—sexual opportunity for me.

Over the last fifteen years, the only place in Russia that's felt some improvement is Moscow. Moscow is decadent and terrifying, but until the crisis hit in the summer of 1998, it wasn't desperate. Up to 85 percent of the nation's wealth is sucked into Moscow. It's a lamprey, a school of liver flukes, bleeding the Russian corpse dry. Moscow only holds 10 of the nation's 145 million . . . which leaves . . . hold on a sec . . . 135 million wretched souls. Half of whom are women. A significant number of whom are young and attractive.

Alyona came from one of the many cities and towns whose few resources had been sucked dry in order to enrich Moscow. Her "options" are limited, galley-slave options. It's either sewing oven mitts in some freak's garage-dungeon, or sleeping with Mark Ames, Joe Blow, or a thousand other unappealing American expats who represent a kind of lottery ticket out of that dead end and into hope.

Nothing signified her desperate fate more than the evening of our first "date." She and a friend took a train from Kirov to Moscow to meet Andy and me. We took them for a walk on the Arbat, then to a shitty, dilapidated laser tag club in some overheated building basement. They couldn't get enough. Later, we took them to Planet Hollywood for dinner and afterward, to the Chuck Norris Beverly Hills Club, a casino nightclub infrequented by hookers and semi-respectable thugs. We were seated in a special balcony area for the concert—the Zaitsev Sisters: a grotesquely saggy,

MOSCOW BABYLON by Roman Papsuev & Mark Ames *note: based on a true story (see "Innovative Management" in Death Porn)

heavily made-up forty-something twin-sister duo lip-synching the shittiest Russian pop Muzak I'd ever heard in my life.

During the show, Alyona could barely contain her joy. The Zaitsev Sisters were one of her favorites! She sighed and squealed. Finally, she grabbed my hand, kissed me, bounced in her seat, and told me, "This is the best night of my life, Mark. Thank you so much!" Later, at Andy's, with the Kremlin lit up in the background, Alyona returned the favor.

In the provinces, not only is life maximally shitty, but chances of escape are almost nil. A provincial isn't even allowed into Moscow, where the old Soviet pass-system to control the population inflow is still in effect. The few Westerners who do go out to a region on business are bound to be grubby oil-worker types or chinless suits looking to squeeze out a last easy buck. They usually don't have the strategic sophistication to tap into the unspoiled beauty; instead, they'll head into their hotel lobby and pick up a 100-dollar whore for the night. Leaving all those nonwhores stranded. Which, ah shucks, leaves a lotta pickins for fellers like me.

It's not as if you have to search hard for attractive *dyevs* when you leave Moscow. You just need to have a sharper eye, since the provincials dress less fashionably. My eye is pretty well-trained: I actually dislike the local equivalent of sorority girls, and prefer the more awkward ones. I find the provincial far more attractive.

Andy and I wasted little time taking advantage of the gross overvaluation of our stocks relative to their real underlying value. We set out exploit as much regional desperation as possible. We called these "provincial runs."

We set a course for Kirov.

Andy and I found Owen sitting at a table with four teenagers. He made a bitter quip about us being scavengers, which wasn't far from the truth: using Owen as the Marines to soften up the enemy was pretty effective. Any girl who has been railroaded into a corner with Owen for 20 minutes is ripe for comparatively decent guys like Andy and me. That was when I met Alyona. I left her my phone number in Moscow and told her to call me if she ever came to town.

Later on, I met one of the stage dancers, Natasha. She came off the stage to talk and dance with me. I was surprised—I'd underestimated the White God Factor. I was also feeling more and more acutely ill, although I tried not to let it slow me up.

Natasha left by 3 A.M., but not before writing down her address on a card for me. Most people in Kirov don't even have their own phones, so you just have to show up at their house. She lived on Industrial Lane (*Ulitsa Industrialnaya*).

Feeling woozy, I soon left the disco. Headache and nausea expanded until it became almost unbearable. My neck muscles tightened up. I returned to my hotel room, took two aspirins, then fell asleep in a kind of delirium. I started shivering and sweating. My whole body convulsed. At some point I lost track of where I was. Then I awoke, and ran to the toilet, violently vomiting, then turning over for an explosion of diarrhea. They were practically concurrent. I was spraying out of both ends, a sprinkler of shit and vomit! The bathroom walls were splattered with half-digested slop. I'd just be wiping my ass for the eighth time with Kirov's finest sandpaper/toilet paper, when . . . WHOOSH!—out comes a gelatinous chunk of yesterday's pulled pork sandwich. But the worst of all was the pain—the neck pains and the headaches. I fell back into delirium, not sure when I was dreaming the pain, dreaming the vomiting, and actually

CHAPTER SIX

5/20/98

Dear Mark!

How are things?
It's my third letter to you. I hope, you have got my last letter.
I don't know what to begin with.
At first, about your trip to California.
How did you spend your time? How did Bob feel after wedding? How did you relax
~~на~~ НА МАЛЬЧИШНИКЕ?

And as for me I didn't waste my time too.
On the 16th of April I was celebrating my birthday.
So now I quite „большая" and in year I shall be allowed to have strong drinks!
I was thrown down with presents, as you know I had a jubilee.
Recently my fellow-friend watched TV-programme on НТВ, which is called „ПРО ЭТО" and she saw Matt and you taking part in it. That's a pity, I didn't have an opportunity to see you again.
I want to tell you ~~(about)~~ some words about myself.
As for my work, now I don't work в „КАЛИНКЕ" (ЭТО ФИРМА С КОТОРОЙ Я ЕЗДИЛА В МОСКВУ),
I returned to place, where I had worked before.
And I don't regret!
My study at the University is going on! Oh!
Of course it is difficult. My session begins in June
It will last from 10 till 28.
~~Ію~~ Truly speaking I have a little fear!
These are my latest news.

I'm eager to find out about your life.
ОЧЕНЬ ЧАСТО ДУМАЮ О ТЕБЕ И
СОЖАЛЕЮ, ЧТО МЫ НЕ СМОГЛИ УВИДЕТСЯ ЗИМОЙ.
Я СКУЧАЮ!

So, I finish my letter and send you photos.
And I hope you will like them.
Also I send my new address:

One of several desperate letters sent by Alyona, from her miserable village, "Raduzhny" (meaning "happy"), to the Big City in Moscow, where there lived a hairy, sleazy, desperate old American named Mark.

doing it. At some point I'd pass out for what seemed like days, only to wake up twenty minutes later, run to the toilet, and vomit up a few drops of bile. Then turn over in a hurry—but there's nothing left to diarrhea, just colon pains, and a squirt or two.

Finally I passed out again, and awoke at around 1:30 in the afternoon. I felt like I'd sparred ten rounds with Tex Cobb. Nothing but body blows. At least I was alive. After showering and shaving, I realized that I even had a little strength in me. Enough strength to meet the dancer before my train left.

She'd left me her address on a napkin. "17 Industrialnaya Ul. Dom 16. Kv. 68." I had a taxi driver take me there, to Industrial Lane. It was a lane like a zillion others in the provinces: ten or so dilapidated block-style apartment buildings painted a weak shade of blue, peeling plaster, muddy roads, a small "park" that usually meant more mud, a couple of dead trees, twisted metal, trash . . . I walked up the stairwell—their building had no elevator—and rang the doorbell. She greeted me, and introduced me to her mother, a quiet, polite woman. They had bright red oriental carpets hanging everywhere in their cramped apartment. There was an odor of cheap perfume, talcum, and some kind of buttery soup. The mother offered me tea and we spoke a little bit about music, San Francisco, journalism. Natasha took my hand and we went for a walk toward the center. She said she wanted to show me a church, her favorite church in Kirov. I bought her a canned Gin & Tonic at a kiosk, and we hopped in a trolley bus. Unfortunately, the church was closed, but she then pointed to my hotel and, as if surprised, said, "Aren't you staying there?"

"Yeah."

"Well, what should we do?" she said, disappointed but smiling.

"I don't know. Do you want to see my hotel?"

"Sure," she said.

I guess I was lucky. The dancer didn't expect much more than a sexual experience with an American.

It was interesting. She was only eighteen, but she was already a fully bloomed whore. She wanted me to hit her in the face while we fucked. I slapped her hard, and her whole body rippled. I smacked her again. I was worn out, but I wasn't going to let her get the best of me, this provincial bitch. I didn't know that they were such decadent beasts, way out here in the middle of nowhere. It says a lot about human nature. . . .

I drove her back to her house on the way to the train station. She was sad to see me go. You could see it written on her face: *"Golly, when will I ever get the chance to get beaten by an American again?"* I was too wiped out to feel much but vague self-pity. I'd made a pretty impressive comeback from the toilet to the bed. I promised to write her. I never did.

When we returned to Moscow, Owen wrote up a feature piece in the *Moscow Times* called "Fear and Loathing in Kirov," even quoting the same Samuel Johnson line that HST used. He portrayed my friend Andy as a loser, and him-

The White God Factor

by Mark Ames

When I was checking out of my hotel in Minsk earlier this month, one of the cleaning women approached me with an obsequious steel-toothed smile.

"You're leaving already?" she asked.

"Yeah, I'm sorry to go," I answered.

"I wanted to introduce you to one of my daughters. I brought pictures... Well, the oldest one is twenty-eight. Maybe... she's too old for you? She has a young boy. I also have an eighteen-year-old daughter. I can introduce you to either one. Which would you prefer?"

"They both sound nice."

She was persistent about pimping one of her daughters off on me. She wouldn't rest until at least one of her daughters had the honor of being sodomized by me, a red-blooded American. After all, I was a White God, and these days in Minsk, White Gods are few and far between. She showed me a pair of black and white neo-Soviet passport photos: Sveta, the 28-year-old, and Anna, the 18-year-old. H'm. This was a tough choice. Should I take door number one—fresh, nubile, easily-impressed; or door number two—divorced, with child... Damn, this was a real brain teaser...

How did I wind up with this steel helmet and sword, wading onto the shores of a wheel-less Indian settlement, way out here in Eastern Europe?

Even though Minsk is actually a clean, quiet, friendly city—a jewel by provincial Russian standards—it is almost totally devoid of foreigners. Ever since Lukashenko came to power, greedy, underqualified Western "entrepreneurs" saw their gold-plated lollypops snatched from their mouths. So they split town, realizing that their chances of participating in the economic rape of Belarus was next to nil: Lukashenko had basically cancelled "privatization" and "foreign aid," the stuff we live by.

There's a lot of good going on there that never gets reported, in part because Westerners haven't made a killing, and in part because Lukashenko doesn't use journalists well the way Chubais & Co. do. For example, did you know that Belarus posted a 2.6 percent gain in GDP last year, and a massive 11 percent gain in the first half of this year-all achieved in total defiance of World Bank and IMF advice? Of course not-reporting that kind of good news about Belarus, or the fact that Lukashenko's approval rating among the population would make any world leader drool with envy, might confuse our sense of good and bad, right and wrong. So he's a "tyrant," and Belarus is an "economic basket case." Consider this recent editorial, "Russia and Its Tyrant Neighbor," from that ultimate paper of record, the New York Times: "Belarus's economy, which looks the same as it did 10 years ago, is so feeble that it makes Russia's economy look robust." Well, there's some truth to this: ten years ago, the economies of both countries were about double the size of what they are today—meaning if Belarus's economy looks like it did ten years ago (and indeed it is getting there faster than its "booming" neighbor Russia), it is the envy of nearly all of the FSU. Belarus doesn't have wage arrears problems and miners' wives laying down on railroad tracks like Russia. In fact, Russia only paid off its arrears by changing the terms of its gas supply agreements, squeezing Belarus for a huge sum of cash (at the advice of anti-Belorussian Western advisors).

If Lukashenko could run in a free and fair Russian election, he could possibly win—which means Chubais' friends would lose everything they've been amassing. That's why the "Russian liberals"—the *English-speaking* thieves—despise him. (One minor point: the opposition press IS alive in Belarus. The *Minsk News*, the only English-language newspaper in Belarus, is rabidly anti-Lukashenko—in comparison, the *Moscow Times* reads as though Chubais himself edits it. *Imya*, the popular Minsk weekly, not only savages Lukashenko with words, but always prints a brutal, hilarious eXile-esque full page picture of the president in highly unflattering poses.)

Grim portrayals mean people are loathe to even visit, much less invest, in Belarus. Almost everyone here asked me, before I left for Minsk, if I wasn't worried about getting arrested. Not at all—hell, if anything, I'd happily offer my services as a kind of Goebbels to the Lukashenko regime, should they ever need a PR guy. The way I see it, thanks to Lukashenko's badboy rhetoric, the cleaning woman offered me her daughters. So he's all right by me. And this is the point I want to get across here. If a poll were held today, I would be one of the 55 percent of Belorussians who recently gave their leader a thumbs-up of approval, and not one of the nine percent of Russians who approve of Yeltsin. Why? Because frankly, I like being a White God. It feels good walking down the street and having people throw themselves at your feet. I had no fewer than three marriage proposals, including one from a "virgin." It was hilarious and gratifying and I never expect to experience that again in Europe.

Men dream of being White Gods because, more than anything, it is sexually appealing. For women, it's a bit different. Women generally aren't turned on by desperate male losers the way men get excited by desperate girls. But this doesn't mean that the White God Factor doesn't appeal to women as well—only for them, it's usually a sentimental thing. Women also like being in the position of strength—in this case, to "help the needy."

When I was in Laos, this German Greens type complained that the White God Factor was already receding. "It's not so good in Laos anymore," she said with a hint of frustration. "The people aren't as poor as they used to be. Four or five years ago it was better." She didn't even realize how evil that was—wishing that the locals were more poor, only in order to satisfy her sentimental desire to be "helpful." Whatever—the point is, it's almost ALWAYS good for us when others suffer and we don't.

So thank you Mr. Lukashenko for saying the wrong things in the wrong way to the wrong people. And a big thank you to you, *The New York Times*, for spreading cheap Cold War lies about an alleged tyrant and his allegedly basket-case nation. And oh yes, to you as well, all the aggrieved bankers, IFIs (international finance institutions) and human rights activists for helping to scare all the White People away from Belarus. All of you helped make my five days in Minsk among the most memorable of my recent life.

Alive & Yellow

by Mark Ames

There's this new Moscow City advertisement in the metro—I can't remember the words exactly, but it's from a letter Chekhov had written, in which he says that once you've grown used to Moscow, you'll never leave. I started thinking about how true that was, in a twisted sort of way. It's not a healthy, heartwarming Sleepless in Seattle kind of love-more like an abusive relationship, the kind so emotionally damaging that it can only be cured with heavy shock treatment and Prozac.

Somehow in my mind, the Chekhov postcard got transformed into: "If you've grown used to Moscow, you're damaged forever." All of us who have begun to think that Russia makes sense, are damaged forever—and, I would argue, for the better. After all, the alternative is much worse. Only an asshole would dedicate his life to his career and ESPN—which is why America is filled with so many assholes. I could have been one of those assholes-instead, I became THIS kind of asshole. Follow me.

Exactly two weeks ago, I saw another corpse-my tenth since arriving. Even before I got a good look, I knew he'd been thrown out of a window from the seven-story Stalin-era building...

I stopped before the corpse to, as MT Out would say, "check it out." It wasn't as nasty as I'd expected. Except for the left tibia, which poked out of his knee like a giant pink turkey bone, he looked like he'd died with some dignity. People passed by, pakyeti in hand, casting a nonchalant glance on their way to the metro. Even the cops seemed bored, waiting for the ambulance to come. The ambulance wasn't in any hurry.

I proudly realized that my own reaction was anything but horror, and I that I'd acquired some of the Russian "rovnodushnost'," or indifference.

At least, I thought so. Last Friday night, I met up with Polina, a Latvian girl whom I'd got to know a few nights before in a drunken haze at Jacko's bash. We headed out to Maks-Club, a flathead-infested disco that she described as "solidny." She paid for nearly everything, making her a winner in my eyes.

Later, we headed back to her apartment (on her coin), way out in the distant suburbs. She had a large selection of videos, and asked me which one I wanted to watch. I suggested "Anal Kanal 3," a German porn flick featuring a black man with an fourteen-inch tool. I guess this is how Germans purge themselves of Nazi war guilt—letting Helga get sodomized by all the untermenschen. What's next? Anal Kanal 4: featuring Rabbi Schlong spraying face paint on a group of Hitlerjugen?

Just as we were crawling into bed, Polina got a phone call. It was her husband, or ex-husband... He said he'd seen us at the Maks-Club, and he wanted to meet with her and talk. Polina hung up, and told me a few interesting tidbits: such as, her husband Seryozh is a serious bandit who is on Russia's wanted list for selling illegal weapons, and that he's a major coke head. "If he gets ten grams, he just snorts it all up and goes crazy," she told me. "I'm afraid he's coked up right now." My first thought was, gee, I'd like to get to know this guy.

Seconds later, Seryozh called again. He was raging jealous. He wanted to come over that second and see her. She told him no again, that her father was staying with her. He told her something that made her blanch, her eyes bugged out. She held her hand over the phone, and whispered, "He's right outside my window! He's calling from his mobile phone from right out the window. Stay down!"

Here's where things get ugly. She agreed to meet him out on the street, and told me to stay in bed, not to move. But I didn't listen. The minute she walked out of the door to meet him, I got up and dressed, just in case. What a horrible way to go: a victim of "domestic violence," six bullet holes in my gut. No glory in that. My pretzel corpse in a suburban Moscow podyezd...

I waited. An hour had gone by, an hour of terror and cowardice. I decided to act. I moved from the bedroom and crawled up to the window to look down onto the street. No one was there. I sat down on the couch in the TV room and went over my options. Either she took off with him, or he killed her. Either way, I figured, I was fucked. My selfish instincts, perfected over the years in California, seized control. I had three options: either stay in the apartment and wait, hoping that the steel door would protect me; sneak out, run up the stairwell, and hide; or make a sprinting "Run, nigga! RUN!" break for it.

Just then, a car pulled up. It stopped below her window. I heard her voice, and that of another man. It was too late. They came up the stairs, then stopped outside the front door. I bet a bullet hurts a lot worse than they make it look in the movies. I hid in the back room, in the dark, looking out the 2nd floor balcony, wondering if I should jump. The image of the defenestration guy flashed... that snapped tibia sticking out of his knee.

She opened the door, and closed it. Then checked the bedroom. I wasn't there. She stopped. I didn't hear Seryozh's voice. Did he leave? Yes! She's alone! When she saw me in the back room, I tried to pretend as though I'd just tied up my shoe laces, that I wasn't afraid of nuthin'.

"I was about to leave," I said, taking little notice of her swollen red face. She was crying and shaking.

Then she told me what had happened. When she walked out of the door, Seryozh grabbed her by the hair, got her in a headlock, and tried dragging her into a car driven by his crony. She finally broke free and ran out onto the main street, where an unmarked militsia car happened to be passing by. They saved her, but naturally, they didn't lock Seryozh up-after all, it was just a "domestic dispute." She was disappointed by my cowardice, but hey, as the 70s California anthem goes, "You can't please everyone/ so you've got to please yourself."

When it was all over, we crawled back into bed, and, in a way I can't explain, reenacted some of the violence of the evening. It was... interesting. When I left the next morning, I saw that metro ad again, and thought, "Yep, I'm damaged for the better."

Needless to say, I'll be seeing Polina again real soon.

self as a suave, detached lady-killer. I didn't get it: there were witnesses who could testify to the contrary!

We also learned what my illness was from. One of the Americans on that doomed Kirov trip, the soccer-hairdo guy, died of meningitis. Based on the symptoms of my illness, it was thought that I may have been the carrier.

So Kirov provided me with cheap, colonialist sex, Owen with invented memories of ribaldry, and Chris, the soccer-hairdo guy, with a brutal death.

A couple of months later, Owen was hired out by *Newsweek*. Just in time to write their cover story on "Decadent Moscow."

By the late summer, I was off to Belarus, the country with the highest White God factor in all of Europe. There, all of the necessary elements converge: economic desperation, a complete dearth of Americans, and, worst (or best) of all, political oppression in the form of dictator Alexander Lukashenko. I hadn't actually experienced a White God reading like that since I was a tourist in 1991. A good salary there was $70 a month. Clubs and restaurants were a fifth or less the price of Moscow's. My instruments were going haywire. The needles vibrated wildly in the red danger zone of White God-ness.

On my first day, I was nearly raped by a beefy Ukrainian girl who worked for the government tax inspectorate. I thought she looked sort of like Laura Dern, but when I looked closer, I realized that she was a tank. When we kissed, she rammed her tongue into my teeth so hard that she nearly loosened two of them. I feigned exhaustion and took a taxi home, but I was impressed with the level of desperation, and what that meant for my personal prospects. The next night, I got a call in my hotel room offering me a whore for $35 an hour, or $100 for the night. I foolishly took her for the night and drank myself silly, even though I had an interview with the finance minister the following morning.

The next day, sitting on some steps next to a freeway, a 19-year-old girl introduced herself to me. She wondered if I was Arab—Arabs were apparently hot items in Minsk until Lukashenko tossed them out. They were shocked that I was an American—wow! A real American!? No Americans come here anymore!

The girl introduced me to her younger sister, Yulia, a short little punkish type who had just turned 17. I took them for a walk. We ate a snack at McDonald's. They were clearly destitute. Poor but alive and playful. They inhaled their milkshakes and french fries, while I looked on. Then we bought some beers and walked to the Park Janki Kupali, a pleasant, green park full of bright red flowers and healthy grass and a variety of deciduous trees. Much greener than any Moscow park. We sat on a bench and talked. Their parents had died in a car accident several years earlier. Yulia was in the car at the time, and they thought she'd died too. Now they lived with their aunt, whom they called their mother, and their cousin, who was an asshole of some kind. I got the feeling that he was raping the older one, while he abused Yulia by telling her that she was fat and ugly and she'd never find a decent man.

I took them out to a "high-class" Uzbeki restaurant for dinner—at ten bucks a head, they were in shock. We drank a few bottles of wine and chowed down some *plov*. That was when I found out that Yulia was a virgin. At that point, her sister ceased to exist in my eyes. Vanished, just like that. Yulia understood, and so did her sister, who quietly accepted it. Yulia and I walked her older sister back home, then I took Yulia back to the Minsk Hotel, where a six-dollar bribe got us past security. Yulia lost her playful edge. She quietly took off her clothes and lay on her back, legs slightly apart. She was my first virgin ever, and it wasn't an easy job. She insisted that I not wear a condom. We spent the next couple of days hanging out and trying mostly in vain to consummate. When she saw me off at the train station, she said to me, "Can you promise me one thing? Please don't forget me, if only for a few days more." I still call Yulia periodically—I'd like her to come out and stay with me, but for some reason she won't. I may have transmitted something from the whore to her.

When I left the hotel, one of the steel-toothed maids from my floor told me that she had wanted to introduce me to her daughters, but then . . . well, she'd seen me with so many women.

I was embarrassed, expecting to get into trouble. I apologized, and told her that I regretted not meeting her daughters.

"Well, you still can!" she beamed. "One is a little older, twenty-eight, with a child. My youngest is eighteen. Are you interested? I could show you their pictures first."

"I'll come back," I promised. "I'll meet you then."

She wrote out her phone number and begged me to call when I returned.

The last provincial run of 1997 that Andy and I took was to Yaroslavl, one of the oldest cities in Russia, part of the famed Golden Ring. We figured that basically, any place outside of Moscow would offer up a high White God factor, and since Yaroslavl's population was 600,000, there had to be at least one equivalent disco-range to Kirov's *Zapretnaya Zona*. On our first night out Andy I and decided to take a walk. A

CHAPTER SIX

few steps outside of our hotel room, we ran into two teenage girls who were being heavily harassed by rapist-packed cars, horns a-honkin'. The girls were strolling, not innocently, scouting for the best deal when we arrived. When the girls saw us, they ran up and asked us to save them. Andy and I turned to each other and burst out laughing: we knew exactly what this meant. It was already in the bag. We took them out to the "coolest" club in Yaroslavl, some sad little bar with cheesy Formica and a small disco area. We fed them shrimp and cocktails, then took them back to our hotel.

Andy's girl was 17, and mine had just turned 18 that night. Andy's was far more attractive, I thought. There was something about her I really liked. He didn't appreciate her, because Andy has a penchant for Playboy-type women. Personally, I don't like them too magazine-pretty.

Mine, Alla, was a chunky redhead, but that was fine with me. Up to 18, their bodies are as taut as volleyballs, from head to foot. None of the stitching has loosened or unraveled. It's not fair that such flesh is wasted on drunken, ungrateful dirtheads. Only a man over 30 can truly appreciate the value of an 18- or a 17- or a 15-year-old's body. As it turned out, Alla was also a virgin. Her hymen must have had thorns on the inside: she screamed bloody murder at any thrust. My hotel room was right next to the floor watch, who must have heard everything.

Alla wasn't yelling sexlike yells—these were bloodcurdling screams that would have brought in a SWAT team back home. Right after I came, she rolled on her back, let out two small burps, then got up and ran to the bathroom and spent the rest of the night puking, while I slept. . . . It's kind of a strange feeling, when a girl starts puking the minute you come inside of her. Puking all night long. For some reason, she drew water in the bathtub and did most of her puking in there. But forgot to drain it. When I pissed the following morning, I noticed the tub all brown, little undigested shrimps floating near the top.

Andy and I met in L'vov, in western Ukraine, the following spring. The woman at the front desk asked us, after we checked in, if we were interested in "brides." She smiled knowingly. A crusty Soviet man in a suit straddled up to our side, squinting intently.

"Of course, we plan on meeting some beautiful brides here," we joked.

"But why go out, when you can have them brought here," the woman said knowingly.

"So you have some brides for us?" we asked.

"Only the best," she said.

"But what if we want to meet some nice girls at a disco or on the street," we suggested. "Can we bring them back?"

"But why do that?" the woman protested. "We'll bring you *our* girls. It's *safer,* they won't steal from you or poison your drink."

"No, but we want to meet regular girls, in a disco."

The old Soviet man shook his head, confused, while the woman smiled condescendingly. Her expression said, "There are no 'normal' girls in this part of the world. They're all whores."

I'm writing this chapter a month after Lena left me. A different Lena—Lena number nine. Russian creativity wilts when it comes to the difficult task of naming their children. Lena was my closest Russian girlfriend. We didn't make it very far: three hell-bent weeks of body fluids, hard drugs, and veneral disease. All that's left is a cheap black duffel bag, the kind shuttle-traders and third-world types use, and a few scars on my dick. Our last sexual blowout left my prick looking like it got destroyed in a fifty-car pileup. She'd fucked probably ten or twenty other men during the three weeks we lived together. That's a thought that's jolted me upright in bed more than a few times. Best to hire the censors to edit that memory.

I met her the night of the *eXile*'s first anniversary party. We held it at an underground squat club called Titan. A ripped-out basement underneath a Stalin-era residential building in downtown Moscow, just off Tverskaya Street. Titan is just about the only club in Moscow that isn't packed with gauche overstock Italian-style furniture in a sad attempt to appear respectable and modern. In fact, there's no furniture whatever. Not even a floor. Some throwaway grammar school desks, a few bent chairs, some tables. . . . Only the small dance hall has a floor as such: a stretch of cement. The walls of the club are covered in Day-Glo orange and green spray paint and graffiti.

Most of the patrons at Titan are orphans, street punks, skinheads, white power bikers who couldn't afford a Big Wheel. The night of our *eXile* first-year anniversary bash, the bikers and skins lifted purses, cameras, anything they could get their hands on. One after another, some middle-class *eXile* invitee would come running up to me or Taibbi with tears in his eyes, wondering what happened to his watch, her bracelet.

Lena had just been released from a prison near Berlin, and deported for good from Germany. She'd spent three and a half years in jail there for drug trafficking. It wasn't the first jail she'd lived in: she'd briefly spent time in jails in Belgium and Poland, too.

She arrived with police escort in Moscow on the evening of our anniversary party, February 6, 1998. She got a ride from the airport to downtown Moscow by sucking off one of the taxi drivers and his dispatcher at the airport. They convinced her to leave her bags with them, probably hoping to coax her into another barter deal later on. She had two bags at the time—all of her belongings were stuffed into them.

Somehow she wound up at the Karusel Club, on Tverskaya Street. The Karusel is a swank flathead nightclub/casino that boasted $75 cocktails and a $200 cover charge. She was tanked by the time she arrived. After getting it on with one or two of the security staff, they led her around the corner, to the basement club Titan, and dumped her there.

At the club, she met a friend of mine, who introduced me to her. She had thick, curly, long golden braids, and sly, Asiatic eyes, chestnut-colored. Her puggish nose and oval face were decidedly Slavic, but her bronze complexion was Caucasian.

After she sucked off one of my friends right in the center of the club, I wound up with her at closing time. I was tanked on cheap vodka and riding the first phenamine waves. Lena attacked me. She hugged and kissed me, and asked me if she could stay at my place for the night. I let her stay with me; I was suckered.

The following evening, when we met up with my friend Andy, she tried to climb a rung up the ladder. Andy had wheels: a Mercedes-Benz . . . she did everything to seduce him, and when he didn't respond, she flat-out told him that she was ready to dump me and move in with him. Andy split, leaving us at a club, and I threw her out of the house. That's when she pulled one of her many film noir femme fatale moves on me.

As she grabbed her bag and purse to leave for good, she whispered, "Can't we just fuck one more time before I go? I promise I'll leave after that."

I was a sucker. I always am.

The next day, she disappeared. I didn't hear from her, and wondered if she had gone forever. Then at around ten at night, someone rang my doorbell. Usually that terrifies me: it's got to be someone I don't want to see. An angry neighbor or reader, or an ex-girlfriend holding our baby. So I didn't answer. A neighbor, the half-French guy who lives across the hall, banged on my door.

"She's ringing my doorbell, Mark," he said, pointing down the hallway. "You answer it."

There, I saw Lena slumped against the entranceway wall, held up by a well-dressed young Russian man. Another woman was with them: they apologized to me, and handed Lena over to me. They were old friends of Lena's, from childhood, before she moved from Moscow to Germany. They'd just seen one another that day for the first time in years. It was the last time they ever wanted to see her.

Lena stumbled into my apartment, then slumped against the wall and fell to the floor.

"You're on heroin?" I asked her.

She nodded yes. It was the best heroin she'd ever had. And she'd saved me a little. Ah, the savage little princess! She wasn't so bad after all! I snorted up the line, and we spent the entire evening drooling, floating, and fucking. It was one of the most wonderful nights of my life.

After that, Lena and I had a certain connection, something beyond the pale of love. Uncut. No impurities. The next day, I woke up late in the afternoon, tossed Lena out, and stumbled to work. We were supposed to meet at my house at midnight, but I was late. She decided that I'd stood her up. And went drinking in Gorky Park with a pair of guys. She fucked one of them, and was almost raped by the other. Maybe she was just out earning money as a hooker. I still don't know.

After that, she stood out in front of my apartment, trying to flag a car down. I saw her there when I returned home at around 2 A.M. She looked like a common whore, the way she held her hand out on the street, shifting from one foot to the other the way other street whores do. I wasn't sure it was Lena—she wasn't wearing the same jacket I saw her in earlier in the day, so I figured it must be someone else. I walked right past her. We looked each other in the face. But the combination of my bad vision and the heroin still affecting me . . . I didn't believe it could be her, so I walked past, and home. She told me she thought that I'd simply decided to ignore her. So she went home with another guy that night, fucked him, and smashed a vodka bottle into the head of yet another man who tried raping her. The next afternoon, she slept with the man's wife as well, before reaching me. I was out of my mind by that time.

Lena was unlike any woman I'd ever known. So many times, I've been told by women here, "Russian girls do what they want. We aren't like Westerners in that way. When we want something, we do it, and worry about the consequences later."

In that sense, Lena was a grotesque of a Russian woman's soul. If she wanted to fuck, she fucked everyone and everything in sight. If she wanted to get high, she'd go to the point of OD-ing. In Germany, she had been interred in a psychiatric hospital for borderline-insanity because it was determined that she had no inhibitions.

Her mother died of cancer while she was in jail. Her brother died in her arms of a heroin overdose, while she was on furlough, shortly after their mother died. And her Azerbaijani

A Nihil Strain of Nationalism

by Mark Ames

"You Americans are stupid. I hate you and your country."

I heard it but didn't pay attention: my head was pounding, and I'd barely slept.

"You dirty Americans," he continued. "I hate you. You have no culture and no history."

If he's talking to me, he's got a point. I smelled like shit after a night of downing gin and tonics, chasing a pair of giraffes around a Kursk disco, then passing out in my clothes. I hadn't showered, and worst of all, I'd been stuck on the overnight train with the most noisome collection of black earth peasants the world has ever known. The pungent odor of cheesy feet and cheap tobacco billowed out of every compartment, sticking to my clothes.

"You are a stupid country, America is." This hangover apparition sounded realer and realer—and it spoke good English too.

I was walking on the platform at Kursky Vokzal, heading back home with my mentor, Dr. John Dolan, while this voice hassled me.

"What's going on?" I mumbled.

The professor nervously laughed. "Uh, I think this guy's a nationalist nut. Let's hurry."

"No! I am no nationalist nut!" the nut screeched.

I turned to get a good look. He was dressed like a Swede in his green and brown patterned sweater, wire-rimmed glasses and fresh haircut, wife-in-arm. Hardly your typical, pasty nationalist nut.

"Russia is a great country," he said, fighting to control his anger.

"I agree," I honestly replied.

"I hope we throw all you dirty Yankees out of Russia."

"What a great idea," I said. "Throw everyone out. Then Russia will be an economic powerhouse." I understood that I might get into a fistfight. It would be ugly: rolling on the slushy platform, slugging it out with some middle-aged Russian couple... booting the husband and wife into human kasha... it might not be very honorable, but it's better than getting purse-whipped to death.

"No, just throw dirty Americans out. Not Europeans. Only Americans. I hate you all."

Now it was getting downright embarrassing. Dr. Dolan fled the scene, leaving me alone. People were staring, including the militsia.

"America is the stupidest country on earth."

"Yeah, I guess that's why we won the cold war," I said. "If we were a little smarter, we might have wound up like you."

His wife cringed and grabbed his arm.

"I hope we throw you dirty Yankees out!" he screeched.

"So do I!" I said.

The nationalist turned back to me with a look of puzzled horror, but his wife pulled him away, melting into the crowd.

"What was wrong with that asshole?!" I asked.

"Uh, Mark, don't you remember..." Dr. Dolan slapped his head and squinted nervously.

"Remember what?"

"Like, uh, all those things you were saying on the train? I think we should get out of here quick before they arrest us." He wasn't joking. He picked up his pace, powerwalking towards the metro. Then he snapped: "That guy understood what you were saying. Everything!"

"Oh. Oops."

Now that I think about it, yeah, I was pretty bad on the train. Like when the sort-of-youngish conductor woman walked by, and I'd say straight to her face, "I bet you've fucked so many passengers in your day that you lost count fifteen years ago." She didn't understand me—she smiled dumbly, two front teeth missing. "It's true, isn't it? You can't even remember the last guy you boned." Dr. Dolan yelped nervously, which only egged me on. "You know the Georgian joke about why Russians have patronymics—so the mothers can remember who the father of their child is. This conductor here has probably squatted out a few rats whose patronymics are *'ya-ne-znayu-vich'* or *'ya-ne-vspomnyuvich.'* Think about it. All a guy has to do is barge into her compartment with a bottle of vodka, and within seconds her panties are hanging from the curtain rod."

Eesh. I guess the middle-aged nationalist heard every word. He was probably a decent, polite man with kind feelings towards Americans before I arrived. It would be hard to explain that it was all affectionate humor on my part. It would be harder to explain the long episode with the three-year-old girl. She came out to play with us in the corridor, sitting on my lap. I held her on my knee and said, in English, "Ah, let me guess what you're going to be when you grow up... h'm... a slut? A prostitute? An amoral money-grubber? Can you say 'slut'?" Little Katya smiled and giggled, and I giggled back.

Dr. Dolan backed away at the time, panting nervously. "Uh, I don't know, Mark. This is where my nihilism ends."

"Come on, she doesn't understand yet, do you?" I bounced the little peasant girl on my knee while her grandmother—who stank like a slaughterhouse—smiled at me. "Let me guess, Katya. You lost your virginity in the maternity ward, didn't you? Dragged one of the orderlies into your crib. Couldn't hold out a few years for a horny old foreigner like myself, huh?"

It's true, I was a real bastard. Four straight hours of this, laughing at my own jokes. What a card! A quip-o-matic! And that old nut probably sat in his compartment, hearing every word, wringing his hands, plotting his revenge, too cowardly to break a bottle over my head. Instead, he cringed, complaining bitterly to his wife, plotting and plotting... he practiced those pathetic nationalist lines in English, for hours, to impress upon me how intelligent he, a Russian, was in comparison to me, the vulgar American imperialist... and the worst part was, I agreed with most of what he had to say. His poor wife...

He'd have never understood if I told him that it was all done out of love. That my sick jokes proved more than sentimental words my affection for Russia. "Kill Your Idols"—that was Sonic Youth's motto. A good motto. But I could never explain it. So I've tried making up for it. I tried being a good nationalist. I went to the Gamaun demonstration that was supposed to take place at the Chisty Prudy metro station last Tuesday at 4:00. I was the only sucker who showed. Then I published a piece in Limonka. Let's see, what else? Well, here, this column is sort of my confession to the Truth Commission. I know, I'm leaving a lot out. Even I can't print most of the things I said on that train ride. Take it from me, it was bad. That poor old bastard had every right to attack me. I should be more careful.

father had been poisoned by her jealous stepmother. Her only surviving relative was a grandmother in Astrakhan, on the Caspian Sea. You can't blame her for taking life a day at a time after all that.

I finally booted Lena out of my house. All those drugs, all that fucking, it was one big distraction. I started noticing flaws, too. A little mustache that I'd never seen. And her hands: coarse, rough fingers, like a man's. Then it started hurting when I pissed. I went in for tests, and although they came up negative, I was sure there was some kind of monster setting up an amusement park in my urethra. Finally, one of the doctors prescribed Azitromitsin, an all-purpose super-antibiotic. Within a month, I was healed. The sores took a bit longer. I thought those might have been syphilis or herpes sores, but they turned out to be abrasions from too much roughhousing. The prick is a sensitive organ, all capillaries, veins, and skin as thin and delicate as butterfly wings. I had her treat it like ground meat, and the results were something like Stalingrad.

Lena finally ditched me, taking one of the two black duffel bags with her, and leaving the other one behind, nearly emptied. She left a few pair of underwear, some socks, a T-shirt, a cheap tracksuit, and some documents in German, her deportation papers, I suppose. I haven't heard from her ever since I threw her out for good. Having a disease-ridden whore lying in bed next to me could only lead to worse and worse things. One of her lovers was an officer of some kind in the OMON paramilitary troops. She'd call his pager under the pseudonym "Sergei," so that his jealous wife wouldn't find out; then he'd call back to my apartment asking for Lena. God knows why she sucked his dick: probably she needed a Moscow registration stamp.

I miss her sometimes. I guess that's why I haven't thrown that ridiculous Blue Ocean duffel bag of hers away. I still think there's a chance she'll call me to claim it.

When Lena moved into my apartment, I was seeing about six other girls. Lena always answered my phone. If a woman called, she'd chew her out and threaten her life if the girl ever called again.

"It'll be cunts for you," she'd growl. Lena meant it too. All those years in prison made her pretty damn tough. She'd tell me bedtime stories of the women she'd raped. There was a thin 19-year-old Bulgarian girl who became her bitch. The story of how Lena cornered her in the shower, beat and kicked her for ten minutes, then made her lick her under threat of pain, was my favorite.

Around that time, I had an article published in the techno-hip magazine *Ptyutch* about an Ugly American running around Moscow like a baseball-capped Hun. It led to an embarrassing television appearance on the show *Pro Eto*, a cheesy, sex-obsessed, *Oprah*-esque talk show. The young, attractive mulatto emcee clearly had it in for Taibbi and me. She led us with questions making us out to be vulgar foreigners taking advantage of Russians. She brought an obese, spinster feminist, Jean MacKenzie, on to the show to counter our arguments. The whole thing was embarrassing—Jean is so frighteningly fat, and the makeup people turned her into a kind of grotesque Cesar Romero—that we pulled our punches.

We didn't come off looking too good. I never saw the actual show, but it's what I've heard. Nevertheless, it did pump up the fame bubble. I've signed several autographs since.

Just the other night, I was on the Old Arbat with Owen, when a sudden downpour forced us to take refuge under a colonnaded roof in front of a theater. Sitting on the cement steps were two punk girls, one with a baseball cap that said "Skinhead," the other with a nose ring.

Owen and I moved close to the girls to get a better look. They were cute, my type. Orphans? Runaways?

Out of nowhere, some egg-shaped beast with a cavewoman's face, dressed in a motorcycle jacket and black jeans, approached me and said, in good English, "I saw you on television."

I hesitated, and mistakenly acknowledged that yes, it was me she saw.

"Get away from these girls," she said indignantly. "You are here to get free Russian girls, aren't you? Well, get away from these ones. I know what you want."

"I came here to get out of the rain," I said, laughing.

"No you didn't. You came here for free Russian girls. I saw you on television. Go away."

I made some lame attempt at confronting her. But, in fact, I was unnerved. The week before, I'd received a pretty valid-looking death-threat fax from somebody calling himself "H8 RED." He wrote, in his two-page rant, "One of us has to leave, Marky, and it's not gonna be me. Remember your article about 'Dying Here'? That's gonna be you if you don't get the fuck out now."

People were getting to know me. And they were on to me. If Russia was going pitchfork, that could mean bad news for me. When people go pitchfork, guys like me—who have been running around their country, whoopin' it up and raping their womenfolk—wind up skewered and posted on the city gates, stake through the ass, out the mouth, organs dripping like jelly onto the blood-caked earth.

Amen.

HA-HA-HA-HA-HA

BY MARK AMES

CHAPTER SEVEN: VANITY AND SPLEEN

"Someday this war's gonna end . . . "
Robert Duvall, *Apocalypse Now*

hen I received my first hate-mail letter, I was terrified. Not just ordinary-terrified, but the kind of undignified panic that they never show in the movies: I was the guy on the sinking ship screaming like a bitch . . . kicking mothers in the teeth for their life jackets, tossing their children overboard to make legroom for myself in the lifeboat.

It came via land mail to the *Living Here* offices. I didn't know that land mail actually made it anywhere in Russia. Especially into the Soviet tangle of buildings and annexes in which our office was hidden. Even the crusty, hunched security guards who stood inside the double-doored entrance in their worn gray Soviet suits, army stripes pinned to the breast, reeked of peeled yellow Brezhnevian incompetence: there's no fucking way on earth they'd let a piece of mail get through the door. *Living Here* was located on Gazetny Pereulok, dom 3 (just down the street from my first office, where I'd sold wine and Seagram's liquor in late 1993), a huge yellow and white turn-of-the-century building that the government leased out for free to the Gaidar Institute.

In turn, the Gaidar Institute leased out space to businesses for its own profit. The Gaidar Institute was set up as a Russian think tank to assist the government in its economic reforms. The Institute was founded by Yegor Gaidar, the first Prime Minister of Russia, the frog-faced architect of "reform" and "shock therapy" and every other curse word associated with capitalism in Russia. Gaidar is the guy responsible for shaking down the entire Russian population, and handing over their belongings to a few well-placed comrades. He will go down in Russian folklore as one of the most terrifying villains ever to set foot on Mother Rus—his name will be invoked by parents to scare their children into going to bed and brushing their teeth.

And now, he was *Living Here*'s landlord. For the small two-room space, no more than twenty square meters in all, we paid a whopping $1,500 a month. And to top it off, the fucker never fixed our heating or faulty telephone lines. Gaidar was learning the landlord trade quickly. A real reformed kinda guy, that Gaidar: from *Homo Sovieticus* into *Homo Mr. Roperius* of *Three's Company.*

CHAPTER SEVEN

How could a hate-mail letter actually make it from one place in Moscow to another, then into a mail slot for *Living Here*'s offices in the Gaidar Institute, all on account of me? You always heard rumors here that no one ever received anything more than a postcard. All the enveloped mail was taken to some location (in Moscow, the mail dump was reportedly somewhere near Sheremetyevo Airport), torn open by the half-starving, unpaid postal service employees, and stripped of any valuables. Then the remains were dumped in a huge, open lot, and that was that.

I stormed into the office and grabbed the letter from

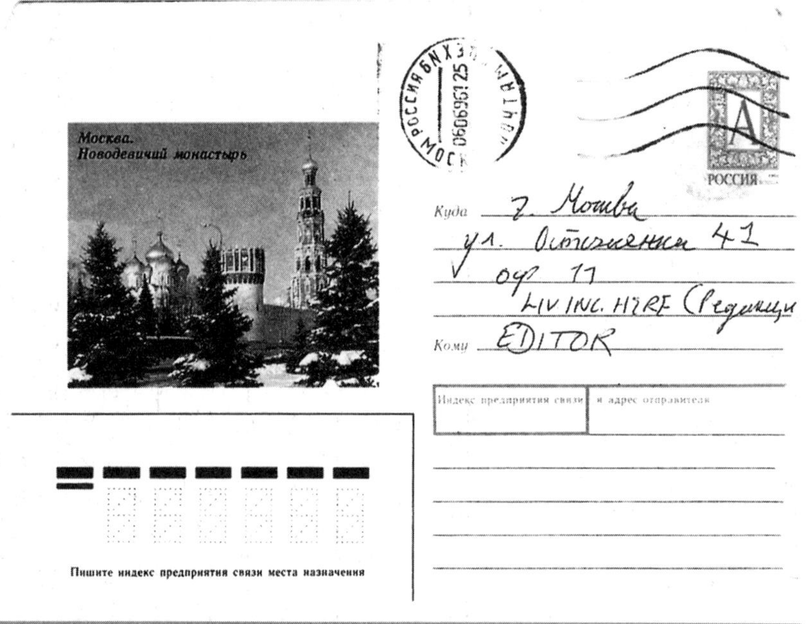

Perhaps the only letter in 1996 to have been successfully transferred from one point within the Russian Federation to another. It still burns to the touch.

Manfred's hands, noticing a strange, cringing expression on his face. I read the first paragraph, then looked up and tried to force a laugh. But it didn't come out. Just a squeak of some kind.

The dignified thing would have been to laugh it off, make a light James Bond-ish quip, then move on to some administrative matter. But instead, I panicked, and it showed.

"Who do you think sent this?!" I demanded.

Manfred shrugged. He didn't seem to want to talk about it much, although he did clearly enjoy seeing me panic.

"It was Owen, don't you think?" I said. "Or maybe Genine. Yeah, she's pissed off because I made fun of her cat in my column. You know how women are about their cats. Especially overweight, lonely American women. No wait, this was written by a Brit, and Genine isn't a Brit, so it had to be Owen."

Manfred didn't reply. He just smiled with that feckless, Amsterdam-café-toothed expression of his. I think Andrei was in the office at the time too. Andrei was an effeminate street kid whom Manfred had "hired" to help design advertisements. He had wavy dark hair and the soft features and crooked white teeth of a prepubescent. Andrei could barely speak a word of English. He tried hard, but he couldn't. He had a learning disability of some kind. Probably Manfred's domineering way of dealing with Andrei didn't help. There was something unpleasant about their relationship. I hated being in that office. Manfred was always more than willing to pile his own work on the poor kid so that he could go out drinking with his friends, making quirky, witty, Social Democratic wisecracks around the *stolovaya* or spouting Beigeist alterno-guy opinions on quirky underground bands. A bunch of fucking Schweiks, all of 'em.

I couldn't read the whole thing until I got home. I stuffed it into my bag and turned to leave. Manfred made me go eat a meal with him in the cockroach-infested Gaidar Institute cafeteria (the real Gaidar was dining down the road at the 5-star Metropol Hotel). I couldn't eat my cabbage soup. My heart was beating into my ears. I slung my bag over my shoulder and headed home, dry mouth, pouring sweat. It was a thirty-minute walk home, down the poplar and birch-lined promenade on

Dutchman Manfred Witteman eyes his advertising underling Andrei like a toasted Gouda sandwich.

the Bulvar Ring, past the statue of Gogol, whom I reverentially bowed to as always on my way past. I lived in a tilted studio apartment in the Kropotkinskaya district. My building even had a name, "Bolshevika," in honor of the lower-level functionaries who were rewarded for their quiet, unflinching servitude by getting apartments in this prestigious region. It wasn't the highest quality building: although only 20 years old, the brick apartment block already had its problems. Wall plaster crumbling and peeling. Doors that didn't close. Balconies giving way. The Stalin-era buildings are the only quality ones in Russia. After that, everything went downhill.

The elevator in my apartment building was broken, so I had to march up seven flights of stairs. By the time I got into my apartment, I was a human amphibian—a terrified human amphibian... it was all too familiar, like being back in the suburbs of California: scared and sweaty. Intellectually, I had to tell myself, no, this isn't the suburbs, this isn't California. But I wasn't convincing.

I opened the letter and read.

It hurt. It hurt even worse than I feared it would. Because I knew I'd have to publish it. Manfred had seen the letter. To attempt a cover-up, after he'd seen it, would be worse than fleeing. Much worse. That wasn't even an option. Was this how Nixon felt, opening the papers every morning? ... 25,000 readers. *25,000!* O, the humiliation! I was sure that the backlash was about to begin, that publishing it might bring other angry, disgruntled readers out of the woodwork. As in, the entire expat community. They'd gather below my window with torches and rakes and hoes! They'd drive me out of *Living Here* and out of town!

For the first eight months of *Living Here*'s existence, I'd sort of lived the literary equivalent of a Serbian sniper overlooking Sarajevo, taking the odd potshot at old ladies shopping for a loaf of bread, blowing the top of their skulls off... then taking long breaks to pound a bottle of *sljivovice* and chew the fat with Miloslav and Bosko. I didn't worry about the consequences of what I wrote because I spent most of my first year hiding. I mean *literally hiding.* I'd sneak up on the community with a couple of articles, whack them on the head with the proverbial rubber chicken, then flee back to my apartment. It was always the same: come production day, I'd get the courage up to write the kinds of things I'd always written for my own private pleasure: pure bile, unchecked invective. Then, the day the newspaper would come out, I'd suddenly be struck with a loss of courage: Why did I just do that?! They'll kill me! So I hid. And when no backlash came, I'd crawl out of my hole, slowly build up my courage again, fire at defenseless civilians from my totally secured nest high up in the hills, flee back to the bunker, and brag to the partisans about the kid on the bicycle and how he rode around in a circle after I blew his head off . . . "Like a headless circus bear! Ha-ha-ha!" "Oh Ames, you're a card!"

My first direct target in the expat community was a Canadian photographer, Heidi Hollenger. She gained a crust of fame in Moscow by photographing the far-right

Vadkovsky per.
d. 3/4 kv. 76

June 1st 1996

Dear Sir/Madam,

Consider the thought-provoking opinion piece from issue 14 of Living Here, written by People's Columnist Mark Ames. It dealt with the fascinating demi-monde of the Moscow expatriate literati, auspicious journalists from that august publication, the Moscow Times, and the esteemed editor-in-chief of Living Here himself.

On the one hand, the article railed against the inconsequential parochialism of features in the Moscow Times, whilst, on the other hand, emulating that very same thing.

When Living Here first appeared, we welcomed a refreshing alternative to the established English-language press, only to find that by its fourteenth issue it had become the antithesis of its former self. Perhaps the change in editorship is a fundamental reason for this. Mr Ames has metamorphosed into Jean MacKenzie. In a country which bombs its own citizens and in which the minimum wage cannot assure survival, he considers the reduced spending power of its expatriate community to be a "painful issue".

We wait with bated breath for issue 15. What burning questions will be on the agenda - shopping for cleaning products, tracking down Pampers, or maybe even interviewing nannies and maids?

Joanna Lillis
Paul Bartlett

opposition. She sweet-talked her way into the bedroom of Vladimir Zhirinovsky and got him to take off his pants for a photograph. She had been interviewed in the local press about her photos, and came across as a complete moron.

"I hate Americans," she was quoted as saying. "I was always a Marxist. I'd never date a Republican."

One expat invited me to her photography exhibition, at a gallery off Gogolevsky Bulvar. Why I went, I don't know—one of those masochistic thrills, I suppose. We came to the opening night party. The gallery was impressive in a kind of central European way, newly remodeled, white-painted walls, lacquered parquet floor, expensive industrial light fixtures that hung down from the ceilings. Most in attendance were sub-middlebrow expat barons, dressed as they thought they should for a photo exhibit: tweedy sports coats, moddish skirts, lots of African silver on the necks and wrists. Free wine and cheese and crackers.

The expats crowded into the large room, talking, occasionally whispering about how bad they thought the pictures were, only to hush up if Hollenger rushed up to introduce someone to them. On the other side of the gallery, a small, shady group of fascists, the subjects of her photos, gathered, nervous and out of place. One was bearded and heavy. A few wore Soviet suits and stood uncomfortably, shifting from foot to foot, afraid to go near the wine and Brie, because the expats were gathered there. The only one who moved with ease from fascist to expat was Nazi-lite Sergei Baburin, the suave nationalist Duma deputy.

One of Heidi's friends, an American redhead grad student from Duke, bounced up and down when she saw Baburin. "Introduce me, introduce me!" I heard her cry.

She wore a tight black miniskirt with a skimpy tank top and black pumps, a halfway attempt at playing the *dyevushka,* very out of place on an angry-looking, makeup-less American grad student. Her corpse-white legs were covered in bright red mosquito bites. She didn't even try hiding them. When she met Baburin, he was cordial. He smiled blankly and held out his hand, bored and halfheartedly enjoying the attention. The expat men, for their part, were nervously discussing business and their planned vacations to Italy and Spain, keeping an eye out for Heidi, just in case they had to reiterate, in their loud, positive voices, how much fun they were having.

Heidi was dressed up in a peach dress and pearl necklace, like some sorority girl, entertaining everyone and guffawing in that loud, obnoxious way of hers. She acknowledged me once. "Who's this tall, handsome man?" she said, ironically.

It hurt bad, and triggered my worst panic attack since my stepfather's death. How was it that she—SHE—this MORON—got famous! She didn't deserve it! She'd never paid a red cent for that fame! She did nothing to *earn* it. It wasn't fair, wasn't fair at all. Fame of that sort wasted on a dumb, talentless dilettante who didn't mean a thing she said or did. Stolen from under my feet, scooped, scooped again!

I held that hatred of Hollenger as something sacred, a rallying point for my mind's troops. And issued my own internal *fatwah* to never forget her, to never let her get away with it. "The Hollenger Must Pay!" was chanted at many an angry student demonstration inside of my head, late at night.

So a year and a half after her photo exhibit, I held to my promise and wrote a column slamming her. Then hid. And nothing happened. I expected to run into her somewhere, but didn't. I expected a lawsuit, or a phone call. Instead, I even got a few compliments. As it turned out, most people who knew Hollenger even agreed.

Later, I hurled invective at the editors of the *Moscow Times,* particularly opinion page editor Michael Kazmarek, who'd banned me from ever writing for the *Moscow Times.* He told another journalist friend of mine, "Mark Ames is *exactly* the kind of writer whom I'd never publish in my opinion pages."

Like most cowards, I was emboldened by the lack of violent backlash. My strategy of keeping myself safe, up to that time, had been pretty foolproof. I had a small circle of acquaintances—about two or three—and my Belgian girlfriend.

Now, after getting that piece of hate mail, the honeymoon with Moscow's expat community had ended.

After receiving that letter, I hid for three days inside of my apartment, only slipping out to buy the basics, or to scurry down the block to Suzanne's apartment for some bland, boyfriend-girlfriend sex. The sex only increased the panic. I felt betrayal everywhere. I'd sulk back to my apartment and work and rework my editor's reply to the poison letter, but each one came off as serious and hurt and defensive. So I had to come up with a better response, if I wasn't going to look like an asshole. I had to mask my hurt, and go on the offensive. I couldn't fake James Bond nonchalance, but I could definitely try to fire a salvo of GRAD missiles.

In the next issue, I published the hate letter. And my reply. I was cheap and unfair. I picked apart the grammar mistakes, then, in a cheap shift to racism, accused the authors of hiding the fact that they were really just a lone, envious African student from the People's University in Southeast Moscow. *Fuck you, nigger! Learn how to write grammatical English, or shut the fuck up!* That was my response.

After printing it, I ran back and hid in my apartment, waiting for the building to be burned to the ground. I tried closing my curtains—until I remembered that in my studio, there wasn't even a curtain to close. Just some dark orange cloth hanging from a broken curtain rod. So I left the open part in the far corner, and quickly scuttled past it on my way from bathroom to bed. I waited for several days for the flames to rise, the windows smashed, smoke pouring in. . . . But the days went by, and nothing happened. Nothing at all.

My heroes were always hated figures. When I was seven years old, I discovered the old Oakland Raiders, the Jack Tatum and Kenny Stabler Raiders. Everyone in the suburbs where I lived rooted for the San Francisco 49ers. Declaring your allegiance to the 49ers wasn't just a shallow Sunday afternoon hobby. The 49ers were, in the besieged '70s, the glue that held the white suburban Bay Area together. Like having a Mexican maid and dragging yourself out for a game of tennis. Everything about the 49ers was Eisenhower-America: the red and gold uniforms, the quarterbacks with 4-H Club names like John Brodie and Steve Spurrier. . . . They were the kind of people you'd have a Sunday bar-b-que with. Even their black players were "good" blacks. They were golden retrievers with red bandanas, great for taking into the park and throwing the Frisbee to, harmless and friendly to everyone.

The Raiders, on the other hand, represented the threat to suburbia. In the early and mid-'70s, white suburbia was under siege in California from all sides. With Zebra killers and Black Panthers creeping around, whitey wasn't safe.

The Raiders played dirty, gratuitously—even stupidly so. They'd slug opponents in the head or bite their exposed flesh during a pileup. Jack Tatum put Daryl Stingley in a wheelchair for life after spearing him in the spine. They came from Oakland, home of the Black Panthers. Even the white people on the Raiders didn't look like "our" whites: unshaven, scraggly, overweight, crude, they looked more like truck drivers or Hell's Angels than grown-up homecoming kings. The Raiders didn't do charity functions or bar-b-ques. They banged speed and planted coke on unfriendly journalists. They wore black and silver. And their fans wore shower caps and Activator. They were gods to me. People from the suburbs didn't dare go to the Oakland Coliseum. My great-uncle, a selfless old ham, took me once. He was terrified, and so was I. He stopped making wisecracks the minute we stepped out of his convertible Cadillac in the parking lot, and absorbed the bloodshot stares of 50,000 Schlitz-soaked Negroes. I was eight years old, and I was sure we were both going to die. We escaped alive. It was the only Raiders game I ever went to.

The Raiders were just part of my problem. I was a curious child who always got into trouble. I started down that route at age seven. We broke into a neighbor's stash of Scotch whiskey, and drank so much that the youngest guy in our group nearly died from alcohol poisoning. A few months later, I convinced the same kid to help me try to light a neighbor's estate on fire. She was a crippled widow who lived on a huge hill surrounded by 50-foot high pines and eucalyptus trees. The fire destroyed a shack at the bottom of the hill and about a half acre of land before the firemen put it out. I got off with a warning. A couple of months later, we took sharpened rocks and destroyed the car that belonged to the woman who had called the neighbors on us. Again, a warning, a few tears, and I was off scot-free.

At age eight, I was already a pothead and a kleptomaniac. I stole from every store I could—usually cigarettes, but also candies, posters, trinkets. I could never figure out why they never busted me. . . . The other kids always seemed to get busted. Maybe I was more slippery back then. Another time we went on a joyride in a neighbor's parents' car. The local sheriff ran us off the road. The car reeked of Panama Red. My brother and I got off with warnings; the others were put on probation.

My parents enrolled me in St. Andrews, a private Episcopalian school, in second grade. Two years later, after terrorizing the teachers and students, I was thrown out, and told that I was never allowed back on their property again.

That was when my parents divorced and we dropped a few socioeconomic rungs down the middle-class ladder. The American dream we had tried to live out had been under siege for years by hippies and intellectuals. By the mid-'70s, it was dead, for us at least. The hippies had won. Everything was turning upside down. Even my baby-sitters were fucked-up hippies. They were always wigging out on some drug or other when they came over. My parents had no idea: they were just getting used to the new world of singles bars and group therapy. Sometimes the baby-sitters' hippie boyfriends would come over and chew me and my brother out for molesting their teenage girlfriends. They were real disgusting trolls, those hippie boyfriends. One of them even smacked me. He's one smelly, hairy reason why I joined the Republican Party in the mid-'80s.

By high school, my spleen kicked into high gear. After getting stomped by jocks, I withdrew into the hills of my mind and trained. I learned how to be far meaner than the inarticulate surf-rats. How to hurt without getting hurt. It earned me the reputation of a real jerk. People talked about my problems at home. They talked a lot back then, about things I'd rather not get into. Let's just say that I took it all out on those who a) were meanest to me, and b) least likely to beat me up. That is: popular girls. I sent at least three of them packing from our high school, and helped trigger bulemia complexes in a few others.

I played football and tried to live out my heroes' lives

from the Raiders of my childhood. I played defensive end, and I played cheap. My trademark was my "rip": I'd swat the opposing lineman's helmet with my padded fist, ringing his ears long enough for me to slip by.

In the last game of my my junior season, playing against Monte Vista High, a 225-pound black tight end complained to me. He told me to stop swatting him in the head. I didn't. Then the ref told me to stop. And I didn't. So the next play, he grabbed me by my jersey, ran me out near the sideline, lifted up the breast plate of my shoulder pads, and peppered me in the diaphragm with his fists, about thirty lightning blows, until I was blue and sucking for air. I lay on my back like a roach soaked in Raid, twitching. The ref watched the whole thing. I crawled up to the ref, and, gasping, wheezed, "He . . . *hhhie!* . . . can't . . . *hhhie!* . . . do . . . *hhhhhhiieee!* . . . that . . . *hhhie!*" The ref shrugged. Ending my dreams of becoming Jack Tatum.

These incidents are the exciting parts, the bad-boy ones. But the other 99 percent of the time I spent playing the coward and collaborator, trying and failing to fit in with middle-class suburban California, vacillating between repeated failed attempts at trying to fit in, shame, and raw hatred.

No matter how much I tried stirring things up, I couldn't even make a tiny ripple in the waters. The flat suburbs couldn't be shaken. Not even the San Andreas Fault could fuck my suburb up.

My imagination, by most standards, was starting to take a major detour. The "R"-rated violent movies that they began showing in the early-'70s gave form to dormant fantasies. The earliest one I remember seeing was *Bluebeard,* a B-movie which graphically showed each mistress getting murdered in her own special way. Those murders were catalogued in my memory, and slated for permanent rerun on the local syndicate.

When *Jaws* came out, I was eight years old. I was so enthralled by the movie—particularly the scene where the half-eaten head floats out from under a boat wreck—that I bought the book and devoured it. I'll never forget the way that Peter Benchley described that first shark mauling of the hippie girl in the surf: "crushing her organs like jelly . . . "

When I started writing, it was because I wanted to reproduce that effect on myself that Benchley had produced on me. Most of the rest of the book was oddly bland, suburb-bland: adult relationships, affairs, divorce . . . familiar stuff, filler between the shark's mangle-feasts. My attitude was, why not make the shark maulings the main part of the book, while the other stuff, the boring humans with their little, boring problems, just glossed over?

Years later, in a creative writing course at Berkeley, our teacher, Thom Gunn, asked us all to say why we chose to be writers. All of the students gave pretentious answers that they'd probably read in *Paris Review* interviews or literary biographies. My own, which I thought was honest, was:

"I write because everything I read sucks, so I hope one day to write something readable."

I told that to Dr. Dolan, who was at the time a Rhetoric professor of mine. "Why didn't you just tell them the truth?" he said. "Tell them the reasons you write are vanity and spleen."

I remember being shocked. I'd never thought about it from that angle. I admired Dolan's cynicism, but I took it as just that: reactionary nihilism colder and cleverer than my own. I couldn't believe that the only reason I'd write was to become famous. The spleen part—yeah, that was obvious. But vanity? If I was merely vain, then I'd write vaguely sentimental workshop fiction stuff, quiet, diminished Raymond Carver stories with ever-so-slight epiphanies. But what I was writing—it was bound to get me nowhere.

Then I graduated. And that's when I ran into that massive, scary wall of Beigeism. It was so large and immovable that it couldn't even be measured. A wall impossible to breach.

I met Edward Limonov nine months after moving to Moscow. Limonov had been one of the reasons I chose to move to Russia. Two of Limonov's books in translation, *Memoirs of a Russian Punk* and *His Butler's Story*, are, in my opinion, the best works of fiction published in the '80s. The former book painted a portrait of provincial Soviet Russia that made me salivate: violent, cruel, and yet full of possibility for a kind of minor epic life. The latter book made me writhe in envy for being about the only honest, nonliterary account of modern America I'd read. What really drove me crazy was *His Butler's* plot: would Limonov get published and famous, thus allowing him to get laid more easily, or not? It was so cynical and antithetical to everything that 20th-century literature had preached, and yet, it was . . . honest. For the sheer bravery of it all, he deserved my awe.

I had heard about Limonov's lecture through his former publisher, the gay journalist and poet, Sasha Shatalov. I knew Shatalov because, a few months after moving to Moscow, I decided that I had to ingratiate myself into Limonov's circle. I tracked Sasha down at the Writer's Union; we met, and became friends. Shatalov is a shaven-headed, bucktoothed intellectual with a penchant for scandal. When I met him, his former lover, the young journalist Yaroslav Mogutin, had just dumped him for an American artist, Robert Fillipini. I had the sense, in my meetings with Shatalov, that he was hoping to score me and get back at his old lover. And I led him on a little bit, never making clear my aversion to cock until I was able to get close enough to his star writer, Limonov.

It was at a library lecture that I met Limonov. The library was well lit and not too different from any neighborhood library in America, except that it was in the bottom floor of one of the zillions of block apartment buildings. The audience ranged from old literary ladies dressed to the hilt to younger, half-nerdy college-age girls. Shatalov brought me backstage, into a small square office with a couple of librarians. Limonov paced back and forth, in his black leather jacket, black jeans, and black boots. He was, of course, "smaller than I'd expected," which is to say, as tall as every star ever is. When Sasha introduced me, he told Limonov that I wasn't a "typical American." I clumsily broke into an anecdote about seeing the Grazhdanskoye Oborona riot, and told him that *Podrostok Savenko* was my favorite novel. He seemed mildly impressed. I realized that I was light-years away from his plane of fame, that we were communicating from different universes.

Limonov was cordial, if a little nervous, around me. I was completing a manuscript at the time, *Skin Plows*, about my bout with the worst episode of scabies that anyone had ever suffered in modern medical history. It's still not the kind of book that I'd like to show to anyone I know.

A nervous middle-aged woman with huge horn-rimmed glasses and red hair piled up into a bun stuck her head into the room and announced that the lecture should begin. I nearly bumped into Limonov trying to walk through the door—like one of those slapstick scenes where the big guy and little guy get squeezed in the doorframe . . . "Uh, heh-heh, you first . . . "

When we walked out into the main hall, I couldn't believe how many people had shown up: there must have been almost a hundred, seated in cheap plastic or wooden chairs arranged in rows. A hundred people, almost all women! In a library! In Russia! I took a seat near the back, and scanned the faces, noticing, to my further horror/envy, that at least one-quarter of the hall consisted of attractive student types, who had taken the time to make up their eyes and cheeks and lips, set their hair, and wear their finest respectable lace and faux-silk blouses.

Limonov stuck to political issues, although most in the crowd wanted to talk about his writing. He paced back and forth, making little eye contact. He told the crowd that literature was, for him, too effete, that his only interest was politics and revolutionary struggle. He compared himself to George Orwell and Ernest Hemingway, recounting, in his half-bored, half-raspy voice, his battle experiences starting in Yugoslavia, where he fought on the side of the Serbs in Bosnia and Krajina, up to the last, failed battle at the White House in 1993. The day after that White House battle, there had been rumors that Limonov had been killed. Or that he'd been wounded. . . . Then came news that Limonov had gone underground. After the Duma granted an amnesty to those who had taken part in the uprising, Limonov came out of hiding. It was an epic story that I was determined to deflate.

During the question and answer part, I rocked nervously in my seat, thinking about how I could penetrate his fame-shield. "*The slow blade penetrates the shield* . . . " No, I never believed that line. Too Zen for my tastes. I knew what to ask him—Dr. Dolan and I had discussed this issue many times.

Finally, after getting the Russian words properly arranged in my head, I stood up and asked: "You said in your book *His Butler's Story* that you wanted to die in a hail of bullets, in a great battle. But you wanted to wait until you were famous enough to make your death worthwhile, so that your death would be reported on the front pages. When I read that you were in the White House during the battle in October, I admired and even envied you, until I found out that you survived. So my question is: *Why didn't you die?*"

He was stunned. A low rumble of laughter rippled in the audience. A few turned and stared at me. Limonov stumbled, then offered a weak answer, about how a comrade had died in his arms and bled on his jacket. He knew I was right: By his own aesthetic standards, he should have been killed in the White House and been made a martyr of the Dark Side. He claimed to have nearly died, but that wasn't good enough, not for an envious lit-twerp like me.

Afterward, Limonov sat at a table to sign books. People lined up a mile long to get their book signed. One girl, young and attractive, asked me for my autograph, thinking I was a writer. She approached me with large, wet brown eyes and an inviting smile. I fled. Later, much later, when I sat alone in my communal apartment room, punching my pillow and biting my knuckles, I regretted—no, not just regretted, I *denounced* that. I denounced that and denounced myself and promised both to punish the guilty (me) and replace myself with a new, quick-thinking, brighter version of me. I replayed that foolish reaction, that simpering "aw-gee-shucks" idiocy, and realized, no, I hadn't changed.

The Limonov X-Files

In Praise of a Sick Punk Newspaper

by Edward Limonov

I have met Mark few years ago, in apartment of my publisher Alexander Schatalov, or to be precise, at Schatalov's kitchen. Most of a Russian's friendships are started in kitchens, no doubts. Mark appeared to me as American should be - a huge, big man, wearing a boots of fifties size, or at least size forty eight. Mark said that he read few of my books published in the United States, and that he liked my books. Then we lost each other for a few years.

One day somebody gave me a newspaper called if I am not mistaken *Novaya Gazeta* with an article signed by Mark. It was entitled "Limonov is not punk, but Zhirinovsky is rotten." In his article Mark wanted to say that Zhirinovsky is more punkish than me, Limonov. I was offended at that statement, as I believe that I am most punkish person on whole territory of Russian Republic and probably on all territory of ex-Soviet Union also. Maybe Shamil Basaev is comparable with me. So, for a while I was angry at Mark, for his preferring Zhirinovksy. Then we have met again when Mark came to my party "bunker" accompanied by a man called Manfred, they together wanted to publish newspaper and they wanted me to collaborate, to write some articles for their newspaper.

I said "Yes", I will write in my broken English, boys, and you will type it, preserving my terrible Russian English style, please. Mark was surprised that I wasn't angry at him anymore for his preference of Zhirinovsky. Meanwhile, as time have passed, Mark understood by himself that Zhirinovsky is much less punk than Limonov is. To be a chairman of National Bolshevik's Party is tougher occupation than to be a chairman of Liberal Democratic Party, isn't it?

After some time Mark splitted from Manfred and started to publish *eXile*. For some time I wrote for two competing English language newspapers, then Manfred gave up, and now *eXile* is only one of its kind on the Moscow's market.

I should say that Mark's paper is probably the freest English language publication in whole world. And craziest as well. I am sure that such publication is impossible to publish and maintain in the United States or elsewhere. Only in Moscow's climate of permanent revolution of conscience is possible to publish such a sick, crazy and funny paper as *eXile* or my National Bolshevik's *Limonka*. I imagine that in ten years time some American and Russian university professors will be studying *eXile* as a cultural and political phenomenon. The changing of one political regime by another one is profitable to incredible freedom. Such freedom will not last for long. But I am happy to live now, to be an editor of a revolutionary *Limonka* and to collaborate in extravagant *eXile*. Your hand, Mister Mark! Troublemakers of the whole world, unite you!

But it will be fair to repeat, Mark, that Limonov is more punkish than Zhirinovsky is.

After the lecture, I followed Limonov out of the library and walked him to the metro stop. On the way down that long, deep escalator, designed to protect the population from nuclear-bombing raids, I asked him how he copes with being a hated, controversial writer. I wouldn't let him leave until I got some answers. He was, after all, the only writer who served as a sort of light for me.

"When you get published, people don't judge you anymore in that way. They sense you have some power," Limonov explained in that emotionless tone he adopts with strangers. "It doesn't matter if you write disgusting things. What matters is if you are published and seen as being powerful. Then everyone treats you with respect."

Afterward, he disappeared in a metro car, not too happy to have a big, hairy American fan stalk him with questions. Not after the way I'd treated him in the lecture. He disappeared into his parallel fame-plane, in that inaccessible dimension so many dimensions above my own. He was untouchable up there.

A few months later, in a glowing example of my gratitude, fulfilling the Sonic Youth ethic of "Kill Your Idols," I wrote a vicious attack on Limonov's incarnation as a fascist, accusing him of being a cynical marketing whiz looking to move more product and maintain his fame. I published it in both the English-language and Russian-language press, and it eventually made it into Limonov's hands.

I tried converting that one article into a permanent position as a humor columnist for the *Moscow Times*, particularly since their other columnists were so bland. Marc Champion, the pencil-necked Brit editor, agreed that it might be a good idea to have a more "humorous, colorful" writer like myself, so he asked me to send him some column-samples. The next week, I sent him three samples. I read the columns over and over, imagining how he might react, eagerly anticipating a new life.

That's when Champion stopped taking my calls.

Finally, I barged into the *Moscow Times* offices and demanded an explanation. He sat me down in his glass-enclosed, Ben Bradlee–editor's office, overlooking the newsroom, and delivered his "fuck off and leave me alone" address to me in his quiet, deliberate, educated British voice: "The problem is that the Moscow community doesn't want or need a Hunter Thompson, which is how I see your columns. Your writing is trenchant but *too violent*." He paused, sighed, then continued with the condescending tone of a high school counselor. "If this was the sixties, a really crazy time, then you could justify that sort of wild Hunter Thompson style of writing [!]. But Moscow is a business community. There's just no market for your style of writing. It's not—how do I say this?—it's not *appropriate* to Moscow."

Oh my, what could I say? If he didn't see it, there was no chance of opening his eyes. In fact, Moscow was a thousand times more wild and violent than the '60s of San Francisco. I was awake at the tail end of that period: It was nothing, a family argument, a few plates tossed against the cupboard, compared to Moscow.

But I lost. I thanked him in my twerpish way, then sulked down the hallway of editor's offices, doors half-open, heads leaning to get a peak at me. That was it. Game's up. It was my first reencounter with the local Beigeists' colonial representative, and I lost. I was routed, in fact, by their age-old weapon: silencers. Their twisted, hyper-edited, Orwellian view of the world even applied to Russia. Here we were, living in the vortex of one of the century's greatest cataclysms, an economic and social apocalypse, in the capital of one of the world's last great empires . . . but according to Champion, it's "not the sixties," that "really crazy time" . . .

I wanted to hang myself—if it wasn't going to happen here, it wasn't going to happen anywhere. I gave up writing, and took the job as the personal assistant to a rich Pakistani businessman. In a matter of a few months, I got caught up in the high world of finance. I was wearing a suit every day to work, power lunching with bankers from Credit Suisse First Boston, Morgan Stanley . . . going to conferences in London . . . helping to manage Russia's first private placement, working with Deutsche Morgan Grenfell, Norton Rose law firm . . . a world I'd never be allowed access to in America had I stayed (and never would have wanted access to) was suddenly mine, in the same way that a baron's lackey was allowed into the aristocracy—a physical, though not spiritual, presence. It was bizarre, that rise of mine into the world of finance—a sort of late-20th-century Moll Flanders, I guess. I made it through for almost two years. I had to do a lot of lying, to wear a mask heavy and thick. It grew more and more uncomfortable as time went by.

Then, unexpectedly, the *Times* printed a second "opinion piece" that I'd written but which Champion had shelved for almost eight months, for fear of alienating "the community." It was titled, "The Rise and Fall of Moscow's Expat Royalty"; in it, I wrote about how once-condescending expats had been overthrown by a new elite of rich Russians, leading to a severe case of "fiscal envy," and causing resentment and bitterness. Expats had fallen from the status of local aristocrats who had once scorned the natives into the role of a kind of petite bourgeoisie, complaining about the high prices and the vulgar wealth. And they couldn't take it on the chin with dignity.

The piece was a sensation by local standards; Champion himself admitted that the *Times* had never printed anything that drew so many letters. When I went to pick up my $125 from the *Moscow Times,* I poked my head into Champion's office to thank him again. He looked stunned—and thinner. Giardia-thin, not healthy-thin. He'd cut his hair and dyed it a sort of dirty yellow, and changed wire-rimmed glasses frames to something a little hipper.

"I heard you guys got a lot of letters from my article," I bragged.

He grimaced, and admitted that he'd never seen an article draw such a reader response. "You really touched a nerve," he said, jabbing his editor's pen into the air for emphasis. It sickened me to get that little concession out of him. He swept back behind some deputies, reverse-fog following him like some caped villain, and that was the last we ever saw of each other.

They were still publishing hate mail a month and a half after the article. But all that hate mail only scared Champion and his new über-Beigeist opinion page editor, Michael Kazmarek. Kazmarek told me that he didn't agree with my article, and, therefore, he wouldn't be looking for any future pieces from me. He also said that he had received a letter in support of my article from a Russian office manager. "I didn't believe it was real, so I called her up. I thought you'd planted it," he said.

That article led to the community's hating me, to expats sneering at me everywhere I went. I was even stopped on the streets twice by expats who noticed me, just to tell me what an asshole I was for writing that piece. . . .

"I'm soooooo jealous of the New Russians and their wealth," one American real estate woman sarcastically screeched into my face when we passed on Kutuzovsky

Prospekt. I got phone calls from people asking, "Did you write that? Aren't you . . . embarrassed?"

A few weeks later, I was offered my very own column at *Living Here*, and eventually, having earned enough fame and enmity, it led to the *eXile*.

I didn't expect much from *Living Here*. I thought I might, if I was lucky, get a few compliments from some greasy student-nerds. Maybe a line of free coke, an inviting smile from some half-attractive Russian literary student, the kind with long, oily hair and a sallow complexion, whose lithe body, trapped in bland *Univermag* clothing, showed promise. What I did expect was a violent backlash; or, if not violent, then at least the kind of weaponry used on me back home: the quiet closing down of my one venue. The silence-bomb.

Neither happened. In fact, the more I hammed it up, the more popular I became.

Anyway, it wasn't as if I'd had a choice. I started writing my *Living Here* columns at the age of 30. It's a little late to change and try to write "responsible," Beigeist articles when you're 30 years old and for the previous 23 years, you've been pretty much isolated from and in opposition to the mainstream reader, working on coming up with a line as memorable as "crushed her organs like jelly . . . "

So, as Jake La Motta might have said, I wrote the only way I knew how to write. Strangely enough, the more repulsive my first-person romps through the epic flames and torn panties of Moscow, the more free drugs and willing girls came my way. Lots of them. I didn't expect it, because my heroes, mostly punks and cult writers, never told me that there were regular perks to irregular aesthetics. Dolan tried to tell me, but I didn't take him seriously. I thought it was just more envy-inspired cynicism on his part, and not kind words of advice from a mentor.

I found out the positive meaning of fame at *Living Here*'s first year anniversary party, on September 20, 1996. We held it at the Duck, knowing that a party at the Duck couldn't possibly fail. Even if *Living Here* couldn't attract more than the five or six friends and hangers-on, the Duck was guaranteed to attract its usual, motley sardine-can crowd of second-rate Russians, alcoholics, sluts, off-duty cops, drug dealers, and rednecks.

It was the first *Living Here* party that I attended. I usually avoided them because I was afraid that either they'd fail, or I'd get attacked. Not physically attacked—that I could deal with—but verbally attacked. So I got blistered drunk beforehand, and emceed the event. Afterward, something happened that I'd never experienced before: Girls made themselves easily available, not for who I was, but for what I was. Several of them, including a young married Russian girl who worked at *Elle*, some other teenager type, and Lyuda, a sort of chunky "Westernized" Russian who worked at the International Medical Clinic. I was still seeing Suzanne. She was in Belgium at the time, and I was supposed to fly out and meet her the next day.

I took full advantage. I must have rammed my tongue down three or four girls' throats, before grabbing Lyuda and leading her out on the balcony of the Duck. You reach the balcony by crawling through the windows on the side of the bar—it's actually a flat roof more than a balcony, and this night was a little too cold for people to use it. When I led her through the window, we were alone on the balcony, kissing.

Wednesday, October 4, 1995

The Rise an

By Marc Ames

My first day in Moscow was a shock. Not because of the dirty streets, the rude clerks or other banal inconveniences (which I'd expected), but rather because of the foreigners themselves. I was standing in the lounge of Park Place with a group of Americans in September 1993 when the manager introduced himself: "I'm sorry I'm late for the softball tournament, but my Russian workers are pathetic." When he heard that I'd just arrived in Moscow, he shook his head, put his hand on my shoulder and said, "You know, the difference between Russian workers and children is that at least you can teach children."

His attitude was the rule, not the exception — at least among those Westerners in the overwhelmingly expat softball tournament. At night, a group of Americans took me to all-expat bars; later, in Western conveyances, they raced back to their Western-standard apartments under fear of the night. It was like an automated 18th century, with the expats as a kind of functional aristocracy, and the Russian masses as — the masses.

In the modern mind, the aristocracy is marked by two characteristics: birthright and downfall. It is due to their birthright, to the fact that the aristocracy didn't have to earn its exalted place in society, that they eventually grew complacent, dull-witted — and were toppled by those who had to work harder, who understood reality a bit better. Right up to and beyond their downfall, the aristocrats are known to have shown a deep contempt for the masses — a contempt in which, considering the French or Russian revolutions, the last blood-stained laugh was on them.

We Westerners who showed up in Moscow in the early dawn of postcommunism were elevated to a sort of aristocracy merely because of a kind of birthright: our passports. In keeping with the script, it didn't take long for most Westerners here — particularly those who came to make a buck — to develop a condescending attitude towards the

OPINION The Moscow Times ✦ 9

nd Fall of Moscow's Expat 'Royalty'

natives, a condescension that often slipped into sheer contempt.

Contempt, though, often leads to tragedy, and complacency leads to the final chapter of the nobility's script: the downfall. Nowhere has this been more evident than in that most blue-blooded branch of Moscow's expat aristocracy, the American Expat. We Americans were granted an exalted status the minute we landed, something we're not used to in Europe. So when the red carpet was pulled from under our feet, we fell hardest.

American expatriates can be divided into two easily recognizable categories. The first is the Ugly, or "typical," American: the culturally insensitive vulgarian — the briefcase-toting bull in World Culture's china shop. The other is the Ugly American's awry twin, the Bohemian American: pious public-television types in thrift-store uniforms who tend to define themselves in inverse proportion to the Ugly American. Russia has been inhabited mostly by Ugly Americans, the sort of creature who will endure the most savage conditions in order to buff up his or her resume. Your average Bohemian American cannot sustain a progressive world view in Russia.

Something awful has happened to Americans in the last year. We've become nastier, wounded. We've taken a fall in economic prestige.

A few months back, I was at an American timeshare dacha for a little get-together with a bunch of young expats, the type for whom a special discount really is better than sex.

Out of the blue, one of the guests launched into an invective against the Russian mafia — not because of anything they'd done to his business but because of what they'd done to his self-esteem. "This so-called mafia is a complete joke," he sneered. "In America, we'd just call them 'gangs.'"

He was, of course, completely wrong. The real joke — as the so-called mafiosi cruise past our Nivas in their 600-series Mercedes and sit atop unimaginable piles of offshore wealth — is on us, and any ambitious American businessman who dares to acknowledge this fact inevitably suffers from a severe case of fiscal envy. For any decent American, fiscal envy is the final pit stop before an open Prozac prescription.

What interested me most was the instinct that clouded the embittered American's perception. He reflected not at all the aristocrat's contempt he was trying to market to us (a contempt that we desperately wanted to buy), but rather a deep resentment. Resentment is perhaps the single ugliest human emotion, more unappealing than raw hatred or Chess King clothing. But after all, resentment and contempt are nearly biochemical twins, differentiated only by point of view. Contempt reflects a position of strength and resentment, a position of weakness. This means that we expatriate Americans are today perceiving Russia from an altogether different frame. Now we American expats are the economically vanquished, priced out of our palaces, which makes holding the title *de l'America* painfully humiliating. What happened?

When I first arrived, real condescension and contempt dominated the typical American-expat operating system. But it was clear I'd arrived at the end of our reign: 1789, 1917, 1993.

Moscow reminded me a lot of the Arnold Schwarzenegger film *Total Recall*: In raising the *Total Recall* analogy to today's Russia, I am not referring to the outdated Marxist metaphor of capitalist exploitation, but rather to very concrete similarities: The film's depiction of the Terran monopoly over the Mutants' oxygen supply is roughly similar to today's precious Western aid that is carelessly dangled before a desperate Russian populace. Terran (Western) businessmen act out the white-collar fantasy equivalent to action-adventure heroes, leading a life among the elite 1 percent of the economic aristocracy in a way that would never have been possible on Terra (in the West).

The only part of the *Total Recall* plot that's missing is the ending: a brutal, flesh-ripping uprising against the Terrans, and the ultimate victory of the Mutants.

But wait: The uprising came after all, although the blood has only been metaphorical — an economic bloodletting, in which most Westerners got left in the gold dust. Most of my friends from 1993, including the American entrepreneur who first invited me to Russia, have returned home with little to show but chronic heart palpitations and a falsified paragraph in their resumes.

It's painful to admit how far we fell — but what really stokes my latent paranoia is what the future holds. Imagine this: American expats peering longingly into the windows of overpriced Moscow restaurants and whining bitterly about the prices while the garish all-Russian clientele, with a mixture of unease and contempt, whispers, "Hey, if these Americans are so great, why did they have to leave home in the first place?"

Marc Ames is a writer living in Moscow. He contributed this article to The Moscow Times.

"I'll do anything you want," she tells me.

Lyuda immediately undoes my pants, then drops to her knees. I saw, through the window, a group of nerds pointing at us and trying to break through their window. They rallied their other friends, and pointed excitedly. Then I grabbed Lyuda and dragged her to the far end of the balcony, turned her around, pulled her pants down, and fucked her in the ass.

CHAPTER SEVEN

That was when I understood, in the most clear, unmediated sort of way, what it was to be famous. It was, frankly, better than any drug or sexual experience: Fame is the sum of those experiences. Later, on my flight out to Paris to meet my girlfriend, I began to rue, well in advance, the fact that I could easily lose this fame. It was so tenuous. It was, I felt, "out of my hands." That's when I first recalled that moment in *Apocalypse Now*, when the Robert Duvall character surveys the falling shells, the lilting helicopters, the bursts of machine-gun fire, the screaming wounded, and the smell of napalm, then says sadly, to no one but himself, "Someday, this war's gonna end . . . "

In the months before *Living Here* collapsed and we started up the *eXile,* I was really riding on the clouds of small-time fame. The money was bad, but the perks were good. I'd split up with my girlfriend, I was meeting women with relative ease, I was getting treated to free drinks and plenty of heroin. It was the most valuable lesson in my life, and the moral was: Anyone who settles for less is an asshole.

When Matt and I first agreed to work together, I blew a huge sigh of relief. The greatest threat to having my perks pulled had been removed. I'd still have my Black Sea dacha, my ZiL and Moscow apartment—that is, I'd have my little plot of fame.

In Matt, I detected, with some unease, that underneath his jock-ish, unpretentious exterior, there lurked gargantuan Ego dying to be noticed. You could hear it every time Taibbi laughed. Anywhere you go with him—restaurants, bars, business meetings—that laugh of his turns heads. At first, people laugh in response. Then they start to complain. In the case of our former partners, they grew to despise him, and did anything to get away from that laugh—even returning to America.

But I heard that laugh, and I thought—*there's my Hitler!*

In our first meeting, I got the sense that Taibbi was sort of dicking around. He talked about "just having a good time" and "going out there and having fun," sports clichés that he'd carried with him from his days as a jock. One thing I liked about Taibbi was that he was an unabashed jock. Few intellectuals have the courage to be authentic jocks. When I arrived at Berkeley, I spent two years slimming down to that punk-poet bony affectation before realizing, Oh shit, I've fucked up! Being in strong physical shape is much better than being a thin jerk, and I threw it all away just so none of these frog-faced shits would accuse me of being a jock. Yet another bad career move, on par with moving into the European Care Home.

Taibbi clearly never suffered from those complexes. And he didn't seem to take this whole thing quite as seriously as I did. The main thing, from his point of view, was that he didn't want to go back to the *Moscow Times.* We were on the same page there.

I told him that he should write a book on his experience as a professional basketball player in Mongolia. But he soon gave that up. "I can't stand writing about myself," he said, cringing at the thought. "I get a chapter into it, and I can't go on. I make myself sick."

The good thing about that was, as I saw it, Taibbi would be one of those hustlers who works "behind the scenes," who gives it a hundred 'n ten percent, but leaves the glory part to the quarterback. Sounded fine with me.

What I didn't expect after hooking Taibbi was that he'd start to steal my thunder. Within a couple of weeks, he had TV cameras in the office interviewing him, radio stations calling him . . . while Kara was telling me that word on the

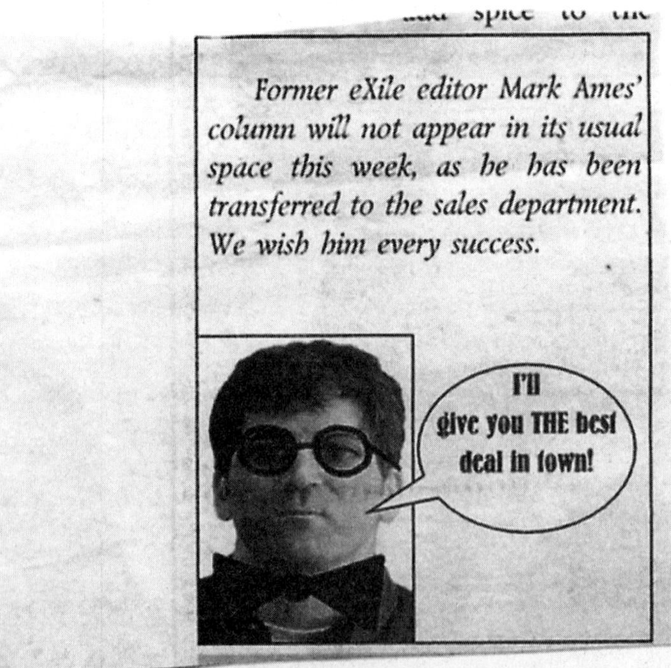

Former eXile editor Mark Ames' column will not appear in its usual space this week, as he has been transferred to the sales department. We wish him every success.
I'll give you THE best deal in town!

There's probably nothing more sickening than the Anglo-American tradition of "laughing at yourself." But sometimes, there's no other choice. After Taibbi joined the *eXile*, word on the street was that Ames had been axed.

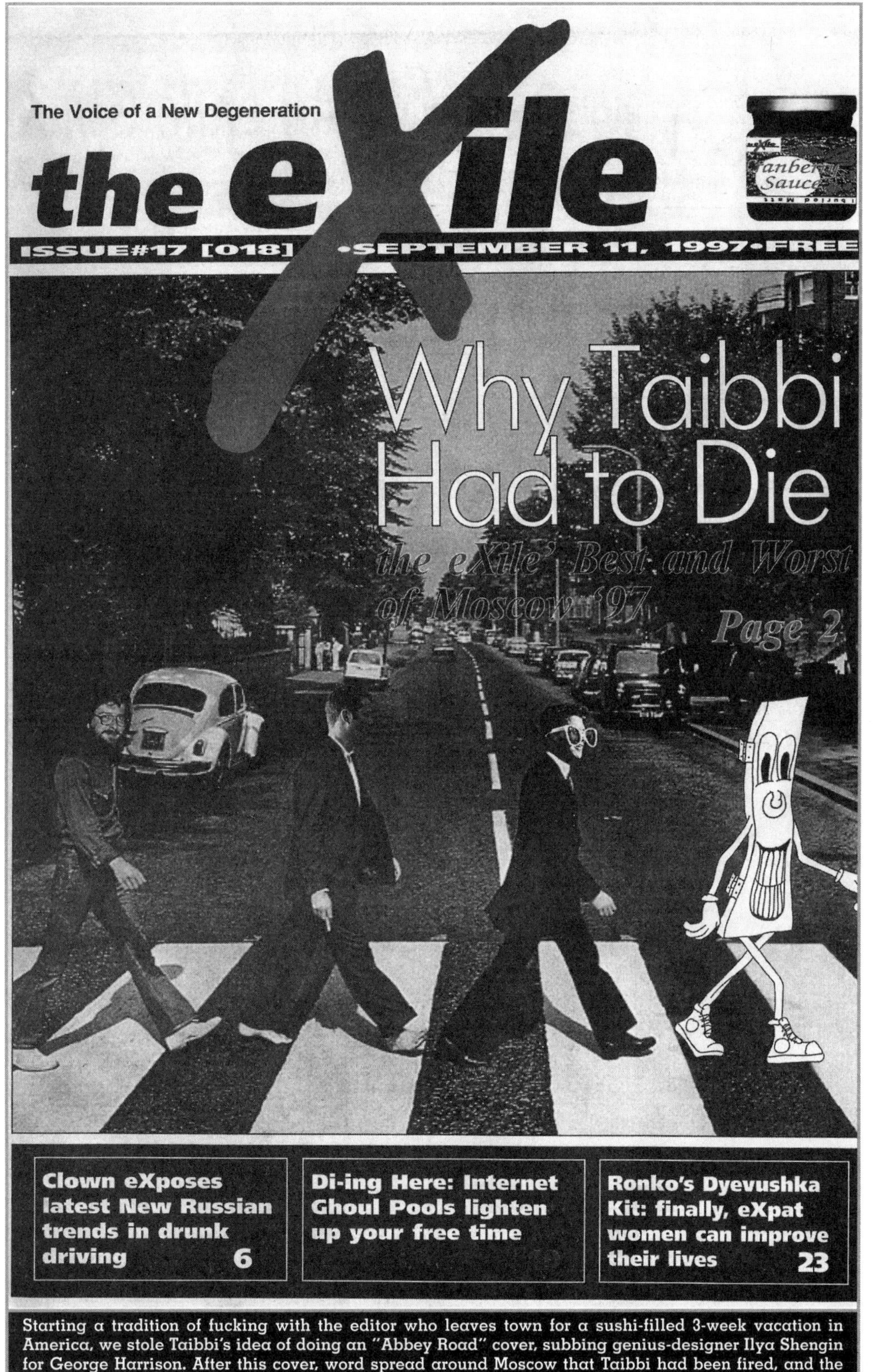
The Voice of a New Degeneration

the eXile

ISSUE#17 [018] •SEPTEMBER 11, 1997•FREE

Why Taibbi Had to Die

the eXile' Best and Worst of Moscow '97

Page 2

Clown eXposes latest New Russian trends in drunk driving 6

Di-ing Here: Internet Ghoul Pools lighten up your free time

Ronko's Dyevushka Kit: finally, eXpat women can improve their lives 23

Starting a tradition of fucking with the editor who leaves town for a sushi-filled 3-week vacation in America, we stole Taibbi's idea of doing an "Abbey Road" cover, subbing genius-designer Ilya Shengin for George Harrison. After this cover, word spread around Moscow that Taibbi had been fired, and the *eXile* was going downhill. It was the third of about ten periods when the *eXile* had "gone downhill."

street had it that I'd quit the newspaper, that Taibbi was running everything. Worse, everyone said the paper improved after Taibbi joined. I had agreed with him that we needed to add respectability and credibility to the paper, precisely so that we could hit bigger targets and make it hurt (we shared a loathing for journalists in particular). The problem was, all that respectability we acquired was chalked up to his joining.

At first, I'll admit it was tough to swallow. I hope, looking back, I didn't make too much of a jealous ass of myself. Before he joined, I knew this might happen. But my choices were limited: I could fight Taibbi and possibly lose everything, or join up with him, the way the Russian mafia joined up with the Cosa Nostra, and divide up the fame dividends between us. Also, I figured the competition and new blood would be good for me—it would discipline my own writing.

But what I didn't realize was how eager Taibbi was to take the self-promotion shtick and run with it. He'd already been on three TV programs before I'd finished tying my shoes in the

20 Years of Humor Conquest

In the year 2017, the eXpats were demonstrating outside the eXile corporate headquarters in Brussels

eXile

Sirs, the readers are revolting again!

Get there!

AMES

TAIBBI

Assholes. Should we pour the molten lead?

Are you crazy, Mark? That's way too expensive! Let's use bullets

BAM!

BAM!

eXile

Your turn

I count six, Matt

ZING

Man, this has been going on for months now

Jesus... How did it come to this?

the eXile

LES N

Xmopolitan

XBoy

XWeek

When we collapsed right after the launch of our weekly issue in 1998, we had no idea we'd ever be in this position...

Christ, those idiots still can't proofread

eXile

NIDE WERK

We were willing to do anything to promote the cause of independent journalism

You understand that our loan is contingent upon a radical change in your editorial policy

IMF LOAN

No problem

We were just about to suggest that ourselves!

After we secured the loan, we went right back to work fighting hypocrisy

the eXile

GO CHUBAIS!

Public funding forced us to take a more professional approach

FWHHHT!

As long as we kept downsizing every year, the IMF kept giving us emergency loans

You're all fired, but here's a free copy of the eXile

You can stay-- with a pay cut

the eXile

Market economy. No pain no gain

We moved on to attract top-flight corporate sponsors

The realist uses... Tide!

Death porn brought to you by Union Carbide

From there, we only needed one more investor to complete our expansion...

The eXile business plan

Just take a look at the bottom line

H'm. I'll have Stan Grossman take a look at these numbers

With His help, we were able to control the entire world's output of humor. And we kept it all for ourselves

HA-HA-HA-HA

I don't know what they're complaining about

It's just good business

OH-OH!

ROMAN 98

morning. His articles were getting reprinted in the Russian press. One morning I walked into the office, and there was an entire TV crew surrounding Matt, with the lights on. I didn't exactly see him, but I heard him yell out in a cheerful voice: "Hey, Mark! Sorry about this! Do you wanna just come back in about a half hour? I'll be done by then!" I heard his trademark laugh bellow—I couldn't see him, but I could pinpoint him aurally—somewhere behind the lights and the guy with the mike and tape recorder. I rolled my sorry ass out of there, and took a long walk. . . . If my ego was Jabba the Hut, then his was the Death Star itself. I was already yesterday's news. Everyone was referring to him as "the editor of the *eXile*." We even received a few calls. "Is Ames still with the paper?" "The *eXile* sure got better since Ames left."

This couldn't go on. I started thinking of "accidents" that might happen to him on one of his crazy "Working Here" stories. . . .

(AP) MOSCOW—A Boston-born journalist was killed in Moscow yesterday during a freak accident at the Moscow City Zoo. Superintendents found the body of Matt Taibbi, 27, torn to shreds in the orangutan park. The orangutans were seen playing catch with his head, while his femur bone was being used as a weapon by another orangutan to establish dominance during this, the traditional mating season.

Taibbi's partner, deputy editor Mark Ames, was the first to arrive on the scene.

"I'm shocked and saddened by this tragic event," Ames said, clutching a photograph of the deceased editor and wearing a black armband over his brand-new suit. "But we will go on. Matt would have wanted it this way."

On the other hand, the *eXile*'s popularity really began to take off, and since I was strapped in for the ride, I had to be grateful to Taibbi for that.

Sometimes I wonder if I've betrayed my own revolution. Is this what it was all about? Is this why I paid all those years? Just for sex and drugs? Well—yeah, what the fuck! And lemme tell ya: The People in me are grateful. Grateful for The Revolution that freed them from the bonds of American banality. They're marching in formation down Red Square, having replaced "Land, Bread and Peace" with "Sex, Drugs and Fame." And "Death to the Paradigm Blob," referring of course to that monstrous universe I escaped from. When you have Sex, Drugs and Fame, when you've escaped the bondage of centrist serfdom, you don't need land, bread, or peace. Or rather, you have land, bread, and peace.

Still, Ours is a totally unfinished revolution. It will never be safe so long as that Paradigm Blob in America and its agents—those well-meaning, pious, cruel expatriates—are pushed back far enough that they cannot threaten the superior counterparadigm that Russia offers.

Actually creating a rival superpower, a competing context—that's another task. The only *real* task that the *eXile* has.

When Taibbi joined the *eXile*, we finally had the possibility to freeze The Blob, to hurt the people who would, with the best intentions, destroy everything unfamiliar in Russia. We'd agreed, in our policy discussions, that we wanted to give the newspaper more surface respectability, in order to expand our influence. Matt insisted that we adhere to a few basic journalistic tenets, such as never misquoting anyone. Facts would be double-checked. Targets carefully chosen. Matt was right: we didn't want to give people a chance to dismiss us easily, which many people could while I was editor. We'd adhere to some of the basic rules of journalism and establish ourselves as better than them even at their own game. That way, we'd really be able to fuck up the party.

Our first victims were the local petty shopkeepers—restaurant and bar owners who feared getting trashed in our club and restaurant guide. They'd bow obsequiously to us when we'd enter their restaurants, especially the desperate expat entrepreneurs. They'd pull aside the Russian wait staff, nervously warn them that if they fucked anything up, their jobs would be lost, then send them out to meet us. Then they'd feed us free food, in the hope that we'd go lighter on them. The Russian wait staff inevitably fucked every order up. That would send the expat entrepreneur into bloodshot rages: They'd shake at the table, trying desperately to act hip in order to court us, then finally burst out of their seats, give a pained smile, explain that their Russian staff was hopeless, and rush into the kitchen, where plates and pots crashed. . . .

Those experiences were usually more unpleasant than anything else. I'd never talked to these kind of people before coming to Moscow, and I certainly didn't come to Moscow and lay my literary rep on the line just to eat free meals with low-rent entrepreneurs. But it was part of the job, and free meals became one of the perks, particularly since we couldn't afford to eat out much. Moscow being as expensive as it was, and our newspaper paying as little as it did, we had to go leeching free meals. Even so, we'd still slam their restaurant or bar.

Being a savage newspaper had its commercial advantages.

"Andrew Paulson. This name should henceforth force any investors, even those who don't have clean hands, to cross themselves and avoid him like the plague. Because the disease which they risk catching from contact with him is called 'financial ruin.'"

Moskovsky Komsomolets, April 8th, 1998.

Three weeks ago, one of *the eXile's* designers came to our offices with the latest rumor surrounding *eXile* suspect Andrew Paulson. Paulson had found another sucker. None other than Derk Sauer's Independent Media had

One Bad Apple...

apparently agreed to fund Paulson to head a revamped *Vechernaya Moskva*.

For the most part, the rumor mills in our collective Ne Spat'/eXile offices tend to swing on the side of truth, so we were a little nervous. Especially since we'd just ran a "we told you so" piece in the previous issue celebrating not just the unceremonious collapse of Paulson's nightlife guide magazine, but more importantly to us, the fact that we'd picked 'em right again. It's called "Bragging Rights," the printed media's version of spiking the ball in the endzone and doing a slow moon walk from one sideline to the other. The article had a gratuitously smarmy tone even by our own standards—which, we realized too late, meant that we'd carelessly set ourselves up for serious public embarrassment if we'd tooted our horns a bit too early.

Sauer had already kindly taken the time to tell us twice, on the record, that he had no interest in doing either a *Time Out* guide or working with Andrew Paulson, even though he expressed his admiration for the *Vechernaya Moskva* editorial team. So if the most recent rumor about the Independent Media acquisition turned out to be true, it could only mean one thing: Sauer had contracted syphilis and the debilitating disease had entered its third and most dangerous phase: brain decay.

Sighs of relief spread throughout our offices after the appearance on April 8th of an article in Moscow's largest daily newspaper, *Moskovsky Komsomolets*, entitled "The American Builder of Potemkin Villages." We immediately canceled those penicillin ampules we had ordered delivered to Sauer's offices, and returned to our usual gross displays of self-congratulation by issuing this, the third, and hopefully last, installment in the saga of eXpat Huckster and Wanted Man Andrew Paulson.

To recap: Paulson first made local publishing history in early 1996 after launching, to great fanfare, *Ponedelnik*, a sort of *Newsweek*-style weekly. While the concept and editorial team were impressive, Paulson proved to have the business acumen of an Ike Turner. The magazine collapsed after three issues, and the diminutive former fashion photographer fled town for rural France, abandoning the superstar journos and staff, and leaving burned investors wondering how they'd been duped.

So when Paulson swept back into town last year on a Bank of Moscow caravan and claims to the Time Out throne, we were convinced that either it was a (not very funny) hoax, or else it was a sign that Armageddon was at hand, and Jesus Christ would finally return to earth to lead us all to a better place. Indeed, we were right on both counts, although the hoax was on investors and staff, while Armageddon was confined to the *VM-Time Out* relationship, which broke off abruptly after Paulson decided that it would work against him. This was a disaster for several

reasons, not least of which because now Paulson had smeared his name in the Western publishing world, thereby nullifying his worth to the Bank of Moscow. Unless he proved to be a good publisher. *VM* came out, but Paulson's Ike Turner management skills meant *Moscow Tribune*-level revenues and allegations of soliciting kickbacks from bank officials to keep the magazine afloat. Paulson was fired in March, the staff quit, and all seemed a sad repeat of his last venture.

As it turns out, things aren't ending quietly. First, the Bank of Moscow succeeded in salvaging *Vechernaya Moskva*, under new staff and management. The magazine looks the same as the original, and although many say the editorial quality has declined, it appears to be on its feet and running.

More ominously, the heat is on Paulson. The aforementioned *Moskovsky Komsomolets* article savaged the Franco-American expat to such a degree that even *we're* inclined to feel sorry for him. His name has been smeared across the Russian capital like few foreigners before. Radio ads the day of the April 8th issue told readers to pick up *MK* and read about how a sweet-talking American huckster had screwed Russian investors and Russian journalists alike.

The key thing to remember is that, from Paulson's point of view, this was no longer an issue of being victimized by a pair of hairy, spiteful Americans. *MK* is known to be backed by Mayor Luzhkov, who in turn is considered the patron of the Bank of Moscow. So Paulson has landed himself on the Mayor's shit list. Hell, Paulson may as well cruise Compton in a red Chrysler LeBaron convertible, top down, blasting Marc Almond and honking his horn at every ho' that walks by...

After seeing the *MK* article, we decided not even bothering to ask Sauer if the rumors of his Paulson buyout were true. We'll spare him the denial.

The article was brutal but well-written—leading us to wonder if it wasn't ghosted by one of Paulson's many victims in the journalism community—two-thirds personal invective, and one-third reporting of roughly the same facts we reported going back to our "Expat Hucksters" issue last November. In fact, in an allusion to the *eXile*, *MK* noted, "Those people, having known the ways of the huckster Paulson, understood that not only would the project collapse, but they could even foretell when the collapse would take place—give or take a few weeks."

When an American entrepreneur gets attacked like this in Russian print, it's bad for all of us, because it only adds to latent Russian suspicions and resentment towards expats whom they increasingly see not as do-gooder missionaries of capitalism, but half-baked swindlers exploiting a gullible people. Paulson is just the latest in a string of Ugly Americans targeted by *Moskovsky Komsomolets*. Not long ago, they ran a story on Jonathan Hay's clique of Americans, and how they swindled millions earmarked for defrauded Russian investors, a story that the *eXile* has been covering since last summer; a few months before that, *eXile* pinup Michael Bass made *MK's* pages, picture and all. Which makes us wonder: what do Russians really think of us these days?

While Hay and Bass may still be keeping afloat, Paulson is clearly up *shite* creek. Any sane person in his shoes would by now have flown to Germany, underwent major plastic surgery and reappeared as a busty Puerto Rican bitch working a cheap brothel in Hamburg.

For the rest of you decent, well-meaning eXpat entrepreneurs, Paulson's costly one-act dramas mean that things are only gonna get tougher in this town for the rest of us. Your savvy may become a liability, as the MK article warns: "...Led astray by the manners of a patent Wall Street businessman with the gift of the gab, the investor somehow, without even realizing it himself, winds up in a Potemkin Village."

A huckster, a builder of Potemkin Villages, a communicable disease...these are the modifiers most Muscovites will remember Paulson by. Perhaps it's a good lesson to the rest of us, that we are not immune from the consequences of our actions.

The article ends with these words of caution: "Be careful, investors!" Which is to say, "Be careful of sweet-talking foreigners!" Really, who can blame them?

Such as when we ran a piece savaging Andrew Paulson, a former drama club flake who, at the age of 35, came to Moscow with dreams of becoming a publishing magnate. I personally couldn't stand the fucker, going back to the days when I worked for the Pak. Paulson tried hitting us up for money. He called me all the time, and I was put in the ugly position of having to cover for my boss. Paulson finally put together a *Newsweek*-style magazine, *Ponedelnik*, that crashed after four issues. Paulson was another one of these oily entrepreneurs with "the gift of the gab." I found him physically repulsive in his publisher's wear: button-down dress shirts without a tie, tweed jacket, and slacks. His pudgy hands and pudgy face and endless schmoozing and power lunching somehow really rubbed me the wrong way. Even his voice—squeaky TV anchorman—made my skin crawl. When *Ponedelnik* fell apart, he fled to France for a year, working as an editor for a fashion magazine. Somehow, while there, he'd ingratiated himself into the Bank of Moscow's upper echelons, and convinced them to launch a media empire—with Andrew Paulson as their Rupert Murdoch–for-hire. It was incredible! Mayor Luzhkov's own bank, financing this clown!

Paulson's first Bank of Moscow project was to launch a *Time Out Moscow*, with the full consent and backing of *Time Out London*. He'd hit the big time! Owen Matthews gleefully accepted the title of deputy editor of *Time Out Moscow*, if only to fuck with Matt and me in his eternal quest to play the "morally ambiguous" double agent. The problem was that our publisher, *Ne Spat'*, might be directly affected by a *Time Out Moscow*.

So we decided to fuck up Paulson's action with a gratuitous investigative article.

As expected, the *Time Out* JV fell apart just before printing time, as Paulson's web of lies began to unravel. Even with all the money that the Bank of Moscow committed to the project, it still wouldn't be enough to cover the costs of buying a *Time Out* franchise. So he broke the agreement. Some of the staff was let go. The *Time Out London* people were shocked and embittered by the way Paulson canceled their agreement at the last second.

I called his thuggish bank's press secretary to quiz him about Paulson's fuck-ups and his past with the bank, and found out—that the bank denied ever knowing him! Within three months, Paulson's newest project, which Owen had promised would "sink" our publisher, collapsed. Paulson later blamed the *eXile* article for souring his relationship with the bank and advertisers.

Terrorizing the local petite-colonialists was mildly satisfying, but the front that Taibbi had opened up against the local Western press corps yielded far more significant victories.

I saw this for the first time at a dinner party Owen held after he'd taken a job at *Newsweek*. He'd invited both Matt and me to attend. Once we got there, Owen, with mischievous pleasure, told us who the preppy guest sitting on his couch was. "His name is Andrew Meier, and he's scared shitless of you guys. He thinks you'll write him up."

Andrew pointedly avoided us for the first hour. I didn't mind: In general, I try to avoid personal confrontations.

Finally, Owen introduced us with a mischievous smile on his face.

"Oh, you're the Mark and Matt from the *eXile*?" Andrew blurted out awkwardly. Andrew looked well paid: pressed button-down Polo shirt, Dockers slacks, and those brown leather hiking boots that make the yuppie look sporting and mountain-climbing happy. "I tell everyone I meet: If you read one newspaper about Russia, read the *eXile*! No, it's true! Ask anyone!" He jabbed his finger at the air for emphasis. I sat in a chair, listening to this guy, thinking, *You've got a real job! . . . you write for* Time*-fucking-magazine! . . . why are you bothering to make a fool of yourself? Don't you realize that this is all just more comic material? . . .*

"I was on the phone with David—David Remnick," Andrew continued. "You know, the funniest thing you guys ever did was when you pretended that you were Remnick. I sent him that piece. I told Remnick what I tell everyone—the *eXile* is the only newspaper that tells it like it is!"

On the next couch over, Taibbi was getting serviced by Andrew's wife. She'd done some freelance work for *L.A. Times* bureau chief Carol J. Williams, the single biggest target of the *eXile* in our war against the foreign press corps. "You guys are right on—dead on!" she said.

Afterward, Matt and I were laughing at the ridiculousness of it all. Why were they trying to defect to our camp?

In time, we attracted more and more foreign press. We'd appeared in articles and news programs. We made appearances on Russian television, and attracted Russian journalists to write for our newspaper. All of this pulled us out of the margins and into the world of legitimacy.

Something had happened. The Beigeists' most powerful weapon—ignoring and silencing the opposition—was no longer effective. The two-front approach we led had earned us an officially recognized seat in the General Assembly.

They were lumbering and clumsy and slow to act. When they finally retaliated, it only worked to our advantage, the way hatred and violence increases the power of the Devil. Kathy Lally of the *Baltimore Sun* argued that the *eXile* should be banned from a popular and highly influential Internet forum for Russia-watchers, the Johnson's List. We retaliated by playing one of our most devastating practical jokes of all: We caught her agreeing to back a boycott of the *eXile*'s sponsors, and considering acting as a witness in what our phone caller claimed was a criminal investigation into our alleged "hate crimes." We printed the conversations, and she never bothered us again.

In the summer of 1998, as Russia's financial crisis spun totally out of control, a truly formidable Beigeist opened up a new front against us, arguing that we should be banned from the same Internet list because we allegedly supported violence against women. His name was Michael McFaul, and he boasted an armory of credentials—Stanford associate professor, leading Carnegie Endowment

By Johnny Chen

I woke up last Friday morning with a screaming woodie. Johnny Jr. popped up bright and early that morning, and he wasn't in a good mood. "Get your clothes on, jack," he snarled. "Hey! Didja hear me?! I said GET YOUR FUCKING CLOTHES ON! It's been six weeks since I've been in the Temple of Doom, Chen, and I'm through waiting. Tonight, we're gonna do things MY way, understand?"

I'd never seen it so pissed off at me before. He wasn't in a mood for compromises or negotiations. He laid an ultimatum on me that if I didn't get him laid that night, it was off to Whores R Us for some toxic, unprotected sex that was sure to land both of us in the morgue within six months.

I took his threats pretty seriously. If there's one thing I've learned, it's that Johnny Jr. doesn't fuck around.

So I took him for a walk on Independence Day, Friday, June 12th: the day that Russia freed itself from half of its own conquered territory. The weather was boiling hot, as you know: sticky, sweaty. We walked up the promenade from Gogolevsky Bulvar to Pushkinskaya Ploschad, then turned down Tverskaya towards the Manezh.

"Jesus Christ," Johnny Jr. barked, "I've never seen so many sluts in my life!"

He was right: girls either wore see-through shirts with see-through bras, or see-through shirts with no bras AT ALL. How does a man keep from going mad here? It just ain't fair. I've been suffering through a sexual famine lately. I have only myself to blame, but knowing that doesn't help me through it. Walking alone down Moscow's streets, past rows of arm-locked dyev-babes, I began to ponder the life of a molester. A sexual offender. Anything but this, walking alone among all this sexual energy, this human pollen, the only idiot not getting any for six straight weeks, like the Boy in the Plastic Bubble or something.

There was only one answer for me: The Duck. I went there Friday night for the sweatiest, ugliest Ladies' Night yet. It was horrible. Every person was a human sprinkler system of slime, sweat, semen and b.o. Sweat dripped from the ceiling. Slavic pheromones burned your nose. Under such circumstances, I knew that I, Johnny Chen, had a pretty good chance of scoring. And I did. In fact, I never made it more than half-way in. Literally within four minutes of arriving, some teenager with a face like Muttley's from Laff-A-Lympics fell off the bar and onto my shoulders. I carried her almost straight out to the coat check, then hurried her down to a taxi, ran her home, up my stairs, and into my apartment. The whole time she was begging me to take her back, to be careful, she was drunk, bla-bla-blah... After we were through, I had no idea what to do with her. She was bleeding and crying. As for me, I was depressed. I'd just shot a load large enough to repopulate North Korea. So I walked her over to my balcony, and held her in my arm, leaning her over the ledge.

"Throw her over," Johnny Jr. advised me.

"What?"

"You know you want to," he said. "Just pick her up and throw her over. You'll feel better, I promise."

But I didn't have the energy. Instead, I passed out on the floor, and woke up the next morning, with Muttley beside me. It took me a long time to get rid of her, but I did. You know how that is. It always works out that you have horrible poo cramps the morning after, and all you want to do is dump a huge shit, but you've got this humiliated, skanky bitch tagging around. Girls, if I can give you one piece of advice to win a man's heart, it's to get up bright and early the morning after, and leave before he even wakes up. Because despite what the song says, There Ain't No Morning After.

This is the infamous Johnny Chen "rape" column that drove Dr. McFaul to advocate censoring the *eXile*, and started a second "boycott the *eXile*" grassroots movement in Moscow's expat community.

A Confederacy of Dunces

By Mark Ames

Boy have Americans done a great service in showing the Russian savages how much better our culture is than their old, evil, oppressive Soviet culture. During those Cold War years we were feeling mighty superior to the "Orwellian" Soviets for suppressing anything they found offensive, while we, God Bless Us, had built our culture on the very concept of tolerance and free speech.

Free speech for everyone, that is, except when it offends you.

Last week, yet another "Burn the eXile!" scandal erupted, first touched off by an anonymous letter to the Johnson's Russia List, an internet forum for thousands of Russia-oriented scholars and journalists the world-over. The anonymous letter—which, incidentally, most local Western correspondents believe was written by a certain colleague of theirs who has come under heavy criticism in these pages—claimed that the eXile should be banned from the JRL because, based on out-of-context quotes from twerp-O-matic Johnny Chen's last club review, the newspaper has gone rape-mad:

"The Exile's editorial stance, which both condones and celebrates rape, needs to be brought to the attention of the readers of the Johnson list and needs to be considered when deciding whether or not to include their submissions any longer," the anonymous poison pen claimed, using the convenient veil of anonymity. The letter was clearly written by an American, in American prose, the product of a brain not merely washed, but scrubbed, pressed, and bleached in the factory tubs of political correctness.

Russian readers might be confused by the inanity of it all, but brace yourselves for the real shocker. Professor Michael McFaul—henceforth referred to as Dr. McFaulwell—of Stanford University, basing his stance purely on the anonymous letter, raised her one by announcing his immediate vote for censoring the eXile:

"I was appalled by the quote from Johnny Chen's article in Exile sent by 'anonymous' to your list. The Exile writers and editors occasionally have some interesting insights about Russia. I am glad that Exile has the right the publish its views both here and in Russia, but must such a valuable publication as the Johnson List dupe so low as to propagate the ideas and promote the reputations of people who celebrate rape? Why dont you suggest that Exile set up their own list. Those who want to support the open propagation of violence against women can then subscribe to this list, and spare the rest of us from having to tacitly condone these views by subscribing to your list."

Dr. McFaulwell then apparently leaned hard on Johnson to impose a blanket censorship ban on the eXile, even using his position as a heavy hitter in the Carnegie Foundation and a board member of another Johnson project that Carnegie is helping to fund to pressure Johnson to comply—at least, that's how we interpreted subsequent email exchanges. For our Russian readers, we want to emphasize again that **THIS IS NOT MADE UP.** Americans—First Amendment-proud Americans—were **REALLY** having this debate. A Stanford Professor tried to have us censored and banned from an internet list based on an anonymous poison letter. Of course, the fact that Dr. McFaulwell is both a former USAID consultant and a regular contributor to *The Moscow Times* might help put his ketamine-logic and eerie, Zhdanov-esque reaction into perspective, but it still doesn't say much about Americans setting a fine example when it comes to showing Russians about tolerance and free speech.

The next day, scores of postings were sent to Johnson urging him not to listen to Dr. McFaulwell, and to keep publishing the eXile. Supporters included several foreign correspondents, academics, a representative from the Kennan Institute, and two outspoken feminists, CBS News's Beth Knobel, and Masha Gessen—that's right, Masha Gessen. We have to tip our hats to you for your principled courage on that one, Masha, after all the shit you've taken from us. Perhaps your experience as both a Russian and American has made you a little more tolerant than pampered uber-geeks like Dr. McFaulwell.

On a minor note, a nerd-infested internet list for Americans-without-lives-in-Moscow also ran the anonymous letter, which provoked half-literate community service dropouts to post their own version of a baloney-sandwich lynch mob. One woman wrote, "My husband has begged me to stop reading the Exile, as it only raises my bloodpressure [...] They are an embarrassment to me as an American in Russia." Fair enough. But not far enough for Ian Schier—whose name we will print because he posted to the list a private e-mail sent to him by Matt Taibbi. Schier courageously wrote, "I'm afraid that a warning of a boycott of advertisers may be in order. As it is, I had thought about placing an advertisement in the Exile and have decided not to do so. There is a fine line between acceptable humor and unacceptable insults, and the Exile crosses it far too many times." Interestingly, we remember the ad Ian wanted to place. We've still got a copy. It goes: "I am: a middlebrow tub of lard Jew with stained underwear. You are: still alive. Let's get together at my place and watch old 'Friends' reruns! Email me for a fun time at nxrprim@cityline.ru." Ian complained that he hadn't received a personal insult since elementary school. We're sorry to hear that kids avoided you in junior high and high school, but we'll make up for lost time, Ian.

So there you have it, Russians. All that malarkey we Americans told you about tolerance and free speech? We didn't **REALLY** mean it. What are you, fools or something? Ha-ha-ha!

This July 4th is dedicated to all those Americans who have gone public in calling for the eXile to be censored and boycotted. It's an eXile Fourth of July and what better way for an eXile to act than to act as... well, an eXhole!

As for us, we're offering to all those offended by Johnny Chen's article—and to the community at-large—a human sacrifice of sorts. See, in order to make Chen feel the pain that he inflicted on others, we arranged for him to be gang-raped by the cast of Ian Schier's favorite television sitcom, "Friends."

And as you'll see in the comix strip to your left, there's a warm, happy, Spielbergian moral to it all.

And if that's not enough, you can even win a "Death Porn" T-shirt if you send us a photograph of yourself defacing or burning the eXile in your own special way. After all, what does an American stand for, if not the pursuit of liberty, justice... and the right to burn anything he or she disagrees with?!

analyst, Hoover Institute tool (note the squeaky Clinton-like synthesis of liberal Carnegie and conservative Hoover creds), and the Clinton administration's most relentless academic propagandist in favor of its near-genocidal reformophilia. As McFaul's SimCity global-village-paradigm crumbled around him in a reality of corruption, cynicism, and destruction, he decided that taking on voices of opposition was more important to The Cause than writing truthfully about Russia. As he wrote more than once, "The facts on the ground are often not as important as the perception of those facts."

McFaul pressured David Johnson, who ran the Internet list, to ban the *eXile*, based on the now-infamous "rape" article by Johnny Chen. He argued that a publication that glorifies rape in its pages should not be allowed a forum on a "serious" academic list, even if the editor of that list, David Johnson, only reprinted relevant and serious political

One way to annoy the hell out of our under-sexed, hysterical P.C. detractors was to publish comix, placing their arguments in the "mouth" of Johnny Chen's dick. Roman, the artist, forgot to make Chen's eyes slanted—because the editors forgot to tell him that "Chen" is a Chinese name.

articles from our newspaper. McFaul argued that by posting our "serious" pieces, Johnson was "tacitly condoning rape and violence against women." Of course it was an absurd argument. Johnson had posted several articles from fascist and radical communist Russian publications.

In another time, we would have lost without a fight. McFaul expected it to end that way: His ugly confidence showed through in his postings to the list. In the world he came from, you won debates by flashing your credentials, and that was that. A show-trial display of debate might be allowed—the kind of false, cringing, shamefully polite debates that his people conduct. In his Stanford/Carnegie world, a pair of wounded tweaks like Taibbi and me would simply get zapped by 100 rectons of McFaul voodoo-rays, and that would be it. You'd never hear a peep out of us again.

I was terrified and seething mad when he first tried to silence us. Night after night, McFaul and I squared off via email. It got nastier and nastier. I'd whiff out, pound the computer, and curse in my ovenlike box-sized apartment during those long July nights. I could imagine where McFaul was, on the other end of this Information Superhigh-way: either in his quiet office on the Stanford campus, in that quaint, nauseating ranch-setting in the

CONGRESS GETS [SIC]!

Dear eXile,

I've been following your wonderful exposes via Johnson's Russia List and giving them added circulation in a bulletin I write from our foundation for U.S. policymakers in Congress and in government. You are coming up with some excellent material — the Hinshtein reprint in addition to your original investigative pieces — that are provoking much-needed discussion in Washington. I just ran a one-paragraph summary of the Hinshtein article and another of Hoagland's response. It seems that Mr. Hoagland provokes more questions than he answers, and I hope you keep digging.

I can tell you from my conversations with senior congressional staff of both parties that they do read your work and have followed up on some of it with inquiries to the government.

Keep it up!

Sincerely,

J. Michael Waller, Ph.D.
Vice President
American Foreign Policy Council
1521 16th Street NW
Washington, DC 20036 USA
202-462-6055
mike@salnet.net
jmwaller@aol.com

Proof that the *eXile* "mattered." Waller's right-wing think-tank was the arch-enemy of McFaul's, and since the enemy of our enemy was our friend, we liked Waller.

rolling peninsula foothills, where robins and bluebirds chirp in the oak trees outside of his open window. . . . Or, if he wasn't on the Stanford campus, playing god to the sons and daughters of America's oligarchy, then he was reading some comforting Daniel Boorstin book in the study of his two-story Palo Alto home, oblivious to the low background hum of lawn mowers and weed-eaters, as a crew of illegals from Guatemala manicures his front yard. I can picture it perfectly because I was reared not far from there, in the San Jose suburbs, about 20 miles south of and 20 degrees hotter than the bay-cooled Palo Alto. McFaul's golden retriever, inevitably named Pasha or Sasha, gnaws on an expensive handmade Earth Toy underneath the mahogany wood desk. His Volvos—both of them—are safely parked in his neatly organized garage, oil trays beneath the chassis. A police patrol car slows before his home to make sure that the Guatemalan gardeners are staying clear of the doors and windows to the McFaul manor. The Guatemalans obligingly cower before the cop. Satisfied, the patrol car moves on to check up on the next two-story beyond the hedges. Mrs. McFaul, who chairs a domestic violence support foundation, returns home late. Over a skinless chicken dinner, she talks about her good fight, while Dr. McFaul, an agitated vein bulging in his forehead, recounts his battle against the *eXile*, the very incarnation of the McFaul-ian bogeyman.

Taibbi and I kept quiet at first. Johnson queried his subscribers as to whether or not McFaul's ban should be enforced. The response was overwhelming: Tens of letters representing local bureau chiefs, Russian journalists, and various academics, as well as others, came to our aid. We'd become too famous to fuck with. Banning us would mean violating another one of those sacred Beigeist tenets: Thou Shalt Not Censor. It was sweet. We piped in, renaming McFaul "McFalwell" and abusing him from every angle possible.

Eventually, he sent an email saying, "Okay, you win, I'm exhausted. I give up."

Shortly after, his colleague at Stanford, Gordon Hahn, also of the Hoover Institute, started another email war with Taibbi and tried to have us banned. Within a week, he also surrendered and even apologized.

Afterward, the whole tale was written up in both the *Scotsman* and *Frankfurter Allgemeine Zeitung*, making us out to look like victims of an evil mainstream plot to censor one of the most important, honest sources of information from Russia. The Beigeists were in a bind: If they ignored us, we'd roll right over them. But if they attacked us openly, they risked making us more famous—and thus more firmly entrenched.

So if The People of My Mind are wondering whether or not their revolution has been corrupted by hedonism, the answer is, not at all. (After all, when The People were stuck in the baking Santa Clara Valley suburbs, they bewailed the famine of pleasure, and the famine of possilibity.) We're taking the revolution out of our tiny republic and spreading it as far as we can. We're radicalizing the revolution. No more cringing in the Sarajevo hills, picking off old ladies, and fleeing, screaming, back to the safety of the bunker.

With Matt, I had a formidable ally, one who'd been on the other side, who saw and studied how they worked, came back with the intelligence reports, and struck at their very hearts. Now, we were more like those Somali warlords, whipping up dust in our machine-gun-mounting Toyota pickups, wreaking havoc against a lumbering Superpower. We dragged McFaul's and Hahn's and Lally's charred corpses through the dust-and-fly-infested streets of our newspaper for all to have a laugh. We forced them into a hasty retreat. Now, the goal is to make a landing on American soil—after all, we are Americans—and to make them surrender at least some piece of real estate in American Letters to us.

But even if my sex and drugs supplies were slashed to pre-Revolutionary levels—which, in the last few months, has happened—I wouldn't leave Russia. Those are the perks, well-deserved perks, but no longer essential perks. They aren't the reason I came.

The most important thing is protecting Russia from going the way of Prague. From becoming a domesticated, obedient member of the Global Village. This paradigm, this counteruniverse, so fragile, must be preserved, if only because my very health depends on it. Russia is my home. I have never, not once since moving here, thought about returning to America. Or anywhere else.

As this chapter is being written, the Yeltsin regime responsible for creating this horrible, bizarre, and yet epic paradigm is cracking apart. I have no idea what will come next, but my instincts tell me that I'll have to be more careful if I want to stay, and avoid getting nailed to the side of a church. Can't have the Russians thinking I'm merely here to rape and pillage. Wouldn't be prudent—or safe. "Uh, guys . . . heh-heh . . . it was a joke, get it? Yeah?" No, the next people in power won't get it much at all.

Anyway, the best thing is to aim our guns Westward and Westward only. If only to keep them off our property.

Every other Sunday, I go to Limonov's apartment to pick up his article for the *eXile*. I usually drop by at around noon or 1 P.M. Sometimes I wind up staying for hours. He makes tea, boiling water and tea leaves in a dented tin cup over the stove top, then pouring it into a tea mug and handing it to me.

He lives on the sixth floor, in apartment 66, just off the Old Arbat. There are two doors: one on the sixth floor corridor, which leads to three apartments, then one to his apartment. When I press the buzzer to 66, Limonov is always just a few seconds from the door. I'm usually late—California time—but he rarely complains. I press the buzzer, and Limonov opens the upper bolt lock. He looks down at the ground as he approaches me, sighing ironically. He comes up to the glass-paneled door in the corridor, opens it, lets me in, and shakes my hand. He usually wears a torn black sleeveless T-shirt or a button-down black T-shirt, black fake jeans unraveling at the seams, and Keds-like shoes. And his trademark heavy, plastic Soviet glasses. His gray hair is always done up like an older, fascist James Dean.

We go back into his kitchen/reading room. More often than not, Limonov has some girl sitting quietly in a divan-chair underneath the bookshelves, while we sit at the kitchen table, talking in English. He likes to practice his English with the *eXile* boys. Every half hour or so, he'll lean over to the girl and make some quip, asking her if she understands. She usually lies and says she does.

Once, in mid-June 1998, I came over to pick up an article he'd written on the Russian intelligentsia, whom he has always loathed for their masochism.

He offered me the usual cup of tea. I told him how McFaul and others were trying to get us remarginalized.

"Well, that means you're famous now," he said, approvingly. "You should be happy."

"It's better than not being famous," I said, looking over at his new girlfriend. Her name was Nastya. She was a little punkette, dressed adoringly in a spiked dog collar, thrashed boots, army coat, and Grazhdanskoye Oborona T-shirt. Limonov claimed that she was 16—or rather, that Nastya told him she was 16.

She squinted at me with sly, Asiatic eyes and said, "He doesn't look American."

Limonov laughed. "No, he's a Chechen," he said.

When Nastya spoke, I noticed her two front teeth, slightly crooked and too large for her mouth. No fucking way she was 16. More like 14, tops. She slumped back into the divan, boots pigeon-toed, fumbling restlessly with a strand of hair. She stared at me like a little child, unabashed. Limonov pointed to a *Pulp Fiction* poster that she had defaced by erasing Uma Thurman's eyes and drawing devil's horns on her head. He was annoyed, but clearly proud.

One of Limonov's skinhead bodyguards from his National-Bolshevik Party came by at 2 P.M. Sasha had been a champion judo expert in the Soviet Army when he was stationed in East Germany. He was shorter than me,

Doctor Limonov's Advices For Traveling In A Cattle Vagon

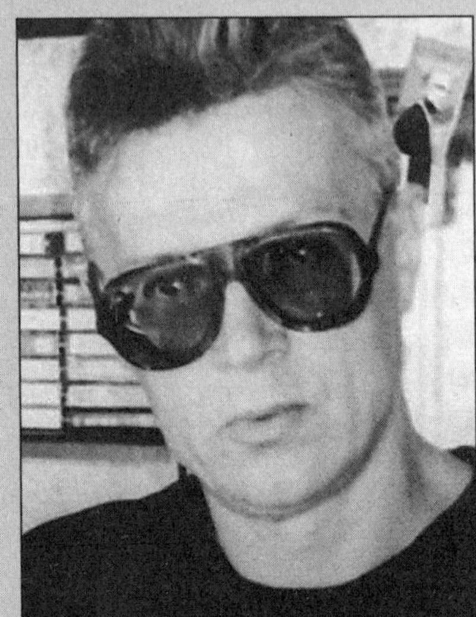

By Dr. Limonov

Current situation in Russia can be identified as very tense. Russians are extremely angry at its own politicians. Russians are extremely angry at its own politicians. They also very angry at Westerners whom they consider or a villains and thieves and responsible for the fall of Mother Russia. It is very probable that anti-Western pogroms would occur at big Russian cities. On another hand any government after Yeltsin's would use Westerners as scapegoats for the deeds of last decade. So, Westerners should prepare themselves to arrests, interrogations and difficult trips to Siberia in a cattle wagons. Following are advices, based on personal experience and on my father Veniam Ivanovich's experience.

My father Veniam Ivanovich was an NKVD [the KGB's predecessor under Stalin-Ed.] officer and during the 50s regularly made trips to Siberia as a chief of military convoy unit. At his charge he have had a few wagons filled up with convicted prisoners, who were sent to different Siberian camps. My father would dispose of his human merchandise on different Siberian stations. His final destination was a rail station and port "Sovietskaya Gavan," located on Pacific Ocean coast, near Japan. On his way back to Kharkov my father collected some prisoners in order to transport them to European Russia's prisons and camps.

Once, as a kid of 13, I went to Kharkov's railway station to meet my father, who arrived from Sovietskaya Gavan. Narve, at first I have looked for him among crowd of passengers. He wasn't there. Finally I found my father on outskirts of Kharkov's railway station. Semicircle of soldiers with a rifles (bayonets facing prisoners, descending from wagon into "Black Maria's" automobile), was breaked at one place. My father was staying there, reading the names of prisoners. Holster of his was opened and naked pistol's body was shining at spring sun. So, I am descendent of professional caretaker of prisoners. I know well how to take care of them. My father taught me.

Before to get into details about how to equip oneself to trip to Siberia I should say that my father was a dangerous, good, honest, almost ascetic type of officer, not drinking, not smoking. I suppose he was a difficult bastard as well as for his subordinate soldiers, as to prisoners. No weakness, metal, harsh, disciplined man, who lived on his trips no better than his soldiers, little better than his prisoners.

At his travels, they lasted few weeks, because Russia is very big country, my father would always take his suitcase. Or, rather it wasn't suitcase. It cannot be called suitcase-it was Russian "chemodan." On its cover was glued forever a list of items that my father carried with him to Siberia. He would take aluminum mug, spoon and fork. My father carried with him a pocketknife with as many as eleven items, including scissors. He would take also few needles, black and white threads. He would take four sorts of brushes: one for his teeth, one for his boots, one for his uniform and one for his uniform's buttons. Buttons he would at first cover with stinking liquid called "osedal," and then brush them to shining state. My father always carried with him at least ten white cotton pieces to sew it to his collar. (You don't bother yourself with it, you will be in no need for white collar) every morning. He also carried many pieces of soft cloth, "portiankas", to wrap it around his feet. Portiankas are much better than sock, they can be used much longer. Of course portiankas can be used only with a boots, no shoes can survive on a trip to Siberia anyway.

You may need also wooden spoon. It's much better in eating hot "balanda"-prisoner's soup, what usually served in mugs. With a wooden spoon you can eat faster, and it will not burn your lips. The only food to be recommended to take with you are dried up bread and "salo," salted pork fat. Tea and sugar are luxuries, so you should hide it on your body somewhere, in order that your fellows travelers will not rip-off you. Don't carry many things. Anyway, soldiers or fellow prisoners criminals of common law will take them from you. For the same reason don't wear good clothes.

If you can snatch some money in cattle wagon, then from time to time you will be able to ask soldiers to buy some food for you. Old-timers highly recommend to fold money, as many times as you can, to state of a small ball or little cube. Then you can color it on surface with a dirt and sew it on your clothes as if it is a button. Many buttons made of one and five dollar bills, and Siberia will be a little warmer for you.

I highly recommend to stop smoking now. Then in a cattle wagon you will be suffering less.

Edward Limonov is the chairman of an up and coming nationalist political party, the National-Bolshevik Party, and author of several books.

but about three times wider, with hands that swallowed mine when we shook.

They invited me to take a walk with them. They were planning to meet with a group of striking miners from Vorkuta who had just recently begun a sit-in at the White House, demanding that Yeltsin and his government resign and that their months of unpaid wages be paid. I agreed to go. Nastya found it all boring. She ran out ahead of us, and we didn't see her again.

The three of us walked down the Old Arbat, past a group of middle-aged American tourists.

"Promise me you'll let me load them all in the cattle wagons myself if you take over," I joked to Limonov. He laughed, and assured me at least a post on a commission to deal with the colonialist occupiers.

"You have the right attitude," he told me, laughing.

We crossed to the Smolenskaya metro station, just behind the McDonald's. As we stepped onto the escalator, a tall, attractive woman, with long blond hair and an intelligent face, quickly caught up to us and stared at Limonov.

"Are you . . . are you Edward Limonov?" she asked, excited.

"Yes," he said calmly.

She nodded, then, half-confused, turned and quickly made her way down the escalator.

"Wait!" he called after her. "Who are you? Where are you going?" Sasha and I laughed, but Limonov lost her.

We got on the metro, changed on the ring line, and got out at Barrikadnaya, the closest stop to the White House. On the way, two or three more people stared knowingly at Limonov. He half-ignored them, speaking to me in English, and keeping an eye out for girls.

Limonov was telling me that I might want to start worrying about the CIA. "Your newspaper is dangerous," he said. "You and Matt may have problems getting back into America. Have you ever thought of that?"

I had a hard time imagining that, but from his point of view, our problems with McFaul and Hahn were exactly that: the beginning of a war with the CIA. They are Stanford boys, Clinton people, and they work at the Hoover Institute, a known breeding ground for spook propagandists. "Ideas are very dangerous," Limonov said. "Your newspaper is showing a side of Russia that these people don't want out."

It was boiling hot that day, about 95 degrees and humid. We walked quietly down Konyushkovskaya Ulitsa. On the east side of the street, a row of makeshift monuments to those who fell in the battle at the White House in 1993. Red ribbons tied to the sickly birch trees. Black-and-white photos of the fallen: young and old, grim Soviet-looking passport photos blown up to life-size. A few were even young women, dressed in blouses and hair neatly combed for the photographs, now dead. Dozens of people, with their names, dates of birth and death written below. Flowers are laid at the places where some fell in battle. As comical as that October uprising may have been, you really had to pause to respect the fallen.

Painted on the fences are slogans denouncing the Yeltsin regime and their attack on the White House. That the Yeltsin regime even allowed this seething display of dissent, just a couple hundred meters from the White House, showed how they'd learned from the American oligarchy that silence is the best weapon against dissent.

Police in uniform walked past us and stared menacingly. A little farther down, there was a water truck, and several dozen *militsioneri*, some with AKs slung around their shoulders.

We approached a gated area on the eastern side of the White House, next to Gorbuty Bridge, where hundreds of miners, mostly topless with their T-shirts wet and wrapped on their heads, lazily paced around, pounding bottles of *kvas*.

The police stopped us, but then, recognizing Limonov, turned their heads and let him pass. Limonov barely acknowledged their presence.

We stepped over a barrier, and for the next two hours, we were assaulted by groups of miners, all of whom wanted to speak to Limonov. Miners! Talking literature and politics with a writer! Limonov tried to convince them to radicalize, to join with his National-Bolshevik Party, because everyone else, the Communists, Zhirinovsky, whoever, they didn't give a fuck about the miners. Every other word was *blyad* and *khui*, cuss words. They came in crowds to speak to him.

After some time, we joined a group of miners who had laid out a large sheet on the lawn. We shared some more *kvas*—donated by Mayor Luzhkov—and they crowded around Limonov to talk with him.

Then they asked who I was.

Limonov proudly put his hand on my shoulder and said, "My American friend who writes for a newspaper that we consider a fraternal newspaper, the *eXile*. The only good, anti-bourgeois Western newspaper I know."

I get uneasy when Limonov calls me anti-bourgeois. A context-clash: my reactionary politics and bourgeois blood, versus his reactionary politics and lumpenprole blood.

CHAPTER SEVEN

ЛИМОНКА

№77

ГАЗЕТА ПРЯМОГО ДЕЙСТВИЯ

О К Т Я Б Р Ь 1 9 9 7 г.

Цена договорная.

ТРЕТИЙ ГОД ИЗДАНИЯ

Выходит с ноября 1994 г. каждые 2 недели

В номере:
- КТО ИМЕННО ДАЕТ ДЕНЬГИ КПРФ
- ГОЛОВИН/УРЛА
- ДУГИН/О ЖЕНЩИНЕ
- НБП И СОРОС
- КОМУ ПОДРАЖАТЬ РУССКОЙ ДЕВОЧКЕ
- ПАВЛА I КАЗНИЛ ЗАПАД
+ ЗАМЕТКИ АМЕРИКАНСКОГО ДРУГА

РОССИИ

Правильный ответ, пацан!

Limonov's extremist newspaper, "Limonka," is named both after him and the slang word for hand grenade. Here is an article "from our American friend" Ames, telling his skinhead readers how painfully boring life in the West is, and why they should stay in Russia.

Mark Ames, гл. редактор газеты Exile, выходящей в Москве на английском

СКУКА ПОРОЖДАЕТ РУСОФОБИЮ

Популярная в кругах иностранцев в Москве поговорка звучит приблизительно так: "Проблема с Россией в том, что она населена русскими."

Парень, который сообщил мне эту поговорку, —

Единственное "происшествие" за мою десятидневную поездку случилось, когда я перебрался в отель в районе Бастилии, известный местным как "опасный". "Опасный" — относительное определе-

вызывая французов на поединок. Два араба пониже вылезли из "Рено", расхрабрившиеся, смеясь, один размахивал небольшим лезвием... Это был самый унизительный расовый инцидент, который я когда-либо наблюдал, хуже даже, чем Беркли (Калифорния) — известный тем, что там разозленные черные охотятся за тщедушной белой добычей. Араб медленно, неспеша прошел к своему авто. Никто ничего не сделал. Хиппи собрали свои манатки, пересекли улицу и занялись своими ранами, боясь даже оглянуться.

После этого я представил, что половина свидетелей происшествия будет, вероятнее всего, голосо-

"America, huh?" said one miner, a huge, mustached jerk from Vorkuta, browned from the sun. "Isn't it true that America is shit? Huh?"

I kept quiet.

"America is shit, huh? Is that why you left?"

"It's just that no one does anything there," I answered, finally forced to. "Russians live more intensely. That's how it should be."

The miner seemed somehow offended. He tried hitting me up for money. I balked, like an idiot. I thought he was just fucking with me. Limonov intervened and explained that I wasn't a rich American, that not all of us were rich. If I was smart, I would have given the money, scored points. But I'm always slow to the mark in these things. And anyway, fuck him for asking a shitty American for money.

At one point, because of the heat, Limonov took off his shirt. The miners started to make fun of him.

"Why did you take off your shirt?" one said. "You want to show off your muscles?" A few laughed.

"No," Limonov replied. "It's hot."

But he's clearly proud of being the sort of Iggy Pop of the right-wing literary world.

I kept my shirt on. These Slavs—they have mostly bald chests. They were already making quips about the "kike-masonic" conspiracy to sink Russia. My North African chest and stomach and back could be sheared and made into pillows for these guys. Best to keep the shirt on and sweat puddles instead. . . .

State Nihilism Rules Russia

by Mark Ames

Why aren't there any political assassinations in Russia today? On paper, it makes no sense. The nation has gone from a great empire to a kind of banana republic sucking loans out of organizations that were originally set up to assist the Third World, while millions of workers go unpaid for months because the structures (government/banking) that are supposed to pay them are busy siphoning their wages off to Cyprus... You couldn't ask for more perfect conditions for political instability. So why isn't anyone getting killed over it? (Indeed, the only assassinations are ones that involve mafia-style hits over valuable assets-the haves getting capped by the have-mores.) Why isn't there a Zapatista-style guerrilla movement? A single political assassination?

The argument that Russians are passive and enjoy "feeling the sting of the knout," as the last Empress put it a few years before being bayoneted, shot, rifle-butted and necro-sodomized by not-so-passive Russians, is not only racist but also false. For several decades leading up to the 1917 revolution, Russia was plagued by political terrorism. Even during Soviet times people rose against their oppressors. The Kengir uprising against Stalin's GULAGs ended with some 600 deaths, and over 1,000 Russians were gunned down in the suppression of a worker's uprising in Novocherkassk in 1964. Today, we can only count one uprising as such—the 1993 revolt, which led to somewhere between 150 and 500 deaths. It was actually the perfect uprising, from the point of view of the power structures (and comically moronic on the opposition's part). It concentrated the entire opposition movement inside of one building in the center of the capital, instead of dispersing throughout the nation. Thus it was easy not only to crush the opposition, but also to marginalize them, and therefore—and this is the key—completely discredit armed opposition as an option.

That the Russians are reacting passively—or rather, not reacting at all—to the present national calamity is obvious; what isn't obvious is *why*. The reason, I believe, is that Russians are oppressed by a kind of State Nihilism so comprehensive and effective that people have lost not only their will to fight, but even the ability to conceive that active opposition is an option. It is a nihilism that is imposed from above, a nihilism that grew organically around the activities of those in power, until it became a symbiotic force intertwined with the power structures. State Nihilism has proven to be a far more potent tool to control the populace than State Terror, which has failed as a power-strategy in late-20th century politics. State terror calls too much attention to itself and to the structures behind it—terror focuses people's attention on who they should oppose, and what they would gain by overthrowing them. But what if the populace could be inversely-terrorized? What would they be fighting for if they were convinced that nothing could be changed?

In order to rally even a vanguard to action, there has to be a kind of binding ideology. When the People's Will activists tossed bombs at Alexander II's passing carriage, they weren't killing a man and the innocents surrounding him-they were advancing the cause of Righteousness. The same with the Israeli settler who sprays kneeling worshippers with bullets, or the Palestinian who walks into a yellow schoolbus with a bomb attached to his chest. Who in today's Russia has that kind of fervent *belief in something*?

Almost no one. Marxism-Leninism is dead; Orthodox religion is mostly a fashion trend/ cigarette importer; Western liberalism turned out to be a cruel hoax, although some grotesque form reigns today if only by default. The one movement which could have rallied a powerful opposition—nationalism—has been effectively declawed and debased, particularly by the disastrous war in Chechnya, but also by the clowns who coapted nationalism, such as Zhirinovsky (who was probably created by the KGB precisely to cheapen and control nationalism) and Yeltsin. Chechnya in many ways posed the greatest threat to those in power, not because of the danger of the dissolution of the Russian Federation, but because it could have whipped up real nationalist sentiment among the Russian masses. Nationalism would have given people purpose, and national purpose is the enemy of those who are today ruling. Losing a drawn-out war against a tiny guerrilla movement turned out to be the perfect strategy—even if it wasn't planned that way—to discredit the possibility of Russian national glory and further the sense of hopelessness. *Paradoxically, the loss in Chechnya actually strengthened the regime.*

Every action that reinforces the national despair and nihilism also reinforces the position of those in power. Each obvious case of corruption and cronyism only reminds the public of how helpless they are, and how little they can do. The more blatant the theft, the more demoralized the public; the more demoralized the public, the more powerful the rulers; and the more powerful the rulers, the more assets they can steal. It's an amazing circular equation of State Nihilism that would cause a revolution in almost any other country where ideology, religion or nationalism still existed. In a way, the Russians are innovators in this. But Russians have been innovators in the realm of ideas for quite a while—indeed, the word "nihilism" was first coined by Turgenev in Father's and Sons to describe his character Bazarov, although that was used in an entirely different, more "positive" sense. There's no reason why State-imposed "negative" Nihilism won't become an alternative power-strategy to liberalism in the 21st Century, just as communism opposed liberalism.

If anyone denies that Russia is gripped by a state-controlled, all-encompassing nihilism, then just look to that most telling symptom of all: earlier this year, Russians were asked (via government organs), What does Russianness even mean? The answer is irrelevant; the answer lies in the need to ask the question. The question caused a stir, then frustration, then passive despair. And, not surprisingly, an answer never arrived. We barely hear it asked today. The answer was *nihil*.

CHAPTER SEVEN

The leader of the striking miners from Vorkuta, as well as the head of the union for disabled miners, met with Limonov to lay out their positions. They weren't ending their sit-in until Yeltsin resigned. "Let them try to force us out with troops. If they do, if they spill blood, all fucking hell will break loose. None of us are afraid to die."

I sat on the lawn, in the shadow of that massive white government building, built like a huge concrete and granite car muffler standing up on the flat end, listening to this talk of revolution and bloodshed. Inside there, hundreds of *apparatchiki* were robbing the nation and hitting up the IMF for more loans to avert a revolution. Four and a half years earlier, I was a fresh defector, walking through the gunfire in this very district, with my head in the clouds, and absolutely no plans for the future except never to return to America. Now, I had access to the very gated lawn. And was being introduced to strike leaders by Limonov as a comrade.

After a few hours, we shook hands with the miners and left. Limonov bought himself a beer. I demanded an ice-cold Coca-Cola, to make a point. Limonov paid for it.

Then we got on the metro. At Kievskaya, he and Sasha got out to switch to another line. We said good-bye. After the doors closed, a young girl and a middle-aged man in glasses approached me, smiles on their faces, and, pointing to Limonov, asked, "Was that . . . was that him?"

10/12/01 05:48 FAX 02

Stop that whining, Mark. Didn't you get it from what that bright Briton told you? Ask your ma before selling us your shit, man. Cause WE ARE NOT BUYING. Wanna abuse people? Get a bit yourself. And please, take it like a man.

Suck my fucking dick. And hello from the gutter.

To be continued... **H8 RED**

10/12/01 05:48 FAX 01

Congratulations, Mark, I am back. You know me.

How will you swallow this, Marky? IMF has signed away its billions. You wanna talk crisis now? Fuck you and your cocksucking investment houses of all sorts. You want an explanation why it happened? Well, because the chicks are not the only fucking problem you have to deal with back home. You biggest problem is your greedy government that wants to control everything. Would you please fucking agree with that? I know you agree, no matter what you say. With the government like that everyone who is 10% sane would agree. The problem is, you are greedy, too. For many of your fellow citizen motherfuckers the only way to get back part of what they are giving away in taxes to your cocksucking government is to play Russian Shares Roulette. The problem here is that too many of your USAID-type assholes got involved with playing it. They feel a bit more than disappointed actually LOSING their money instead of earning. What do you think they care about, the Russian people? Hoarseshit. What they care about is their greenbacks, cause that is all they got to compensate for their small, lame dicks. They need to stuff chicks with dough to keep them interested. These guys are good at lobbying things, aren't they? They simply lobbied for these billions. Do they give a shit that the most of it will go for big four-wheel-drive vehicles and huge, pompous palaces all around Moscow? No, they don't. What they care about is that THEY get a tiny part of it. Could you just fucking imagine that? Take a few jumbo jets full of money; throw it for the profit of a bunch of thieves just to ensure that your shares don't tumble too much.

Don't piss me off, Mark. Remember what I told you before? I said leave it here RIGHT NOW. You've lost your privileges, man. No laughing matter, you dickhead.
Come on, motherfucker. Face it.

Talking shite? Talk no more. You will get enough shite from me to be real concerned, Mark. What a lovely creator of words you are, Marky. Don't turn your shit into shite, man. You will deceive no one. Listen, it's you who are so full of shite that your eyes are brown, man.

Talking some K-Y jelly stuff? You gotta be kidding, man. K-Y is shite. Every American sucker knows that. You need to get Slippery Stuff. You know exactly what part of yours you need to lube up. Cause that is exactly the part I am going to drive my Grand Cherokee into.

Let me ask you a few questions, Mark. What do you know about our culture? What do you know about Moscow? What do you know about Russians except for the fact that our Moscow got more hot chicks than your whole cocksucking land of USA?

I gonna scream it in your fucking face.

The last death-threat letter sent by the Russian nerd-stalker. The letters stopped after a column that dared the stalker to "get it over with or shuttup." The stalker shuttup, and reappeared as an angry email letter freak named Alexei who demanded a free "Death Porn" T-shirt from the *eXile*, and threatened to beat Johnny Chen to a bloody pulp if he ever saw him. While getting a death threat is not exactly flattering, it is a sign that you're a big enough asshole to matter. And it's not as scary as it seems at first, either. As a recent study showed, all major presidential assassins were characterized by one common denominator: They didn't start off by faxing written threats to the victim.

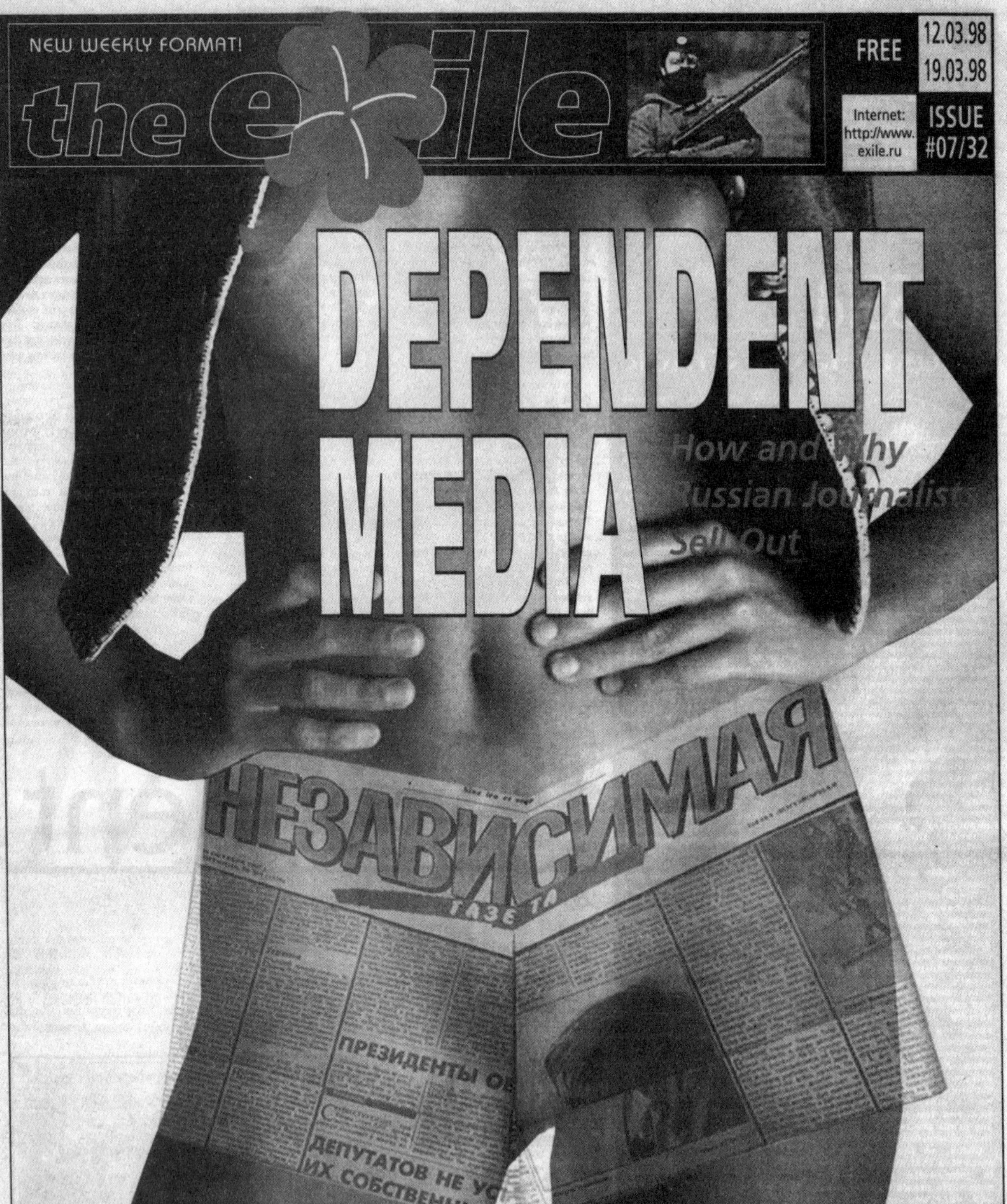

NEW WEEKLY FORMAT!
the exile
FREE
12.03.98
19.03.98
Internet: http://www.exile.ru
ISSUE #07/32
DEPENDENT MEDIA
How and Why Russian Journalists Sell Out
НЕЗАВИСИМАЯ
ГАЗЕТА

By Boris Kagarlitsky/ Westerners who want to be glad they won the cold war invariably believe the multitudinous news reports that describe Russians basking in a sea of new personal liberties—freedom to do business, freedom to practice religion, freedom to read an uncensored press. They want to believe that the collapse of communism really brought the goodies the West promised democracy would bring./ *Continued on page 2*

ROBBER BARON DENIED NBA TIX P.4

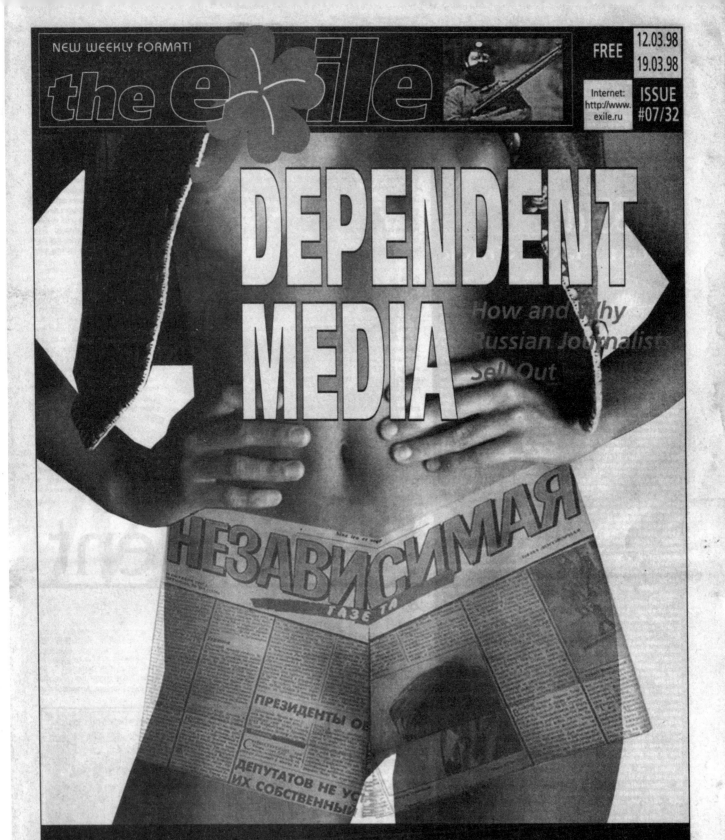

BY MATT TAIBBI

CHAPTER EIGHT: HACKS

Part I: The Hacks on Paper

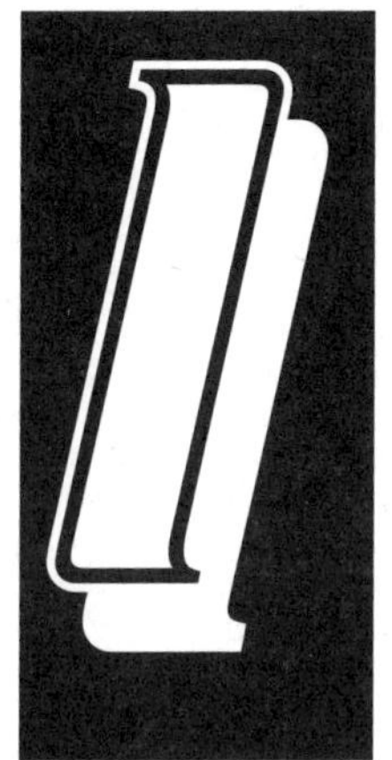

don't know Richard Paddock, the *Los Angeles Times* Moscow correspondent, beyond what I've read under his bylines. But I do know a story *about* him. A freelancer who worked with him told it to me.

Paddock, a semi-recent transfer to Moscow from California, had apparently been frustrated since his arrival in Russia. Carol Williams, his modifier-happy bureau chief, was the office's big star. He wasn't getting much play. And even the *Times*'s bold Russian containment policy, which specified that no Russian employee may enter a staffer's office without permission (although even nonpaid Western interns may), had failed to cheer him up. He was unhappy and had become philosophical. And one day he decided to share his thoughts with the freelancer.

"Do you see this?" he said to the young photographer, waving his hand. He was standing in front of a giant map of Russia. "Do you see it?"

The photographer nodded. "In all of this," he said, "there's no story. There's just no story here."

As the photographer backed up, letting this sink in, Paddock pressed on.

"Do you remember Humphrey the whale? That thing in California?"

"Sure," the photographer said.

"I did that story for a *whole week*," he said. "A whole week!"

Reliable sources confirm this story.

Reporters have changed over the years. I should know. My father, my stepmother, my godfather, my godmother—half my family works in the press. I spent my entire life hanging around press people. In my experience, they all had a few things in common: miserable personal lives, money problems, and a profound antipathy for public figures and celebrities.

Most of the reporters I knew were conspicuously difficult people. You always had to push them pretty hard to get them to give anyone, even a little kid, a break. My father's reporter friends never said, "Hey, Matt, you've grown since I last saw you!" They said, "Hey, you're still pretty short, you little fuck." Or: "I can still take you."

When I was seventeen, I worked as an intern for the *Village Voice.* I shared a tiny office with the novelist Tom Robbins, a young wiseass named Bill Bastone, and my boss, Wayne Barrett. Barrett was one of the most boring writers in the city, but also one of the most feared investigative journalists around. He was also a horrible-*looking* guy, balding, with long brittle copper hair, crooked teeth, and always dressed in half-tucked-in yellowing Arrow shirts. He was obsessed with unraveling municipal scandals like Queens Borough President Donald Manes's suicide, the Parking Violations Bureau scam in the Bronx—stories that took weeks of digging around in grim public records halls and hundreds of phone calls a week to make any progress at all on.

I remember coming to work and telling him that I'd seen someone jump off a building the day before. The jumper had left an enormous human pizza on the corner of Bleecker and Christopher after finally giving in to a crowd that was chanting, "Jump! Jump! Jump!"

"Freaked me out," I said to Wayne, shaking my head.

Hats Off To Hack Writers

By Abram Kalashnikov
the eXile

The American comedian Richard Pryor once questioned America's traditional fear of Russia. "I don't know what the big deal about Russia is," he said. "I mean, if a Russian walk down the street,

and he don't got that hat on, I don't know who the fuck he is."

Western journalists come up against that problem all the time. In order to sell their stories to the home audience, they go to great lengths, when they describe Russians, to put that *hat* on so that their readers can recognize them. It is a technique that Soviet journalists writing about America used to use; in every interview with an American, accessories ranging from cheeseburgers to burning crosses tended to figure heavily in the portraits, to help prevent communist readers from mistaking Americans for human beings like themselves.

Western journalists find the hat especially necessary when they toss in "man on the street" quotes to flesh out their text. No Russian mentioned in a Western article who doesn't have a government title can afford to be without his "hat"— otherwise, the folks at home won't know why he's being quoted. Michael Gordon of the *New York Times* demonstrates in a recent article in which he interviews Moscow housewife "Tanya Yesin" about housing subsidies:

"It is absolutely absurd," she sniffed, as she offered a cup of steaming tea and black currant jam to a visitor [which one? Gordon? Is he afraid of admitting to drinking tea? A.K.]. "They have to raise our wages and salaries if they want us to pay more."

Would Gordon write the same way at home? For instance: "I totally disagree with the OJ verdict," said Hick McFlabb, as he munched from a plate of crispy fried chicken and stared proudly out the window at his Ford Pickup truck. "I think he was probably guilty."

Who knows. Anyway, sometimes even the President needs a "hat," as *Reuters* proved last week:

"He [Yeltsin] said the water was cold but he warmed up in a Russian 'banya' steam bath, wielding traditional twig switches to invigorate the blood circulation."

So that's what those switches are for! Silly me— all these years I've been beating myself with them, and it turns out that all you need to do is *wield* them to get the blood flowing. Well, at least the President knows how to use them, and that's reassuring.

When Western journalists leave the hat off, it's usually because they want to write something nice about a Russian. In her recent bio on Boris Nemtsov, Carol J. Williams of the *Los Angeles Times* made sure there were no hats within a 10-mile radius of the Deputy Prime Minister, as it was important for her to convey Nemtsov's traditionally non-Russian qualities of honesty, youth, and charisma:

"NIZHNI NOVGOROD— He calls himself a kamikaze, and, indeed, many expect the brash Boris Yefimovich [Williams leaves the hat off but makes sure to keep the sidelocks on; subsequent Russians are identified in the article without patronymics] Nemtsov to quickly crash and burn.

"In the four months since he left the helm of this prosperous Volga river reform showcase to become first deputy prime minister in Moscow, the charismatic crusader has taken aim at the corrupt and the greedy who have made post-Soviet Russia a vast and terrifying gangland.

The 37-year old former physicist has presided over the first promising signs of economic recovery since Russia jettisoned communism, and, to the cheers of the struggling masses, has waged war against government fat cats junketing in imported luxury cars and chartered planes."

I think I must not be getting out enough since I bought that VCR from Andrew Kramer of the San Francisco *Chronicle.* Where are these cheering, struggling masses Williams refers to? My own street is pretty quiet. In fact, I would be content with this story so far if there were one person somewhere in Russia who was actually physically cheering Nemtsov— someone besides Ms. Williams, that is. I somehow doubt it. She goes on:

"'First of all, kamizazes don't always end up dead,' Nemtsov said, fixing his interlocutor [maybe it was Williams Gordon saw receiving steaming tea and jam!] with the wide-eyed ebony gaze that has made him the darling of Russian politics, at least among Russian women."

Good thing Williams is at least clear on Nemtsov's good looks. She's a little murkier on his record against corruption. Interestingly, her belated effort to stick a fig-leaf of a "hat" on Nemtsov in order to prove her pro-Russian-ness ends in spectacular failure:

"Nemtsov was among the first to bare his personal finances, disclosing ownership of a two-room apartment here, a 5 year-old Russian-made Zhiguli compact, savings of $1,300 and a 1996 income of less than $16,000."

Never mind that Nemtsov's anti-corruption drive has widely been accepted to be a fraud: Williams forgot to check the trunk of Nemtsov's "Russian-made" Zhiguli. According to *Kommersant Daily*, Nemtsov's declaration actually listed an income of 853 million rubles, or more than $150,000.

My award for this issue, for Best Unsubstantiated Assertion, goes to John Grimond of the *Economist.* In an article in which hats are jettisoned for antennae as Russians from the town of Vorkuta become "Vorkutians," Grimond spends more than 1,000 words describing the horror of life in the arctic city. Vorkuta boasts "black smoke which belches into the air," "swirling coal dust," mafia wars, stalled factories, and a population so poor that they can't even afford to have sex— "I wouldn't have the 5,000 rubles for a packet of condoms," one Vorkutian is quoted as saying. In the second-to-last paragraph, we are still in a land of "excess vodka and early death"— "In Vorkuta," said one local, "we have twelve months of winter. The rest is summer."

Then, suddenly, in the last graph, Grismond defies the laws of rhetoric and changes his mind, seemingly without any reason.

"Vorkuta...voted to re-elect President Boris Yeltsin last year...It would not back him today. Is reform therefore doomed to fail? This survey would argue that, despite all the evidence of misery and despair, it is not. It may even succeed."

Well John, I take my hat off to that.

Few things outraged Moscow's Western press corps more than the *eXile* Press Review, written by the pseudonymous misanthrope Abram Kalashnikov. Originally written by a xenophobic Russian reporter who had extensive experience working with criminally lazy Western journalists, the Press Review later turned into a platform for *eXile* staffers to out specific Western reporters for specific stylistic and factual mistakes, using the same acerbic, anti-Western voice of the original Kalashnikov.

He paused and looked at me, then handed me a scrap of paper. "Go to this address in Queens," he deadpanned. He thought I was kidding, bringing that suicide up. "I want you to do a public-records search. Find the building plan for Donald Manes's house. And hurry back."

Barrett and Bastone never had a good word to say about anyone. They abused me savagely every time I came into the office, usually for nothing in particular, but violently if there was so much as the slightest reason. Once, after telling them I'd been an All-Star baseball player, I actually struck out at a *Voice* softball game. I heard about that every day for the next two months, at times as often as every five minutes. Those guys hated *everyone.* Photographs grew on the walls like moss and were instantly defaced the instant they were up there, particularly if they featured public officials or women. It was my understanding then that this was a healthy atmosphere for a newsroom. My father told me it was normal, nothing to worry about.

A few years later, I worked as a stringer for a little newspaper in New Bedford, Massachusetts, called the *Standard-Times* (my father called it the "Substandard-Times"). I worked nights, covering town meetings and other little bullshit community news events. The night editor there was a young guy named Chris who sat at his desk with his ear pressed up against the police radio, swearing at everyone who walked past him. One night, he came up to me wringing his hands and grinning from ear to ear. He wanted me to go to nearby Marion, the town with the highest per-capita income in all of elitist Massachusetts.

"They've got some problem with their water," he laughed. "This is great. I love it when those rich fucks get E. coli in their water!"

I later realized that if, as a consumer, you want good newspapers, you're not going to get them if the reporters are people who only reluctantly tell you the truth. Ideally you have a bunch of people who are outcasts, even sociopaths, who get off on telling people the blunt truth, because that's the whole point: The other parts of society—government, business, etc.—have to be able to function while trusting the public to know the worst.

When people in power behave badly, and are greedy and acquisitive and don't do their jobs, things in society go wrong and the chickens eventually come home to roost. The press is supposed to be one of the ways that boomerang comes back. And it's supposed to come back *hard.* At least, that was what my school of thought had taught me.

By the time I joined the *eXile,* I had a different idea about the press, formed as a result of working for years in the Western press corps in Moscow. My American and British colleagues there weren't the same contentious, foul-mouthed reporter types I'd grown up around. They were a bunch of corrupt, cheerleading patsies, from the same species of predictable, obedient moron that Joe McCarthy had twisted around his finger in the fifties to serve the cause of terrorizing free-thinking America. The only difference was that these people were, if anything, more effective than the McCarthy-era journalists had been in preempting public debate through name-calling and labeling. They were subtler, and more thorough. And creepily enough, they did what they did on their own, for the fun of it apparently, without any McCarthy figure egging them on.

To really understand just how completely the Western press corps failed to cover the Russia story in the mid-1990s, and how insidious the actual reporting they did was, you need first to understand some of the peculiarities in the Western approach to foreign journalism which make it easy for reporters to avoid doing their jobs correctly. There were several specific conditions which made this possible, including:

The lack of competition.

Most of the major American cities have only one newspaper large enough to warrant keeping a reporter permanently posted in Moscow. Take Richard Paddock's *Los Angeles Times* Moscow bureau, which has to be one of the most notorious sources of wrong and stupid gibberish in the entire world of print journalism. Because the *L.A. Times* is the only L.A. paper with a Russian bureau, *Times* correspondents know that they're likely to be the only regular print sources of information about Russia for their readers outside of the wire services. As a result, any spin they put on their stories, or any ludicrous inaccuracy, is likely to go unchallenged—and they know it.

In particular, the papers that tend not to send reporters to places like Moscow are the ones that act as working-class alternatives to elite papers, i.e., the *Boston Herald* to the *Boston Globe,* the *Post* to the *New York Times,* and so on. So you tend to see coverage of one type all across the board.

As a journalist, there are two things you know you never need to do when you have no competition. The first is break news. The second is come up with original feature ideas more than once in a Martian year. Regarding breaking news: In 1997, the year covered by this book, foreign reporters in Moscow only broke about a half-dozen important stories.

Make Me Pukh

Barometer (n): An ingenious device for telling us what kind of weather we're having.
*** Ambrose Bierce, the Devil's Dictionary***

$55,000 (n): About how much it costs to hire someone in Moscow to tell you what kind of weather you're having.
*** The eXile Dictionary***

No, you weren't hallucinating last week. In the middle of the biggest socioeconomic crisis to befall Russia since 1991, reporters from several major news services, as well as the Moscow Times, published lengthy features on—you guessed it—*pukh*.

Far eclipsing even the Mir Space Station, *pukh*—the annoying white shit that falls from trees one week a year here, making journalists sneeze— has long been recognized by foreign editors in Europe and America as the Ultimate Article Subject for Russia-based reporters. Editors love *pukh* because it boasts all the qualities that make a truly saleable Russia news article.

For one thing, in the endless parade of "Those Russians have a different word for everything!" foreign-color stories which allow reporters to avoid complex or unwelcome news (like the financial crisis), *pukh* reigns supreme as the dumbest, least informative, most defiantly irritating news option out there. *Pukh* is more irrelevant than falling icicles, more distracting than Mir, and every bit as cliche as the birch branches Russians beat themselves with in the banya to "improve the flow of blood." It's literally the ultimate puff piece—an easy score for a hack looking to get out of work early.

Pukh stories also give reporters a chance to castigate Russians for their stupidity (the excess *pukh* in Moscow is a result of a Stalin-era urban planning mistake, in which too many female poplars were planted) and to gloat over American dominance of Russia (the offending species of poplar comes from America).

The mileage newspaper editors get out of the *pukh* story is an amazing testament to the grotesque laziness of their reporters. Instead of leaving their offices and going out in search of facts and revealing material, reporters will take *pukh*, an insanely dull story topic that literally drops in their laps, and embellish it with 800-1000 words of 8th-rate lyrical wordsmithing. Here, for instance, is a passage from a recent story by the AP's Maura Reynolds:

"Although it looks and acts a lot like it, it's not snow. It's `*pukh*.' And it marks the arrival of summer in the Russian capital as surely as its colder cousin marks the winter."

Wow...that's deep. Folks, this is journalism on the level of local TV live sports standups. As in: "Well, Chet, some fans here at the Delta Center feel the Bulls are going to win tonight's game. Others, however, feel they are going to lose."

(Bronwyn McClaren of the Moscow Times even out-banaled Reynolds in her *pukh* story, the Times's third in one week, with the line, "It seems, however, that for each *pukh* detractor, there is a *pukh* supporter.")

Reynolds didn't do much with her subject, but she at least left some clues as to where she got her story idea:

"It floats into eyes, noses, and morning cups of coffee..."

Whose cup was that, Maura? The rest of her piece was pretty much standard *pukh* literature: quotes from complaining pedestrians, the "weren't the Stalin-era-communists-stupid" historical background, the assertion that *pukh* this year is worse than ever (if you look back, you can find this element somewhere just about every year), and the tried-and-true straight-press tool, the "One thing's for sure: Life goes on" conclusion:

"In the end, many Muscovites agree with her. In fact, most seem to take much the same attitude toward their summer snow as they do toward their winter snow: Resignation.

"'It's part of nature,' says 45-year-old Natalia Dvoyeva. 'We just have to put up with it.'"

Well...that's great. If you're wondering what you're supposed to do with that information, you're not alone. It almost makes you glad that some writers, like the Knight-Ridder service's Inga Saffron, took the time out to be offensive in addition to inane:

"MOSCOW —Mention these things to a disaster-weary Russian and you're likely to get no more than a shrug: Chernobyl, nuclear subs rusting in Baltic Sea fishing grounds, fountains of dioxin- laced soot spewing forth on Russian towns, drinking water that makes Geiger counters ring like lost alarm clocks.

"Of all the environmental catastrophes the communists foisted upon this suffering land, the one that really gets Russians going is `*pukh*,' the cottony spores of the female black poplar tree."

Okay, so from this we're supposed to infer that Russians are more upset about *pukh* than they are about Chernobyl and irradiated drinking water. That is, the ones that survived, right? Actually, this passage is almost correct, except Saffron has her subject wrong. Substitute "Western journalists living in Moscow" for "Russians" in that last sentence, and you've got a solid piece of reporting there.

Saffron goes on to prove that even a story about *pukh* can be a fitting vehicle for heavyhanded hack propaganda and stereotyping:

"I hate it. ... You can try to mop it up with a wet cloth, but afterward it just flies around again," complained an exasperated Olga Andreyeva, 48, a building caretaker who makes extra money cleaning the apartments of Moscow's new middle class.

Even here, under all this *pukh*, we're slipping in a line about the mythical middle class! Imagine a Russian version of the same passage:

"Sometimes pigeon shit lands on my forehead, and when I try to brush it off, it just smears," said Ricardo Lopez, a taxi driver who makes extra money chauffeuring the wealthier members of New York's acquisitive yuppie class.

It's ridiculous, isn't it? Of course, even Saffron didn't go as far as the Moscow Times's Jean MacKenzie, who last week lapped the *pukh* field with her boldly hyperbolic puff piece, "A Riddle Wrapped in *Pukh*." That piece began:

"Better minds than mine have struggled with the question of what makes Russia the way it is. Just what combination of historical, geographical, meteorological and anthropological conditions formed the popular id?"

The answer to that question, incredibly, is:

"But since it's June, it's hot, and I'm going on vacation soon, I'll take a shortcut. The answer, in a word, is *pukh*."

MacKenzie goes on to maneuver *pukh* into the role of proving that Russia is a "nation of extremes", where it is too hot when it's hot, and too cold when it's cold...rhetorically, this moves the narrative on to a quote by a MacKenzie friend, who then says that Russians should "cherish the golden mean — but instead we put it in jail or drive it into exile."

Pukh, responsible for the purges! Woodward and Bernstein couldn't have solved it better. Then again, they didn't have so much free time...

Steve Liesman of the *Wall Street Journal* uncovered conflicts of interest between the Institute For a Law-Based Economy (ILBE), a key recipient of USAID money, and a private mutual fund run by the girlfriend of the ILBE chief, Jonathan Hay. Chrystia Freeland of the *Financial Times* published a link between a major Russian bank, which had recently won a state auction, and a Swiss publishing house which had paid a suspiciously large advance to the Russian state official in charge of holding auctions. Dima Zaks of the *Moscow Times* broke the story about the size of that official's advance. And I broke a couple of stories, one of them in conjunction with *Boston Globe* bureau chief David Filipov, in which we linked a prominent American banker to that Swiss publishing house. And that was it. There were hundreds of reporters in the city, and that was their gross investigative output for 1997.

If you wrote for a Moscow bureau, other reporters for other papers not only weren't your enemies, they were your friends. If you worked at AP, every time Reuters did a feature story somewhere, well, there was a feature you could do, too—even using the same interview subjects. And once you did your story, the guy down the hall from *Time* could do the same story . . . at which point it could be handed off to the guy from the *L.A. Times*, and so on, and so on. In this way, the same features were regurgitated over and over, with the absolute bare minimum of effort, year after year after year.

Covering the news in Moscow was like going to college; the press corps was like a frat that stole the answers to exams and passed them around to all the brothers. Seniors and freshmen shared alike in the spoils. Pop quiz: Which of the following was written by the lowest-paid American reporter in Moscow in December 1996—and which was written by the city's highest-paid British reporter in December 1997?

a) MOSCOW—After one of the balmiest autumns on record, winter has blown into Moscow with a vengeance, putting lives at risk and the goodwill of Muscovites to the test.

By late Thursday afternoon, the temperature had dropped to minus 24 degrees Celsius, a numbing cold that immediately began taking its toll on the city's less fortunate residents.

On Thursday alone, 40 frostbite sufferers were taken to hospitals, where two of them died . . . 38 people were hospitalized for hypothermia, or severe exposure, and five deaths since the cold snap began last weekend.

Many of the victims are *bomzhi*, or homeless drifters, among them a nameless man whose lonely death on a Moscow street Tuesday was recorded by the newspaper *Komsomolskaya Pravda*. "Eighteen degrees of frost turned out to be too strong for the sick old man with neither a passport nor a hope in life," the paper said.

b) MOSCOW—Muscovites yesterday were locked in a bitter battle with the elements, as extreme cold gripped the capital, causing deaths and injuries and forcing most people to stay indoors.

As temperatures fell to -30C, the coldest recorded December for nearly a century in the capital, hospitals reported a flood of victims, including 50 people suffering from frostbite and hundreds more admitted with hypothermia or fractures caused by slipping on the icy pavements.

At least nine people have died since the cold weather set in at the weekend, one when he was struck on the head by a giant icicle which fell from the top of a high-rise building.

Most of the victims, however, were from the ranks of the thousands of homeless and alcoholics in Moscow, who have little chance of survival unless they can find warmth and shelter for the night.

The correct answers are a) entry-level *Moscow Times* reporter Greg Miller, December 1996, and b) *Times of London* bureau chief Richard Beeston, December 1997.

December 1999 will feature dozens of stories with that exact same Miller/Beeston lead, with that same line about the "ranks of the homeless,"and that same cloying, hypersentimental tone. Only the bylines will change, although it isn't uncommon for reporters to write the same lead year in and year out. That's how these reporters collect their salaries; by rehashing the appropriate old story at the appropriate time.

December in Moscow is frostbite and "falling icicle" month, as well as "Santa Claus competes with Ded Moroz, the Russian Santa Claus" month. June is the month for lengthy stories about *pukh*, the annoying fluffy pollen which fills the air in the city every summer, making reporters sneeze on their way to work. August is the month for the "[insert number] years after the August 1991 coup, Russia is [level of progress Russia has made in developing into a democratic state]" story. And so on.

Reporters, in addition, have a ready-made playbook for visits to any province or ex-Soviet territory. As a Moscow hack, every time you go on the road somewhere, you write the same stories every other journalist has written when they visited that place. You can even look up the same interview subjects (when they aren't fictional) and obtain the same quotes.

I myself did this, when I wrote for the *Moscow Times* and freelanced for other Western papers. For instance, when I went to Uzbekistan, I had a list of stories to do ready in advance, before I got on the plane. In fact, I could have written the stories before I went on the trip, and just filled in the names of the people eventually quoted later. I knew, for instance, that I had to do the "resolute Bokhara Jew" story, about the gritty race of Bokhara Jews. This was one of the oldest tribes in the whole history of Judaism, which had survived adversity and anti-Semitism to maintain a small but tightly knit community in the central Asian steppe.

That story, I knew, would have to be led by a description of a wizened old Jew resting on the Sabbath (or doing something else "Jewish") in his humble Uzbek home. Ideally, the lead is accompanied by a photo. The rest of the story would be a rehash of population statistics and historical data about Bokharan Jewish migration and other stuff that I could cull from other stories already published by the AP or the *New York Times* or whatever. Since they weren't competitors, they wouldn't care.

Going to the Russian territory of Kalmykia, the only Buddhist territory in Europe? Look up Telo Rinpoche, the ethnically Kalmyk American who is now the region's lama. Everybody else has done a story on him, so you might as well, too. Visiting Astrakhan? Join 400 others and do a story about the "colorfully corrupt caviar trade." Destination, Vorkuta? The "life in a desolate coal-mining shithole" story is required of every visiting hack. Vladivostok even has a particular supermarket, of all things, that every visiting reporter does a story on: It was created with USAID funding.

Since they don't compete in the area of subject matter, most journalists advance their careers by striving to be wordier, more pretentious, or more racist than their colleagues. These qualities tend to impress editors. A few even attempt to embellish their regurgitated stories with a peculiar brand of newspaper humor, which industry standards dictate must never actually make you laugh. Alessandra Stanley of the *New York Times* provided a good example in 1997 in her own "December-death-by-exposure" story, which she published just after Beeston's:

"When the flaps are down, it is too cold for Russian-made cars, Zhigulis and Ladas, to start. Which means that the streets of Moscow, normally as jammed and brutish as downtown Lagos, Nigeria, are miraculously free and clear: Only Volvo and Mercedes engines can rev themselves awake in this kind of weather. When it is really freezing, foreigners and rich Russians rule the highways—winter joy rides for the Happy Few. The outer lanes are littered with stalled cars, looking a little like carrion abandoned in the desert."

"The City Ambulance Service announced today that last week three people died of exposure and another 138 were rushed to the hospital. Russians read between the lines and find some solace in the sobering news: At least the ambulances are working."

You have to be very bold to make a joke out of the fact that owners of Western cars live like human beings, while silly Russians who haven't gotten the hang of the free market die like dogs. But that's what the *New York Times* pays its foreign correspondents the big money for.

Oddly enough, the ability to tease Russians for their failure to effectively remain alive seems to be a quality the most prestigious papers actively seek in their writers. Here's another bit by Beeston, who scored a minor innovation in 1997 by writing not one, but two "December-death-by-exposure" stories:

"Freezing Russians put their trust in vodka."
FROM RICHARD BEESTON IN MOSCOW
"Flying in the face of scientific research and basic common sense, millions of Russians, including some of their pets, are getting through the cold snap with the help of the country's favorite drink."

It would be easy enough, of course, to point out that many homeless people are homeless precisely because they're alcoholics, and that dead drunks in winter are something you can find in any northern city anywhere in the world—New York, for instance, or Beeston's own London.

The problem is, Beeston and his competitors, people like Chrystia Freeland of the *Financial Times* or Helen Womack of the *Independent*—they're all friends. They have lunch together, spend weekends at one another's dachas, compare notes. There's no competition there, not even of the friendly sort. Collusion and mutual support is the rule.

There are a few other reasons why herd reporting is so widespread among Moscow reporters. Among them is the fact that the editor is dependent upon the reporter as an information source.

The Moscow-based correspondent, particularly the one who speaks Russian, has his boss by the balls. It's an advantage he has over reporters at home. That's because a domestic editor at an American paper—say, a city editor—always knows when his reporter is indulging in rhetorical excess, simply by virtue of his proximity to the story. For instance, no *New York Post* city hall writer will ever describe Rudy Giuliani as a gay Trotskyite who's soft on crime. That's because he knows no *Post* editor would ever let that through.

There are no such guarantees in Russia. The foreign editor knows nothing that his reporter doesn't tell him. He can't put interview subjects in context, because he often doesn't know who they are—whether they're gay Trotskyites or "reformers" or, more importantly, well-known bullshit artists in the business of providing sexy but misleading or meaningless quotes for the benefit of lazy foreign journalists. The foreign editor can't read the Russian press to check the veracity of his reporter's stories, and, knowing so little, he can't even spot a story that's patently ridiculous or offensive.

An out-of-the-loop editor is the only way to explain how *New York Times* bureau chief Michael Specter got away with writing, in August 1997, one of the most preposterous stories ever to come out of post-communist Russia, a classic entitled "In Moscow Baby Boom, a Vote for the Future." In the piece, Specter, citing statistics from one private obstetrics ward in Moscow, argued that the capital was undergoing a baby boom that signaled widespread optimism under the democratic government.

Russia at the time had a birth-to-death rate of one-to-two—the worst replacement rate in the world outside of Rwanda and Lebanon, and among the worst civilian birth rates ever observed in modern society. It was (and still is) a country so devastated and depressed, its citizens so unwilling to mate and invest in the future despite having not long ago enjoyed all the benefits of life in an advanced and powerful industrial state, that you could almost say it stood as the ultimate monument to the hopelessness and existential despair of the human race at the end of the 20th century. And yet Specter somehow got away with telling America's largest newspaper audience that there was a baby boom under way. It was insane.

Specter in his piece even added the following incredible bulletin: The boom had started "immediately after President Boris Yeltsin defeated his communist challenger in a presidential election widely seen as a turning point for Russia."

Now, when you get right down to it, words mean what they mean. It's hard to see how the word "immediately" in that last sentence could have been meant to mean anything except "immediately." There are no stats on the subject available, but I sure as hell didn't notice millions of people jumping in the sack the minute the polls closed.

The only way you can explain this piece making it into print is by the distance separating Specter's editors from the story. As far as they knew, if Michael says so, it's so.

Before the baby boom piece, incidentally, Specter had also written a "drug plague spreading across Russia" story (one of the many standards; all the big bureau hacks did this piece at least once), which listed the absence of a needle-exchange program as one of the causes behind the spread of AIDS. Had Specter been accountable to an editor in the know, someone might have pointed out to him that, unlike the United States, syringes can be bought freely at any Russian pharmacy or streetside kiosk—making an exchange program unnecessary.

This kind of shit made it past American editors and into print on an almost daily basis.

A corollary to the editor's dependence upon the reporter for information is the fact that Russians don't read the Western press very much. As a foreign reporter in Moscow, you can write the most wildly inaccurate and derogatory things about your interview subjects without any fear of reprisal, since the people you're writing about as a rule neither read English, nor have access to your newspaper/magazine. This is the main reason Western articles filed from Russia often feature a suspiciously harmonious narrative, in which the quotes support the lead thesis with a sort of beautiful, Euclidean precision.

I might as well admit right now that when I was a reporter for the *Moscow Times*, I frequently fudged "man-on-the-street" color quotes. I did this in order to keep my narrative line clean enough to satisfy my editors, which allowed me to get out of the newsroom at a decent hour. I hated my job and took no pride in my work, so unfortunately I was willing to do quite a lot to get out of the office early. At the time, I tried unsuccessfully to mitigate my guilt by fudging quotes in a way that made my articles more entertaining. In retrospect, I'm amazed my editors never caught on. On almost a daily basis, I was filing stories as ridiculous as this post-parliamentary-election wrap-up:

Tuesday, December 19, 1995
Political Verdict: Kolbasa Up, Cutlets Down
By Matt Taibbi

Ruling parties may change, and elections come and go, but for Volodya Terekhin, a packer at the Businovsky Meat-Processing Factory in northern Moscow, there's only one political principle that matters.

"Cows don't vote," he said. "And we still have jobs."

I have enough of these misdemeanors on my conscience that I'm now acutely sensitive to the presence of false quotes in news articles, so much so that I find it difficult to read anything about Russia these days. That's because almost every reporter in Moscow is doing the same thing I did.

Now, I have no proof that other reporters in town fudged quotes in the same way. But I can provide some examples of articles that set alarm bells off when I read them. Here's one by Maura Reynolds of the Associated Press. You be the judge:

"The winter dawn comes swiftly in Siberia. By the time a vague yellow glow appears behind the clouds, Leonid Ivanov is already knee-deep in the river.

"He stands near shore in a black sheepskin coat and green waders, casting slowly for arctic trout. He is the only point of color against the vast whiteness of the shore, the sky and the steam that rises in sheets from the swift-running water.

"Gently, he dips his 30-foot fishing rod toward where the current runs faster, his lure seeking the prey that provides his margin of survival.

" 'I come here every day,' he says. 'There's no work, so I come here.' "

Folks, people just don't talk like that. Imagine how ridiculous an article by a Russian reporter about American kids would read if it included a passage like this:

"3 P.M. comes swiftly after a day of non-learning in America's ravaged school system. By the time the microwave oven finishes heating his yellowing bread-and-processed cheese sandwich, Johnny Smith is already on his knees in front of his 30-inch television.

" 'I come here every day,' he says. 'I have no life, so I come here.' "

Another sign that something might be wrong with this quote is the quotee's name, Ivanov. Ivanov is the Russian equivalent of Smith or Jones, and is a conspicuously over-represented name in articles filed by Western reporters. For some mysterious reason, those interview subjects whom reporters meet by chance, outside, miles from a telephone and/or other verifiable witnesses, tend very often to be named Ivanov. And when he isn't Ivanov, he has a pretty good chance of being a Sidorov or a Petrov—the Joneses and Davises of the Russian language.

One *Moscow Times* reporter, a former colleague of mine who unfortunately has to remain nameless, was very proud of his prowess at fabricating quotes. The crowning achievement of his career at the MT was the day in which he quoted a Petrov, a Sidorov, and an Ivanov, all in the same article. He was a master who made my quote-massaging look by comparison like a cheap attempt at brown-nosing my editors.

CHAPTER EIGHT

He was known to have gone for a beer in the neighboring *Pravda* building instead of out on a story, pocketing the taxi money and making up even the geographical details in the pieces he eventually filed.

Sometimes all it takes is a semester or two of Russian-language courses to spot suspicious quotes. One reporter whom it helped to study up for was the above-mentioned Specter of the *New York Times.* A note on Specter's background: In the fall of 1997, he competed in an online contest called the "Hackathion" which was sponsored by Slate Press. In this contest, reporters were asked to demonstrate "greed under pressure" by putting together news features from cheat-sheets of facts and manufactured quotes in under two hours. Online readers voted for the contestant who produced the most convincing article out of thin air.

Specter won the thing running away.

Here's a passage from his real professional life, culled from an ice-fishing story he wrote in early 1998:

"Asked if he thought it was a rather extreme way of getting to know himself, Shubov laughed.

" 'This is how Russians relax,' he said. 'Who said it's supposed to be comfortable?' "

Let's leave aside for a moment the damning fact that the very same quote appeared, attributed to a different name, in a similar piece about ice fishing filed weeks before Specter's by David Filipov of the *Boston Globe.* That's something you could miss, if you weren't looking. But as far as I'm concerned, the real giveaway in this passage is the quotee's name. The name "Shubov" is derived from the word *shuba,* or fur coat. Specter ostensibly conducted this interview out on the ice, in subzero temperatures. It gets damn cold out there in the Russian north, and if you're going to be out there all day, the way ice fishermen are, you've got to dress warmly. Like in a fur coat.

Suspicious quotes aren't the only reason Western reporters should be thankful Russians don't read their work. There are some who'd probably have to fear for their lives if Russians were actually shown their articles.

In March 1998, Adam Tanner of Reuters did something few Western reporters have had the opportunity to do—he visited a Russian prison. For years, virtually every request by a Westerner to see the inside of a prison was rejected by Russian authorities, and for good reason: The conditions inside Russian prisons are below subhuman. Human-rights groups like Helsinki Watch have even gone so far as to describe incarceration in Russian prisons as violations of the Geneva convention on torture. Prisoners are packed like sardines into ancient cells without ventilation, sleeping in shifts because there isn't room for everyone to lie down at the same time. Seventy-five square centimeters per prisoner is the norm.

An example of how bad things are behind Russian bars: In 1995, two prisoners in the Altai Krai cooked and ate a third prisoner in an attempt to be reclassified as insane and transferred to a mental ward, where there was more space. Ironically, the victim in that story was originally a conspirator who had planned, along with the other two, to cook and eat a different prisoner. Unfortunately for him, though, he fell asleep too early, and was himself diced up by impatient accomplices. Judges reviewing the case declared both killers sane and gave them both the death penalty. They were shot a year later after a stint in relatively roomy death row.

Tanner was another old coworker of mine from the *Moscow Times.* He was a tall guy with a year-round tan and a perfect head of shiny dark Prell-commercial hair who wore ties and pressed chinos in an office where jeans were the norm. His talent for radiating negative energy was legend. The Russian staff in particular went into fits over his hideously wooden Russian and his utilitarian attitude toward their culture as subject matter. In one incident that became quite famous in the office, Tanner was assigned to write about a serial killer who'd been captured in Siberia somewhere. Anxious to fill out the journalism-school list of required story elements, Tanner went to extra lengths to get a "man-on-the-street" reaction to the arrest, even though he was only about an hour from deadline and yet still inconveniently located many time zones away from the story. So what he did was call the interregional operator and have her dial numbers at random, using the exchange of the city where the killings had taken place. Apparently you can do that, if you're an American. . . . Basically he was calling random apartments to ask for their opinion about the news. The only problem was, the line was bad, and Tanner was forced to shout into the phone, in his atrocious Russian, the question, "Have you heard about the maniac who killed people?" Except that the way he said it, it came out as "Maniac killed people! Maniac killed people!"

"*Manyak,*" he screamed, "*ubil ludei! Ubil ludei!*"

He had some poor old *babushka* on the line for that one, and I wouldn't be surprised if she died of an aneurysm on the spot.

In any case, years later, I spotted Tanner's name over this Reuters story about conditions in the Medyn prison in the Moscow region. A few paragraphs into the piece, I realized Adam hadn't changed:

"MEDYN, Russia, March 27 (Reuters)—Murderer and thief Viktor Kolganov, sitting on a bunk bed in the room he shares with about 40 other men, says life in Russian prisons is no longer the brutal ordeal of Soviet times.

" 'Conditions are day and night compared to what they were,' " said Kolganov, who served 11 years for murder in the 1980s and returned to jail last year after a robbery conviction.

" 'It used to be hard back then. In the pre-trial detention centers they used to feed us just once a day. Now everyone eats three times daily.' "

Even beyond the obvious problem of an interview subject who serves 11 years in a ten-year span, Tanner's lead is a disgrace, an affront not only to Russian prisoners, but to common decency. After all, it doesn't take much thinking to see that the first prisoner allowed to speak with a Western reporter after a multiyear all-Russian embargo on prison press coverage is not likely to have too much negative to say. When you're dealing with interview subjects who have it so rough that they'd sell out their own mothers for an extra bowl of oatmeal, you've got to be a little discriminating about what you end up publishing.

But Tanner, whose Reuters bureau had been

Hacks Head Hack-To-School

BY ABRAM KALASHNIKOV
the eXile

Back in the days when I was an exchange student in New Jersey, I used to spend a lot of time in the basement. The reason was that the father in my host family had built an expensive bar and pool room in the basement and wanted everyone to use it as much as possible. That he had almost no friends who drank seriously or played pool was something that hadn't occurred to him until his $8,000 investment was history. So the family was subject to endless games of compulsory eight-ball.

Foreign journalists don't have pool rooms. What they do have are $80,000 liberal arts educations. And they're herding us into the basement for compulsory lectures every chance they get.

A pool room is a great thing, if you know how to play pool. It's the same with education. If you're a thinker rather than a careerist, exposure to arts and literature at a young age can actually be worth all that money your parents spent on it. But if you don't like to think, you're just stuck with a bad investment—unless you can find other uses for it.

Vanora Bennett of the *Los Angeles Times* made a valiant effort a few weeks ago to make alternate use of her education. Her piece, entitled "Sobchak Fall from Grace Takes Page From Novels," should actually have been entitled "I Went to College," since that was what the article was really about.

Bennett's article is a literary Evel Knievel act—an attempt to ride a feverish narrative up the ramp of Anatoly Sobchak's career, leap over a chasm of improbabilities, and land safely in a nest of pretentious literary allusions. The distance of the gap should have daunted even the most daring hack, but Bennett plunged ahead, with disastrous results. She starts off with a confident rev of the engines:

"ST. PETERSBURG— The fall of Anatoly Sobchak, a one-time democratic hero, has been as darkly fantastic as any of the classical Russian literature written in this imperial capital that he ran for five post-Soviet years."

So far, so good. But the "literary" angle Bennett stuck in the lead is so obscure that she is forced to dispense with it for the first 500 words of her article, returning to her theme only near the end. The final leap, when she makes it, is a freakish spasm of illogic:

"If anything does make people in St. Petersburg feel a twinge of sympathy for Sobchak, it is the extraordinary circumstances in which he fell ill Oct. 3, an episode in the tradition of the city's 19th century writers Alexander Pushkin and Nikolai Gogol.

"Russia's classical literature [why not liter*ary*?] heroes are little men-youths pursued through freak floods by nightmarish bronze czars on horseback; or downtrodden bureaucrats dying while their empty overcoats carry on, writing meaningless chits at their desks."

I don't remember Akaky Akakiyevich's overcoat continuing to work after his death, but we'll give Bennett the benefit of the doubt as she struggles to tie all of this to Sobchak. Her incredible summation:

"In Sobchak's case, an ambulance was called to the city prosecutor's office to take him to the hospital only after his wife rushed in to save her husband from what she called 'Communists and Gestapo'."

What? Did we miss something? I may be wrong, but that segue seemed to me to make *no sense at all*.

After all, only a madman could compare the destitute, balding, dull-witted, socially inept, incorruptible low-level-clerk/simpleton hero of Gogol's "Overcoat" story with the flamboyant, obscenely wealthy, silver-haired, glib, amoral, bloated ex-political boss Anatoly Sobchak. The one thing the two might have in common is hemhorroids, and even there we'd be relying on unnamed sources.

Bennett figures she can get away with this because she knows American readers don't know any better. If she were a Russian reporter, she'd be comparing Huck Finn to Richard Nixon, with smooth-talking Chuck Colson as Nixon's stuttering Jim.

Sovietology is another favorite source of inappropriate hack cliches. Michael Specter of the *New York Times* came back from vacation recently with a classic effort in absurd journalistic imagery, in a story about the new "drug plague" in Russia:

"For decades," Specter writes, "the kitchen has been the central symbol of this communal society, a place where dozens of neighbors forced to live together would grumble, grab some vodka and try to make it through the night. When the Communists ran Russia, the kitchen dissident was regarded with esteem and his fevered plots gave rise to collective insubordination that most people welcomed.

"But the communal kitchen — and the culture of sharing that it represents — has taken on a sinister new role: It is the center of a new home-brewed drug culture that threatens to decimate the country's youth while fueling a wave of crime that has already put the country's partial democracy at risk."

Doubtless Specter in college was forced to write a term paper of some kind about "kitchen dissidents" and has been struggling to build an article around the phenomenon ever since.

Reread Specter's comparison carefully. His sole link between "kitchen dissidents" and the new drug plague is the fact that both dissident insubordination and drug cookery take place in a kitchen.

Most Russian apartments have one or two rooms, plus a kitchen and a bathroom. Given that, we can conclude that about a fourth of all indoor residential activity in Russia takes place in a kitchen. I read, eat, work, and even sometimes do my nails in the kitchen. Drug brewing happens in a kitchen because that's where the stove is. Dissidentism took place in the kitchen because that's where intellectuals bided their time while normal Russians were having sex in the bedrooms.

I don't see too much "culture of sharing" here. Then again, I didn't have the benefit of being educated about Russia in American universities...

told by authorities the previous year that one of their own would have to "commit a crime" if they wanted to see the inside of a Russian jail, clearly wanted the coup of a prison visit badly enough that he was willing to play ball with the warden. As a result, millions of readers around the world now think that Russian prisons aren't so bad after all. This is despite countless testimonials from recently freed convicts (including an American named Stanley Williams, who did two years in remand for drug dealing before the charges were dropped and wrote about it for the *eXile*), which describe today's Russian jails as hell on earth, and a worthy cause for an international uproar.

Fortunately for Tanner, no convict who will ever see freedom is likely to read that piece. The only Russian who'll get a copy is, I'm sure, the prison bureaucrat who set up the visit, who'll read it carefully before considering the next Reuters interview request.

If undercutting Russians behind bars wasn't bad enough, some Westerners went one step further and brutalized Russians who not only had no access to their newspapers, but weren't even on the Planet Earth.

The near-disintegration of the Mir space station was easily the most popular story among Western reporters in 1997. This was mainly because it had all the qualities Western editors found most attractive in Russia features: a dramatic story line, a high level of irrelevance to real political events, and a steady stream of compelling visual evidence of Russia's inferiority to the West. Western *Schadenfreue* in the scores of stories filed daily about the "crippled Mir Space Station" was so obvious that at times it was embarrassing. Thesauruses all over the city were ravaged as reporters sought to find new and thrilling ways to portray Russia's national shame and despair over its troubled spaceship.

But when the ship itself began to lose its knee-slappin', finger-wavin' appeal for gloating jingoistic reporters, attention was suddenly focused on the foibles and failures of Russia's cosmonauts.

For example, the AP on August 13, 1997, ran an unbylined story which suggested that Russian cosmonauts were making questionable procedural decisions in order to earn more money in bonuses:

"Moscow (AP)—Cosmonaut Anatoly Solovyev switched his Soyuz capsule to manual control as he approached the Mir Space Station, then guided the ships into a gentle embrace—and earned himself a hefty cash bonus."

"Russian and U.S. space officials," the mystery AP writer went on, "agreed that Solovyev's decision to go manual last week was the best way to get the job done. But" [note how the word "But" here expresses the author's relief that his theory that Russians are making irresponsible decisions might still be plausible] "the episode highlights the unusual reward system which Russian news media say also pays $1,000 for each spacewalk."

Those cosmonauts had to be some of the bravest people alive. To willingly fly up to deep space to live on a ship that the whole world knows is falling apart requires more guts than the entire international community of journalists has combined. And now the AP was giving one of them a hard time over a lousy thousand bucks.

No wonder the AP writer left his byline off. If I were a cosmonaut and came back to earth after nearly dying a slow death in deep space to find out that some *American reporter*, of all things, had been nosing around Star City, asking my superiors if maybe I was doing spacewalks in order to pad my pocket, I'd be wanting to pay that writer a little visit— and make sure that he was thereafter referred to as "crippled AP correspondent."

These were just a few of the ways Western reporters stuck it to Russia because the system allowed them to. But there were other ways they got around doing their jobs, like the most common excuse of all—that the audience was too far away and supposedly too uninformed about Russia to understand any story that couldn't be explained in three words or less.

If you ever want to see an example of a group of people who are just a little bit too willing to accept the unpleasant realities of capitalism with a smile, then go to Moscow and start visiting the press bureaus. Reporters there may not know a whole lot about Russia—in fact, they may not even speak the language, or know the names of anyone in government except the president and the prime minister—but, to the last man, they sure as hell know one thing: Journalism is a *business*, and in order to stay competitive, they have to keep things simple for their readers.

Ask any Moscow-based reporter why he didn't write about something called the "loans-for-shares" scandal, or about the improprieties connected with USAID bigwig Jonathan Hay, or about the loopholes in Boris Nemtsov's anticorruption drive, and he's bound to say the following: "It's too complicated. My readers wouldn't understand. I've got to keep it simple."

The sad thing is, he's right. His readers really *wouldn't*

understand. In fact, after being fed a steady diet of his newspaper's reports for ten or twenty years, a reader is usually a drooling buffoon who's lucky if he can understand anything more complicated than a cereal box.

These days I'm constantly amazed, when I visit the States, by how little people know about Russia. Seven years after the collapse of communism, I still have people ask me whether Russians still have to wait on line for bread, or whether you can make a Russian cry with the gift of a pair of old blue jeans, and so on. Americans have been so thoroughly trained to view the world in visual clichés that when the press fails to provide them with a compelling new one for a new society, they're unable to move beyond the old one for the old world.

All of which is a result of an evil little thing I call the "elementary school" test. When I worked for the *Moscow Times*, my managing editor—a kindly, misguided old wire-service hack named Jay Ross whose farts were audible throughout our spacious newsroom—used to insist that every article that went into his newspaper had to be simple and self-explanatory enough that an elementary school student (read: Jay himself) could understand it. This was standard not only for the *Moscow Times*, but for straight newspaper reporting as a whole.

When I joined the *eXile* and could finally write whatever way I wanted, this was the first bad habit I parted with. Mark and I made it a point never to talk down to our readers. Our attitude was, *fuck* the reader—if he doesn't understand something, he can ask someone. Because once you start applying the Jay Ross "elementary school" test to every story you write, you enter a whole new realm of subjective judgment as to what's newsworthy and what isn't. In other words, you give reporters another way to be biased without their readers knowing it.

For instance, when handsome young Deputy Prime Minister Boris Nemtsov took office, virtually every Western bureau—in an effort to build up a pro-democratic,

#13 • July 31 - August 13, 1997 • P. 22

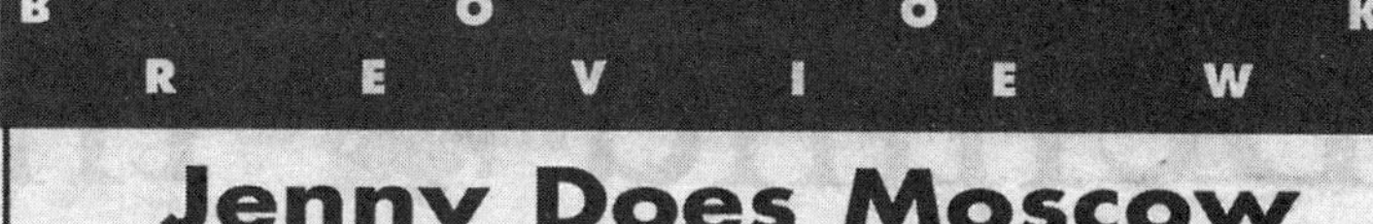

BOOK REVIEW

Jenny Does Moscow

Vodka, Tears, and Lenin's Angel
by Jennifer Gould
354 pages
St. Martin's Press 1997
$25.95

By Matt Taibbi

First of all, let's start with the title. Jennifer Gould's nickname at the Moscow *Times* was not "Lenin's Angel." I know. I worked with her there. Her real nickname, whether she knew it or not, was "Ты моя комната!"— "You my room!"—which was the only way she knew how to tell her drivers to bring her home at night.

I nearly collapsed dead when I heard Jennifer Gould had published a book. It was like hearing that ear mites had developed the gift of speech, or that horses had gotten together and opened a bar called "Steve's" in lower Manhattan. Jennifer Gould was not a bad journalist in the usual sense. She had a certain narrow, squishy, banal style that fit well with the narrow, squishy, banal format standard for most mass-market newspaper features. But if she wasn't an incompetent feature writer, there was one thing she certainly was: a moron of rare intensity.

Gould was so dumb that, even drunk, the men at the Moscow *Times* were too embarrassed to try to fuck her. They knew that by morning she'd have composed an entire Sylvia-Plath-style epic about the whole incident, devoting two dozen pleading metrically-confused stanzas to the vomit scene. She was a legend at the office. Every unassisted hour she escaped alive, every time she managed to open her own car door or negotiate a sidewalk without a map—each of these instances were regarded as a stunning supernatural interventions that the MT drivers, of whom she writes so fondly as friends, never stopped recounting with amazement.

And God, does it all show in her book. I don't know how she convinced a major publishing house like St. Martin's Press to print her, but their compliance makes "Lenin's Angel" a criminal conspiracy, unlike books by vanity-published-authors like Rick Furmanek where there is just one lone mediocrity to blame.

Meant to be the intimate journal of a young reporter in the "Wild and Wooly" former Soviet Union, Gould's book is actually the ultimate exercise in non-introspection—a record of a person whose exposure to one of the most violent and turbulent periods in history did not cause her to question herself or her beliefs, but instead allowed her to make a montage of banal impressions perfectly serviceable for the goal of publishing a glossy book with a smiley, pinup cover.

How bad is Gould's book? She devotes an *entire chapter* to her taxi drivers. Whereas most journalists feel queasy devoting a single quote to a taxi driver in something as inconsequential as a general-interest feature article, Gould sees no problem in devoting a whole *chapter* of a *book* to her drivers as a method of describing her Russian experience. The driver chapter is 16 pages long; the book, 354. Given that this is Gould's definitive account of her three-year trip, we can deduce that 4.5% of her Russian experience was centered around people who were paid to hang around her.

Gould's book is, I suppose, one thing that can happen when you pump $200,000 of Ivy League education (Gould had a Columbia Journalism School pedigree, another mystery) into a the body of a young woman who is full of gall, ambition and vague sexual narcissism (see the jacket photo) but has been otherwise completely lobotomized. Her prose reads like standard Maileresque j-school descriptive technique, with the crucial caveat that the things she describes are extraordinarily inappropriate to the gritty blood-and-guts style she attempts (was it Mailer who taught her to describe forks and knives as "the tools of food"?). I mean, how gritty can you really be when 41 pages into the book you're still looking for an apartment, for God's sake?

Open any page of "Lenin's Angel" and you will find classic instances of unintentional humor. You read and smack your forehead in astonishment, thinking, "Did she really write that?"

For an example, let's open to a random page— 153:

"It's a busy month for freelancers," she writes, "some of whom live in authentic Russian flats." *Authentic Russian flats?* How does one distinguish an authentic Russian flat from a non-authentic one? And aren't all flats in Russia Russian?

Okay, maybe that was a typo—let's try again. Let's flip to page...310:

"The outskirts of Grozny are sprayed with bullets...Nothing, though, prepares me for the city center, which looks like a late twentieth-century version of Dante's Inferno after a nuclear attack."

Hell after a nuclear attack? A late-twentieth century nuclear attack? Looks like Gould flunked the "redundancy" section of her last composition exam at Columbia.

And so on and so on. It would be easy to keep going from page to page in Gould's book and brutalizing her awful prose and startling lack of awareness. But there is a larger issue here, and that is what the publication of Gould's book says both about the publishing industry and the American/Canadian reading public. Take the back jacket blurb: "In 1994, 24 year-old Jennifer Gould left an aspiring reporter's dream job on the Philadelphia Inquirer, and flew to Moscow. The young Canadian spoke no Russian, knew no Russians, and had no job waiting. Three years later, she was not only fluent, but mixing with Russians and 'ex-pats'..."

Now, if the American reading public is genuinely going to be impressed that Gould learned a foreign language after three years [a shameless lie, incidentally; Gould never once worked without a translator] or that, once in Moscow, she "mixed" with Americans and Europeans, then there is simply no chance in hell that they will ever grasp something like, for instance, loans-for-shares. I mean, the rest of us working here just might as well go home right now, and only the few of us who can afford liposuction will have any hope of ever getting published.

Beyond that, Gould's book will serve as incentive for more hyperambitious mediocrities like her to eschew their rightful profession, television, and go into print journalism.

The result will be more self-promoting books that are tremendously patronizing and insensitive to foreign peoples, who will see their misfortunes used to drive the careers of bimbos, and, conversely, fewer books in which someone actually has something to say. When print becomes a place to be dumb and have a pretty face, we're all in a lot of trouble.

pro-Western political icon—made it a point to praise his anticorruption bill, which was one of his first accomplishments as a cabinet member. Carol J. Williams of the *Los Angeles Times* gave a typical write-up:

"In the four months since he left the helm of this prosperous Volga river reform showcase to become first deputy prime minister in Moscow, the charismatic crusader has taken aim at the corrupt and the greedy who have made post-Soviet Russia a vast and terrifying gangland.

"The 37-year-old former physicist has presided over the first promising signs of economic recovery since Russia jettisoned communism and, to the cheers of the struggling masses, has waged war against government fat cats junketing in imported luxury cars and chartered planes."

The "war" Carol J. was talking about was Nemtsov's anticorruption bill, which was ostensibly intended to put a stop to rigged insider auctions of state properties. Now, a cartoonish phrase like "waged war against government fat cats" passes the simplicity test, so it can safely be squeezed into a light, mass-market profile story like Williams's. But explaining the particulars of that "war" would make the piece too complicated, so the reader is left with the generality.

Which is too bad, because, as always, the devil was in the details. The April 8 decree, entitled "On high-priority measures for preventing corruption and reducing budget expenditures in the purchase of products for state needs," was actually a masterpiece of legal chicanery. It mandated that auctions of state properties had to be open and transparent in every instance—except when a closed tender was judged to be the "best possible method" for carrying out the sale! Furthermore, there was no mechanism in the decree for determining who would decide when auctions should be open, and when they should be closed. The result was a legal absurdity: a law which is irrefutable, except when you want to refute it.

The decree went on to provide another set of exceptions to the open-tender rule, and finished with a flourish: Tenders need not be held at all—meaning contracts can be directly granted to contractors *without competition*—if there's an "urgent need" for a product! The Nemtsov decree therefore provided the legal basis for significantly expanding the scope of the insider dealing it was supposed to be eliminating.

Los Angeles Times

CAROL J. WILLIAMS
CHIEF OF BUREAU

Sadovaya-Samotechnaya 12/24, Kv. 57
103051 Moscow, Russia

Office: 200-0204
299-0486
Fax: 299-2304
Home: 230-2749

Though the loopholes in Nemtsov's corruption drive were widely publicized (by us, among others), the *L.A. Times* never bothered to correct or amend its lionization of Nemtsov. Which made sense, in a way. After all, what *Los Angeles Times* reader could possibly care about the fine print in a relatively obscure Russian presidential decree governing auction procedure? None of them, of course.

Still, in a just world, Williams would have compensated for not publishing that information by also not publishing a story calling Nemtsov a "crusader" against corruption, a story which she knew to be false. But Nemtsov had the good fortune to be a glamorous, young, pro-Western politician with a long record (as governor of Nizhni Novgorod) of passing legislation easing restrictions on foreign investment, so Williams took the opportunity to write the "simple" story on his behalf.

All in all, the Williams piece was a classic example of how to achieve bias through the selective use of objective facts, and it was facilitated by the need to be "simple" for readers who were perceived to be stupid and uninformed.

A TYCOON OF THE TIMES

F Scott Fitzgerald was wrong—there was one more. One big and especially nasty one, if the *Moscow Times* is any guide. While tycoons as a class have been making a comeback for ages now, the word "tycoon" as a propaganda tool apparently required the emergence of Boris Berezovsky as a prominent public figure before it could be successfully revived.

After having used the word fewer than 30 times in each of the years 1994, 1995 and 1996, the Moscow Times in the month of May, 1998 alone used the word "tycoon" 25 times. In 23 of those instances, they were describing Berezovsky. In almost every instance, they used the word with the same darkly disapproving tone that, ironically enough, Soviet propagandists used to bring to its closest Russian translation, *magnat*— suggestive of a callous, fatbodied exploiter of vast kingdoms of natural riches for his own personal use, a man in a tall black top hat who walks past the pits with his nose scrunched up on his way to telling the foreman that coffee break is hereafter canceled in favor of longer work days.

Like a top hat and a pencil moustache in cartoons, the word "tycoon" in a news article is a great identifier of villians. Once you've got that tycoon tag firmly stuck on someone, readers will be ready to blame him for almost everything—and let everyone else off. Which means you can blame him for anything. Or try, anyway. In any case, here's a quick rundown on the mileage the MT got out of the ty-word in May:

Date: May 30
Headline: President Asks TV to Toe State Line.
Tycoon: Boris Berezovsky
Other tycoons mentioned without being called tycoons ("non-tycoon tycoons'): Vladimir Gusinsky
Berezovsky blamed for: manipulating public opinion
Not blamed for: the 1986 Red Sox, measles

Date: May 29
Headline: Yeltsin Backs Ruble, Market Steadies
Tycoon: Boris Berezovsky
Non-tycoon tycoons mentioned: Vladimir Potanin, Mikhail Khordakovsky, Alexander Smolensky

Date: May 28
Headline: Big Loan Needed to Save Ruble
Tycoon: Boris Berezovsky
Berezovsky blamed for: Being a "proponent of devaluation", "actively stoking rumors of a ruble crash"
Not blamed for: Shyness in adopted children of lesbians, Scatman John record sales

Date: May 27
Headline: Media Chiefs Accuse Kremlin of Meddling
Tycoon: Boris Berezovsky
Berezovsky Blamed For: Controlling ORT even though he doesn't hold the majority stake
Not blamed for: Hogging the remote, World Wars One and Two

Date: May 26
Headline: Yeltsin Lashes Out at Media
Tycoon: Boris Berezovsky
Berezovsky Blamed For: Being a "worst censor"
Not blamed for: Keanu Reeves's acting in "Devil's Advocate", *pukh*, gnats

Date: May 26
Headline: Star Tokobank Falls Down
Tycoon: Boris Berezovsky
Berezovsky Blamed For: "Stalking Tokobank"
Not blamed for: Stalking Valerie Bertinelli

Date: May 25
Headline: Russia Far From Indonesia Scenario
Tycoons: Boris Berezovsky, Vladimir Potanin
Berezovsky alone implicitly blamed for: Aiding communists by allowing his media outlets to provide alarmist coverage of crisis
Implicitly exonerated of: Most of the Atlanta child murders, man's helplessness to know his true role in creation

Date: May 21
Headline: General Rolls Forward
Tycoon: Boris Berezovsky
Non-tycoon tycoons mentioned: Vladimir Potanin

Date: May 19
Headline: Government Tightens Control of TV
Tycoon: Boris Berezovsky
Non-tycoon tycoons mentioned: Vladimir Gusinsky

Date: May 19
Headine: Next Step Could Be Kremlin
Tycoon: Boris Berezovsky
Berezovsky Blamed For: Supporting Lebed, possibly considering talking Lebed out of reversing the results of privatization sometime way, way in the future
Not blamed for: OJ getting off, greenhouse gases, the phenomenon of farting, subpar nursing in volunteer field hospitals

Date: May 15
Headline: Tycoon's Daughter Charged
Tycoon: Who else?
Berezovsky blamed for: Siring drug-taking degenerate
Not blamed for: The way Hitler turned out, the way Stalin turned out

Date: May 14
Headline: American Appraiser to Evaluate Svyazinvest
"Tycoon-turned politician": Boris Berezovsky
Berezovsky blamed for: Complaining that Svyazinvest auction was rigged
Not blamed for: Questioning the officiating in Bulls-Pacers game, complaining loudly in English at French restaurants, blaming it all on abduction by Satanists in youth

Date: May 6
Headline: Russia Plans to Unite Infrastructure
Tycoon: Boris Berezovsky
Berezovsky blamed for: Displaying eagerness to "wrangle control over Russian Media"
Not blamed for: Wearing Wranglers, Charles Rangel's accent

To give you an idea of just how lenient Western journalists could be with the facts in order to maintain a simple story line, let's take a look again at those two small paragraphs from Williams's Nemtsov piece:

"In the four months since he left the helm of this prosperous Volga river reform showcase to become first deputy prime minister in Moscow, the charismatic crusader has taken aim at the corrupt and the greedy who have made post-Soviet Russia a vast and terrifying gangland.

"The 37-year-old former physicist has presided over the first promising signs of economic recovery since Russia jettisoned communism and, to the cheers of the struggling masses, has waged war against government fat cats junketing in imported luxury cars and chartered planes."

Aside from the central mistake of misreporting the "crusader" business, Williams in these two little graphs takes liberties with the truth no fewer than three other times.

The first gray area comes in the phrases "prosperous Volga river reform showcase" and "first promising signs of economic recovery." Williams here is referring to Nemtsov's record as governor of Nizhni Novgorod, a region whose capital is the former Soviet city of Gorky, which was widely touted as an economic success story and a "crucible of

The *Moscow Times* was one of the major offenders in the area of using insidious labels like "Technocrat" and "Reformer" to describe Russian politicians.

Technocrats Dominant In Cabinet

By David McHugh
STAFF WRITER

The new-look Cabinet confirms that President Boris Yeltsin intends to remodel the government not as a force in its own right, but as a nonpolitical economic bureau of the Kremlin, analysts said Wednesday.

reform." While it was true that Nizhni pursued free-market reforms more aggressively than almost any other region in the country, its reputation as a success story came about largely as a result of Nemtsov calling it one. In fact, Nizhni in 1996 ranked exactly in the middle of Russia's 89 regions in terms of median income, and was only slightly above average for industrial output. Though it received a disproportionately large amount of foreign investment—it ranked fifth out of 89 regions in 1996, according to the State Statistics Committee—Nizhni was just another region in terms of economic performance.

Also, what exactly did Carol J. mean when she used the word "prosperous"? Prosperous like Kuwait? Like Switzerland? Did it mean Carol J. would have wanted to take Russian citizenship and move there herself? You know, I somehow don't think so. The average monthly salary in the Nizhni region is something like three hundred dollars, and the vast majority of people there live like . . . well, they live like Russians. In shitty concrete apartment buildings with roaches. On a diet consisting mainly of potatoes and kielbasa. And in daily anticipation of their six-months-or-more backlogged wages. No, you couldn't drag Carol J. Williams into permanent Nizhni residence with a Bradley tank.

Carol J.'s next gaffe was the "junketing in imported luxury cars" bit. Here she was referring to the fact that Nemtsov, when he took federal office, called for all state employees to ride in Russian-made Volga cars, instead of Volvos or Mercedes. Only Western reporters actually bit on this crude piece of would-be populist grandstanding. Russian reporters saw right through it. The fact is, Volga automobiles are manufactured in Nemtsov's native Nizhni region. Calling for the state to purchase them was really just classic porkbarrel politics. Furthermore, Volgas were comparable in price to Volvos, but broke down considerably more often. It was one of the world's most overpriced products. The move would have been a terrible buy for the cash-strapped state. Nemtsov backed off that campaign well before Carol J. published her piece. She lauded it anyway.

Lastly, and least subtly of all, there is the bit about the "cheers of the struggling masses." Again, as was the case with Specter's "immediately" phrase, there really isn't any way to take this passage except to mean that there were struggling masses somewhere that were actually, physically cheering for Nemtsov.

I defy Williams to pinpoint that moment. It didn't happen. Not anywhere, not anytime. Trust me. In fact, Nemtsov was unpopular enough in his own region that in the election to fill his seat after he moved to federal government, Nizhni residents voted in a communist over Nemtsov's handpicked candidate. And a year later, in the election for mayor of the city of Nizhni Novgorod, voters elected Andrei Klimentiyev, a sworn enemy of Nemtsov, despite the fact that he was a convicted felon.

But the very worst crime reporters committed in the name of "simplicity" was the use of labels to identify politicians and their policies.

In late April, I called up *New York Times* reporter Michael Gordon as part of a poll I was doing among Western reporters in the city. The poll question was: What do you think the word "technocrat" means? I was calling Gordon because he'd used the word in a recent story about new Prime Minister Sergei Kiriyenko.

Use of words like "technocrat" and especially "reformer" was a pet peeve of the *eXile*. It reduced coverage of Russian politics to the level of a cowboy-movie plot, where everyone wore either a black hat ("communist," "Soviet-style bureaucrat") or a white hat ("young reformer," "young technocrat"). "Technocrat" in particular is a word that's practically meaningless in itself, but is always loaded with bias. If you used it in a negative way, it meant a bloodless automaton who pursued policies that callously ignored the needs of the populus (it was, in fact, frequently used in the fifties by American reporters to describe Soviet politicians). But if you used it in a positive way, it ostensibly meant a person who was more problem-solver than ideologue. It meant a person who sought "technical" solutions to sociopolitical problems, rather than solutions based on ideology.

Don't know what the hell the word "technocrat" means? Well, we didn't either, until we read chapter three of the exciting new eXile publication, "How to win friends and gain influence by surfing the Moscow Times website." As it turns out, a technocrat is a fella with a broader character than Noah Webster would have you believe. In fact, it even seems that the technocrat might be defined just as easily by what he wears on his nose as by the politics he preaches. Here's a short list of some of the people the Moscow Times has called technocrats over the years:

Sergei Kiriyenko, Prime Minister
Crat-entials: "young technocrat", 4/28/98; "whiz-kid technocrat", 4/24/98; purveyor of "technocratic economic sludge", 4/11/98;
Is also a(n): "market-oriented reform figure", 5/5/98;
"Bespectacled": yes
Redundancy factor: 0

Costas Simitis, Greek Premier
Crat-entials: "technocrat", 2/1/96;
"Bespectacled": when he reads
Redundancy factor: "a pragmatic technocrat", 2/1/96

Dmitri Vasiliyev, Federal Securities Committee Chief
Crat-entials: "quixotic technocrat", 3/31/98
Is also: "reform-minded", 3/22/97
"Bespectacled": yes

Anatoly Chubais, loans-for-shares architect
Crat-entials: "technocrat who is also a symbol of reform", 11/27/97
"Bespectacled": no

Maxim Boiko, former State Property Chief
Crat-entials: "boyish, bespectacled technocrat", 8/14/97
Is also a(n): "reformer", 8/14/97
"Bespectacled": see above

Sergei Witte, doomed Tsarist Minister of Finance
Crat-entials: "consummate technocrat", 1/30/96
Is also a(n): "autocrat", 1/30/95; "nationalist" 1/30/95
"Bespectacled": yes

Tiit Vahi, absurdly-named Estonian Premier
Crat-entials: "technocrat", 1/27/96
Redundancy factor: "a moderate technocrat", 1/27/96
"Bespectacled": when he reads

Anatoly Dyakov, former head of UES
Crat-entials: "quintessential Soviet technocrat", 2/3/98
Is also a(n): "hardliner", 2/3/98
"Bespectacled": no
Redundancy factor: "prosaic" technocrat, 2/3/98

Viktor Chernomyrdin, mumbling ex-Premier
Crat-entials: "subsidy-friendly Soviet technocrat", 1/27/96
Is also: "all things to all people", 3/24/98; "likely to compromise the program of economic reform", 1/12/94; a "reformer" 12/18/97

Robert Kocharyan, President of Armenia
Crat-entials: "technocrat", 4/28/98;
Is also a(n): "nationalist", 4/28/98
"Bespectacled": no
Redundancy factor: 0

Boris Yeltsin
Crat-entials: "A typical technocrat", 4/25/96
Is also a(n): "hardliner", 11/3/95; "democrat", 10/17/94; "reformer", 10/17/94
"Bespectacled": no

The latter usage was the one Western reporters in Moscow favored when describing pro-Western politicians. They used it despite compelling historical evidence that the very idea of a "technocrat" was totally ridiculous. Nowhere was there more evidence of that, in fact, than in ex-communist Moscow. These reporters obviously all knew that one of the pillars upon which Marxist theory rests is its insistence on being not ideology, but science. Marx, the ultimate "technocrat," very volubly detailed all the ways in which the seizing of the means of production by the proletariat was a proven historical inevitability, not a political platform. The result of all this "science," of course, was a 20th century full of enough politics to last mankind until the next ice age. And what politics!

Reporters in Moscow could hardly walk five feet without being reminded of that, but the instant bespectacled (people described as "technocrats" by Western reporters almost always wore glasses, for some reason) young Sergei Kiriyenko was nominated as Prime Minister by Boris Yeltsin, reporters started stepping over each other to call him a "technocrat." It was like a fashion craze, where you wake up one day to find everyone wearing baggy shorts. Gordon was one of the first hacks to ride the wave.

I'd never met Gordon before, and when I reached him by phone, I nearly burst out laughing. He sounded like a caricature of a TV anchorman, a hurrumphing, baritone cross of Dan Rather and Howard Beale. His reply to the question of what "technocrat" meant was staggeringly verbose and convoluted, so much so that I couldn't print it (which may have been the idea). Still, he hovered close to the consensus definition, using the phrase "more of a problem-solver than ideologue," among others. But the most interesting thing he said addressed not the word itself but his reasons for using it:

"Look, I'm doing my best to sum this person up for my reader in a way he'll understand, give him a catchword that makes sense," he said. "I need to keep things simple."

Gordon had laid that "catchword" business on me in a tone of self-congratulatory innocence, as though he'd just done a service for his poor, ignorant reader by keeping things simple. But when you thought about it, there was a completely different process at work.

The thing is, when you call someone a "problem-solver" rather than an ideologue, you're implying that social problems have natural, preexisting solutions, like the sculpture that already existed, uncarved, in

Michelangelo's block of stone. Or like a chess problem. You're implying that there are methods of dealing with social problems which are objectively right, or objectively wrong. And when you use the word "technocrat," those objectively right solutions suddenly become the exclusive province of your problem-solving "technocrat" subject.

In other words, you're deciding for your reader what is objectively right and what is objectively wrong. Use of the word "technocrat" is a step beyond labeling politicians according to their ideological beliefs. It labels them according to their proximity to the truth—your truth.

Journalists' misuse of the word "technocrat" was nothing compared to the things they did with the word "reform." A vast and insidious effort at political disinformation rivaling the anticommunist crusade of the McCarthy era was hidden in their manipulation of this one seemingly bland little word.

Ostensibly, "reform" was supposed to describe the whole process of dismantling the remains of Soviet government and rebuilding government, and society, in the West's law-based, democratic, capitalist image. A "reformer" was therefore always a democrat and a staunch advocate of free trade. Bearers of the tag tended to include the most radically pro-Western of the new class of Russian politicians, most notably onetime Prime Minister Yegor Gaidar, property chief–turned–Deputy Prime Minister Anatoly Chubais, and the above-mentioned Nizhni Novgorod governor–turned–Deputy Prime Minister Boris Nemtsov.

The implicit opposite of a reformer, of course, was a communist reactionary, someone who wanted to go back to the old system. The word "reformer," therefore, was a bastard post-communist offspring of old Cold War language. The Western propaganda machine which had once been geared toward deconstructing "reds" in power was now shifted slightly to support the "reformers" who'd taken their place.

The only problem with this formula is that the political enemies of the people Western journalists called "reformers" were, by the mid- and late nineties, not always communists. They included nationalists, authoritarians, even other democrats like Grigory Yavlinsky. They included industrialists who disapproved of World Bank structural adjustment policies toward Russia, and ordinary Russians who simply resented Western and particularly American influence on Russian life. In short, by 1997, they included just about everyone in Russia outside of a few shrewdly self-promoting Machiavellian bureaucrats in Yeltsin's administration.

Use of the word "reform" went beyond simple anticommunism. It was more like corporate p.r. In fact, by the time the *eXile* came on the scene, "Reform" really only described one of many teams competing for the few remaining slices of pie that were left to be divvied up in the Russian privatization process. Called "reformers," Chubais and his ilk were really the team that would let Western businessmen in on the action.

That reform no longer had anything to do with creating a law-based society, furthering democracy, strengthening the right to free speech, or even pushing the cause of fair business practice could be seen clearly in Western coverage of the giant "Svyazinvest" auction, which was held in late July 1997.

That auction, in which the state sold off 25.1 percent of the state telecommunications monopoly Svyazinvest, was won by a consortium that included big loans-for-shares winner Oneximbank, American investor George Soros, and Deutsche Morgan Grenfell. These were allies of Chubais, the leading "reformer" of the time. The losing bid came from shady industrialists Boris Berezovsky and Vladimir Gusinsky. God knows what actually went on behind the scenes on both sides in preparation for this auction, but one thing that came out after the auction was that State Property Chief Alfred Kokh—another official frequently referred to as a "reformer"—had accepted a $100,000 book advance from a Swiss publishing house called Servina that news reports had connected to Oneximbank. Kokh, a protégé of Chubais and a member of the so-called St. Petersburg Mafia of old Chubais acquaintances from his native Leningrad, had been in charge of running the auction, under Chubais's supervision.

Now, there was plenty of evidence to support the conclusion that the advance was a bribe. For one thing, Kokh had never written a book before, and advances of that size are unusual for anyone except for the most famous authors or well-anticipated manuscripts. Secondly, the book would have been Servina's first in four years of existence. And lastly, Servina was headed by a former employee of the Oneximbank Swiss office; that employee had told muckraking Russian reporter Alexander Minkin of *Novaya Gazeta* that he'd commissioned the Kokh book because he thought it "would be interesting to the Oneximbank people."

As a result of those news reports about Servina—first by Minkin, and then, in a rare act of sound Western investigative reporting, by Chrystia Freeland of the *Financial Times*—Kokh was fired from government and placed under investigation by the Moscow Prosecutor's Office for misuse of public office. Various Russian news reports subsequently speculated that Kokh had passed false insider information to the Berezovsky team prior to the auction about the size of Oneximbank's bid, leading Berezovsky to bid lower than he'd planned and allowing Onexim, Soros et al. to walk away with the victory.

Oddly, though, the Kokh firing went virtually unmentioned in the Western press, and on the heels of the Soros victory, Svyazinvest was hailed as a breakthrough for fair business in Russia. Chubais, who as Deputy Prime Minister and Finance Minister had overseen the auction, was widely praised for finally helping the Russian government earn some real money. In September, in fact, the influential *Euromoney* magazine even named him "Finance Minister of the Year":

"The relative transparency of the Svyazinvest deal," the magazine wrote, "was in marked contrast to Russia's earlier 'loans-for-shares' scandal in which the government was accused of handing over valuable state assets at rock-bottom prices to well-connected insiders."

The magazine failed to mention that the "loans-for-shares" auctions they railed against had been overseen and designed by Chubais himself. Then there is the curious phrase "relative transparency." What exactly is a "relatively transparent" auction? Clearly the insertion of the word "relative" was meant to address the whole issue of the Kokh firing and the apparent bribe.

But from where I sat, an auction was either fair or it wasn't. Either the team submitting the highest bid in absolutely free and fair conditions won, or it didn't. If you just used a little insider information, or just bribed one government official, well, that's still insider dealing or bribery. You couldn't have a "relatively fair" auction any more than you could be "relatively" pregnant. As my friend Jonas Bernstein wrote in one of his columns for the *Moscow Times*, subtler didn't necessarily mean cleaner.

But that was the way the Western press played it. Just a week after the *Euromoney* piece came out, Daniel Hoffman of the *Washington Post* wrote a piece in which he parroted the "relatively fair" concept:

"Some analysts," he wrote, "said it [the Svyazinvest auction] was a relatively fair sale because unlike most tenders, it went to the highest bidder and earned a bundle of cash for the government."

Hoffman hadn't done his homework. Even during the overtly bogus loans-for-shares auctions, the property always went to the highest bidder—no bids were awarded without at least nominal competition. Here again the word "relatively"—which other thesaurus-bearing reporters replaced with phrases like "fairest yet"—was inserted in answer to the Kokh business, but this time the justification was that the government had made a lot of money.

While the herd was frantically trying to apologize for the Svyazinvest auction, it left unreported a huge subplot to the entire story, which was that there were major Western financiers securing outrageous bargains on this deal which had apparently hinged on bribery and insider dealing. By most conservative estimates, the Svyazinvest packet that the Onexim–Soros consortium won was worth at least three times the $1.8 billion it was eventually sold for. So George Soros—the same financier who had spoken out, in a well-publicized article for the *Atlantic Monthly*, against "robber-baron capitalists"—gets in bed with the ultimate robber-baron, Vladimir Potanin of Oneximbank, and walks away with a fantastic investment! And this was thanks, apparently, to a few shady deals which the Western press not only ignores but praises as the "fairest yet."

Another Westerner who made out on the Svyazinvest deal was Boris Jordan, the head of MFK-Renaissance, the investment wing of Oneximbank. Jordan, an American of Russian heritage, had merged his Renaissance investment company with Oneximbank just prior to the Svyazinvest bid and was said to have been instrumental in securing Western financing for the deal (his brother Nick worked at Deutsche Morgan Grenfell).

Just after the *Euromoney* piece came out, I heard that the once-mighty newspaper *Pravda*—by now one of the deadest, most unreadable publications in Russia, with a minuscule circulation and a staff of near-illiterate, ex-communist corpses—had published a story to the effect that Boris Jordan had an uncle named "Troyansky" who worked in the Servina publishing house in Switzerland.

A series of phone calls to Switzerland and to various Moscow sources confirmed that a law firm called Secretan Troyanos had incorporated Servina publishers four years before, and that the head of that firm, Tikhon Troyanos, was a cousin of Jordan's. In itself, the story proved nothing, but given all the other information already out there—Jordan's connection to Oneximbank, Oneximbank's connection to Servina, Kokh's connection to Servina, the Svyazinvest connection between Kokh, Oneximbank, and Jordan—it was definitely an interesting and newsworthy piece of a larger puzzle, and the first piece that involved a Westerner.

Not wanting anyone to have the excuse to ignore the

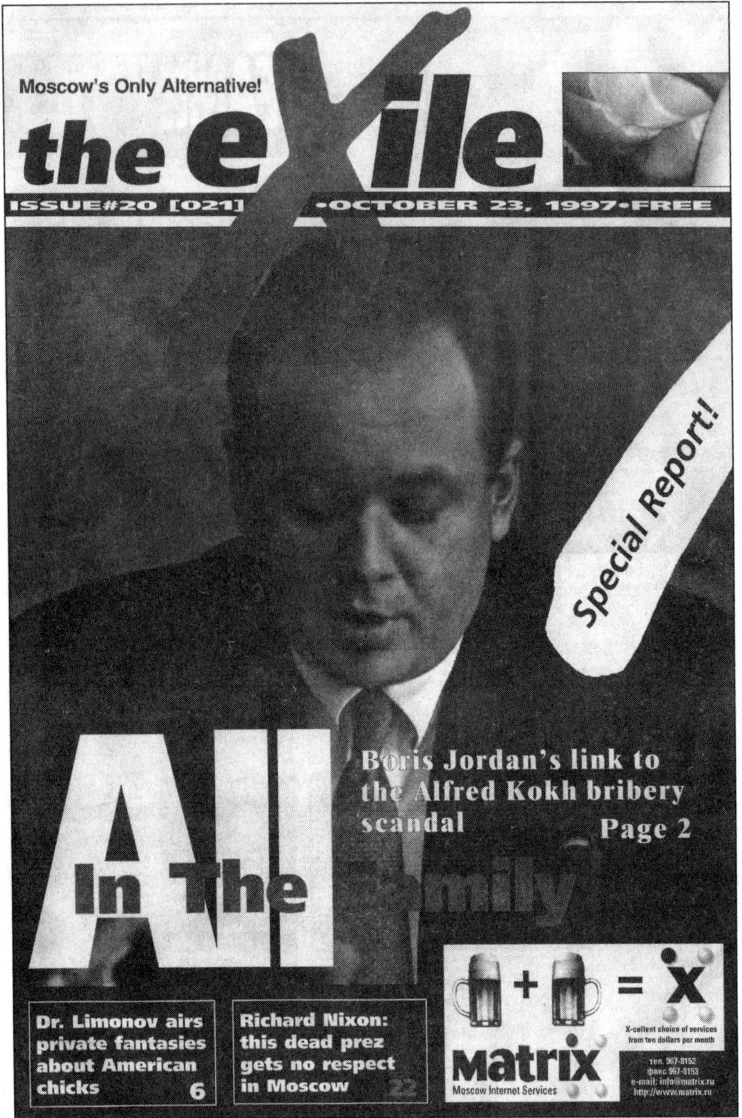
Moscow's Only Alternative!

the eXile

ISSUE#20 [021] •OCTOBER 23, 1997•FREE

Special Report!

Boris Jordan's link to the Alfred Kokh bribery scandal Page 2

All In The Family

Dr. Limonov airs private fantasies about American chicks 6

Richard Nixon: this dead prez gets no respect in Moscow 22

story because it appeared in the disreputable *eXile* first, I called up David Filipov, an ex-coworker from the *Moscow Times* and a friend who was now the bureau chief of the *Boston Globe*, and pitched the story to him.

Filipov, incidentally, was the only bureau head in the city I felt I could trust with a story like this. It was well-known among freelancers that stories you pitched to the "big guys" like the *Los Angeles Times* or the *New York Times* would often be rejected, only to be done soon afterward by the bureau's own lazy staffers. So if you had something interesting or confidential you wanted to sell, you couldn't bring it to someone you didn't know personally and trust. And even though I'd known David since 1992, and even though we'd gone to high school in the same town, played basketball together, and had lunch just a few weeks before, we still had a pretty shaky phone call.

"David," I said. "The reason I'm calling is that I have a pretty good story. It's this thing I'm going to do in my paper, but would also like to publish somewhere else so that there would be a better chance someone would pick it up."

"Okay," he said. "And you want to run it past me, but you want a guarantee that if I turn you down, I won't do it myself."

"Right," I said. Hackworld ethics were so moronic that even two friends had to have conversations like this.

"Okay, I agree," he said.

I told David the Jordan business, he went for the story, and we ran it in the *Boston Globe* under a double byline, concurrently with an *eXile* cover story, in early October. Crediting the *Boston Globe*, the Russian press picked it up—the National News Wire Service, *Nezavisimaya Gazeta*, the Moscow radio station *Radio Rocks*, *Moskovsky Komsomolets*, and others. The list of Russian outlets who repeated the story included blatantly anti-Chubais, anti-"reformer," Boris Berezovsky–controlled papers, but it also included more politically ambiguous publications like *Moskovsky Komsomolets*.

On the other hand, not a single Western publication or news service picked up the Jordan story—not even the *Moscow Times*, which supposedly covered the expatriate community. The omission might have been understandable had it not been for the fact that the very week before the story broke, numerous Western publications, including the *Wall Street Journal*, the *Chicago Tribune*, and the *Christian Science Monitor*, had run stories about the fact that Jordan had been denied a visa into Russia. That story had been sold in the West as yet another "the Russians are heathens who can't do business" tale, a story about how Russians had not yet matured to the point where they could do business with respectable Westerners.

Even with heavy coverage of the visa incident, no one returned to the Jordan story after our *Globe* piece broke, despite the obvious possibility that the two incidents were related. After all, it made sense that someone on the losing side of Svyazinvest—particularly Boris Berezovsky, who also happened to be Deputy Secretary of the Russian

Embattled Banker Denied McMuffin

By Mark Whitehouse
STAFF WRITER

American investment banker Boris Jordan has again been denied full service in a restaurant, MFK-Renaissance Bank officials said Monday. Yesterday morning, the prominent businessman attempted to purchase an Egg McMuffin at the McDonald's restaurant on Gazetny Pereulok in central Moscow, but was denied.

"Boris was told that he couldn't purchase the Egg McMuffin because he arrived after 10:30 a.m. However, we've been down this road before," said a spokesman for the Moscow-based investment bank Jordan founded in 1995 and recently merged with the Uneximbank-backed MFK.

The breakfast snafu is a virtual repeat of a similar scene last August, when Jordan was denied a membership at the prestigious El Dorado Restaurant located across the river from the Kremlin. Some suggested at the time that Jordan's attempts to secure board seats at one of Russia's largest steel factories prompted the factory's management to pull political strings to keep him from being accepted as a full-time member of the El Dorado restaurant. To this day, Jordan can only be served there if there is available seating.

> It is too early to tell whether politics played a role in the Egg McMuffin incident.

The Renaissance official said it is too early to tell whether politics played a role in the Egg McMuffin incident. Jordan claims that according to his watch, he arrived at 10:23 a.m., well before the breakfast menu ends. However, the McDonald's server who handled Jordan alleges that the restaurant's clock read 10:36. Her shift manager, Valery Tyatchkov, agreed.

"I wouldn't be surprised if this was part of some larger shoving match," said the Renaissance spokesman. "We've got to exhaust the possibility that it's a technical problem and that the next time Boris returns to McDonald's, they'll give him his breakfast during regular breakfast hours."

Jordan's close relationship with Uneximbank and its president Vladimir Potanin could have invited the wrath of Russia's other powerful bankers, some of whom have criticized Uneximbank for using its political influence to win recent privatization auctions.

This is the latest hurdle Jordan has faced during the past year as he sought to complete a merger of his investment bank Renaissance Capital and MFK. Just last week, the esteemed banker, who is seen as a pioneer and trailblazer in the Western financial community, was turned away from the Jazz Kafe for not dressing "properly," on the same day that the Central Bank refused to grant Jordan a license to head the new MFK-Renaissance bank.

Last October, Jordan's visa was revoked for what authorities described as "technical reasons." But Jordan maintained that the visa scuffle was orchestrated by banking competitors.

Jordan is formally head of the Renaissance Capital investment company and executive chairman of MFK bank, which merged in January 1998.

Uneximbank was one of the original investors in Renaissance, and the two banks worked together last summer to put together the winning $1.9 billion bid for a piece of Svyazinvest, Russia's telecommunications network. That auction was hailed as the first example of an open auction and the opening shot in the reformers' war against "crony capitalism," the sort of insider dealing that marked previous auctions. It is thought that bankers unhappy with the results, namely Boris Berezovsky, have since retaliated by arranging various annoying incidents for Jordan. The Egg McMuffin incident is just one in a series of similar upsetting incidents. Others in the Western investment community expressed some concern, noting that if today he is denied an Egg McMuffin, tomorrow, he could be denied a Happy Meal.

In our phony April 1 issue of the *Moscow Times*, we parodied the Western press's inexplicable concern over Boris Jordan's visa troubles with a sensational article blasting McDonald's for denying the super-rich banker an Egg McMuffin.

Security Council at the time—got upset with Jordan and decided to return a little fire. Of course, that might have been just because of Jordan's formal alignment with Oneximbank; in fact, Jordan himself said that his visa was denied as part of the "Banker's War" between Berezovsky and Oneximbank's Potanin. But if there was something else in Jordan's relationship with Potanin, well, then, that would be all the more reason for a jilted rival to strip his visa and call attention to him.

Who knew? There was almost no way of ever finding out. But it certainly didn't make sense to publish one side of the story, i.e., the visa incident, and not publish the other. And if it didn't make sense for the *Chicago Tribune* or the *Christian Science Monitor*, it made no sense at all for the *Moscow Times*. After all, Jordan, whose Renaissance firm managed over $1 billion in assets, was the most conspicuous foreigner living in Moscow, the very beacon of the expatriate community. As distasteful as the idea of crediting me or the *eXile* for a story must have been for the *Moscow Times*, I felt that it was totally unthinkable that they would not run the story. It was just outside the realm of possibility, like the *Carmel Gazette* not reporting Clint Eastwood's birthday.

But when a few days passed and the story still hadn't run in their paper, I realized that Jordan was safe. So I called up the few reporter friends I had left on the *Times* staff to find out what was going on. Erin Arvedlund, one of the token humans on the paper's business desk, whispered into the phone that she had no idea what had happened.

"It was a great story," she said. "I don't know why they didn't do it. I think it's because Geoff likes Jordan."

"Geoff *likes* Jordan?" I asked. "How can anybody *like* Jordan?"

"I don't know, but I think he does," she said.

Erin quit the MT staff that weekend, so on Monday I called up Mark Whitehouse, the paper's gaunt young melanin-deprived business reporter who had been perfecting a cringing, originality-free professional persona for years and was clearly angling for Winestock's job. He'd already ripped off a couple of my *eXile* pieces that year and I figured that he would have been the one to do the story, if anyone had. But he seemed surprised when I asked him what had happened to the Jordan story.

"Oh, well, I don't know," he said. "I wouldn't know anything about that. I'm not covering it."

"Why not?"

"Oh, well, I don't know," he said. "I suppose it's interesting, but . . . I don't know."

CHAPTER EIGHT

The next day, in the midst of a huge world financial crisis that had been triggered by the crash of the Asian markets, Whitehouse did a front-page story on the Russian market that featured a portrait of an unruffled Jordan heroically braving the storm. It was a classic example of what journalists call a *blow job:*

"But when 2 P.M. rolled around, an eerie calm reigned on the trading floor of the investment bank Renaissance Capital. 'Did it open?' asked Boris Jordan, the bank's 31-year-old head, as he strolled into the equities department."

So much for the Jordan story. If Jordan was going to come off looking like John Wayne in MT coverage just a few days after a story like David's and mine broke, there wasn't much chance of us getting picked up anywhere.

As it turned out, we'd been fucked from the start. Some eight months later, I got a tip that the *Moscow Times*'s publisher, Derk Sauer, had been in negotiations with Jordan during the time period in question to purchase provincial Russian newspapers together. Sauer himself later admitted to me that he had had meetings with Jordan's Renaissance bank shortly before my Servina story broke. Under those circumstances, there was no way the MT was going to pick us up.

But the Jordan story wasn't the Western press's worst display of blind advocacy. They were saving that for a story which broke about a month later, in November 1997—the so-called Writer's Union scandal.

What happened was that Chubais and a team of his closest advisers all got caught in what appeared to be a bribery scam. The Deputy Prime Minister admitted, following a report by that same Minkin of *Novaya Gazeta*, to having accepted a $90,000 book advance for a history of privatization. The advance came from "Segodnya" publishers, a company which was controlled by Oneximbank, the same bank which had profited enormously from a series of auctions over the past two years that Chubais played a key part in. Chubais admitted to receiving his advance, all but conceding that he had been caught in a blatant conflict of interest. Yeltsin fired the three associates which were still in government—Maxim Boiko (the original "Harvard-educated economist"), Pyotr Mostovoi, and Alexander Kazakov—but kept Chubais on.

This was not the first time Chubais had been in trouble. On the contrary, in his relatively short career in government, he'd already racked up a list of improprieties even Marion Barry would envy. Earlier that summer, Chubais had admitted to receiving a $3 million interest-free loan from Stolichny Bank, apparently in exchange for Stolichny's victory in the auction of AgPromBank, the state agricultural bank, which controlled the second-largest banking network in Russia. He had also been caught failing to pay taxes the year before. Furthermore, the income he did later report was due to investments through a shady investment company called Montes Auri which was raided the same day Kazakov was fired, using money from the Stolichny loan. Chubais had also been caught on audiotape in fall 1996, in a story that was reported by *Moskovsky Komsomolets*, discussing how best to suppress the criminal investigation into the activities of his associates Vladimir Yevstafiyev and Sergei Lisofsky. He'd also been questioned as to his possible involvement in improper campaign practices as a result of an incident in which the former Lisofsky and Yevstafiyev were caught hauling a half million dollars in cash out of the White House in the middle of the night. That money had come from Yeltsin's reelection campaign fund: Chubais had been the campaign manager. Chubais also reportedly far exceeded legal spending limits as campaign manager; the obvious spending gap had been a key in Yeltsin's victory over the communists.

There had been other incidents. Under pressure to put an end to duty-free privileges for the notorious National Sports Fund and for the Afghan Veterans Association, Chubais in 1995 scored a major p.r. victory by revoking their special statuses. A month later, he personally reinstated them. Chubais in 1995 also brokered the loans-for-shares auctions, which even according to the most conservative estimates cost the Russian state billions of dollars. Other scandals included the fudged USAID-funded voucher commercial, which Chubais turned into a commercial for his political party, Russia's Choice, and the closing of the investigation into the Investor Protection Fund.

Last but not least, Chubais was also a notorious enemy of free speech. In September 1996, when he was head of a Presidential Commission on media issues, and the second most powerful man in Russia after Boris Yeltsin, he chaired a meeting with the editors of Russia's most influential newspapers. According to various news reports of that meeting, one editor of a major newspaper, whom I feel pretty sure was Igor Golombiyevsky of *Izvestia*, got up to complain that the government was using the Yeltsin-allied oil firm LUKoil (which owned a stake in the paper) to put pressure on him to alter his editorial slant in favor of the government. Chubais reportedly replied: "You will write what you are told to write, or bones will crack."

Golombiyesky eventually got a taste of the "Bonecracker" spirit firsthand. He was fired a little less than a year later when his paper published an exposé which demonstrated that Chubais had accepted the $3 million no-interest loan from Stolichny Bank. Chubais was widely accepted to have been the impetus behind the firing, which was considered a sort of Alamo for the free press in Russia.

Despite all of this, the Western press, to the last man, treated the "Writer's Union" scandal as Chubais's christening into the world of scandal. Inga Saffron of the *Philadelphia Inquirer* provided a typical account a few days after the scandal broke:

"Anatoly B. Chubais isn't just the idea man behind Russia's economic reforms, he's the tough-as-nails enforcer who made them happen. . . . Once considered a squeaky clean free marketeer, Chubais was revealed last week to be as unprincipled as the average Russian bureaucrat."

Last week? Was she kidding? No, she wasn't, and neither were any of the other reporters in town: There wasn't a single writer from a major paper who touched upon any part of Chubais's scandalous past while covering this story.

But some outlets did more than just leave out important background. Reuters, for instance, failed to report even the most basic elements of the near-firing story.

The book-advance story was about bribery. It was not a story about unreported income or inflated literary fees. Reuters left the bribery angle out. In the most misleading story it released, correspondent Adam Tanner, that same old coworker of mine from the *Moscow Times*, cast the story in a light that implied that Chubais was in trouble simply for making a lot of money:

"Boiko and Mostovoi, both close allies of Chubais, the father of Russia's privatization program, lost their jobs for splitting a $450,000 book advance from a Russian publisher with Chubais and three other associates.

"The issue is a delicate one because Yeltsin himself has written two volumes of memoirs, the most recent of which was written during his first term and came out in 1994.

"Yeltsin earned $280,000 in royalties in 1994 and 1995 for his second memoir, he said during the presidential campaign last year. In an income declaration earlier this year, Yeltsin said he was still earning bank interest on the book earnings."

Yelstin's royalties came from a book that actually sold well enough to earn $280,000. Chubais took an advance—not royalties—from a company that directly benefited from his policies for a book that even under a once-in-a-millennium convergence of favorable planets would not earn more than $10,000. The comparison to Yeltsin was absolutely preposterous and totally misleading. Reading it, you wonder why he wrote it that way, until you get to the end:

"Economics Minister Yakov Urinson said Chubais must be retained as he was essential to keep economic reforms going.

"'I'm completely sure that he is needed today in the Russian government and by the Russian people, not just for investment but to resolve all the questions before us,' Urinson told Reuters.

"Chubais conceded Friday that he and his allies received excessive fees for the proposed book on Russia's privatization campaign. But he said the bulk of the advances were given to a charity promoting small businesses."

The Urinson quote—which left out the critical addition "a close Chubais ally" (Urinson was one of Chubais's closest advisers)—capped a rhetorical flourish which ended in another misleading sentence. After all, when you end by saying "he said the bulk of the advances were given to a charity promoting small businesses," and don't challenge it, the reader is likely to accept it as true.

The minimum standard of journalistic ethics here would have required that Tanner point out that no one in the Russian press corps had yet been able to find that "charity," that former Prime Minister Yegor Gaidar, who was supposed to be heading the charity, changed his story about that charity the next day, and that the money had not, after all, even been paid to this same nonexistent charity!

The maximum standard, which he was obviously never in danger of approaching, would have required here that he point out that the alleged "charity," the "Fund for the Defense of Private Property," bore the same name as the fictional organization through which Chubais had processed his $3 million interest-free loan from Stolichny Bank earlier that year. That fact would have helped the reader understand that the charity was almost certainly a front. But then, no Western reporter got that right—not one. Only the Russians brought that up.

I called Tanner myself to find out what had happened. We chatted for a minute, then I abruptly told him I was interviewing him. Why, I asked, hadn't he included Oneximbank in his story?

He was silent for about ten whole seconds, taking in the treacherous fact that I was actually putting him on the record. Finally he said, "Well, it's impossible to explain everything . . . "

"No one's asking you to explain *everything*," I said. "I'm just saying that before you report anything else, you have to report the link to the bank. It's the most important part of the story."

"Well, the story is there," he said. "I think the main question is whether or not there was influence-peddling, or a conflict of interest."

"Right," I said quickly. "So why wasn't that in your story?"

Suddenly there was silence on the phone. I hadn't realized it yet, but my interview with Tanner was over; he was pawning me off on his superior, chief correspondent Martin Nesirky, who called me back a few minutes later and gave an amazing and revealing interview.

Moscow's Only Alternative!
the eXile
ISSUE#22 [023] -NOVEMBER 20, 1997-FREE
Guess who's driving the getaway car...
Former Moscow World Bank chief tries his hand at meteorology 22
Faith No More storms into Moscow this Sunday, and the eXile cares a lot!
Edward Limonov is an extremist, but really, can you blame him? 21

In our cover story about the "Writer's Union" scandal, we tried to put the appropriate spin on the true meaning of Anatoly Chubais's $90,000 book advance.

A quick note about interviewing reporters. From experience I know that journalists in private complain constantly about the way various public figures refuse to answer questions posed by the press, about the lame denials they make, the total lack of openness in their speech, and, more importantly, their hostility to reporters.

Pre-emptive Shutdown Has Traders On Edge

By Mark Whitehouse
STAFF WRITER

As Moscow's brokers arrived at work Tuesday morning, the stage was being set for a massacre. Wall Street had fallen, Hong Kong was a bloodbath, and price quotes for Russian shares were already showing a massive drop in the market.

Fearing a debacle, officials shut down the Russian Trading System, the computer-based trading system that is the lifeblood of the Russian stock market, postponing the opening of trade by three hours, until 2 p.m. NTV television issued a nationwide warning against panic.

But when 2 p.m. rolled around, an eerie calm reigned on the trading floor of investment bank Renaissance Capital. "Did it open?" asked Boris Jordan, the bank's 31-year-old head, as he strolled into the equities department.

The sell orders from London did not flood in. Nobody jumped out any of the giant windows overlooking the Moscow River. Nobody even broke a sweat.

While some $88 million in Russian shares did trade hands Tuesday, most of them were apparently bought and sold by so-called traders, who differ from brokers in that they specialize in speculating on daily fluctuations in the market.

As Kirill Maltsev, sales director at Rye, Man & Gor securities, watched the

See MOOD, Page 2

But the funny thing is that if you call up any reporter and put him on the other side of the deal, when he's suddenly the one being interviewed, he'll inevitably transform into the kind of evasive, hostile, doublespeaking twit even the p.r. department of Exxon would be glad to hire.

I asked Nesirky why Oneximbank had been left out of the story.

"Too much detail," he boomed, in a bellicose British lilt. "Our work stands for itself. We try to tell each story as objectively and as simply as possible, taking into account what would be of interest to our readers. Believe me, nothing was consciously left out. There was just so much information . . . "

"But," I said, "I just spoke with Adam Tanner, and he said the real issue was whether or not there was influence-peddling—"

"Whatever Adam told you is not relevant," he barked, interrupting me. "You can't quote Adam."

"What are you talking about?" I said. "Of course I can. I talked to him."

"No you can't. I'm the one responsible for this story," he said.

"Yes, I can," I said. "I identified myself, I told him I was working on a story, and he never indicated to me that he didn't want to be quoted for the record."

"He indicated to me that he didn't want to be quoted for the record," Nesirky said firmly. "And I'm telling you that you *can't* quote him."

Now, even the greenest cub reporter knows an interview subject can't claim off-the-record privileges ex post facto. If you know you're talking to a reporter—and Tanner definitely did —it's your own goddamn fault if you say something dumb.

For Nesirky to insist otherwise to another professional was ridiculous, like a presidential candidate insisting to his opponent on election night that votes from Texas count twice.

He went on:

"There is no conspiracy here. . . . That that aspect of the story was not in the piece does not have any other meaning. . . . We're just trying to tell the story simply and objectively. Also, and this is something you're probably not aware of, we're dealing with a legal minefield here. If someone wants to proceed against our news organization, then I need not remind you that the UK libel laws are among the most stringent in the world."

What was he talking about? I said nothing, deciding to let him run with the line for a while. After a brief silence he continued:

"Of course," he added, speaking up, "that has nothing to do with our coverage of the Chubais story."

"Then why bring it up?" I asked.

"Look," he said. "If in the heat of the moment, details were left out of a story, that absolutely does not mean that the story was intended to favor anybody. . . . The story we were trying to tell was that Chubais was kept on not because any scandal was being swept under the rug, but because it was economically and politically expedient. Look, whether you like it or not, Chubais is a well-known figure in the West, a person without whom Russia would have a terrible time dealing with the IMF. . . . It would be nothing short of suicidal for Russia to remove him."

I said nothing. He was swimming in deeper waters by now.

"Of course," he quickly broke in, recovering himself, "this is not *my personal opinion,* but the opinion of various named sources which were quoted in the article."

Here Nesirky reiterated his commitment to objectivity, called me "pathetic" for continuing to "hammer away" at this issue, and finally, saying that we were going "round and round in circles," tried to conclude:

"Look, all I can say is, if you are going to mention Reuters in your article, you must quote

the eXile

NATURAL BORN
DEPUTY PRIME MINISTERS

"TERRIFYING! OLIVER STONE TAKES THE VIEWER TO WHERE FEW DARE TO GO: THE EVIL HEART OF MAN!" *JOEL SIEGEL, GOOD MORNING AMERICA*
"CHUBAIS IS A NATURAL BORN ACTOR... HIS 'REFORMER' CHARACTER IS SURE TO EARN HIM AN OSCAR!" *GENE SISKEL, AT THE MOVIES*
"A THINKING-MAN'S BLACK COMEDY... SURREAL, SEXY, DIACHROMATIC... GODARD MEETS FREDDY KRUEGER!" *JOSE ALINEZ, THE BAKHTIN BUGLE*

the eXile

VOX POPULI

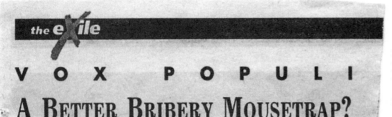

A Better Bribery Mousetrap?

One thing that struck us about the Anatoly Chubais "Writer's Union" Scandal was how crude and ill-considered the method Chubais, Boiko et al had chosen to take their bribes was. Why receive an inflated book advance and openly declare it to the public? Why not find some other, less conspicuous way to cheat the law? We asked prominent Muscovites their opinion: Since the current Chubais method for taking bribes has proved inefficient, which method would you suggest be use next time?

VADIM MIKHAILOV, HEAD, DIGGER UNDERGROUND SOCIETY: I don't have any experience with either paying or receiving bribes. But basically, you've got to get right up close to someone in power, get to know them real well, and then blackmail them. That's the best way by far.

KLARA KASPAROVA, MOTHER, WORLD CHESS CHAMPION GARRY KASPAROV: Gosh, I don't know. I don't think I should answer that question. That's not the kind of thing one jokes about.

VLADIMIR POLYAKOV, PRESS SPOKESMAN, GORBACHEV FUND: I don't know. We don't have any experience with that. And besides, we've reached a point where we can't even deal with humor anymore.

NIKOLAI PANSHEV, FORMER DETECTIVE, MOSCOW CRIMINAL INVESTIGATION DEPARTMENT: You leave a whole bunch of money in some place where your guy will find it.

ALEKSANDR TKACHENKO, PSYCHOLOGIST, EXPERT ON SERIAL MURDER: I would think there would be some ingenious way to do it so that no one would find out, ever.

VIKTOR FILATOV, SPOKESMAN, LDPR: Watch CNN. They'll tell you everything you have to know.

me as saying that if this aspect of the story was left out of our coverage, it was either due to an oversight, or to the sheer volume of information—"

"Wait," I said, trying to follow him. "Now it's an oversight?"

That sent us flying into another heated exchange. Afterward, he clarified the quote:

"That is, if you think that information should have been in the story, it was an oversight."

So if I think it was an oversight, it was an oversight, but since he doesn't think it was an oversight, it wasn't an oversight. For the record, I think it was an oversight.

Nesirky, Tanner, and co. weren't alone in failing to report the Oneximbank link accurately. No less an authority than the *Washington Post*, in the person of correspondent David Hoffman, carefully avoided the implication that Chubais had been involved in influence-peddling. The lead from the piece sets the tone appropriately:

"President Boris Yeltsin fired two more top aides to Deputy Prime Minister Anatoly Chubais Saturday but refused to accept Chubais's resignation, leaving Russia's leading economic reformer still in office but dealing a major setback to the prospects for further liberalization of the economy."

Obviously this was going to be an "isn't this scandal a shame" story. There were a lot of those. Hoffman came closest to actually telling the story when he wrote:

"But the uproar grew more intense because the source of payments appears to be one of the most influential and wealthy of the tycoons who have been feuding with each other and with Chubais in recent months."

No mention of the fact that the payment came from someone who benefited from Chubais's actions as Vice-Premier. It just came from some guys who were feuding. That omission, plus the key omission of the history of Chubais's other improprieties, allowed Hoffman to include the following quote without making it seem ludicrous:

" 'The different political forces involved in the attacks on Chubais understood that this is a team which is preventing stealing public money, and stops unfair rules of the game,' said Leonid Gozman, a Moscow State University political psychology professor who has been close to Chubais and Gaidar."

Chubais, the architect of loans-for-shares, heading the team which stops unfair rules of the game? When I called Hoffman to ask him how he had let that through, he snapped at me:

"I know what you're trying to do, and you know what you're trying to do," he said. "Obviously you haven't read my pieces on this."

It didn't occur to me at the time, but I had. In fact, in the *eXile*'s Press Review column, we'd pointed out that Hoffman was one of the first Western journalists to coin the phrase "relatively fair auction" with regard to the Svyazinvest auction.

A quick note on Chubais. Because he pushed through loans-for-shares, and because he brokered the "group of seven" deal for banker support of Yeltsin prior to the 1996 election, a deal which left the bankers immensely powerful following the election, he can easily be said to have created, almost single-handedly, the Russian tycoon class. You can't separate Chubais and the tycoons; they have each been equally responsible for the other's rise to wealth and prominence.

When Chubais was finally fired, we tried to reassure the Western business community that, contrary to all expectations, the world hadn't ended with his dismissal.

Given that, two of the four additional pieces Hoffman sent me can be classified as hogwash on the basis of the headlines alone: "Yeltsin Aides Take On the Moguls" (Sept. 26) and "Kremlin Reformers Take on the Money Magnates" (Sept. 9). A third, "Yeltsin Seeks Halt in Attacks on Reformers," gave the same Chubais vs. Tycoons line in the body of the piece:

"Chubais had also publicly taken on some of the new oligarchs, saying the government would not be pushed around by them."

Not only did Chubais create the oligarchic class, he was, even through the week the Writer's Union story broke, right up to the time he was nearly fired, still working actively to enrich one of the tycoons—Vladimir Potanin. Just a few weeks prior to the breaking of the scandal, Chubais was in London, meeting with British Petroleum which—surprise!—subsequently announced a deal to buy a stake in the Potanin-controlled Sidanko oil company as soon as Chubais returned.

Hoffman's only solid piece of reporting on Svyazinvest came in a lengthy Oct. 26 piece, which at least partially described Chubais's true role in the proceedings. By then, the Alfred Kokh story, which demonstrated to every Moscow reporter with a pulse that Svyazinvest was probably a faked auction, was over two months old. In the meantime, Hoffman had whiffed three times in three separate pieces.

Including this new piece, that means Hoffman blew 4 out of 5 stories on Chubais in the two months preceding and including the Writer's Union scandal. That's a batting average of .200—what baseball players call the Mendoza line. In baseball, you can't even stay in the big leagues as a good-fielding shortstop with a .200 batting average. But in journalism, apparently, you can write for the *Washington Post.*

Reuters and the *Washington Post* weren't alone in blowing their Chubais/Svyazinvest coverage. Patricia Kranz of *Business Week*, in a swooning profile of Potanin published a few weeks before the Writer's Union story, offered the following nugget of wisdom high up in her piece:

"Potanin had angered his rivals by refusing to play by normal Moscow rules, where state assets would be divvied up among tycoons at private sessions. Instead, he had insisted on a competitive auction for Svyazinvest and had paid a princely sum, breaking the game wide open."

This was after former state property chief Alfred Kokh had already been fired for, as Yeltsin said, "favoring one side too much" in the Svyazinvest auction! Even Hoffman's "relatively fair" was better reporting than that. When I called Kranz about that story, she made a smarter move than her colleagues at Reuters and the *Washington Post*: she freaked out off the record, then called me back with a prepared on-the-record statement, which was:

"I've done a lot of reporting, and the story reflects my conclusions. I spoke with one of the losers in the auction, Mikhail Freedman of Alfa-Bank, and he told me that he believed that the actual auction was fair, and that the bidder that made the highest bid won. His only quarrel was that Oneximbank had had more government accounts to work with, and therefore had more cash with which to bid."

"Okay," I said. "So why didn't you put that in the story?"

"I don't have to tell you why I put anything in my story!" she snapped, then hung up.

Here's another example of the Western press's favorable treatment of Chubais. Just before the Writer's Union scandal broke, Fred Coleman of *USA Today* interviewed the Deputy Prime Minister, and when he said, "I think Yeltsin has the historical right to name his successor," Coleman didn't even ask him what he meant, as though it didn't matter that a democrat is not supposed to believe in a ruler's right to name his successor.

Going back into more ancient history, almost no one (with the conspicuous exception of the then Marc Champion–run *Moscow Times*) in the Western press criticized Chubais for his role

World Defies Pundits, Does Not End

X 26.03.98 31.03.98 www.exile.ru #09 P.3

For almost a year now, Western journalists have been predicting widespread catastrophe in the event of an Anatoly Chubais firing. Were they right? In a panic, we called around Moscow to find out:

Timur Ivanidze, Director, International Weather Department, State Meteorological Service (Gidromettsentr)

eXile: Did the sun rise on time today?

Ivanidze: Um...why do you ask?

eXile: Well, Chubais was fired yesterday, and we just wanted to make sure everything is okay.

Ivanidze: (laughing) Oh, well, in that case, yes, it did rise on time. And it will probably set on time.

eXile: Were there any natural disasters as a result of his firing?

Ivanidze: Actually, it's a funny thing. There was almost no bad weather anywhere in the world today.

Vera Alekseyeva, Public Relations Secretary, Mytishinsky Dairy Factory:

eXile: Since the firing of Anatoly Chubais, have cows stopped giving milk?

Alekseyeva: Of course not. Cows have not stopped giving milk. What did you think, that cows are made so that they would give milk until Chubais was fired?

eXile: It's sort of a humorous question.

Alekseyeva: In that case, I don't want to answer it.

Galina Vavilova, Director, Moscow Puppet Theater:

eXile: How's business?

Vavilova: Fine.

eXile: So since Anatoly Chubais was fired, people haven't been coming to your theater and saying, "Hey, why should I watch this? They're just puppets"?

Vavilova: We have a popular theater. And 90% of our clients are children. And children are not politicians.

Unnamed Spokesman, Australian Embassy:

eXile: Say, how are you guys?

AUS: Fine.

eXile: We have a question. Have you been in touch with Australia today?

AUS: Yes.

eXile: Everything okay down there?

AUS: Sure. Why?

eXile: Well, Anatoly Chubais was fired yesterday, and we just want to make sure the world didn't end.

AUS: (laughing) No, Australia's okay.

eXile: Continent still intact? Still surrounded by water?

AUS: Yes, you could say that.

eXile: You folks still saying "G'day" around the office there?

AUS: Yes, people are still saying "G'day" around here.

eXile: May we use your name?

AUS: (laughing) No way.

Vladimir Khairetgainov, Chief Investigator, Moscow UNON (Illegal Narcotics Distribution Directorate):

eXile: Are people using drugs more now that Anatoly Chubais has been fired?

Khairetgainov: I don't see the connection at all.

eXile: People have been saying that all kinds of bad things will happen when he gets fired, and we just wanted to know how you're holding up.

eXile: I still don't understand the connection. We have nothing to do with that business.

Vladimir Goncharov, IB Undertakers:

eXile: Since Chubais got fired, have the dead been rising and running around the city, causing trouble?

Goncharov: No, they're still dead.

Unnamed spokeswoman, Moscow Patriarchy:

eXile: Have people stopped believing in God since Anatoly Chubais got fired?

Patriarchy: (angrily) Of course not. What, did people believe in the God Chubais? No, they believe in God.

in the phony "loans-for-shares" auctions until years after the fact, and even then only mildly.

All throughout his career, Anatoly Chubais demonstrated that he is not only antidemocratic, but anti–fair play, anti–clean business, totally contemptuous toward the concept of free speech and a law-based society, and not, in any way, antioligarchic.

And yet, for some reason, the Western press corps still insisted, after years of examining his multitudinous Machiavellian warts under a microscope, on making him out, in its coverage, to be the champion of democratic, anti-oligarchic, free-and-fair business reform. It didn't make any sense.

What I found most incredible about the Chubais story was the degree to which Western reporters were willing to dispense with their traditional independent role and attack other journalists who were out there trying to uphold the basic tenets of the profession. The *Moscow Times*, for instance, was one of many press outlets to discount the Writer's Union story because of the likelihood that the Russian journalist Minkin, who broke the story, had been handed the material by Chubais's

And Another Thing...

On Friday, November 14, the day Alexander Kazakov was fired in the wake of the "writer's union scandal," word got back to us at the *eXile* that Moscow Times interim editor Geoff Winestock was planning to write an editorial calling, at last, for the dismissal of Anatoly Chubais.

We were thrilled. Finally, we thought, even the *Moscow Times* was coming around. Something that we'd been saying for six, seven months, in virtually every issue, was going to be supported by the mainstream press. We were impressed. Geoff Winestock had seen the light.

So the next day we open up the *Moscow Times*, and what do we find? An editorial entitled "Yeltsin Faces Ugly Choice on Chubais." An editorial of the type we at the *eXile* call an "Africa: At a Crossroads, Facing Tough Choices" piece. A case study in vacillation. Winestock had backed off.

Here's what we can now definitively say about Geoff Winestock: he will never commit himself to any moral position unless it is meaningless. Want proof? On Tuesday, November 4, Winestock wrote an editorial entitled, "Don't Let Corruption Ruin Russia," about the results of a survey by the British security agency Control Risk which named Russia the most corrupt country in the world.

That editorial finished with the following strong declarative sentence: "The government must take the obvious steps now to turn this around: Write simple and clear laws, reduce the power of government to interfere in purely commercial decisions and start punishing those who treat the laws on corruption as a joke."

Two weeks later, when Anatoly Chubais virtually admits in public (for the umpteenth time, incidentally) to treating the corruption laws as a joke, by showing (in Winestock's own words) "arrogance and contempt for the principles of honest government," Winestock concludes that the question of whether or not to dismiss him is "a hard choice."

But Winestock's Tuesday, November 18 editorial, "Sleaze War Deals Blow to Reform," was an act of treachery against his fellow journalists so outrageous that that it outshines even his obvious favoritism toward Chubais. He writes:

"The nature of the expose and the campaign that has followed it leave little doubt that this was more than simply a lucky piece of investigative journalism. Alexander Minkin, the journalist who spilled the beans, is known for working closely with the heavies of Kremlin intrigue, especially business tycoon Boris

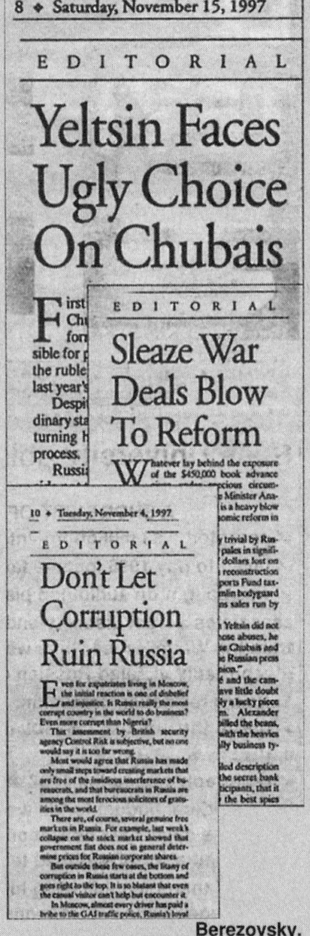

8 ◆ Saturday, November 15, 1997

EDITORIAL

Yeltsin Faces Ugly Choice On Chubais

EDITORIAL

Sleaze War Deals Blow To Reform

Whatever lay behind the exposure of the $450,000 book advance

10 ◆ Tuesday, November 4, 1997

EDITORIAL

Don't Let Corruption Ruin Russia

Even for expatriates living in Moscow, the initial reaction is one of disbelief and injustice. Is Russia really the most corrupt country in the world to do business? Even more corrupt than Nigeria?

That assessment by British security agency Control Risk is subjective, but no one would say it is too far wrong.

Most would agree that Russia has made only small steps toward creating markets that are free of the insidious interference of bureaucrats, and that bureaucrats in Russia are among the most ferocious solicitors of gratuities in the world.

There are, of course, several genuine free markets in Russia. For example, last week's collapse on the stock market showed that government fiat does not in general determine prices for Russian corporate shares.

But outside these few cases, the litany of corruption in Russia starts at the bottom and goes right to the top. It is so blatant that even the casual visitor can't help but encounter it.

In Moscow, almost every driver has paid a bribe to the GAI traffic police, Russia's loyal

Berezovsky.

"Minkin gave such a detailed description of the affair, complete with the secret bank account details of all the participants, that it was certain that he was helped by the best spies within the Kremlin. Who they were working for is a mystery but Berezovsky, Chubias's bitter enemy, is the obvious candidate."

First of all, none of this disgraceful invective against arguably Russia's best investigative journalist, a man who to judge by his professional contribution is worth a thousand Winestocks, is even relevant. Where a journalist gets his story is not relevant, as long as it's true—and Minkin's was. Chubais admitted it was.

Let me repeat that. Where a journalist gets his story is not relevant, as long as it is true. If the ghost of Adolf Hitler himself walks into your office and drops Nixon's secret tapes on your desk, your source doesn't matter if you check them out and find they're genuine.

But that's only a logical reason to be disgusted by Winestock's editorial. What should be emotionally unacceptable to anyone who works in this profession is the thought of Geoff Winestock stooping to what amounts to calling Alexander Minkin an errand boy for spies.

Investigative reporting in Russia is a very dangerous game, and Minkin is one of the few people in this city who has emerged with both his life and any kind of public dignity from the practice of it. He has been repeatedly beaten, sometimes savagely, for speaking out in public against corruption. A few years ago, two thugs in ninja suits leaped through his window into the room where he was asleep with his wife and attacked him with a crowbar.

I was one of the first reporters to reach him in the hospital. When I asked him who did it, he answered angrily, "Who did this? Yeltsin, Gaidar, Chubais, Grachev, Korzhakov..." And he proceeded to name every official in Russia.

Jay Ross, the Moscow Times's managing editor, edited that quote out when I wrote the story of the attack on Minkin.

While Alexander Minkin was out looking both ways every time he left his podyezd, literally putting his life on the line to try to get the truth about corruption out in print, Geoff Winestock was quietly moving up the career ladder, moving from business correspondent to business editor to managing editor and finally to Editor-in-chief. He reached his current comfy green office above the Moscow Times newsroom, and the $5K salary that goes with it, without so much as a bruise.

And then he turns around and has the balls to say that Alexander Minkin is a stooge for spies! There's no doubt that Minkin uses ready-made kompromat, and cavorts with "spies." But he appears to play both sides of the fence. He chooses what material to use or not use—and doesn't seem to take orders. He published a damaging transcript of a Boris Nemtsov phone conversation back when Nemtsov was still a Berezovsky protege. He's also a self-aggrandizing prick in person. But that doesn't matter. He survives without being an outright whore like Mikhail Berger, Sergei Markov, Yuliya Latynina and most of the other Russian commentators Winestock publishes. And that's a hard thing to pull off in modern Russia, much harder than anything Geoff Winestock will ever have to do in his miserable professional life.

Minkin will be receiving a copy of the Winestock piece by fax in the upcoming days. It will be interesting to hear what he has to say in return.

—Matt Taibbi

political enemies. That that didn't matter as long as the story was true—and Chubais himself admitted it was—didn't seem to occur to most of the folks in the Western press corps. They forgot that a true journalist shouldn't care where a story comes from, as long as it's true. If Adolf Hitler himself handed me the Writer's Union story, I would have run it—if it checked out. But my colleagues were more concerned with finding a way to discredit this blow to their hero than they were with showing solidarity with this daring Russian journalist, a survivor of multiple beatings, who'd had the guts to stand up to authority in the name of free speech.

Throughout the *eXile*'s long campaign against the Western press for its knee-jerk support of "reform" and its adherents, neither Mark nor I could really come up with a good reason for why our colleagues were acting the way they were. The obvious explanation was that "reform" benefited the Western business community, and positive coverage of it was a great boon to the Western corporations in town. But the people in the press corps weren't businessmen. They weren't getting a return out of fudging the story. So what was the explanation?

One good theory a friend of mine came up with was that Chubais appealed to the intellectual snobbery of the predominantly liberal arts–educated press corps—like Trotsky, Marx, and other academic heroes, Chubais was a socially awkward egghead who used inaccessible, lofty formulae to dictate the fate of millions. He appealed to the inner geek of the Western reporter (who usually also, of course, featured an outer geek in his actual person).

That seemed to us the best explanation, until we got, through a series of unpleasant confrontations with big-bureau hacks, a closer look at the reporters we were criticizing. As it turned out, assigning rational explanations to anything the press corps did was simply giving them too much credit. The dynamics at work were much closer to a high school popularity contest than to a political cabal. With journalists, it turned out, there was always a lot less there than meets the eye.

Part II: The Hacks in Person

"A Russian, I'm afraid, is like that: he has a passionate desire to bolster up his own importance by striking up an acquaintance with a count or a prince who is at least one rank above him, and a nodding acquaintance with a count or a prince is much more important to him than the most intimate relationship with people of his own class."

Nikolai Gogol, *Dead Souls*

In late March 1998, the following letter appeared on the "Johnson's List," an influential Internet newsgroup for some 2,000 prominent professors, journalists, and other Russia enthusiasts. The letter was part of an online debate over the merits of the *eXile* Press Review column, which had been featured regularly on the list. After a series of yays, it was the first real "nay," and it was a good one:

From: Baltimore Sun *(Moscow Bureau) <baltimore @glas.apc.org> Subject:* eXile

Let a thousand flowers bloom, let Matt Taibbi print whatever he wants. After all, it's a free country. And we all can use some help keeping on our toes. But why reprint it? All of us who need this message about our shortcomings can pick up an eXile *and read it. Reprinting only the press reviews deprives the reader of necessary context. In a recent* eXile, *the editor wrote about how he dealt with his pregnant girlfriend when she refused to get an abortion. She wouldn't listen to reason, so he threatened to kill her. That worked! Then he muses on forever about another pregnant acquaintance who aborted and about his relief that this child—who would have been a sloped-head idiot—was instead a dead fetus properly wallowing in the sewers. I don't know how it all turned out, I didn't read further. But it did help me understand the mean-spirited and mindless attack on Fred Hiatt. So don't just reprint part of the* eXile. *Give us all or nothing.*

Kathy Lally
The Baltimore Sun
Moscow

Lally, the wife of Pulitzer Prize–winning *Baltimore Sun* reporter Will Englund, was writing in response to a recent column of mine in which I'd attacked *Washington Post* reporter Fred Hiatt for giving suspiciously positive coverage of slimy Oneximbank chief Vladimir Potanin. Her point was that since Mark had written what she'd considered a sexist column about threatening to kill his girlfriend, my column shouldn't be reprinted on the Internet.

Lally was clearly calling for our material to be censored, but she stopped just short of overtly saying so. Instead, she was asking list guru David Johnson to either print the entire *eXile* along with the press review, or nothing at all. Which was ridiculous, of course—following the same logic, Johnson would have to print the *Boston Globe* Help Wanted section along with Moscow bureau chief David Filipov's articles, the entire daily Interfax wire with every Interfax story, and so on.

We'd always played by the rules with the Johnson's List. Since the Press Review was appropriate to its civil tone, we sent it regularly. But knowing Mark's column wasn't family reading, actually far from it, we'd rarely sent that.

Neither Mark nor I had ever met Lally, but we could guess what she was like, since we'd had many detractors like her: a fat-ankled middle-aged American woman who resented the *eXile* for its cheerful advocacy of the kind of raucous sex she probably wasn't having with her husband. That was our instinctive, childish estimation of who she was. Our more mature, adult guess was based on her articles, and placed her somewhere near the bottom of the heap among even the most jingoistic, reactionary, and uninformed reporters the Western press corps had to offer.

To see her in her proper context, one need only read an article she wrote about protesting Russian coal miners.

In late spring 1998, coal miners across Russia sat on railroad tracks in spots all around the country to block train travel. This was done in protest over the nonpayment of their wages. Some of these guys hadn't received their salaries for over a year, and they were working in ancient mines with equipment so outdated and unsafe that regions like arctic Vorkuta were seeing about two fatalities a week. Proceeds from sales of the coal mined with their unpaid labor were being swallowed up by despotic government bureaucrats, mafia middlemen, and the mine owners themselves: The protests were aimed at forcing the government to cough up its share of the payroll debt. After grinding railroad travel to a virtual halt all over the country, and helping trigger a massive stock market crash, they managed to extract some money out of Yeltsin's administration, then dispersed.

The lead of Kathy Lally's story about the end of those protests reads as follows:

"With the ruble strengthening and stock prices rising yesterday, the latest Russian economic crisis began to subside. Ordinary citizens returned to what they do best—persevering and hoping for the best."

That was Lally's take on the miners—that "what they do best" is "persevering and hoping for the best," even though "persevering and hoping for the best" had already won them a year of unpaid labor in the world's most treacherous hellholes. The article might as well have been headlined, "Hey, Miners: Eat Shit and Like It!" In any case, you get the point: Lally was hardly a Russophile.

Lally's letter about us to the list clearly called for a response, and the one we thought of was typically hostile: We decided to make a prank phone call, catch Lally saying something dumb, and publish it. It was a decision that very nearly sank our newspaper.

Our initial plan was standard *eXile* prank material. We would call and represent ourselves as a community action committee interested in instituting a boycott of our newspaper. Our "committee" would describe a three-prong plan of attack: number one, a general boycott of restaurants and clubs which distributed the *eXile*; number two, a boycott of all products and services advertised in the *eXile*; and finally, number three, a campaign to bring criminal charges against the *eXile* for "incitement of hatred and violence" under the Russian criminal code.

What we planned to do was tell Lally that our "committee" had already contacted FAPSI, the Federal Agency of Governmental Media, and say that FAPSI had told us that they needed testimony from three "independent experts"

before they could determine whether or not to bring charges. We would then ask our fat-ankled foe to act as one of these independent experts and testify against our paper.

FAPSI was a notorious gang of thugs which regulated telephone, telegraph, and fax communications, and was best-known for its control over the phone lines between government departments. Out of all the pseudo-secret services in the government, FAPSI was probably the most enthusiastic of phone-tappers, and in general it had a reputation for being a reactionary force on par with the old KGB. Including the bit about FAPSI in our little phone prank was like a control question in a customer survey. There was no way, we figured, that even someone as thick-headed as Lally would even consider cooperating with Russian spies to prosecute American journalists. Still, we were interested in hearing what she had to say.

From the tone of Lally's letter, it was clear we would have a much better chance of fooling her if a woman made the phone call. So we had a friend make the call from her home, posing as the wife of a Christian missionary who'd also written Johnson to complain about us. The result of the call was extraordinary:

eXile: May I speak to Kathy Lally, please?

Lally: This is she.

eXile: Hi, Mrs. Lally, my name is Wendy Helleman, and I'm calling because I'm part of a group that is working to close down the *eXile* newspaper. I read your name on the Johnson's List, where my husband published a critique of the *eXile*, and I thought I'd try to enlist your support.

Lally: I completely sympathize with you. Frankly, I wish they'd just go away. That . . . the newspaper is an awful thing, they give the Western press a bad name. What they publish is just dreadful!

eXile: Well, that's why we're working to get them closed down. We're sort of working on doing a two-front approach. One is that we're trying to organize a boycott, and the other is that I'm working with some officials from FAPSI and they said that they could go ahead and press charges against the editors under article 117 of the criminal code, but that they'd need three experts for what they call "independent opinions." Since I saw your piece on the Johnson's List, I thought you might be willing to help us out and appear as an expert witness for FAPSI's case.

Lally: H'm, I'll have to think about it. I'm not sure how my newspaper would feel about it if I acted in such a role, but I certainly do sympathize with you.

eXile: Well, if not, would you be willing to participate in an organized boycott of the newspaper? We're going to start by boycotting the *eXile*'s advertisers and distribution points to force people not to carry or sponsor the newspaper.

Lally: You know, I've spoken to someone about that—I've personally thought about calling advertisers myself. Although I don't read the newspaper myself [!], I have heard that they used my name as a phony byline in an article last week. I'm outraged. . . . As for participating in the FAPSI investigation, what exactly would one need to become an "expert" or offer an "independent opinion"? What do I need to do, exactly?

eXile: They just need an independent opinion, you know, to get another Western journalist to testify on the language, since it's in English. We're trying to convince them that the *eXile* broke the criminal code which bans literature that incites hatred or violence.

Lally: Well, I'll think about it. Please call me tomorrow.

When we heard this, we figured we had Lally beat, hands down. Here was an American journalist on the recordsaying that she "completely sympathized" with an effortto have other American journalists thrown in a Russian jail by secret services just for publishing something shedidn't like.

In any normal set of circumstances, that would be enough to blackball her for life in the journalism profession. Writers and editors tend to take a dim view of censorship advocates. The news wouldn't make it back home, but in Moscow, at least, we thought we had what it took to make her a pariah in her field.

Following the usual playbook, we published the transcript of the call, high-fived each other, and started work on the next issue, figuring we'd won that battle.

A few days later, Mark and I were out eating breakfast in town when we ran into Fred Weir, the correspondent for the *Hindustan Times.* Fred was one of the city's few excellent Western reporters and we got along with him very well, although we teased him for being the prototypical "bearded lefty." He had the full lefty uniform: messy head of thinning gray hair, tinted glasses, ratty sweater, salt-and-pepper beard, sensitive opinions, patient bearing, Canadian citizenship, and a taste for modest diversions like his daily egg breakfast at the Starlite. A longtimer in Moscow, he was one of the elder statesmen of the local press community. He knew everybody, a one-man grapevine.

At the sight of us, he rolled his eyes.

"Oh, Jesus," he said. "You know, Kathy Lally called me yesterday. She was in tears . . . "

Mark and I looked at each other and burst out laughing.

"Good!" I shouted.

"Fuck her!" said Mark.

"She was really broken up," he said. "I think she may have a nervous breakdown. She's really on the edge."

"That's great!" shouted Mark, eyes glowing with what to Fred must have seemed disturbingly genuine happiness. "We'll push her over."

"It's her own fault," I said. "What was she thinking, writing what she did?"

"Well," said Fred, still looking nervously at Mark's smiling face. "I think the basic thing is . . . she thinks you guys are sexist."

"What the hell does that matter?" I said. "That's no reason to go around advocating throwing reporters in jail, for Christ's sake."

"Well, I tried to explain that to her," said Fred, picking at his eggs. Then he looked up at us and in a philosophical voice said, "You see, I think when it gets down to is. . . . She just feels that since she's with the *Baltimore Sun,* and you guys aren't a major bureau, that she's automatically right. I tried to explain to her that America has a long tradition of innovations starting in small independent papers, but her feeling is that you guys . . . that you're in the swamp and should know your place."

I spent all night thinking about what Fred had said. If he was right, this really was like high school all over again: the popular kids giving the nerds a hard time just for getting too close to their lockers. The Johnson's List criticism now made me feel like I'd just had my books dumped.

It got worse the next day. On that same Internet list, a letter appeared from *Newsday's* Susan Sachs, a close friend of Lally's. In it, she regaled us for our attack on Lally, called for us to be excluded from the list, and accused us of having fabricated our phone prank.

This was too much. Of all the things the *eXile* was guilty of—and we were guilty of a lot—we'd never fabricated a story. Advocating censorship was one thing, but accusing a reporter of fabricating a story is, if anything, worse. Ask any journalist: It's the worst thing one reporter can do to another. And coming from a *Newsday* staffer on a forum as influential as the Johnson's List, our reputation was now sure to take a huge dive.

I rushed over to Sachs's office to demand an apology, this time with a tape recorder in my pocket. I was sure she knew that the Lally interview had really happened as we'd reported it, and I wanted to catch her on tape admitting as such.

It is hard for me now to find the words to describe just exactly how condescending Sachs was during my interview with her. Like Lally, her mind apparently divided people up according to what sort of job they had, and when she received me, she carried herself as though I had called not to accuse her of libel, but to ask her for a job. Rather than answer my questions, she instead took out a notepad, adopted a detached schoolmarm tone, and tried to "interview" me about the *eXile*. She apparently believed that I would be so flattered by the attention of a *Newsday* staffer that I would forget what I'd come to her office for—a move so puerile and transparent that for a moment I thought she was kidding:

eXile: I don't know where you got the idea that we fabricated quotes. . . . Probably you're a friend of Kathy Lally's, I have no idea. But as a reporter, you should have at least called us before you did that. But you didn't do that, did you?

Sachs (frowning, taking out notebook) : Tell me a little bit about the *eXile*. How long has it been around?

eXile: It's been around a year, but let's get back to my question. Did you call us?

Sachs: How long have you worked there?

eXile (incredulous): No, no, no, did you answer my question?

Sachs: What was your question?

eXile: Did you call us before you wrote that?

Sachs: Before I wrote what?

eXile: That we had fabricated quotes!

Sachs: Before I wrote what was on the Johnson's List.

eXile: Right.

Sachs: Did I call you?

eXile: Yeah.

Sachs: I did call you?

eXile(slapping forehead): No, you didn't!

Sachs: Well, there's your answer then.

As she spoke, Sachs—a plump, dark, unsmiling woman around forty—reclined in her chair and regarded me with a lazy, self-satisfied expression. If you'd tossed her a fluffy Persian to stroke, she would have made a perfect B-movie villain. The whole scene was so unreal I had to pinch myself to keep from getting dizzy. And then the conversation got even stranger, as it turned out that Sachs and I were, rhetorically, not even in the same country:

eXile (talking about Lally): This is a journalist who said, "I completely sympathize with what you're doing . . . "

Sachs: What was it she was supposedly sympathizing with?

eXile: With the instigation of a criminal investigation by FAPSI . . .

Sachs: What's FAPSI?

eXile: FAPSI is the federal organ which controls the use of communications machines and equipment, and . . .

Sachs: In what country?

eXile (startled): In Russia!

A moment later, Sachs popped a still weirder question, asking if Taibbi was an Armenian name. I stared at her in disbelief before whispering that, no, it was an Italian name. The thing is, all Armenian names end with "-ian"—Petrosian, Manukian, etc. In fact, for anyone who's lived in the former Soviet Union for any length of time, almost nothing sounds less like an Armenian name than mine. Sachs's question was akin to asking someone named Rodriguez what province of China he comes from.

After that exchange, she kicked the B-movie villain act into high gear:

eXile: Well, it certainly matters to me why . . . I mean, are you comfortable with the fact that you've printed a false accusation? That doesn't bother you at all?

Sachs: Did I print a false accusation?

eXile: Absolutely!

Sachs: Where did I print it?

eXile: Okay, you didn't print it. You aired it on a public forum. A false accusation.

Sachs: Well (yawning) . . . You know. Am I uncomfortable? I'm feeling pretty comfortable these days.

Frustrated, I decided to call Sachs's editor in Long Island.

If Sachs wouldn't apologize, I felt sure her editors would at least publicly disavow themselves from her statement. After all, Sachs had invoked *Newsday*'s name in her letter. But I was too late; when I reached *Newsday*'s foreign editor, Sachs had apparently already spoken to him. Before I'd said a word, he identified himself as "a friend of Kathy Lally's."

"Well, then I'm probably out of luck," I said. "All the same, you should know that your correspondent publicly accused me of fabricating quotes. It's not true, and I think she will admit as much if you ask her."

"My position," he replied coldly, "is that *Newsday* does not approve of misrepresentation of the sort you practice."

"But misrepresentation is legal," I said. "I can identify myself as anyone I want in an interview, as long as I don't do so to defraud someone out of money. You know that. Libel, on the other hand . . . "

"Susan is our bureau chief and she can do anything she wants," he said, and then hung up.

The next day was production day at the *eXile*, and I'd just about forgotten the whole matter when suddenly I got a frantic phone call from my friend Matt Bivens, the editor of the *St. Petersburg Times*.

"Matt," he said. "I thought you should know. Kathy Lally just sent me an email, asking me questions about your visa status."

"What?" I asked.

"She claims she's doing a story on you guys, and needed some information. But some of the questions were pretty strange."

They sure were. Aside from a very ominous question about the type of visas *eXile* employees used, the questions included, "Which of the anti-Chubais oligarchs do you think might be financing them?" and "Where do they get their money?" They were questions that virtually any American who's lived in Russia knows had only one purpose—to obtain information to get us in trouble. It was like a Mexican alien asking about another Mexican's INS status.

Suddenly Mark and I found ourselves faced with the reality that fat-ankled Kathy Lally, the schoolmarmish former guardian of the *Baltimore Sun*'s local education beat, was going to send the tax police or the immigration service storming into our offices after ourselves and our employees. And soon more reports were coming in: David Filipov of the *Boston Globe* and the above-mentioned Fred Weir both called to report that Lally had sent them similar questionnaires. For all we knew, she'd sent queries to every multicelled organism in the city.

Again, like almost any business in Russia, we were totally vulnerable to bureaucratic attack. Even though our visas were in order, the authorities could have shut us down with the blink of an eye for any one of a million reasons, mainly because we weren't backed by any heavy people.

In a panic, I called the *Baltimore Sun* headquarters in the States, hoping without much confidence that I'd get a better audience than Sachs's editor. When *Sun* deputy foreign editor Myron Beckenstein got on the phone, I informed him, as calmly as I could, that we had gotten word that his reporter was doing a story on us, and that she hadn't called us.

"I'm calling you to ask you to communicate to Kathy that if she is indeed doing a story on us, we would be happy to answer any questions she has," I said.

"Of course," he said, sounding shocked. "I'm sure she'll call. I know Kathy, she doesn't do grudge stories."

"Well, there's definitely a personal conflict here," I said. "She's welcome to write whatever she wants about us, we don't mind. In fact, we don't even mind if she doesn't call us. We just—"

"Well, *we* would mind if she didn't call you," he said.

Relieved to finally have a human being on the phone, I told Beckenstein about the visa questions, and explained that I was concerned his reporter might be looking for a way to close my newspaper down. He seemed horrified and promised to look into it. I hung up the phone encouraged that he might stop the bleeding.

But no sooner had I put the phone down than it rang again. It was my father, calling from New York.

"Matt," he said, in a concerned voice. "I just got a message on my machine from Will Englund. He says you're stalking his wife."

For a moment I was too shocked to answer. "*What?*" I said finally.

"The message went like this: 'Mike, hi, this Will Englund. I just thought I'd give you a call . . . I'm in town to pick up my Pulitzer Prize. I just thought I'd let you know that your son has been harassing my wife to a degree that borders on stalking. I'd like to speak with you about it . . . ' That's it. Then he left his number."

I couldn't believe it. What kind of sick maniac calls up someone he's never spoken to before, and leaves a message on an answering machine saying, "*Hello, I just won the Pulitzer Prize, your son is stalking my wife?*"

I was, to put it mildly, enraged that Englund had had the nerve to call my father without calling me first, but at the same time, I knew it made sense in the weird high school popularity contest dynamics of the world these people lived in. My father, a correspondent for *NBC Dateline* and the owner of a closetful of Emmys, was a fellow "popular kid" whose support they thought they could safely enlist. These people were so steeped in careerism that they actually thought that family ties came second after allegiance to the elite.

The irony of the whole thing was that Englund had won his reputation by being jailed by the Russian secret services in 1995 for writing an exposé on the Russian chemical-weapons program. The guy was a champion of free speech, somebody who would otherwise have been a hero of mine. The whole thing was incredibly depressing.

Concerned that Lally might follow through with some sort of action against the paper, I decided against confronting Englund myself. In person, I would almost certainly lose my temper, maybe even beat him up. That would solve nothing, and would probably result in the closure of the paper. So I let my father handle it, sending him all the relevant materials, articles, etc., letting him judge for himself.

A few days later, my father called me back.

"I reached Will Englund," he said. "He sounded reasonable."

"What did you say?"

"Well, we talked for a long time," he said. "But among other things, I told him that if he had a problem with you in the future, he should call you himself. I told him that you're basically reasonable in the end." He laughed. "I asked him—what the hell did he want me to do, take away your allowance?"

"What else?"

"Well, I told him that he had to try to understand that from your point of view, given his history, it was ironic, to say the least, that his wife would talk about working with something like FAPSI to close you guys down."

I wished Susan Sachs were listening, so that she could hear a real reporter in action. My father didn't even live in Russia, but he familiarized himself with something as obscure as FAPSI, once it became his business to know what he was talking about. That it was family business didn't matter.

The Sachs-Lally-Englund matter ended with that phone call.

The *eXile* was the first experience I'd ever had with taking life seriously. I partied my way through high school, slept through college, and in my professional career . . . well, the things in my past that I'd put the most effort into—playing pro basketball in Mongolia, playing baseball for the Red Army—had been based upon openly self-promoting and frequently overtly stupid publicity stunts. When I did these things, I was being ridiculous and I knew it. And even though the magazine pieces I'd written about those experiences had been written honestly, the narrative still was always ironic and self-mocking.

After all, it was sort of a joke in itself that an educated, literate person would run off to the steppes to play basketball rather than do something serious with his life like the rest of his peers. In fact, that was where most of the humor came from in those pieces—the fact that it was a person who was actually not a clown, writing what were in essence clown diaries. Like all things that are inherently sad, it was funny when written a certain way.

For a while, I thought that this was going to be my whole career: traveling around the world, putting on silly costumes, and providing mainstream American magazines with lengthy tracts of straight weatherman humor—phony, "nutty" asides to accompany the phony, vacuous, dull "straight" news pieces they all featured in the pages closer to the front.

I'd embarked on that career path with the guilty understanding that derisive humor about foreign peoples would be welcomed by editors, while humor that in any way exposed America would not. I was aware of this—and, to be completely honest, I had chosen those projects partly on the basis of that knowledge, because I knew that they would sell. The Mongol-basketball

ЭКЗОТИКА

Чтобы поразить монголов, я стал косить под Родмана

Как американский журналист покорял баскетбольный Олимп в... Монголии

С окончанием прошлогодних президентских выборов я заскучал в Москве. Писать стало не о чем, все развлечения уже приелись. Пораскинув хорошенько мозгами, я решил уехать. Выбор пал на Монголию - там, говорили мне, зарождается баскетбол. А баскетбол я любил всегда, журналистику же - уже не очень. Я попрощался с коллегами по газете «Москоу Таймс», надел кроссовки и сел в поезд, направляющийся в Улан-Батор. Степь, юрты, баранье мясо и невысокие азиаты в смешных головных уборах - вот и все, что было мне известно о Монголии. Осталь-

усилить состав руководство «Орлов» обратилось к самому крупному человеку в Монголии - борцу по имени Оргилболда. Это был настоящий монстр - ростом 219 см и весом 155 кг, из которого собрались сделать монгольского Шакила О'Нила.

Но в переговорах с Оргилболдой не повезло. Борец признался, что он монгол несовременного типа и не очень понимает «сагсан бомбог». Мол, мяч летает по площадке слишком быстро, да и баскетбольное кольцо хоть висит невысоко, но до него еще допрыгнуть надо. А вот в борьбе все ясно. Соперник стоит перед тобой, и нужно только

рушилась слава, хотя особыми баскетбольными талантами я похвастаться не мог. «Мэт Таибби, - писал один газетчик, - принес своими сумасшедшими выходками дух NBA в Монголию». «Он играет с волосами, как у Денниса Родмана и показывает характер Чарльза Баркли», - писал другой. Меня останавливали на улицах, просили автографы. Знакомые монголы приводили в гости своих детей, чтобы показать живую «звезду». А на телевидении мне предложили вести новую англоязычную

передачу «Утро с Мэтом Таибби».

Тем временем «Алтайские Орлы» в начале чемпионата выиграли четыре игры подряд. Нас стали сравнивать с непобедимыми «Чикаго Буллз»...

Но с наступлением зимы все рухнуло.

Мэтт ТАЙББИ.
Бостон – Москва.

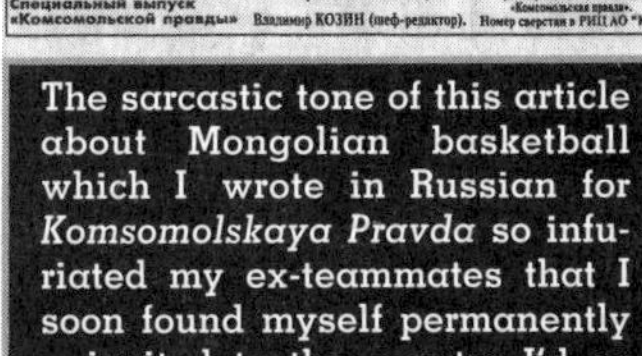

Спорт
Специальный выпуск «Комсомольской правды»

The sarcastic tone of this article about Mongolian basketball which I wrote in Russian for *Komsomolskaya Pravda* so infuriated my ex-teammates that I soon found myself permanently uninvited to the country I'd so enjoyed living in.

story, in fact, was really a story about the triumph of American values in a culture that was ancient and highly resistant to change. It was a story I could tell with enthusiasm and a clear conscience because the American values in question were really some of the ones I liked best—high-flying, slam-dunking, elbows-first, low-post physical basketball; trash-talking, flashiness, exuberance, style. It was an act—Charles Barkley in the land of Genghis Khan. I idolized Charles Barkley; he had been one of my biggest heroes growing up. So why not write that story—even if it meant also taking advantage of a natural American editorial prejudice in favor of jingoistic stories?

But I felt guilty about the whole thing. There had to be something else to do in life. But what?

It wasn't even that I would have been afraid to take the risk of not getting published to go do a story that took on America. I just didn't know where that story was. Washington? NRA headquarters? I'd once had the idea of planting myself as a mole in all sorts of loathsome American organizations, e.g., the campaign staff of Phil Gramm, and writing a book about the experience called *Dumb Like Me.* But I never did that, for the same reason I hadn't been able to settle down at home: I felt like a geek in the United States. In Russia I was leading an adventurous, romantic life, seeing the world, whereas at home, even if I had done that *Dumb Like Me* book, I'd have just been another careerist flunkie out of college trying to get published.

Why? Because deep down, I didn't really care about Phil Gramm, the NRA, or anything else. I was an upper-middle-class kid with not much to complain about. Life had treated me pretty well. Intellectually, I was repulsed by guns and supply-side economics and all of that, but my own physical life had been very insulated from hardship caused by any of it. *Dumb Like Me* would have been a fake book. The moral outrage I would have needed to sell it would have all been decorative.

But in examining the Western press for the *eXile* I had found, for the first time, *real* outrage. The people I was writing about were people I knew. I had worked with them. I knew how they worked, how easy their lives were. I knew how much money they made. And I knew how pompously they had all reacted, first when I'd quit to move to Mongolia, and then when I came back to edit *Living Here.* They all talked about *Living Here* and then the *eXile* as though they were beneath them intellectually. Their attitude was a *personal insult* to me. Moscow's foreign press corps was the first arm of society to really hit me where I lived—even if where I lived was actually a world of privilege and conceit.

The Thesaurus Wars: At the Front

General Alexander Lebed's victory in the Krasnoyarsk gubernatorial elections sent reporters scrambling for their Thesauruses as they never had before. Formula journalism dictates that all storied include required elements, and the required element for any story about Lebed is a catchy modifying phrase to go with the General's actual name. Reporters seem to go through an extraordinary amount of effort to avoid copying one anothers' catchwords, but through no effort at all to avoid grasping for new ways to avoid using the same 7-8 words to describe one man. The only difference is in the phrasing:

"Tough-talking former paratroop commander." Gleb Bryansky, *Reuters*
"The plain-speaking Lebed," Celeste Bohlen, *New York Times.*
"Square-jawed war hero," *Moscow Times* editorial.
"Gravel-voiced war hero," *Times of London* editorial.
"Gruff paratroop commander," *Reuters*
"Gruff Afghanistan war hero,".David Filipov, *Boston Globe.*
"Tough-talking reserve general, " *Reuters.*
"Napoleon-in-waiting, maverick General," Fred Weir, *Hindustan Times.*

A year later, I found that taking on all of these people had put my life into focus. I was no longer angry because these people had insulted me. I was angry because they were wrong. My colleagues weren't just stupid and petty. They were shilling for the rich and sucking up to tyrants, teaming up to squelch dissent, keeping the world, and particularly rich America, isolated from desperate emergencies. Anatoly Chubais and his ilk were the Marie Antoinettes of our day, and the Western press was happy to trail along in their carriage, and even lie on their behalf.

Working for the *eXile* made me realize that right and wrong really do still exist, that the struggle between good and evil hadn't been phased out of existence. The fundamental things really *did* apply, as time goes by. All the rights that I'd enjoyed growing up—free speech, the rule of law—they were all tenuous and fragile, constantly in danger of being taken away. And everybody, even people working in professions as seemingly stupid and inane as newspaper writing, was playing a part in determining whether we kept them or lost them. I didn't need to go away to Mongolia anymore. There was a big enough story right where I was, within my own circle of acquaintances.

Then again, there were days when I felt like people would be better off without news at all. Sometimes there wasn't even a wrong to fight. There was just a void.

Just after New Year's 1998, my old roommate Owen Matthews, now of *Newsweek,* invited me to a dinner party at his place. I was a little hesitant to go. Mark had been to Owen's earlier that week, and two of Owen's female friends, Laura and "Steve" (as she liked to call herself)—both of them upper-class Brits with profound psychological problems ensconced in an ugly public flirtation with bisexuality—had tried to rape him in Owen's bedroom, resorting to a nauseating amateur lesbian sex show when Mark tried to escape. I was expecting an ugly scene and got one. When I showed up with a date, I found Owen, Laura, the saggy-breasted, crew-cutted "Steve", and a third woman—a disheveled brunette with frightened eyes and wizened skin, sitting grimly at his living-room table.

"Matt," Owen said, indicating the brunette. "This is Anne Panzer of the [name of newspaper deleted at the insistence of the publisher]."

I smiled. This was pure Owen—setting up an entertaining conflict in his apartment that he could sit back in his silk robe-skirts and watch. Panzer had been repeatedly savaged in our Press Review column, and any conversation with her was likely to be unpleasant.

I knew Owen's old friend Laura, but the butched-out "Steve" I had only seen, although Owen had told me proudly —proudly because someone in his circle of friends was sleeping with her—that her father was the "Head of the House of Commons," whatever that meant.

"You work with Mark, right?" she said, lazily looking me up and down, stray index finger fiddling with her (obviously new) nose-ring. "You work for that little paper—what's it called?"

"The *eXile*," I said, smiling. Was she serious? Was anyone really that lame? I shook her hand and we sat down.

In this sad love-starved power-worshiping crowd the usual Owen Matthews–style party unfolded. Owen's parties were always eventful—someone was always liable to vomit,

Ironhead Turns Prophet

On March 29, 1997, Carol J. Williams of the *Los Angeles Times* wrote what we thought at the time was the dumbest lead in the history of Moscow journalism. Decrying the ragged state of Russia's roads and the general atmosphere of anarchy she'd observed through her window at the *Times* bureau, Carol J. wrote about a Moscow plagued by "car bombs, speed demons, and potholes wide enough to swallow a whole chassis." Not having ever seen a pothole in this city big enough to swallow a cocker spaniel, let alone a chassis, we ridiculed Williams for over a year for that lead. But lo and behold, last week, on Bolshaya Dmitrovka Ulitsa, a water pipe burst and the road opened up—swallowing, among other things, an entire chassis. Hey, she was a year early, but prescience counts for something. So we're sorry, Carol J. We had you all wrong.

or perform cunnilingus for the crowd, or beat up someone's father, or something, before it was all over. This time we ended up with a gram of cocaine. Around midnight Mark came over. It was around then that Anne, a lonely 35-year-old divorcée who obviously hadn't gotten out much in her life, started to talk animatedly to us. She'd been ignoring me all night but now seemed anxious to get something off her slight chest.

"Why do you guys always go after Carol J. Williams all the time?" she said, suddenly immensely concerned with our attacks on her fellow inept female hack from the rival *L.A. Times.*

We'd noticed that a lot of women, particularly lonely middle-aged women, objected to our brutal treatment of Carol J.—they seemed to think there was an unnecessary element of gleeful misogynystic enthusiasm in our criticism of her work. They were right, of course, but we denied it as long as it annoyed people to do so—and it clearly annoyed Panzer, who was losing her cool in advance. She was holding the mirror of giant coke lines in one hand as she talked, letting it wobble above the table.

"Anne," I said. "Put the mirror down. You're going to spill it!"

"Let me do what I want!" she shrieked.

"Put it down!" I said. "Jesus!"

"No, I'm fine!" Then, without putting it down, she crudely snorted half a line, blowing particles all over the mirror. "So why do you go after Carol so much? Why?"

We didn't know it, but that would only be the third of about a hundred and fifty times she would ask that question.

"Because." I laughed. "She's a moron."

"Why is she a moron?"

"Anne," Mark said, snatching the coke-mirror away from her. "Carol once wrote that Moscow's potholes swallow whole chassis and that the city is littered with flaming automobile hulks from terrorist bombs. That was last spring. It was the dumbest lead I've ever seen. We *have* to attack her."

"But why Carol?"

Mark and I looked at each other. "Because she's a terrible writer," I said, "in addition to being a moron and a terrible reporter."

"Why is she a terrible writer?"

We went back and forth like this for nearly an hour. At one point Panzer said that Carol's writing wasn't her fault, because she doesn't speak Russian very well.

"Well, there you go!" I said. "If her writing's bad because she doesn't speak Russian, then that's not our problem! It's her *job* to know Russian!"

"But none of her researchers speak Russian, either!" Panzer said, spastically half-snorting another line.

"Then why did she hire them?" Mark asked.

"I just don't understand why you go after Carol!"

Mark and I tried to get her off the subject. We ignored her, joked with her, did everything we could to get her to stop, but she wouldn't let up. It was really embarrassing. After enough of this, no amount of cocaine could rescue our mood. Crippling despair set in over the entire room. At one point, Anne got up to go to the bathroom.

"She can't handle her coke," Owen said sagaciously.

At 2 A.M. we all got up to go to a club, a new *eksklusivny* hangout called Angels—a place so exclusive, in fact, that you couldn't get in. The only way to get in was to have a personal invitation, which we did. We went in to find about eight people there on a Saturday night. By then I was just hoping to get my girlfriend Masha home and into bed as soon as possible, but we weren't that lucky. Inside, she whispered to me:

"Looks like Anne's making a move on Steve."

"No way," I said. The idea was so twisted and sad that I couldn't believe it.

But in fact Anne, once inside the club, really was sticking to Steve like a remora. They were dancing together on the empty dance floor, standing together and exchanging glances while stirring their drinks, and chatting. . . . The vibe was there. It was *true.*

I was down from the coke by now and feeling sick. We decided to split. By the time I'd gotten my things, it looked as though Steve was already searching for a plan B, a hunch confirmed by Mark's experience with them later on, when Steve made another play for him. Anne Panzer, separated from the group, caught us at the door.

"Nice to have met you," she said, looking down.

"Nice to have met you," I said. "Listen, I'm sorry we trashed you in the paper. It was nothing personal."

"No, it's okay," she said. "Besides, I think that you were really right both times you picked on me. And I really think your paper is brilliant. I really do."

Before I left, I shook her hand and looked at her. She looked so lost, I really felt sorry for her. She had no idea what she was supposed to be doing here—absolutely none. Except explain Russia to the West.

EPILOGUE

pilogue time. . . . Take out your harmonica and play a slow, doleful Civil War melody. . . . Let the camera pan across the bodies at Appomatox; peer through the smoke and step over the debris. Take a seat on a tree stump and catch your breath. . . . Now, pull our finger.

No, really, pull it. We promise, nothing will happen.

Go ahead.

Go ahead, pull it.

Fine, if that's the way you're gonna be. . . . We'll just put that finger away. In any case, unless our lawyers have held back the manuscript again, it is now the fall of 1999— meaning that the events described in this book mostly took place at least two years ago. A lot has happened in that time; Moscow isn't the same place anymore. We like to talk a lot about the "mojo" being gone; the days of heathen libertine expat excesses are long over, having been brought to an abrupt end by Russia's economic collapse in August 1998. The August events also ushered in the official death of the "reform"effort—even the *New York Times* pronounced Western-sponsored market reform a failure after the August crash. The *eXile*, which for over a year had been the only Western paper to point out the absurdity of a country featuring simultaneously the world's most pronounced depression and its best-performing stock market, had predicted the crash—but was denied the pleasure of gloating when it happened. That's because most of the people who were responsible for the whole mess—the journalists, the brokers, the aid workers, the consultants, and all the rest of the *eXile* villains—had all either been forced out of town or placed under investigation by the time the crisis hit.

Jonathan Hay, for instance, found himself in trouble when Veniamin Sokolov of the Accounting Chamber (one of those very same "communists" whom Charles Blitzer denounced in his clashes with the *eXile*) visited the U.S. Attorney's office in Boston in early 1998. About a year after Sokolov's visit, Hay was questioned by a federal grand jury which had been convened to determine whether or not the Harvard whiz kid should be indicted on conversion charges, i.e., for misuse of government funds. The U.S. government was also reportedly (the reports appearing the the *Wall Street Journal*) considering suing Harvard for the $58 million it had given to Hay's HIID to distribute as aid in Russia.

Anatoly Chubais was been forced out of government in early 1998, but soon reappeared on the national scene in a hilarious new costume. The erstwhile "hero of privatization," the man the entire Western press community had bent over backwards to defend as Russia's best hope for free and fair capitalism, was named CEO of RAO-UES, Russia's conspicuously un-privatized state power company, which has yet to free energy prices. Although he still has the ear of President Yeltsin and new Treasury Secretary Lawrence Summers, Chubais is no longer the icon of the free market he once was: His reputation has slipped to the point where famed Russian anchorman Yevgeny Kiselov of the NTV network could get away with calling him an "oligarch" to his face on live TV in June 1999.

Carol J. Williams was one original *eXile* foe who managed to reenter our lives long after leaving Russia. After we came out against the NATO bombing in Yugoslavia, even organizing a pathetically attended demonstration in front of the U.S. Embassy in Moscow, we noticed a familiar name attached to some of the more preposterous news reports out of the Balkans. Williams had managed to get herself assigned to the war; her articles took this fresh route back into the *eXile* press review.

New York Times correspondent Michael Specter left Moscow in 1998 in the wake of relentless abuse in our newspaper. After the NATO bombing of civilian populations in Serbia, Specter was moved to write an op-ed piece for the *Times* which argued that the difference between Americans and other peoples was that Americans care more about preserving individual lives than the rest of the world.

Michael Bass started a new glossy English-language magazine, *Metropolitan*, which died shortly after its launch. He then started up a restaurant/nightclub called Lips, which died soon after its opening. He then opened a new restaurant/nightclub called Catwalk, which . . . well, you get the idea. He's still in town and has some new gig going.

Geoff Winestock turned out to be an interim editor after all. He left the *Moscow Times* in April, 1999. The mock MT issue which his employees made for him as a going-away present was filled with phony *eXile* pieces (including a piece by "Abram Kalashnikov") which were, apparently, meant to amuse him. He left town quietly, his job taken by a left-leaning young friend of Taibbi's, Matt Bivens.

The Oligarchs survived the crash, but had a bad year. Relatively. Five Russians made the annual Forbes list of billionaires in 1998; none made it in 1999. Nevertheless, it is difficult to imagine that any of them will be forced to seek a wage-earning job anytime soon.

Two of the *eXile*'s staunchest enemies, Michael McFaul and Kathy Lally, have hit snags in their careers. Lally left briefly from the *Baltimore Sun*'s Moscow bureau, but returned ignominiously to pen pieces on Russians' primitive flu-fighting remedies, among other stories. McFaul ominously moved from Palo Alto to Washington, D.C., the very year that he was rumored to be considered for tenure at Stanford. He now spends most of his time working for the Carnegie Endowment, shuttling between Moscow and Washington. We wish him all the success. While nothing has been heard from either Kara, Marcus, or Nicole, Manfred Witteman has weathered the storm pretty impressively. He had worked at *Elle* in Moscow as their computer specialist, but after the crisis, he left Moscow, married his pregnant teenage Russian girlfriend, and returned to Holland. Martin MacLean abandoned Moscow all the way back in 1998, his coupon book scheme having totally failed.

The *eXile*'s rogue columnist, Edward Limonov, is still trying to overthrow the Russian government and impose a Stalinist regime with himself as head. His party was essentially banned from participating in the Duma elections after the Justice Ministry refused to register them. One of his party members, Dmitry Bakhur, spent four months in Butyrka Prison for throwing an egg at Oscar-winning film director Nikita Mikhailkov. He was given a two-and-a-half-year suspended sentence for hooliganism and then released in late June of this year.

Johnny Chen, the other *eXile* rogue, left Moscow in January of 1999 after getting the pink slip from his Big Five accounting firm. He was replaced by a bearded, center-left, progressive Canadian nightlife reviewer, Stuart Pratt, whose schtick is to promote "fun with a social conscience." Shortly after that, the Hungry Duck was closed down after repeated raids by various Russian police and security forces. Doug Steele was tossed out, and the club reopened under the name "Fiesta." Steele now works at the Moscow Chesterfield's and is trying to open a new Hungry Duck in Minsk, capital of Europe's last police state, Belarus. Craig Richter left the Duck the previous summer and, after failing to land a decent job, moved out to a ranch he'd bought near Yaroslavl. The new post-crisis Hungry Duck, like the new post-crisis Moscow, lacks the rape-camp mojo that once made it so special.

Many friends of the *eXile* fared even worse. Andrei Turkin died in December 1997 after falling from his balcony during a birthday celebration. Kolya's drug habit and desperation became so legendary after Jennifer Biggs left Moscow for good that he wound up living near train stations, muling drugs, and getting into near-death situations. Once, he told a story of how he was thrown into the trunk of a car by his drug pusher bosses, driven out to a forest, beaten, and left for dead. He has not been heard from since December 1998.

Owen Matthews's hairline continues to recede.

NOTES

CHAPTER ONE

Owen Matthews of *Newsweek* was one of the journalists present in the room when Marina threatened to have Ames either killed or crippled.

CHAPTER TWO

The *eXile*'s sources for its writings about loans-for-shares and the oligarchy included both Western and Russian newspapers. The particulars of the loans-for-shares auctions were widely reported in the Russian press in papers like *Izvestia* (the specific source for the reports that some of the auction winners had used Ministry of Finance funds to make their bids) and *Moskovsky Komsomolets*; there were also very well reported in the then Marc Champion–run *Moscow Times*, by staffers Anton Zhigulsky, Yulia Tolkacheva, and particularly Jonas Bernstein. Reporting on the backgrounds of the oligarchs came from a disparate set of sources, including the Russian magazines *Profil* and *Sovershenno Sekretno*, as well as the above-mentioned *Moskovsky Komsomolets* (which has published a number of exposés on Boris Berezovsky; its reporter Alexander Khinshtein also wrote a number of stories outlining Anatoly Chubais's connection to the oligarchs), *Segodnya*, *Nezavisimaya Gazeta* and others. An interview with Boris Berezovsky in the *Financial Times* in the fall of 1996 originally identified the oligarchs as a group; subsequent news reports by Western reporters, including David Hoffman of the *Washington Post*, consistently listed the seven bankers/industrialists listed in the text as a self-contained unit. MK was also a source on things like the Dmitri Kholodov murder (Kholodov was an MK staffer) and some of the reporting about the Igor Golombiyevsky/*Izvestia* affair. In the latter matter, interviews with Leonid Krutakov, the reporter whose article, "Kredituí Ili . . .," resulted in Golombiyevsky's firing, were a major source of information. Also, information about Alexander Minkin's beatings came from interviews with Minkin himself; he was briefly a contributor for the *eXile*.

CHAPTER THREE

The assertion that the late Victor Louis was a Soviet double agent has been made publicly a number of times, most recently by Senators John McCain and Jesse Helms during the Strobe Talbott deputy Secretary of State confirmation hearings in February, 1994. Writings about Burson-Marsteller were influenced by conversations with current *Moscow Times* editor Matt Bivens, a former B-M employee (Bivens also wrote an article about B-M for the American *Harper's* magazine), and by articles like "The Zapatistas vs. the Spin Doctors" in the *Canadian Forum*; there were also a number of other B-M employees who spoke with the *eXile* off the record. The Hay-Schleifer HIID scandal was a well-documented news story, written about in the most detail by Steve Liesman of the *Wall Street Journal*; the Investor Protection Fund story was original *eXile* reporting, based entirely on reports obtained from the Russian Accounting Chamber. The NII-Grafit story was first reported by *Komsomolskaya Pravda* on November 18, 1994, in an article entitled "Did the CIA Privatize Our Secret Factory?" Hay was mentioned explicitly in that piece. Subsequently, the Russian Accounting Chamber in December, 1997 sent a report to then-Prime Minister Viktor Chernomyrdin asserting Hay's involvement in the purchase of shares in the NII-Grafit factory. Assertions that the U.S. government funded Anatoly Chubais's political career were based mainly on the writings of George Washington University Professor Janine Wedel, who published her reports in the magazine *Demokratizatsia* and subsequently in her book *Collision and Collusion.* She quotes top U.S. aid official Richard Morningstar: "When you're talking about a few hundred million dollars, you're not going to change the country, but you can help Chubais." Our source for the "Loans-for-squares" cover story shown, about U.S. consultants collecting salaries paid for with World Bank money folling World Bank-inspired layoffs of Russian workers, was also based on reports from the Accounting Chamber.

CHAPTER FOUR

A simple Lexus/Nexus search provided most of our background information on Michael Bass. His criminal record we found documented in several places: Among other things, a December 10, 1985, article on the UPI wire describes Bass's sentence for mail fraud by U.S. District Judge Andrew Hauk. Bass had been convicted and sentenced to two years in prison for obtaining a line of credit under false pretenses for a dummy electronics company, buying television sets and other merchandise from companies like Sony and Samsung, and dumping the merchandise in South America at cut-rate prices. According to the *Los Angeles Times*, in an article published November 12, 1988, Bass eventually served 13 months in Lompoc Federal Penitentiary. Bass's involvement with Don King and Julio Cesar Chavez was documented in a November 8, 1988, article in the *New York Times.* The book *You'll Never Make Love in This Town Again* was put out by Dove Books in 1989, eventually reaching the *New York Times* best-seller list.

CHAPTER FIVE

The arrest of Liza Berezovsky, daughter of Boris Berezovsky, for cocaine possession, and her subsequent release and abrupt acquittal, were widely reported in the local press, including in the popular daily *Moskovsky Komsomolets*, and in the *Moscow Times.*

CHAPTER SEVEN

Alexander Minkin wrote an article for *Novaya Gazeta* detailing exactly how Yegor Gaidar was handed this prime piece of centrally located real estate for his Gaidar Institute, and how, in turn, he has been able to turn around and rent the space for exorbitant market rates.
Andrew Paulson's downfall was the subject of a few articles, including those published in the *Moscow Times* and *Moskovsky Komsomlets.*

CHAPTER EIGHT

The original source for the story about Chubais's "bones will crack" statement came from *Nezavisimaya Gazeta* editor Vitaly Tretyakov, who was widely quoted in the Russian press after the media conference; Jonas Bernstein of the *Moscow Times* re-reported the incident. Boris Jordan was widely quoted after his visa was denied as saying that his treatment by the customs committee was likely connected to the "banker's war"; numerous Western publications, including the *Wall Street Journal* and the *Christian Science Monitor*, speculated that Boris Berezovsky might have been responsible for the incident. None of those publications, however, put forth any theories as to why Jordan might have been targeted, outside of his association with Oneximbank. The original reporting uncovering the book advances of Chubais and his aides came from Alexander Minkin of Novaya Gazeta. Chubais's acceptance of a $3 million interest-free loan, his tardiness in paying taxes, and his use of the Montes-Auri fund for his declared income all came from an article by Leonid Krutakov in Izvestia entitled "Kreditui Ili . . . " Other Chubais improprieties reported by Jonas . . . " Bernstein in the *Moscow Times*, and Berstein with Matt Bivens in *Demokratizatsia*, in an article entitled "Russia Never Knew."

EPILOGUE

The incident in which two National-Bolshevik youths threw eggs at Nikita Mikhalkov was widely reported in the Russian press (*Moskovsky Komsomolets*, *Novaya Gazeta* and *Megapolis,* to name a few) as well as in the *Moscow Times*. TV 6 news cameras even caught Mikhalkov kicking one of the egg-throwers in the face as his personal bodyguards held him down. The video stills were reprinted in several newspapers. Mikhalkov called the egg-throwing incident a "terrorist" act.